Edwards

Disaster
Recovery
Directory™

The professional's resource for business continuity and emergency preparedness

Letter from the Publisher

Dear Subscriber,

"What's next?" In our 15 years of disaster recovery publishing, we've never been asked this question so often and with such urgency. We've all seen the devastation that both natural and man-made disasters can cause. With instant on-the-scene reporting the physical and emotional damage has been brought directly into our homes via television – and in all too many cases into our homes literally.

While we often hear about what could have been done to prevent certain disasters, the sad fact is that we cannot possibly prevent all disasters. If Mother Nature decides it's time for an earthquake or a hurricane, we cannot request a pass. And despite the best of our preventive measures, our free and open society almost guarantees that not every terrorist will be stopped at our borders.

The 15th Anniversary Edition of Edwards Disaster Recovery Directory marks a milestone in our publication's history. In this edition you'll see our title change from The Disaster Recovery Yellow Pages to Edwards Disaster Recovery Directory. The many suggestions we received in 2005 led to a reorganization of category sections, as well as an increase in the number of sections, making our directory easier than ever to navigate. We've also grown our vendor listings by more than 33% from last year's edition.

The year 2005 has seen a turning point in both the perception and the reality of the importance of effective disaster recovery planning. Being prepared and staying prepared is no longer the purview of just disaster recovery professionals—it is the responsibility of all of us.

Now more than ever, we know that our readers are counting on us to provide the most accurate information possible and we accept our responsibility eagerly. As members of the disaster recovery community, we are committed to improving our product every year. We welcome your suggestions so that we will be able to continue to improve Edwards Disaster Recovery Directory in the editions to come.

Sincerely,

Doug

Douglas H. Tanger
Publisher

2006
15th Edition

Edwards
Disaster
Recovery
Directory™

The professional's resource for business
continuity and emergency preparedness

Published by

Edwards
Information

Edwards Information LLC, P.O. Box 1600, Brookline, MA 02446, tel: 800-990-9936, fax: 617-264-2323
www.EdwardsInformation.com

Edwards Disaster Recovery Directory™
2006 15th Edition

Copyright © 2005 by Edwards Information, LLC

ISBN 0-9759662-2-7
Library of Congress Catalog Card Number HV-5512-D57
ISSN 1074-0112

Trademarks

EDWARDS DISASTER RECOVERY YELLOW PAGES and EDWARDS DISASTER RECOVERY DIRECTORY, graphics, logos, taglines, page headers, trade names, trade dress, service marks, service names and other marks indicated in this publication are trademarks of Edwards Information, LLC. All other trademarks not owned by Edwards Information, LLC that appear in this publication are the property of their respective owners. All trademarks and/or trade dress are protected by state, federal and local laws of the United States and international laws protecting trademarks and/or trade dress. The trademarks and/or tradedress appearing in this publication may not be used in connection with any product or service that is not the respective trademark or trade dress owner's, in any manner that is likely to cause confusion among existing or potential customers, or in any manner that disparages or discredits the respective owners of such trademarks and/or trade dress.

Disclaimer

Information contained in Edwards Disaster Recovery Directory (the "Directory") is provided by suppliers of disaster recovery products and services ("Suppliers"), and the Directory is not responsible for the truth or accuracy of any claims made by Suppliers either in the Directory or otherwise. Suppliers may place a single listing in the Directory without charge, but may add additional listings or enhanced features to their listings, for which they compensate Edwards Information, LLC (the "Owner"). The Directory is not a licensing agency, professional organization, trade association, or independent testing service, makes no investigation into the qualifications of Suppliers, and does not warrant the quality of services provided by any Supplier. Owner provides the information contained in the Directory "as is" and without warranty or representation, express or implied, and specifically disclaims any implied warranty of merchantability or fitness for a particular purpose. Each user of the Directory (a "User") waives any claim he, she or it may have against the Owner, its officers, directors, employees, equity holders, agents, attorneys and contractors arising out of the use by such User of the information contained in the Directory or provided to them by any Suppliers, and each User agrees to indemnify such persons and hold them harmless against any claim made by any third party on account of the use by such User of any information contained in the Directory or any services provided by any Supplier.

Printed in The United States of America

Publisher
Douglas H. Tanger

Editor-in-Chief
Dr. Steven Lewis, C.I.S.A.

Technology Director
Mitch Rosenbaum

Marketing Director
Amy Paxson

Business Manager
Susan E. Broderick

Regional Listing Manager
Jeremy Siegel

Regional Listing Manager
Lindsey Mark

Advertising Sales
Charlotte Lane
Tammy A. Spencer
Keith O. Taunton
Longshore Media Development

Cover Design
Brad Pruett

Proofreader
Michele Bush

Composition
Bookmasters, Inc.

Table of Contents

COMMUNICATIONS SYSTEMS

EQUIPMENT

General Equipment **6**-9

MATERIALS & PUBLICATIONS

Films/Videos **7**-1

Miscellaneous Materials **7**-1

Books, journals, newsletters, general **7**-2

MOBILE FACILITIES & EQUIPMENT

SERVICES

TRAINING & CONFERENCES

COMPANY LISTING, ALPHABETICALLY

How to Use Edwards Disaster Recovery Directory.

Edwards Disaster Recovery Directory is designed to be a useful reference both before and after a disaster.

It may sound obvious, but the best time to deal with a disaster is before it happens. Yet so many companies wait until a disaster strikes to try and plan around the consequences. To that end, Edwards Disaster Recovery Directory can be an invaluable tool in getting your company's disaster plan underway.

We suggest you start by simply looking through the directory. A quick scan of the table of contents will stimulate thinking about areas that your organization may not have considered, and provide a starting point for exploring additional local resources. You may also find that the sheer breadth of categories will provide insight into just how many potential disasters there are.

But lest you become overwhelmed with trying to plan for them all, the helpful planning guides in Edwards Disaster Recovery Directory should help clarify how your organization can develop a disaster recovery plan of its own, and put your mind at ease.

Begin with the article titled "Getting Your Disaster Plan Going." There you'll find a top-level view of disaster planning, including important things to remember, whether you already have a plan in place or not.

Once your planning is underway, or if your organization already has a disaster recovery plan, read through "Items Often Overlooked in Disaster Planning." This piece outlines a number of things forgotten by many organizations—even those that already have plans in place.

Then, to broaden your view, read the articles on "workplace violence," "the effects of bioterrorism," and important issues involved in "crisis communications."

Following this begin to work on locating "second-sources" and "out-of-region" suppliers. The reason for this is straightforward but not immediately obvious. Typically, most businesses have a group of local vendors who they rely on in an emergency. However, when a large-scale disaster or event occurs, these local contacts may be destroyed themselves, or at least, overwhelmed with work. This is where it is crucial to be able to quickly turn to out-of-region vendors to get help. As an example, after one recent hurricane, one of our readers in South Carolina used our directory to obtain electric generators from Texas, since there were none to be had along the entire south-east seaboard.

But beyond planning—what if you actually have a disaster?

In the event of a disaster, simply find the category or multiple categories that pertain to your disaster. Or if you already know the name of a vendor, you can find their contact information in the alphabetical index in the back of the directory.

Order additional copies of EDRD.

Order additional copies of Edwards Disaster Recovery Directory. It's always helpful to have an extra copy around the office, or safely stored off site. You may choose book or CD.   Simply copy, complete and fax this page to **617-264-2323** or call us at **800-990-9936** or go to our website at www.EdwardsInformation.com.

Your order

Please send me _____ copies of EDRD Book: **$149 each**   _____

Please send me _____ copies of EDRD on CD-ROM: **$149 each**   _____
(contains online links to vendor websites)

Order both, and save! _____ Book/CD-ROM sets : **$189 each set**   _____

Shipping and handling: **$8.95 PER ITEM**   _____
(Outside US: **$18.50**)

                                                                 Total: _____

Your shipping information

Name
_____

Company Name
_____

Address
_____

Address
_____

City, State, Zip
_____

E-mail
_____

Telephone
_____

Your payment information

❑ **Enclosed is my check for** _____
(Make payable to Edwards Disaster Recovery Directory and mail to address below.)

❑ **Please invoice me: Purchase order #:** _____

❑ **Credit card:**   ○ Visa   ○ Mastercard   ○ American Express   ○ Discover

_____
Card Number   Expiration Date

_____
Cardholder's Name (please print)

_____
Cardholder's Signature

DISASTER PLANNING

Disa

Reco

Dire

Getting Your Disaster Recovery Plan Going!

Many organizations make the recovery process harder for themselves—or even impossible—by not planning ahead for disaster recovery. While they may take steps to try to *prevent* disasters, they ignore the reality that prevention won't always work.

Creating a disaster recovery plan can seem overwhelming, given the complexity and demands of even the smallest organizations. We have found it helpful to keep the following points in mind as you proceed.

Remember, a disaster plan is never a fixed, finished document. A good plan evolves and improves over time. Therefore, it doesn't have to be perfect the first time you do it. The important thing is to get started!

Be systematic in your plan. Don't try to outguess Nature and plan for a flood, a hurricane, or a fire. You'll quickly become overwhelmed by the possibilities. Instead, look at the common results from *any* disaster:

- Loss of *information*
- Loss of *access* to information, people and/or facilities
- Loss of *personnel*

Make a matrix, with these three items as the columns, and each of your activities as a row. (Beyond the obvious, your activities include things like "accounts receivable," "payroll," "real estate management," etc., depending on your situation.) Then determine how you would respond to loss of information, access, and/or personnel for each function.

RECOVERY TIME PERIODS

Following any disaster, there will be two time periods that must be planned for. First will be the immediate, disorganized, "limited-operations" time span, which will then be followed by a period of "makeshift-operations," which can be quite lengthy until normal operations can be resumed.

Typically, following a physical disaster, the limited-operations time span can extend for up to a week or more, while the makeshift-operations time span can last for several months until normal operations are restored.

This need to recover in phases is typically very difficult for top management to accept. Often, when asked to prioritize among the organization's services or products, management's first reaction is to consider them all equal. Following that, people are often unrealistic in their estimation of how quickly departments can accomplish their tasks. In one example, the organization had planned to relocate a key department to a hotsite four hours away—without realizing that most of the affected people were single parents, who couldn't possibly go there!

A good plan evolves and improves over time. Therefore, it doesn't have to be perfect the first time you do it. The important thing is to get started!

People are often unrealistic in their estimation of how quickly departments can accomplish their tasks.

THE DISASTER RECOVERY PLANNING PROCESS

Once management has a proper mindset to build upon, the objective of the planning process is to systematically sort out the various issues and priorities so that a cost-effective plan can be developed which is in perspective to the level of loss exposure that the organization is risking.

The process itself can be summarized in the following steps:

- Provide top-management guidelines
- Identify serious risks
- Prioritize the operations to be maintained and decide how to maintain them
- Assign the disaster team
- Take a complete inventory
- Know where to get help
- Document the plan
- Review the plan with key employees, test the plan, and train all employees

Top management has to indicate the length of time the organization is willing to accept disruption of each of its key functions.

Provide top management guidelines

Top management has to indicate the length of time the organization is willing to accept disruption of each of its key functions, and the amount of money the organization is willing to invest in procuring standby equipment, paper forms, testing, etc., as part of being prepared for an emergency.

Identify serious risks

This is a "brainstorming" process, which is best accomplished by working with the employees themselves during department or group meetings. It serves the dual role of building the awareness of the employees to the issue of disaster planning as well as surfacing potential risk areas about which management may not have been aware.

Prioritize the operations

Most managers never think about it, but for the typical organization, the highest priority is payroll.

As an example of prioritizing, most managers never think about it, but for the typical organization, the highest priority is payroll. Even if this is performed by an outside service, there is usually a terminal for remote input of the payroll data. So, in the event of a disruption, either at the source of the data or at the payroll processor, there must be a delegation of authority to someone (remember, the president, owner, etc. may well not be available) to be able to issue substitute manual advance checks.

In general, top management will have to decide how long they are willing to operate without being able to perform each of their daily operations, such as accepting customer credit applications, receiving deliveries, etc., in addition to their more obvious operations such as buying and selling. Banks need to create policies on accessing safe deposit boxes, sending out mortgage bills, commercial night depository, etc., in addition to just worrying about deposits and withdrawals. Based on its priorities, the organization can plan out how long to suspend each operation, and designate either a manual backup mode or a longer lead-time approach for each function.

Assign the disaster team

Disasters always seem to happen at the worst possible times, when the fewest personnel are available. Therefore, it is crucial that as part of the disaster plan, management appoint one person in charge of recovery and one person as second-in-command. Following this, as many specific tasks as possible within the plan should be pre-assigned. In the wake of hurricane Hugo, with most telephone service knocked out, one company in South Carolina that had not pre-assigned tasks reported that it took four days just to assemble their key personnel.

> **Disasters always seem to happen at the worst possible times, when the fewest personnel are available.**

Take a complete inventory

While most organizations have records covering the make and model numbers of their equipment, they are usually not updated and almost never kept off-site. Inventory information should include emergency vendor contacts for all equipment (including microfilmers, specialty mailing and manufacturing equipment—not just computer hardware and software), descriptions and formats of all data files, and copies of all business forms used, along with the vendor contact for each.

> **While most organizations have records covering the make and model numbers of their equipment, they are usually not updated and almost never kept off-site.**

Know where to get help

Actively collect any additional names of service or equipment providers as you come across them.

Document the plan

The plan should be written down—remembering that if the core document is longer than 15-20 pages it will never be read or used—along with the various assignments, updated inventory, and all key phone numbers. Key personnel should have a copy of this documentation at home.

Review, train, and test

The key types of tests applicable to contingency planning include:

- Blink test
- "Independent" expert assessments/structured walk-through
- Component tests
- "Pull-the-plug" evaluation

By assigning specific people to each of the key task areas, it is possible to generate the most useful and least expensive of these tests—the "blink" test.

> **By assigning specific people to each of the key task areas, it is possible to generate the most useful and least expensive of these tests—the "blink" test.**

This is where personnel speak up and simply say "I can't do that," or "I don't retain that information," etc. This can include a yearly review with experienced employees and can be part of the introductory training for new employees.

Following this, non-assigned employees will be asked to review the plan as it pertains to them. As part of this process, they will be encouraged to provide their independent comments on the plan, based on their detailed expertise and familiarity with the daily ebb and flow of their specific operations.

The next step is to test those plan components which can be tested independently of one another. Specifically, this includes items such as the recovery of back-up files and the procurement and testing of dial-up backup links to hotsites, etc.

With respect to "pull-the-plug" exercises, it may not be feasible to bring the entire organization "down"; however, the typical day-to-day mini-disasters which knock out installations and affect the entire organization should be treated as this type of a test. Following the recovery from these events, the results as well as lessons learned should be documented as if the event were a planned test, and any corrective actions warranted should then be taken.

Conclusion

At minimum, you should do the following:
- Designate a second-in-command,
- List individual responsibilities ahead of time, and assign specific people to each task,
- Protect critical paper records,
- Keep copies of all of your forms off site—especially checks and purchase orders,
- Set clear priorities among your activities and specify beforehand the longest amount of time you are willing to be "dead in the water" for each of your activities,
- Have backup communications, including dial-up to replace "leased-lines" and radios to replace telephones and cell-phones,
- Keep a copy of your disaster plan at home

Don't try to go it alone. People throughout your organization may have dealt with disasters before and may have their own good ideas.

Finally, don't try to go it alone. People throughout your organization may have dealt with disasters before and may have their own ideas about what they'd do in an emergency. Beyond that, your competitors and colleagues at other companies in the region can be resources in the planning process. If you include their input and advice you'll not only benefit from their experience, but also find it easier to gain their cooperation for mutual assistance when the inevitable disasters actually happen!

Items Often Overlooked In Business Continuity And Disaster-Recovery Planning—Even By Experienced Planners

In building the Edwards Information Disaster Recovery Yellow Pages(tm) over the last 15 years, we have worked with organizations ranging from retailers, universities, banks and dairies to insurance companies, local governments and more. Even with experienced and systematic planners, certain items are often overlooked. Some of these are small but crucial items which simply compound problems when disaster occurs; others can threaten the survival of the organization. These are discussed in turn, below.

1. Vulnerability of telephone and network terminators to falling water

Most facilities have a panel on a wall where the telephone wires enter the building. Typically this is not covered, and in the event of water coming down the wall, they "burn out" and are destroyed. Similarly, most computer networking racks are exposed in order to reduce heat buildup. However, they are not shielded from nearby sprinkler heads or water coming from above the ceiling and following the cables down to the rack. When they are hit by water, they also burn out.

Most facilities have a panel on a wall where the telephone wires enter the building. Typically this is not covered, and in the event of water coming down the wall, they "burn out" and are destroyed.

2. Doors that need a key to open from the inside

Particularly in older buildings, many external doors have deadbolts which need a key in order to exit. Often institutions that are open to the public, such as banks and government offices lock their doors but remain open for many hours after their public hours have ended. For everyone's safety, every exit door needs to be operable from the inside without a key.

3. Assuring all safes are fireproof

A frequent problem is the use of non-fireproof safes to protect key documents. Safes are designed to be burglar-proof; however, most are not insulated, and in a fire, the contents are incinerated.

4. Familiar, everyday, "low-tech" paper items

The two most important documents in any disaster are company checks and purchase orders. A supply must be kept off-site, ready to purchase critical equipment and supplies.

5. Insurance coverage for the "decorations"

Many organizations have valuable paintings, displays, and antiques in their facilities. Often these are not covered by insurance riders for danger or loss.

6. Employees' relevant personal-life situations

Often, an organization's disaster plan requires key employees to relocate to a computer hotsite for the duration of an emergency. In a number of situations we've found that those employees were single parents, with no ability to even work emergency overtime, much less relocate out of the region to a hotsite. Other employees may rely exclusively on public transportation to get to and from work, and may not be able to get to a site requiring a car for transport.

You can help uncover such situations by having all employees sign a form on a yearly basis indicating that they have read and understood the disaster plan as it pertains to them, and asking them to note any limitations they may have in carrying it out. Then plan around those limitations, possibly by selecting an alternative backup site solution or assign other staff to cover.

> **Some employees may rely exclusively on public transportation to get to and from work, and may not be able to get to a site requiring a car for transport.**

7. Temporary, out-of-the-ordinary, situations which can affect plan execution

One of the most common atypical situations is that of temporarily disabled employees who require special assistance to exit the facilities, or are perhaps unable to carry key materials while using crutches. Planners need to identify these employees and task someone with ensuring their safety and ability to be effective during a disaster.

> **One of the most common atypical situations is that of temporarily disabled employees who require special assistance to exit the facilities, or are perhaps unable to carry key materials while using crutches.**

8. Familiar departments whose functions seem intuitively obvious

All organizations depend on a series of support functions, including mail delivery, check printing, voicemail, janitorial, and personnel. Because these functions are so familiar, planners often don't spend the time to go through the details of these operations to understand how they really operate.

9. Planning for after-hours operations

Many organizations operate around the clock. An example of this would be a bank with night depositories for large commercial customers. Often, there are no offsite lists of contact numbers, which are needed to notify these important customers if the facility becomes unavailable.

10. The needs of outside emergency organizations

Particularly in this age of consolidation, many organizations have far-flung locations. Many times local fire and police departments covering these locations do not have up-to-date contact information or copies of the building plans in the event of a disaster at their local facility. As part of their periodic disaster plan review, planners should obtain a confirmation from each local site that all relevant information has been communicated to the local authorities.

> As part of their periodic disaster plan review, planners should obtain a confirmation from each local site that all relevant information has been communicated to the local authorities.

11. A "second set of eyes"

After conducting all the emotional negotiations with various "stakeholders" throughout the organization, and finally finishing the plan, it's hard for planners to believe that the result can still be myopic–too inward-oriented. What is needed throughout the process and especially at the end, is an occasional informal "outside audit" by a knowledgeable person from outside of the organization. This person can be a disaster-planning colleague from another organization, or someone from the organization's external auditors, parent organization, etc.

12. Out-of-region back-up vendors for key support services

When large-scale disasters strike, the vendors of many common items such as electric generators and common services such as "pumping-out flooded basements" can become overwhelmed with the demands of the disaster's victims. Planners need to have out-of-region backup second-sources located beforehand.

13. Lessons from past crises

Almost all organizations we've worked with have had major disasters that have entered into their corporate lore. However, these organizations typically fail to document the details of what went wrong, what went right, what they've learned, and what they need to change for the future.

14. External factors—nearby risks and limitations

Many organizations don't realize they are located near areas that can be a focus of demonstrations or potential targets of violence. Locations near abortion clinics are familiar examples of this situation. In an unusual example of this dilemma, after September 11, 2001, an organization was unable to get access to their back-up office and storage site, located on an Air Force base, which was closed to the non-military public.

> Many organizations don't realize they are located near areas that can be a focus of demonstrations or potential targets of violence.

Planners should acquire a wider perspective on these sensitive sites from region-wide contingency management organizations such as NEDRIX (New England Disaster Recovery Information Exchange) in New England www.nedrix.com, the Business Recovery Managers Association in California www.brma.com, or the Business Continuity Planners Association in the Midwest www.bcpa.org. (See others in the "Associations" sections in the table of contents.)

15. Verifying that your company's "outsourcing" provider has not become a terror target

In this age of outsourcing, it has become very common for companies to move key components of their operations to foreign countries, but the chosen sites are often not monitored for political and social instability. Recently, a popular outsourcing city in one of those foreign countries turned up on the "attack list" of one of the terror organizations.

16. Making unjustified assumptions:

16a. Assuming that all of your people will survive the disaster

> One of the cruelest consequences of the 9/11 terrorist attack was that while many organizations had provided for backup operations, the employees they needed to operate them had all perished in the attack.

One of the cruelest consequences of the 9/11 terrorist attack was that while many organizations had provided for backup operations, the employees they needed to operate them had all perished in the attack and there were no provisions for temporary workers. You need to know where to get replacement employees or contract workers who can take up the slack in such a situation. If your systems are so customized that such workers can't be found, then you've identified another key vulnerability for your organization.

16b. Assuming your organization is important to the utility companies

Many planners simply assume that because of the nature of their organization (bank, nursing home, etc.), the utility companies will assign them a high priority in their recovery operations. During the 2004 hurricane devastation in Florida, many nursing home operators—who simply assumed that they had the same priority as hospitals—found out that they were actually lower-level in priority than most businesses.

16c. Assuming that your generator's fuel supply will outlast the disaster

> Most diesel-powered generators only have about a three-day supply of fuel in their supply tanks.

Most diesel-powered generators only have about a three-day supply of fuel in their supply tanks. Often, during a disaster, areas become inaccessible to fuel trucks for longer periods of time than that, and alternate plans need to be drawn up for that eventuality.

16d. Assuming that airplanes and specialty transportation will always be available

Many organizations are dependent upon air deliveries of key items. An example would be drug companies who are delivering test samples for clinical trials. These deliveries were completely disrupted after 9/11 when the entire air fleet of the country was grounded. Another example would be organizations who have arranged for air delivery of replacement computers in a disaster—just the time when airports might be closed. Alternative means of transportation need to be identified in advance to cover these eventualities.

17. Neglecting to test the plan and do what it says

A well thought-out plan does put a company in a good position, but it's very important to execute the plan and make sure all the parts are in place. Actually buy the back-up generator listed in the plan. Be sure the off-site copies of the computer back-ups are tested on a regular basis. Also, be sure your overall plan is tested and distributed to all the people who need it.

Be sure your overall plan is tested and distributed to all the people who need it.

Bioterrorism: The Impact of its Psychological Effects on Business Continuity

The impact of such an event will certainly reach far beyond the immediate incident and focus of attack.

Business interruptions due to a biological attack could alter normal activity for months after and shake employee confidence in management.

Of major concern would be companies' possible loss of large groups of key personnel to illnesses resulting from bioterrorism.

Much attention has been directed recently regarding the potential for terrorist attack using Weapons of Mass Destruction. The impact of such an event will certainly reach far beyond the immediate incident and focus of attack. Some of the spread of damage will be due to the nature of the specific bioterrorist material used such as chemicals, biologicals or nuclear matter and the path of potential contamination each of these would follow.

The risk of business disruption due to an actual bioterrorist event is small, however, compared to the psychological impact that will affect employees in a wide range of businesses on an ongoing basis. One major aim of terrorism is to induce long-term fear and anxiety in individuals, a community, or a nation. Terrorists hope that the fear of future attacks will become crippling, thus maximizing the impact of the direct damage. Business interruptions due to a biological attack could alter normal activity for months after and shake employee confidence in management and the very safety of the environment in which they have to work because of fears of possible continuing contamination.

In the past, descriptions of a typical scenario for a bioterrorist attack often involved a small plane, like a crop duster, spreading a biological agent over a large city or stadium in such a fine aerosolized form that those affected might not be aware of the immediate contamination. No one imagined the method of distribution would be the US Postal Service. Anthrax laden letters were discovered in Florida, Washington DC, New York City, and New Jersey.

Along with anthrax, there are many other ways bioterrorism can strike a business. Howard Steinberg, the Morris County New Jersey Health Department bioterrorism coordinator, suggested that plans should be developed for the different biological agents and posted for employees in case a disease bearing bacteria or virus is introduced into the workplace through the mail, or a contagious employee or any other avenue. Employees should know these plans as well as they know the plans for fire evacuation.

At the micro level, a business should take a realistic look at their facility infrastructure, plans and procedures. Of major concern would be companies' possible loss of large groups of key personnel to illnesses resulting from bioterrorism. Resulting possible lawsuits could reach millions in damages. Other bioterrorism threats such as Plague or SARS, diseases that the FBI ranks as a probable events, or agents such as Ricin, VX and Sarin gas could be devastating. While they may be very difficult to inflict on a large scale, they can be dispersed in small areas of buildings through the HVAC (Heating, Ventilation and Air Conditioning) systems causing illness, psychological harm and costing a company hundreds of thousands of dollars to mitigate.

What should companies be doing to reduce business risks associated with Bioterrorism:

Update all Business Continuity and/or Crisis Management plans by creating a special section for Terrorism, and more specifically Bioterrorism, including developing a list of key company contacts as well as a list of the appropriate government authorities with protocols for dealing with these types of possible threats.

Maintaining a dialogue with appropriate community leaders, emergency first responders, relevant government agencies, community organizations and utilities is crucial. These should include police, fire and emergency medical services agencies, emergency management agencies, Public Works Department, hospitals, Electric and Telephone companies, and the American Red Cross.

Maintaining a dialogue with appropriate community leaders, emergency first responders, relevant government agencies, community organizations and utilities is crucial.

Maintain contact with the company's HVAC vendor, learn about and assess what security measures they have in operation and what procedures are used to recruit and screen their employees.

Assure that your Facilities Management contingency plan includes procedures to coordinate management of HVAC systems. No unauthorized contractors should have access to them. At a minimum, if actual threats are made against a company or any signs of unusual illness present in office areas, facility engineers should shut down HVAC systems immediately. There are also sensors that can be installed for HVAC systems that can detect chemical agents which would obviously be most valuable to your preparedness if appropriate and necessary.

Highly visible companies must invest in more sophisticated physical security procedures; checking IDs is not enough. Physical security should consist of checking packages of any sort brought into a building. Security cameras, turnstiles, communication devices for security personnel, and even metal detectors in some cases, are all strong preventative measures to protect businesses.

The Emergency Management Team or business continuity planners in the organization should develop a process of communication with Human Resources and the Medical Department to identify unusual trends or clusters of illness that may occur in the organization. Simple indicators like the number of cars in the employee parking lot may provide an index of employee absence.

Review the fire evacuation procedures. Make sure the Fire Wardens have been clearly identified and trained, and conduct evacuation drills on a consistent basis. Each warden should also have access to emergency kits and

Make sure the Fire Wardens have been clearly identified and trained, and conduct evacuation drills on a consistent basis.

accessories readily available at their desk or at other locations on each floor. If at all possible, some relationship with local Fire officials may be very important and useful.

Keep portable battery operated radios, flashlights, extra batteries and first aid kits available on each floor in a high-rise building and designated areas in smaller structures. Fluorescent exit signs as backup to battery operated emergency lights, and fluorescent tape to rope off dangerous areas could also be helpful.

Provide continuing training for key staff members in crisis management, business continuity and general services. Local or federal authorities, for example, the Red Cross, FEMA, State Police, Office of Emergency Management, or the Department of Health, may provide training on bioterrorism or other threats to facilities or staff.

Procedures need to be developed for employees to report an emergency and a warning system established to notify personnel should any action be necessary such as evacuation.

Communications are crucial to any organization and even more so in an emergency. Procedures need to be developed for employees to report an emergency and a warning system established to notify personnel should any action be necessary such as evacuation. It would also be important to prepare communications to both employees and their families in advance that would consider the possible human effects as well as the legal liabilities.

Also helpful in this effort would be developing a relationship with a Mental Health Professional trained in crisis/disaster response to help with prevention and preparedness services . According to the American Psychological Association, the unknowns regarding bioterrorism as well as the regular news coverage on this topic contribute to the feelings of anxiety and fear. Individuals having a difficult time coping with their reactions to this threat can be identified and offered referrals for follow-up counseling.

Employees who were not contaminated may experience psychosomatic reactions that mimic the symptoms of those exposed to the health threat.

Should an event occur, the Mental Health Professional can help with the diagnostic assessment of employees in the contaminated work environment. Employees who were not contaminated may experience psychosomatic reactions that mimic the symptoms of those exposed to the health threat. The company's designated Mental Health Professionals can also provide acute on-site intervention after an event. Employees may experience symptoms of agitation and panic if they believe they are in continued or potential danger.

On site support and defusings can help normalize psychological reactions and calm employees. Stress management and other techniques for coping can be facilitated until the workplace is stabilized. In the aftermath, before a return to work is possible, debriefing services with ongoing crisis counseling can be available at the workplace for employees trying to regain their typical business functioning. These crisis support services were available at many businesses in Manhattan when company executives realized that employees were often afraid to return to work or could not focus on their tasks. After the business equipment was returned to functioning, many companies found that important and key personnel needed to access those systems were not performing effectively at all and needed psychological intervention to enable them to return to work.

For further information, see the directory sections on "Training," as well as "Associations—Public information and awareness." Also, see the Center for Disease Control's website at: www.cdc.gov/niosh/topics/prepared/.

Author: Dr. Jakob Steinberg, PhD is the President of Crisis Recovery Services L.L.C., a consulting firm specialized in managing the human impact of crisis. He is a licensed psychologist in private practice and a tenured full Professor of Psychology at Fairleigh Dickinson University. He is also Clinical Associate Professor in the Department of Psychiatry at the New Jersey Medical School and a Staff Privilegee in the Department of Psychiatry, Morristown Memorial Hospital, Morristown, NJ.

DISASTER PLANNING

After the business equipment was returned to functioning, many companies found that important and key personnel needed to access those systems were not performing effectively at all and needed psychological intervention to enable them to return to work.

Is a violence-free workplace in your forecast?

By: Larry J. Chavez, B.A., M.P.A.

Since 9-11, a total of 87 fatal incidents of workplace violence have occurred, resulting in the deaths of 139 people and the wounding of 95 more.

Workplace violence sits on the extreme end of the scale of problems involving people.

Concern for workplace security peaked in the days following September 11, 2001. People began to fear the foreign terrorist threat—but no such attacks ever materialized in the American workplace. Workplace violence incidents, on the other hand, occurred with regularity. Since 9-11, a total of 87 fatal incidents of workplace violence have occurred resulting in the deaths of 139 people and the wounding of 95 more—not at the hands of foreign terrorists, but at the hands of people within our own ranks, those we trusted with the key to the office, the password to our computer system and the right to be among us.

Workplace violence sits on the extreme end of the scale of problems involving people. Like a stored up charge of energy, it waits for certain conditions to exist to unleash its destructive force. A single act of workplace violence exposes innocent people to unimaginable horrors, and leaves its host organization reeling in an aftermath of legal problems that can endure for years. One such incident occurred on the morning after Christmas in the year 2000.

The offices of Edgewater Technologies of Wakefield, Massachusetts were disrupted by a deafening succession of blasts from the muzzle of an AK-47 assault rifle, something employees in a high-tech firm would never expect to hear. This awesome and destructive weapon of war was in the vengeful and merciless hands of Michael McDermott, a 46-year-old software engineer. He was on a mission to punish members of Edgewater's human resource and accounting staff for a recent IRS wage garnishment that had been imposed upon him. This was a matter over which his intended victims had no control, but McDermott's perception was his reality and he viewed these innocent employees as collaborators with his federal foe. So, with each pull of the trigger, a fellow employee fell until the number tolled seven. Within minutes, those McDermott had selected for execution lay dead at or near their desks. An eerie silence followed, broken only by the occasional sound of an employee scampering to safety. Typical of most workplace killers, McDermott did not kill any more than those he had targeted. Spent from his ordeal, he sat in the company's reception area waiting for the inevitable. Like so many other workplace killers, McDermott crossed the line into darkness, never to return to the world of relative civility he had known. Life as he knew it was over. As police approached, McDermott offered no resistance.

As if things were not chaotic enough at Edgewater that morning, the media descended with the singular purpose of fulfilling the demand for information by those who find workplace violence cases sensational, spectacular and, sadly, intriguing. Within an hour of McDermott's shots, millions of people were being informed of the events as they unfolded. People, many time zones away, were viewing real-time images of SWAT teams and ambulances attending to the bloody aftermath. As the sun set that day, the names "Wakefield", "Edgewater" and "McDermott" were echoed hundreds of times until they became linked, intertwined and inseparable. As horrifying as the Wakefield incident was, there are cases on record that exceed it in terms of loss of life and sheer destructive force. But, what is most disheartening is the fact that scenes such as this have been repeated hundreds of times across the American landscape and are continuing with no end in sight.

People, many time zones away, were viewing real-time images of SWAT teams and ambulances attending to the bloody aftermath.

Where have organizations gone wrong? As a professional violence prevention trainer, I have made some observations. There is first good news. Thankfully, the human resource profession has taken the issue seriously and has made some strides in dealing with the problem through the establishment of policy and the application of sound employee acquisition practices. As a result, many organizations are beginning to screen applicants with violence prevention in mind.

Now the bad news—it is not enough to have an antiviolence policy on the wall and an employee manual on the shelf that purports to address the problem. There is a woeful lack of violence prevention awareness where it counts the most—among first-line supervisors.

It is not enough to have an antiviolence policy on the wall and an employee manual on the shelf.

These people are the eyes and ears of every organization. They see every person within their area of responsibility every single day and are more likely than anyone else to observe a potentially violent situation in its earliest stages. But they cannot do what's expected of them without proper training.

According to a 1999 study conducted by the Society for Human Resource Management, only 35% of organizations train managers and supervisors to identify warning signs of violent behavior. While basic workplace violence awareness training would suffice for employees, first-line supervisors should be provided formal instruction and the opportunity to take part in hypothetical, problem-solving scenarios. They must be trained to identify the warning signs of impending violence and to conduct basic threat assessment to support the documentation and reporting of potentially dangerous situations.

Only 35% of organizations train managers and supervisors to identify warning signs of violent behavior.

They must also be trained to recognize, identify and eliminate organizational risk factors that could lead to violence and, equally important, supervisors should be given instruction on how to defuse hostile or potentially violent employees.

There are many cases on record in which supervisors had advance knowledge of an employee's dangerous tendencies, yet failed to act to protect innocent employees.

Unfortunately, too many organizations have failed to provide workplace violence prevention training for supervisors and this has led to some tragic outcomes. There are many cases on record in which supervisors had advance knowledge of an employee's dangerous tendencies, yet failed to act to protect innocent employees. One of the most chilling examples came from a quote of a retired supervisor of a Mississippi-based U.S. defense contractor following a workplace massacre.

"When I first heard about [the shootings], he [Williams] came to my mind—he had talked about wanting to kill people saying "I am capable of doing it." (Source: Associated Press and Clarion-Ledger, Jackson, Mississippi, July 8, 2003)

The supervisor was referring to Doug Williams, an employee with whom he had worked prior to retirement. Williams was responsible for the July 8, 2003 shooting of 14 co-workers, killing 6, before committing suicide. With the knowledge this supervisor possessed, it is reasonable to assume that some effort could have been made to protect innocent employees. Whether this was a case of supervisory negligence or a lack of training, lawyers of the aggrieved families will no doubt pursue the matter further.

No organization can afford to maintain a climate of negligence where lives of innocent people hang in the balance. In 1999, a jury awarded $7.9 million dollars to the families of two men killed in a workplace violence incident in North Carolina. According to the attorney for the family:

". . . This man was a ticking time bomb and the management knew it, yet they did nothing to protect their employees . . ." (Associated Press, May 5, 1999).

No executive would relish having to take the witness stand to defend such a failure.

The cost of a single fatal incident of workplace violence far exceeds the minor cost of the training that may have prevented it.

The cost of a single fatal incident of workplace violence far exceeds the minor cost of the training that may have prevented it. Although declining budgets are often blamed for training cutbacks, a new application of an old concept in training can be employed to resolve the problem—regional training cooperatives. Used extensively by the public sector, they can also serve the private sector. These are informal alliances of regional training coordinators who pool their resources to bring quality training to a large number of organizations within a geographical area. In this manner, small organizations receive the same quality training as their larger counterparts.

With executive emphasis on workplace violence prevention, coupled with the commitment to provide training, it is possible to establish a safe and peaceful work environment. Once achieved, employees are free to be productive, knowing that their safety is your concern. Managers and supervisors are transformed into valuable problem-solvers, part of the solution to workplace violence and not part of the problem.

Larry J. Chavez, B.A., M.P.A. is the head of Critical Incident Associates (www.workplaceviolence101.com). He is a long-time trainer and consultant on workplace violence, a graduate of the FBI's Hostage Negotiation School, a law enforcement veteran, and was the Senior Hostage Negotiator for the Sacramento Police Department. He can be reached at: endwpv@aol.com.

11 Steps of Crisis Communication

By: *Jonathan Bernstein*

Every organization is vulnerable to crises. As a reader of the Edwards Disaster Recovery Directory, you're well aware that the days of playing ostrich are gone. You can play, but your stakeholders will not be understanding or forgiving because they've watched what happened with Bridgestone-Firestone, Bill Clinton, Arthur Anderson, Enron, Worldcom, 9-11, The Asian Tsunami Disaster and—even as I write this—Hurricane Katrina.

If you don't prepare, you WILL take more damage. And when I look at existing "crisis management" plans when conducting a "crisis document audit," what I often find is a failure to address the many communications issues related to crisis/disaster response. Organizations do not understand that, without adequate communications:

- Operational response will break down.
- Stakeholders (internal and external) will not know what is happening and quickly be confused, angry, and negatively reactive.
- The organization will be perceived as inept, at best, and criminally negligent, at worst.

The basic steps of effective crisis communications are not difficult, but they require advance work in order to minimize damage.

The basic steps of effective crisis communications are not difficult, but they require advance work in order to minimize damage. The slower the response, the more damage is incurred. So if you're serious about crisis preparedness and response, read and implement these 11 steps of crisis communications, the first eight of which can and should be undertaken before any crisis occurs.

The 11 Steps of Crisis Communications

1. Identify Your Crisis Communications Team

A small team of senior executives should be identified to serve as your company's Crisis Communications Team. Ideally, the team will be led by the company CEO, with the firm's top public relations executive and legal counsel as his or her chief advisers. If your in-house PR executive does not have sufficient crisis communications expertise, he or she may choose to retain an agency or independent consultant with that specialty. Other team members should be the heads of major company divisions, to include finance, personnel and operations.

2. Identify Spokespersons

Within each team, there should be individuals who are the only ones author-ized to speak for the company in times of crisis. The CEO should be one of those spokespersons, but not necessarily the primary spokesperson. The fact is that some chief executives are brilliant business people but not very effective in-person communicators. The decision about who should speak is made after a crisis breaks—but the pool of potential spokespersons should be identified and trained in advance.

Not only are spokespersons needed for media communications, but for all types and forms of communications, internal and external, including on-cam-era, at a public meeting, at employee meetings, etc. You really don't want to be making decisions about so many different types of spokespersons while "under fire."

> **Within each team, there should be indi-viduals who are the only ones authorized to speak for the company in times of crisis.**

3. Spokesperson Training

Two typical quotes from well-intentioned company executives summarize the reason why your spokespersons should receive professional training in how to speak to the media:

- "I talked to that nice reporter for over an hour and he didn't use the most important news about my organization."
- "I've done a lot of public speaking. I won't have any trouble at that public hearing."

All stakeholders—internal and external—are just as capable of misunder-standing or misinterpreting information about your organization as the media, and it's your responsibility to minimize the chance of that happening. Spokesperson training teaches you to be prepared, to be ready to respond in a way that optimizes the response of all stakeholders.

> **"I talked to that nice reporter for over an hour and he didn't use the most impor-tant news about my organization."**

4. Establish Communications Protocols

Initial crisis-related news can be received at any level of a company. A janitor may be the first to know there is a problem, or someone in personnel, or noti-fication could be in the form of a midnight phone call from an out-of-town executive. Who should be notified, and where do you reach them?

An emergency communications "tree" should be established and distrib-uted to all company employees, telling them precisely what to do and who to call if there appears to be a potential for or an actual crisis. In addition to appropriate supervisors, at least one member of the Crisis Communications Team, plus an alternate member, should include their cellphone, office and home phone numbers on the emergency contact list.

Who are the stakeholders that matter to your organization?

5. Identify and Know Your Stakeholders

Who are the stakeholders that matter to your organization? Most organizations, for example, care about their employees, customers, prospects, suppliers and the media. Private investors may be involved. Publicly held companies have to comply with Securities and Exchange Commission and stock exchange information requirements. You may answer to local, state or federal regulatory agencies.

6. Decide on Communications Methods

For each stakeholder group, you need to have, in advance, complete emailing, snail-mailing, fax and phone number lists to accommodate rapid communication in time of crisis.

For each stakeholder group, you need to have, in advance, complete emailing, snail-mailing, fax and phone number lists to accommodate rapid communication in time of crisis. And you need to know what type of information each stakeholder group is seeking, as well as the best way to reach each of your contacts.

Another thing to consider is whether you have an automated system established to ensure rapid communication with those stakeholders. You should also think about backup communications options such as toll-free numbers for emergency call-ins or special Web sites that can be activated in times of crisis to keep various stakeholders informed and/or to conduct online incident management.

7. Anticipate Crises

If you're being proactive and preparing for crises, gather your Crisis Communications Team for long brainstorming sessions on all the potential crises which can occur at your organization. There are at least two immediate benefits to this exercise:

You may realize that some of the situations are preventable by simply modifying existing methods of operation.

- You may realize that some of the situations are preventable by simply modifying existing methods of operation.
- You can begin to think about possible responses, about best case/worst case scenarios, etc. Better now than when under the pressure of an actual crisis.

In some cases, of course, you know that a crisis will occur because you're planning to create it—e.g., to lay off employees, or to make a major acquisition. Then, you can proceed with steps 9-11 below, even before the crisis occurs.

8. Develop Holding Statements

"Holding statements"—messages designed for use immediately after a crisis breaks—can be developed in advance.

While full message development must await the outbreak of an actual crisis, "holding statements"—messages designed for use immediately after a crisis breaks—can be developed in advance to be used for a wide variety of scenarios to which the organization is perceived to be vulnerable, based on the assessment you conducted in Step 7 of this process. An example of holding state-

ments by a hotel chain with properties hit by a natural disaster—before the company headquarters has any hard factual information—might be:
"We have implemented our crisis response plan, which places the highest priority on the health and safety of our guests and staff."

"Our hearts and minds are with those who are in harm's way, and we hope that they are well."

"We will be supplying additional information when it is available and posting it on our Web site."

The organization's Crisis Communications Team should regularly review holding statements to determine if they require revision and/or whether statements for other scenarios should be developed.

9. Assess the Crisis Situation

Reacting without adequate information is a classic "shoot first and ask questions afterwards" situation in which you could be the primary victim. But if you've done all of the above first, it's a "simple" matter of having the Crisis Communications Team on the receiving end of information coming in from your communications "tree," ensuring that the right type of information is being provided so that you can proceed with determining the appropriate response.

10. Identify Key Messages

With holding statements available as a starting point, the Crisis Communications Team must continue developing the crisis-specific messages required for any given situation. The team already knows, categorically, what type of information its stakeholders are looking for. What should those stakeholders know about "this" crisis? Keep it simple—have no more than three main messages for all stakeholders and, as necessary, some audience-specific messages for individual groups of stakeholders.

The Crisis Communications Team must continue developing the crisis-specific messages required for any given situation.

11. Riding Out the Storm

No matter what the nature of a crisis . . . no matter whether it's good news or bad . . . no matter how carefully you've prepared and responded . . . some of your stakeholders are not going to react the way you want them to. This can be immensely frustrating. What do you do?

- Take a deep breath.
- Take an objective look at the reaction(s) in question. Is it your fault, or their unique interpretation?
- Decide if another communication to those stakeholders is likely to change their impression for the better.

Decide if another communication to those stakeholders could make the situation worse.

- Decide if another communication to those stakeholders could make the situation worse.
- If, after considering these factors, you think it's still worth more communication, then take your best shot!

"It Can't Happen To Me"

When a healthy organization's CEO or CFO looks at the cost of preparing a crisis communications plan, either a heavy investment of in-house time or retention of an outside professional for a substantial fee, it is tempting for them to fantasize "it can't happen to me" or "if it happens to me, we can handle it relatively easily."

Hopefully, that type of ostrich-playing is rapidly becoming a thing of the past. Yet I know that thousands of organizations hit by Hurricane Katrina will have, when all is said and done, suffered far more damage than would have occurred with a fully developed crisis communications plan in place.

Jonathan Bernstein is the President of Bernstein Crisis Management (www.bernsteincrisismanagement.com); he can be reached at: jonathan@bernsteincrisismanagement.com.

ASSOCIATIONS

YOU HAVE THE KNOWLEDGE.
YOU HAVE THE EXPERIENCE.

Isn't it time you received the recognition?

Distinguish yourself in the business continuity field with professional certification through the DRI International.

Professional certification will:

- Validate your knowledge and expertise
- Highlight your skills to employers and clients
- Demonstrate your commitment to high ethical and professional standards
- Increase your professional value

Put Your Career on the Fast Track with Professional Certification

DRII certification is recognized worldwide. Make a commitment to certification today. Select your level of certification based on current knowledge and experience, then build toward becoming a Master Business Continuity Professional.

Four Levels of Certification	Required Work Experience	Certification Exam
Associate Business Continuity Planner (ABCP)	None required	DRI International certification examination
Certified Functional Continuity Professional (CFCP)	2 years minimum, in at least 5 Professional Practice subject areas	DRI International certification examination
Certified Business Continuity Professional (CBCP)	2 years minimum, in at least 5 Professional Practice subject areas	
Master Business Continuity Professional (MBCP)	5 years minimum, in at least 7 DRII subject areas	DRI International master case study examination

DRI International: The Leader in Business Continuity Education and Professional Certification

Since 1989, DRI International has provided top quality educational opportunities for business continuity and disaster recovery professionals. To date more than 12,000 professionals have participated in our copyrighted educational curriculum, and more than 5,700 practitioners have become certified business continuity professionals. DRI International provides basic, experienced, and master level industry certification that is recognized worldwide.

DRI International — The Best Instruction in the Field of Business Continuity Planning

Learn the best practices in the field with continuing education from DRII. DRII courses are packed with case studies and interactive problems to teach you the best, most cost-effective methods in business continuity planning today. DRII instructors are certified, experienced professionals who average over 20 years' experience in the field.

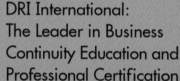

Now you can learn at your desk, at your convenience, and take certification tests locally! DRII now offers on-line courses, and you can take certification exams locally at Prometric testing centers!

Visit **www.drii.org** for more information and a schedule and listing of DRII classes for 2005 or call 703-538-1792.

ASSOCIATIONS

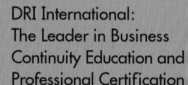

ASSOCIATIONS

Cleaning & restoration associations

American Industrial Hygiene Association
2700 Prosperity Ave
Suite 250
Fairfax, VA 22031
703-849-8888
www.aiha.org

Association of Specialists in Cleaning & Restoration (ASCR)
8229 Cloverleaf Dr.
Suite 460
Millersville, MD 21108
800-272-7012
www.ascr.org

Building Service Contractors Assn. Intl.
10201 Lee Highway
Suite 225
Fairfax, VA 22030
703-359-7090
800-368-3414
www.BSCAI.org

Carpet & FabriCare Institute, The
P.O. Box 2160
Mission Viejo, CA 92690
800-227-7389
www.CARPET9.org

First General Enterprises
2455 E Sunrise Boulevard
Suite 1201
Fort Lauderdale, FL 33304-3115
954-537-5556
800-523-3680
www.CLAIMSSUPPORT.com/firstgen.htm

International Society of Cleaning Technicians
1355 Saybrook Crossing
Thompson Station, TN 37179
615-591-9610
800-949-4728
www.ISCT.org

MasterPros Emergency Services Consortium
270 Sheldon Avenue, Suite 405
Toronto, ON M8W4M1
Canada
416-822-3334
http://www.MasterPros.com

Nat. Assoc. Waterproofing & Struct. Repair Contrctrs
8015 Corporate Drive
Suite A
Baltimore, MD 21236
410-931-3332
www.nawsrc.org

National Air Duct Cleaners Association (NADCA)
1518 K Street N.W.
Suite 503
Washington, DC 20005
202-737-2926
www.NADCA.com/index.htm

Xtreme Team / Bolden's Mfg
20799 Riverwood Ave
Building B
Noblesville, IN 46062
888-776-6708
317-776-8787
www.hydro-systems.com

Computer security associations

AFCOM
742 East Chapman Avenue
Orange, CA 92866
714-997-7966
www.afcom.com

Computer Security Institute
600 Harrison Street
San Francisco, CA 94107-1387
917-305-3390
866-271-8529
www.GOCSI.com

ISSA Information Systems Security Association
7044 S. 13th Street
Oak Creek, WI 53154
414-908-4949
800-370-ISSA
www.issa.org

The SANS Institute
8120 Woodmont Avenue
Suite 205
Bethesda, MD 20814
301-654-7267
www.sans.org

Disaster assistance associations

American Red Cross National Headquarters
Preparedness Dept. Community Disaster Ed.
2025 E Street, NW
Washington, DC 20006
202-303-4498
www.REDCROSS.org/services/disaster

Nechama - Jewish Response to Disaster
4330 S. Cedar Lake Road
Minneapolis, MN 55416
763-732-0610
612-490-5848
www.nechama.org

ground breaking association

Who Is AFCOM?

Industry Leader

An industry leader since 1980, AFCOM is the only association that brings IT management resources and information to the data center field. Through articles, local chapters, conferences, web seminars and an on-line resource center, AFCOM has created an innovative medium for data center professionals to interact and exchange ideas.

What AFCOM Offers You

Here are some of the benefits of an AFCOM membership that help members reach their objectives:

Data Center Message Board

Messages are posted and answered by members daily

Communiqué Newsletter

Learn new management strategies and read what's new in the industry in this monthly html newsletter

DCM Magazine

Disaster recovery plans, security, facilities management and disaster preparedness are just a few of the topics that are covered in each issue of this bimonthly publication

Two Annual Conferences

The only educational experience dedicated to the needs of data center professionals with over 100 educational sessions, a tradeshow and networking.

For more information, logon to
www.afcom.com or call 714.997.7966

A F C O M

UNPARALLELED RESOURCES UNPARALLELED SUPPORT

The Association of Contingency Planners

The Association of Contingency Planners (ACP) is a non-profit professional association dedicated to fostering continued professional growth and development in effective contingency and business resumption planning.

Benefits of ACP Membership

- *Introduction to peers and a network of resources that specialize in Emergency Response, Business Continuity and Technology Recovery*

- *Attendance to chapter meetings for education credits*

- *Association sponsored networking and professional development opportunities*

- *Discounts on products, services, conference fees, and training materials*

- *Members only website section for access to presentations, templates, etc.*

1-800-445-4ACP

MEMBERSHIP
Membership is open to industry professionals and individuals interested in the fields of continuity planning and emergency management. Each ACP Chapter establishes their own chapter dues which range from $60 to $110. Unaffiliated general US membership is available for $75 for those located 50 miles or more from a chapter. International memberships are available for $100.

www.acp-international.com

ASSOCIATIONS

Emergency preparedness & disaster recovery associations

America Prepared Campaign
45 Rockfeller Plaza
New York, NY 10111
212-332-6302
www.americaprepared.org

**American Bio-Recovery Association
P.O. Box 828
Ipswich, MA 01938
888-979-2272
www.americanbiorecovery.com**

American Planning Association
122 S Michigan Avenue
Suite 1600
Chicago, IL 60603-6111
312-431-9100
312-786-6704
www.PLANNING.org

American Public Works Association
2345 Grand Boulevard
Suite 500
Kansas City, MO 64108-2641
816-472-6100
www.APWA.net

American Red Cross BICEPP Program
3747 Euclid Avenue
Cleveland, OH 44115
216-431-3311

American Society for Industrial Security (ASIS)
1625 Prince Street
Alexandria, VA 22314-2882
703-519-6200
www.ASISONLINE.org

American Society of Safety Engineers
1800 E Oakton Street
Des Plaines, IL 60018-2100
847-699-2929

Association of Contingency Planners National HQ
7044 S 13th Street
Oak Creek, WI 53154-1429
414-768-8000 x116
www.ACP-INTERNATIONAL.com

Association of Contingency Planners (ACP)
Arkansas Chapter
P.O. Box 17587
Little Rock, AR 72222-7587
501-220-6258

Association of Contingency Planners (ACP)
Central Arizona (Phoenix) Chapter
P.O. Box 67434
Phoenix, AZ 85026-7434
480-557-1132
www.acp-international.com

Association of Contingency Planners (ACP)
Los Angeles Chapter
669 Pacific Cove Drive
Port Hueneme, CA 93041-2171
805-984-9547
805-495-7335
www.acp-international.com

Association of Contingency Planners (ACP)
Orange County (California) Chapter
P.O. Box 1842
Orange, CA 92856-1842
626-537-2712
www.acp-international.com

Association of Contingency Planners (ACP)
San Diego (California) Chapter
P.O. Box 420722
San Diego, CA 92142
858-385-2700
www.acp-international.com

Association of Contingency Planners (ACP)
Colorado Rocky Mountain Chapter
P.O. Box 3943
Englewood, CO 80155-3943
720-889-2020
303-794-2729
www.acp-international.com

Association of Contingency Planners (ACP)
N.E. Florida (Jacksonville) Chapter
P.O. Box 23556
Jacksonville, FL 32241-3556
904-281-3271
www.acp-international.com

Association of Contingency Planners (ACP)
Greater Tampa Bay Area Chapter
P.O. Box 17761
Clearwater, FL 33762-0111
727-567-4777
www.acp-international.com

Association of Contingency Planners (ACP)
Mid-Florida (Orlando) Chapter
340 S. Lakeside Drive
Satellite Beach, FL 32937
321-554-1922
www.acp-international.com

Association of Contingency Planners (ACP)
South East Florida Chapter
P.O. Box 291214
Davie, FL 33329
954-383-4031
www.acp-international.com

Association of Contingency Planners (ACP)
Central Illinois (Bloomington) Chapter
PMB 104, 1701 E. Empire St., Suite 360
Bloomington, IL 61704
309-828-1313
www.acp-international.com

Association of Contingency Planners (ACP)
Greater Chicago Chapter
233 S. Wacker Dr., Suite 3530
Chicago, IL 60606
312-875-1069
www.acp-international.com

Association of Contingency Planners (ACP)
Oklahoma Chapter
1215 S Boulder Ave, P.O. Box 776
Tulsa, OK 74101-0776
918-835-0435
918-560-2137
www.acp-international.com

Association of Contingency Planners (ACP)
Liberty Valley (Philadelphia) Chapter
3925 Dartmouth Lane
Bethlehem, PA 18020
610-867-9839
www.acp-international.com

Association of Contingency Planners (ACP)
Sioux Empire (South Dakota) Chapter
P.O. Box 884
Sioux Falls, SD 57101-0884
605-782-5020
www.acp-international.com

Association of Contingency Planners (ACP)
Middle Tennessee (Nashville) Chapter
P.O. Box 198050
Nashville, TN 37219-8050
615-401-2275
www.acp-international.com

Association of Contingency Planners (ACP)
North Texas (Dallas) Chapter
P.O. Box 167751
Irving, TX 75016
214-820-0899
www.acp-international.com

Association of Contingency Planners (ACP)
P.O. Box 13371
Austin, TX 78711-3371
512-473-4072
www.acp-international.com

Association of Contingency Planners (ACP)
South Texas (Houston) Chapter
7710T Cherry Park, Suite 206
Houston, TX 77095
281-550-4995
www.acp-international.com

Association of Contingency Planners (ACP)
Utah Chapter
P.O. Box 11434
Salt Lake City, UT 84147-1434
801-902-4508
www.acp-international.com

Association of Contingency Planners (ACP)
Washington D.C. Mid-Atlantic Chapter
P.O. Box 17402
Arlington, VA 22216
301-931-2050
www.acp-international.com

Association of Contingency Planners (ACP)
Washington State Chapter
P.O. Box 2346
Redmond, WA 98073-2346
425-580-8095
www.acp-international.com

Association of Contingency Planners; LA Chapter
2087 Channelford Road
Westlake Village, CA 91361-3508
805-332-5400
www.acp-international.com/la

Association of State Floodplain Managers (ASFPM)
2809 Fish Hatchery Road
Madison, WI 53713
608-274-0123
www.floods.org/home/

Business Continuity Planners Association
P.O. Box 75930
St. Paul, MN 55175-0930
651-223-9801
www.bcpa.org

Business Disaster Preparedness Council, The
Lee County Emergency Mgmnt.
P.O. BOX 398
Ft. Myers, FL 33902-0398
941-477-3600
www.leegov.com

Business Network of Emergency Resources, Inc.
551 Fifth Ave
Suite 3025
New York, NY 10176
888-353-BNET
212-599-1599
www.bnetinc.org/home.html

Business Recovery Managers Association
P.O. Box 2184
San Francisco, CA 94126-2184
925-355-8660
www.BRMA.com

Business Recovery Planners Assoc of WI
5910 Mineral Point Road
Madison, WI 53705-4456
608-231-7502

Business Recovery Planners Association of SE WI
1957 S 81st Street
West Allis, WI 53219-1011
414-543-8100

ASSOCIATIONS

Canadian Centre for Emergency Preparedness
860 Harrington Ct
Burlington, ON L7N 3N4
Canada
905-331-2552
www.CCEP.CA

Canadian Emergency Preparedness Association
6715 Henry Street
Chilliwack, BC V2R 2C2
Canada
604-858-7092
www.cepa-acpc.ca

Catholic Relief Services
209 West Fayette St
Baltimore, MD 21201-3443
410-625-2220
800-736-3467

Center for Domestic Preparedness
P.O. Box 5100
Anniston, AL 36205-5100
256-847-2225
866-213-9551
cdp.dhs.gov

Centre for Emergency Preparedness and Response
860 Harrington Court
Burlington, ON L7N SN4
Canada
905-331-2552
www.ccep.ca

Church World Service Emergency Response Program
475 Riverside Drive
Suite 700
New York, NY 10115
212-870-3151

Contingency Planners of Ohio
P.O. Box 340825
Columbus, OH 43234-0825
614-249-9339
614-331-8417
www.CPOHIO.org

Contingency Planning Association of the Carolinas
P.O. Box 32492
Charlotte, NC 28232-2492
704-906-1158
www.CPACCAROLINAS.org

Contingency Planning Exchange
11 Hanover Square
Suite 501
New York, NY 10005
212-344-4003
www.CPEWORLD.org

Disaster Forum Association
11215 Jasper Avenue
Suite 437
Edmonton, AB T5K 0L5
Canada
780-424-8742

Disaster Recovery Info Exchange-Ottawa
P.O. Box 20518
390 Rideau Street
Ottawa, ON K1N 1A3
Canada
613-238-2909
www.drieottawa.org

Disaster Recovery Info. Exchange (DRIE-SWO)
P.O. Box 27035
Kitchener, ON N2M 5P2
Canada
519-895-1213
www.drie-swo.org/

Disaster Recovery Information Exchange (DRIE)
157 Adelaide St. W
P.O. Box 247
Toronto, ON M5H 4E7
Canada
647-299-9743
www.DRIE.org

Disaster Recovery Information Exchange (West)
P.O. BOX 1557 Station M
Calgary, AB T2P 3B9
Canada
403-543-4695
www.DRIE.org/west/

Disaster Recovery Institute
2175 Sheppard Avenue East
Suite 310
Toronto, ON M2J 1W8
Canada
416-491-5335
888-728-3742
www.dri.ca

DR Information E-Change Group
CVS Pharmacy, Inc.
1 CVS Drive #1
Woonsocket, RI 02895
401-765-1500

DRI International
201 Park Washington Court
Falls Church, VA 22046-4527
703-538-1792
www.DRII.org

Electric Power Research Institute (EPRI)
3412 Hillview Avenue
Palo Alto, CA 94304-1395
650-855-2000
www.EPRI.com

Emergency Management Association of Texas
P.O. Box 424
Richmond, TX 78611
512-473-4072

Erie County Emergency Services
95 Franklin Street
Room 270
Buffalo, NY 14202
716-858-8477
www.erie.gov

Florida Emerg. Prep. Assn.
3015 Shannon Lakes North
Tallahassee, FL 32309
850-906-0779

Great Lakes Business Recovery Group
1647 Dancer Drive
Suite 102
Rochester Hls, MI 48307-3312
248-650-9900

Great Plains Contingency Planners
P.O. Box 33
Omaha, NE 68101-0033
402-633-1192
www.greatplainscontingencyplanners.com

Health Canada, Centre for Emergency Preparedness and Response
100 Colonnade Road, PL6201A
Ottawa, ON K1A 0K9
Canada
613-954-8498
http://www.phac-aspc.gc.ca/new_e.html

Humane Society of the United States, The
700 Professional Drive
Gaithersburg, MD 20879
301-258-3103

International Assn of Emergency Managers (IAEM)
201 Park Washington Court
Falls Church, VA 22046-4527
703-538-1795
www.IAEM.com

International Association of Fire Chiefs
4025 Fair Ridge Drive
ste 300
Fairfax, VA 22033-2868
703-273-0911
www.IAFC.org

Iowa Contingency Planners
P.O. Box 249
Des Moines, IA 50301
515-246-7059
www.iowacontingencyplanners.org

ISA International Society of Arborculture
P.O. Box 3129
champaign, IL 61826-3129
217-355-9411
www.isa-arbor.com

Kentuckiana Contingency Planner's Users's Group
Jefferson County School System
Louisville, KY 40233
502-485-3948

Mid-America Contingency Planning Forum
P.O. Box 38112
St. Louis, MO 63138
314-466-3509
www.brookstech.net/mcpf/index.html

Mid-Atlantic Disaster Recovery Assoc., Inc., MADRA
4500 Paint Branch Parkway
College Park, MD 20743
301-226-9900
703-456-5744
www.madra.org

Mid-Island Emergency Coordinators and Managers
#210 - 660 Primrose Street
Qualicum Beach, BC V9K 1S7
Canada
250-752-6921
www.qualicumbeach.com

Midwest Contingency Planners
P.O. Box 1632
Indianapolis, IN 46206-1632
765-778-8758

National Defense Industrial Association
2111 Wilson Boulevard
Suite 400
Arlington, VA 22201-3061
703-522-1820
www.NDIA.org

National Emergency Management Association (NEMA)
P.O. Box 11910
Lexington, KY 40578
859-244-8000
www.nemaweb.org

National Fire Protection Agency (NFPA)
1 Batterymarch Park
Quincy, MA 02169-7471
617-770-3000
800-344-3555
www.NFPA.org/catalog/home/index.asp

National Funeral Directors Assn.
13625 Bishops Drive
Brookfield, WI 53005
800-228-6332
262-789-1880
www.NFDA.org

NEDRIX - New England Disaster Recovery Information Exchange
P.O. Box 52120
Boston, MA 02205
781-485-0279
www.NEDRIX.com

Northeast Florida Association of Contingency Planners
P.O. Box 23556
Jacksonville, FL 32256
904-281-3271
www.ACP-INTERNATIONAL.com/neflorida

ASSOCIATIONS

Northeast States Emergency Consortium
1 West Water Street
Suite 205
Wakefield, MA 01880-1301
781-224-9876
www.NESEC.org

Ontario Association of Emergency Managers
P.O. Box 67043
2150 Burnhamthorpe Road W.
Mississauga, ON L5L 5V4
Canada
www.oaem.ca

Ontario Funeral Service Association (OFSA)
300 North Queen St
Suite 205N
Etobicoke, ON M9C 5K4
Canada
416 695 3434
800 268 2727
www.ofsa.org

Partnership for Emergency Planning
c/o Sprint MS:KSOPHM0106-1B402
6480 Sprint Parkway- Truman C
Overland Park, KS 66251
913-315-8224
www.PEPKC.org

PSEG
80 Park Plaza L1a
Newark, NJ 07102
973-430-6725
www.pseg.com

Puerto Rico Info Security Emergency Mgmt Assoc.
John Robles adn Associates
P.O. Box 29715
San Juan, PR 00929-0715
787-768-1115
787-647-3961

Responder Knowledge Base
5765-F Burke Centre Parkway
PMB 331
Burke, VA 22015
703-641-3731
www.rkb.mipt.org

Society of Fire Protection Engineers
7315 Wisconsin Ave.
Suite 620 E
Bethesda, MD 20814
301-718-2910
www.SFPE.org

The American Civil Defense Assn. (TACDA)
P.O. Box 1057
Starke, FL 32091-1057
904-964-5397
800-425-5397
www.TACDA.org

The Center for Biosecurity of UPMC
The Pier IV Building
621 E. Pratt Street, Suite 210
Baltimore, MD 21202
443-573-3304

www.upmc-biosecurity.org

The Infrastructure Security Partnership (TISP)
1801 Alexander Bell Drive
Reston, VA 20191
703-295-6231
http://www.tisp.org

Three Rivers Contingency Planning Association
620 Liberty Avenue
Pittsburgh, PA 15222-2722
412-762-2614

Tree Care Industry Association
3 Perimeter Rd
Unit 1
Manchester, NH 03031
603-314-5380
800-733-2622
www.TCIA.org

Equipment rental associations

American Academy of Sanitarians
720 South Colorado Blvd
Suite 960-S
Denver, CO 80246
678-584-9127
www.sanitarians.org

California Rental Association
4640 Northgate Blvd. Suite 160
P.O. Box 348420
Sacremento, CA 95834
800-272-7400
916-922-4222
www.craonthenet.org

Portable Sanitation Association International
7800 Metro Parkway
Suite 104
Bloomington, MN 55425
952-854-8300
800-822-3020
www.psai.org

Facility management associations

Association for Facilities Engineering
8160 Corporate Park Drive
Suite 125
Cincinnati, OH 45242
513-489 2473
www.afe.org

**Building Owners & Managers
Association (BOMA)
1201 New York Avenue N.W.
Suite 300
Washington, DC 20005
202-408-2662
www.BOMA.org**

International Facility Management Association
1 E. Greenway Plaza
Suite 1100
Houston, TX 77046
713-623-4362
www.IFMA.org

Insurance associations

American Risk & Insurance Association
716 Providence Road
Malvern, PA 19355-3402
610-640-1997
www.ARIA.org

American Society of Appraisers
555 Herndon Parkway
Suite 125
Herndon, VA 20170
703-478-2228
www.APPRAISERS.org

Institute for Business and Home Safety
4775 E. Fowler Avenue
Tampa, FL 33617
813-286-3400
www.ibhs.org

Insurance Information Institute
110 William Street
New York, NY 10038
212-346-5500
www.iii.org

National Assn. of Public Insurance Adjusters
21165 Whaitfild Pl #105
Potomac Falls, VA 20165
703-433-9217
www.NAPIA.com

New York Public Adjusters Association
299 Broadway
New York, NY 10007
212-285-0510
www.NYPAA.com

Professional Insurance Agents Association
25 Chamberlain Street
Glenmont, NY 12077
800-424-4244
www.PIAONLINE.com

Property Loss Research Bureau (PLRB)
3025 Highland Parkway
Suite 800
Downers Grove, IL 60515-1291
888-711-PLRB
630-724-2200
www.PLRB.org

Quarles & Brady LLP
1395 Panther Lane
Suite 300
Naples, FL 34109-7874
239-262-5959
www.quarles.com

Wall Street Technology Association
241 Maple Ave
Red Bank, NJ 07701
732-530-8808
www.wsta.org

ASSOCIATIONS

Windstorm Insurance Network, Inc.
P.O. Box 30486
Pensacola, FL 32503
850-473-0601
www.windnetwork.com

Public information & awareness associations

American Association of Homeland Security Professionals
1717 K Street NW Suite 600
Washington, DC 20036
866-722-4774
http://www.aahsp.org

American Industrial Hygiene Assn
2700 Prosperity Avenue
Suite 250
Fairfax, VA 22031-4340
703-849-8888
www.AIHA.org

American Red Cross National Headquarters
2025 E Street, NW
Washington, DC 20006
202-303-4498
www.REDCROSS.org/services/disaster

Assoc. of State & Territorial Health Officials
1275 K Street N.W.
Suite 800
Washington, DC 20005-4006
202-371-9090
www.astho.org

Association of State Dam Safety Officials
450 Old Vine Street
2nd Floor
Lexington, KY 40507-1544
859-257-5140
www.DAMSAFETY.org

Atlantic Oceanographic and Meteorological Laboratory
4301 Rickenbacker Causeway
Miami, FL 33149
305-361-4450
www.aoml.noaa.gov

California Seismic Safety Commision, The
1755 Creekside Oaks Drive
Suite 100
Sacramento, CA 95833
916-263-5506
www.seismic.ca.gov

Canadian Environmental Auditing Association
1-6820 Kitimat Road
Mississauga, ON L5N 5M3
Canada
905-814-1160
www.ceaa-acve.ca

Caribbean Disaster Emergency Response Agency
Manor Lodge
Building #1
Lodge Hill, St. Michael
Barbados
246-425-0386
www.CDERA.org

Chemical Manufacturers Association
1300 Wilson Boulevard
Arlington, VA 22209-2323
703-741-5000

ComCARE Alliance
1701 K St. NW
12th Floor, Suite 400
Washington, DC 20006
202-429-0574

Congressional Hazards Caucus
4220 King St
Alexandria, VA 22302
703-379-2480
http://www.hazardscaucus.org

Disability Preparedness Center
1010 Wisconsin Avenue N.W.
Washington, DC 20007
202-338-7158

Earthquakes Canada (East)
Natural Resources Canada
7 Observatory Crescent
Ottawa, ON K1A 0Y3
Canada
613-995-5548 [en]
613-995-0600 [fr]
www.seismo.nrcan.gc.ca

Earthquakes Canada (West)
P.O. Box 6000
9860 West Saanich Road
Sidney, BC V8L 4B2
Canada
250-363-6500
www.pgc.nrcan.gc.ca

Electrical Safety Foundation International
1300 N. 17th Street
Arlington, VA 22209
703-841-3229
www.electrical-safety.org

Home Safety Council
1725 Eye Street, NW
Suite 300
Washington, DC 20006
202-349-1100
www.homesafetycouncil.org

Industrial Accident Prevention Association
207 Queens Quay West
Toronto, ON M5J 2Y3
Canada
416-506-8888
www.IAPA.ca

International Hurricane Protection Assciation World Office
2501 Floral Road
Lantana, Fl 33462
561-433-2101

Multihazard Mitigation Council of the National Institute of Building Science
1090 Vermont Avenue, NW
Suite 700
Washington, DC 20005-4905
202-289-7800
www.nibs.org/MMC/mmchome.html

National Association for Search and Rescue
P.O. Box 232020
Centreville, VA 20120-2020
877-893-0702
703-222-6277
www.nasar.org

National Association of County and City Health Officials
1100 17th Street, NW
Second Floor
Washington, DC 20036
202-783-5550
www.naccho.org

National Association of Environmental Professionals
P.O. Box 2086
Bowie, MD 20718
888-251-9902
301-860-1140
www.naep.org

National Association of Flood and Storm Water Management Agencies
1301 K Street, NW
Suite 800 East
Washington, DC 20005
202-218-4122
www.NAFSMA.org

National Drought Mitigation Center - University of Nebraska, Lincoln
239 L.W. Chase Hall
P.O. Box 830749
Lincoln, NE 68583-0749
402-472-6707
drought.unl.edu

National Safety Council
1121 Spring Lake Drive
Itasca, IL 60143-3201
800-621-7619
800-845-4672
www.NSC.org

National Voluntary Organizations Active in Disaster
P.O. Box 151973
Alexandria, VA 22315
703-339-5596
www.nvoad.org

Public Risk Management Association
500 Montgomery Street
Suite 750
Alexandria, VA 22314
703-528-7701
www.PRIMACENTRAL.org

Society of Fire Protection Engineers
7315 Wisconsin Ave.
Suite 620 E
Bethesda, MD 20814
301-718-2910
www.SFPE.org

Southern California Earthquake Center
University of Southern California
3651 Trousdale Parkway
Los Angeles, CA 90089
213-740-5843
www.scec.org

Texas Severe Storm Association
P.O. Box 122222
Arlington, TX 76012
www.tessa.org

The National Environmental Services Center
West Virginia University
P.O. Box 6064
Morgantown, WV 26506
800-624-8301

Records management associations

ARMA International
13725 W. 109th Street
Suite 101
Lenexa, KS 66215
913-341-3808
www.arma.org

Association for Information & Image Mgmt. (AIIM)
1100 Wayne Avenue
Suite 1100
Silver Spring, MD 20910-5616
301-587-8202
www.AIIM.org

Information Technology Association of America
1401 Wilson Boulevard
Suite 1100
Arlington, VA 22209-2318
703-522-5055
www.ITAA.org

PRISM International: Professional Records & Information Services Management
605 Benson Road #B
Garner, NC 27529-3905
800-336-9793
919-881-0677
www.PRISMINTL.org

Productivity Inc.
100 Commerce Drive
Shelton, CT 06484-6255
860-225-0451
800-966-5423
www.productivityinc.com

ASSOCIATIONS

ASSOCIATIONS

Society for Information Management
401 N Michigan Avenue
Chicago, IL 60611-4267
312-527-6734
www.SIMNET.org

Risk management associations

Canadian Society for Industrial Security Inc.
141 Bentley Avenue
Unit B
Ottawa, ON K2E 6T7
Canada
613-274-3022
800-461-7748
www.csis-scsi.org

Certified Risk Managers Intl.
Austin, TX 78755
800-633-2165
www.thenationalalliance.com

Global Disaster Information Network GDIN
26128 Talamore Drive, Suite 201
South Riding, VA 20152
202-647-5070
www.gdin.org

Institute of Hazardous Materials Management
11900 Parklawn Drive
Suite 450
Rockville, MD 20852-2676
301-984-8969
www.IHMM.org

International Association of Professional Security
525 SW 5th Street
Suite A
Des Moines, IA 50309-4501
515-282-8192
www.IAPSC.org

Ontario Environment Industry Association
2175 Sheppard Avenue East
Suite 310
Toronto, ON M2J 1W8
Canada
416-531-7884
www.ceia.on.ca

Public Entity Risk Institute
11350 Random Hills Road
Suite 210
Fairfax, VA 22030
703-352-1846
www.riskinstitute.org

Risk and Insurance Management Society(RIMS)
655 3rd Avenue
New York, NY 10017
212-286-9292
www.RIMS.org

Security Industry Association
635 Slaters Lane
Suite 110
Alexandria, VA 22314
703-683-2075
866-817-8888
www.siaonline.org

Society for Risk Analysis
1313 Dolley Madison Boulevard
Suite 402
McLean, VA 22101
703-790-1745
www.sra.org

Society of Risk Management Consultants
P.O. Box 510228
Milwaukee, WI 53203
800-765-7762
www.srmcsociety.org

Terrorist Incident Response Association
234 West Dixie Avenue
Marietta, GA 30060
678-640-9743
www.tiraonline.org

The National Burglar & Fire Alarm Association
8380 Colesville Road
Suite 750
Silver Spring, MD 20910
301-585-1855
www.alarm.org

The Risk Management Association
One Liberty Place
1650 Market Street, Suite 2300
Philadelphia, PA 19103
215-446-4000
www.rmahq.org

Safety associations

Academy of Certified Hazardous Materials Managers, Inc.
P.O. Box 1216
Rockville, MD 20849
800-437-0137
301-916-3306
www.achmm.org

International Safety Equipment Association
1901 North Moore Street
Arlington, VA 22209
703-525-1695
www.safetyequipment.org

Spill Control Association of America
32500 Scenic Lane
Franklin, MI 48025
248-851-1936
313-849-2333
http://www.scaa-spill.org

The National Environmental, Safety & Health Training Association - NESHTA
2720 E Thomas Road
Suite 253C
Phoenix, AZ 85016
602-956-6099
http://neshta.org

Trauma/counselor associations

American Academy of Experts in Traumatic Stress
368 Veterans Memorial Highway
Commack, NY 11725-4322
631-543-2217
www.AAETS.org

American Psychological Association
750 First Street N.E.
Washington, DC 20002-4242
800-374-2721
www.APA.org

American Trauma Society
8903 Presidential Parkway
Upper Marlboro, MD 20772
301-420-4189
www.AMTRAUMA.org

ASSOCIATIONS

ASSOCIATIONS

ASSOCIATIONS

BACKUP SITES & SERVICES

Restores from tape take time and are often unreliable.

What's worse is that you won't know if a tape set is blank, corrupted or incomplete until you restore.

At that point, it is too late!

ExaGrid's Intelligent Data Protection is an online system that offers a complete primary and second site disaster recovery solution for the same or less than the monthly cost of your current tape solution. ExaGrid can be used to protect: files, email and databases from existing backup applications; archive files from email archive applications; and mission critical files stored directly on ExaGrid for hourly protection.

True online data protection without the limitations of tape.

- ☐ Restore data quickly
- ☐ Restore data that is accurate and reliable
- ☐ Protect mission critical files hourly
- ☐ Enable online data disaster recovery
- ☐ Improve data protection management
- ☐ Eliminate backup window restrictions
- ☐ Improve data security
- ☐ Enhance regulatory compliance and discovery

ExaGrid's Intelligent Data Protection
Can Work for You!

800.868.6985

www.exagrid.com/dr

exagrid.com

BACKUP SITES & SERVICES

Restores from tape take time and are often unreliable.

What's worse is that you won't know if a tape set is blank, corrupted or incomplete until you restore.

At that point, it is too late!

ExaGrid's Intelligent Data Protection is an online system that offers a complete primary and second site disaster recovery solution for the same or less than the monthly cost of your current tape solution. ExaGrid can be used to protect: files, email and databases from existing backup applications; archive files from email archive applications; and mission critical files stored directly on ExaGrid for hourly protection.

True online data protection without the limitations of tape.

☐ Restore data quickly

☐ Restore data that is accurate and reliable

☐ Protect mission critical files hourly

☐ Enable online data disaster recovery

☐ Improve data protection management

☐ Eliminate backup window restrictions

☐ Improve data security

☐ Enhance regulatory compliance and discovery

ExaGrid's Intelligent Data Protection
Can Work for You!

800.868.6985

www.exagrid.com/dr

exagrid.com

BACKUP SITES & SERVICES

Check processing, bank: all vendors

Boston Financial Data Services
2 Heritage Drive
North Quincy, MA 02171
617-483-5000
888-772-2337
www.BOSTONFINANCIAL.com

DRS, Disaster Recovery Services, Inc.
P.O. Box 12293
Charlotte, NC 28220
704-525-0096
www.drs.net

United Recovery Services Co.
100 Dobbs Lane
Cherry Hill, NJ 08034
856-427-5700
www.UCC-URS.com

Coldsite services

Affiliated Warehouses Companies, Inc.
P.O. Box 295
Hazlet, NJ 07730-0295
732-739-2323
www.AWCL.com

bigbyte.cc
123 Central Ave SW
Albuquerque, NM 87012
505-255-5422
www.bigbyte.cc

E.V. Bushoff Company
33 N. Third Street
Suite 500
Columbus, OH 43215
814-221-4736
www.evbco.com

ICS Logistics
2625 W 5th Street
Jacksonville, FL 32254-2066
904-786-8038
904-693-2914
www.ICSLOGISTICS.com

Data center-outsourced continuity & colocation space

**Alicomp
2 Christie Heights
Leonia, NJ 07605
800-274-5556
www.alicomp.com**

bigbyte.cc
123 Central Ave SW
Albuquerque, NM 87012
505-255-5422
www.bigbyte.cc

**Cervalis
1200 Bedford Street
Stamford, CT 06905
866-602-2020
203-602-2044
www.CERVALIS.com**

Collocation Solutions
1950 N Stemmons Freeway
Suite 2033
Dallas, TX 75207-3139
214-231-0162
www.COLLOCATIONSOLUTIONS.com

CompuCom Systems
7171 Forest Lane
Dallas, TX 75230
972-856-3600
www.compucom.com

**Consonus AllWaysOn Data Centers
180 East 100 South
Questar Building
Salt Lake City, UT 84111
888-452-8000
www.consonus.com**

Data393
393 Inverness Parkway
Englewood, CO 80112-5816
303 268-1470
www.data393.com

eGlobalReach, Inc
22 Grasshopper Lane
Acton, MA 01720
978-635-9542
www.eglobalreach.com

FiberMedia Headquarters
2410 Hollywood Boulevard
Hollywood, FL 33020
954-367-0416
www.fibermedia.net

GenTech
5225 Exchange Drive
Flint, MI 48507
810-244-7777
www.gentechmi.com

GoldenGate Software, Inc.
301 Howard Street
Suite 2100
San Francisco, CA 94105
415-777-0200
www.goldengate.com

GramTel USA
316 E Monroe
South Bend, IN 46601
574-472-4726
www.gramtel.net

Herakles, LLC
1100 North Market Blvd.
Sacramento, CA 95834
916-679-2100
www.heraklesdata.com

Infocrossing Inc.
2 Christie Heights
Leonia, NJ 07605-2233
866-779-4369
201 840-4754
www.INFOCROSSING.com

Klein Enterprises Inc
6819 Academy Parkway W NE
Albuquerque, NM 87109
505-344-3960

NCR Business Continuity Solutions
1611 S Main Street
Dayton, OH 45479
800-587-0911
www.NCR.com/services/mgmt_ops_bus.htm

Offsite, LLC
3618 8th Ave
Kenosha, WI 53140
312-off-site
312-633-7483
www.off-site.com

Peak 10
8910 Lenox Pointe Drive
Suite A
Charlotte, NC 28273-3432
866-473-2510
www.peak10.com

SECTOR, Inc.
90 Broad Street
New York, NY 10004
866-383-3315
www.sectorinc.com

Security Center, The
147 Carondelet Street
New Orleans, LA 70130
504-522-1254

Sentinel Data Centers
128 First Avenue
Needham, MA 02494
781-444-4348
www.sentineldatacenters.com

TELEHOUSE America
The Teleport
7 Teleport Drive
Staten Island, NY 10311
718-355-2572
718-355-2525
www.telehouse.com

USG Recovery Services
7831 East Bush Lake Road
Suite 100
Edina, MN 55439
612-874-6500
www.usgrecoverycenter.com

VeriCenter Inc.
757 N Eldridge Parkway
Suite 200
Houston, TX 77079
281-584-4500
www.VERICENTER.com

VLEC Communications Inc.
910 15th Street, Suite 857
Denver, CO 80202
303-530-0206
http://www.vlecom.com

Xand Corporation
11 Skyline Drive
Hawthorne, NY 10532
914-592-8282
www.xand.com

Data General: backup sites & services

Computer Engineering Associates
8227 Cloverleaf Drive Suite 308
Millersville, MD 21108
410-987-7003
www.CEANEWS.com

NPA Computers
751 Coates Avenue
Holbrook, NY 11741
631-467-2500
www.npacomputers.com

River Bend Business Continuity
One Omega Drive
Stamford, CT 06907
203-978-7444
www.riverbend1.com

BACKUP SITES & SERVICES

Data hosting: managed services

Alicomp
2 Christie Heights
Leonia, NJ 07605
800-274-5556
www.alicomp.com

Allstream ITS
370 King Street West, Suite 450
Toronto, ON M5V 1J9
Canada
416-591-7220
613-795-8501
www.allstream.com

Business Recovery Center, Inc.
1259 Route 46 East
Building #1
Parsippany, NJ 07054
973-299-0302
www.businessrecoverycenter.com

Consonus AllWaysOn Data Centers
180 East 100 South
Questar Building
Salt Lake City, UT 84111
888-452-8000
888-311-2600
www.consonus.com

DBSi
3949 Schelden Circle
Bethlehem, PA 18017
610-691-8811
www.dbsintl.com

Fusepoint Managed Services
6800 Millcreek Dr
Mississauga, ON L5N4J9
Canada
905-363-3737
905-363-3796
www.fusepoint.com

Net Telcos, Inc.
4551 Cox Road
Suite 100
Glen Allen, VA 23060
804-270-6063
888-328-2286
www.nettelcos.com

Peak 10
8910 Lenox Pointe Drive
Suite A
Charlotte, NC 28273-3432
866-473-2510
866-4-PEAK10
www.PEAK10.com

SECTOR, Inc.
90 Broad Street
New York, NY 10004
866-383-3315
www.sectorinc.com

VeriCenter Inc.
757 N Eldridge Parkway
Suite 200
Houston, TX 77079
281-584-4500
www.VERICENTER.com

DEC: backup sites & services

Digital Equipment Corp
200 Forest Street
Marlborough, MA 01752
508-467-5111
www.COMPAQ.com

IBM Global Services
10 North Martingale Road
Woodfield Prese
Schaumburg, IL 60173
1-800-IBM-7080
www.ibm.com

BACKUP SITES
& SERVICES

Hewlett-Packard: backup sites & services

Construction Data Service Inc
4989 Santa Anita Avenue
Temple City, CA 91780
626-401-0039
www.CONSTDATA.com

Hewlett-Packard Co
14475 NE 24th Street
Bellevue, WA 98007
425-643-4000

**IBM Canada Ltd.
3500 Steeles Avenue, East
Markham, ON
Canada
905-316-2067**

**IBM Global Services
10 North Martingale Road
Woodfield Prese
Schaumburg, IL 60173
1-800-IBM-7080
www.ibm.com**

SunGard Availability Services
680 E Swedesford Road
Wayne, PA 19087
800-468-7483
800-523-4970
www.availability.sungard.com

Hotsites/warmsites: control data

BlueBridge Networks, LLC
1255 Euclid Avenue
Suite 500
Cleveland, OH 44115
216-621-BLUE
866-990-BLUE
http://www.bluebridgenetworks.com

**River Bend Business Continuity
One Omega Drive
Stamford, CT 06907
203-978-7444**

Titan #1,LLC
4949 Randolph Road NE
Moses Lake, WA 98837
509-762-1332

VeriCenter, Inc.
757 N. Eldridge Pkwy.
Suite 200
Houston, TX 77079
281-584-4500
866-411-8287
http://www.vericenter.com

IBM large systems: backup sites & services

**Alicomp
2 Christie Heights
Leonia, NJ 07605
800-274-5556
www.alicomp.com**

Contemporary Computer Services
200 Knickerbocker Avenue
Bohemia, NY 11716
631-563-8880
www.ccsinet.com

**IBM Canada Ltd.
3500 Steeles Avenue, East
Markham, ON
Canada
905-316-2067**

**IBM Global Services
10 North Martingale Road
Woodfield Prese
Schaumburg, IL 60173
1-800-IBM-7080
www.ibm.com**

BACKUP SITES & SERVICES

BACKUP SITES & SERVICES

Recovery Room Inc.
323 Lake Hazeltine Drive
Chaska, MN 55318
952-361-9355
888-361-9355
www.RECOVERYROOM.com

SunGard Availability Services
680 E Swedesford Road
Wayne, PA 19087
800-468-7483
800-523-4970
www.availability.sungard.com

IBM midrange (System/3x, AS400, etc.): backup sites & services

Application Design Services, Inc.
250 A Centerville Road
Warwick, RI 02886
401-737-2040
866-423-7400
www.adsapps.com

Comlanta
2 Sun Court
Norcross, GA 30092
770-449-6116
800-649-9726
www.COMLANTA.com

IBM Canada Ltd.
3500 Steeles Avenue, East
Markham, ON
Canada
905-316-2067

IBM Canada Ltd.
SERTI - 7555 Ville d'Anjou
Montreal, Quebec H2J 2S5
Canada
905-316-2067

IBM Global Services
10 North Martingale Road
Woodfield Prese
Schaumburg, IL 60173
1-800-IBM-7080
www.ibm.com

SECTOR, Inc.
90 Broad Street
New York, NY 10004
866-383-3315
www.sectorinc.com

SunGard Availability Services
680 E Swedesford Road
Wayne, PA 19087
800-468-7483
800-523-4970
www.availability.sungard.com

Synergistic Online Solutions
6650 Highland Road Suite 219
Waterford, MI 48327
248-666-4590
888-349-2982
http://www.synergisticonline.com

IBM RS-6000: backup sites & services

IBM Canada Ltd.
3500 Steeles Avenue, East
Markham, ON
Canada
905-316-2067

IBM Global Services
10 North Martingale Road
Woodfield Prese
Schaumburg, IL 60173
1-800-IBM-7080
www.ibm.com

Symitar Systems Inc
404 Camino Del Rio S
San Diego, CA 92108
619-542-6700
888-796-4827
www.SYMITAR.com

Multi-vendor hotsites

E. V. Bishoff Company
33 N. Third Street
Suite 500
Columbus, OH 43215
614-221-4736
www.evbco.com

Sentinel Data Centers
128 First Avenue
Needham, MA 02494
781-444-4348
www.sentineldatacenters.com

Networks & PCs: backup sites & services

AccessIT
55 Madison Avenue
Morristown, NJ 07960
973-290-0093
www.ACCESSITX.com

BRM Disaster Recovery Services Inc
1018 Western Avenue
Pittsburgh, PA 15233-2024
412-249-1200
www.businessrecords.com

CAPS Business Recovery Services
2 Enterprise Drive
Suite 200
Shelton, CT 06484
800-542-2773
www.CAPSBRS.com

Continuity Centers
1000 Woodbury Road
Woodbury, NY 11797
516-622-0200
516-704-0021
www.CONTINUITYCENTERS.com

Hitachi Data Systems
750 Central Expressway
Santa Clara, CA 95050
800-227-1930
www.hds.com

IBM Global Services
10 North Martingale Road
Woodfield Prese
Schaumburg, IL 60173
1-800-IBM-7080
www.ibm.com

MCI
1 Digex Plaza
Beltsville, MD 20705
240-264-2000
www.DIGEX.com

MDY Advanced Technologies Inc.
21-00 State Route 208
Fair Lawn, NJ 07410
201-797-6676
www.MDY.com

Safecore Inc.
1 Cabot Road
Medford, MA 02155
781-391-1700
www.safecore.com

Services Conseils
6555 Metropolitan E Blvd
Montreal, PQ H1P 3H3
Canada
514-955-0213
www.rdiinc.com

STS Business Services Inc
241 Main Street
Hartford, CT 06106
800-541-4964

SunGard Availability Services
680 E Swedesford Road
Wayne, PA 19087
800-468-7483
800-523-4970
www.availability.sungard.com

Vanguard Vaults
8151 Fruitridge Road
Sacramento, CA 95865
916-686-8286
888-582-8587
www.VANGUARDVAULTS.com

Office/voice recovery sites

Boston Financial Data Services
2 Heritage Drive
North Quincy, MA 02171
617-483-5000
888-772-2337
www.BOSTONFINANCIAL.com

CAPS Business Recovery Services
2 Enterprise Drive
Suite 200
Shelton, CT 06484
800-542-2773
www.CAPSBRS.com

Cervalis
1200 Bedford Street
Stamford, CT 06905
866-602-2020
203-602-2044
www.CERVALIS.com

IBM Canada Ltd.
227 11th Avenue, SW
Calgary, Alberta T2P 4B4
Canada
905-316-2067

IBM Canada Ltd.
1382 Spruce Street
Winnipeg, Manitoba R3E 2V7
Canada
905-316-2067

IBM Canada Ltd.
3600 Steeles Avenue, East
Markham, ON L3R 927
Canada
905-316-2067

IBM Canada Ltd.
SERTI - 7555 Ville d'Anjou
Montreal, Quebec H2J 2S5
Canada
905-316-2067

IBM Global Services
10 North Martingale Road
Woodfield Prese
Schaumburg, IL 60173
1-800-IBM-7080
www.ibm.com

Offsite, LLC
3618 8th Ave
Kenosha, WI 53140
312-off-site
312-633-7483
www.off-site.com

River Bend Business Continuity
One Omega Drive
Stamford, CT 06907
203-978-7444

Telax Voice Solutions
701 Evans Ave.,
Suite 703
Toronto, ON M9C1A3
Canada
416-207-9936
www.telax.com

Online data disaster recovery systems

Exagrid Systems
2000 West Park Drive
Wesboro, MA 01581
508-898-2872
www.exagrid.com

Servers, general: backup sites & services

Cervalis
1200 Bedford Street
Stamford, CT 06905
866-602-2020
203-602-2044
www.CERVALIS.com

GenTech
5225 Exchange Drive
Flint, MI 48507
810-244-7777
www.gentechmi.com

Sun: backup sites & services

Dynamic Systems, Inc.
5261 W. Imperial Hwy.
Los Angeles, CA 90045
877-DSI-2-BUY
310-337-4400
www.dynasys.com

IBM Canada Ltd.
3500 Steeles Avenue, East
Markham, ON
Canada
905-316-2067

IBM Global Services
10 North Martingale Road
Woodfield Prese
Schaumburg, IL 60173
1-800-IBM-7080
www.ibm.com

BACKUP SITES
& SERVICES

Tandem: backup sites & services

**IBM Global Services
10 North Martingale Road
Woodfield Prese
Schaumburg, IL 60173
1-800-IBM-7080
www.ibm.com**

Telecommunications, misc.: backup sites & services

**IBM Canada Ltd.
3500 Steeles Avenue, East
Markham, ON
Canada
905-316-2067**

Neon Communications, Inc.
2200 West Park Drive
Westborough, MA 01581
800-891-5080
508-616-7800
www.NEONINC.com

River Bend Business Continuity
One Omega Drive
Stamford, CT 06907
203-978-7444

SDN Global
P.O. Box 7787
Charlotte, NC 28241
704-587-4868
704-588-2233
www.sdnglobal.com

Tele-Serve
409 Main Street
Eau Claire, WI 54701
800-428-8159
715-834-3442
www.tele-serve.net

Teloquent Communications Corporation
4 Federal Street
Billerica, MA 01821
800-468-6434
www.TELOQUENT.com

WinStar Communications
2350 Corporate Park Drive
Herndon, VA 20171
877-WIN-4GSA
www.WINSTAR.com

Unisys: backup sites & services

FirstMerit Corporation
6625 W Snowville Road
Brecksville, OH 44141
440-838-4044
www.FMDRS.com

**IBM Global Services
10 North Martingale Road
Woodfield Prese
Schaumburg, IL 60173
1-800-IBM-7080
www.ibm.com**

Open Solutions
3098 Piedmont Road NE
Suite 200
Atlanta, GA 30305
404-262-2298
800-275-4374
www.OPENSOLUTIONS.com

Voice recovery services

GemaTech
10981 San Diego Mission Rd
Suite 210
S, CA 92108
619 283 3765
www.gematech.com

Taction
251 Jefferson Street
Waldoboro, ME 04572
207-832-0800
800-258-4100
www.taction.net

**Teltone Corporation
P.O. Box 945
Bothell, WA 98041
800-426-3926
425-487-1515
www.teltone.com**

COMMUNICATIONS SYSTEMS

COMMUNICATIONS SYSTEMS, Software & Equipment

Command-center equipment

American LaFrance Corporation
8500 Palmetto Commerce Parkway
Ladson, SC 29456
888-253-8725
843-486-7400
www.americanlafrance.com

Communications-Applied Technology
11250-14 Roger Bacon Dr.
Reston, VA 20190-5202
800-229-3925
www.c-at.com

Diversified Telecom Solutions-DTS
612 Antelope Trail
Temple, TX 76504
254-760-7710
http://www.dtstx.com

LDV Inc.
180 Industrial Drive
Burlington, WI 53105
800-558-5986
www.ldvusa.com

The Winsted Corporation
10901 Hampshire Avenue South
Minneapolis, MN 55438
800-447-2257
952-944-9050
www.WINSTED.com

Wright Line LLC
160 Gold Star Blvd.
Worcester, MA 01606
800-225-7348
508-852-4300
www.wrightline.com

Zetron Inc.
12034 134th Ct NE
Redmond, WA 98052
425-820-6363
www.zetron.com

Computer channel extension equipment

CNT
P.O. Box 440
Lumberton, NJ 08048
609-518-4000
800-222-5482
www.cnt.com

Consulting services: telecomunications

BWT Associates
P.O. Box #4515
Shrewsbury, MA 01545
508-845-6000
www.bwt.com

CapRock Communications
4400 S Sam Houston Parkway E
Houston, TX 77048
832-668-2300
888-482-0289
www.caprock.com

Federal Engineering Inc.
10600 Arrowhead Drive
Fairfax, VA 22030
703-359-8200
www.FEDENG.com

Homisco Inc
99 Washington Street
Melrose, MA 02176
781-665-1997
www.HOMISCO.com

Koxlien Group The
800 Wisconsin Street
Unit 103
Eau Claire, WI 54703
715-831-5581
www.KOXLIEN.com

PanAmSat Corporation
20 Westport Road
Wilton, CT 06897
203-210-8000
http://www.panamsat.com

SECTOR, Inc.
90 Broad Street
New York, NY 10004
866-383-3315
www.sectorinc.com

Dispatch software

Intergraph Public Safety
241 Business Park Blvd.
Madison, AL 35758
256-730-8911
877-818-4170
www.publicsafety.intergraph.com

Streem Communications
4201 Galleria Drive
Loves Park, IL 61111
800-325-7732
815-639-1100
www.streemalert.com

Email backup systems

MessageOne Inc.
11044 Research Boulevard
Building C - Fifth Floor
Austin, TX 78759-5328
512-652-4500
888-367-0777
www.MESSAGEONE.com

TriAxis Inc.
23 Midstate Drive
Suite 106
Auburn, MA 01501
508-721-9691
www.triaxisinc.com

Emergency notification software

Advanced Continuity
5909 Flynnsbrooke Terrace
Haymarket, VA 20169
800-299-5235
www.advcontinuity.com

Alpha Communications
42 Central Dr.
Farmingdale, NY 11735
631-777-5500
secure.alpha-comm.com

Amcom Software Inc
5555 W 78th Street
Minneapolis, MN 55439-2702
952-829-7445
800-852-8935
www.AMCOMSOFT.com

Amtelco
4800 Curtin Dr.
McFarland, WI 53558
800-356-9148
608-838-4194
www.amtelco.com

AudienceCentral
1319 Cornwall Ave
Bellingham, WA 98225
360-756-9090
360-920-5105
http://www.audiencecentral.com

Dialogic Communications Corp
730 Cool Springs Boulevard
Suite 300
Franklin, TN 37067
615-790-2882
800-723-3207
www.DCCUSA.com

Enera Inc
1525 E 55 St.
Chicago, IL 60615
866-463-6372
773-955-4475
www.enera.com

EnvoyWorldWide Inc
100 Crosby Drive
Bedford, MA 01730-1438
781-482-2100
www.ENVOYWORLDWIDE.com

MadahCom, Inc.
540 Interstate Court
Sarasota, FL 34240
941-342-9022
http://www.madah.com

MessageOne Inc.
11044 Research Boulevard
Building C - Fifth Floor
Austin, TX 78759-5328
512-652-4500
888-367-0777
www.MESSAGEONE.com

MIR3
11455 El Camino Real
San Diego, CA 92130-2022
858-724-1200
www.MIR3.com

Net Synergistics LLC
Basking Ridge, NJ 07920
908-719-9873
http://www.alertearth.org

RecoveryPlanner
2 Enterprise Drive
Shelton, CT 06484
203-925-3950
866-925-3950
www.RECOVERYPLANNER.com

Reverse 911
6120 Parkdale Place
Indianapolis, IN 46254
800-247-2363
317-631-0907
www.reverse911.com

Send Word Now
224 West 30th Street
Suite 301
New York, NY 10001
800-388-4796
www.sendwordnow.com

Streem Communications
4201 Galleria Drive
Loves Park, IL 61111
800-325-7732
815-639-1100
www.streemalert.com

Emergency notification systems

Cornell Communications
7915 North 81st St.
Milwaukee, WI 53223-3830
414-351-4660
800-558-8957
www.cornell.com

Emergin, Inc
6400 Congress Ave
Suite 1050
Boca Raton, FL 33487
866-eme-rgin
561-361-6990
www.emergin.com

Enera Inc
1525 E 55 St.
Chicago, IL 60615
866-463-6372
773-955-4475
www.enera.com

MIR3
11455 Elcamino Real Suite 360
San Diego, CA 92130
858-724-1200
www.MIR3.com

Send Word Now
224 West 30th Street
Suite 301
New York, NY 10001
800-388-4796
www.sendwordnow.com

Streem Communications
4201 Galleria Drive
Loves Park, IL 61111
800-325-7732
815-639-1100
www.streemalert.com

Warning Systems, Inc.
6767 Old Madison Pike
Suite 110
Huntsville, AL 35806
256-880-8702
www.warningsystems.com

Fault-tolerant communications

CUBIX Corp
2800 Lockheed Way
Carson City, NV 89706
775-883-7611
www.CUBIX.com

Mobile communications centers

AllTech Communications
2830 Charles Page Blvd.
Tulsa, OK 74127
918-576-0000
www.goalltech.com

CapRock Communications
4400 S Sam Houston Parkway E
Houston, TX 77048
832-668-2300
888-482-0289
www.caprock.com

Inmarsat, Inc.
1100 Wilson Blvd
Suite 1425
Arlington, VA 22209
703-647-4760
703-647-4778
www.inmarsat.com

NACS
North American Catastrophe Services, Inc.
864-B Washburn Rd.
Melbourne, FL 32934
888-595-6227
321-259-0888
www.nacs1.com

OnScreen Technologies Inc.
200 9th Avenue North, Suite 210
Safety Harbor, Fl 34695
727-797-6664
www.onscreentech.com

Mobile satellite communications

CapRock Communications
4400 S Sam Houston Parkway E
Houston, TX 77048
832-668-2300
888-482-0289
www.caprock.com

IBM Global Services
10 North Martingale Road
Woodfield Prese
Schaumburg, IL 60173
1-800-IBM-7080
www.ibm.com

Inmarsat, Inc.
1100 Wilson Blvd
Suite 1425
Arlington, VA 22209
703-647-4760
703-647-4778
www.inmarsat.com

COMMUNICATIONS SYSTEMS

Mobile Satellite Ventures
10802 Parkridge Blvd.
Reston, VA 20191
613-742-4168
www.msvlp.com

Rentsys Recovery Services
200 Quality Circle
College Station, TX 77845-4468
800-955-5171
www.RENTSYS.com

ViaSat, Inc.
On-The-Move & Portable Terminals
6155 El Camino Real
Carlsbad, CA 92009
760-476-4796
760-476-4738
www.viasat.com

Network monitoring equipment

Ameritec Corp
760 Arrow Grand Circle
Covina, CA 91722
626-915-5441
www.AMERITEC.com

Concord Communications Inc.
600 Nickerson Road
Marlborough, MA 01752
508-460-4646
800-851-8725
www.CONCORD.com

Fluke Corporation
P.O. Box 9090
Everett, WA 98206
425-347-6100
800-443-5853
www.fluke.com

Mindready Solutions Inc(HQ)
2800 Marie-Curie Ave
Saint-Laurent, QC H4S 2C2
Canada
514-339-1394
877-636-1394
www.MINDREADY.com

Phonetics Inc
901 Tryens Road
Aston, PA 19014-1597
610-558-2700
610-558-0222
www.SENSAPHONE.com

Network/communications equipment

Canvas Systems, Inc.
3025 Northwoods Parkway
Norcross, GA 30071
770-662-1881
http://www.canvassystems.com

IC Engineering, Inc.
P.O. Box 321
Owings Mills, MD 21117
410-363-8748
http://www.ICengineering.com

Patriot Antenna Systems
704 North Clark Street
Albion, MI 49224
800-470-3510
517-629-5990
www.sepatriot.com

Telecom Source, Inc.
387 Codell Dr.
Lexington, KY 40509
800-770-6183
859-422-2500
http://www.telecomsourceinc.com

The Adtran Store
35 Wilson Drive
Sparta, NJ 07871-3427
973-940-7351
866-423-8726
http://www.adtranstore.com

TriAxis Inc.
23 Midstate Drive
Suite 106
Auburn, MA 01501
508-721-9691
www.triaxisinc.com

U.S. Netcom Corp.
710 S Maiden Lane
Joplin, MO 64801
417-781-7000
800-835-7788
www.usnetcomcorp.com

Notification & dispatch services: phone, fax, etc.

Amcom Software Inc
5555 W 78th Street
Minneapolis, MN 55439-2702
952-829-7445
800-852-8935
www.AMCOMSOFT.com

Boomerang.com
2450 Embarcadero Way
Palo Alto, CA 94303
800-779-7792
www.BOOMERANG.com

COMMUNICATIONS SYSTEMS

Community Alert Network Inc.
255 Washington Avenue Extension
Suite 105
Albany, NY 12205-6000
800-992-2331
518-862-0987
www.CAN-INTL.com

**Dialogic Communications Corp
730 Cool Springs Boulevard
Suite 300
Franklin, TN 37067
615-790-2882
800-723-3207
www.DCCUSA.com**

**Digital Courier Systems
P.O. Box 20522
San Jose, CA 95160
877-WARNFAST
408-927-6327
www.criticalert.com**

**EnvoyWorldWide Inc
100 Crosby Drive
Bedford, MA 01730-1438
781-482-2100
www.ENVOYWORLDWIDE.com**

Global Link Communications Inc.
3448 Progress Drive
Suite A
Bensalem, PA 19020-5813
215-633-0300
800-494-5465
www.GLINKCOMM.net

Information Station Specialists(ISS)
Broadcast Systems
P.O. Box 51, 3368 88th Avenue
Zeeland, MI 49464-0051
616-772-2300
www.THERADIOSOURCE.com

**National Notification Network (3N)
505 North Brand Blvd
Suite 700
Glendale, CA 91203
818-230-9700
888-366-4911
www.3NONLINE.com**

Streem Communications
4201 Galleria Drive
Loves Park, IL 61111
800-325-7732
815-639-1100
www.streemalert.com

Strohl Systems
631 Park Avenue
Kng of Prussa, PA 19406
610-768-4120
800-634-2016
www.strohlsystems.com

**Teltone Corporation
P.O. Box 945
Bothell, WA 98041
800-426-3926
425-487-1515
www.teltone.com**

VERSO Technologies
400 Galleria Parkway SE
Atlanta, GA 30339
678-589-3500
www.verso.com

VoiceGate Corporation
550 Alden Road
Suite 112
Markham, ON L3R 6A8
Canada
800-668-2387
905-513-1403
www.VOICEGATECORP.com

Wallace Wireless
1576 Sweet Home Road
Amherst, NY 14228
716-583-1604
416-971-4310
www.WALLACEWIRELESS.com

Notification/dispatch systems

**Amtelco
4800 Curtin Dr.
McFarland, WI 53558
800-356-9148
608-838-4194
www.amtelco.com**

City Watch by AVTEX
5775 West Old Shakopee Road
Suite 160
Bloomington, MN 55437
952-831-0888
800-323-3639
www.avtex.com

Critical Situation Management Inc.
3 Bala Plaza
Suite 102E
Bala Cynwyd, PA 19004
610-617-9988
www.criticalsituationmanagement.com

Digital Courier Systems
P.O. Box 20522
San Jose, CA 95160
877-WARNFAST
408-927-6327
www.criticalert.com

Exacom, Inc.
99 Airport Road
Concord, NH 03301
603-228-0706
www.exacom.com

COMMUNICATIONS SYSTEMS

Intelligent Wireless Solutions
33635 Ansley Road
Magnolia, TX 77355
281-356-5689

Streem Communications
4201 Galleria Drive
Loves Park, IL 61111
800-325-7732
815-639-1100
www.streemalert.com

Teltone Corporation
P.O. Box 945
Bothell, WA 98041
800-426-3926
425-487-1515
www.teltone.com

Power on/off remote telephone control

Dataprobe
11 Park Place
Paramus, NJ 07652
201-967-9300
www.DATAPROBE.com

Gordon Kapes Inc
5520 W. Touhy Avenue
Skokie, IL 60077
847-676-1750
www.GKINC.com

Server Technology Inc
1040 Sandhill Dr.
Reno, NV 89521
408-988-0142
800-835-1515
www.servertech.com

Radios & walkie-talkies

Amerizon Wireless
3512 Cavalier Drive
Fort Wayne, IN 46808
260-484-0466
800-336-6825
www.amerizonwireless.com

Communications-Applied Technology
11250-14 Roger Bacon Dr.
Reston, VA 20190-5202
800-229-3925
www.c-at.com

David Clark Company Incorporated
360 Franklin Street
P.O. BOX 15054
Worcester, MA 01615-0054
508-751-5800
800-900-3434
http://www.davidclark.com

Eton Corporation
1015 Corporation Way
Palo Alto, CA 94303
800-872-2228
650-903-3866
www.etoncorp.com

First Alert
140 Pennsylvania
Bldg. #5
Oakmont, PA 15139
800-345-7462 x1217
www.simacorp.com

Icom America Inc
2380-116th Ave NE
Bellevue, WA 98004
425-454-8155
www.ICOMAMERICA.com

Information Station Specialists(ISS)
Broadcast Systems
P.O. Box 51, 3368 88th Avenue
Zeeland, MI 49464-0051
616-772-2300
www.THERADIOSOURCE.com

Motorola Inc Special Business Unit
1303 E Algonquin Road
Schaumburg, IL 60196
847-576-5000
800-668-6765
www.MOT.com

PROTOCOL
15635 Saticoy Street
Unit A
Van Nuys, CA 91406
818-782-5705
800-400-5705
http://www.walkietalkie.com

Satellite communications

ViaSat, Inc.
Mobile & Fixed Site Terminals
6155 El Camino Real
Carlsbad, CA 92009
760-476-4796
760-476-4738
www.viasat.com

Telecommunications, continuous uptime

Ascendent Systems
181 Metro Drive
Suite 410
San Jose, CA 95110
888-507-1777
www.ascendenttelecom.com

CapRock Communications
4400 S Sam Houston Parkway E
Houston, TX 77048
832-668-2300
888-482-0289
www.caprock.com

SECTOR, Inc.
90 Broad Street
New York, NY 10004
866-383-3315
www.sectorinc.com

Telecommunications, lost-power bypass units

Viking Electronics Inc
P.O. Box 448
Hudson, WI 54016
715-386-8861
www.VIKINGELECTRONICS.com

Telecommunications, voice continuity

CapRock Communications
4400 S Sam Houston Parkway E
Houston, TX 77048
832-668-2300
888-482-0289
www.caprock.com

Freels Enterprises Inc.
2523 Route 50
Mays Landing, NJ 08330
609-965-7666
800-234-7229
www.freelsonline.com

Voice Continuity Services, Inc.
15707 Vista Vicente Dr.
Ramona, CA 92065
866-415-2185
760-787-0865
www.voiceserv.net

Voice Continuity Services, Inc.
120 Kelly Glen Lane
Sonoma, CA 95476
707-939-6707
www.voiceserv.net

Voice Continuity Services, Inc.
8449 Flagstone Dr.
Tampa, FL 33615
813-887-1070
www.voiceserv.net

Telecommunications, wireless

Aluma Tower Company Inc.
P.O. Box 2806 - DR
Vero Beach, FL 32961-2806
772-567-3423
www.ALUMATOWER.com

Bearcom Wireless Worldwide Inc.
4009 Distribution Drive
Suite 200
Garland, TX 75041
800-541-9333
www.BEARCOM.com

Braley Communication Systems Inc
1760 E Hubert Rd
Midland, MI 48640
989-687-6319
www.EJOURNEY.com/~braley

C-COM Satllite Systems Inc.
2574 Sheffield Rd
Ottawa, ON K1B3V7
Canada
877-463-8886
613-745-4110
www.c-comsat.com

Cell-Tel Government Systems
8226 Philips Highway
Jacksonville, FL 32256
904-363-1111
800-737-7545
www.CELL-TEL.com

Con-Space Communications Ltd.
505-5600 Parkwood Way
Richmond, BC V6V 2M2
Canada
800-546-3405
604-244-9323
www.conspace.com

Inmarsat, Inc.
1100 Wilson Blvd
Suite 1425
Arlington, VA 22209
703-647-4760
703-647-4778
www.inmarsat.com

Moblie Enhanced Situation Network
1500 Eckington Place, N.E.
Washington, DC 20002
202-380-4171
www.xmradio.com

Signal Mountain Networks, Inc.
30000 Mill Creek Avenue
Suite 425
Alpharetta, GA 30022
678-867-0793 x102
www.signalmountain.com

Talk-A-Phone Co.
5013 N Kedzie Ave
Chicago, IL 60625
773-539-1100
www.talkaphone.com

Telesat Canada
1601 Telesat Court
Ottawa, ON K1B 5P4
Canada
613-748-0123
800-267-1870
www.TELESAT.ca

TESSCO Technolgies Incorporated
11126 McCormick Rd.
Hunt Valley, MD 21031
410-229-1000
www.TESSCO.com

ViaSat, Inc.
Satcom VoIP
6155 El Camino Real
Carlsbad, CA 92009
760-476-4796
760-476-4738
www.viasat.com

Telephone answering

TEL-US Message Center
400 S Beverly Drive
Beverly Hills, CA 90212
310-552-6000
800-223-1000
www.TEL-US.com

Telephone dialing equipment, automated

Amtelco
4800 Curtin Dr.
McFarland, WI 53558
800-356-9148
608-838-4194
www.amtelco.com

Enera Inc
1525 E 55 St.
Chicago, IL 60615
866-463-6372
773-955-4475
www.enera.com

VoiceGate Corporation
550 Alden Road
Suite 112
Markham, ON L3R 6A8
Canada
905-513-1403
800-668-2387
www.VOICEGATECORP.com

Warning systems

OnScreen Technologies Inc.
200 9th Avenue North, Suite 210
Safety Harbor, Fl 34695
727-797-6664
www.onscreentech.com

Streem Communications
4201 Galleria Drive
Loves Park, IL 61111
800-325-7732
815-639-1100
www.streemalert.com

Wireless communications

Amerizon Wireless Communication Service
3512 Cavalier Drive
Fort Wayne, IN 46808
260-484-0466
www.AMERIZONSATELLITE.com

ANVIL Technologies Inc.
1210 Sheppard Avenue East
Suite 507
North York, ON M2K 1E3
Canada
905-887-7535
336-545-8140
www.anviltech.biz

Arch Wireless
7090 Samuel Morse Drive
Suite 500
Columbia, MD 21046
800-340-4732 x8555
410-872-8555
www.arch.com

Atilla Technologies, LLC
Castle Point on Hudson
Hoboken, NJ 07030
201-216-5029
www.attila-tech.com

Cornell Communications
7915 North 81st Stt.
Milwaukee, WI 53223-3830
414-351-4660
800-558-8957
www.cornell.com

Daycom Systems Inc.
6759 Mesa Ridge Road
Suite 150
San Diego, CA 92121
858-200-3100
www.DAYCOMSYSTEMS.com

COMMUNICATIONS SYSTEMS

Dialogic Communications Corp
730 Cool Springs Boulevard
Suite 300
Franklin, TN 37067
615-790-2882
800-723-3207
www.DCCUSA.com

EnvoyWorldWide Inc
100 Crosby Drive
Bedford, MA 01730-1438
781-482-2100
www.ENVOYWORLDWIDE.com

Fortress Technologies
4023 Tampa Road
Suite 2000
Oldsmar, FL 34677
813-288-7388
888-4-privacy
www.fortresstech.com

GlobalCom Satellite Communication
2709 Compton Drive SW
Decatur, AL 35603-2641
256-432-2685
www.GLOBALCOM-USA.com

Inmarsat, Inc.
1100 Wilson Blvd
Suite 1425
Arlington, VA 22209
703-647-4760
703-647-4778
www.inmarsat.com

Maritime Telecommunications Network
3044 N. Commerce Pkwy
Miramar, FL 33025
954-538-4000
954-538-4023
http://www.mtnsat.com

Motient Corporation
300 Knightsbridge Parkway
Lincolnshire, IL 60069
800-668-4368
www.MOTIENT.com

New England Satellite Systems Inc
786 Hartford Turnpike
Shrewsbury, MA 01545
508-842-4328
www.NESATELLITE.com

Outfitter Satellite
2911 Elm Hill Pike
Nashville, TN 37214
615-889-8833
www.OUTFITTERSATELLITE.com

Rajant Corporation
148 E. Lancaster Ave.
Wayne, PA 19087
484-582-2200
www.rajant.com

Remote Satellite Systems
10 4th Street
Suite 208
Santa Rosa, CA 95401
707-545-8199
www.REMOTESATELLITE.com

SES America
2010 Corporate Ridge
McLean, VA 22102
703-610-1000
www.ses-america.com

Sola Communications LLC
113 North Pat
SCOTT, LA 70583
337-232-7039
www.solacom.com

St. Louis Electronics Inc
148 Welden Prkwy
Maryland Heights, MD 63043
314-615-3131

COMMUNICATIONS SYSTEMS

COMMUNICATIONS SYSTEMS

COMMUNICATIONS SYSTEMS

COMMUNICATIONS
SYSTEMS

COMMUNICATIONS SYSTEMS

EQUIPMENT

EQUIPMENT, Computer - New, Used, Refurbished & Rental

3-Com equipment

The Newman Group
7400 Newman Boulevard
Dexter, MI 48130
734-426-3200
www.tng.com

AT&T

AT&T
One AT&T Way
Bedminster, NJ 07921
800-222-0400
www.business.att.com

Gower Technical Services Inc
2740 Sawbury Boulevard
Columbus, OH 43235
614-764-2224
www.GOWERTECH.com

ATMs

ATM Exchange Inc. The
3930 Virginia Avenue
Cincinnati, OH 45227
513-272-1081
www.atmex.com

Diebold Inc
5995 Mayfair Road
North Canton, OH 44720
330-490-4000
www.DIEBOLD.com

Basic-4

Retrofit Technologies
455 Fortune Boulevard
Milford, MA 01757
508-478-2222

Cable & wiring connectors

Black Box Corp
1000 Park Drive
Lawrence, PA 15055
724-746-5500
800-552-6816
www.BLACKBOX.com

Black Box Corp.
2707 Main Street
Duluth, GA 30096
678-475-5500
www.blackbox.com

Cisco Systems

Canvas Systems, Inc.
3025 Northwoods Parkway
Norcross, GA 30071
770-662-1881
http://www.canvassystems.com

High Point Solutions Inc
5 Gail Court
Sparta, NJ 07871
973-940-0040
www.highpoint.com

Zycko
7667 Cahill Road
Suite 400
Minneapolis, MN 55439
952-944-3440
800-832-6539
www.zycko.com

Computer & electronic hardware, emergency replacement & rental

Canvas Systems, Inc.
3025 Northwoods Parkway
Norcross, GA 30071
770-662-1881
http://www.canvassystems.com

Data General

Computer Wholesalers
2831 Ringling Blvd.
Sarasota, FL 34237
800-229-2897
www.COMPUTERWHOLESALERSINC.com

Hanson Data Systems Inc
249 Cedar Hill Street
Marlborough, MA 01752
508-481-3901
800-879-4374
www.HANSONDATA.com

International Computing Systems
P.O. Box 343
Hopkins, MN 55343
952-935-8112
800-522-4272

Sysgen Data Marketing Ltd
12 Elkland Road
Melville, NY 11747
631-491-1100
www.SYSGEN.com

TriAxis Inc.
23 Midstate Drive
Suite 106
Auburn, MA 01501
508-721-9691
www.triaxisinc.com

Data storage devices

Media Mastr Computer Products, Inc.
7A Marlen Drive
Robbinsville, NJ 08691-1604
609-856-7576
800-522-4274
www.mmcpi.com

Qualstar Corporation
3990 Heritage Oak Ct.
Simi Valley, CA 93063
805-583-7744
www.qualstar.com

Quantum Corporation - Storage Devices
4001 Discovery Drive
Suite 1100
Boulder, CO 80303
720-406-5700
www.dlttape.com

StorageTek
One Storagetek Drive
Louisville, CO 80028
303-673-5151
800-877-9220
www.STORAGETEK.com

TriAxis Inc.
23 Midstate Drive
Suite 106
Auburn, MA 01501
508-721-9691
www.triaxisinc.com

Dataproducts printers

Dataco DeRex Inc
2280 NW 33rd Court
Pompano Beach, FL 33069
954-977-6362
800-825-1262
www.DATACO.com

DEC

ABS Associates Inc
2100 Golf Road
Rolling Mdws, IL 60008
847-437-8700
www.ABS-INC.com

Compurex Systems Inc(CSI)
35 Eastman Street
South Easton, MA 02375
508-230-3700
800-426-5499
www.compurex.com

Computer Clearing House
246 Commerce Drive
Rochester, NY 14623
585-334-0550
www.COMPUTERCLEARINGHOUSE.com

Dataware Systems Lease Inc
30 Bay Street
Staten Island, NY 10301
718-447-4911
www.DATAWARESYSTEMS.net

Decision One
2323 Industrail Parkway West
Hayward, CA 94545
800-345-7950

Na Technologies
2197 Canton Road
S-112
Marietta, GA 30066
770-449-8000
www.na-tech.com

TriAxis Inc.
23 Midstate Drive
Suite 106
Auburn, MA 01501
508-721-9691
www.triaxisinc.com

Xerxes Computer Corp
5735 W Old Shakopee Road
Minneapolis, MN 55437
952-936-9280
800-328-3884
www.xcc.com

Hewlett-Packard

ABTECH Systems Inc.
2730 Loker Avenue W
Carlsbad, CA 92008
760-827-5110
800-474-7397
www.abtechsys.com

AltaTech Technologies Inc
3850 Annapolis Ln N
Plymouth, MN 55447
763-475-2900
800-546-2582
www.ALTATECHNOLOGIES.com

Canvas Systems, Inc.
3025 Northwoods Parkway
Norcross, GA 30071
770-662-1881
http://www.canvassystems.com

Computech Systems Corp.
11421 NE 120th Street
Kirkland, WA 98034
800-882-0201
www.COMPUTECH.com

EQUIPMENT

CSU Industries
395 Pearsall Avenue
Cedarhurst, NY 11516
516-239-4310
www.CSUINDUSTRIES.com

Cypress Technology Inc.
8565 Sommerset Drive
Suite A
Largo, FL 33773
727-557-0911
www.CYPRESS-TECH.com

Eurodata Inc
2574 Sheffield Rd
Ottawa, ON K1B 3V7
Canada
613-745-0921
www.EURODATA.ca

Hardware & Peripherals Inc.
4920 Commerce Parkway
Cleveland, OH 44128
216-292-9200
www.HPI-COMPUTERS.com

Hewlett-Packard Canada, Ltd.
5150 Spectrum Way
Mississauga, ON L4W 5G1
Canada
905-206-4725
www.hp.com

Hewlett-Packard Company
3000 Hanover Street
Palo Alto, CA 94304-1185
650-857-1501
www.hp.com

Lynne Company
P.O. Box 339
Grover Beach, CA 93483
805-489-1564

Monterey Bay Communications
1010 Fair Avenue
Santa Cruz, CA 95060
831-429-6144
www.MONTBAY.com

NorCo Computer Systems Inc
2888 Nationwide Parkway
Brunswick, OH 44212
800-892-1920

Paramount Computer
6301 E Stassney Lane
Suite 200
Austin, TX 78744
512-263-7010
www.pmount.com

P-SPAN
131 Birch St.
Amery, WI 54001
715-268-8106
www.p-span.com

Source Systems Inc
9043 Dutton Drive
Twinsburg, OH 44087
330-963-1001
www.sourcesys.com

World Data Products
121 Cheshire Lane
Minnetonka, MN 55305
952-476-9000
800-553-0592
www.WDPI.com

IBM midrange (System/3x; AS400, etc.)

Canvas Systems, Inc.
3025 Northwoods Parkway
Norcross, GA 30071
770-662-1881
http://www.canvassystems.com

Champion Solutions Group
791 Park of Commerce Boulevard Suite 200
Boca Raton, FL 33487
561-997-2900
www.CHAMPIONSG.com

DD1 Computers
4120 Finley Road
Irving, TX 75062
972-570-1227

East Coast Computer Inc
1350 S Cypress Road
Pompano Beach, FL 33060
954-463-7300
954-783-1771
www.ECC400.com

Express Computer Systems
1733 Kaiser Avenue
Irvine, CA 92614
800-327-0730
www.ECSUNIX.com

System ID Warehouse
1400 10th Street
Plano, TX 75074
972-516-1100
888-648-4452
www.SYSTEMID.com

IBM point-of-sale equipment

Illinois Wholesale Cash Register (IWCR) Corp
2495 Pembroke Avenue
Hoffman Estate, IL 60195
800-544-5493
www.ILLINOISWHOLESALE.com

EQUIPMENT

IBM RS-6000

Canvas Systems, Inc.
3025 Northwoods Parkway
Norcross, GA 30071
770-662-1881
http://www.canvassystems.com

Datatrend Technologies Inc
121 Cheshire Lane
Minnetonka, MN 55305
952-931-1203
800-367-7472
www.datatrend.com

Evolving Solutions, Inc
3989 County Road 116
Hamel, MN 55340
800-294-4362
763-516-6500
www.evolvingsol.com

MSI: Minnesota Systems International. Inc
1701 American Boulevard E
Minneapolis, MN 55425
952-883-0808

Penn Computer Corporation
2940 Turnpike Drive
Hatboro, PA 19040
215-444-9999
888-510-5700
www.penncomputer.com

Worldwide Trade Corp
1363 Park Road
Chanhassen, MN 55317
952-474-0322
www.WORLDWIDETRADECORP.com

ISC teller equipment & branch controllers

Benchmark Technology Group
1665 Bluegrass Lakes Parkway
Alpharetta, GA 30004
678-319-3999
www.BENCHMARK-US.com

Keyboards, ruggedized

Advanced Input Systems
600 W. Wilbur Avenue
Coeur d'Alene, ID 83815
800-444-5923
www.advanced-input.com

Input Technologies LLC
842D South Sierra Madre
Colorado Springs, CO 80903-3314
719-475-7223
www.INPUT-TECH.com

Marquardt Switches Inc
2711 Rt. 20 E.
Cazenovia, NY 13035
315-655-8050
www.SWITCHES.com

Macintosh

Pre-owned Electronics Inc
125 Middlesex Turnpike
Bedford, MA 01730
781-778-4600
800-274-5343
www.Preowned.com

Misc., all computer equipment

Agility Recovery Solutions
7621 Little Ave
Suite 218
Charlotte, NC 28226
866-364-9696
www.AGILITYRECOVERY.com

BootSector Industries
180 Great Neck Road
Farmingdale, NY 11735
631-249-2700
800-568-2668
http://www.bootsector.com/

C&T Systems
150 State Street
Saint Paul, MN 55107
800-472-2081
www.ASSETRECOVERYCORP.com

Data Exchange Corporation
3600 Via Pescador
Camarillo, CA 93012
805-388-1711
800-237-7911
www.DEX.com

Electronic Renaissance Corp.
104 Sunfield Avenue
Edison, NJ 08837
732-417-9090

Insight Public Sector
6820 S. Harl
Tempe, AZ 85283
800-467-4448
480-333-3000
www.ips.insight.com

NACOMEX USA
P.O. Box 394
Tivoli, NY 12583
845-757-2626
212-808-3062
www.NACOMEX.com

EQUIPMENT

Quantum Technology Inc
7939 Montgomery Avenue
Elkins Park, PA 19027
215-635-2650

Rapid Technologies LLC
10130 SW Nimbus Avenue
Portland, OR 97223
503-968-3125
www.RAPID-TECH.com

Rentsys Recovery Services
200 Quality Circle
College Station, TX 77845-4468
800-955-5171
www.RENTSYS.com

Rentsys Recovery Services
6700 Hollister
Houston, TX 77040
800-955-5171
www.RENTSYS.com

NCR

ABEC
P.O. Box 862
McMinnville, OR 97128
503-434-9100
800-255-8064
www.ABEC.biz

BankSystems
1253 Eagan Industrial Road
Eagan, MN 55121
651-686-1400
www.BANKSYSTEMSMARKETING.com

Computer Connection Corp
1101 W 80th Street
Minneapolis, MN 55420
952-884-0758
www.cccmn.com

Harwood International Corp
100 Northshore Office Park
Chattanooga, TN 37343
423-870-5500
www.HARWOOD-INTL.com

UNI-COMP Equipment Corp
108 Mid Town Court
Hendersonvlle, TN 37075
615-822-8484
www.unicompeq.com

Network backup/recovery equipment

IMS Systems Inc
12081 Tech Road
Silver Spring, MD 20904
301-680-0006
800-526-0791
www.IMSS.com

MiraLink Corp
28 SW 1st Avenue
Suite 410
Portland, OR 97204
503-419-1660
www.MIRALINK.com

TriAxis Inc.
23 Midstate Drive
Suite 106
Auburn, MA 01501
508-721-9691
www.triaxisinc.com

Network equipment, LAN/WAN

Adtranstore, Inc.
35 Wilson Drive
Sparta, NJ 07871
888-328-2266
www.1-888-DATACOM.com

Canvas Systems, Inc.
3025 Northwoods Parkway
Norcross, GA 30071
770-662-1881
www.canvassystems.com

Ryder Communications Inc
35 B Wilson Drive
Sparta, NJ 07871
877-RYDRCOM
877-793-7266

The Newman Group
7400 Newman Boulevard
Dexter, MI 48130
734-426-3200
www.tng.com

TRS Rentelco
90 Brunswick Blvd.
Dollard Des Ormeaux, QC H9B 2C5
Canada
514-683-9400
800-874-7123
www.trs-rentelco.com

XRoads Networks
Von Karman Commerce Center
17165 Von Karman Ave - Suite 112
Irvine, CA 92614
888-9-XROADS
949-477-6100
www.xroadsnetworks.com

Network security, hardware

Resilience Corporation
510 Clyde Ave
Mountain View, CA 94043
888-297-8515
650-230-2200
www.resilience.com

EQUIPMENT

Network security, software

Resilience Corporation
510 Clyde Ave
Mountain View, CA 94043
888-297-8515
650-230-2200
www.resilience.com

Nixdorf

National Business Systems
2919 W Service Road
Eagan, MN 55121
651-688-0202
www.NBSUSA.com

Online tape replacement systems

Exagrid Systems
2000 West Park Drive
Wesboro, MA 01581
508-898-2872
www.exagrid.com

PCs (IBM & compatibles)

ACP
1317 E Edinger Avenue
Santa Ana, CA 92705
714-558-8822
800-347-3423
www.ACPSUPERSTORE.com

GE Financial Services
3000 Lakeside Drive
Suite 200 N
Bannockburn, IL 60015
847-615-0992
800-323-6217
www.GE.com

Nexcom International Corp. LTD.
46706 Fremont Blvd.
Fremont, CA 94538
510-656-2248
www.nexcom.com

Rent-a-PC
10391 Jefferson Blvd.
Culver City, CA 90232
310-237-5324
www.Rent-a-PC.com

Rent-a-PC
1913 NW 40th Court
Pompano Beach, FL
954-979-8300
www.Rent-a-PC.com

Rent-a-PC
2135-G Defoor Hills Road
Atlanta, GA 30318
404-352-0900
www.Rent-a-PC.com

Rent-a-PC
60 Howard St
Watertown, MA 02472
617-926-2266
www.Rent-a-PC.com

Rent-a-PC
600 Sylvan Avenue
Englewood Cliffs, NJ 07632
201-568-6555
www.Rent-a-PC.com

Rent-a-PC
4110 Butler Pike, Suite 100
Plymouth Meeting, PA 19462
610-940-9500
www.Rent-a-PC.com

Rent-a-PC
2738 Gallows Road
Vienna, VA 22180
703-207-0550
www.Rent-a-PC.com

Rent-A-PC / All Service Computer Rentals
265 Oser Avenue
Hauppauge, NY 11788-3609
631-273-8888
800-R-E-N-T-A-P-C
www.Rent-a-PC.com

Rentex
337 Summer Street
Boston, MA 02210-1732
617-423-5567

Point-of-sale equipment, misc.

Chicago Cash Register
6300 Oakton Street
Morton Grove, IL 60053
312-666-5555
800-227-6386
www.CHICAGOCASHREGISTER.com

Electronic Systems International
22532 Avenida Empiesa Rancho
Santa Margarita, CA 92688
800-843-7749

ERC Parts
4001 Cobb International Boulevard N
Kennesaw, GA 30152
770-984-0276
800-241-6880
www.ERCONLINE.com

EQUIPMENT

MCR Technologies
6 Greenwood Street
Wakefield, MA 01880
781-438-7801
www.MCRTECHNOLOGIES.com

Retail Control Solutions Inc
460 Hillside Avenue
Needham, MA 02494
781-444-7300
800-767-2212
www.WEFIXMICROS.com

Printers, plotters, misc.

Source Graphics
1530 N Harmony Circle
Anaheim, CA 92807
714-939-0114
www.sourcegraphics.com

TallyGenicom
4500 Daly Drive
Suite 100
Chantilly, VA 20151
800-436-4266
www.tallygenicom.com

Trilogy Magnetics Inc
424 N Mill Creek Road
Quincy, CA 95971
800-873-4323
www.TRILOGYMAG.com

Ruggedized computers

308 Systems, Inc
2637 Wapiti Rd
Fort Collins, CO 80525
970-282-7006
www.308systems.com

Bizco
7950 'O' Street
Lincoln, NE 68510
877-2B-TOUGH
877-228-6844
www.toughonline.com

Portable Computer Systems, Inc.
12851 W. 43rd Drive
Unit 2
Golden, CO 80403
303-346-2487
888-836-7841
www.portablecomputersystems.com

Prosys Information Systems
4900 Avalon Ridge Parkway
Norcross, GA 30071
888-337-2626 x9011
678-268-9011
https://panasonic.prosysis.com

Sun

Advantec Computer Company
48989 Milmont Drive
Fremont, CA 94538
510-440-9700
www.ADVANTECO.com

Ames Sciences Inc.
507 Dover Road
Easton, MD 21601
410-820-8100
www.ANYTHING4SUN.com

Atlantix Global Systems Inc
1 Sun Court
Norcross, GA 30092
770-248-7700
888-786-2727
www.ATLANTIXGLOBAL.com

Can Am Computer Inc.
300 Route 17 South
Mahwah, NJ 07430
201-512-1414
201-512-1763
www.CANAM-SYSTEMS.com

Canvas Systems, Inc.
3025 Northwoods Parkway
Norcross, GA 30071
770-662-1881
http://www.canvassystems.com

Centurian Surplus Inc.
375 Tennant Avenue
Morgan Hill, CA 95037
408-778-2001
www.CENTURIANSURPLUS.com

Computer Connection of NY Inc.
11206 Cosby Manor Road
Utica, NY 13502
315-724-2209
800-566-4786
www.CCNY.com

CRA Inc.
11011 N 23rd Avenue
Phoenix, AZ 85029
602-944-1548
www.CIT.com/CRA

Flagship Technologies Inc
3939 County Road 116
Hamel, MN 55340
800-416-8900
www.FLAGSHIP.com

Minicomputer Exchange
610 N Pastoria Avenue
Sunnyvale, CA 94085
408-733-4400
www.MCE.com

EQUIPMENT

QUEST International Inc
65 Parker
Irvine, CA 92618
949-581-9900
www.questinc.com

Radiant Resources Inc
10 Smallbrook Circle
Randolph, NJ 07869
973-442-5555
www.radiantresources.com

Relational Technology Services
12821 Starkey Road
Largo, FL 33773
727-524-9668
www.gcw.com

Security Computer Sales
2340 County Road J
White Bear Lk, MN 55110
651-653-5200
www.SecurityComputer.com

Solar Systems Inc & Peripherals
8134 304th Ave SE
Preston, WA 98050
800-253-5764
425-222-7588

**TriAxis Inc.
23 Midstate Drive
Suite 106
Auburn, MA 01501
508-721-9691
www.triaxisinc.com**

Vernon Computer Rentals & Leasing
77 Selleck Street
Stamford, CT 06902
800-827-3434
800-386-1282

Virtual Group The
25307 Dequindre Road
Madison Heights, MI 48071
248-545-3100
www.VirtualAutomotive.com

West Coast Computer Exchange Inc
10980 Gold Center Drive
Rncho Cordova, CA 95670
916-635-9340
www.wccx.com

WTE/Worldwide Technology Exchange
315 W Ponce DeLeon Ave
Suite 957
Decatur, GA 30030
404-378-0990
888-983-7866
www.wtesystems.com

Tandem

CDS
P.O. Box 400
Oakhurst, NJ 07755
732-517-0919
www.CDS.net

NCD: Medical Corporation
33801 Curtis Boulevard
Suite 100
Eastlake, OH 44095
440-953-4488
www.NCDMEDICAL.com

Tape backup units, portable

Advanced Digital Information Corp. (ADIC)
P.O. Box 97057
Redmond, WA 98073
425-881-8004
800-336-1233
www.ADIC.com

Exabyte Corp
2108 55th Street
Boulder, CO 80301
303-442-4333
www.EXABYTE.com

Tape replacement systems

Exagrid Systems
2000 West Park Drive
Wesboro, MA 01581
508-898-2872
www.exagrid.com

Teller equipment, misc.

New England Bank Equipment
160 Oak Street
Glastonbury, CT 06033
800-842-9985

Texas Instruments

Capital Data
3300 W Main Street
Lansing, MI 48917
517-371-7100
800-999-4409
www.CAPITALDATAUSA.com

Lake Erie Systems and Services Inc
5321 Buffalo Road
Erie, PA 16510
814-898-0704
www.fastprinters.com

EQUIPMENT

Unisys/Burroughs

Ceva Computer Corp
100 Hayes Drive
Brooklyn Heights, OH 44131
216-749-7300
www.CEVACOMPUTER.com

Concept Computer Inc
1665 Main Street
Buffalo, NY 14209
716-884-8220
800-561-5852

Hardware Technology
16160 Caputo Drive
Morgan Hill, CA 95037
408-776-9920

LNJ Enterprises
4225 SW57 Avenue
Davie, FL 33314
954-525-7339
www.LNJE.com

Partners Remarketing Inc.
5637 La Ribera Street Unit A
Livermore, CA 94550
925-449-2120
www.PARTNERSREMARKETING.com

Symco
105 Satellite Blvd
Suite I
Suwanee, GA 30024
770-451-8002
www.symco.com

Worldwide Financial Systems
165 Rano Street
Buffalo, NY 14207
716-877-3213
800-782-5224
www.worldwidefinancialsys.com

Wang

ELI Systems Inc
288 Northfolk Street
Cambridge, MA 02139
617-547-1113
800-447-1156
www.ELI.com

Item Inc
5509 Vine Street
Alexandria, VA 22310
703-971-5700
800-367-4836
www.ITEMINC.com

National Data Systems
1077 Aaron Avenue NE
Bainbridge Island, WA 98110
206-780-5700

Network Management Corp.
210 Washington Street
Chardon, OH 44024
440-285-8400
www.NETMAN2000.com

Wyse

Micro Technologies International
2590 Shell Road
Georgetown, TX 78628
800-288-1487
www.MTICOM.com

EQUIPMENT, General

Access flooring

Computer Site Technologies Inc
3130 SE Indian
Stuart, FL 24997
954-425-0638

Computex Support Services
1601 E Plano Parkway
Plano, TX 75074
972-424-4011
www.COMPUTEXINC.com

Air cleaning equipment

Air Systems International, Inc.
829 Juniper Crescent
Chesapeake, VA 23320
800-866-8100
757-424-3967
www.airsystems.com

AllerAir Industries Inc.
2049 Le Chatelier
Laval, QC H7L 5P1
Canada
888-852-8247
www.allerair.com

Erlad Inc.
1980 Turnpike Street
North Andover, MA 01845
978-975-3336
www.CAPTAIR.com

Failsafe Air Safety Systems Corp
79 Fillmore Ave
Tonawanda, NY 14150
716-694-6390
www.fasscorp.com

EQUIPMENT

Air testing equipment

Draeger Safety Inc.
101 Technology Drive
Pittsburgh, PA 15275
412-787-8383
800-615-5503
www.DRAEGER-SAFETY.com

Industrial Scientific Corporation
1001 Oakdale Road
Oakdale, PA 15071
412-788-4353
www.indsci.com

Zellweger Analytics
400 Sawgarss Corp Parkway
Sunrise, FL 33325
954-514-2700
800-538-0363

Alarms & warning systems, misc.

American Science and Engineering Inc.
829 Middlesex Turnpike
Billerica, MA 01821
978-262-8700
800-225-1608
www.AS-E.com

American Signal Corp.
4801 W Woolworth Avenue
Milwaukee, WI 53218-1417
800-243-2911
www.AMERICANSIGNAL.com

CANBERRA Co. - Canada
West -50B Caldari Rd
Concord, ON L4K 4N8
Canada
905-660-5373
www.canberra.com/canada/

Federal Signal Corporation
2645 Federal Signal Drive
University Park, IL 60466
800-548-7229
708-534-3400
www.federalwarningsystems.com

Potter Electric Signal Co
2081 Craig Road
Saint Louis, MO 63146
800-325-3936

Quest Technologies, Inc.
1060 Corporate Center Dr.
Oconomowoc, WI 53066
262-567-9157
800-245-0779
www.quest-technologies.com

Warning Systems Inc.
2225 Drake Avenue SW
Suite 2
Huntsville, AL 35805-5189
256-880-8702
877-218-9506
www.WARNINGSYSTEMS.com

Wheelock
273 Branchport Ave
Long Branch, NJ 07740
800-631-2148
732-331-2419
www.wheelockinc.com

Whelen Engineering Co.
Route 145 Winthrop Rd.
Chester, CT 06412
860-526-9504
www.whelen.com

Alarms, earthquake

Earthquake Safety Systems Inc
2550 Bay Vista Lane
Los Osos, CA 93402
805-534-1582
www.eqsafetysys.com

Earthquakes Canada (East)
Natural Resources Canada
7 Observatory Crescent
Ottawa, ON K1A 0Y3
Canada
613-995-5548 [en]
613-995-0600 [fr]
www.seismo.nrcan.gc.ca

Earthquakes Canada (West)
P.O. Box 6000
9860 West Saanich Road
Sidney, BC V8L 4B2
Canada
250-363-6500
www.pgc.nrcan.gc.ca

Alarms, fire

Environment One Corp.
2773 Balltown Road
Niskayuna, NY 12309
518-346-6161
www.EONE.com

NOTIFIER/Fire-Lite Alarms Inc
1 Fire-Lite Place
Northford, CT 06472
203-484-7161
www.NOTIFIER.com

Safety Technology International Inc
2306 Airport Road
Waterford, MI 48327-1209
800-888-4784

EQUIPMENT

SimplexGrinnell
100 Simplex Dr.
Westminster, MA 01441
978-731-2500
www.simplexgrinnell.com

Vision Systems Inc.
700 Longwater Dr
Norwell, MA 02061
781-740-2223
800-229-4434
www.VSL.com.au

Alarms, hydrogen chloride gas detection

Biosystems
651 South Main Street
Middletown, CT 06457
860-344-1079
www.biosystems.com

Fike Corporations
704 S.10th St.
Blue Springs, MO 64015
816-229-3405
410-893-2999
www.FIKE.com

General Monitors
26776 Simpatica Circle
Lake Forest, CA 92630
866-686-0741
949-581-4464
www.generalmonitors.com

NanoScake Materials, Inc.
1310 Research Blvd
Manhattan, KS 66502
785-537-0179
877-fast-act
www.fast-act.com

Nextteq, LLC
8406 Benjamin Rd.
Suite J
Tampa, FL 33634
877-312-2333
www.nextteq.com

Proengin, Inc.
405 NE 8th Street
Fort Lauderdale, FL 33304
954-760-9990
www.proengin.com

RAE Systems
3775 North First Street
San Jose, CA 95134
408-952-8200
www.raesystems.com

EQUIPMENT

RKI Instruments, Inc.
33248 Central Ave.
Union City, CA 94587
800-754-5165
510-441-5656
www.rkiinstruments.com

Thermo Electron Corporation
355 River Oaks Pkwy
San Jose, CA 95134
408-965-6022
www.thermo.com

Alarms, radiation

Aramsco
1655 Imperial Way
Thorofare, NJ 08086
856-848-5330
800-767-6933
www.aramsco.com

CANBERRA Co. - Canada
West -50B Caldari Rd
Concord, ON L4K 4N8
Canada
905-660-5373
www.canberra.com/canada/

General Atomics Electronic Systems, Inc.
4949 Greencraig Lane
San Diego, CA 92123
858-522-8300
www.ga-esi.com

KI4U, Inc.
212 Oil Patch Lane
Gonzales, TX 78629
830-672-8734
www.nukalert.com

Pulcir Incorporated
9209 Oak Ridge Highway
Oak Ridge, TN 37830
800-862-1390
865-927-6358
http://www.pulcir.com

Teletrix
P.O. Box 14209
Pittsburgh, PA 15239
412-798-3636
http://www.teletrix.com

Alarms, water

Dorlen Products
6615 W Layton Avenue
Milwaukee, WI 53220-4564
262-282-4840
800-533-6392
www.WATERALERT.com

Barriers, temporary

AccuForm Signs
16228 Flight Path Drive
Brooksville, FL 34604
800-237-1001
www.accuform.com

Temporary Perimeter Systems
19784 Kenrick Ave
Lakeville, MN 55044
952-469-5101
866-469-5101
www.smartbarrierusa.com

Biodetection, suspicious powder analyzer

GenPrime, Inc.
157 S. Howard
Suite 605
Spokane, WA 99201
866-624-9855
509-624-9855
www.genprime.com

Construction equipment rental

Aerial Access Equipment
13764 Airline Highway
Baton Rouge, LA 70817
225-753-2332
www.aae-la.com

Airworx Construction Equipment & Supply
501 W. Raymond St.
Indianapolis, IN 46225
317-471-1272
574-268-9664
www.airworxcorp.com

Bierschbach Equipment & Supply
1101 S. Lyons
Sioux Falls, SD 57106
605-332-4466
www.bierschbach.com

Gorman-Rupp Company
P.O. Box 1217
Mansfield, OH 44901
419-755-1011
419-755-1213
www.gormanrupp.com

Hertz Equipment Rental
225 Brae Blvd.
Park Ridge, NJ 07656
888-777-2700
www.hertzequip.com

EQUIPMENT

Hi-Way Equipment Co., Inc.
6203 Long Drive
Houston, TX 77087
713-649-0940
www.HI-WAYEQUIPMENT.com

Johnson Machinery Co.
800 E. La Cadena Drive
P.O. Box 351
Riverside, CA 92501
951-686-4560
www.johnson-machinery.com

NationsRent
450 East Las Olas Blvd.
Ft. Lauderdale, FL 33467
800-667-9328
www.NATIONSRENT.com

NES Rentals
8770 W. Bryn Mawr
4th Floor
Chicago, IL 60631
773-695-3999
800-NES-RENT
www.nesrentals.com

Spider, a division of SafeWorks, LLC
365 Upland Drive
Seattle, WA 98188
877-774-3370
www.spiderstaging.com

Sunbelt Rentals
1337 Hundred Oaks Drive
Charlotte, NC 28217
866-786-2358
704-348-2676
www.sunbeltrentals.com

Trico Equipment
Rental Headquarters
Vineland, NJ 08360
800-468-7426
www.tricoequipment.com

Trinity Rentals/D-C Electric, Inc.
1403 W. Washington
Pittsfield, IL 62363
217-285-5566
217-430-1200

Tyler Rental Inc
3838 Maytown Road S.W.
Olympia, WA 98512
800-772-0237
360-786-1441
www.tylerrental.net

United Rentals Inc
2138 Espey Ct
Crofton, MD 21114
301-864-5100
301 943 7081
http://www.unitedrentals.com

Victor L. Philips Co., The
1305 SW 42nd St.
Topeka, KS 66609
800-878-4345
785-267-4345
www.vlpco.com

Victor L. Philips Co., The
3250 N. Hydraulic St.
Wichita, KS 67219
800-878-3346
316-838-3346
www.vlpco.com

Victor L. Philips Co., The
2203 W. Jones Ave.
Garden City, KS 67846
800-511-1435
620-275-1996
www.vlpco.com

Victor L. Philips Co., The
6330 W. Highway 60
Brookline Station, MO 64120
800-955-2729
417-887-2729
www.vlpco.com

Victor L. Philips Co., The
3205 E. 20th St.
Joplin, MO 64802
800-878-8223
417-781-8222
www.vlpco.com

Victor L. Philips Co., The
4100 Gardner Avenue
Kansas City, MO 64120
800-878-9290
816-241-9290
www.vlpco.com

Continuous up-time computers

MessageOne Inc.
11044 Research Boulevard
Building C - Fifth Floor
Austin, TX 78759-5328
512-652-4500
888-367-0777
www.MESSAGEONE.com

Cooling equipment, mobile

Adapt Inc.
888 Shenandoah Shores Road
Front Royal, VA 22630
800-243-2665
www.COOLESTSPOT.com

Aggreko Rental
4607 W. Admiral Doyle Drive
New Iberia, LA 70560-9134
800-258-4874
www.aggreko.com

AirPac Inc.
AirPac Technology Park
888 Shenandoah Shores Road
Front Royal, VA 22630
888-324-7722
540-635-5011
www.AIRPACINC.com

Cat Rental Power
AC6109
P.O. Box 610
Mossville, IL 61552
1-800-RENT CAT
847-749-0797
www.catrentalpower.com

Foley Rents
833 Centennial Ave
Piscataway, NJ 08855
732-885-5555
www.Foleyinc.com

MovinCool
Denso Sales California, Inc.
3900 Via Oro Avenue
Long Beach, CA 90810
800-264-9573
www.movincool.com

TOPP Potable Air
12 Crozerville Road
Aston, PA 19014
800-892-8677
www.etopp.com

Washington Air Compressor Rental Co.
1800 4th Street, NE
Washington, DC 20002
202-635-1500
240-832-7500
www.washair.com

Washington Air Compressor Rental Co.
41096 John Mosby Hwy (Rt. 50)
Chantilly, VA 20105
703-742-6200
240-832-7500
www.washair.com

Defibrillators, external

Cardiac Science
1900 Main Street
Suite 700
Irvine, CA 92614
949-797-3800
888-274-3342
www.cardiacscience.com

Defibtech, LLC
753 Boston Post Road
Suite 102
Guilford, CT 06437
203-453-6654
866-333-4248
www.defibtech.com

HeartSine Technologies, Inc.
940 Calle Amanecer
Suite E
San Clemente, CA 92673
949-218-0092
866-HRT-SINE
www.heartsine.com

LifeSavers, Inc.
759 Bloomfield Ave
#102
West Caldwell, NJ 07006
866-641-1200
www.lifesaversinc.com

Medtronic Emergency Response Systems
11811 Willows Road NE
P.O. Box 97006
Redmond, WA 98073
800-442-1142
425-867-4000
http://www.medtronic-ers.com

Philips
3000 Minuteman Road
Andover, MA 01810
800-934-7372
www.MEDICAL.PHILIPS.com

SOS Technologies
1401 Franquette Avenue
Suite A3
Concord, CA 94520
925-691-9335
www.sostechnologies.net

Zoll Medical Corporation
269 Mill Road
Chelmsford, MA 01824
800-348-9011
978-421-9655
www.zoll.com

Diverters, falling water

Facility Supply
81 Loudville Road
Easthampton, MA 01027
800-981-8128
413-527-6265
www.FACILITYSUPPLY.com

Sulmac Inc
1115 Main Street
Holyoke, MA 01040
413-533-5347
800-773-3929
www.SULMAC-DEWAY.com

Drying & dehumidification equipment

Aggreko Rental
4607 W. Admiral Doyle Drive
New Iberia, LA 70560-9134
800-258-4874
www.aggreko.com

Bolden's Mfg / Xtreme Products
20799 Riverwood Ave
Building B
Noblesville, IN 46062
888-776-6708
317-776-8787
www.hydro-systems.com

Interlink Supply
542 W. Confluence Ave.
Salt Lake City, UT 84123
800-660-5803
800-794-7425
www.interlinksupply.com

Paul Davis Restoration of Akron
2735 Second Street
Cuyahoga Falls, OH 44221
330-920-1936
330-920-4201
www.pdrestoration.com

Paul Davis Restoration of Central CT
107 M Oakwood Drive
Suite 107M
Glastonbury, CT 06033
860-633-7733
www.pdrestoration.com

RentalMax
908 E Roosevelt Road
Wheaton, IL 60187
630-221-1133
888-462-9736
www.RENTALMAX.com

ServiceMaster by Gaudet
6 Jefferson Avenue
Woburn, MA 01801-4325
781-932-1171
800-281-0072
www.servicemasterbygaudet.com

Sunbelt Rentals
1337 Hundred Oaks Drive
Charlotte, NC 28217
866-786-2358
704-348-2676
www.sunbeltrentals.com

Temp-Air
One Rupp Plaza
3700 West Preserve Blvd.
Burnsville, MN 55337
952-707-5050
800-836-7432
www.temp-air.com

United Rentals Pumps, Power, HVAC
1730 North Powerline Road
Pompano Beach, FL 33069
800-462-0994
954-917-5440
www.unitedrentals.com

United Rentals Pumps, Power, HVAC
371 Taft Vineland Road
Orlando, FL 32824
888-269-8292
407-854-6061
www.unitedrentals.com

United Rentals Pumps, Power, HVAC
3990 Jonesboro Road
Forest Park, GA 30297
800-506-5831
404-363-4503
www.unitedrentals.com

United Rentals Pumps, Power, HVAC
30A Independence Road
Kingston, MA 02364
866-544-7867
781-585-7881
www.unitedrentals.com

United Services DKI
130 Skipjack Road
Frederick, MD 20678
800-644-8658
410-414-3195
www.unitedrentals.com

Washington Air Compressor Rental Co.
1800 4th Street, NE
Washington, DC 20002
202-635-1500
240-832-7500
www.washair.com

Washington Air Compressor Rental Co.
41096 John Mosby Hwy (Rt. 50)
Chantilly, VA 20105
703-742-6200
240-832-7500
www.washair.com

Electronics cleaning & drying equipment

Odell Electronics Cleaning Stations
1061 Bradley Rd.
Westlake, OH 44145
440-365-5910
888-779-0011
www.odellstations.com

EQUIPMENT

Environmental cleanup equipment rental & supplies

A Royal Wolf Portable Storage
23422 Clawiter Rd
Hayward, CA 94545
800-447-7223
www.ROYAL-WOLF.com

AlturnaMATS, Inc.
POB 344
Titusville, PA 16301
888-544-6287
814-827-8884
www.Alturnamats.com

Austin Power Equipment
10749 E. Crystal Falls
Legander, TX 78641
512-260-3333
www.APETAD.com

Bolden's Mfg / Rent-X
20799 Riverwood Ave
Building B
Noblesville, IN 46062
888-776-6708
317-776-8787
www.hydro-systems.com

CDCLarue Industries, Inc.
7 West 40th Street
Sand Springs, OK 74063
866-954-9700
918-245-5034
www.cdclarue.com

Curtis L.N. & Sons
1800 Peralta Street
Oakland, CA 94607
800-443-3556

Hertz Equipment Rental
225 Brae Blvd.
Park Ridge, NJ 07656
888-777-2700
http://www.hertzequip.com

Jon-Don
400 Medinah Road
Roselle, IL 60172
800-556-6366
www.JON-DON.com

PND Corporation
14320 NE 21st St.
Suite 6
Bellevue, WA 98007
425-562-7252
425-562-7254
www.plugndike.com

Rex Spencer Equipment Company
323 N. Mullen Road
Belton, MO 64012
800-878-6078
816-331-6078

SafetyHQ.com
68 Allen Road
Bow, NH 03304
603-226-7233
http://www.safetyhq.com

Sorbent Products Company, Inc.
645 Howard Avenue
Somerset, NJ 08873
800-333-7672
732-302-0080
www.sorbentproducts.com

The Hertz Corp.
225 Brae Boulevard
Park Ridge, NJ 07656
201-307-2000
www.HERTZ.com

The New Pig Corp
1 Pork Avenue
Tipton, PA 16684
800-468-4647
www.NEWPIG.com

Environmental controls

INTRA Computer Inc
16115 Rockaway Boulevard
Suite 210
Jamaica, NY 11434
718-805-3911
www.INTRACOM.com

Evacuation equipment

Aiex Co.
1210 Avon Street
Belmont, CA 94002
650-591-3700

AOK Global Products Limited (RESCUE CHAIRS)
940-D Grand Blvd
Deer Park, NY 11729
631-242-1642
800-649-4265
www.rescuechairs.com

Baker Safety Equipment
4369 S Dupont Hwy
Townsend, DE 19734
302-652-7080
www.LIFECHUTE.com

Criterion Strategies Inc
580 Broadway
Suite 305
New York, NY 10012
212-343-1134
www.criterionstrategies.com

Evac+Chair Corporation
17 E 67th Street
New York, NY 10021-5818
212-734-6222
www.EVAC-CHAIR.com

Garaventa (Canada) LTD.
7505-134A St.
Surrey, BC V3W 7B3
Canada
604-594-0422
800-663-6556
www.GARAVENTA.com

HMP Industries
4 Hershey Drive
Ansonia, CT 06401
203-734-8201
800-208-8201

OnScreen Technologies Inc.
200 9th Avenue North, Suite 210
Safety Harbor, Fl 34695
727-797-6664
www.onscreentech.com

THE RESCUE CHAIR

Is Your Building Safe?
Fire, Power Outage, Terrorist Attack, Gas Leak, Hurricane, Tornado

Available on GSA*
#GS-07F-9037D
(For government
orders only)

A MUST in any
High-Rise Emergency

It rides the stairs

* Opens in Seconds

* Carry 2 Children or 1 Adult (up to 300 lbs.)

* Weighs only 25 lbs.

The Safest and Easiest way to Transport the Disabled in an Emergency

NO **FACILITY SHOULD BE WITHOUT THE**
AOK
RESCUE CHAIR

AOK GLOBAL
Products, Ltd.

940-D Grand Blvd
Deer Park, New York 11729
Toll Free: 1-800-649-4265
Tel: 631-242-1642
Fax: 631-242-4564
e-mail: sales@rescuechair.com
www.rescuechair.com

O-Two Medical Technologies Inc
7575 Kimbel Street
Mississauga, ON L5S1C8
Canada
905-677-9410
800-387-3405
www.otwo.com

Fire fighting equipment

Ansul Inc.
1 Stanton Street
Marinette, WI 54143
715-735-7411
800-862-6785
www.ansul.com

Flexlite Inc.
P.O. Box 175
Red Bank, NJ 07701
732-263-1771
www. flexliteusa.com

FoamPro — Hypro/Pentair Water
375 Fifth Avenue
New Brighton, MN 55125
651-766-6300
800-533-9511
www.foampro.com

Intelagard, Inc.
590 Burbank Street
Suite 220
Broomfield, CO 80020
303-309-6309
303-410-1565
www.intelagard.com

Mainstream Dry Hydrants Inc.
6 Neely St. R.R. #1
Dunrobin Shores, ON K0A 1T0
Canada
613-832-0300
613-299-7712
www.dryhydrants.ca

Metro Fire & Safety Equipment
Jomike Court
489 Washington Ave.
Carlstadt, NJ 07072
201-635-0400
800-226-9324
www.metrofire.com

Safeware
3200 Hubbard Road
Landover, MD 20785
800-331-6707
www.safewareinc.com

UK
13400 Danielson Street
Poway, CA 92064
858-513-9100
800-327-7388
www.ukbright.com

EQUIPMENT

Fireproof safes, files, & containers

DEW Filing Systems and Storage
1525 E. Apache Blvd.
Tempe, AZ 85281
877-933-7238
480-858-0024
www.thefilestore.com

FireKing International Inc.
101 Security Parkway
New Albany, IN 47150
812-948-8400
800-227-7513
www.FIREKING.com

FireSafe Innovations LLC
4 Elmwood Hill Lane
Rochester, NY 14610-3446
585-385-9007
www.SAFESUPPLIES.com

Safetyfile, Inc.
23075 Highway 7
Excelsior, MN 55331
800-700-8025
952-908-3160
www.safetyfile.com

Fuel cells, power, portable

MagPower Systems Inc
Suite 330
6165 Highway 17
Delta, BC V4K 5B8
Canada
604 940-3232
www.magpowersystems.com

Furniture rental, commercial/residential

CORT Furniture Rental - Commercial/Residential
11250 Waples Mill Road
Suite 500
Fairfax, VA 22030-7400
703-968-8500
800-962-CORT
www.CORT1.com

Deskco Office Furniture
910 Rt 110
Farmdale, NY 11735
631-753-3601
www.BECKOFFICEFURNITURE.com

National Business Services Inc
1601 Magoffin Avenue
El Paso, TX 79901
800-777-7807
www.NBSINC.com

Office Furniture Rental Alliance
2100 E. Fullerton Drive
Unit C
Fullerton, CA 92831
714-447-4023
888-318-6372
www.OFRA.com

Office Furniture Rental Alliance
1049 Montague Expressway
Milpitas, CA 95035
408-719-3217
415-760-7752
www.SHOPOFRA.com

Office Furniture Rental Alliance
71 George Street
East Hartford, CT 06108
860-528-2000
www.OFRA.com

Office Furniture Rental Alliance
1075 Florida Central Parkway
Suite 2100
Longwood, FL 32750
407-260-5048
www.ofra.com

Office Furniture Rental Alliance
5080 N. Royal Atlanta Drive
Tucker, GA 30084
770-491-8896
www.OFRA.com

Office Furniture Rental Alliance
397 South Glen Ellyn Road
Chicago, IL 60108
630-790-9740
888-318-6372
www.OFRA.com

Office Furniture Rental Alliance
8800 Lottsford Road
Largo, MD 20774
301-333-4116
888-318-6372
www.OFRA.com

Office Furniture Rental Alliance
838 West Goodale Blvd.
Grand View, OH 43212
614-469-7950
888-318-6372
www.OFRA.com

Office Furniture Rental Alliance
Stemmons Cornerstone Crossing
9761 Clifford Drive, Suite 180
Dallas, TX 75220
214-358-5990
888-318-6372
www.OFRA.com

EQUIPMENT

Office Furniture Rental Alliance
6000 E. Marginal Way
Seattle, WA 98108
206-768-8000
888-318-6372
www.OFRA.com

Palmer Snyder
1050 Chinoe Road
Suite 106
Lexington, KY 40502
800-762-0415
800-535-4519
www.palmersnyder.com

RBF Interiors
5055 Natural Bridge Avenue
Saint Louis, MO 63115
314-383-7003
www.rbfinteriors.com

WEHSCO Bed Products
146 Campanelli Parkway
Stoughton, MA 02072
800-225-8680
781-344-8676
www.WEHSCO.com

Generators, electric

A Rental Service Division of Wirtz Rentals
1045 W. 47th
Chicago, IL 60609
773-247-2443
www.wirtz.com

A to Z Equipment Rentals & Sales
15634 N 32nd Street
Phoenix, AZ 85032
602-992-1150
www.A-ZEQUIPMENT.com

AAR Divison Indeck Power
1111 Willis Avenue
Wheeling, IL 60090
847-541-8300
800-446-3325
www.INDECK.com

Ace Tool Rental
7131 Lee Highway
Falls Church, VA 22046
703-532-5600
www.toolrental.com

Aggreko Rental
4607 W. Admiral Doyle Drive
New Iberia, LA 70560-9134
800-258-4874
www.aggreko.com

Air & Electric Equipment Co.
2314 N 2nd Street
Philadelphia, PA 19133
215-425-8500
www.AIRANDELECTRIC.com

ASCO Power Techonologies
50 Hanover Rd.
Florham Park, NJ 07932
800-800-2726
www.asco.com

Atlantic Detroit Diesel Allison Inc
180 State Hwy./Rt. 17 S
Lodi, NJ 07644
718-665-1500
www.ATLANTICDDA.com

Aura Systems, Inc.
2335 Alaska Ave.
El Segundo, CA 90245
310-643-5300 x213
www.aurasystems.com

Barco
2205 S Industrial Boulevard
Dallas, TX 75207
214-428-5691
www.barcopump.com

Bayside Equipment Co.
3562 Haven Avenue
Redwood City, CA 94063
650-368-3955

Belyea Company Inc
2200 Northwood Avenue
Easton, PA 18045
610-515-8775
www.BELYEAPOWER.com

California Diesel and Power
150 Nardi Lane
Martinez, CA 94553
925-229-2700
www.gotpower.com

Castay Inc
900 E Airline Highway
La Place, LA 70068
504-524-8444
985-652-9722

Cat Rental Power
AC6109
P.O. Box 610
Mossville, IL 61552
1-800-RENT CAT
847-749-0797
www.catrentalpower.com

CESCO
7251 Cross County Rd
North Charleston, SC 29418
888-772-3726
843-760-3000
www.blastandpaint.com

Controls & Power Systems
P.O. Box 183
Boxford, MA 01921
978-887-8525

Cummins NPower LLC
7145 Santa Fe Drive
Hodgkins, IL 60525
651-636-1000
800-642-0085
www.CUMMINSNPOWER.com

Cummins Rocky Mountain LLC
601 North 101st Ave.
Avondale, AZ 85323
800-800-2345
www.cummins.com

Curtis Engine & Equipment Inc
3918 Vero Road
Baltimore, MD 21227
410-536-1203
800-573-9200
www.CURTISENGINE.com

Cycle City
2555 W Chester Pike
Broomall, PA 19008
610-356-2662
www.CYCLE-CITY.com

DeFranco True Value/Rental
3105 Pine Avenue
Niagara Falls, NY 14301
716-285-3393

Duthie Power Services
2335 E Cherry Industrial Circle
Long Beach, CA 90805
562-432-3931
www.DUTHIEPOWER.com

Electric Tool & Supply Co.
7910 W Market Street
Peoria, AZ 85345
623-878-0777

Energy Systems
7100 S Longe St STE 300
Stockton, CA 95206
209-983-6900
www.energysystem.net

Enviro-Energy Technologies
4981 Hwy 7 East
Suite 12A-271
Markham, ON L3R 1N1
Canada
416-927-7690
www.enviro-energytech.com

FM Emergency Generator
35 Pequit Street
Canton, MA 02021-2502
781-828-0026
www.FMGENERATOR.com

Foley Machinery Co.
978 State Hwy 33 E
Monroe Township, NJ 08831
609-443-1991
www.foleyinc.com

Foley Power Systems
855 Centennial Avenue
Piscataway, NJ 08855
732-885-5555
www.foleyinc.com

Foley Rents
833 Centennial Ave
Piscataway, NJ 08855
732-885-5555
www.Foleyinc.com

Forces Inc
31 W. 350 Diehl Rd.
Naperville, IL 60563
800-222-1195
630-369-4100
www.forcesinc.com

Generac Power Systems, Inc
P.O. Box 8
Waukesha, WI 53187-0008
262-544-4811
www.GENERAC.com

Gulf Electroquip Inc
425 N Wayside Drive
Houston, TX 77020
713-675-2525

H O Penn Machinery
660 Union Ave
Hoitsville, NY 11742
631-654-4400
www.hopeonmachinery.com

Hahn Equipment Co.
5636 Kansas Street
Houston, TX 77007
713-868-3255
www.HAHNEQUIPMENT.com

Hercules Portable Power Co.
24000 Broad Street
Carson, CA 90745
310-830-2254
www.herculesportablepower.com

Hertz Equipment Rental
225 Brae Blvd.
Park Ridge, NJ 07656
888-777-2700
www.hertzequip.com

Holt Cat Power Systems
2001 N Loop 12
Irving, TX 75061
972-721-5800
210-648-8407
www.holtcat.com

Huntington Power Equipment Inc
8 Algonkin Road
Shelton, CT 06484
203-929-3203
www.huntingtonpower.com

Ingersoll-Rand Equipment and Services
10430 Drummond Road
Philadelphia, PA 19154
800-679-1951
215-632-4200
www.irco.com

Ingersoll-Rand Equipment Sales
300 Turnpike Road
Southborough, MA 01772
508-481-1350
www.IRCO.com

iPower Systems
1307 Brentwood Hills Blvd
Brandon, FL 33511-6157
813-685-2424
813-789-2121
www.i-power-systems.com

Johnson Power Systems
656 East La Cadena Drive
P.O. Box 357
Riverside, CA 92502
951-683-5960
951-686-4560
www.JOHNSON-POWER.com

Kawasaki Portable Generators
Route 44
Punnam, CT 06260
860-928-7565

Kelly Generator & Equipment Inc
8431 Old Marlboro Pike
Uppr Marlboro, MD 20772-2614
301-420-3983
800-677-3815
www.kge.com

Keystone Pump & Power, LLC
1480 S. Mountain Road
Dillsbury, PA 17019
717-502-8500
www.keystonepumpandpower.com

Kinsley Power Systems
14 Connecticut South Drive
East Granby, CT 06026
860-844-6100
www.kinsleypower.com

Kraft Powerr
199 Wildwood Avenue
Woburn, MA 01801
781-938-9100
800-969-6121
www.KRAFTPOWER.com

Leppert Nutmeg Inc.
113 W Dudley Town Road
Bloomfield, CT 06002
860-243-1737
www.LEPPERTNUTMEG.com

Louisiana Machinery
4727 N W Evangeline Thwy
Carencro, LA 70520
337-896-7211
www.louisianamachinery.com

Louisiana Rents
38294 hwy 30
Gonzales, LA 70737
225-644-6600
http://louisiana.cat.com

Mack Boring & Parts Co.
2365 Route 22
P.O. Box 3116
Union, NJ 07083
908-964-0700
800-622-5364
www.MACKBORING.com

McQuade & Bannigan Inc.
1300 Stark St.
Utica, NY 13502
315-724-7119
www.MQB.com

Milton Cat, Power Systems Division
101 Quarry Drive
Milford, MA 01757-1733
508-634-3400
www.MILTONCAT.com

Mitsubishi Generators and Pumps
6525 Daniel Burnham Drive
Suite C
Portage, IN 46368
888-387-3464
219-764-5400
www.mitsubishi-generators.com

NationsRent
450 East Las Olas Blvd.
Ft. Lauderdale, FL 33467
800-667-9328
www.NATIONSRENT.com

NationsRent
91 N 12th Street
Brooklyn, NY 11211
718-387-4872
www.NATIONSRENT.com

Nickell Equipment Rental & Sales
3261 East Highway 34
Newnan, GA 30265
770-253-4242
www.nickellrental.com

Patten Power Systems
615 W Lake Street
Elmhurst, IL 60126
630-530-2200
www.pattenpower.com

EQUIPMENT

Peterson Power Systems Inc
2828 Teagarden Street
San Leandro, CA 94577
510-895-8400
www.PETERSONPOWER.com

Pinckney Tru-Value Hardware
114 W. Main
Pickney, MI 48169
734-878-2000
www.PINCKNEYHARDWARE.com

Power Equipment Co
7 Franklin R McKay Road
Attleboro, MA 02703
508-226-3410

Power Plus
1850 West Pinnacle Peek Rd.
Phoenix, AZ 85027
480-951-9116
623-434-0389

Quinn Power Systems
10273 Golden State Blvd.
Selma, CA 93662
559-891-5447
559-896-4040
www.QUINNGROUP.net

Reliable Electric Motor Inc
285 Murphy Road
Hartford, CT 06114
860-522-2257
www.reliableelectricmotor.com

Rental Motors Sports
Rt. 202
Gorham, ME 04038
207-839-5522
www.rentalmotorssports.com

Rent-a-Tool Inc
777 N Shore Road
Revere, MA 02151
781-289-3800
800-272-8484
www.rentatool.com

RP RENTALS INC
1855 Stanhope St.
Ridgewood, NY 11385
718-456-7397
www.rprentals.com

Rudox Engine & Equipment Co.
765 State Route 17
Carlstadt, NJ 07072
201-438-0111

Russelectric Inc.
99 Industrial Park Rd
Hingham, MA 02043
781-749-6000
www.russelectric.com

SML Industries Inc.
2001 N. 17th Avenue
Melrose Park, IL 60160
800-730-3927
708-338-9900
www.voltmaster.com

Stewart & Stevenson
1631 Chalk Hill Road
Dallas, TX 75212
866-782-8660
214-623-1655
www.ssss.com

Stewart & Stevenson Services
1400 Destrehan Avenue
Harvey, LA 70058
504-347-4326
www.ssss.com

Sunbelt Rentals
1337 Hundred Oaks Drive
Charlotte, NC 28217
866—786-2358
704-348-2676
www.sunbeltrentals.com

Sunbelt Scaffolding and Supply, Inc.
2090 N. Orange Blossom Trail
Orlando, Fl 32804
407-244-5556
www.sunbeltscaffolding.com

Sunstate Equipment Co.
5425 E. Washington Street
Phoenix, AZ 85034-2106
888-456-4560
www.SUNSTATEEQUIP.com

Sweinhart Electric Co. Inc
7425 Orangethorpe Avenue
Suite E
Buena Park, CA 90621
714-521-9100

Taylor Rental Center
67 NH Route 11
Farmington, NH 03835
603-332-0911

Tool and Equipment Service Solutions LLC
5 Manila Avenue
Hamden, CT 06514
203-248-7553

Tradewinds Power Corp.
5820 NW 84th Ave
Miami, FL 33166
305-592-9745
800-223-3289
www.TRADEWINDSPOWER.com

TriAxis Inc.
23 Midstate Drive
Suite 106
Auburn, MA 01501
508-721-9691
www.triaxisinc.com

EQUIPMENT

United Rentals Pumps*Power*HVAC
3400 NW 15 Street
Lauderhill, FL 33313
954-797-3867
http://www.unitedrentals.com

United Rentals Pumps*Power*HVAC
9375 Boggy Creek Rd.
Orlando, FL 32824
888-269-8292
http://www.unitedrentals.com

United Rentals Pumps*Power*HVAC
3990 Jonesboro Rd.
Forest Park, GA 30297
800-506-5831
www.unitedrentals.com

United Rentals Pumps*Power*HVAC
30 A. Independence Rd.
Kingston, MA 02364
866-544-7867
www.unitedrentals.com

United Rentals Pumps*Power*HVAC
130 Skipjack Rd.
Prince Frederick, MD 20678
800-544-8658
http://www.unitedrentals.com

United Rentals Pumps*Power*HVAC
82 East Browning Rd.
Bellmawr, NJ 08031
610-972-3642
www.unitedrentals.com

United Rentals Pumps, Power, HVAC
40 Industry Drive
West Haven, CT 06576
203-937-9953
866-742-0434
www.unitedrentals.com

United Rentals Pumps, Power, HVAC
1730 North Powerline Road
Pompano Beach, FL 33069
800-462-0994
954-917-5440
www.unitedrentals.com

United Rentals Pumps, Power, HVAC
371 Taft Vineland Road
Orlando, FL 32824
888-269-8292
407-854-6061
www.unitedrentals.com

United Rentals, Inc.
40 Industry Drive
West Haven, CT 06516
866-742-0434
www.unitedrentals.com

United Services DKI
130 Skipjack Road
Frederick, MD 20678
800-644-8658
410-414-3195
www.unitedrentals.com

Vaughn's Power Equipment Inc
412 Veterans Memorial Boulevard
Kenner, LA 70062
504-466-8568

Washington Air Compressor Rental Co.
1800 4th Street, NE
Washington, DC 20002
202-635-1500
240-832-7500
www.washair.com

Washington Air Compressor Rental Co.
41096 John Mosby Hwy (Rt. 50)
Chantilly, VA 20105
703-742-6200
240-832-7500
www.washair.com

Waverly Tool Rental & Sales Inc
20 Cedar Street
Framingham, MA 01702
508-872-8880
www.waverlytool.com

Weld Power Service Company
14 Technology Drive
Auburn, MA 01501-3211
508-832-3550
800-288-6016

Wheeler Machinery Co.
4901 W. 2100 So.
Salt Lake City, UT 84120
801-974-0511
www.wheelermachineryco.com

Winco Inc
225 S Cordova Avenue
Le Center, MN 56057-1805
507-357-6821
800-733-2112
www.wincogen.com

Lighting, emergency

Airstar America, Inc.
10950 Burbank Blvd
N. Hollywood, CA 91601
800-217-9001
818-753-0066
www.airstar-lighting.us

EQUIPMENT

Allmand Bros., Inc.
1502 West 4th Ave
Holdrege, NE 68949
800-562-1373
308-995-4495
www.allmand.com

American Permalight Inc
2531 W 237th St #113
Torrance, CA 90505
310-891-0924
www.americanpermalight.com

Foley Rents
833 Centennial Ave
Piscataway, NJ 08855
732-885-5555
www.Foleyinc.com

Hertz Equipment Rental
225 Brae Blvd.
Park Ridge, NJ 07656
888-777-2700
www.hertzequip.com

Industrial Services, Inc.
P.O. Box 4595
Chatsworth, CA 91313
818-822-7529
661-251-5312
www.isirentals.com

OnScreen Technologies Inc.
200 9th Avenue North, Suite 210
Safety Harbor, Fl 34695
727-797-6664
www.onscreentech.com

PowerFlare
6489 Camden Ave. Suite 108
San Jose, CA 95120
408-323-2371
877-256-6907
www.powerflare.com

Prism - Emergency Inflatable Lighting
8131 Baymeadows WEST STE 202
JACksonville, FL 32257
904-880-9900
www.prismcs.net/eil.html

Simpler Life Emergency Provisions
2035 Park Avenue
Suite 1
Redlands, CA 92373
909-798-8108
800-266-7737
www.simplerlife.com

SOLAR INC
3210 SW 42nd Avenue
Palm City, FL 34990
772-286-9461
www.solarlighting.com

The Keystone Group
FlareAlert
P.O. Box 509
Niwot, CO 80544
888-652-6164
www.flarealert.com

Tower Solutions
1150 Hostein Drive NE
Pine City, MN 55063
480-315-8830
www.towersolutionsinc.com

UK
13400 Danielson Street
Poway, CA 92064
858-513-9100
800-327-7388
www.ukbright.com

Underwater Kinetics
13400 Danielson Street
Poway, CA 92064
800-327-7388
858-513-9100
www.UWKINETICS.com

Washington Air Compressor Rental Co.
1800 4th Street, NE
Washington, DC 20002
202-635-1500
240-832-7500
www.washair.com

Washington Air Compressor Rental Co.
41096 John Mosby Hwy (Rt. 50)
Chantilly, VA 20105
703-742-6200
240-832-7500
www.washair.com

Will-Burt Company
169 S. Main St.
P.O. Box 900
Orriville, OH 44667
330-682-7015
www.wilburt.com

Mailing equipment

Automated Mailing Systems Corp.
10730 Spangler Road
Dallas, TX 75220
800-527-1668
www.AMSCODALLAS.com

EQUIPMENT

Medical equipment, emergency

Aramsco
1655 Imperial Way
Thorofare, NJ 08086
856-848-5330
800-767-6933
www.aramsco.com

Chinook Medical Gear, Inc.
120 Rock Point Drive
Unit C
Durango, CO 81301
970-375-1241
800-766-1365
www.chinookmed.com

Emergency Preparedness Systems
21279 Protecta Dr.
Elkhart, IN 46516
800-478-2363
574-522-7201
www.tempsbed.com

Galls Incorporated
2680 Palumbo Drive
P.O. Box 54308
Lexington, KY 40509
800-477-7766
859-266-7227
www.galls.com

Johns Hopkins Lifeline
600 North Wolfe Street
Jefferson B1-104
Baltimore, MD 21287
410-502-7415

LifeSavers, Inc.
759 Bloomfield Ave
#102
West Caldwell, NJ 07006
866-641-1200
www.lifesaversinc.com

Lifesaving Systems, Inc.
485 Abbeywood Drive
Roswell, GA 30075
866-OXYLATE
770-552-8696
www.lifesavingsystemsinc.com

Pacific Consolidated Industries (PCI)
12201 Magnolia Avenue
Riverside, CA 92503-4820
951-479-0860
www.pci-intl.com

Philips
3000 Minuteman Road
Andover, MA 01810
800-934-7372
www.MEDICAL.PHILIPS.com

Simpler Life Emergency Provisions
2035 Park Avenue
Suite 1
Redlands, CA 92373
909-798-8108
800-266-7737
www.simplerlife.com

U O Equipment Co.
5863 W 34th St
P.O. Box 924615
Houston, TX 77292-4615
800-231-6372
713-686-1869

World Prep Inc.
2620-T Centennial Road
Toledo, OH 43617
419-843-3869
www.worldprep.com

Zoll Medical Corporation
269 Mill Road
Chelmsford, MA 01824
800-348-9011
978-421-9655
www.zoll.com

Moisture meters

Delmhorst Instrument Co.
51 Indian Lane East
Towaco, NJ 07082-1025
973-334-2557
877-335-6467
www.delmhorst.com

Power line analyzers & monitors

Dranetz Technologies
1000 New Durham Road
Edison, NJ 08817-2216
732-287-3680
800-372-6832
www.DRANETZ-BMI.com

Pearson Electronics Inc
4009 Transport St
Palo Alto, CA 94303
650-494-6444
www.pearsonelectronics.com

EQUIPMENT

Power protection & continuation devices

ALSO SEE UPS IN GENERAL EQUIPMENT SECTION

American Superconductor
8401 Murphy Drive
Middleton, WI 53562
608-831-5773
www.superbuc.com

BLI International, Inc. - Priority Start!
17939 Chatsworth St.
Suite 521
Granada Hills, CA 91344
818-363-5390
www.PRIORITYSTART.com

Clary Corp
1960 Walker Avenue
Monrovia, CA 91016-4847
800-442-5279
www.CLARY.com

Cummins Power Rent
1400 73rd Avenue N.E.
Minneapolis, MN 55432
623-572-4940
877-769-7669
www.cumminspower.com/rental

Dependable Power Systems
P.O. Box 339
Fredericktown, OH 43019
740-694-0496

Dynamic Systems
Nesconset, NY 11767
800-422-0708

Eaton Corp Powerware
2727 Kurtz Street
San Diego, CA 92110
619-291-4211
800-854-2658
www.POWERWARE.com

Eaton Corporation Powerware
8609 Six Forks Road
Raleigh, NC 27615
919-872-3020
800-554-3448
www.powerware.com

Kaydon Filtration Group
1571 Lukken Industrial Drive W
Lagrange, GA 30240
706-884-3041
800-241-2342
www.kaydonfiltration.com

Kussmaul Electronics Co., Inc.
170 Cherry Avenue
West Sayville, NY 11796
800-346-0857
631-567-0314
www.kussmaul.com

Majorpower Corporation
7011 Industrial Drive
Mebane, NC 27302
800-931-4919
www.majorpower.com

Minuteman UPS
1455 Lemay Drive
Carrollton, TX 75007
972-446-7363
800-238-7272
www.MINUTEMANUPS.com

Oneac Corp
27944 N Bradley Road
Libertyville, IL 60048
847-816-6000
800-327-8801
www.ONEAC.com

Power & Systems Innovations, Inc.
P.O. Box 590223
Orlando, FL 32859-0223
407-380-9200
http://www.psihq.com

Powervar
1450 Lakeside Drive
Suite C
Waukegan, IL 60085
847-816-8585
800-369-7179
www.powervar.com

Powerware
N 9246 Highway 80
Necedah, WI 54646
608-565-7200
800-356-5794
www.powerware.com

Price Wheeler Corp.
3800 31st St
San Diego, NJ 92011
800-528-0313

SmartPower Systems
1760 Stebbins Drive
Houston, TX 77043
800-882-8285
www.SMARTPOWERSYSTEMS.com

Staco Energy Products
301 Gaddis Boulevard
Dayton, OH 45403-1391
937-253-1191
866-261-1191
www.stacoenergy.com

EQUIPMENT

SunWize Technologies Inc
1155 Flatbush Road
Kingston, NY 12401
800-817-6527

Universal Power Systems Inc
4230 Lafayette Center Drive
Suite G
Chantilly, VA 20151
800-438-8774
703-378-6100
www.upsi.com

Rental equipment, all types

4 - Star TrueValue Builing Center
P.O. Box 309
455 Highway C
Seymour, MO 65746
417-935-4384

410 Rentals
25018 Hwy 410 E
Buckley, WA 98321
253-826-7671
http://www.410rentals.com

All in One Rentals
2095 Jericho Turnpike
East Northport, NY 11731
631-499-5151
www.ALLINONE.com

AlturnaMATS, Inc.
POB 344
Titusville, PA 16301
888-544-6287
814-827-8884
www.Alturnamats.com

Ankeny Rental Center
1617 S. Ankeny Blvd
Ankeny, IA 50023
515-964-5400
515-554-2365
www.ankenyrentalcenter.com

Auto Supply True Value
2876 Maybank Highway
Johns Island, SC 29455
843-559-1555
843-559-2579

Birch Equipment Rental & Sales
1619 Kentucky St
Bellingham, WA 98226
866-722-4724
360-734-5744
http://www.birchequipment.com

Blanchard Machinery Inc.
14301 N.E. 19th Avenue
North Miami, FL 33181
305-949-2581
www.blanchardmachinery.net

California Rental Association
4640 Northgate Blvd. Suite 160
P.O. Box 348420
Sacremento, CA 95834
800-272-7400
916-922-4222
www.craonthenet.org

Canvas Systems, Inc.
3025 Northwoods Parkway
Norcross, GA 30071
770-662-1881
http://www.canvassystems.com

Carr Hardware
547 North St.
Pittsfield, MA 01202
413-443-5611
413-243-2541
www.CARRHARDWARE.com

City TrueValue Just Ask Rental
750 Farmington Avenue
Bristol, CT 6010
860-582-7166

Clark - Devon Hardware Co.
6401 N. Clark Street
Chicago, IL 60626
773-764-3575
773-764-RENT
www.CLARKDEVON.com

Cleveland Brothers Equipment Company
5300 Paxton St
Harrisburg, PA 17111
800-482-2378
www.clevelandbrothers.com

Corey InduServe
407 Washington Street
Williamston, NC 27892
252-809-9022
www.INDUSERVE.com

Crete True Value Just Ask Rental
1122 Main Street
Crete, NE 68333
402-826-3397

Dripping Springs Hardware & Rental
28000 Ranch Road N., Suite 12
P.O. Box 1184
Dripping Springs, TX 78620
512-858-5601

Festvities, LLP
P. O. Box 6275
1374 Carley Road
Springdale, AR 72766
866-549-7368
479-750-8981
www.efestivities.com

EQUIPMENT

Godwin Pumps of America, Inc.
One Floodgate Road
Bridgeport, NJ 08014
856-467-3636
http://www.godwinpumps.com

Grand Rental Station
1541 S. Calumet Avenue
Chesterton, IN 46304
219-395-9797
219-405-3327
www.nwigrandrental.com

Hertz Equipment Rental
225 Brae Blvd.
Park Ridge, NJ 07656
888-777-2700
www.hertzequip.com

JBK True Value & Just Ask Rental
18 Washington Square Shopping Center
Chestertown, MD 21620
410-778-9600
www.jbkhardware.com

Journagan True Value
1200 E. Church
Aurora, MO 65605
417-678-4488
www.TRUEVALUE.com/journagan

Keystone Building Center
200 N.E. Commercial Circle
P.O Box 1249
Keystone Heights, FL 32656
352-473-9991
352-473-9983

Lampe True Value and Just Ask Rental
220 South Riverview Drive
Bellevue, IA 52031
563-872-4459

Longeneckers Just Ask Rental
127 Doe Run Road
Manheim, PA 17545
717-665-2020
717-665-2491
www.LONGENECKERSTV.com

Lorleberg True Value & Just Ask Rental
900 E. Wisoncsin Avenue
P.O. Box 603
Oconomowoc, WI 53066
262-567-0267

Magnolia Rental & Sales, Inc.
175 Hwy 51 South
Batesville, MS 38606
662-563-9373
662-934-3000

Magnolia Rental & Sales, Inc.
Hwy 6 West
P.O. Box 518
Oxford, MS 38655
662-236-7368
662-934-3000

NationsRent
450 E. Las Olas Blvd.
Ft. Lauderdale, FL 33301
800-667-9328
www.nationsrent.com

Nickell Equipment Rental & Sales
1507 Highway 16 West
Griffin, GA 30223
770-227-9122
678-776-4214
www.nickllrental.com

Plantation True Value Hardware
1221 FM 359
Richmond, TX 77469
281-342-5207
www.TRUEVALUE.com/plantation

Price & Gannon True Value & Just Ask Rental
2448 Centreville Rd.
Centreville, MD 21617
410-758-0730

Rental Works
6520 West Broad Street
Richmond, VA 23230
804-288-0018
www.rentalworks.com

Rental World
1020 E Business 83
McAllen, TX 78501
956-630-5222
www.RENTALWORLD.com

Samuelson True Value & Just Ask Rental
456 Breeze Street
Craig, CO 81625
970-824-6683
970-824-4200

Sarver TrueValue Just Ask Rental
551 S. Pike Road
Sarver, PA 16055
724-295-5131

Steele's Hardware
Route 611 Main Street
Tannersville, PA 18372
570-629-3406
www.STEELES-HARDWARE.com

Sun Rental Center
380 South Main
Colville, WA 99114
509-684-1522
509-684-2501
www.sunrentalcolville.com

EQUIPMENT

Sunbelt Rentals
1337 Hundred Oaks Drive
Charlotte, NC 28217
866—786-2358
704-348-2676
www.sunbeltrentals.com

Taylor Rental
118 Daniel Webster Hwy
Nashua, NH 03060
603-888-1670
www.TAYLORRENTALNASHUA.com

Taylor Rental
255 Route 31 South
Warren City
Washington, NJ 07887
908-689-4666

Taylor Rental
205 North Avenue
Webster, NY 14580
585-872-2770
www.TAYLORRENTALCENTERS.com

Taylor Rental
394 Oriskany Blvd.
Whitesboro, NY 13492
315-736-3232
www.taylorrentalcenters.com

Taylor Rental
136 N. Jensen Road
Vestal, NY 13850
607-729-7156

Taylor Rental, Sales & Service
1321 N. Spring St.
Beaver Dam, WI 53916
920-887-7142
920-887-1321

Ted's Rental & Sales Inc.
26344 U.S. Highway 160
Durango, CO 81303
970-247-2930
970-247-8665
www.TEDSRENTAL.com

Tri-Lift NC Inc.
2905 Manufacturers Rd
Greensboro, NC 27406
336-691-1511
www.tri-lift.com

Tri-Supply & Equipment
831 S. DuPont Parkway
New Castle, DE 19720
302-838-6333
302-697-0300
www.TRISUPPLYANDEQUIPMENT.com

United Rentals Inc. (HQ)
5 Greenwich Office Park
Greenwich, CT 06831-5128
203-622-3131
www.UR.com

Viking Rentals Inc
138 Society Drive
Telluride, CO 81435
970-728-0101
www.vikingrentals.biz

Wesco Rental Businesses, LP
Wesco Tool & Equipment
19106 S. Normandie Avenue
Torrance, CA 90502
310-538-2958
www.wescocompanies.com

Whitehead's Grand Rental Station
1620 State Street
Blair, NE 68008
402-426-9011

Sandbag filliing equipment

Alexander Equipment
4728 Yender Avenue
Lisle, IL 60532
630-663-1400
www.alexequip.com

Hogan MFG Inc.
P.O. Box 398
Escalon, CA 95320
209-838-7323
209-838-2400

The Sandbagger Corp.
P.O. Box 607
Wauconda, IL 60084
815-363-1400
www.THESANDBAGGER.com

Security & authentication systems

America's Personal Security, Inc.
228 Dolphin Point
Suite 3
Clearwater, FL 33767
727-443-6603
www.americaspersonalsecurity.com

Capital Card Systems
7613 Standish Place
Rockville, MD 20855
888-645-0727
301-545-0727
www.CapitalCardSystems.com

Fargo Electronics, Inc.
Secure Card Identity Systems
6533 Flying Cloud Drive
Eden Prairie, MN 55344
952-941-9470
800-459-5636
www.fargo.com

EQUIPMENT

Global ePoint, Inc.
339 S. Cheryl Lane
City of Industry, CA 91789
909-869-1688
http://www.globalepoint.com

ViaSat, Inc.
Type 1 IP Encryption Technology
6155 El Camino Real
Carlsbad, CA 92009
760-476-4796
760-476-4738
www.viasat.com

Site control

360 Surveillance, Inc.
11-625 Alpha Street
Victoria, BC V8Z 1B5
Canada
250-388-7232
www.360surveillance.com

Smoke & odor counteracting products

Air Quality Engineering
7140 Northland Dr N
Brooklyn Park, MN 55428
763-531-9823
800-328-0787
www.AIR-QUALITY-ENG.com

**ServiceMaster by Gaudet
6 Jefferson Avenue
Woburn, MA 01801-4325
781-932-1171
800-281-0072
www.servicemasterbygaudet.com**

Vaportek Inc.,
P.O. Box 148
W226 N6339 Village Drive
Sussex, WI 53089
800-237-6367
262-246-5060
www.vaportek.com

Steam cleaners & pressure washers

Foley Rents
833 Centennial Ave
Piscataway, NJ 08855
732-885-5555
www.Foleyinc.com

Mi-T-M Corporation
8650 Enterprise Drive
Peosta, Iowa 52068
563-556-7484
www.MITM.com

Sioux Steam Cleaner Corp
1 Sioux Plaza
Beresford, SD 57004
605-763-2776
605-763-3333
www.sioux.com

Surge protectors

Atlantic Scientific
4300 Fortune Place
Suite A
Melbourne, FL 32904
800-544-4737
321-725-8000
www.atlanticscientific.com

Atlantic Scientific Corp
4300 Fortune Place
Suite A
West Melbourne, FL 32904-1527
321-725-8000
800-544-4737
www.ATLANTICSCIENTIFIC.com

Banaher Power Solutions
5900 Eastport Boulevard
Richmond, VA 23231
804-236-3326
805-968-3551
www.banaherpowersolutions.com

Belkin Components
501 W Walnut Street
Compton, CA 90220
310-898-1100
www.BELKIN.com

Bravo Communications, Inc.
3463 Meadowlands Ln
San Jose, CA 95135
408-297-8700
800-366-0297
www.BRAVOBRAVO.com

EQUIPMENT

CITEL Inc
1515 NW 167th Street
6-303
Miami, FL 33169-5100
305-621-0022
www.citelprotection.com

EFI Electronics Corp
1751 S 4800 W
Salt Lake Cty, UT 84104
801-977-9009
800-877-1174
www.EFINET.com

Geist Manufacturing Inc.
1821 Yolande Avenue
Lincoln, NE 68521
402-474-3400
www.GEISTMFG.com

Innovative Technology Inc
15470 Flight Path Drive
Brooksville, FL 34604
352-799-0713
800-647-8877
www.INNOVATIVETECHNOLOGY.com

L.E.A. International
10701 Airport Drive
Hayden, ID 83835
800-881-8506
www.leaintl.com

Patton Electronics Co
7622 Rickenbacker Drive
Gaithersburg, MD 20879
301-975-1000
www.patton.com

Zero Surge Inc
889 State Route 12
Frenchtown, NJ 08825
908-996-7700
800-996-6696
www.ZEROSURGE.com

Tanks, storage

ConVault Florida
1410 Industrial Dr.
Wildwood, FL 34785
352-748-6462
www.OldCastleTorecest.com

Rain for Rent
3404 State Road
Bakersfield, CA 93308
661-399-9124
800-742-7246
www.rainforrent.com

Transformers, electric

AMS Alltronics Inc.
60013 Pro Glen Abbey
Oakville, ON L6M 3H2
Canada
905-844-5772
877-228-8612
www.hard-to-find.net

Electronic Specialists Inc
P.O. Box 389
Natick, MA 01760-0004
800-225-4876
508-655-1532
www.ELECT-SPEC.com

EMSCO, Electric Motor Supply Co.
4650 Main Street
Fridley, MN 55421
800-328-1842
763-571-9005
www.emscomn.com

Foley Rents
833 Centennial Ave
Piscataway, NJ 08855
732-885-5555
www.Foleyinc.com

Sunbelt Transformer Inc
1922 S Martin Luther King Dr
Temple, TX 76504
800-433-3128
www.sunbeltusa.com

Unison Transformer Svc Inc
3126 Brinkerhoff Road
Kansas City, KS 66115-1202
913-321-3155

UPS-uninterruptible power supplies

ALSO SEE **POWER PROTECTION & CONTINUATION** IN GENERAL EQUIPMENT SECTION

Alpha Technologies
3765 Alpha Way
Bellingham, WA 98226
360-671-7703
www.ALPHA.com

American Power Conversion Corp
132 Fairgrounds Road
West Kingston, RI 02892
401-789-5735
800-788-2208
www.apcc.com

Ametek HDR Power Systems
3563 Interchange Road
Columbus, OH 43204
614-308-5500
www.hdrpower.com

EQUIPMENT

Behlman Electronics
4532 Telephone Road
Ventura, CA 93003
805-642-0660
800-456-2006
www.BEHLMAN.com

Cables-to-go
2351 South 2300 West
Salt Lake City, UT 84119
801-973-6090
www.cablestogo-oem.com

**Cat Rental Power
AC6109
P.O. Box 610
Mossville, IL 61552
1-800-RENT CAT
847-749-0797
www.catrentalpower.com**

**Caterpillar Power Quality Protection
Systems
100 NE Adams Street
Peoria, IL 61629-0001
309-578-6298
800-947-6567
www.CATUPS.com**

Computer Air and Power Systems, Inc.
2372 Walsh Ave
Santa Clara, CA 95051
408-748-0200
800-800-4ups
www.caps4ups.com

Controlled Power Company
1955 Stephenson Highway
Troy, MI 48083
248-528-3700
800-521-4792
www.CONTROLLEDPWR.com

Cyberex Inc
5900 Eastport Boulevard
Bldg V
Richmond, VA 23231
800-238-5000
www.CYBEREX.com

General Atomics Electronic Systems, Inc.
4949 Greencraig Lane
San Diego, CA 92123
858-522-8300
www.ga-esi.com

Hitran Corp
362 State Route 31
Flemington, NJ 08822
908-782-5525
www.hitrancorp.com

Instrumentation & Control Systems(ICS)
520 W Interstate Road
Addison, IL 60101
630-543-6200
www.ics-timers.com

International Power Technologies
1129 s 300 W
Orem, UT 84058
801-224-4828
www.iptinc.com

Kelly Generator & Equipment Inc
8431 Old Marlboro Pike
Uppr Marlboro, MD 20772-2614
301-420-3983
800-677-3815
www.kge.com

Liebert Corp
1050 Dearborn Drive
Columbus, OH 43085
614-888-0246
800-877-9222
www.LIEBERT.com

Majorpower Corporation
7011 Industrial Drive
Mebane, NC 27302
800-931-4919
www.majorpower.com

MGE UPS Systems
1660 Scenic Avenue
Costa Mesa, CA 92626
714-557-1636
800-523-0142
www.MGEUPS.com

Myers/Abacus Power Products Inc.
2000 Highland Avenue
Bethlehem, PA 18020
610-868-3500
800-526-5088
www.ABACUSCONTROLS.com

Philtek Power
P.O. Box 1
Blaine, WA 98231
360-332-7252
360-332-7253
www.philtek.com

Power Systems Specialists, Inc.
103 Rt 6
P. O. Box 1216
Milford, PA 18337
888-305-1555
570-296-4573
www.p-s-s.com

Superior Electric
383 Middle Street
Bristol, CT 06010
860-582-9561
www.superiorelectric.com

Toshiba International Corp
13131 W Little York Road
Houston, TX 77041
800-231-1412

EQUIPMENT

Total Concept Sales
501 W Glenoaks Boulevard
Glendale, CA 91202
818-547-9476
www.SMARTUPS.com

Tracewell
9962 Route 446
Cuba, NY 14727
585-968-2400
www.TRACEWELL.com

TriAxis Inc.
23 Midstate Drive
Suite 106
Auburn, MA 01501
508-721-9691
www.triaxisinc.com

Tripp Lite
111 W. 35th St
Chicago, IL 60609
312-329-1777
www.TRIPPLITE.com

Warning signs

AccuForm Signs
16228 Flight Path Drive
Brooksville, FL 34604
800-237-1001
www.accuform.com

LabelMaster
5724 North Pulaski Road
Chicago, IL 60646
800-621-5808
773-478-0900
www.labelmaster.com

Legible Signs, Inc.
2221 Nimtz Road
Rockford, IL 61111
888-Legi-Sign
815-654-0100
www.legiblesigns.com

Temporary Perimeter Systems
19784 Kenrick Ave
Lakeville, MN 55044
952-469-5101
866-469-5101
www.smartbarrierusa.com

The Nutheme Company
1461-D Lunt Avenue
Elk Grove Village, IL 60007
847-952-1870
www.nutheme.com

Washing equipment, truck wheels & tires

Wheelwash Division, Global Equipment
P.O. Box 810607
Boca Raton, FL 33481
561-750-8662
www.wheelwash.com

Water purification equipment

Global Water Group Inc
8601 Sovereign Row
Dallas, TX 75247
214-678-9866
www.GLOBALWATER.com

Hydration Technologies, Incorporated
2484 Ferry St SW
Albany, OR 97322
541-917-3335
www.hydrationtech.com

Isonics Corporation
6851 Oak Hall Lane
Suite 119
Columbia, MD 21045
410-381-5254
www.ISONICS.com

EQUIPMENT

EQUIPMENT

EQUIPMENT

EQUIPMENT

EQUIPMENT

MATERIALS & PUBLICATIONS

Films/Videos

Production

remote-i
81 David Love Place
Goleta, CA 93117
805-683-3738
http://www.remotei.com

The MARCOM Group, Ltd.
20 Creek Parkway
Boothwyn, PA 19061
800-654-2448
610-859-8989
www.marcomltd.com

Rental & sale

BCP Media
P.O. Box 510754
St. Louis, MO 63151
314-894-0276
www.BCPMEDIA.com

Coastal Training Technologies
500 Studio Drive
Virginia Beach, VA 23452
800-767-7703
www.COASTAL.com

Commonwealth Films Inc
223 Commonwealth Avenue
Boston, MA 02116-1700
617-262-5634
www.COMMONWEALTHFILMS.com

Emergency Film Group
140 Cooke St P.O. Box 1928
Edgartown, MA 02539
508-627-8844
http://www.efilmgroup.com

FSP Books and Videos
577 Main Street
Hudson, MA 01749
978-562-1289
www.FIRE-POLICE-EMS.com

Spanish language

Long Island Production
dba TheTraining Network Inc
106 Capitola Drive
Durham, NC 27713
800-390-8283

National Instructors Resource Center
4148 Louis Avenue
Holiday, FL 34691
800-246-5101
www.nirc.biz

Miscellaneous Materials

Crisis response kits

Lutheran Disaster Response of New York
22 Cortlandt St.
New York, NY 10007
866-864-1600
212-406-9736
www.LDRNY.org

Quake Kare, Inc.
P.O. Box 13
Moorpark, CA 93020-0013
800-2pre-pare
800-277-3727
www.quakekare.com

Planning & 'how to' manuals

American Water Works Association, AWWA
6666 W. Quincy Ave.
Denver, CO 80235
800-926-7337
303-794-7711
www.awwa.org

Assisting People with Disabilities in a Disaster
FEMA 500 C Street SW
Washington, DC 20472
202-566-1600
www.FEMA.gov/rrr/assistf.shtm

Bioterrorism Preparedness Program
3 Capitol Hill
Room 309
Providence, RI 02908
401-222-6868
401-222-6953
www.health.ri.gov/environment/biot

Coping With Technological Disasters
Prince William Sound Regional Advisory Council
3709 Spenard Road
Anchorage, AK 99503
907-277-7222
www.pwsrcac.org

Fedhealth
7739 E. Broadway
Tucson, AZ 85710
888-999-4352
520-290-0929
www.fedhealth.net

GENESYS Software Systems Inc
5 Branch Street
Methuen, MA 01844
978-685-5400
www.genesyshcm.com

InfoEdge
P.O. Box 391619
Cambridge, MA 02139
800-363-7150
617-628-0481
www.infoedge.com

National Association of County and City Health Officials
1100 17th Street, NW
Second Floor
Washington, DC 20036
202-783-5550
www.naccho.org

Rothstein Catalog on Disaster Recovery
4 Arapaho Road
Brookfield, CT 06804
203-740-7400
www.DisasterRecoveryBooks.com

Planning & 'how to' manuals, foreign languages

American Red Cross Disaster Services
2025 E Street NW
Washington, DC 20006
703-206-6000
www.REDCROSS.org/disaster/index.html

American Red Cross National Headquarters
2025 E Street, NW
Washington, DC 20006
202-303-4498
www.REDCROSS.org/services/disaster

Pan American Health Organization
Emergency Preparedness Program
525 Twenty-third Street, NW
Washington, DC 20037
202-974-3520
202-974-3399
www.paho.org/english/ped/pedhome.htm

Training materials

US, EPA: Chemical Emergency Preparedness and Prevention Office
Ariel Rios Federal Building (5104A)
1200 Pennsylvaina Avenue, NW
Washington, DC 02460
1-800-424-9346
1-703- 412-9810
www.epa.gov/swercepp/

Publications

Books, journals, newsletters, general

"Vital Records Programs: Recovering Business Critical Records"
Available via: ARMA International
13725 W. 109th Street, Suite 101
Lenexa, KS 66215
913-341-3808
800-422-2762
www.arma.org

9-1-1 MAGAZINE
18201 Weston Pl.
Tustin, CA 92780
714-544-7776
800-231-8911
www.9-1-1magazine.com

Altered Standards of Care in Mass Casualty Events
Agency for Healthcare Research and Quality (AHRQ)
540 Gaither Rd.
Rockville, MD 20850
800-358-9295
www.ahrq.gov/research/altstand

'An Ounce of Prevention: Disaster Planning for Archives'
Available via: ARMA International
13725 W. 109th Street, Suite 101
Lenexa, KS 66215
913-341-3808
800-422-2762
www.arma.org

Applied Technology Council
201 Redwood Shores Parkway
Suite 240
Redwood City, CA 94065-1191
650-595-1542
www.ATCOUNCIL.org

Applied Technology Council
2111 Wilson Blvd.
Suite 700
Arlington, VA 22201
703-351-5052
www.atcouncil.org/index.html

Avoid Disaster: Keep Your Business Going
Avail. via John Wiley & Sons
10475 Crosspoint Blvd.
Indianapolis, IN 46256
877-762-2974

Bank Administration Institute
1 N Franklin Street
Chicago, IL 60606
312-553-4600
800-323-8552
www.BAI.org

Bioterror Preparedness, Attack and Response
Elsevier
11830 Westline Industrial Drive
St. Louis, MO 63146
800-545-2522

Bomb Threat Management and Policy
Elsevier
11830 Westline INdustrial Fulfillment Drive
St. Louis, MO 63146
800-545-2522

Business Continuity: Best Practices
Avail. via Rothstein Assoc. Inc.
4 Arapaho Rd
Brookfield, CT 068094-3104
203-740-7444
888-768-4783

'Claims Magazine'
Available from: The National Underwriter Co.
5081 Olympic Boulevard
Erlanger, KY 41018
800-543-0874
www.CLAIMSMAG.com

Cleaning Specialists Magazine, ICS
22801 Ventura Blvd #115
Woodland Hills, CA 91364
818-224-8035
800-835-4398
www.icsmag.com

Contingency Planning & Recovery Institute (CPR-I)
P.O. Box 81151
Wellesley Hills, MA 02481
781-235-2895
www.CONTINGENCYPLAN-INST.com

Contingency Planning and Disaster Recovery
Avail. via John Wiley & Sons
10475 Crosspoint Blvd.
Indianapolis, IN 46256
877-762-2974

Continuity Insights
301 South Main St.
Doylestown, PA 18901
215-230-9556
www.CONTINUITYINSIGHTS.com

'Data Center Management Magazine' (DCM)
Available via: Afcom
742 East Chapman Avenue
Orange, CA 92866
714-997-7966
www.afcom.com

Definitive Handbook of Business Contingency Management
Avail. via John Wiley & Sons
10475 Crosspoint Blvd.
Indianapolis, IN 46256
877-762-2974

SUBSCRIPTION OFFER

FREE - if you subscribe now

 Official Publication of the Canadian Centre for Emergency Preparedness

EmergencyManagement Canada

Emergency Management Canada (EMC) is published on a quarterly basis and is distributed to more than 3,000 Emergency Preparedness Professionals across Canada. *EMC* is dedicated to providing informative and practical information on federal and world events.

A subscription to *Emergency Management Canada* is absolutely FREE if you subscribe before 31 December 2005!

To take advantage of this FREE subscription to *EMC*, please fill out the form below and return to:

Emergency Management Canada

AJP ANDREW JOHN PUBLISHING INC.

c/o Andrew John Publishing Inc., 115 King Street West, Suite 220 Dundas, ON L9H 1V1
brobinson@andrewjohnpublishing.com

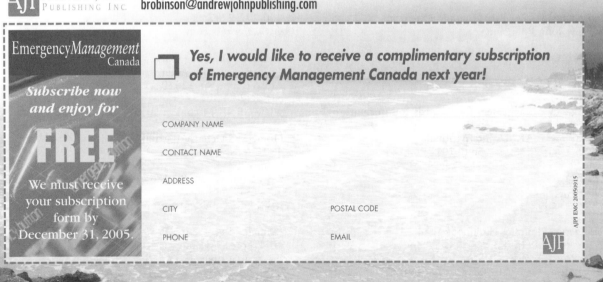

EmergencyManagement Canada

Subscribe now and enjoy for

FREE

We must receive your subscription form by December 31, 2005.

Yes, I would like to receive a complimentary subscription of Emergency Management Canada next year!

COMPANY NAME

CONTACT NAME

ADDRESS

CITY   POSTAL CODE

PHONE   EMAIL

AJP EMC 20050915

Disaster Management in Telecommunications
Avail. Via John Wiley & Sons
10475 Crosspoint Blvd.
Indianapolis, IN 46256
877-762-2974

Disaster Recovery Journal
P.O. Box 510110
Saint Louis, MO 63151
314-894-0276
www.DRJ.com

Disaster Recovery Testing
Avail. via Rothstein Assoc. Int'l
4 Arapaho Rd
Brookfield, CT 06804-3104
203-740-7444
888-768-4783
www.rothstein.com

Disaster Research Center
University of Delaware
87 East Main Street
Newark, DE 19716-2581
302-831-6618
www.UDEL.edu/DRC

Disaster Resource Guide
P.O. Box 15243
Santa Ana, CA 92735
714-558-8940
800-826-2201
www.DISASTER-RESOURCE.com

E-commerce Security: Weak Links, Best Defenses
Avail. via John Wiley & Sons
10475 Crosspoint Blvd.
Indianapolis, IN 46256
877-762-2974
www.wiley.com

Emergency Management Canada Magazine
Andrew John Publishing
115 King Street
Dundas, ON L9H 1V1
Canada
905-628-4309

'Emergency Management for Records & Information Programs'
Available via: ARMA International
13725 W. 109th Street, Suite 101
Lenexa, KS 66215
913-341-3808
800-422-2762
www.arma.org

Emergency Planning Handbook, 2nd
Avail. Via ASIS Int'l
1625 Prince Street
Alexandria, VA 22314-2818
703-519-6200
www.asisonline.org

Emergency Response Planning
Elsevier Science, Health Sciences Division
11830 Westline Industrial Drive
St. Louis, MO 63146
800-545-2522

Emergency Services Magazine
800-224-4EMS
www.emsmagazine.com

'Every Second Counts' Emergency Response Magazine
Available from: National Safety Council
1121 Spring Lake Drive
Itasca, IL 60143-3201
630-285-1121
www.nsc.org/pubs/esc.htm

Explosion Protection
Elsevier
11830 Westline Industrial Drive
St. Louis, MO 63146
800-545-2522

Frontline First Responder Magazine
7626 Densmore Ave
Van Nuys, CA 91406
800-224-4367
818-786-4367
http://www.ffrmagazine.com

FrontLine Magazine
2150 Fillmore Cr.
Ottawa, ON K1J 6A4
Canada
613-747-1138
www.frontline-canada.com

Fundamentals of Aquatic Toxicology
CRC Press, LLC
2000 NW Corporate Blvd.
Boca Raton, FL 33431
800-272-7737
www.crcpress.com

Genium Publishing Corp
1171 Riverfront Center
Amsterdam, NY 12010
518-842-4111
www.GENIUM.com

Homeland Defense Journal
4301 Wilson Boulevard
Suite 1003
Arlington, VA 22203-1867
301-455-5633
www.homelanddefensejournal.com

Homeland Protection Professional
4057 Forest Avenue
Western Springs, IL 60558
708-246-2525
www.hppmag.com

Hurricane Protection Magazine
840 US Highway One
Ste. 330
North Palm Beach, FL 33408
561-627-3393
773-425-9542
http://www.HPmag.com

Indoor Enviroment Connections
12339 Carroll Ave
Rockville, MD 20852
301-230-9606
www.ieconnections.com

Institute of Internal Auditors Inc
247 Maitland Avenue
Altamonte Springs, FL 32701
407-830-7600
www.THEIIA.org

'IT Handbook InfoBase: Bus. Continuity Planning'
Available via: FFIEC
3501 Fairfax Dr., Room 3501
Arlington, VA 22226
703-516-5588
www.ffiec.gov

Janes
110 N. Royal Street
Suite 200
Alexandria, VA 22314
703 683-3700
www.janes.com

Journal of Emergency Management
470 Boston Post Road
Weston, MA 02493
781-899-2702
www.emergencyjournal.com

Lessons from Oklahoma City Bombing
Avail. via American Society of Civil Engineers
1801 Alexander Bell Drive
Reston, VA 20191-4400
800-548-2723
703-295-6163

Lightning Strikes: Staying Safe Under Stormy Skies
Mountaineers Books
1001 SW Klickitat Way, Suite 201
Seattle, WA 98134
206-223-6303

Manager's Guide to Contingency Planning for Disasters
Avail. via John Wiley & Sons
10475 Crosspoint Blvd.
Indianaoplis, IN 46256
877-762-2974
www.wiley.com

'Mngr's Guide to Contingency Planning-Disasters'
Available via: Arma International
13725 W. 109th Street, Suite 101
Lenexa, KS 66215
913-341-3808
800-422-2762
www.arma.org

National Association of County and City Health Officials
1100 17th Street, NW
Second Floor
Washington, DC 20036
202-783-5550
www.naccho.org

'National Fire Protection Association Journal'
Available Via: National Fire Protection Assoc.
1 Batterymarch Park
Quincy, MA 02169-7471
617-770-3000
www.nfpa.org/NFPAJournal/index.asp

'Natural Hazards Observer'
Avail. via: Natural Hazazards Center, Univ. of CO
482 UCB
Boulder, CO 80309-0482
303-492-6818
303-492-6819
www.Colorado.edu/hazards

'NFPA 1600: Standard for Disaster Planning'
Available via: NFPA
1 Batterymarch Park
Quincy, MA 02169-7471
617-770-3000
www.nfpa.org

North Safety Products
2000 Plainfield Pike
Cranston, RI 02921
800-430-4110
www.northsafety.com

'Preparing for Trial'
Available via: James Publishing
3505 Cadillac Avenue. Suite H
Costa Mesa, CA 92626
800-394-2626
714-755-5450
www.JAMESPUBLISHING.com

'Risk Management Magazine'
Available via: Risk Insurance Management Society
655 3rd Avenue
New York, NY 10017
212-286-9292
www.rmmag.org

Rothstein Catalog on Disaster Recovery
4 Arapaho Road
Brookfield, CT 06804-3104
203-740-7444
888-768-4783
www.DisasterRecoveryBooks.com

Safe Supervisor
20 Kernan Road
Unit 101
Oroville, WA 98844
800-667-9300
www.SAFESUPERVISOR.com

'Safety & Health Magazine'
Available via: National Safety Council
1121 Spring Lake Drive
Itasca, IL 60143-3201
630-285-1121
www.nsc.org/pubs/sh.htm

'SC Magazine'
Available via: Haymarket Media Inc.
114 W. 26th St., 3rd Floor
New York, NY 10001
646-638-6000
www.scmagazine.com

'Security Magazine'
Available via: Business News Publishing
1050 IL Rt. 83, Suite 200
Bensenville, IL 60106
630-616-0200
www.securitymagazine.com

'Security Management Magazine'
Available via: Security Management
1625 Prince Street
Alexandria, VA 22314
703-518-1455
www.securitymanagement.com

'Storage Magazine'
Available from: TechTarget
117 Kendrick St., Suite 800
Needham, MA 02494
781-657-1000
www.storagemagazine.techtarget.com/

Technology Law Bulletin
40 Broad Street
Boston, MA 02109
617-350-6800
www.gesmer.com

The BIC Alliance
6378 Quinn Drive
Baton Rouge, LA 70817
800-460-4242
225-751-9996

The Disaster Recovery Handbook
Avail. via AMACON
800-714-6395

'The Law and Procedure of Insurance Appraisal'
Available from: Wilkofsky, Friedman, Karel&Cummins
299 Broadway, Suite 1700
New York, NY 10017
888-791-7781
212-285-0510

The Risk Management Association
One Liberty Place
1650 Market Street, Suite 2300
Philadelphia, PA 19103
215-446-4000
www.rmahq.org

Voices of Safety International
264 Park Ave.
N. Caldwell, NJ 07006
973-228-2258
www.voicesofsafety.com

When Their World Falls Apart: Helping Families and
Children Manage the Effects of Disaster
National Association of Social Workers Press
750 First Street NE, Suite 700
Washington, DC 20002
800-227-3590
www.naswpress.org

Earthquake-specific

Commercial Property Guide: Earthquake Safety
Avail. online via: Seismic Safety Commission
1755 Creekside Oaks Drive, Suite 100
Sacramento, CA 95833
916-263-5506
916-263-0594
www.seismic.ca.gov/sscpub.htm

Earthquake Anxiety in Children
Central United States Earthquake Consortium
2630 East Holmes Rd
Memphis, TN
901-544-3570
800-824-5817
www.cusec.org

Earthquake Preparedness Handbook (online, PDF)
Avail. online
www.lafd.org/eqindex.htm

Earthquake Preparedness: for Childcare Providers
Avail. via FEMA, online (PDF)
500 C Street
Washington, DC 20472
202-566-1600
www.fema.gov/kids/daycare.pdf

Living with Earthquakes in California
Oregon State University Press
102 Adams Hall
Corvallis, OR 97331
541-737-3166
800-426-3797
www.oregonstate.edu

The National Tsunami Hazard Mitigation Program
International Tsunami Information Center
Bishop St., Suite 2200
Honolulu, HI 96813
808-532-6416
www.pmel.noaa.gov/tsunami-hazard/

U.S. Army Corps of Engineers
211 Main Street
Room 302
San Francisco, CA 94105-1905
415-744-2809
www.spd.usace.army.mil/earth.html

U.S. Geological Survey
119 National Center
Reston, VA 20192
703-648-4447
www.usgs.gov

Human factors

A Practical Guide for University Crisis Response
Avail Via. A.A. of Experts in Traumatic Stress
368 Veterans Memorial Highway
Commack, NY 11725
631-543-2217
www.aaets.org

Anniversary Reactions to a Traumatic Event
National Mental Health Information Center
P.O. Box 42557
Washington, DC 20015
800-789-2647
301-443-9006
www.mentalhealth.samhsa.gov

Be Alert, Be Aware, Have a Plan: Guide to Safety
Lyons Press
P.O. Box 480
Guilford, CT 06437
203-458-4500
http://www.bealertbeaware.com/

Blindsided: Managers Guide to Catastrophic Incidents
Portfolio Publishing Company
P.O. Box 7802
The Woodlands, TX 77387

Center for Development and Disability
2300 Menaul Boulevard NE
Albuquerque, NM 87107
505-272-2990
cdd.unm.edu

Centers for Disease Control and Prevention
1600 Clifton Rd
Atlanta, GA 30333
800-311-3435
404-639-3311
www.phppo.cdc.gov/phtn/stress-05/default.asp

Crisis Management: Planning for the Inevitable
520 Bellmore Way
Pasadena, CA 91103
626-683-9200

Crisis Response in Our Schools
Avail Via. A.A. of Experts in Traumatic Stress
Commack, NY 11725
631-543-2217
www.AAETS.org

Dealing with Problem Employees: A Legal Guide
Avail. via Nolo Press
950 Parker Street
Berkeley, CA 94710-2524
800-728-3555
www.nolo.com

Developing Mental Health Crisis Response Plan
Avail. via: NYS Psychological Assn.
6 Executive Park Drive
Albany, NY 12203
800-732-3933
518-437-1040
www.nyspa.org/specialty/disaster.htm

East Hazel Crest P.D.
17223 S. Throop
East Hazel Crest, IL 60429
708-798-2186
ehc506@hotmail.com

Eye of the Storm, Inc
4635 Hillview Drive
Nazereth, PA 18064
610-614-1860
www.eyeofthestorminc.com

Jane's Crisis Communications Handbook
Avail. via: ASIS International
1625 Prince St
Alexandria, VA 22314-2818
703-519-6200
www.asisonline.org

NY State Psychological Assn.
6 Executive Park Drive
Albany, NY 12203
800-732-3933
www.nyspa.org

Training Manual: Mental Health/Human Serv Workers
National Mental Health Information Center
P.O. Box 42557
Washington, DC 20015
800-789-2647
301-443-9006
www.mentalhealth.samhsa.gov

Trauma Pages, Post Traumatic Stress Disorder
Baldwin David V PHD Psychologist
3003 Williamette St. Suite D
Eugene, OR 97405
541-686-2598
www.trauma-pages.com

Online & electronic

'Anthrax Video'
Available Via: National Resource Safety Center
3621 South Harbor Blvd.
Santa Ana, CA 92704
800-468-4296
www.nrsc.com

ATF Bomb Threat and Detection
Avail via online
www.atf.gov/explarson/index.htm

Continuity Central
www.ContinuityCentral.com

Continuity Insights
301 South Main St.
Doylestown, PA 18901
215-230-9556
www.CONTINUITYINSIGHTS.com

ContinuityPlanner.com
New Focus
208-1063 King S
Hamilton, ON L8S 4S3
Canada
800-461-3095
www.CONTINUITYPLANNER.com

CPM Group
20 Commerce Street
Flemington, NJ 08822
908-788-0343
www.CONTINGENCYPLANNING.com

Disaster Mitigation Guide
Avail via FEMA online
www.fema.gov/library/biz4.shtm

Disaster News Network
9195-C Red Branch Road
Columbia, MD 21045
410-884-7350
888-203-9199
www.DISASTERNEWS.net

Disaster Recovery for LANS
Avail. via: TC International
Phoenix, AZ 85076-1108
800-322-2202
602-777-7992

'Earthquake Safety Video-reducing employee expos.'
Available via: National Resource Safety Center
3621 South Harbor Blvd.
Santa Ana, CA 92704
800-468-4296
www.nrsc.com

Effective Physical Security
Elsevier
11830 Westline Industrial Drive
St. Louis, MO 63146
800-545-2522

'Emergency Preparedness at Work Video'
Available via: National Resource Safety Center
3621 South Harbor Blvd.
Santa Ana, CA 92704
800-468-4296
www.nrsc.com

Fire and Explosion Planning Matrix
Avail. online
www.osha.gov/dep/fire-expmatrix/index.html

IT Business Edge
124 N. First Street
Louisville, KY 40202
502-583-8024
www.itbusinessedge.com

Lightning Strike Emergencies
Goldhil Home Media Int'l
Camarillo, CA 93012
800-737-1825
www.goldhil.com

MasterWorks Communications
3223 Brushwood Lane
Fallbrook, CA 92028-8040
760-723-8897
www.mwc.cc

Repairing Your Flooded Home
Avail. via: Red Cross
www.redcross.org/services/disaster

'SearchStorage.com Compliance Infoguide'
Available from: TechTarget
117 Kendrick St., Suite 800
Needham, MA 02494
781-657-1000
searchstorage.techtarget.com/

Security and Loss Prevention
Elsevier
11830 Westline Industrial Drive
St. Louis, MO 63146
800-545-2522

Surviving the Storm: Guide to Hurricane Preparation
Avail. via: FEMA, 500 C Street,
Washington, DC 20472
202-566-1600
www.fema.gov/hazards/hurricanes

xynoMedia Technology
One Saw Mill River Road
Suite 190
Yonkers, NY 10701
866-4-TECH-PLAN
914-377-0600
www.zynomedia.com

Your Family Disaster Plan
Avail. via: FEMA, online
www.fema.gov/library/famplan.shtm

Security

PentaSafe Security Technologies Inc.
1233 West Loop S #1800
Houston, TX 77027-9106
713-860-9390
www.netiq.com

Disa

Reco

Dire

CHRONICLING
DISASTER RELIEF EFFORTS, INDUSTRY NEWS & SERVICES
FOR OVER 20 years

The BIC Alliance is a business and industrial communications alliance of more than 200 companies that helps connect key energy, construction and governmental decision makers with one another and industrial suppliers of related products and services.

Our company publishes the Business & Industry Connection — the nation's largest multi-industry newsmagazine with more than 90,000 readers each issue. We also produce The Leisure Connection — the Gulf South's leisure source for business and industry. We recently published "It's What We Do Together That Counts" — a book about faith over adversity.

Our sister company, Ind-Viro Search, offers executive recruiting and merger and acquisition intermediary services.

As we have helped others build, clean up and make America safe for two decades, we are now focusing our efforts on four primary areas in the aftermath of Hurricane Katrina:

1. **We will work with people displaced by Hurricane Katrina to help them find jobs. We will also work with energy-related companies to help them find personnel.**

2. **We will assist industrial, construction, maintenance, safety, environmental and disaster-response companies in getting their message out to those in business, industry and government who are rebuilding areas devastated by Hurricane Katrina.**

3. **We will help energy-related companies find investment partners to relocate, rebuild and respond to industrial, construction and government needs.**

4. **We will encourage others in business and industry to volunteer their time and resources to help those affected by the hurricane.**

For more information on the BIC Alliance and our services, please call Earl Heard in Baton Rouge at (225) 751-9996 or toll-free at (800) 460-4242 or Thomas Brinsko in Houston at (281) 486-1500. Visit our Web sites at www.bicalliance.com, www.bicpublishing.com and www.theleisureconnection.net.

Bank buildings & interiors

Bank-In-A-Box
5435 Claybourne Street
Suite 606
Pittsburgh, PA 15232
412-681-1091
800-653-0896
www.bank-in-a-box.com

Newground Resources Inc
15450 South Outer 40 Rd. Suite 300
Chesterfield, MO 63017
314-821-2265
www.NEWGROUND.com

Boilers: Mobile

Wilkinson Mobile Boilers
P.O. Box 890147
East Weymouth, MA 02189
800-777-1629
www.gtwilkinson.com

Decontamination equipment, portable

ArmaKleen Company, The
469 North Harrison Street
Princeton, NJ 08543
800-332-5424
609-497-7220
www.armex.com

FSI North America
311 Abbe Rd
Sheffield Lake, OH 44054
440-949-2400
http://www.fsinorth.com

FSI North America(r)
311 Abbe Rd.
Sheffield Lake, OH 44054
440-949-2400
www.fsinorth.com

Intelagard, Inc.
590 Burbank Street
Suite 220
Broomfield, CO 80020
303-309-6309
303-410-1565
www.intelagard.com

Powell Decontamination Systems
402 McKinney Parkway
Lillington, NC 27546
800-800-6296
910-893-9132

RMC Medical
3019 Darnell Road
Philadelphia, PA 19154-3201
215-824-4100
800-332-0672
www.rmcmedical.com

STERIS Corporation
5960 Heisley Road
Mentor, OH 44060
440-354-2600
800-548-4873
www.steris.com

TVI Corporation
7100 Holladay Tyler Road
Glenn Dale, MD 20769
301-352-8800
www.TVICORP.com

Zumro Inc
P.O. Box 696
Hatboro, PA 19040
800-932-6003
215-957-6502
www.zumro.com

Food, lodging, & sanitary services, mobile

Carlin MFG., LLC
1391 W Shaw Avenue Suite D
Fresno, CA 93711-3602
559-276-0123
www.CARLINMFG.com

Kitchens to Go
1070 Whirlaway Ave
Naperville, IL 60540
630-305-6147
www.K-T-G.com

Long Life Food Depot
P.O. Box 8081
Richmond, IN 47374-0081
800-601-2833
765-939-0110
www.LONGLIFEFOOD.com

New England Rest Room's Inc.
POB 555
North Reading, MA 01864
877-883-5874
978-664-3993
www.187788flush.com

The Gardner Stern Company
1945 S Halsted Street
Suite 202
Chicago, IL 60608
312-733-0401
800-738-0401
www.GARDNERSTERN.com

Hazardous materials storage buildings

Safety Storage Inc.
2301 Bert Drive
Hollister, CA 95023
831-637-5955
www.safetystorage.com

Heating equipment, mobile

Hertz Equipment Rental
225 Brae Blvd.
Park Ridge, NJ 07656
888-777-2700
http://www.hertzequip.com

Sunrise Energy Systems Inc.
620 West Coliseum Blvd
Fort Wayne, IN 46808
260-482-1764
800-762-4128
www.heaterguys.com

World Marketing of America Inc.
P.O. Box 192
Mill Creek, PA 17060
800-233-3202
814-643-6500
www.WORLDMKTING.com

Hewlett Packard: mobile computers delivered onsite

SunGard Availability Services
680 E Swedesford Road
Wayne, PA 19087
800-468-7483
800-523-4970
www.availability.sungard.com

Housing, temporary

A. L. E. Mobile Housing
POB 117715
Carrollton, TX 75011-7715
888-921-5749
www.govcon.com

Able Mobile Housing
4101 W. Pierson Rd
Flint, MI 48504
800-273-5774
888-222-2253
www.ablehousing.com

Blu-Med Response Systems
5808 Lake Washington Blvd
Suite 215
Kirkland, WA 98033
425-739-2795
888-680-7181
www.blu-med.com

CRS Temporary Housing
800-968-0848
800-659-2727
www.crstemphousing.com

Disaster Services, Inc. (Temporary Housing)
1009 Bay Ridge Ave #152
Annapolis, MD 21403
410-974-8090
800-547-7749

DMA Insurance Housing Assistants, National HQ
140 Marine View Ave. Suite 218
Solana Beach, CA 92075
800-550-1911
800-206-9425
www.dmahousing.com

Housing Headquarters, Inc.
1850 W. Winchester Ct. Suite 217
Libertyville, IL 60048
866-918-RELO

Instant Offices
48 Wall St. Suite 1100
New York, NY 10005
212-918-4640
www.instant-offices.com

Interim Housing Solutions
866-279-4471
703-893-1901
www.interimhousingsolutions.com

Marriott Execustay Insurance Housing Solutions
Nationwide Service
1020 Serpentine Lane
Pleasanton, CA 94566
800-990-9292
www.marriottinsurancehousing.com

NACS
North American Catastrophe Services, Inc.
864-B Washburn Rd.
Melbourne, FL 32934
888-595-6227
321-259-0888
www.nacs1.com

Oakwood Worldwide Headquarters
2222 Corinth Ave
Los Angeles, CA 90064
310-478-1021
www.oakwoodworldwide.com

Office Suite s PLUS
2333 Alexandria Dr.
Lexington, KY 40504
800-316-7950
859-514-2000
www.officesuitesplus.com

Pacific Corporate Housing
POB 1059
Corona Del Mar, CA 92625
949-425-9127
www.PacificCorpHousing.com

MOBILE FACILITIES & EQUIPMENT

Relocation Housing Specialists
1337 Howe Ave
Suite #104
Sacramento, CA 95825
800-690-0070
www.rhstemphousing.com

Resun Leasing Inc.
22810 Quicksilver Dr.
Dulles, VA 20166
866-772-2328
703-661-6190

Temporary Housing Directory
3308 Preston Rd
Suite 350-341
Plano, TX 75093
800-817-3220
www.temporaryhousingdirectory.com

Totus Business Continuity Centers
105 Maxess Road
Melville, NY 11747
631-574-4400
www.totusoffice.com

IBM-midrange: mobile computers delivered onsite

SunGard Availability Services
680 E Swedesford Road
Wayne, PA 19087
800-468-7483
800-523-4970
www.availability.sungard.com

Lighting, emergency

PATLITE USA Corp.
3860 Del Amo Blvd.
Suite 401
Torrance, CA 90503
310-214-3222
888-214-2580
www.patlite.com

Miscellaneous mobile units & facilities

Clamshell Buildings Inc
1990 Knoll Drive
Ventura, CA 93003
805-650-1700
800-360-8853
www.CLAMSHELL.com

Kitchens to Go
1070 Whirlaway Ave
Naperville, IL 60540
630-305-6147
www.K-T-G.com

Resun Leasing
22810 Quicksilver Drive
Dulles, VA 20166
703-661-6190
866-772-2328
www.resunleasing.com

Mobile administrative offices

Angelus Mobileasing Co. Inc
1134 Santa Anita Avenue
South El Monte, CA 91733
626-443-1715

Bennett's Trailer Co.
3655 Market Street
Aston, PA 19014
800-735-5820
www.MODULARNOW.com

Delmarva Trailer Rentals
7431 Washington Blvd.
Baltimore, MD 21227
410-799-1185
800-544-0745
www.delmarvatrailers.com

Dick Moore Housing
6565 US Highway 51 N
Millington, TN 38053
901-873-4663

GE Capital Modular Space
7100 District Boulevard
Bakersfield, CA 93313
661-397-3833
www.MODSPACE.com

GE Capital Modular Space
7700 Matapeake Business Drive
Brandywine, MD 20613
301-372-1282
www.MODSPACE.com

Golden Office Trailers Inc
18257 Grand Avenue
Lake Elsinore, CA 92530
909-678-2177

Kullman Industries
1 Kullman Corporate Drive
Lebanon, NJ 08833-2163
908-236-0220
www.KULLMAN.com

McGrath RentCorp
5700 Las Positas Road
Livermore, CA 94551
510-276-2626
www.MGRC.com

Miller Building Systems
58120 C.R. 3 South
Elkhart, IN 46517
800-423-2559
www.MBSIONLINE.com

Mobile Mini Storage Systems
2660 N Locust Avenue
Rialto, CA 92377
909-356-1690
800-288-5669
www.MOBILEMINI.com

Mobile Modular
5700 Las Positas Road
Livermore, CA 94551
800-944-3442
925-606-9000
www.MobileModularRents.com

Mobile Modular
11450 Mission Boulevard
Mira Loma, CA 91752
951-360-6600
800-944-3442
www.MOBILEMODULARRENTS.com

Mobile Modular
1180 Celebration Blvd.
Suite 102
Celebration, FL 34747
321-939-2142
www.MOBILEMODULARRENTS.com

Mobile Modular
4445 E Sam Houston Prkwy S
Pasadena, TX 77505
281-487-9222
800-944-3442
www.MOBILEMODULARRENTS.com

NY Grace Realty
38-08150 Street
Flushing, NY 11354
718-358-6100
www.nygracerealty.com

Portable Space
201 Schooley Avenue
Exeter, PA 18643
570-655-4501

Resun Leasing
22810 Quicksilver Drive
Dulles, VA 20166
703-661-6190
866-772-2328
www.resunleasing.com

Satellite Shelters Inc
2530 Xenium Lane N
Minneapalis, MN 55441
763-551-7219
www.satellite.co.com

Sommer and Sons Mobile Leasing Inc
1800 Lorain Boulevard
Elyria, OH 44035
800-826-5654

Tactron Inc
Sherwood, OR 97140
800-424-8228
www.TACTRON.com

Williams Scotsman
1625 Western Drive
West Chicago, IL 60185
630-293-0095
800-782-1500
www.WILLSCOT.com

Williams Scotsman
8211 Town Center Drive
Baltimore, MD 21236
800-782-1500
www.WILLSCOT.com

Williams Scotsman
170 Central Avenue
Kearny, NJ 07032
973-589-1234
800-782-1500
www.WILLSCOT.com

Williams Scotsman
13932 Woodbine
Aurora, ON L0H 1G0
Canada
905-726-3551
800-782-1500
www.willscot.com

Williams Scotsman
1271 Confederation St
Sarina, ON N7S 4M7
Canada
519-336-1010
800-782-1500
www.WILLSCOT.com

Williams Scotsman Du Canada Inc.
715 Rue Dubois
St Eustache, QC J7R 4Z1
Canada
514-634-1220
800-782-1500
www.WILLSCOT.com

WMI Services Corp. HQ
1411 Opus Place
Downers Grove, IL 60515
708-656-5350
www.wm.com

Mobile bank branches

Bank-In-A-Box
5435 Claybourne Street
Suite 606
Pittsburgh, PA 15232
412-681-1091
800-653-0896
www.bank-in-a-box.com

DRC Inc
3677 Park Ave
Ellicott City, MD 21023
410-750-7131
www.DRCONSITE.com

Engage Technologies Inc.
8419 Sunstate Street
Tampa, FL 33634
813-885-6615
www.engagetech.net

New England Security
200 Myles Standish Boulevard
Taunton, MA 02780
508-823-6531
www.nes-group.com

Rentsys Recovery Services
200 Quality Circle
College Station, TX 77845-4468
800-955-5171
www.RENTSYS.com

Mobile cargo storage space

A Royal Wolf Portable Storage
23422 Clawiter Rd
Hayward, CA 94545
800-447-7223
www.ROYAL-WOLF.com

Portable Storage Corp
835 W State Street
Ontario, CA 91762
800-527-8673
909-986-7577
www.storagecontainer.com

Wells Cargo, Inc.
1503 W. McNaughton St.
P.O. Box 728
Elkhart, IN 46515
800-348-7553
574-264-9661
http://www.wellscargo.com

Williams Scotsman
2960 Arnold Tenbrook Road
Arnold, MO 63010
636-296-1500
www.williamscotsman.com

Mobile classrooms

Mobile Modular
5700 Las Positas Road
Livermore, CA 94551
800-944-3442
925-606-9000
www.MobileModularRents.com

Mobile Modular
11450 Mission Boulevard
Mira Loma, CA 91752
951-360-6600
800-944-3442
www.MOBILEMODULARRENTS.com

Mobile Modular
1180 Celebration Blvd.
Suite 102
Celebration, FL 34747
321-939-2142
www.MOBILEMODULARRENTS.com

Mobile Modular
4445 E Sam Houston Prkwy S
Pasadena, TX 77505
281-487-9222
800-944-3442
www.MOBILEMODULARRENTS.com

Resun Leasing
22810 Quicksilver Drive
Dulles, VA 20166
703-661-6190
866-772-2328
www.resunleasing.com

Mobile computer rooms & data centers

APC
128 Fairgrounds Rd.
West Kingston, RI 02892
877-272-2722
877-800-4272
http://www.apc.com

IBM Global Services
10 North Martingale Road
Woodfield Prese
Schaumburg, IL 60173
1-800-IBM-7080
www.ibm.com

Rentsys Recovery Services
200 Quality Circle
College Station, TX 77845-4468
800-955-5171
www.RENTSYS.com

Stockwood W.B. Inc
31 6th Road
Woburn, MA 01801
781-935-8181

Mobile decontamination shelters

Blu-Med Response Systems
5808 Lake Washington Blvd
Suite 215
Kirkland, WA 98033
425-739-2795
888-680-7181
www.blu-med.com

Burch Manufacturing Company, Inc.
618 First Ave. North
Fort Dodge, IA 50501
515-573-4136
www.burchmfg.com

Zumro Inc
P.O. Box 696
Hatboro, PA 19040
800-932-6003
215-957-6502
www.zumro.com

Mobile homes

After Disaster Housing Co
640 W Commodore Boulevard
Jackson, NJ 08527
732-928-8100

American Mobile Homes Inc
51 Moore Road
East Weymouth, MA 02189-2305
781-331-0333

Marriott Execustay Insurance Housing Solutions
Nationwide Service
1020 Serpentine Lane
Pleasanton, CA 94566
800-990-9292
www.marriottinsurancehousing.com

Mobile hospitals

Blu-Med Response Systems
5808 Lake Washington Blvd
Suite 215
Kirkland, WA 98033
425-739-2795
888-680-7181
www.blu-med.com

Mobile kitchens

Bishop Companies, The
P.O. Box 11
Goldendale, WA 98620
800-443-3473
www.BISHOPSERVICES.com

Bishop Services
P.O. Box 11
221 W. Main
Goldendale, WA 98620
509-773-4707
509-773-5597
www.bishopservices.com

Kitchens to Go
1070 Whirlaway Ave
Naperville, IL 60540
630-305-6147
www.K-T-G.com

United Rentals
811 Post Street
Greensboro, NC 27405
336-379-9757
800-852-9441
www.UR.com

United Rentals Inc.
130 Skipjack Road
Prince Frederck, MD 20678
800-544-8658
www.UR.com

Mobile restrooms

Alpine Portable Restrooms
43925 Beaver Meadow Rd
Sterling, VA 20166
540-905-0847
540-338-8914

American Innotek Inc.
501 S Andreasen Drive
Escondido, CA 92029
760-741-6600
800-366-3941

Cascade - Phillips Co.
P.O. Box 1459
Clackamas, OR 97015
800-726-4768
www.sanipot.com

Kitchens to Go
1070 Whirlaway Ave
Naperville, IL 60540
630-305-6147
www.K-T-G.com

Mobile Modular
5700 Las Positas Road
Livermore, CA 94551
800-944-3442
925-606-9000
www.MobileModularRents.com

Mobile Modular
11450 Mission Boulevard
Mira Loma, CA 91752
951-360-6600
800-944-3442
www.MOBILEMODULARRENTS.com

Mobile Modular
1180 Celebration Blvd.
Suite 102
Celebration, FL 34747
321-939-2142
www.MOBILEMODULARRENTS.com

Mobile Modular
4445 E Sam Houston Prkwy S
Pasadena, TX 77505
281-487-9222
800-944-3442
www.MOBILEMODULARRENTS.com

Modoc Sanitation
14371 County Road 1
POB 658
Eagleville, CA 96110
530-279-2025
530-640-2944

New England Rest Room's Inc.
POB 555
North Reading, MA 01864
877-883-5874
978-664-3993
www.187788flush.com

Phillips Environmental Products, Inc.
290 Arden Drive
Belgrade, MT 59714
406-388-5999
877-520-0999
www.thepett.com

Roadmaster LLC
310 Steury Ave
Goshen, IN 46514
574-537-0669
www.roadmasterllc.com

Suburban Sanitation Service, Inc.
P.O. Box 307
18 Colonial Road
Canton, CT 06019
860-673-3078
800-899-4337
www.suburbansanitationservice.com

Mobile security units

CM Services & Security
306 Winthrop Street Unit 150
Taunton, MA 02780
508-989-3528
www.CMServices-Security.com

New Heights Manufacturing
P.O. Box 57
Ellaville, GA 31806
800-826-2844
www.SKY-WATCH.net

Selectron, Inc.
7225 SW Bonita Road
Portland, OR 97224
503-639-9988
800-547-9988
www.selectron.com

US Bunkers, Inc.
13836 S.W. 142 Avenue
Miami, FL 33186
305-971-2511
305-803-6434
www.usbunkers.com

Mobile showers

Celebrity Services Group, LLC.
P.O. Box 111
Fishers, IN 46038
317-578-2822
www.celebrityservicesgroup.com

Kern Valley Portable Showers, Inc.
P.O. Box 535
Wofford Heights, CA 93285
760-376-3145
760-376-6626
www.kernvalley.com/kvps

Kitchens to Go
1070 Whirlaway Ave
Naperville, IL 60540
630-305-6147
www.K-T-G.com

Mobile sinks

AAA Commercial Products
P.O. Box 241308
5815 Landerbrook Dr.
Mayfield Hts, OH 44124
877-536-0808
www.aaacommercialproducts.com/

Britz-Heidbrink, Inc.
1302 9th St.
Wheatland, WY 82201
307-322-4040
cages-bh.com

Kitchens to Go
1070 Whirlaway Ave
Naperville, IL 60540
630-305-6147
www.K-T-G.com

Modular buildings

Butler Manufacturing Co.
1540 Genessee Street
Kansas City, MO 64102
816-968-3000
www.BUTLERMANUFACTURING.com

Jim's Mobile Offices
P.O. Box 547
Marion, IL 62959-9801
618-997-6072

Kitchens to Go
1070 Whirlaway Ave
Naperville, IL 60540
630-305-6147
www.K-T-G.com

Kullman Industries Inc
1 Kullman Corporate Campus Drive
Lebanon, NJ 08833
908-236-0220
www.KULLMAN.com

Mobile Modular
5700 Las Positas Road
Livermore, CA 94551
800-944-3442
925-606-9000
www.MobileModularRents.com

Mobile Modular
11450 Mission Boulevard
Mira Loma, CA 91752
951-360-6600
800-944-3442
www.MOBILEMODULARRENTS.com

Mobile Modular
1180 Celebration Blvd.
Suite 102
Celebration, FL 34747
321-939-2142
www.MOBILEMODULARRENTS.com

Mobile Modular
4445 E Sam Houston Prkwy S
Pasadena, TX 77505
281-487-9222
800-944-3442
www.MOBILEMODULARRENTS.com

Mobile Office Inc
4845 W 111th Street
Alsip, IL 60803-2897
773-735-6500
708-636-5400
www.MOBILEOFFICEINC.com

Modtech Holdings
310 Gibbs Boulevard
Glen Rose, TX 76043
254-897-3072
800-225-4909

Morgan Building Systems Inc
2800 McCree Road
Garland, TX 75041
972-840-1200
www.MORGANUSA.com

MPA Systems Inc.
P.O. Box 838
Sanger, TX 76266-0838
888-233-1584
940-458-2600
www.MPASYSTEMS.com

Porta-King Building Systems
4133 Shoreline Drive
Earth City, MO 63045
314-291-4200
800-284-5346
www.porta-king.com

Resun Leasing
221 South Street
New Britain, CT 06051
800-692-1234
www.resunleasing.com

Sprung Instant Structures
1001 10th Ave SW
Calgary, AB T2R 0B7
Canada
403-245-3371
800-528-9899
www.disasterecovery.com

Sprung Instant Structures
5711 Dannon Way
West Jordan, UT 84088
801-280-1555
800-528-9899
www.disasterecovery.com

Outsourced continuity & colocation space

Collocation Solutions
1950 N Stemmons Freeway
Suite 2033
Dallas, TX 75207-3139
214-231-0162
www.COLLOCATIONSOLUTIONS.com

ColoSpace Inc.
1050 Hingham Street
Rockland, MA 02370
888-583-9200
781-383-9200
www.Colospace.com

Computer Horizons - Headquarters
49 Bloomfield Avenue
Mountain Lks, NJ 07046
973-299-4000
800-321-2421
www.computerhorizons.com

IBM Global Services
10 North Martingale Road
Woodfield Prese
Schaumburg, IL 60173
1-800-IBM-7080
www.ibm.com

Recovery trailers

Base-X Expedition Shelters
6051 North Lee Highway
Fairfield, VA 24435
800-969-8527
www.base-x.com

IBM Canada Ltd.
3500 Steeles Avenue, East
Markham, ON
Canada
905-316-2067

IBM Global Services
10 North Martingale Road
Woodfield Prese
Schaumburg, IL 60173
1-800-IBM-7080
www.ibm.com

Rescue U Disaster Systems
1887 Laurelwood Court
Thousand Oaks, CA 91362
805-492-0393
www.RESCUEU911.com

Refrigeration and freezing

Americold Logistics Inc. Headquarter Office
10 Glenlake Parkway South Tower
Suite 800
Atlanta, GA 30328
678-441-1400
www.americold.net

Kitchens to Go
1070 Whirlaway Ave
Naperville, IL 60540
630-305-6147
www.K-T-G.com

Nordic Cold Storage Inc.
4300 Pleasantdale Road
Doraville, GA 30340
770-448-7400
www.nordiccold.com

Shelters, portable

ALSO SEE COTS, TENTS IN SUPPLIES SECTION

Base-X Expedition Shelters
6051 North Lee Highway
Fairfield, VA 24435
800-969-8527
www.base-x.com

Blu-Med Response Systems
5808 Lake Washington Blvd
Suite 215
Kirkland, WA 98033
425-739-2795
888-680-7181
www.blu-med.com

Design Shelter Inc.
P.O. Box 1445
STN B
Mississauga, ON L4Y 4G2
Canada
604-921-8805
905-564-1761
www.DESIGNSHELTER.com

Holliday Canopies
141 Woodbridge Drive
Charleston, WV 25311
800-788-3969
www.canopyguy.com

Mahaffey Fabric Structures
5094 East Shelby Drive
Memphis, TN 38118
800-245-8368
901-363-6511
www.fabricstructures.com

Motala Tents Inc.
P.O. Box 3295
Mission, BC V2V-4J4
Canada
604-826-8368
http://www.motalatents.com

Sprung Instant Structures
1001 10th Ave SW
Calgary, AB T2R 0B7
Canada
403-245-3371
800-528-9899
www.disasterecovery.com

Sprung Instant Structures
5711 Dannon Way
West Jordan, UT 84088
801-280-1555
800-528-9899
www.disasterecovery.com

Weatherhaven
5700 Marine Way
Burnaby, BC V5J 5C8
Canada
604-451-8900
www.weatherhaven.com

Shelters, radiation

Survivor Depot Inc.
P.O. Box 551957
Fort Lauderdale, FL 33355
954-382-3323
http://www.survivordepot.com

Temporary water chillers, heaters, a/c

**Aggreko Rental
4607 W. Admiral Doyle Drive
New Iberia, LA 70560-9134
800-258-4874
www.aggreko.com**

**Cat Rental Power
AC6109
P.O. Box 610
Mossville, IL 61552
1-800-RENT CAT
847-749-0797
www.catrentalpower.com**

**Caterpillar Power Quality Protection
Systems
100 NE Adams Street
Peoria, IL 61629-0001
309-578-6298
800-947-6567
www.CATUPS.com**

Foley Rents
833 Centennial Ave
Piscataway, NJ 08855
732-885-5555
www.Foleyinc.com

Louisiana Machinery Co., LLC
38294 Hwy 30
Gonzales, LA 70737
1-800-685-4228
225-268-9922
http://louisiana.cat.com

MagPower Systems Inc
Suite 330
6165 Highway 17
Delta, BC V4K 5B8
Canada
604 940-3232
www.magpowersystems.com

United Rentals
4900 Upshur Street
Bladensburg, MD 20710-1116
301-864-5100
800-521-5138
www.unitedrentals.com

Trading room recovery sites

Eagle Rock Alliance LTD.
80 Main Street
Floor 3rd
West Orange, NJ 07052
973-325-9900
800-277-5511
www.EAGLEROCKALLIANCE.com

**IBM Global Services
10 North Martingale Road
Woodfield Prese
Schaumburg, IL 60173
1-800-IBM-7080
www.ibm.com**

MOBILE FACILITIES & EQUIPMENT

MOBILE FACILITIES & EQUIPMENT

SERVICES

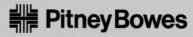

SERVICES, Cleanup & Restoration

Air duct cleaning

Action Pro Air Duct Cleaning
1513 E. Woodlawn St.
Allentown, PA 18109
610-821-8338
908-850-0551

Board-up services

1-800-BoardUp Inc.
9420 Watson Industrial Park
St. Louis, MO 63126
800-585-9293
www.1-800-BoardUp.com

A-1 Glass Services Inc
1247 N Collins Boulevard
Covington, LA 10433
985-892-5312
800-394-8881

A-AAACORN Glass & Board Up Service
4552 S Kedzie Avenue
Chicago, IL 60632
773-776-5000

Diamond National Glass Co.
6800 De Bie Drive
Paramount, CA 90723
562-634-2100

First General Services of Central Pa, Ltd.
227 Springdale Ave
York, PA 17403
717-845-7391
800-669-7391

First General Services of Fort Bend County
10055 Becknap #120
Sugar Land, TX 77478
281-933-1244
800-Boardup
www.firstgeneralfortbend.com

First Response
1919 South Michigan Street
South Bend, IN 46613
574-288-0500
www.firstresponseDRS.com

Paul Davis Restoration
1325 Whitlock Lane
Suite 108
Carrollton, TX 75006
972-323-6565
866-PAUL-DAVIS
www.pdrestoration.com

Paul Davis Restoration & Remodeling of Tarrant County
1663 Hickory Drive
Suite B
Fort Worth, TX 76117
817-759-2600
877-PAUL-DAVIS
www.pdrestoration.com

Paul Davis Restoration of Northeast New Jersey
110B Route 46 E
Saddlebrook, NJ 07663
973-546-0203
877-WE-DRY-NJ
www.pdrestoration.com

Paul Davis Restoration of Volusia County
2330 S. Nova Road
Suite 1
South Daytona, FL 32119
386-760-8959
www.pdrestoration.com

USA Glass & Mirror
207 9th Street
San Francisco, CA 94103
415-285-1110

Carpet cleaning

ALSO SEE DRY CLEANING/LAUNDRY IN CLEANUP
AND RESTORATION SERVICES SECTION

Action Chem-Dry
4855 Creek Road
Lewiston, NY 14092
716-754-7700
www.chemdryusa.com/action.ny

American Classic Chem-Dry by Morley
P.O. Box 8702
Moreno Valley, CA 92552
951-601-3775
909-820-0949

ChemDry of Long Beach
2143 Studebaker
Long Beach, CA 90815
562 437-7000
310 530-7989

Chemdry Tricity Carpet Cleaning
1513 E. Woodlawn St.
Allentown, PA 18109
610-821-4916
908-475-8916

Duraclean Professional Services
P.O. Box 1845
Irmo, SC 29063
803-732-2000
www.duraclean.net

SERVICES

SERVICES

Hobbs Ultra-Clean Service
141 Desert Rd.
Corapeake, NC 27926
252-465-8297
888-462-2744
hobbs@coastalnet.com

Paul Davis Restoration of Akron
2735 Second Street
Cuyahoga Falls, OH 44221
330-920-1936
330-920-4201
www.pdrestoration.com

Rainbow International
P.O. Box 3146
Waco, TX 76707
254-745-2444
800-583-9100
www.raimbowintl.com

Sahara Chem-Dry
4616 W. Sahara Ave. #370
Las Vegas, NV 89102
702-242-0500
702-458-0050
http://www.saharachemdry.com

Sargeant Steam Clean
64 Thomas Crescent
Huntsville, ON P1H 2M3
Canada
705-789-2289

Stanley Steemer International, Inc.
5500 Stanley Steemer Parkway
Dublin, OH 43016
800-783-3637
800-STEEMER
www.stanleysteemer.com

Steamatic Inc. International Headquarters
303 Arthur Street
Fort Worth, TX 76107
817-332-1575
800-527-1295
www.steamatic.com

Cleaning companies, data processing sites

Cleaning Services Group CSG
230 North Street
Danvers, MA 01923
800-683-6572
978-750-8900
www.CLEANINGSERVICESGROUP.com

Dalworth Restoration
12750 S. Pipeline Road
Euless, TX 76040-5250
817-355-8625
www.DALWORTH.com

Data Clean Corp
1033 Graceland Avenue
Des Plaines, IL 60016-6511
847-296-3100
800-328-2256
www.dataclean.com

Data Clean Inc.
740 East Debra Lane
Anaheim, CA 92805
800-328-2256
www.dataclean.com

Cleanup, dry-ice blasting

Granite State Environmental LLC
7 Colby Ct.
#104
Bedford, NH 03110
800-448-2024
603-622-1650
www.moldboston.com

Cleanup, medical: post crime/trauma

Action Cleaners Restoration
925 Seton Court
Wheeling, IL 60090
847-658-8988
www.ACR.com

American Bio-Recovery Association
P.O. Box 828
Ipswich, MA 01938
888-979-2272
www.americanbiorecovery.com

BioCare Inc.
P.O. Box 817
Easley, SC 29641-0817
864-855-3400
800-875-9396

BIOPRO, LLC
1015 North McQueen Road, #166
Gilbert, AZ 85233
877-492-7549
602-234-6856
dcillian@aol.com

Crime and Death Scene Cleaning
POB 828
Ipswich, MA 01938
877-366-8348
978-356-7007
www.cadsc.com

New England Crime Scene Clean-up and Safety Consulting Services
P.O. Box 896
Hampton, NH 03843
800-524-9591
www.necsc.com

ServiceMaster Clean At Irvine
33 Hammond Street
Suite 208
Irvine, CA 92618
949-586-5919
949-279-2339

ServiceMaster Cleaning & Restoration
1105 Yuba Street
Marysville, CA 95901
530-741-8178
800-RESPOND
www.servicemasterclean.com

ServiceMaster Cleaning & Restoration
1105 Yuba Street
Marysville, CA 95901
530-741-8178
www.servicemasterclean.com

ServiceMaster of Germantown
715 Chaney Cove
Suite 102
Collierville, TN 38017
901-854-6225
901-853-3748

ServiceMaster Professional Cleaning
7350 N.W. 7th Street
Suite 106
Miami, FL 33126-2976
305-264-8999
786-486-2526

ServiceMaster Professional Restoration
3869 Norwood Drive #3
Littleton, CO 80125
720-981-8809

Damage assessment

ALSO SEE INSURANCE ADJUSTERS PUBLIC IN
MISC. SERVICES SECTION

Borden/Lee Consulting
16335 Londelius Street
North Hills, CA 91343
818-893-2552

Continental Restoration Consulting
P.O. Box 550340
Dallas, TX 75355
214-342-8910
800-616-8600
www.continentalconsulting.com

The Price-Hollingsworth Company
96 Riverbrook Ave.
Lincroft, NJ 07738
732-530-9863
800-568-5865
www.pricehollingsworth.com

URS Corporation
200 Orchard Ridge Dr.
Suite 101
Gaithersburg, MD 20878
301-258-6554
www.urscorp.com

Debris removal

AshBritt Environmental
P.O. Box 3150
Lake Arrowhead, CA 92532
909-336-6464
954-545-3535
www.ashbritt.com

Cat 5 Disaster Services / Nationwide
154 Campground Road
Decaturville, TN 38329
731-852-2560

Horizon Contracting Inc.
43925 Beaver Meadow Rd
Sterling, VA 20166
540-338-8989
703-675-5399

K Manley Trucking
25096 Drewry Rd
Drewryville, VA 23844
434 658-9349
757 630-0206

Phillips and Jordan Inc
8940 Gall Blvd
Zephyrhills, FL 33541
813-783-1132
www.PANDJ.com

Phillips and Jordan Inc
8245 Chapel Hill Rd
Cary, NC 27513
919-388-4222
919-388-4225
www.PANDJ.com

Phillips and Jordan Inc
16 Court St
Robbinsville, NC 28771
828-479-3371
828-479-3010
www.PANDJ.com

RJS Landscaping
115 Washington Valley Rd.
Warren, NJ 07059
908-917-9221
908-251-2642

Tidy Coast Containers, Inc.
P.O. Box 8322
Hobe Sound, FL 33475
772-545-4000
tidycoast@tidycoast.com

Treescaps Inc.
618 Winwood Rd.
Gastonia, NC 28052
704-867-4100
704 598-6641
www.treescapeonline.com

Underwood DisasterRecovery, LLC
1032 South Mildred Avenue
Brooksville, FL 34601
352-279-1767

Decontamination, biological

ACSI - Advanced Containment Systems
8720 Lambright Rd
Houston, TX 77075
800-927-2271
713-987-0336
www.acsi-us.com

Allen-Vanguard Corp.
5459 Canotek Rd
Ottawa, ON K1J 9M3
Canada
613-747-3590
866-747-3590
www.pwallen.com

First Line Technology
POB 58111
Washington, DC 20037
202-249-8480
866-556-0517

Demolition specialists

BELFOR
185 Oakland Avenue
Suite 300
Birmingham, MI 48009
800-856-3333
www.belfor.com

RL Construction.com
23851 HWY 385
Hill City, SD 57745
605-574-9550
www.rlconstruction.com

Robinette Demolition Inc.
0 S. 560 Highway 83
Oakbrook Terrace, IL 60181
630-833-7997
www.RDIDEMOLITION.com

Washington Air Compressor Rental Co.
1800 4th Street, NE
Washington, DC 20002
202-635-1500
240-832-7500
www.washair.com

Washington Air Compressor Rental Co.
41096 John Mosby Hwy (Rt. 50)
Chantilly, VA 20105
703-742-6200
240-832-7500
www.washair.com

Disposal, electrical equipment

TCI Inc.
P.O. Box 765
Pell City, AL 35125
205-338-9997
www.TCI-PCB.com

TCI Inc.
39 Falls Industrial Park Road
Hudson, NY 12534
518-828-9997
www.TCI-PCB.com

TCI Inc.
455 Archer Dr.
Kirkland Lake, ON P2N 3J5
Canada
705-567-9997
www.TCI-PCB.com

Disposal, hazardous waste

Amec Earth & Environmental
221 18th St. SE
Calgary, AB T2E 6J5
Canada
403-248-4331
www.amec.com

Chemical Waste Management
1550 Balmer Road
Model City, NY 14107
716-754-8231
www.CWMMODELCITY.com

Clean Harbors Environmental
1501 Washington Street
Braintree, MA 02184-7599
781-849-1800
800-282-0058
www.CLEANHARBORS.com

Keith Industries
248 Astor Street
Newark, NJ 07114
973-642-3332
www.keithindustries.com

Laidlaw Inc.
P.O. BOX 5028
Burlington, ON L7R 3Y8
Canada
905-804-0449
800-563-6072
www.LAIDLAW.com

Safety-Kleen System Inc.
5400 Legacy Drive Cluster Building 3
Plano, TX 75024
972-265-2000
www.SAFETY-KLEEN.com

Shaw Environmental
P.O. Box 551
Findlay, OH 45839
800-537-9540

SUNPRO
7392 Whipple NW
North Canton, OH 44720
330-452-0837
www.sunproservices.com

Waste Management of Canada
5045 South Service Rd Suite 300
Burlington, ON L7L 5Y7
Canada
905-633-3999
www.wm.com

Waste Management(National HQ)
1001 Fannin Street
Houston, TX 77002
713-512-6200
www.WM.com

Dry cleaning/laundry, emergency & specialty

Betty Brite Cleaners
P.O. Box 47
Windsor, NJ 08561
609-426-4600
800-543-8787
www.bettybritecleaners.com

Brown's Cleaners
270 City Centre Avenue
Ottawa, ON K1R 7R7
Canada
613-235-5181
www.BROWNSCLEANERS.on.ca

Certified Restoration Drycleaning Network (CRDN)
3948 Ranchero Dr.
Ann Arbor, MI 48108
888-379-2532
www.CRDN.com

Certified Restoration Drycleaning of Denver
6086 E. County Line Road
Highlands Ranch, CO 80126
303-991-0600
303-906-7784
www.crdn.com

Cleary Cleaners
187 Gonic Road
Rochester, NH 03839
603-332-2374

Clothes Call
2421 Crofton Lane, Unit 4
Crofton, MD 21114
877-721-7445
410-721-7445

CRDN of the Midsouth
456 Distribution Parkway
Collierville, TN 38017
901-850-1611
901-387-7442
http://www.crdn.com

Custom Commercial Fabric Restoration Services
3201 Suite A Investment Blvd.
Hayward, CA 94545
510-723-1000
800-80S-MOKE
www.CCFRS.com

First Response
1919 South Michigan Street
South Bend, IN 46613
574-288-0500
www.firstresponseDRS.com

FSW Cleaners
7535 W 99th Place
Bridgeview, IL 60455
708-598-4158

Huntington Cleaners
26822 Coolidge Highway
Huntington Wd, MI 48070
248-541-6038
888-266-3208
www.HUNTINGTONCLEANERS.com

Kent Cleaners Ltd
183 Lansdowne St East
Peterborough, ON K9J 7P7
Canada
705-745-7904

Lansing Cleaners
18210 Torrence Avenue
Lansing, IL 60438
708-474-2459

Milto Cleaners
459 State Rd
Greenwood, IN 46142
317-888-7396
800-720-9122

Rainbow International Carpet Care & Restoration
1010 N University Parks Drive
Waco, TX 76707
254-745-2444
800-840-7404
www.rainbowinternational.com

The Clothes Doctor
27132 Burbank
Foothill Rnch, CA 92610
949-206-1557

Widmer's
2016 Madison Road
Cincinnati, OH 45208
513-321-5100
www.widmerscleaners.com

Drying & dehumidification

Action Catastrophe
4640 Lipan Street
Denver, CO 80211
303-964-1188
www.ACTIONCATASTROPHE.com

All Care Chem-Dry
13727 S.W. 152 Street
#273
Miami, FL 33177
305-969-3733
305-213-8505

Bay Area Disaster Kleenup
390 Scarlet Blvd
Oldsmar, FL 34677
800-362-8453
813-835-1445
www.bayareadk.com

**BELFOR
185 Oakland Avenue
Suite 300
Birmingham, MI 48009
800-856-3333
www.belfor.com**

C & E Services Inc.
P.O. Box 14566
Phoenix, AZ 85063
602-246-2483
www.CESRVS.com

Chem Dry - By Moore
8 Glen Road
Yonkers, NY 10704
914-843-8062

Clean Care of New England
C & C Construction
Warwick, RI 2886
401-736-5420

Colorado Catastrop[he Inc.
5150 Havana St Suite F
Denver, CO 80209
303-333-0392
1-888-88COCAT
cocat.com

Con-Tech Restorations Ltd.
425 A Midwest Rd.
Toronto, ON M1P 3A6
Canada
416-288-9932
1-866-388-9488

Dehumidification Technologies, Inc.
6609 Ave. U
Houston, TX 77011
713-939-1166
www.RENTDH.com

Disaster Services, Inc.
3030 Amwiler Road
Atlanta, GA 30360
1-800-669-1411
770-446-5300
www.disasterservices.com

Dri-Eaz Corp.
15180 Josh Wilson Road
Burlington, WA 98233-9656
800-932-3030
www.DRI-EAZ.com

EnviroDri, Inc.
17431 Alico Center Rd
Suite 1
Fort Myers, FL 33912
239-482-2169
800-830-0067
www.wateroutswfl.com

First General Services Canada
Div. of First General Enterprises (Ontario) Ltd.
437 Flint Road
Toronto, ON M3J 2T7
Canada
416-736-0395
877-888-9111
www.firstgeneral.ca

First General Services of Fort Bend County
10055 Becknap #120
Sugar Land, TX 77478
281-933-1244
800-Boardup
www.firstgeneralfortbend.com

First General Services of the Quad Cities
958 E. 53rd St. Suite 5
Davenport, IA 52807
563-386-7220

First Response
1919 South Michigan Street
South Bend, IN 46613
574-288-0500
www.firstresponseDRS.com

First Restoration Services of Ashville
12 National Avenue
Fletcher, NC 28732
800-537-6151
828-684-1582
www.firstrestoration-avl.com

Ideal Drying
432 N Canal Street
Suite 16
South San Fran, CA 94080-4666
800-379-6881
650-873-3229
www.IDEAL1.com

SERVICES

Munters
6810 Kitimat Rd.
Mississauga, ON L5N 5M2
Canada
905-858-5894
www.muntersmcs.com

Munters Corporation
79 Monroe Street
P.O. Box Box 640
Amesbury, MA 01913
800-MUNTERS
www.MUNTERSAMERICA.com

Paul Davis Restoration
315 Trane Drive
Knoxville, TN 37919
865-584-0216
www.pdrestoration.com

Paul Davis Restoration
27 Water Street
Wakefield, MA 01880
781-224-3475
781-245-0003
www.pdrestoration.com

Paul Davis Restoration
1325 Whitlock Lane
Suite 108
Carrollton, TX 75006
972-323-6565
866-PAUL-DAVIS
www.pdrestoration.com

Paul Davis Restoration & Remodeling
141 Main Street
Indian Orchard, MA 01151
413-543-5001
www.pauldavisofwesternmass.com

Paul Davis Restoration & Remodeling of Tarrant County
1663 Hickory Drive
Suite B
Fort Worth, TX 76117
817-759-2600
877-PAUL-DAVIS
www.pdrestoration.com

Paul Davis Restoration & Remodeling, Mid-Mich
881 Hull Road
Suite 100
Mason, MI 48854
517-676-8000
www.pdrestoration.com

Paul Davis Restoration of Akron
2735 Second Street
Cuyahoga Falls, OH 44221
330-920-1936
330-920-4201
www.pdrestoration.com

Paul Davis Restoration of Lehigh Valley
626 East Cedar Street
Allentown, PA 18109
610-433-2212
www.pdr-usa.net

Paul Davis Restoration of Northeast New
Jersey
110B Route 46 E
Saddlebrook, NJ 07663
973-546-0203
877-WE-DRY-NJ
www.pdrestoration.com

Paul Davis Restoration of S.W.
Chicagoland
1335 Lakeside Drive
Unit 1
Romeoville, IL 60446
630-378-9011

Paul Davis Restoration of Tucson
2555 North Coyote Drive
Suite 113
Tucson, AZ 85745
520-624-4560
www.pdrestoration.com

Paul Davis Restoration of Volusia County
2330 S. Nova Road
Suite 1
South Daytona, FL 32119
386-760-8959
www.pdrestoration.com

Paul Davis Restoration of Western Michigan
1730 Olson Street N.E.
Suite C
Grand Rapids, MI 49503
800-676-9118
www.pdrestoration.com

Paul Davis Restoration of Western NY
P.O. Box 1984
Buffalo, NY 14231
716-824-2230
800-836-8910
www.pdrestoration.com?bfny

Regency Construction Corporation
DKI of Clinton Township
35240 Forton Court
Clinton Township, MI 48035
586-741-8000
888-41Regency
www.regencyconstruction.com

Restoration Rental Equipment
4402 S. Danville Dr.
Abilene, TX 79605
325-692-1818
www.a-town.net/rental.asp

Restorx Northern Illinois
4497 S Park Road
Freeport, IL 61032-9327
815-235-9606
630-512-9690
www.lossreduction.com

SERVICES

SERVICES

ServiceMaster Advanced Restorations
565 Commerce Street
Southlake, TX 76092
817-481-0664
817-808-3791

ServiceMaster by Gaudet
6 Jefferson Avenue
Woburn, MA 01801-4325
781-932-1171
800-281-0072
www.servicemasterbygaudet.com

Servicemaster by Professional Clean
119-14 14 Rd.
College Point, NY 11356
718-762-5566
866-466-7668
www.servicemaster-ny.com

ServiceMaster Clean At Irvine
33 Hammond Street
Suite 208
Irvine, CA 92618
949-586-5919
949-279-2339

ServiceMaster Cleaning & Restoration
1105 Yuba Street
Marysville, CA 95901
530-741-8178
800-RESPOND
www.servicemasterclean.com

ServiceMaster Cleaning and Restoration
P.O. Box 2192
Suite D
Merced, CA 95344
209-726-9182
888-726-9182

ServiceMaster of Germantown
715 Chaney Cove
Suite 102
Collierville, TN 38017
901-854-6225
901-853-3748

ServiceMaster of Tehachapi
20571 SAnta Lucra
Tehachapi, CA 93561
661-822-9408
661-333-3396

ServiceMaster of the Lake
360 Business Park Road
Linn Creek, MO 65052
573-365-4688
573-346-3585
www.svmlake.com

ServiceMaster Professional Cleaning
7350 N.W. 7th Street
Suite 106
Miami, FL 33126-2976
305-264-8999
786-486-2526

ServiceMaster Professional Restoration
3869 Norwood Drive #3
Littleton, CO 80125
720-981-8809

Servpro of Seal Beach/Cypress/Los Alamitos
3267 Katekka Avenue
Los Alamitos, CA 90720
562-431-9400
714-236-9599

The Fire Works Restoration Co./1-800BOARDUP
9420 Watson Industrial Park
St. Louis, MO 63126
314-961-3473
www.1-800Boardup.com

Water Out
375 Faraday Avenue
Jackson, NJ 08527
800-848-1761
732-942-6278

Water Out - Atlanta
3455 Peachtree Ind. Blvd.
Suite 305-219
Duluth, GA 30096
770-613-9525
www.WATEROUT.com

World Wide Drying Inc.
P.O. Box 750
Taunton, MA 02780-0750
508-823-0189
800-442-1911
www.WORLDWIDEDRYING.com

Electronic equipment & PCs, cleaning

Asset Recovery Technologies Inc.
1580 Louis Avenue
Elk Grove Village, IL 60007
847-758-1985
800-805-0644
www.disasterhelp.com

BELFOR
185 Oakland Avenue
Suite 300
Birmingham, MI 48009
800-856-3333
www.belfor.com

Comservco Ent. Corp
2920 Avenue R. PMB #304
Brooklyn, NY 11229-0702
718-332-2300

RescueTech
10343 Federal Blvd
#J423
Denver, CO 80260
303-380-1708
866-380-1708
www.rescuetech.us

Restoration Technologies Inc
3695 Prairie Lake Court
Aurora, IL 60504
630-851-1551
800-421-9290
www.RESTORATIONTECHNOLOGIES.net

Restronic
113 S Market Street
Frederick, MD 21701
301-682-9887
www.RESTRONIC.com

V & M Restoration
2341 N Pacific Street
Orange, CA 92865
714-970-9140
800-451-5380

Environmental cleanup

ALSO SEE REMEDIATION SERVICES IN CLEANUP
& RESTORATION SERVICES SECTION

Allied Environmental Group Inc
2163 Merrick Avenue
Merrick, NY 11566
516-867-6452
800-969-3478

Allstate Power Vac
928 E Hazelwood Avenue
Rahway, NJ 07065
908-862-3800
800-876-9699
www.ALLSTATEPV.com

Anco Environmental
35 Russo Place
Berkeley Heights, NJ 07922
908-464-3511
www.ANCOENV.com

Cans-To-Go, LLC
11410 W. Brown Deer Rd. Suite 1
Milwaukee, WI 53224
414-447-9000
414-788-4269
canstogo.com

Carner Brothers Environmental Excavating
P.O. Box 116
Roseland, NJ 07068
973-226-1840
973-226-5872

Clean Harbors Environmental
1501 Washington Street
Braintree, MA 02184-7599
781-849-1800
800-282-0058
www.CLEANHARBORS.com

Clean Harbors Environmental Services, Inc.
1501 Washington Street
P.O. Box 859048
Braintree, MA 02184-9048
781-849-1800
800-282-0058
http://www.cleanharbors.com

Commercial Paving & Recycling Company LLC
2 Gibson Road
Scarborough, ME 04074
207-883-3325
www.CPCRS.com

Cura Emergency Services
6205 Chapel Hill Boulevard
Suite 100
Plano, TX 75093
800-486-7117
972-378-7333
www.SPILLSOLUTIONS.com

CYN Environmental Services
100 Tosca Dr
Stoughton, MA 2072
781-341-1777
www.CYNENV.com

Edwards & Cromwell Spill Control
11519 Investor Ave.
Building B
Baton Rouge, LA 70810
225-292-3377
www.edwardsandcromwell.com

ENPRO Services Inc
12 Mulliken Way
Newburyport, MA 01950
800-966-1102
978-465-1595
www.enpro.com

Environmental Products & Services of Vermont Inc.
532 State Fair Boulevard
Syracuse, NY 13204-1129
315-471-0503
800-THE-TANK
www.EPSOFVERMONT.com

Environmental Quality Company
36255 Michigan AV
Wayne, MI 48184
734-329-8000
www.eqonline.com

Environmental Services Inc.
90 Brookfield Street
South Windsor, CT 06074
1-800-486-7745
1-860-528-9500
www.e-s-i.com

Lincoln Environmental Inc.
333 Washington Highway
Smithfield, RI 02917
401-232-3353
www.LINCOLNENV.com

Locus Technologies
1333 N California Boulevard
Walnut Creek, CA 94596
925-906-8100
www.locustec.com

MACTEC Inc
1105 Sanctuary Parkway
Suite 300
Alpharetta, GA 30004
770-360-0600
www.MACTEC.com

Marine Pollution Control Corp.
8631 W. Jefferson Ave.
Detroit, MI 48209
313-849-2333
www.marinepollutioncontrol.com

MECX, L.L.C.
6300 W. Loop S.
Suite 500
Bellaire, TX 77401
713-585-7000
www.mecx.net

National Response Center
c/o United States Coast Guard(G-OPF)-Room 2611
2100 2nd Street, Southwest
Washington, DC 20593-0001
800-424-8802
202-267-2165
www.NRC.USCG.mil/nrchp.html

Paul Davis Restoration of Sacramento
4751 Pell Drive, Suite #2
Sacramento, CA 95838
916-648-2040
916-416-5138
PDRestoration.com

Protect Environmental Services, Inc.
6504 Midway Road
Haltom City, TX 76117
817-589-9005
www.protectusa.net

Ross Environmental Services Inc
150 Innovation Drive
Elyria, OH 44035
440-366-2000
www.ROSSENVIRONMENTAL.com

ServiceMaster Clean At Irvine
33 Hammond Street
Suite 208
Irvine, CA 92618
949-586-5919
949-279-2339

TEAM-1 Emergency Services
Head office 1650 Upper Ottawa Street
Various Ontario Locations
Hamilton Ontario, ON L8W 3P2
Canada
905-383-5550
1-800-32-SPILL
www.team-1.com

Tri-S Inc. Environmental Services & Consulting
25 Pinney Street
Ellington, CT 06029
860-875-2110
www.TRI-SENVIRONMENTAL.com

Fire & water damage restoration
(Canadian entries followed by U.S. entries)

Fire & water damage restoration-Alberta

First General Services (Edm) Inc.
7311 - 77 Avenue
Edmonton, AB T6B 0B7
Canada
780-463-4040

Servicemaster of Red Deer
6 - 7439 - 49th Avenue Crescent
Red Deer, AB T4N 1X6
Canada
403-341-6072

Fire & water damage restoration-British Columbia

Edenvale Restoration Specialists
5707 Sidley Street
Suite 4
Burnaby, BC V5J 5E6
Canada
604-436-1440
604-590-1440
www.EDENVALE.com

On Side Restoration Services Ltd.
2303 Douglas Road
Burnaby, BC V5C 5A9
Canada
604-293-1596
888-663-6604
www.onside.ca

R.S. Restoration Services, Ltd
786 Fairview Road
Unit - A
Victoria, BC V9A 5V1
Canada
866-313-0030
250-388-0030
www.rsrestorationservices.com

Fire & water damage restoration-Newfoundland

Frontier Cleaning and Restoration
266 Curling Street
Corner Brook, NF A2H 3J7
Canada
709-785-5859
709-632-9567

Fire & water damage restoration-Ontario

Carpet Revival Centre Ltd. The
P.O. Box 711 Coons Industrial Park
Brockville, ON K6V 5T4
Canada
613-342-4967
866-582-6219

Cleancare Services
RR #5
Owen Sound, ON N4K 5N7
Canada
519-376-9932

Disaster Kleenup Canada - Shamrock Services (Sarnia)
1323 Lougar Ave.
Sarnia, ON N7S 5N5
Canada
519-337-4192
877-448-4424
shamrock@xcelco.on.ca

First General Services Canada
Div. of First General Enterprises (Ontario) Ltd.
437 Flint Road
Toronto, ON M3J 2T7
Canada
416-736-0395
877-888-9111
www.firstgeneral.ca

Graham Restorations
55 Unsworth Drive
Hamilton, ON L8W 2T7
Canada
905-574-1210
800-250-2538

BELFOR

Restoration Services

Providing Single Source Recovery Solutions
Offices Across Canada

24/7 Emergency Hotline – 1-866-366-0493

SERVICES

RainbowBrite
270 Sheldon Avenue, Unit 405
Toronto, ON M8W4M1
Canada
416-255-4248
416-822-3334
www.RainbowBrite.ca

Schutt Restoration Services (SRS)
750 harold Cres.
Thunder Bay, ON P7C 5H7
Canada
807-624-9080
866-624-9080

ServiceMaster of Ottawa
768 Belfast Road
Ottawa, ON K1G 0Z5
Canada
613-244-1997
877-209-2997
www.SMOTTAWA.com

Terra Restoration/Steamatic Hamilton
115 Hempstead Drive
Unit 5
Hamilton, ON L8W 2Y6
Canada
905-387-0662

Urban Clean Ltd.
27 Nixon Road
Bolton, ON L7E 1J7
Canada
905-951-2900
800-363-3473
www.bachly.com

Fire & water damage restoration-Quebec

Osler Hoskin & Harcourt LLP
1000 de La Gauchetiere
Suite 2100
Montreal, QC H3B 4W5
Canada
514-904-8159
514-793-8159
www.osler.com

Fire & water damage restoration-Alabama

Paul Davis Restoration of the Wiregrass
336 Simms Road
Dothan, AL 36301
334-702-7379
www.pdrestoration?wire

ServiceMaster Advanced Cleaning
5158 Mobile South St.
Theodore, AL 36582
251-653-9333

ServiceMaster Disaster Services
975 Tate Dr.
Suite 1
Dothan, AL 36301
334-712-1118

ServiceMASTER Restoration & Clean
P.O. BOX 1013
Guntersville, AL 35976
256-582-7778

Fire & water damage restoration-Arizona

AAA Painters
3021 West Heatherbrae Dr.
Phoenix, AZ 85017
602-242-7248
480-650-8206
www.phoenixpaintingcontractors.com

Az Carpet & Restoration Co.
2423 South 17th Street
Phoenix, AZ 85034
602-257-8444
www.AZCARPET.com

East Valley Disaster Services Inc.
257 W Broadway Road
Mesa, AZ 85210
480-833-4538

Paul Davis Restoration of Tucson
2555 North Coyote Drive
Suite 113
Tucson, AZ 85745
520-624-4560
www.pdrestoration.com

Pro Care Services, Inc.
7166 Ed Everett Way
P.O. Box 2839
Carefree, AZ 85377
480-488-7800

ServiceMaster By Ed Smith
755 N. Country Club Dr, ste 1
Mesa, AZ 85201
480-834-5248
www.4servicemaster.com/AZ/3784

Fire & water damage restoration-Arkansas

ServiceMaster Disaster Restoration and Cleaning
144 Wyatt Cove
Hot Springs, AR 71913
501-525-3125
www.4servicemaster.com/ar/6541

Fire & water damage restoration-California

Advanced Restoration Specialists Inc
2548 Strozier Avenue
South El Monte, CA 91733
310-329-2755
www.ADVRESTORE.com

Advanced Restoration Specialists Inc.
2548 Strozier Avenue
South El Monte, CA 91733-2020
626-442-7700
800-310-4911
www.ADVRESTORE.com

Better Floors & Restorations
201 W Santa Fe Avenue
Placentia, CA 92870
714-524-8500
www.dkfs.com

Buzco Construction Co. Inc.
25202 Crenshaw Boulevard Suite 300
Torrance, CA 90505
310-326-8139

Certified Restoration and Construction Inc.
6251 Sky Creek Drive
Suite G
Sacramento, CA 95828-1027
916-386-4811

DK Services
20172 Charlanne Drive
Redding, CA 96002
530-224-2323

Document Reprocessors - West Coast Operations
1384 Rollins Road
Burlingame, CA 94010
650-401-7711
800-437-9464
www.DOCUMENTREPROCESSORS.com

Donjean's Cleaning & Restoration Inc.
1595 W 16th Street
Merced, CA 95340
209-383-2880
800-543-7847
www.DONJEAN.com

Emercon Construction Inc
2906 E Coronado Street
Anaheim, CA 92806-2501
714-630-9615
800-734-9167
www.emercon.com

Four Star Cleaning & Restoration
4302 Solar Way
Suite 1
Fremont, CA 94538-6309
800-255-3333
510-796-5900
www.BAYAREAFOURSTAR.com

Hi-Tech Carpet & Restoration
P.O. Box 2497
Rocklin, CA 95677
916-789-9213
916-624-1225

New Life Service Co.
39 5th Street
Eureka, CA 95501
707-444-8222

Paul Davis Restoration - Peninsula
297 N. Amphlett Blvd
San Matco, CA 94401
650-685-5320
650-642-0480
www.pdrestoration.com

Paul Davis Restoration of San Diego Inc.
9225 Chesapeake Drive
Suite F
San Diego, CA 92123
858-560-0444
www.pdrestoration.com?sdno

Premier Cleaning and Restoration
2985 Dutton Avenue
Suite 14
Santa Rosa, CA 95407
707-522-0198
707-763-5722

Protech Construction
11626 Goldring Rd.
Arcadia, CA 91006
800-884-6999
www.ptech1.com

Restotech Water & Fire Damage Restoration
2201 East Wellow
Long Beach, CA 90755
800-995-8988
562-427-4742
www.dkirestotech.com

ServiceMaster @ Coachella Valley
74990-Joni Dr. #2
Palm Desert, CA 92260
760-568-1227

ServiceMaster Absolute Water and Fire Damage Serv.
6975 North Ave.
Suite B
Lemon Grove, CA 91945-1438
619-287-7070
www.SMSANDIEGO.com

ServiceMaster Allcare Restoration
782 Avzerais Avenue
San Jose, CA 95126
408-885-0280
www.SERVICEMASTERCLEAN.com

ServiceMaster Anytime
2351 W Lugonia Ave.
Redlands, CA 92373
909-796-4939
www.4SERVICEMASTER.com/ca/3602

ServiceMaster Anytime
2351 W. Lugonia Ave. Unit E
Redlands, CA 92373
909-796-4939
http://www.smanytime.com

ServiceMaster At The Valley
5173 N. Douglas Fir Road
Suite 5
Calabasas, CA 91302
818-591-1137

ServiceMaster by Master and Sons
26810 Oak Ave.
Unit F
Santa Clarita, CA 91351
661-299-9090
818-227-3863
www.MASTERANDSONS.com

ServiceMaster by TA Russell
541 South Glendora Avenue
Suite B
Glendora, CA 91741
626-963-4048
800-808-9700

ServiceMaster Clean
13502 E. Whittier Blvd.
Suite H268
Whittier, CA 90605
562-945-2745

ServiceMaster Clean At Irvine
33 Hammond Street
Suite 208
Irvine, CA 92618
949-586-5919
949-279-2339

ServiceMaster Cleaning & Restoration
1105 Yuba Street
Marysville, CA 95901
530-741-8178
800-RESPOND
www.servicemasterclean.com

ServiceMaster Cleaning and Restoration
P.O. Box 2192
Suite D
Merced, CA 95344
209-726-9182
888-726-9182

ServiceMaster Disaster Restoration Services
5650F Imhoff Drive
Concord, CA 94520
800-480-TIDY
925-288-0479

ServiceMaster Disaster Restoration Services
2731 Fair Oaks Ave.
Redwood City, CA 94063
650-299-9080
800-750-TIDY

ServiceMaster Eastern Sierra
401 Commerce Circle Suite #1
Mammoth Lake, CA 93546
760-924-2097

ServiceMaster Napa - Vallejo - Benicia
5431 Napa Vallejo Highway
American Canyon, CA 94503
707-255-5550
707-648-1608

ServiceMaster of Fairfield / Vacaville
1111 - B Western Street
Fairfield, CA 94533
707-428-1608
800-491-1608

ServiceMaster of the Foothills
11229 McCourtney Rd
Grass Valley, CA 95949
530-273-1957

ServiceMaster Sierras
21097 B Longeway Rd
Sonora, CA 95370
209-532-1700
www.4SERVICEMASTER.com/ca/3535

ServiceMaster Total Restoration
42346 Rio Nedo, Unit A
Temecula, CA 92590
800-486-8717
951-296-1919
www.smrestore.com

Servpro of Seal Beach/Cypress/Los Alamitos
3267 Katekka Avenue
Los Alamitos, CA 90720
562-431-9400
714-236-9599

Spiegel Certified Restoration
4299 State Street
Montclair, CA 91763
909-628-8988

Tri-Tech Restoration Co. Inc.
3301 San Fernando Boulevard
Burbank, CA 91504
800-900-8448
818-551-4575
www.TRITECHRESTORATION.com

World Restoration Services Inc.
3900 N State Street
Ukiah, CA 95482
707-485-5441

Zebra Restoration Services
11365 Sunrise Park Dr.
Rancho Cordova, CA 95742
916-635-8571
www.zebrarestoration.com

Fire & water damage restoration-Colorado

Disaster Restoration Inc
4275 Forest St.
Denver, CO 80216
800-475-FIRE
303-657-1400
www.DISASTER-EXPERTS.com

ICA
2090 W Bates Avenue
Englewood, CO 80110
303-806-9090
www.icaco.net

Johnson's Chem-Dry
P.O. Box 1298
Crested Butte, CO 81224
970-349-7052

Kessler Construction Co., Inc.
5809 Wright Drive
Loveland, CO 80538
970-663-4342
970-663-4428
www.kesslerconstructionco.com

Palace Construction
7 South Galapago Street
Denver, CO 80223
303-777-7999
www.PALACECONSTRUCTION.com

Paul Davis Restoration
1602 S. Parker Rd.
Suite 214
Denver, CO 80231
303-338-8232
www.PDRESTORATION.com

Paul Davis Restoration
948 S Santa Fe Ave
Pueblo, CO 81006
719-583-8080

Servicemaster of FT. Collins
912 Smith Field Drive
Suite 5
Ft. Collins, CO 80524
970-484-0588
970-493-2910
www.SERVICEMASTERCLEAN.com

ServiceMaster Professional Restoration
3869 Norwood Drive #3
Littleton, CO 80125
720-981-8809

Fire & water damage restoration-Connecticut

Clean Sweep Restoration Services of New England
63 North Plains Industrial Road
Wallingford, CT 06492
800-952-0556
203-949-8660

Maguire J.P. Associates Inc
266 Brookside Road
Waterbury, CT 06708-1426
203-755-2297
www.JPMAGUIRE.com

Paul Davis Restoration
33 Flax Mill Road
Branford, CT 06405
203-315-1500
pdrestoration.com

Paul Davis Restoration
55 Whiting Street
Suite 1D
Plainville, CT 06062
860-747-6993
800-294-4464
www.pdrestoration.com

SERVICES

Paul Davis Restoration of Eastern CT
P.O. Box 1169
Old Saybrook, CT 06475
860-388-3444
860-388-1706
www.pdrestoration.com

ServiceMaster Clean
455 Main St., Building 1
P.O. Box 306
Deep River, CT 06417
860-388-0440
800-238-4282

Fire & water damage restoration-Delaware

ServiceMaster of Brandywine Valley
P.O. Box 3309
223 Valley Road
Wilmington, DE 19804
302-652-4151
302-338-4151

Servpro
700 Cornell Drive
Suite 3
Wilmington, DE 19801
302-652-1122

Fire & water damage restoration-Florida

AdvantaClean
6831 Edgewater Commerce Parkway
Suite 1101
Orlando, FL 32810-4224
407-839-0088
www.advantaclean.com

All Pro Chem-Dry
360 Lolly Lane
Jacksonville, FL 32259
904-230-9918
904-285-0003

CMS Restoration
3930 Holden Rd
Lakeland, FL 33811
863-644-2958
863-581-2752

First General Services of the Panhandle
1593 Hwy 393 South
Santa Rosa Beach, FL 32459
850-622-9700

Instar Services Group
400 9th Ave S
Safety Harbor, FL 34695-3856
727-726-1357
800-446-1620
www.instarservices.com

Paul Davis Restoration
1 Independent Drive
Suite 2300
Jacksonville, FL 32202-5020
888-907-5907
904-737-2779
www.pdrestoration.com

Paul Davis Restoration Co. of Collier
6200 Shirley Street
Suite 206
Naples, FL 34109
239-598-2426
239-825-2726
www.pdrestoration.com

Paul Davis Restoration of Greater Miami Inc.
7240 S.W. 39 Terrace
Miami, FL 33155
305-260-0034
www.pdrestoration.com

Paul Davis Restoration of Orlando
1155 N. Kentucky Avenue
Winter Park, FL 32789
407-629-6700
www.pdrestoration.com

Paul Davis Restoration of Palm Beach County
1025 N. Florida Mango Rd #9
West Palm Beach, FL 33409
561-478-7272
www.restorepalmbeach.us

Paul Davis Restoration of St. Augustine
2139 Dobbs Road
Unit 1
St. Augustine, FL 32086
904-824-1468
http://www.pdrestoration.com

Paul Davis Restoration of Volusia County
2330 S. Nova Road
Suite 1
South Daytona, FL 32119
386-760-8959
www.pdrestoration.com

Paul Davis Restoration Polk County
308 Commerce Court
Winter Haven, FL 33880
863-299-9688
www.pdrestoration.com

PUROCLEAN OF SOUTH MIAMI
6702 SW 157 Ct
Miami, FL 33193
305-752-4019
305-773-9993
www.purocleanmiami.com

Puroclean of South Miami
6702 SW 157 Ct
Miami, FL 33193
305-752-4019
www.purocleanmiami.com

ServiceMaster Clean 24 Hour
5906 Breckenridge Pkwy.
Suite H
Tampa, FL 33610
813-623-6111
727-258-6111
www.servicemaster.com

ServiceMaster Fire & Water Restoration Inc.
2622 Carolyn Street
Deltona, FL 32738
386-574-4333
386-804-3169

ServiceMaster of Amelia Island
2428 Lynndale Road
Fernandina Beach, FL 32034
904-277-2998

ServiceMaster Professional Cleaning
7350 N.W. 7th Street
Suite 106
Miami, FL 33126-2976
305-264-8999
786-486-2526

ServiceMaster Remediation
933 N.W. 31st Avenue
Pompano Beach, FL 33069
954-969-5906
866-969-6653
www.AOMEGAGROUP.com

ServiceMaster Services
2447 Executive Plaza Road, Suite 3
Pensacola, FL 32504
850-479-6065

Servpro of North Palm Beach
117 Miller Way
West Palm Beach, FL 33403
561-881-8784

Sierra Paul J. Construction Inc
912 W Dr Martin Luther King
Tampa, FL 33603
800-409-5897

The Carpet Market
1655 NW Federal Highway
Stuart, FL 34994
772-692-9970

Fire & water damage restoration-Georgia

Disaster Services Inc
3030 Amwiler Road
Atlanta, GA 30360
770-446-5300
800-669-1411
www.DISASTERSERVICES.com

Disaster Services, Inc.
3030 Amwiler Road
Atlanta, GA 30360
1-800-669-1411
770-446-5300
www.disasterservices.com

FireStar Inc.
206 Wedgefield Crossing
Savannah, GA 31405
912-232-3473

Paul Davis Restoration
1979 A Parker Court
Stone Mountain
Stone Mountain, GA 30047
770-985-1727
www.pdrestoration?gcga

Paul Davis Restoration of N. Fulton & Forsyth
1360 Union Hill Road
Suite 3-D
Alpharetta, GA 30004
770-360-7994
www.pdrestoration.com

ServiceMaster of Decatur
3402 Oakcliff Road
Suite B6
Doraville, GA 30340
770-368-1866
www.4servicemaster.com/ga/3015

ServiceMaster Restoration Services
3355 Oak Dr SE
Conyers, GA 30013
770-483-4414
www.sm-restore.com

Stanley Steemer
3730 Honeysuckle Lane
Atlanta, GA 30340
770-451-3035
www.stanley-steemer.com

Fire & water damage restoration-Idaho

A1 Restoration Inc.
1261 Wilson D2
Pocatello, ID 83201
208-237-0033
208-221-1284

All American Cleaning
P.O. Box 2588
Idaho Falls, ID 83403
208-529-8179

Chem-Dry of Boise
5519 Kendall Street
Boise, ID 83706
208-322-7771
www.CHEMDRY.com

SERVICES

Mr.Steam/Ree-Construction
720 N Main Street
Suite A
Bellevue, ID 83313
208-788-2220
800-222-4068
www.dthe-restores.com

ServiceMaster Cleaning & Restoration
P.O. Box 1731
Idaho Falls, ID 83403
208-524-8262
www.4servicemaster.com/id/1259

Fire & water damage restoration-Illinois

All Clean Restoration Services Inc.
2300 S Illinois Street
Belleville, IL 62220-2803
800-422-3944
618-235-3202

Evans Restoration Services Inc.
2831 N Farmers Market Road
Springfield, IL 62707
217-528-2878
www.EVANSRESTORATION.com

First Advantage Restoration
301 Woodbury Street
South Elgin, IL 60177
800-282-1616
847-931-1600

Forbes Services
702 N Des Plaines Street
Plainfield, IL 60544
708-544-1200

JC Restoration
142 Thorndale Avenue
Bensenville, IL 60106
800-956-8844
630-773-6699
www.JCRESTORATION.com

Metropolitan Fire Restoration Services
729 E Park Avenue
Libertyville, IL 60048
847-367-8500
847-234-0760
www.metrofire.com

Paul Davis Restoration of S.W. Chicagoland
1335 Lakeside Drive
Unit 1
Romeoville, IL 60446
630-378-9011

Peerless Cleaners
519 N Monroe Street
Decatur, IL 62522
217-423-7703
800-879-7056
www.peerlessrestoration.com

ServiceMaster by Armstrong
P.O. Box 353
Wheaton, IL 60189
630-562-0600
800-937-3783

ServiceMaster Chicago Hub
4183 N Elston Ave.
Chicago, IL 60618
800-843-8415
773-583-4300
www.WESERVECHICAGO.com

ServiceMaster Disaster Services
25 W North Avenue
Villa Park, IL 60181-1249
630-833-0888
www.SERVICEMASTER.com

ServiceMaster H.K.H.
508 N. Oak Park Avenue
Oak Park, IL 60302
708-524-7915

ServiceMaster of Effingham
3230 S. Banker
Effingham, IL 62401
217-342-3206
888-812-7290
www.4servicemaster.com/IL/3926

Smoke Services
801 Scheel Street
Belleville, IL 62221
618-234-9696

Spectrum Restoration Services
P.O. Box 318
Sugar Grove, IL 60554
630-557-2621
www.spectrumrestoration.com

Disaster Kleenup International
611 Busse Road
Suite 205
Bensonville, Illinois 60106
630-350-3000
www.disasterkleenup.com

Fire & water damage restoration-Indiana

Chem-Dry of Lafayette
2131 N. Klondike Rd.
West Lafayette, IN 47906
765-423-1166

First Response
1919 South Michigan Street
South Bend, IN 46613
574-288-0500
www.firstresponseDRS.com

Paul Davis Restoration of East Central IN
1300 S. Hoyt Avenue
Muncie, IN 47302
765-284-3737
800-276-9526
www.pdrestoration.com

PCS Restoration
650 East Main St
Whiteland, IN 46184
317-535-7007
1-800-535-9416

ServiceMaster Advantage
6947 W 300 N
Delphi, IN 46923
765-564-1099
888-364-1188
http://www.svmadv.com

ServiceMaster by Fentz
7833 N. Irwin Dr.
Greenfield, IN 46140
317-894-2777
317-352-0031

ServiceMaster by Towne
1405 S. Nappanee St.
Elkhart, IN 46516
574-293-5200
877-625-3639

ServiceMaster Tri-County
1200 Bell Lane
Suite C
New Albany, IN 47150
812-944-5094
502-426-4504
www.4SERVICEMASTER.com/IN/6471

Fire & water damage restoration-Iowa

Paul Davis Restoration
3100 N.W. 101st Street
Suite C
Des Moines, IA 50322
515-252-0600
515-252-0545
www.pdrestoration.com

Paul Davis Restoration of Sioux City
200 South Fairmount Street
Sioux City, IA 51106
712-234-0095
712-234-0096

Paul Davis Restoration of Urbandale
Des Moines, IA
515-334-3473

ServiceMaster by Avenue of the Saints
1831 J St. S.W.
Cedar Rapids, IA 52404
319-365-9265
319-354-6328

ServiceMaster West
7605 University Ave.
Clive, IA 50325
515-274-9109

Fire & water damage restoration-Kansas

Clean Tech Restoration
1060 N West St
Wichita, KS 67203
316-729-8100
www.cleantechrestoration.com

Givens Cleaning Contractors, Inc.
250 Pennsylvania
Wichita, KS 67214
316-265-1315
givenscc@4givens.net

Givens Restoration & Cleaning
250 N. Pennsylvania
Wichita, KS 67214
316-265-1315
www.givenscleaning.com

ServiceMaster Clean In A Wink
4821 N. Hydraulic
Wichita, KS 67219
620-221-1386

ServiceMaster Clean in a Wink - Derby
4821 N. Hydraulic
Wichita, KS 67219
316-788-9654
800-646-2325
www.CLEANINAWINK.com

Fire & water damage restoration-Kentucky

Paul Davis Restoration & Remodeling
224 Ewing Road
Owensboro, KY 42301
270-691-0005
888-390-0005

Paul Davis Restoration of Lexington
230 Industry Parkway
Nicholasville, KY 40356
859-885-7653
800-960-7653
www.pdrestoration.com

R.L. Smith Co. Inc.
2557 Beaver Dam Road
P.O. Box 365
Leitchfield, KY 42755-0365
270-259-5684
270-589-0521
www.RLSCI.com

ServiceMaster by Anderson
3231 Buckriegel Parkway
Suite 119
Louisville, KY 40299
502-261-1755

Fire & water damage restoration-Louisiana

Catalano's Cleaning Services
4525 Airline Drive
Metairie, LA 70001
504-885-7417

Cleaning Unlimited Inc
5009 River Road
Harahan, LA 70123
504-832-1636

ServiceMaster Quality Services
P.O. Box 766
Houma, LA 70361-0766
985-872-1029
985-868-4028
www.S-MQS.com

Weil Cleaners Inc.
508 4th St N.
Monroe, LA 71207
318-325-3162

Fire & water damage restoration-Massachusetts

A.R.S. Services Inc.
612 R. Washington Street
Newton, MA 02458
800-298-6660
617-969-1119
www.arsserv.com

Action Fire InStar Services
30 Haynes Circle
Chicopee, MA 01020
413-594-7800
800-783-7668
www.INSTARSERVICES.com

Bostonian Cleaning Services
26 Quincy Avenue
Braintree, MA 02184-4404
781-340-1252

Demos Restoration Services
30 Haynes Circle
Chicopee, MA 01020
413-594-7801
www.instarservices.com

Disaster Specialists
P.O. Box 480
Sandwich, MA 02563
800-675-3622
508-888-1113
www.disasterspecialists.com

Envirotech Clean Air Inc.
10 Spencer Street
Stoneham, MA 02180
781-279-2900
617-839-7836
www.breatheasier.com

Facility Supply
81 Loudville Road
Easthampton, MA 01027
800-981-8128
413-527-6265
www.FACILITYSUPPLY.com

Fire Restoration Services of New England
90 Kerry Place
Norwood, MA 02062-4765
800-649-5080
www.FIRERESTORE.com

Kennedy Restoration Services
221 Libbey Industrial Parkway
Weymouth, MA 02189
781-335-8000
www.KENNEDYCARPET.com

Master Clean Restoration Services Inc
65 Chief Justice Cushing Highway
Hingham, MA 02043-2028
781-749-2314

Munters Corporation
79 Monroe Street
P.O. Box Box 640
Amesbury, MA 01913
800-MUNTERS
www.MUNTERSAMERICA.com

Oceanside Inc
217 Thornton Drive
Hyannis, MA 02601
508-771-3374
800-464-3318
www.oceansdeinc.com

Paul Davis Restoration
27 Water Street
Wakefield, MA 01880
781-224-3475
781-245-0003
www.pdrestoration.com

Purofirst Div. of Cardan Construction Inc
P.O. Box 290
Pittsfield, MA 01202
413-499-0010

ServiceMaster - Disaster Associates
4 Manison Street
Stoneham, MA 02180
781-438-6033
800-649-6369
www.SUM911.com

**ServiceMaster by Gaudet
6 Jefferson Avenue
Woburn, MA 01801-4325
781-932-1171
800-281-0072
www.servicemasterbygaudet.com**

ServiceMaster Commercial & Residential
21 D Fruean Way
South Yarmouth, MA
800-479-3999
508-398-8000

ServiceMaster Services Inc.
960 Turnpike Street
Canton, MA 02021
800-734-3315
617-323-7516
www.SERVICEMASTERSERVICES.com

**Trefler & Sons Antique/Fine Art
Restoration
29 Tower rd
Newton, MA 02464
617-965-3388
617-590-8676
www.trefler.com**

Fire & water damage restoration-Maryland

Begal Enterprises, Inc. Fire & Water Restoration
Specialists
12300 Carroll Avenue
Upper Level
Rockville, MD 20852
301-984-8566
301-984-8566
http://www.begal.net

Capital City Restorations
1219 Taft St.
Rockville, MD 20850
800-785-8810
301-251-8810
www.CAPITALCITYRESTORATIONS.com

CWK Construction Co. Inc
4512 Buchanan Street
Hyattsville, MD 20781
301-927-7033

Disaster Restoration Solutions, Inc.
10078 Tyler Place Suite D
Ijamsville, MD 21754
301-926-0000
www.drs-usa.com

Paul Davis Restoration & Remoldeling
7913 - D Cessna Avenue
Gaithersburg, MD 20879
301-948-8008
www.pdrestoration.com

Paul Davis Restoration Inc. of Southern MD
7801 Old Branch Avenue
Suite 105
Clinton, MD 20735
301-856-0090
www.pdrestoration.com

ServiceMaster by Singer
4401 Eastern Ave, Bldg 45
Baltimaore, MD 21224
410-563-2600
410-688-0530
www.smsinger.com

ServiceMaster Quality Clean
184 Childs Rd.
Elkton, MD 21921
410-392-4900
877-4NO-DIRT

Fire & water damage restoration-Minnesota

A & M Disaster Services
3010 E Lake Street
Minneapolis, MN 55406
612-722-0137

Advance Companies Inc
6400 Old Central Ave. N.E.
Fridley, MN 55432
763-572-2000

Fire & water damage restoration-Michigan

**BELFOR
185 Oakland Avenue
Suite 300
Birmingham, MI 48009
800-856-3333
www.belfor.com**

Magna-Dry International Inc.
114 Old M 21
Jenison, MI 49428
616-457-6664

SERVICES

Paul Davis Restoration & Remodeling
2222 Glendening Rd.
Suite 11
Kalamazoo, MI 49001
269-388-3700
www.pdrestoration.com/?kalz

Paul Davis Restoration of Macomb & St. Clair Counties
3807 East 10 Mile Road
Warren, MI 48091
586-755-1700
800-770-3170
http://www.pdrestoration.com

Paul Davis Restoration of Northwest Mich
822 Robinwood Court
Traverse City, MI 49686
231-933-9077
800-938-3473

Paul Davis Restoration of Northwest Michigan
822 Robinwood Ct.
Traverse City, MI 49686
231-933-9077
www.pdrestoration.com

**Regency Construction Corporation
DKI of Clinton Township
35240 Forton Court
Clinton Township, MI 48035
586-741-8000
888-41Regency
www.regencyconstruction.com**

ServiceMaster Home & Office
128 E. Grant Street
Alpena, MI 49707
989-358-2600
www.4servicemaster.com/mi/5090

ServiceMaster Lakeshore
P.O. Box 298
536 Oak St.
Ferrysburg, MI 49409
616-842-3131
231-739-7177
www.SERVICEMASTERLAKESHORE.com

**ServiceMaster of Big Rapids West
9415 Northland Drive
Big Rapids, MI 49346
231-823-8300**

ServiceMaster of Grand Traverse Area
5057 Sawyer Woods Dr.
Traverse City, MI 49684
231-943-9191

ServiceMaster of Ingham County
210 State Street
Mason, MI 48854
517-676-1626
800-336-5789
www.SERVICEMASTERCLEAN.com

ServiceMaster of Kalamazoo
3344 Ravine Road
Kalamazoo, MI 49006
800-530-7747
269-344-3600
www.smkazoo.com

Sunrise Cleaning
4100 Hunsaker St.
East Lansing, MI 48823
517-351-4200
www.sunrisecleaning.biz

Fire & water damage restoration-Minnesota

Du All Service Contractors Inc.
636 39th Avenue NE
Columbia Heights, MN 55421
763-788-9411
www.DUALLSERVICES.com

Lindstrom Cleaning & Construction Inc
9621 10th Ave N
Minneapolis, MN 55441
763-544-8761

Quantum Restoration
10525 Hampshire Ave. S.
Suite 100
Boomington, MN 55438
952-943-4357
www.QUANTUMCOMPANIES.com

Scott Construction
720 Walker Street
St. Louis Park, MN 55426
612-721-3311

Service Team of Professionals
6615 - 141st Avenue N.W.
Ramsey, MN 55303
763-753-8080
612-810-2091

ServiceMaster Cleaning Service of Brown Co.
622 N. Franklin St.
New Ulm, MN 56073
507-354-4233

ServiceMaster of Chaska/Shakopee
P.O. Box 64
Chaska, MN 55318
952-445-5233

ServiceMaster of Forest Lake
804 Margaret Street
St. Paul, MN 55106
651-464-1214
www.smstp.com

ServiceMaster of Osseo / Maple Grove
9702 85th Ave. North
Maple Grove, MN 55369
763-424-4100
www.SMOMG.com

ServiceMaster of Rochester
P.O. Box 6434
Rochester, MN 55903
507-282-5747

ServiceMaster of the Lakes Area
203 Lake Street
P.O. Box 714
Alexandna, MN 56308
320-763-5551
320-763-5270
www.SERVICEMASTERBYSTRONG.com

ServiceMaster South Metro
22068 Canton Court
Farmington, MN 55024
651-463-7700

Thunder Restoration, Inc.
2525 Nevada Avenue N.
Suite 208
Minneapolis, MN 55427
800-374-8810
763-323-3139
www.thunder-restoration.com

Ungerman Construction Co
4450 Nicollet Avenue
Minneapolis, MN 55419
612-825-2800

Fire & water damage restoration-Mississippi

Paul Davis Restoratin of Central Mississippi
274 Commerce Park Drive Suite
Ridgeland, MS 39157
601-605-1717

Paul Davis Restoration of Central Mississippi
274 Commerce Park Drive
Ridgeland, MS 39157
601-605-1717
www.pdrestoration.com

ServiceMaster By Chuck Wallace
P.O. Box 3878
Brookhaven, MS 39603
601-835-1000
601-270-2362

ServiceMaster by Reid
270 Highpoint Drive
Ridgeland, MS 39157
601-853-1615
601-992-9700

Fire & water damage restoration-Missouri

Jim Thompson & Co.
1 Jim Thompson Way
Blackwell, MO 63626
636-337-8200
www.disasterjim.com

Paul Davis Restoration & Remodeling
1207 Eaglecrest
Nixa, MO 65714
417-725-7575
www.pdrestoration.com

ServiceMaster CleanWorks, LLC
787 Highway Z
St. Robert, MO 65584
866-336-5994
888-532-3839

The Fire Works Restoration Co./1-800BOARDUP
9420 Watson Industrial Park
St. Louis, MO 63126
314-961-3473
www.1-800Boardup.com

Woodard Cleaning & Restoration Service
9308 Manchester Road
Saint Louis, MO 63119
314-961-9102
www.woodardcleaning.com

Fire & water damage restoration-Montana

DaySpring Restoration
533 W. Franklin Street
Missoula, MT 59801
800-555-3803
406-543-6070
www.dayspringrestoration.com

Fire & water damage restoration-Nebraska

ServiceMaster of Sarpy County
1116 Grenoble Dr.
Bellevue, NE 68123
402-293-1625

ServiceMaster of Sooland
1905 A Street
South Sioux City, NE 68776
402-494-3188
www.4servicemaster.com/ne/2706

Fire & water damage restoration-New Hampshire

Paul Davis Restoration of Central NH
720 East Industrial Park Drive
Unit 1
Manchester, NH 03109
603-622-9800
www.pdrestoration.com

PDR of Southern NH and ME
12 D Elm Rd.
P.O. Box 419
North Hampton, NH 03820
603-964-8484
800-863-7948
pdrestoration.com

ServiceMaster of Carroll & Coos County
16 Saco Pines
P.O. Box 58
Center Conway, NH 03813
603-447-5031
800-734-5031
4servicemaster.com/nh/3259

Fire & water damage restoration-New Jersey

AstroCare Fire & Water
50 S Center Street
Orange, NJ 07050-3529
973-677-1234
www.astrocare.com

Cornerstone Appraisal and Restoration
29 Emmons Drive
Suite G-50
Princeton, NJ 08540
609-520-8877
888-831-5011
www.cornerstone-restoration.com

MaximForce Drying
145 Talmadge Road
Edison, NJ 08817
732-287-3010
www.WaterOutMiddlesexNJ.com

Paul Davis Restoration
586 Route 70
Suite 1-A
Brick, NJ 08723
732-451-1280
www.pdrestoration.com

Paul Davis Restoration of Mercer & Middlesex, Inc.
865 Lower Ferry Road
Suite B-18
Ewing, NJ 08628
609-538-8424
www.pdrestoration.com

Paul Davis Restoration of Morris County
248 Columbia Turnpike
Florham Park, NJ 07932
973-765-9707
www.pdrestoration.com

Paul Davis Restoration of Somerset, Hunterdon, & Warren Counties
158 Cregar Road
Suite 200
High Bridge, NJ 08829
908-638-8440
pdri.net?shwc

ServiceMaster of Cherry Hill
2 Keystone Avenue
Suite 100
Cherry Hill, NJ 08003
856-751-1577
800-686-8919

ServiceMaster To The Rescue
P.O. Box 177
1809 B S. Delsea Drive
Vineland, NJ 08362
856-692-4269
www.servicemaster.com

The ArmaKleen Company
469 North Harrison Street
Princeton, NJ 08543
800-332-5424
609-497-7220
www.armex.com

Fire & water damage restoration-New Mexico

Bear Carpet & Restoration
3400 Girard Boulevard NE
Albuquerque, NM 87107
505-888-1164

Paul Davis Restoration of New Mexico
7820 4th, N.W.
Albuquerque, NM 87107
505-884-5583
505-321-7995
www.pdrestoration.com

ServiceMaster of Albuquerque / West Mesa
3206 Alta Monte N.E.
Albuquerque, NM 87107
505-880-1233

ServiceMaster Quality Restoration
1760 Hadley Avenue
Las Cruces, NM 88005
505-541-0400

Fire & water damage restoration-New York

Advanced Restoration Corporation
151 Lafayette Road
West Babylon, NY 11704-4903
631-422-2100
www.ADVANCEDRESTORATION.com

AllPro Cleaning & Restoration Services
13 Haven St
Elmsford, NY 10523
800-352-7886
914-592-2849
www.ALLPRORESTORATION.com

American Fire Restoration
277 Willis Avenue
Roslyn Heights, NY 11577-2107
516-484-1777
800-777-8116

Bio-Recovery Corporation
33-15 Greenpoint Ave
Long Island City, NY 11101-2011
718-729-2600
877-246-2532
www.biorecovery.com

Certified Restoration Services Inc.
1361 -15 Lincoln Avenue
Holbrook, NY 11741
631-737-5050

D & S Professional Services
P.O. Box 114
Minoa, NY 13116
800-359-2534
315-656-2533
www.DSPROFESSIONALSERVICES.com

Document Reprocessors
5611 Water St
Middlesex, NY 14507
888-437-9464
www.DOCUMENTREPROCESSORS.com

Loss Recovery Systems Inc.
10 Dwight Park Drive
Syracuse, NY 13209
315-451-9111
www.lrs911.com

LVI Services, Inc.
470 Park Avenue South
11th Floor, N. Wing
New York, NY 10016
888-584-2677
www.lviservices.com

Paul Davis Restoration & Remodeling
5681 Zerfass Road
Dansville, NY 14437
585-335-2780
800-836-8910
www.pdrestoration.com

Paul Davis Restoration of N.Y.
2 Pinehurst Ave.
New York, NY 10033
212-740-6611
PDR-USA.NET

Paul Davis Restoration of Rockland and Orange Counties
307 Bloomingburg Road
P.O. Box 277
Middletown, NY 10940
845-361-1840
845-361-1841
www.pdrestoration.com

Paul Davis Restoration of Western NY
61 Archer Street
Buffalo, NY 14120
800-836-8910
www.pdrestoration.com

Restoration Specialists of Greater New York
450 Westbury Ave
Carleplace, NY 11514
631-587-3800

ServiceMaster Complete Restoration
1319 Walden Avenue
Checktowaga, NY 14211
716-893-9797

ServiceMaster of Kingston
41 Greenkill Avenue
Kingston, NY 12401
845-338-4821
877-Klean4U

ServiceMaster of Rochester
2171 Monroe Avenue
Rochester, NY 14618
585-473-3290

ServiceMaster of West Rochester, NY
3011 Edgemere Dr.
Rochester, NY 14612
585-227-9900

Fire & water damage restoration-Nevada

Certified Restoration and Remediation Services
9775 S. Maryland Parkway
Suite F167
Las Vegas, NV 89123
702-837-6653

Fire & water damage restoration-North Carolina

Advantaclean
2953 Interstate Street
Charlotte, NC 28208
704-391-3330
800-948-5329
www.advantaclean.com

SERVICES

First Restoration Services Inc.
1517 N Graham Street
Charlotte, NC 28206-3021
800-743-6717
704-376-6777
www.FIRSTRESTORATION.com

First Restoration Services of Ashville
12 National Avenue
Fletcher, NC 28732
800-537-6151
828-684-1582
www.firstrestoration-avl.com

Paul Davis Restoration
34-A Redmond Dr
Fletcher, NC 28732
828-687-7766
www.pdrestoration\?aanc

Paul Davis Restoration
6600 Windmill Way
Wilmington, NC 28405
910-452-7290
pdrcarolinacoast.com

ServiceMaster of Hendersonville
797 Locust Street
Hendersonville, NC 28792
828-697-9831
800-697-9831
www.4SERVICEMASTER.com/nc/6239

Fire & water damage restoration-North Dakota

Paul Davis Restoration & Remodeling
355 7th St. NW
West Fargo, ND 58078
701-271-4770
www.pdrfargo.com

Fire & water damage restoration-Ohio

Cleaning Genie Inc.
5433 Schultz Drive
Sylvania, OH 43560
419-885-5511
www.cleaninggenie.com

First General Services of Cleveland & Akron
29767 Lafayette Way
Westlake, OH 44145
800-943-7054
440-899-9474
www.firstgeneralservices.com

Harris Fire & Water Cleaning Specialists
26901 Eckel Road
Perrysburg, OH 43551
419-874-9420
877-883-9896
www.HARRISCLEANING.com

Kulis Freeze Dry
725 Broadway Ave.
Bedford, OH 44146
440-232-8352
www.kastaway.com

OmniClean
5205 West 161st Street
Brook Park, OH 44142
216-362-8686
www.OMNICLEAN.com

Paul Davis Restoration & Remodeling of Cleveland Metro West
424 Pearl Road
Brunswick, OH 44212
330-221-2002
877-742-3245
www.pdrestoration.com

Paul Davis Restoration of Akron
2735 Second Street
Cuyahoga Falls, OH 44221
330-920-1936
330-920-4201
www.pdrestoration.com

Paul Davis Restoration of Cleveland Metro
7209-A Chagrin Road
Chagrin Falls, OH 44023
440-247-5122
CMOH@pdr-usa.net

Paul Davis Restoration of Dayton
1960 W. Dorothy Lane
Dayton, OH 45439
937-436-3411
www.pdrestoration.com

ServiceMaster - At Your Service
2150 Baty Road
Lima, OH 45807
419-339-0871
888-258-3280
www.4SERVICEMASTER.com/oh/5268

ServiceMaster by Corbett
92 Shiawassee Avenue
Akron, OH 44333
330-864-7300
www.4servicemaster.com/oh/1305

ServiceMaster Quality Services
8600 Harrison Pike
Cleves, OH 45002
513-353-9238
937-294-8800

Thompson Building Associates, Inc
3333 Refugee Rd
Columbus, OH 43232
614-863-9650
800-BOARDUP (262-7387)
www.THOMPSONBUILDING.com

Wades ServiceMaster Superior Restoration
4700 Caprice Dr.
Middletown, OH 45044
513-424-9487
937-293-3977

Fire & water damage restoration-Oklahoma

Abney Construction Inc.
405 NW JA RiChardson Loop
Ada, OK 74820
580-332-6229

Purified Restoration Fire Smoke & Water
4115 S 72nd East Avenue
Tulsa, OK 74145
918-610-8173

ServiceMaster Advantage
7002 E. 38th Street
Tulsa, OK 74145
918-250-7040
918-852-6702
www.4SERVICEMASTER.com/ok/4212

ServiceMaster by Jeff
9267 E. 58th Street
Tulsa, OK 74145
918-294-8590
918-230-8429
www.4servicemaster.com/ok/5613

TRC
712 S. Wheeling Ave
Tulsa, OK 74104
918-585-1990
www.trcdisastersolutions.com

Fire & water damage restoration-Oregon

Immediate Environmental Recovery Solutions
P. O. Box 18174
Portland, OR 97218
800-369-3214
503-288-4848
www.iersos.com

ServiceMaster by Samburg
58360 Rigdon Rd
Warren, OR 97053
503-366-5390
360-431-0924
www.columbia-center.org

ServiceMaster of Gateway
6605 S.E. 66th Ave
Portland, OR 97206
503-760-2461
503-453-6574

ServiceMaster of LaGrande
P.O. Box 411
LaGrande, OR 97850
541-962-2639
800-573-2575

ServiceMaster of Lake Oswego
P.O. Box 246
Portland, OR 97224
503-636-8720

Fire & water damage restoration-Pennsylvania

ABM/Disaster Recovery SVCS.
420 Feheley Drive
King of Prussia, PA 19406
610-275-6200

Barrett Cleaning and Restoration
P.O. Box 0613
Hatboro, PA 19040
215-715-3544
215-675-1020
http://hometown.aol.com/barrettcleaning/

Cameo Services Inc.
420 S. Sherman St.
York, PA 17403-5303
717-843-8893
www.CAMEOYORK.com

Compleat Restorations
2797 S. Queen St.
Dallastown, PA 17313
800-699-1176
www.compleatrestorations.com

Compleat Restorations
702 Pointview Ave
Ephrata, PA 17522
800-699-1176

Eastern Diversified Services Inc.
89 Allentown Road
Souderton, PA 18964
215-723-1920
800-295-3636
www.easterndiversified.com

FireDEX of Pittsburgh
4030 William Flynn Highway
Allison Park, PA 15101
412-487-3332

First General Services of N.E. PA
31 Ruddle Street
Wilkes-Barre, PA 18702-4309
570-824-0680
800-421-3080
www.FIRSTGENERALSERVICE.com

First General Services of Pen-Mar Inc.
5165 Design Ave
Waynesboro, PA 17268
717-762-0550

SERVICES

Frye Restoration
1000 Sixth & Railroad Street
Monongahela, PA 15063
724-258-7577

G.S. Jones & Sons
8347 Ohio River Boulevard
Pittsburgh, PA 15202-1451
412-766-6886
www.GSJONESANDSONS.com

Insurance Damage Specialist
333 Lexington Street
York, PA 17403
717-718-1969
www.ids-team.com

Insurance Damage Specialists
333 Lexington Street
York, PA 17403
717-718-1969
877-718-1969
www.ids-team.com

Mellon Certified Restoration
611 County Line Road
Huntingdon Vy, PA 19006
215-357-6000
www.meloncr.net

Paul Davis Restoration
34 Yale Avenue
Morton, PA 19070
610-328-5901

Paul Davis Restoration of Bucks County
205 North Main Street
Telford, PA 18969
215-799-0777
www.pdrestoration.com

Paul Davis Restoration of Western PA
1600 West Lawrence Avenue
Ellwood City, PA 16117
724-758-6540
www.pdri.net

Service Master By Artec
150 E Baltimore Avenue
Clifton Heights, PA 19018
610-626-9002

Service Master of Fay-West
112 North Third St.
POB 752
Connellsville, PA 15425
724-628-2122

ServiceMaster
186 Sunset Blvd. East
Chambusburg, PA 17201
717-267-2223
www.4SERVICEMASTER.com/pa/2127

ServiceMaster by Holobinko
465 E. Rolling Ridge Dr.
Bellefonte, PA 16823
814-231-0812

ServiceMaster Cleaning & Restoration
P.O. Box 679
Springtown, PA 18081
610-346-8545
www.ser2rescue.com

ServiceMaster of Allentown
933 Chestnut St.
Emmaus, PA 18049-2098
610-965-6058
800-882-7450
www.4SERVICEMASTER.com/pa/2421

ServiceMaster of Somerset
2312 W. Bakersville-Edie Rd
Suite #2
Somerset, PA 15501
814-445-1380
www.4SERVICEMASTER.com/pa/3749

Total Restoration Contracting
209 W. Main St.
Collegeville, PA 19426
800-734-4100
610-489-1650
www.TOTALRESTORATIONCONTRACTING.com

Unsmoke/Restorx
4660 Elizabeth Street
Coraopolis, PA 15108
412-351-8686
800-332-6037
www.UNSMOKE.com

Fire & water damage restoration-Rhode Island

ServiceMaster Of Bristol County
15 Osage Dr
Middletown, RI 02842
401-274-9500
www.Servicemaster.com

Fire & water damage restoration-South Carolina

Catastrophe Services, Inc. (CSI)
P.O. Box 23551
Columbia, SC 29224
803-788-1800
800-952-6106
www.catastropheserv.com

Fire & water damage restoration-South Dakota

Intek Painting Svc.
505 N Harlem Avenue
Sioux Falls, SD 57104
605-334-9716

ServiceMaster of Aberdeen
P.O. Box 577
Aberdeen, SD 57402
800-700-4528
605-225-4528
www.ABERDEENCLEAN.com

Fire & water damage restoration-Tennessee

Insurance Contractors Inc
648 N Broadway
Portland, TN 37148
615-323-8889
866-656-7790

Paul Davis Restoration
6622 Lee Highway
Chattanooga, TN 37421
423-899-2406

Sean's ChemDry
738 Nissan Blvd
Smyrna, TN 37167
615-890-8055
615-373-4930
www.thecleanest.com

ServiceMaster by Cornerstone
9362 Marbella Cove
Cordova, TN 38018
901-624-9200
901-624-1050

ServiceMaster by Cypress Bend
218 Hub Cir.
Allgood, TN 38506
931-372-8480

ServiceMaster by FloorServe
6250 E. Shelby Dr
Memphis, TN 38141
901-363-1331
866-967-3783

ServiceMaster Clean
P.O. Box 751027
Memphis, TN 38175
800-RESPOND
800-737-7663
www.servicemasterclean.com

ServiceMaster Clean
3839 Forest Hill-Irene Road
Memphis, TN 38125
800-633-5703
901-597-8158
www.servicemaster.com

ServiceMaster Clean by Stechyn and Son
97 Oak Valley Drive
Spring Hill, TN 37174
931-840-0065

ServiceMaster of Chattanooga
P.O. Box 3350
Chattanooga, TN 37404
423-624-0937
www.SERVICEMASTER.com

ServiceMaster of Germantown
715 Chaney Cove
Suite 102
Collierville, TN 38017
901-854-6225
901-853-3748

Servpro
P.O. Box 1978
Gallatin, TN 37066
615-451-0600
800-SER-VPRO

Fire & water damage restoration-Texas

AAAction Cleaning and Restoration
2218 Patterson Industrial Drive
Pflugerville, TX 78660
512-837-1470
www.actionc-r.com

Allen Restoration & Construction
5551 Woodland Hills Drive
Denton, TX 76208
940-320-1900
www.ALLENRESTORATION.com

A-Town Hi-Tech LP
4402 S Danville Drive
Abilene, TX 79605-7238
325-692-1893
800-388-1204
www.a-town.net

Blackmon Mooring Steamatic
303 Arthur Street
Fort Worth, TX 76107
877-730-1948
www.blackmonmooring.com

BMS Catastrophe Inc. (BMS CAT)
303 Arthur Street
Fort Worth, TX 76107-2352
800-433-2940
817-332-2770
www.BMSCAT.com

Boone's Restoration Technologies
27331 Robinson Road
Conroe, TX 77385
281-444-5959
800-450-1265
www.boonesrestoration.com

Continental Machinery Company Inc.
10382 Miller Road
Dallas, TX 75238
800-616-8600
www.CONTINENTALMACHINERY.com

SERVICES

Continental Restoration Consulting
P.O. Box 550340
Dallas, TX 75355
214-342-8910
800-616-8600
www.continentalconsulting.com

First General Services of Northeast Texas
P. O. 9712
Longview, TX 75608
903-759-8803

Hi-Tech Fire & Water Restoration Inc
4402 S Danville Drive
Abilene, TX 79605-7238
915-692-1892
800-388-1204
www.a-town.net

Partners' Restoration & Construction, LLC
2650 Lombardy Lane
Suite S
Dallas, TX 75220-2523
214-366-2528
www.partnersrecon.com

Paul Davis Restoration
7320 Ashcroft Dr.
Suite 201
Houston, TX 77081
713-270-6030
713-545-6082
www.pdrestoration.com

**Paul Davis Restoration
1325 Whitlock Lane
Suite 108
Carrollton, TX 75006
972-323-6565
866-PAUL-DAVIS
www.pdrestoration.com**

Paul Davis Restoration & Remodeling of Tarrant County
1663 Hickory Drive
Suite B
Fort Worth, TX 76117
817-759-2600
877-PAUL-DAVIS
www.pdrestoration.com

Restoration Specialists Inc.
4501 Sunbelt Dr STE B
Addison, TX 75001
214-637-2200

**ServiceMaster Advanced Restorations
565 Commerce Street
Southlake, TX 76092
817-481-0664
817-808-3791**

ServiceMaster Advantage Restoration & Cleaning
P.O. Box 890282
Houston, TX 77289
281-332-3900
www.svmhouston.com

ServiceMaster Clean Quality Restoration
P.O. Box 311294
New Braunfels, TX 78131
830-625-1625
210-658-4881
www.4servicemaster.com/tx/5997

ServiceMaster Professional Services
P.O. Box 203664
Austin, TX 78720
512-249-8710

ServiceMaster Professional Services
P.O. Box 1269
Marble Falls, TX 78654
830-693-3869
www.SERVICEMASTERCLEAN.com

ServiceMaster Quality Restoration
P.O. Box 4514
McAllen, TX 78502-4514
956-686-2907

ServiceMaster Restoration by Carroll
7586 Dillon
Houston, TX 77061
713-667-5052
www.servicemasterrestoration.com

ServiceMaster SouthWest
1723 - B Eldridge
Sugar Land, TX 77478
281-242-5777
www.servicemastersouthwest.com

ServiceMaster Superior Restoration & Cleaning
P.O. Box 3068
McKinney, TX 75070
972-881-2345

Servpro
2623 National Circle
Garland, TX 75041
214-343-3973
972-278-7871

ServPro of El Paso East
232 Peyton Rd.
El Paso, Tx 79928
915-852-0993

Sims City Cleaners Inc
9623 Hillcroft Street
Houston, TX 77096
713-721-3100

Southwestern Restoration, Inc.
11063 Timberline
Houston, TX 77043
713-932-1177
www.smartpages.com/home/southwesternrestoration

Steamatic Inc. International Headquarters
303 Arthur Street
Fort Worth, TX 76107
817-332-1575
800-527-1295
www.steamatic.com

Stefek Restoration Services Inc.
20108 AlGreg St.
Pflugerville, TX 78660
512-837-5774
866-783-3351

Fire & water damage restoration-Utah

Certified Disaster Services
2675 Industrial Drive
Building 1 Suite 3
Ogden, UT 84401
801-399-9996

ServiceMaster of St. George and Cedar City
P.O. Box 395
Washington, UT 84780
435-628-9866
435-867-5321
www.servicemastercleaning.com

ServiceMaster Restoration & Cleaning Services
394 East 400 South
Price, UT 84501
435-637-9165
435-650-1006
www.4servicemaster.com/ut/5855

Utah Disaster Kleenup
13081 Minuteman Drive
Draper, UT 84020
801-553-1010
www.UTDK.com

Fire & water damage restoration-Virginia

A-1 Flood Tech
9111 Centreville Road
Manassas, VA 20110
703-631-0400
703-361-2156
www.a1floodtech.com

Bay Restoration & Air Duct Services
805 Camp Mill Road
Lively, VA 22482
800-438-2436

Paul Davis Restoration of Greater Richmond, Inc.
112 S. Providence Rd.
Suite 103
Richmond, VA 23236
804-330-9500
pdsgrri@worldnet.att.net

ServiceMaster of Chantilly
14325 E Willard Rd
Chantilly, VA 20151
703-968-0505
301-656-8330
www.4SERVICEMASTER.com/va/1976

ServiceMaster Restoration Services
1 W. 4th Street
P.O. Box 954
Salem, VA 24153
540-375-9411
540-375-9410

Servpro
8433 Eucid Ave
Manassas, VA 20111
703-739-2800

United Restoration Inc.
360 Cleveland Place
Virginia Beach, VA 23462
757-490-1966
866-599-8057
www.UNITEDRESTORATION.org

Fire & water damage restoration-Washington

BELFOR
3826 Woodland Park Ave North
Seattle, WA 98103
800-775-0806
www.belfor.com

Coit Restoration Services
16750 Woodinville-Redmond Rd. N.E.
Building C-102
Woodinville, WA 98072
800-367-2648
425-481-9505
www.COIT.com

Columbia Chem-Dry
933 S. Nevada Dr.
Longview, WA 98632
360-423-5754

Holland-Dutch Cleaning/Restoration Services Inc
535 Industry Drive
Tukwila, WA 98188
206-322-7000
www.HOLLANDDUTCH.com

Humidity Control Systems
Vancouver, WA 98668
800-642-7910

Injectidry Systems Inc
825 7th Avenue
Kirkland, WA 98033-5749
425-822-3851
800-257-0793

Servicemaster
2839 W. Kennewick Avenue
Suite 336
Kennewick, WA 99336
509-582-0166
www.4SERVICEMASTER.com/wa/6224

SERVICES

ServiceMaster by J-L
P.O. Box 3002
Everett, WA 98213
425-353-5586
www.SMJL.com

ServiceMaster Professional Cleaning
P.O. Box 10055
Yakima, WA 98909
509-452-8906

Fire & water damage restoration-West Virginia

Mountaineer Chem-Dry
823 Bethel Road
Morgantown, WV 26501
304-598-3691
304-276-5700

ServiceMaster of Martinsburg
7520 Arden Nollville Rd
Martinsburg, WV 25401
304-262-2600
www.cleanonthe.net

ServiceMasterClean of Kanawha Valley
5703 Sissonville Drive
Charleston, WV 25312
304-345-9198
304-542-3163

Captain Clean Inc.
P.O. Box 5081
Sheridan, WY 82801
307-672-0726
www.CAPTAINCLEAN.com

Fire & water damage restoration-Wisconsin

First General Services of Madison
2030 South Park Street
Madison, WI 53713
800-318-3473
608-258-2094
www.FGSMADISON.com

Paul Davis Restoration of Fox Valley
2225 Northern Road
Appleton, WI 54914
920-882-9287
800-491-0552
www.pdri.net/?fxwi

Paul Davis Restoration of Northeast WI
2225 Northern Road
Appleton, WI 54914
920-882-9287
800-491-0552
www.pdri.net/?nowi

Paul Davis Restoration of Southeast Wisconsin
2000 S. 4th Street
Milwaukee, WI 83202
414-383-3131
www.pdrestoration.com

ServiceMaster by Frintz
P.O. Box 2137
Kenosha, WI 53141
262-942-9246
847-855-1900

ServiceMaster of Milwaukee
4141 North Richards Street
Milwaukee, WI 53212
414-962-9910
www.4servicemaster.com/WI/3846/

ServiceMaster Restoration & Cleaning
1200 Silver Drive
Suite 15
Baraboo, WI 53913
608-253-2905
cqserve@yahoo.com

Specialized Services
807 Carol Lynn Drive
Little Chute, WI 54140
920-788-1738

Sullivan's Cleaning and Restoration Service
3065-A Commodity Lane
Green Bay, WI 54304-5666
920-337-1986
920-337-0280
www.sullivanscleaning.com

Flood damage restoration

ABC Chem-Dry
432 Lafayette St.
Utica, NY 13502
800-FOR-ABC1
315-738-1111
www.abcchemcleaners.com

All Care Chem-Dry
13727 S.W. 152 Street
#273
Miami, FL 33177
305-969-3733
305-213-8505

All Ways ChemDry
2303 Randall Rd
Suite 292
Carpentersville, IL 60110
630-377-7417
www.ALLWAYSCD.com

Ayers Professional Services
5400 Elmo Weedon Rd.
College Station, TX 77845
979-776-5800

Bay Area Clean Care
1656 Clarion Avenue
Petoskey, MI 49770-9263
231-347-7707
www.bayareacleancare.com

Bayside Chem-Dry
1065 Cedar Point Blvd
Cedar Point, NC 28584
252-393-7580
252-634-2244

BELFOR
185 Oakland Avenue
Suite 300
Birmingham, MI 48009
800-856-3333
www.belfor.com

Brothers ChemDry & Oceanfront ChemDry
2984 South Lynnhaven Road
Virginia Beach, VA 23452
757-498-3439
757-486-5746
www.CHEMDRYUSA.com/oceanfront.va

C&G Chem-Dry
513 Oakton Road
Odenton, MD 21113
410-674-4240
800-333-4240

Chem Dry - By Moore
8 Glen Road
Yonkers, NY 10704
914-843-8062

Chem-Dry of Brazos County
5400 Elmo Weedon Rd.
College Station, TX 77845
979-776-9833
www.chemdry.com

Chem-Dry of Marin
15 F Pamaron Way
Suite F
Novato, CA 94949
415-382-8196
415-499-8196
chemdryofmarin@earthlink.net

Chem-Dry of North Valley
4243 Keefer Road
Chico, CA 95973
530-891-6747
530-533-2944
www.CHEMDRY.com

Chem-Dry on the No. Shore
329 Franklin St
Reading, MA 01867
781-670-9169
978-774-2705

Coakley & Williams Construction Co Inc
16 S Summit Avenue
Gaithersburg, MD 20877
301-963-5000
www.COAKLEYWILLIAMS.com

DryTech Co, LLC
13419 Fenway Blvd North
Hugo, MN 55038
651-429-8444
651-261-8196

Emergency Restoration Specialists Inc.
1100 Menomonee Ave.
South Milwaukee, WI 53172
414-571-9977
www.removewater.com

Findlay Dinger (Service Master)
670 Cherry Street
Winter Park, FL 32789
800-237-9688
407-678-1808

First Coast Chem-Dry
5605 Florida Mining Blvd S.
Jacksonville, FL 32257
904-262-2322
904-237-0504
www.TOUCHDOWNCLEAN.com

First General Services Canada
Div. of First General Enterprises (Ontario) Ltd.
437 Flint Road
Toronto, ON M3J 2T7
Canada
416-736-0395
877-888-9111
www.firstgeneral.ca

First General Services of Cleveland &
Akron
29767 Lafayette Way
Westlake, OH 44145
800-943-7054
440-899-9474
www.firstgeneralservices.com

First General Services Treasure Valley
16299 Franklin Rd.
Nampa, ID 83687
208-463-2385

First Response
1919 South Michigan Street
South Bend, IN 46613
574-288-0500
www.firstresponseDRS.com

First Restoration Services of Ashville
12 National Avenue
Fletcher, NC 28732
800-537-6151
828-684-1582
www.firstrestoration-avl.com

Flood Rescue
6064 Scanlan Suite #1
St. Louis, MO 63139
314-452-3194

Glenncarey Restoration Contractors Ltd.
4735 Westney Rd.
Claremont, ON L1Y 1A2
Canada
905 428-6327
905 649-3545
www.glenncareygroup.com

Harris Fire and Water Cleaning Specialists
26901 Eckel Rd.
Perrysburg, OH 43551
877-883-9896
419-874-9420
www.harriscleaning.com

MARCOR Environmental
246 Cockeysville Rd.
Suite 1
Hunt Valley, MD 21030
410-785-0001
800-547-0128
www.marcor.com

Munters Corporation
79 Monroe Street
P.O. Box Box 640
Amesbury, MA 01913
800-MUNTERS
www.MUNTERSAMERICA.com

NCRI
8065 Flint Street
Lenexa, KS 66214
913-663-4111
www.NCRICAT.com

New Image Building Services, Inc.
320 Church Street
Mount Clemens, MI 48043
586-465-4420
800-434-4120
www.newimagebldg.com

Paul Davis Restoration
10201 N. 21st Ave Suite 5
Phoenix, AZ 85021
623-445-9922
602-329-2732
http://www.pdrestoration.com

Paul Davis Restoration
399 E Harrison
Corona, CA 92879
909-270-5304
www.pdrestoration.com

Paul Davis Restoration
1979 A Parker Court
Stone Mountain
Stone Mountain, GA 30047
770-985-1727
www.pdrestoration?gcga

Paul Davis Restoration
1325 Whitlock Lane
Suite 108
Carrollton, TX 75006
972-323-6565
866-PAUL-DAVIS
www.pdrestoration.com

Paul Davis Restoration
P.O. Box 5
1323 W. 7900S #204
W. Jordan, UT 84088
801-561-4900

Paul Davis Restoration & Remodeling of Tarrant County
1663 Hickory Drive
Suite B
Fort Worth, TX 76117
817-759-2600
877-PAUL-DAVIS
www.pdrestoration.com

Paul Davis Restoration of Akron
2735 Second Street
Cuyahoga Falls, OH 44221
330-920-1936
330-920-4201
www.pdrestoration.com

Paul Davis Restoration of Greater Phoenix
4607 S. 35th Street
Suite 3
Phoenix, AZ 85040
602-278-8837
602-276-2008
www.pdrestoration.com

Paul Davis Restoration of New Mexico
7820 4th, N.W.
Albuquerque, NM 87107
505-884-5583
505-321-7995
www.pdrestoration.com

Paul Davis Restoration of Palm Beach County
1025 N. Florida Mango Rd #9
West Palm Beach, FL 33409
561-478-7272
www.restorepalmbeach.us

Paul Davis Restoration of S.W.
Chicagoland
1335 Lakeside Drive
Unit 1
Romeoville, IL 60446
630-378-9011

Paul Davis Restoration of Tucson
2555 North Coyote Drive
Suite 113
Tucson, AZ 85745
520-624-4560
www.pdrestoration.com

Paul Davis Restoration of Volusia County
2330 S. Nova Road
Suite 1
South Daytona, FL 32119
386-760-8959
www.pdrestoration.com

Pro-Tech Cleaning & Restoration,LLC
508 Johns Road
Boerne, TX 78006
830-816-3202
www.pro-techrestore.com

Regency Construction Corporation
DKI of Clinton Township
35240 Forton Court
Clinton Township, MI 48035
586-741-8000
888-41Regency
www.regencyconstruction.com

Service Management Group LLC
417 Knowlton Street
Bridgeport, CT 06608
203-333-1707
800-688-1707
www.svcmgmt.com

ServiceMaster by Gaudet
6 Jefferson Avenue
Woburn, MA 01801-4325
781-932-1171
800-281-0072
www.servicemasterbygaudet.com

ServiceMaster Cleaning & Restoration
1105 Yuba Street
Marysville, CA 95901
530-741-8178
800-RESPOND
www.servicemasterclean.com

ServiceMaster Cleaning and Restoration
P.O. Box 2192
Suite D
Merced, CA 95344
209-726-9182
888-726-9182

ServiceMaster of Germantown
715 Chaney Cove
Suite 102
Collierville, TN 38017
901-854-6225
901-853-3748

ServiceMaster Professional Cleaning
7350 N.W. 7th Street
Suite 106
Miami, FL 33126-2976
305-264-8999
786-486-2526

ServiceMaster Professional Restoration
3869 Norwood Drive #3
Littleton, CO 80125
720-981-8809

Servpro of Seal Beach/Cypress/Los Alamitos
3267 Katekka Avenue
Los Alamitos, CA 90720
562-431-9400
714-236-9599

Spectrum Restoration Service
2600 Beverly Dr.
Suite 105
Amora, IL 60501
630-898-3200
www.spectrumrestoration.com

Surfside Chem-Dry
1211 S. Oxnard Blvd
Oxnard, CA 93030
805-485-9595
818-225-2436

The Fire Works Restoration Co./1-800BOARDUP
9420 Watson Industrial Park
St. Louis, MO 63126
314-961-3473
www.1-800Boardup.com

TRC
712 S. Wheeling Ave
Tulsa, OK 74104
918-585-1990
www.trcdisastersolutions.com

Water Out of Fort Wayne
1951 Lakeview Dr.
Fort Wayne, IN 46808
260-489-2070
260-410-2940
www.wateroutfortwayne.com

SERVICES

Full-service restoration, general contractors
(Canadian entries followed by U.S. entries)

Full-service restoration, general contractors-Alberta

First General Services Ltd.
3320 - 17th Ave. SW
Calgary, AB T3E 0B4
Canada
403-229-1479
www.FIRSTGENERAL.net

UNICCO Facility Services Canada Co.
1029006 132 ave
Edmonton, AB T5E 1Y6
Canada
403-660-6873
780-448-9373
www.UNICCO.com

Full-service restoration, general contractors-British Columbia

Clean-Scene Restorations
4640 Minto Rd.
Castlegar, BC V1N 4B3
Canada
800-414-8890
www.cleans.ca

Edenvale Restoration Specialists
5707 Sidley Street
Suite 4
Burnaby, BC V5J 5E6
Canada
604-436-1440
604-590-1440
www.EDENVALE.com

UNICCO Facility Services Canada Co.
318 1199 West Pender St
Vancouver, BC V6E 2R1
Canada
604-682-4442
www.UNICCO.com

Full-service restoration, general contractors-Ontario

Disaster Kleenup Canada
360 Ambassador Drive
Mississauga, ON L53 2J3
Canada
905-564-0188
800-354-8632
www.dkc.ca

First General Services Canada
Div. of First General Enterprises (Ontario) Ltd.
437 Flint Road
Toronto, ON M3J 2T7
Canada
416-736-0395
877-888-9111
www.firstgeneral.ca

Servicemaster of Canada
5462 Timberlea Bvld
Mississauga, ON L4W 2T7
Canada
905-670-0000
800-263-5928
www.SERVICEMASTER.ca

UNICCO Facility Services Canada Co.
411 Richmond St East
Toronto, ON M5A 3S5
Canada
416-369-0040
www.UNICCO.com

SERVICES

UNICCO Facility Services Canada Co.
855 Industrial Ave
Unit 6
Ottawa, ON K1G 4L4
Canada
613-736-5900
www.UNICCO.com

Service Master of Midland/Orilla
425 Cranston Crescent
Midland, Ont L4R4P4
Canada
705-527-5722

Full-service restoration, general contractors-Quebec

UNICCO Facility Services Canada Co.
4180 Thimens Blvd.
St-Laurent, QC H4R 2B9
Canada
514-332-2085
www.UNICCO.com

Full-service restoration, general contractors-Alabama

ServiceMaster Professional Cleaning
608 Old 231
Cropwell, AL 35054
205-525-4663

Therml Abatement, Inc.
15219 CR 70
P. O. Box 207
Andalusia, AL 36420
877-718-5837
334-428-3041

Full-service restoration, general contractors-California

Accurate Construction
1671 Anaheim Street
Harbor City, CA 90710
800-696-1977
310-534-1921
www.ACCURATECONSTRUCTION.com

Bay Metro Corporation
2325 Third St.
#320
San Francisco, CA 94107
415-626-4067
www.Baymetrocorp.com

Britannia Inc.
255 South Maple Avenue
South San Francisco, CA 94080-6305
650-742-6490
www.BRITDKI.com

California Restoraton Contractors
5960 Valentine Road
Suite 4
Ventura, CA 93003-6671
805-650-1209

Corner Construction Co Inc
1035 S La Brea Avenue
Los Angeles, CA 90019
323-965-1999
800-777-9412
www.CORNERCONSTRUCTION.com

Disaster Response
20172 Charlanne Drive
Redding, CA 96002
800-368-3693
www.FIREWINDWATER.com

DKI/Better Floors & Restorations
201 W Santa Fe Avenue
Placentia, CA 92870
800-655-2005
www.DKBF.com

Em & M's Restoration
2509 South Broadway
Santa Ana, CA 92707
714-434-6577
www.EMANDMCORP.com

Emercon
2906 E. Coronado Street
Anaheim, CA 92806
714-630-9615
800-734-9167
www.emercon.com

Immediate Response Service Company
15235 Brand Blvd.
Suite A-108
Mission Hills, CA 91346
800-483-9009
818-898-4055
www.fwdxports.com

Paul Davis Restoration - East Bay
2126 Edison Avenue
San Leandro, CA 94578
510-635-6800
www.pdeastbay.com

Paul Davis Restoration - Peninsula
297 N. Amphlett Blvd
San Matco, CA 94401
650-685-5320
650-642-0480
www.pdrestoration.com

Paul Davis Restoration of Contra Costa & Solano
5013 - C Forni Drive
Concord, CA 94520
925-939-1300
www.pdrestoration.com

SERVICES

Paul Davis Restoration of San Diego Inc.
9225 Chesapeake Drive
Suite F
San Diego, CA 92123
858-560-0444
www.pdrestoration.com?sdno

Paul Davis Restoration of Southern California
14670 Firestone Blvd.
Suite 406
La Mirada, CA 90638
800-325-4636
714-228-0895
www.pdrestoration.com

QwikResponse Disaster Control & Construction
16315 Piuma Avenue
Cerritos, CA 90703
562-809-1532
888-809-1532
www.QWIKRESPONSE.com

Skill Clean
198 Harbor Court
Pittsburg, CA 94565
925-432-4393

Smith & Sons Disaster Kleenup, Inc.
P.O. Box 1447
Arroyo Grand, CA 93421
805-481-2955
800-540-2955
www.SMITHNSONS.com

Thunderbird Catastrophe Services Inc
Alta Loma, CA 91701
800-897-6532

V & M
1575 Alvarado Street
San Leandro, CA 94577
510-352-3900
www.vmrestoration.com

Full-service restoration, general contractors-Colorado

Paul Davis Restoration / Denver West
1602 S. Parker Rd
Suite 214
Denver, CO 80231
303 296-8080
720 280-3900
www.pdrestoration.com

Paul Davis Restoration/Northern Colorado
323 Lincoln Ct.
Fort Collins, CO 80524
970-221-1281

ServiceMaster by Arrigo Restoration
80 Fabrication Drive
Pueblo, CO 81007
719-542-2000
www.arrigo-restoration.com

Full-service restoration, general contractors-Florida

Accutech Restoration & Remodeling
1600 Barber Road
Sarasota, FL 34240
941-378-0700
941-747-5325
www.ACCUTECHRESTORATION.com

First General Services of SW Florida
17431 Alico Center Rd.
Suite 1
Fort Myers, FL 33912
239-454-4402

Paul Davis Restoration
1 Independent Drive
Suite 2300
Jacksonville, FL 32202-5020
888-907-5907
904-737-2779
www.pdrestoration.com

Paul Davis Restoration
8812 Venture Cove
Tampa, FL 33637
813-984-2700
www.pdrtampa.com

Paul Davis Restoration Inc. of Volusia County
2330 South Nova Road
Suite 1
South Daytona, FL 32119
386-760-8959
www.pdrestoration.com

Paul Davis Restoration of Palm Beach County
1025 N. Florida Mango Rd #9
West Palm Beach, FL 33409
561-478-7272
www.restorepalmbeach.us

Paul Davis Restoration of Pensacola-Ft. Walton
101 E. Brainerd Street
Suite A
Pensacola, FL 32501
850-437-0400
www.pdrestoration.com

Paul Davis Restoration of Tallahasse
4948 Six Oaks Drive
Tallahasse, FL 32303
850-576-7901
850-576-9317
www.pdrestoration.com

Paul Davis Restoration of the Space Coast
3815 N. Highway #1
Suite 118
Cocoa, FL 32926
321-690-0000

Paul Davis Restoration of the Treasure Coast
1950 S.W. Biltmore Street
Port St. Lucie, FL 34984
772-340-2080
www.pdrestoration.com

Paul Davis Restoration, Tampa East
8812 Venture Cove
Tampa, FL 33637
813-984-2700
www.pdrestoration.com

Van Sangas General Contractor Inc
1572 SE South Niemeyer Circle
Port St. Lucie, FL 34952
772-335-1526

Full-service restoration, general contractors-Georgia

Alacrity Services LLC
2100 RiverEdge Parkway
Suite 420
Atlanta, GA 30328
770-953-3220
866-953-3220
www.alacrityservices.com

Alvin L Davis Inc
310 E Montgomery Xrd Unit 15
Savannah, GA 31406
912-352-2666

BlueStar Construction Co
4132 Atlanta Hwy
Suite 110-315
Loganville, GA 30052
770-736-9202
850-218-1200

Bowles Construction Inc.
1012 Tindon Street
Augusta, GA 30909
800-738-9446
www.BOWLESCONSTRUCTION.com

Paul Davis Restoration
1979 A Parker Court
Stone Mountain
Stone Mountain, GA 30047
770-985-1727
www.pdrestoration?gcga

Full-service restoration, general contractors-Idaho

Disaster Kleenup Serving Treasure Valley
701 N. Kings Road
Nampa, ID 83687
208-887-0004
800-574-0345
www.IDDK.com

King Services and Construction
2337 3rd Ave North
Lewiston, ID 83501
208-746-4192
www.kingservices.com

Paul Davis Restoration
1510 Robert St., Suite 101
P.O. Box 5346
Boise, ID 83705
208-429-9992
www.pdrestoration.com

Steam/Ree-Construction
Hailey, ID 83333
800-222-4068

Full-service restoration, general contractors-Illinois

Paul Davis Restoration
P.O. Box 1001
2758 - B Yale Blvd.
Springfield, IL 62705-1001
217-544-4667
800-334-8414
www.pdrestoration.com

ServiceMaster Cleaning Services
7245 N. St. Louis
Skokie, IL 60076
847-329-0044
800-843-8415
www.weservcechicago.com

Full-service restoration, general contractors-Indiana

First Response
1919 South Michigan Street
South Bend, IN 46613
574-288-0500
www.firstresponseDRS.com

Paul Davis Restoration of Michiana
2301 N. Bendix Drive
South Bend, IN 46628
574-234-4400
www.pdrestoration.com

United Services DKI
500 E Ridge Road
Griffith, IN 46319-1100
219-972-6300

Full-service restoration, general contractors-Kansas

NCRI
8447 E 35th St. N
Wichita, KS 67226-1344
316-636-5700
800-598-6274
www.NCRICAT.com

Full-service restoration, general contractors-Kentucky

Paul Davis Restoration
914 Searcy Way
P.O. Box 20045
Bowling Green, KY 42103
270-782-0123
www.pdrestoration.com

Purofirst Disaster Services
2251 Stanley Gault Pkwy
Louisville, KY 40223
502-244-1510

ServiceMaster of Bowling Green
1052 - H Searcy Way
Bowling Green, KY 42103-7170
270-782-8500
www.4servicemaster.com/ky/5191

Full-service restoration, general contractors-Louisiana

First General Services of Baton Rouge
6836 Renoir Avenue
Baton Rouge, LA 70806
225-928-7205

ServiceMaster of Lafayette
205 Knobcrest
Lafayette, LA 70507
337-234-1289
www.SMOFLAFAYETTE.com

Full-service restoration, general contractors-Maryland

Paul Davis Restoration of Baltimore
2 West Rolling Crossroads
Suite 210
Baltimore, MD 21228
410-719-8830
800-929-3929
www.pdrestoration.com

RJ Cleaning and Restoration
507 Saltoun Ave
Odenton, MD 21113
410-672-3104
443-336-9493
www.rjcleanrestore.com

Full-service restoration, general contractors-Massachusetts

Able Restoration Inc.
55 Woodrock Road
Weymouth, MA 02189
781-335-0000
617-592-2571
www.able911.com

Paul Davis Restoration
27 Water Street
Wakefield, MA 01880
781-224-3475
781-245-0003
www.pdrestoration.com

Paul Davis Restoration of Cape Cod & The Islands
108 Susan Lane
Brewster, MA 02631
508-896-1799
508-790-0029
www.pdrestoration.com

Paul Davis Restoration of W. Middlesex County
457 Great Road
Acton, MA 01720
978-264-3141
http://www.PDRESTORATION.com

Paul Davis Restoration of Western Mass
141 Main St.
Springfield, MA 01151
413-543-5001
pauldavisofwesternmass.com

UNICCO Service Company
275 Grove Street
Auburndale, MA 2466
617-527-5222
www.UNICCO.com

Full-service restoration, general contractors-Michigan

Hammer Restoration Inc.
3205 Fashin Square Blvd.
Saginaw, MI 48603
989-793-5700
800-601-9925
www.HammerRestoration.com

Paul Davis Restoration
105 Enterprise Dr.
Ann Arbor, MI 48103
734-930-0303
800-550-4042
www.pdrestoration.com

Paul Davis Restoration - Washtenaw County
105 Enterprise Drive
Ann Arbor, MI 48103
734-930-0303
www.pdrestoration.com

Regency Construction Corporation
DKI of Clinton Township
35240 Forton Court
Clinton Township, MI 48035
586-741-8000
888-41Regency
www.regencyconstruction.com

Full-service restoration, general contractors-Minnesota

LeMaster Restoration, Inc.
430 Gateway Blvd
Burnsville, MN 55337
952-707-1256
888-811-0562
www.lemasterconstruction.com

Paul Davis Restoration & Remodeling
23577 Highway 10
Detroit Lakes, MN 56501
218-847-1800
www.pdrfargo.com

Full-service restoration, general contractors-Missouri

The Fire Works Restoration Co./1-800BOARDUP
9420 Watson Industrial Park
St. Louis, MO 63126
314-961-3473
www.1-800Boardup.com

Full-service restoration, general contractors-Montana

Americlean Corporation
1119 Maggie Lane
Billings, MT 59101
406-256-9113
406-256-9111
www.Americleanonline.com

Full-service restoration, general contractors-New Hampshire

Paul Davis Restoration of Central New Hampshire
720 East Industrial Drive
Manchester, NH 03109
603-622-9800
603-361-5456
www.pdrnh.com

Full-service restoration, general contractors-New Jersey

Paul Davis Restoration
586 Route 70
Suite 1-A
Brick, NJ 08723
732-451-1280
www.pdrestoration.com

Paul Davis Restoration of Mercer & Middlesex, Inc.
865 Lower Ferry Road
Suite B-18
Ewing, NJ 08628
609-538-8424
www.pdrestoration.com

Paul Davis Restoration of Northeast New Jersey
110B Route 46 E
Saddlebrook, NJ 07663
973-546-0203
877-WE-DRY-NJ
www.pdrestoration.com

PCI
202 Lexington Avenue
Hackensack, NJ 7601
201-646-9000
www.PCICLEANS.com

Sage Landscaping and Tree Service
P.O. Box 7237
Watchung, NJ 07069
908-668-5858
sagelandscaping@verizon.net

Full-service restoration, general contractors-New Mexico

Paul Davis Restoration of New Mexico
7820 4th, N.W.
Albuquerque, NM 87107
505-884-5583
505-321-7995
www.pdrestoration.com

ServiceMaster of Santa Fe
1291 Clark Road
Suite B
Santa Fe, NM 87507
505-473-7789
505-424-1703
www.4servicemaster.com/NM/1397

Full-service restoration, general contractors-New York

Advanced Restoration Corporation
151 Lafayette Road
West Babylon, NY 11704-4903
631-422-2100
www.ADVANCEDRESTORATION.com

CRYSTAL RESTORATION
450 Westbury Avenue
Carle Place, NY 11514
516-333-7070
800-878-2797
WWW.RESTORATION-SPECIALISTS.COM

Maxons Restorations Inc
280 Madison Avenue
New York, NY 10016-0801
800-362-9667
212-447-6767
www.MAXONS.com

Paragon Restoration Group Inc
5230 Transit Road
Depew, NY 14043
716-685-2775
www.PARAGON-RESTORATION.com

United Restoration Services Inc
1075 Central Avenue
Scarsdale, NY 10583
914-472-5565
www.unitedrestoration.com

Full-service restoration, general contractors-Nevada

GraEagle Consstruction, LLC.
3111 S. Valley View Blvd. # B-108
Las Vegas, NV 89102
702-248-0170
702-353-5327
www.graeagleconstruction.com

GraEagle Construction, LLC.
1380 Greg Street
Suite 237
Sparks, NV 89431
775-851-2722
www.graeagleconstruction.com

Mitigation and Repair Solutions
2901 South Highland Drive Suite 13C
Las Vegas, NV 89109
702-257-3955
www.marsrestoration.com

Full-service restoration, general contractors-North Carolina

A & I Fire & Water Restoration
300 Harley Drive
Wilmington, NC 28405
910-799-5135
www.ai/restoration.com

After Disaster
1130 West Vandalia Road
Greensboro, NC 27404
800-948-0242
www.AFTERDISASTER.com

Allied Restoration Specialists
1317 Pecan Avenue
Charlotte, NC 28205
704-377-1661
704-576-2476

Paul Davis Restoration - Triad
1301 South Park Drive
Kernersville, NC 27284
800-951-7881
336-993-4581
www.pauldavistriad.com

Full-service restoration, general contractors-North Dakota

Paul Davis Restoration and Remodeling
P.O. Box 69
355 7th Street NW
West Fargo, ND 58078
701-271-4770
www.pdrfargo.com

Full-service restoration, general contractors-Ohio

3D Disaster Kleenup of Columbus
4110 Perimeter Dr.
Columbus, OH 43228
614-351-9695
866-449-8740
www.3DDKI.com

CIS Steeplejack
749 Tory Lane
Nationwide Church Steeple Restoration
Medina, OH 44256
216-395-5663
330-461-2655
http://www.steepleusa.com

Cousino Construction Company, Inc.
26901 Eckel Rd.
Perrysburg, OH 43551
800-874-2122
419-874-9500
www.cousinoconstruction.com

First General Services of Cleveland & Akron
29767 Lafayette Way
Westlake, OH 44145
800-943-7054
440-899-9474
www.firstgeneralservices.com

J. Bowers Disaster Restoration Specialists
3113 Mogadore Road
Akron, OH 44312
800-289-9050
330-628-4807
www.j-bowersconst.com

Paul Davis Restoration of Akron
2735 Second Street
Cuyahoga Falls, OH 44221
330-920-1936
330-920-4201
www.pdrestoration.com

Paul Davis Restoration of Western Lake Erie
1035 S. McCord Rd.
P.O. Box 848
Holland, OH 43528
419-866-9844
www.pdrestoration.com

Full-service restoration, general contractors-Oklahoma

Dutil's Home Repair / Water Out of Oklahoma
7203 Cache Road
Lawton, OK 73505
580-536-3649
580-536-3683
www.DUTIL.net

Full-service restoration, general contractors-Oregon

Steamway/Disaster Restorations
500 Pacific AV SW
Albany, OR 97321
541-928-7267
www.disasterrestorations.com

Full-service restoration, general contractors-Pennsylvania

Advanced Restoration Technologies Inc
150 E Baltimore Avenue
Clifton Heights, PA 19018
610-626-9002
800-224-3473

Dynamic Restoration
901 S. Bolmar St.
Suite A
West Chester, PA 19382
888-760-2842
http://www.dynamic24-7.com

First General Services of Central PA, Ltd.
227 Springdale Avenue
York, PA 17403-3927
717-845-7391

Insurance Restoration Services
9189 Marshall Rd
Cranberry TWP, PA 16066
412-322-1135
www.DISASTERCONTRACTOR.com

Mellon Certified Restoration
419 Church Lane
Yeadon, PA 19050
610-622-5860
www.MELLONCR.com

Paul Davis Restoration
115 E. Glenside Avenue
Suite 12
Glenside, PA 19038
215-887-5991
www.pdrestoration.com

Paul Davis Restoration & Remodeling
599 Airport Road
Lititz, PA 17543
717-291-6000
866-765-0773
www.pdr-pa.com

Tuckey Restoration Inc.
12 Stover Drive
Carlisle, PA 17013
717-249-7052
www.TUCKEY.com

Full-service restoration, general contractors-Rhode Island

Insurance Reconstruction Services, Inc.
41 Cedar Swamp Road
Smithfield, RI 02917
401-231-3130
888-231-3130
http://www.insurancerecon.com

Full-service restoration, general contractors-South Carolina

A & I Fire & Water Restoration
1004 Ace Avenue North Ext.
Myrtle Beach, SC 29577
843-448-8485
888-881-FIRE
www.ai-restoration.com

Atlantic Builders
P.O. Box 21587
Charleston, SC 29413
843-554-2065
www.abischn.com

First Restoration Services
7269 Cross Park Drive
Suite A
Charleston, SC 29418
866-844-9FRS
843-552-9377
www.FIRSTRESTORATION.com

Full-service restoration, general contractors-Tennessee

Cypress Bend Construction, LLC
P.O. Box 3291
Cookeville, TN 38502
9313720092

Paul Davis Restoration of the MidSouth
2093 Thomas Road
Suite 6
Memphis, TN 38134
901-373-5394
888-373-5390
www.pdrestoration.com

SERVICES

Full-service restoration, general contractors-Texas

ARS Advanced Restoration Solutions
12811 Duncan Road
Suite J
Houston, TX 77066
281-397-0184
www.ARSRESTORATION.com

Eastco Enterprises Inc.
26605 Bulverde Road
San Antonio, TX 78260
830-980-4771
www.EASTCOENT.com

Interstate Restoration Group, Inc.
8910 Oak Grove Road
Fort Worth, TX 76140
800-622-6433
817-293-0035
www.interstaterestoration.com

Interstate Restoration Group, Inc.
8910 Oak Grove Road
Fort Worth, TX 76140
800-622-6433
817-293-0035
www.interstaterestoration.com

Paul Davis Restoration
7320 Ashcroft Dr.
Suite 201
Houston, TX 77081
713-270-6030
713-545-6082
www.pdrestoration.com

Paul Davis Restoration & Remodeling of Tarrant County
1663 Hickory Drive
Suite B
Fort Worth, TX 76117
817-759-2600
877-PAUL-DAVIS
www.pdrestoration.com

Full-service restoration, general contractors-Utah

Intermountain Construction & Recovery Alliance
13081 South Minuteman Drive,
Draper, Utah 84020
866-483-5911
www.intermountain-recovery.com

Full-service restoration, general contractors-Virginia

First Atlantic Restoration
414 S Parliament Drive
Virginia Bch, VA 23462
757-499-1915
www.FIRSTATLANTICFIRE.com

Paul Davis Restoration & Remodeling of Suburban VA
6886 Wellington Rd
Manassas, VA 20109
703-335-2424
www.PDR-USA.net

Paul Davis Restoration of Greater Tri-Cities
37 Four Winds Road
Bristol, VA 24202
276-669-7208
www.pdrestoration.com

Full-service restoration, general contractors-Washington

Service Master of Greater Tacoma / Bremerton
1016 South 30th Street
Tacoma, WA 98409
800-339-5720
253-383-1776
www.4SERVICEMASTER.com/WA/2271

Full-service restoration, general contractors-Wisconsin

Paul Davis Restoration
1555 S. Commercial St.
Neenah, WI 54956
920-729-1551
www.pdrestoration.com

Furniture restoration

Classic Furniture Services
90 Hayward Street
Franklin, MA 02038
800-834-6016
508-528-6747
www.CLASSIC-FURNITURE.com

Fine Wood Solutions
702 Pointview Avenue
Ephrata, PA 17552
877-837-2105
717-625-3030
www.FINEWODSOLUTIONS.com

First Response
1919 South Michigan Street
South Bend, IN 46613
574-288-0500
www.firstresponseDRS.com

Trefler & Sons Antique/Fine Art Restoration
29 Tower rd
Newton, MA 02464
617-965-3388
617-590-8676
www.trefler.com

Infrared thermography moisture assessment

First Response
1919 South Michigan Street
South Bend, IN 46613
574-288-0500
www.firstresponseDRS.com

Flir Systems, Inc.
16 Esquire Rd
North Billerica, MA 01862
800-464-6372
www.flirthermography.com

Master Contract Services Ltd.
8883 164A Street
Surrey, BC V4N 1A2
Canada
1-604-583-7103
1-877-211-7171
www.mastercontract.net

Paul Davis Restoration of Akron
2735 Second Street
Cuyahoga Falls, OH 44221
330-920-1936
330-920-4201
www.pdrestoration.com

Pro Care Services, Inc.
7166 Ed Everett Way
P.O. Box 2839
Carefree, AZ 85377
480-488-7800

Jewelry replacement

Beverly Bremer Silver Shop
3164 Peachtree Road NE
Atlanta, GA 30305
404-261-4009
800-270-4009
www.BEVERLYBREMER.com

Claimlink
10 Broad Street
Red Bank, NJ 07701
800-537-4700
www.CLAIMLINK.com

Claimlink Jewelry Solutions
Ten Broad Street
Red Bank, NJ 07701
800-537-4700
www.claimlink.com

Lightning damage repair

Nu-Air The Healthy Choice
5626 Rt. 38
Pennsawken, NJ 08109
856-317-0500
800-203-8319

Mold remediation

Abatement Technologies, Inc.
2220 Northmont Parkway
Suite 100
Duluth, GA 30096
800-634-9091
770-689-2600
www.mold-removal.com

Advanced Enviromental Consultants
2908 Oregon Court
Torrance, CA 90503
310-347-3347
www.moldwhatnow.com

Advanced Restoration Specialists Inc.
2548 Strozier Avenue
South El Monte, CA 91733-2020
626-442-7700
800-310-4911
www.ADVRESTORE.com

Alliance Environmental Group
990 W. Tenth Street
Azusa, CA 91702
626-633-3500
888-314-3300
www.alliance-enviro.com

Alpine Air Corp.
543 Ave. 60
Los Angeles, CA 90042
310-862-4019
888-623-8690
http://www.alpineaircorp.com

Basement Systems
60 Silvermine Road
Seymour, CT 06483
800-541-0487
www.basementsystems.com

BELFOR
3826 Woodland Park Ave North
Seattle, WA 98103
800-775-0806
www.belfor.com

Electronic Decontamination Specialists
13081 S Minuteman Drive
Draper, UT 84020
801-553-1087
877-553-1030
www.UTDK.com

First Response
1919 South Michigan Street
South Bend, IN 46613
574-288-0500
www.firstresponseDRS.com

Moldlab
3792 Arapaho Rd
Addison, TX 75001
972-247-9373
www.moldlab.com

SERVICES

Munters Corporation
79 Monroe Street
P.O. Box Box 640
Amesbury, MA 01913
800-MUNTERS
www.MUNTERSAMERICA.com

Paul Davis Restoration of Akron
2735 Second Street
Cuyahoga Falls, OH 44221
330-920-1936
330-920-4201
www.pdrestoration.com

Paul Davis Restoration of Central Orange County
8 Hammond Drive
Suite 114
Irvine, CA 92618
949-859-9515
800-300-9237
www.PDRESTORATION.com

Paul Davis Restoration of Northeast New
Jersey
110B Route 46 E
Saddlebrook, NJ 07663
973-546-0203
877-WE-DRY-NJ
www.pdrestoration.com

Paul Davis Restoration of Palm Beach County
1025 N. Florida Mango Rd #9
West Palm Beach, FL 33409
561-478-7272
www.restorepalmbeach.us

Paul Davis Restoration of Tucson
2555 North Coyote Drive
Suite 113
Tucson, AZ 85745
520-624-4560
www.pdrestoration.com

Regency Construction Corporation
DKI of Clinton Township
35240 Forton Court
Clinton Township, MI 48035
586-741-8000
888-41Regency
www.regencyconstruction.com

TriCounties CRDN
14 West Gutierrez St.
Santa Barbra, CA 93101
805-962-CRDN
805-962-2736
www.tricountiescrdn.com

Overspray removal services

Continental Overspray Rempoval
4475 Mission Boulevard
#224
San Diego, CA 92109
800-459-5772
www.OVERSPRAYREMOVAL.com

Detail Masters Inc
855 Proton Road
San Antonio, TX 78258
210-490-1155
800-634-9275
www.DETAILMASTERS.com

Nationwide Overspray Network
12901 Nicholson Road
Suite 100
Farmers Branch, TX 75234
800-345-1269

Overspray Removal Specialists
8854 S Tamiami Trail
Sarasota, FL 34238
941-966-8600
800-835-5858
www.OVERSPRAY.com

Overspray Removal Specialists
3400 Tamiami Trl N
Suite 204
Naples, FL 34103-3717
239-435-0511

Referral service, disaster cleanup

BELFOR
185 Oakland Avenue
Suite 300
Birmingham, MI 48009
800-856-3333
www.belfor.com

COCAT.INC
5150 Havana St. Suite F
Denver, CO 80237
303-333-0392
www.cocat.com

First Response
1919 South Michigan Street
South Bend, IN 46613
574-288-0500
www.firstresponseDRS.com

STERIS Corporation
5960 Heisley Road
Mentor, OH 44060
440-354-2600
800-548-4873
www.steris.com

Remediation services

3E Company
1905 Aston Ave
Carlsbad, CA 92008
800-360-3220
760-602-8700
www.3ecompany.com

Advanced Engineering Solutions Inc
5820 N Canton Center Road
Suite 150
Canton, MI 48187-2600
734-459-9948
www.AES-INC.com

Alpha Omega Environmental Services Inc.
933 N.W. 31 Avenue
Pompano Beach, FL 33069
954-427-8586
954-410-6281
www.AOMEGAGROUP.com

BELFOR
185 Oakland Avenue
Suite 300
Birmingham, MI 48009
800-856-3333
www.belfor.com

Clayton Group Services Inc.
P.O. Box 8008
Novi, MI 48376-8008
888-357-7020
248-344-8550
www.CLAYTONGRP.com

COCAT Inc.
5150 Havana St.
Suite F
Denver, CO 80239
303-333-0392
1-888-88COCAT
www.cocat.com

D'Ambra Construction Co. Inc
800 Jefferson Boulevard
Warwick, RI 02886
401-737-1300
800-966-7645
www.d-ambra.com

Fleet Environmental Services, LLC
75-D York Avenue
Randolph, MA 02368
888-233-5338
781-815-1100
www.fleetenviromental.com

Groundwater & Environmental Services Inc
1340 Campus Parkway
Neptune, NJ 07753
732-919-0100
www.GESONLINE.com

Laidlaw Inc.
55 Shuman Boulevard Suite 400
Naperville, IL 60563
630-848-3000
800-524-3529
www.laidlawschoolbus.com

Munters Corporation
79 Monroe Street
P.O. Box Box 640
Amesbury, MA 01913
800-MUNTERS
www.MUNTERSAMERICA.com

Simmons Enivronmental Svcs Inc
213 Elm Street
Salisbury, MA 01952
978-463-6669
www.simmons21e.com

STERIS Corporation
5960 Heisley Road
Mentor, OH 44060
440-354-2600
800-548-4873
www.steris.com

Smoke & odor counteracting services

Air Flow Systems
11221 Pagemill Road
Dallas, TX 75243
214-503-8008
800-818-6185
www.AIRFLOWSYSTEMS.com

Aire Master of America Inc.
P.O. Box 2310
Nixa, MO 65714
417-725-2691
800-525-0957
www.AIREMASTER.com

Alan Plummer Associates Inc
7524 Mosier View Court
suite 200
Fort Worth, TX 76118
817-284-2724
www.apaienv.com

All Care Chem-Dry
13727 S.W. 152 Street
#273
Miami, FL 33177
305-969-3733
305-213-8505

Americlean Services Corp.
9201 Enterprise Court
Manassas Park, VA 20111
703-551-2903
301-953-2420
www.americleaniaq.com

SERVICES

BELFOR
185 Oakland Avenue
Suite 300
Birmingham, MI 48009
800-856-3333
www.belfor.com

BELFOR
3826 Woodland Park Ave North
Seattle, WA 98103
800-775-0806
www.belfor.com

Carter Burgess Inc
10816 Executive Center Drive
Little Rock, AR 72211
501-223-0515
www.C-B.com

Clean Aire Inc.
1006 Rabbit Run
Hopkins, SC 29061
803-776-1117

Colorado Catastrophe Inc.
5150 Havana St
Suite F
Denver, CO 80209
303-333-0392
1-888-88COCAT
www.cocat.com

First Response
1919 South Michigan Street
South Bend, IN 46613
574-288-0500
www.firstresponseDRS.com

Global Technologies Inc.
P.O. Box 51005
New Bedford, MA 02745
508-991-3939
800-339-8600
www.globalodorcontrol.com

Johnny's Drycleaning
3414 W Unionhills Dr. #8
Phoenix, AZ 85027
623-582-9261

LS Chemical Services
281 Heather Crest Drive
Chesterfield, MO 63017
314-576-1877
www.LSCHEMICALSERVICES.com

Mateson Chemical Corp
1025 E Montgomery Avenue
Philadelphia, PA 19125
215-423-3200
800-434-0010
www.matesonchemical.com

Munters Corporation
79 Monroe Street
P.O. Box Box 640
Amesbury, MA 01913
800-MUNTERS
www.MUNTERSAMERICA.com

Odor Science & Engineering Inc
1350 Blue Hills Avenue
Bloomfield, CT 06002
860-243-9380
www.ODORSCIENCE.com

Paul Davis Restoration
27 Water Street
Wakefield, MA 01880
781-224-3475
781-245-0003
www.pdrestoration.com

Paul Davis Restoration
1325 Whitlock Lane
Suite 108
Carrollton, TX 75006
972-323-6565
866-PAUL-DAVIS
www.pdrestoration.com

Paul Davis Restoration & Remodeling of Tarrant County
1663 Hickory Drive
Suite B
Fort Worth, TX 76117
817-759-2600
877-PAUL-DAVIS
www.pdrestoration.com

Paul Davis Restoration of Akron
2735 Second Street
Cuyahoga Falls, OH 44221
330-920-1936
330-920-4201
www.pdrestoration.com

Paul Davis Restoration of Johnson Co. Inc.
15050 West 116th
Olathe, KS 66062
913-345-2700
www.pdrestoration.com

Paul Davis Restoration of Northeast New Jersey
110B Route 46 E
Saddlebrook, NJ 07663
973-546-0203
877-WE-DRY-NJ
www.pdrestoration.com

Paul Davis Restoration of Tucson
2555 North Coyote Drive
Suite 113
Tucson, AZ 85745
520-624-4560
www.pdrestoration.com

Restoration Specialists
450 Westbury Ave
Carle Place, NY 11514
800-432-6243

RESTORX-BORDER STATES
203 S Central Avenue
Sidney, MT 59270
800-578-2113

Service Master
3829 Forest Hill Irene Rd.
Memphis, TN 38125
901-597-7500
800-633-5703
www.SERVICEMASTER.com

ServiceMaster Albino Services
579 South Leonard Street
Waterbury, CT 06708
203-753-0666

ServiceMaster Clean At Irvine
33 Hammond Street
Suite 208
Irvine, CA 92618
949-586-5919
949-279-2339

ServiceMaster Cleaning & Restoration
1105 Yuba Street
Marysville, CA 95901
530-741-8178
800-RESPOND
www.servicemasterclean.com

ServiceMaster of Germantown
715 Chaney Cove
Suite 102
Collierville, TN 38017
901-854-6225
901-853-3748

ServiceMaster Professional Cleaning
7350 N.W. 7th Street
Suite 106
Miami, FL 33126-2976
305-264-8999
786-486-2526

ServiceMaster Professional Cleaning Services
P.O. Box 7771
Nashua, NH 03060
603-883-4800
www.SERVICEMASTER.com

ServiceMaster Professional Restoration
3869 Norwood Drive #3
Littleton, CO 80125
720-981-8809

St. Croix Sensory Inc.
3549 Lake Elmo Ave N
Lake Elmo, MN 55042
800-879-9231
www.FIVESENSES.com

Steamco
27 Lakeview Ave
Wakefield, MA 01880
781-391-4133
www.steamcocarpets.com

Tech Environmental
1601 Trapelo Road
Waltham, MA 02451
781-718-9305
www.TECHENV.com

The Fire Works Restoration Co./1-800BOARDUP
9420 Watson Industrial Park
St. Louis, MO 63126
314-961-3473
www.1-800Boardup.com

Webster Environmental Associates Inc
13121 Eastpoint Park Blvd
Suite E
Louisville, KY 40223
502-253-3443
www.ODOR.net

Zorix Consultants Inc.
3425 Semenyk Court Suite 200
Mississauga, ON L5C 4P9
Canada
905-277-1110
www.ZORIX.ca

Textile & garment restoration

Alliance of Professional Restoration Drycleaners
4544 Harding Road
Suite 208
Nashville, TN 37205
615-230-5966
866-313-2773
www.aprd.com

Video tape restoration

Film Technology Company Inc.
726 Cole Avenue
Los Angeles, CA 90038
323-464-3456
www.filmtech.com

NBD International Inc
241 Myrtle Street
Ravenna, OH 44266
330-296-0221
www.NBDINT.com

Specs Bros LLC
1 Mt. Vernon Street
P.O. Box 5
Ridgefield Park, NJ 7660
201-440-6589
www.specbros.com

VidiPax
450 W 31st Street
4th Floor
New York, NY 10001
212-563-1999
800-653-8434
www.vidipax.com

SERVICES

SERVICES

SERVICES, Computer Maintenance/Repair

Hard disk repair

Daisy Disc Corp
19 Graf Road
Newburyport, MA 01950
978-462-3475
www.DAISYDISC.com

Spectrum Computer Inc
12611 Hoover
Stanton, CA 90680
714-799-7345
www.SPECTRUMCOM.com

TIF Data Recovery Service Specialist
9182 Independence
Chatsworth, CA 91311
805-526-1555
www.I-T-S.com

Vics Computer Service
8125 Westglen Drive
Houston, TX 77063
713-789-1888
800-999-1827

Laser printer repair

DEPOT AMERICA
1495 State Route 34
Farmingdale, NJ 07727-1602
732-919-0209
800-648-6833
www.DEPOT-AMERICA.com

Macintosh & Apple equipment repair

ExpressPoint
1109 Zane Ave N
Golden Valley, MN 55422
763-543-6000
www.expresspoint.com

Varitek
1301 S Lewis St
Anaheim, CA 92805
714-283-8980
www.VARITEKINC.com

Misc. peripherals repair

Linco Computer Sales and Service
15518 Silver Ridge Drive
Houston, TX 77090
281 893-8880
800 895-8889
www.lincocomputer.com

Minnesota Computers Inc
9909 S Shore Drive
Minneapolis, MN 55441
763-544-7900
800-544-5345
www.minnesotacomputers.com

Sprague Magnetics Inc
12806 Bradley Avenue
Sylmar, CA 91342
818-364-1800
www.sprague-magnetics.com

Personal computer repair, all types

21st Century Computer
8801 Davis Blvd
Keller, TX 76244
817-379-6603
877-HENSLIN
www.HENSLIN.com

Datatronics Inc
27326 Robinson Road
Conroe, TX 77385
281-367-0562
www.DATRONICSINC.com

Decision One
50 E Swedesford Road
Frazer, PA 19355
610-296-6000
www.decisionone.com

Hartford Computer Group
1610 Colonial Parkway
Inverness, IL 60067
224-836-3550
800-680-4424
www.HARTFORDCOMPUTERGROUP.com

Tailored Technologies Co
622 3rd Avenue
New York, NY 10017
212-503-6300
www.TAILTECH.com

Printer repair

Dataco DeRex Inc
9001 Lenexa Drive
Shawnee Msn, KS 66215
913-438-2444
800-825-1262
www.DATACO.com

Logical Maintenance Solutions Inc.
17551 Von Karman Ave
Irvine, CA 92614
714-549-1608
800-240-8721
www.LMSservice.com

Sun equipment repair

Akibia
4 Technology Drive
Westborough, MA 01581
508-621-5100
www.AKIBIA.com

Sun Valley Technical Repair Inc.
15555 Concord Circle
Morgan Hill, CA 95037
408-779-4115
800-250-5858
www.svtr.com

TriAxis Inc.
23 Midstate Drive
Suite 106
Auburn, MA 01501
508-721-9691
www.triaxisinc.com

SERVICES, Consulting

Appraisers

Antique & Personal Property Appraisals
2650 Jamacha Rd.
Suite 147, PMB 131
El Cajon, CA 92019
619-670-4455
www.personalpropertyappraisals.com

Globe Midwest Adjusters Intl.
25800 Northwestern Highway
Southfield, MI 48075-8403
800-445-1554
248-352-2100
www.globemw-ai.com

Howarth, Keys & Associates Inc.
137 Third Avenue North
Franklin, TN 37064
800-647-2236
615-550-5500
www.hkai.biz

Matrix Business Consulting Inc.
2000 Little Raven Street
Suite 6B
Denver, CO 80202
800-321-5200
303-298-1711
www.MATRIXBUSINESSCONSULTING.com

Professional Loss Adjusters
343 Washington Street
Newton, MA 02458
617-850-0477
www.pla-us.com

Smolian Sound Restoration Studios
1 Wormans Mill Court
Suite 4
Frederick, MD 21701-3022
301-694-5134

Architectural/engineering services

BCI Engineers & Scientists Inc
2000 East Edgewood Drive
Suite 215
Lakeland, FL 33803
877-550-4224
863-667-2345
www.bcieng.com

Black & Veatch
8400 Ward Parkway
Kansas City, MO 64114
913-458-2000
www.bv.com

Dressler Consulting Engineers Inc.
4425 Indian Creek Parkway
Overland Park, KS 66207-4013
913-341-5575
www.DRESSLER.net

Earthquake Engineering Consultants
11 Catskill Court
San Anselmo, CA 94960
415-457-7777

Exponent Failure Analysis Associates
149 Commonwealth Drive
Menlo Park, CA 94025
650-688-6719
www.EXPONENT.com

Freyer & Laureta, Inc.
144 North San Mateo Drive
San Mateo, CA 94401
650-344-9901
www.freyerlaureta.com

Fronte Infrastructure Associates, LLC
57 Holdrum Street
Hillsdale, NJ 07642
201-666-8715
201-326-0106

HDH Associates
400 W Main Street
Christiansbrg, VA 24073
540-381-7999
www.HDHASSOCIATES.com

ISES CORPORATION
2165 West Park Court
Suite N
Stone Mountain, GA 30087
770-879-7376
888-456-ISES
www.isescorp.com

James Cohen Consulting PC
P.O. Box 130
Pennington, NJ 08534
267-757-0710
www.expertpages.com/jccpc

SERVICES

Lockwood Greene Engineers Inc.
1500 International Drive
Spartanburg, SC 29303
864-578-2000
www.LG.com

PAULI ENGINEERING
944 N. VAN NESS AVE.
FRESNO, CA 93728
559-237-4408

Process Results, Inc.
201 South Ann Arbor St.
Saline, MI 48176
734-429-8900
www.processresults.com

Rimkus Consulting Group Inc.
8 E Greenway Plaza
Floor 5
Houston, TX 77046
713-621-3550

Short Elliott Hendrickson, Inc.
Butler Square Building, Suite 710-C
100 North Sixth St.
Minneapolis, MN 55403-1515
612-758-6700
866-830-3388
www.sehinc.com

URS Corp.
200 Orchard Ridge Dr.
Suite 101
Gaithersburg, MD 20878
301-258-9780
www.URSCORP.com

Z.S. Engineering P.C.
99 Tulip Avenue
Suite 102
Floral Park, NY 11001-1927
516-328-3200
www.ZSENGINEERING.com

Bioterrorism response planning

Bioterroism Preparedness and Response Planning
Centers for Disease Control and Prevention
1600 Clifton Rd.
Atlanta, GA 30333
800-CDC-INFO
877-554-4625
www.bt.cdc.gov

Knight-Star Enterprises, Inc.
HUB/Woman-Owned Business
P.O. Box 7873
Waco, TX 76714
866-776-1996
254-776-1996
www.knightstar.us

OptiMetrics, Inc.
3115 Professional Drive
Ann Arbor, MI 48104-5131
734-973-1177
www.optimetrics.org

Response Biomedical Corp.
8081 Lougheed Highway
Burnaby, BC V5J 5J1
Canada
604-681-4101
888-591-5577
www.responsebio.com

University of Pittsburgh Medical Center
Clinicians' Biosecurity Network
200 Lothrop St.
Pittsburgh, PA 15213-2582
443-573-3304
www.upmc-cbn.org/dmz/about_network.html

Business continuation services

Anacomp
15378 Avenue of Science
San Diego, CA 92128
858-716-3400
800-364-9870
www.ANACOMP.com

Barney F. Pelant & Associates
243 Harvard Lane
Bloomingdale, IL 60108-2141
630-894-6989
www.bfpelantassoc.com

Business Recovery Consultants Inc.
27 Westwood Boulevard
Hockessin, DE 19707-2059
800-795-5985
www.BRCRECOVERY.com

CAPS Business Recovery Services
2 Enterprise Drive
Suite 200
Shelton, CT 06484
800-542-2773
www.CAPSBRS.com

CGI-AMS
Enterprise Security Practice
4050 Legato Road
Fairfax, VA 22033
800-255-8888
703-267-8000
www.AMS.com/security

Comprehensive Solutions
250 N Sunny Slope Road
Suite 300
Brookfield, WI 53005
262-785-8101
www.COMP-SOLN.com

Continuity First
P.O. Box 28796
Richmond, VA 23228
804-559-6623
www.continuityfirst.com

Continuous Solutions Inc.
PMB 236
8100 M-4 Wyoming NE
Albuquerque, NM 87113
505-228-2438
www.CONTINUOUSSOLUTIONS.com

Deloitte
180 N Stetson Avenue
Chicago, IL 60601
312-946-3000
312-946-2005
www.DELOITTE.com

Disaster Masters
146-23 61st Road
Flushing, NY 11367-1203
718-939-5800
800-843-7526
www.THEPLAN.com/DISASTER.HTM

EBC Partners, Inc.
6753 Thomasville Rd.
Suite 108
Tallahassee, FL 32312
850-894-4043
www.ebcpartners.com

Globe Midwest Adjusters Intl.
25800 Northwestern Highway
Southfield, MI 48075-8403
800-445-1554
248-352-2100
www.globemw-ai.com

Hannah-Watrous Continuity Strategies
P.O. Box 54
Chester, CT 06412-1345
860-227-5046
www.HANWAT.com

IBM Business Resilience and Continuity Svcs
300 Long Meadow Road
Sterling Forest, NY 10979
800-599-9950
www.IBM.com/services/resilience

IBM Canada Ltd.
3500 Steeles Avenue, East
Markham, ON
Canada
905-316-2067

IBM Global Services
10 North Martingale Road
Woodfield Prese
Schaumburg, IL 60173
1-800-IBM-7080
www.ibm.com

KETCHConsulting
P.O. Box 641
Waverly, PA 18471
888-538-2492
570-563-0868
www.ketchconsulting.com

Lunngroup Consulting Inc
255 Newport Dr
Metrotown RPO
Port Moody, BC V3H SH1
Canada
604-780-4816
www.lunngroup.com

Marsh Inc.
1166 Avenue of the Americas
New York, NY 10036-2774
866-928-7475
www.MARSHRISKCONSULTING.com

Professional Loss Adjusters
343 Washington Street
Newton, MA 02458
617-850-0477
www.pla-us.com

Protiviti Inc.
5720 Stoneridge Drive
Pleasanton, CA 94588
888-556-7420
www.protiviti.com

River Bend Business Continuity
One Omega Drive
Stamford, CT 06907
203-978-7444

Short Elliott Hendrickson, Inc.
Butler Square Building, Suite 710-C
100 North Sixth St.
Minneapolis, MN 55403-1515
612-758-6700
866-830-3388
www.sehinc.com

STERIS Corporation
5960 Heisley Road
Mentor, OH 44060
440-354-2600
800-548-4873
www.steris.com

Trackis
2211 Centerbrook Ln.
Katy, TX 77450
888-693-8426
www.trackis.com

TwoSeven, Inc.
Post Office Box 11064
Norfolk, VA 23517
804-339-5890
804-690-1517
www.twoseven.com

Business continuity planning

AccessPoint Business Recovery Services
1103 Victory Drive
Port Moody, BC V3H 1K3
Canada
604-250-4829
http://www.businessrecovery.ws

Appropriate Systems, LLC
68 Greenrale Ave
Wayne, NJ 07470
973-904-1547
www.a-systems.biz

Assurity River Group
P.O. Box 24506
Minneapolis, MN 55424-0506
612-435-2170
877-572-2170
www.continuitysolutions.net

Bel Esprit Partners
11160 Anderson Lakes Parkway
Suite 208
Eden Prairie, MN 55344
952-223-5404
www.belesprit-inc.com

BRProactive Inc.
1141 E Bennett Ave.
Glendora, CA 91741
626-852-0412
www.brproactive.com

CAPS Business Recovery Services
2 Enterprise Drive
Suite 200
Shelton, CT 06484
800-542-2773
www.CAPSBRS.com

Comprehensive Solutions
250 N Sunny Slope Road
Suite 300
Brookfield, WI 53005
262-785-8101
www.COMP-SOLN.com

Contingency Planners, Inc.
2510 Frederick Dr.
Conway, AR 72032-0958
501-329-0958
www.contingency-planners.com

Continuity Shield
1 Yonge Street
Suite 1801
Toronto, ON M5E 1W7
Canada
416-483-0464
www.continuityshield.com

Continuity Solutions, Inc.
6649 North High Street
Worthington, OH 43085
614-885-5001
www.csigroup.cc

Corby M & Associates
255 Park Avenue
Floor 8th
Worcester, MA 01609-1953
508-792-4320

CorigElan, LLC
1052 W. Fulton Market St.
Suite 2 East
Chicago, IL 60607
312-563-1430
www.corigelan.com

Corporate Risk Solutions, Inc.
8725 Rosehill Road
Suite 450
Lenexa, KS 66215
913-422-0410
www.corprisk.net

CRI Network Inc
suite 401- 901 Gordon Street
Victoria, BC V8L 2K6
Canada
250-889-5030
www.crinetwork.com

**DaVinci Technology Corporation
(DaVinciTek)
89 Headquarters Plaza
North Tower, 14th Floor
Morristown, NJ 07960
973-993-4860
http://www.davincitek.com**

Decisive Technologies Inc.
720 Morewood Crescent
Ottawa, ON K4A 2P8
Canada
613-824-3719
www.decisive.ca

Deucalion, Inc
7456 SW Baseline Road Suite 119
Hillsboro, OR 97123
866-269-2150
206-577-2804
www.deucalion.net

**Disaster Management Inc.
1531 SE Sunshine Avenue
Port St. Lucie, FL 34952-6011
772-335-9750
www.DISASTERMGT.com**

Disaster Preparedness of North Texas
2820 E. University Dr.
Suite #174
Denton, TX 76209
817-271-0077
940-365-3442

Disaster Recovery Consultants, LLC
41 Lenox Court
Montville, NJ 07045
908-328-7719

Disaster Recovery System (DRS)
1732 Remson Avenue
Merrick, NY 11566
516-623-2038
http://www.drsbytamp.com

**Disaster Survival Planning Network
(DSPN)
5352 Plata Rosa Court
Camarillo, CA 93012
800-601-4899
www.DSPNETWORK.com**

DJS Technology Solutions
2725 Advance Lane
Colmar, PA 18915
215-822-5515
800-748-8865
www.djs.com

Don J. Brooks Holdings Ltd.
695 Proudfoot Lane Suite 718
London, ON N6H 4Y7
Canada
519-657-5472
www.B2Bcontinuity.com

**EBC Partners, Inc.
6753 Thomasville Rd.
Suite 108
Tallahassee, FL 32312
850-894-4043
www.ebcpartners.com**

eBRP Solutions
7895 Tranmere Drive
Unit 25
Mississauga, ON L5S 1W9
Canada
905-677-0404
1-888-480-3277 (eBRP)
www.ebrp.net

Emotional Continuity Management
Inner Directions, LLP
2815 Van Giesen
Richland, WA 99354
509-942-0443
509-948-3593
www.emotionalcontinuity.com

EnSafe Inc
5724 Summer Trees Drive
Memphis, TN 38134
800-588-7962
www.ENSAFE.com

Ethix Consulting, LLC
202 Berkley Drive
Suite 210
Harrisburg, PA 17112
717-651-1520
609-315-5263
www.ethixconsulting.com

Hannah-Watrous Continuity Strategies
P.O. Box 54
60 W Main Street
Chester, CT 06412-1345
860-227-5046
www.HANWAT.com

Hitachi Data Systems
750 Central Expressway
Santa Clara, CA 95050
800-227-1930
www.hds.com

HZX Computer Systems Consultants - BCP Services
41 Palomino Cres
Toronto, ON M2K 1W2
Canada
416-221-6603

InfoSENTRY Services, Inc.
434 Fayetteville Street
Suite 2330
Raleigh, NC 27601
919-838-8570
www.infosentry.com

Jack Henry & Associates Inc. - Centurion Disaster Recovery
663 West Highway 60
P.O. Box 807
Monett, MO 65708
800-299-4411
417-235-6652
www.jackhenry.com

Jannaway & Associates
102 Robinson Avenue
Toronto, ON M1L 3T3
Canada
416-694-3274
416-569-3274

Jonathan Ward & Associates
3600 Yonge Street
Suite 625
Toronto, ON M4N 3R8
Canada
416-932-2314
www.wardassociates.ca

KPMG, LLP
Risk Advisory Services
345 Park Avenue
New York, NY 10154
212-872-4380
www.kpmg.com

Mainstay Consulting Group, LLC
20 Calle Pastadero
San Clemente, CA 92672
949-280-8648
949-369-1111
www.mainstayconsulting.com

Meredith Management Group
Station Square Three Suite 202
Paoli, PA 19301
800-981-1283
www.MMG-EMS.com

Praetorian Protective Services LLC
8 Estabueno Drive
Orinda, CA 94563
925-376-7169
www.PRAETORIANPROTECTIVE.com

R&A Crisis Management Services
650 South River Road
#713
Des Plaines, IL 60016-8344
847-827-4267
www.raconsulting.net

Redmond Worldwide, Inc
6637 Bergen Place
Brooklyn, NY 11220
718-545-0582
www.redmondworldwide.com

SBP Consulting Services Inc
97 Dovercourt Road
Toronto, ON M6J3C2
Canada
416-723-7953

Scivantage
110 Wall Street
18th Floor
New York, NY 10005
646-452-0050
http://www.scivantage.com

SECTOR, Inc.
90 Broad Street
New York, NY 10004
866-383-3315
www.sectorinc.com

StoneHenge Partners, Inc.
401 South Boston Suite 400
Tulsa, OK 74103
888-972-1999
918-971-1999
http://www.stonehenge.org

Structured Technical Services, LLC
2850 SW Cedar Hills Blvd. #330
Beaverton, OR 97005-1393
503-449-7703
www.structuredtechnical.com

TAMP Computer Systems Inc.
1732 Remson Avenue
Merrick, NY 11566-2611
516-623-2038
www.DRSBYTAMP.com

The Gimbal Group, Inc.
2111 Wilson Blvd.
Suite 700
Arlington, VA 22201
703-351-5054
www.gimbal.com

THE HOWE PARTNERSHIP
Suite #800 #2 St. Clair Ave East
Toronto, ON M4T 2T5
Canada
416-721-1053

The Penta Network
67 Wall Street
Floor 27th
New York, NY 10005-3101
212-804-5702
www.pentaassoc.com

United Security Group
5775 Wayzata Blvd., Suite 700
Minneapolis, MN 55416
612-874-6500
952-582-2955
www.usg-inc.com

URS Corporation
200 Orchard Ridge Dr.
Suite 101
Gaithersburg, MD 20878
301-258-6554
www.urscorp.com

Venture Resources Management Systems (VRMS)
P.O. Box 340457
Sacramento, CA 95834
800-570-8767
vrm.sys.com

Virtela Communications, Inc.
5680 Greenwood Plaza Blvd.
Greenwood Village, CO 80111
720-475-4000
877-803-9629
www.virtela.net

Virtual Corporation
227 Route 206
Northwest Professional Center, Building 1 Suite 2
Flanders, NJ 07836
973-927-5454
800-944-8478
www.virtual-corp.net

Waypoint Advisory
Post Office Box 984
Concordville, PA 19331
610-358-1202
http://www.waypointadvisory.com

Wester & Associates
22 Laurel Drive
Corte Madera, CA 94925
416-274-8493
415-945-9327

Wester & Associates
172 Joicey Boulevard
Toronto, ON M5M 2V2
Canada
416-274-8493
416-489-9327

Zonecast, Inc.
2021 Peyton Ave
210
Burbank, CA 91504
213-215-2037
http://www.zonecast.com

Business impact analysis

Athena Global
3418 Marcil at Sherbrooke
Montreal, QC H4A 2Z3
Canada
514-488-3867
www.athenaglobal.com/

Attainium Corp
14540 John Marshall Highway
Suite 103
Gainesville, VA 20155
571-248-8200
703-941-8462
www.attainium.net

Business Continuity Planners, Inc (BCPI)
12685 Dorsett Road
#126
Maryland Heights, MO 63043
314-541-4913
www.bus-cont-plan.com/

CAPS Business Recovery Services
2 Enterprise Drive
Suite 200
Shelton, CT 06484
800-542-2773
www.CAPSBRS.com

Comprehensive Solutions
250 N Sunny Slope Road
Suite 300
Brookfield, WI 53005
262-785-8101
www.COMP-SOLN.com

DaVinci Technology Corporation (DaVinciTek)
89 Headquarters Plaza
North Tower, 14th Floor
Morristown, NJ 07960
973-993-4860
www.davincitek.com

Disaster Management Inc.
1531 SE Sunshine Avenue
Port St. Lucie, FL 34952-6011
772-335-9750
www.DISASTERMGT.com

SERVICES

EBC Partners, Inc.
6753 Thomasville Rd.
Suite 108
Tallahassee, FL 32312
850-894-4043
www.ebcpartners.com

IBM Global Services
10 North Martingale Road
Woodfield Prese
Schaumburg, IL 60173
1-800-IBM-7080
www.ibm.com

KETCHConsulting
P.O. Box 641
Waverly, PA 18471
888-538-2492
570-563-0868
www.ketchconsulting.com

PreEmpt Inc.
211 Foxbury Drive
Euless, TX 76040
817-685-9765
www.PreEmptInc.com

Protiviti Inc.
5720 Stoneridge Drive
Pleasanton, CA 94588
888-556-7420
www.protiviti.com

R&A Crisis Management Services
650 South River Road
#713
Des Plaines, IL 60016-8344
847-827-4267
www.raconsulting.net

Strohl Systems
631 Park Avenue
Kng of Prussa, PA 19406
610-768-4120
800-634-2016
www.strohlsystems.com

The Gimbal Group, Inc.
2111 Wilson Blvd.
Suite 700
Arlington, VA 22201
703-351-5054
www.gimbal.com

The Revere Group
325 N. LaSalle
Suite #325
Chicago, IL 60610
888-473-8373
312-873-3400
www.reveregroup.com

Business recovery planning

Associated Records and Information Services
P.O. Box 937
Caddo Mills, TX 75135-0937
214-675-9598
903-527-2156
www.associatedrecords.com

CAPS Business Recovery Services
2 Enterprise Drive
Suite 200
Shelton, CT 06484
800-542-2773
www.CAPSBRS.com

Continuity Solutions Inc
6649 N High Street
Suite 100
Worthington, OH 43085-4004
614-885-5001
www.CSIGROUP.cc

Copper Harbor Consulting, Inc.
12 Grant St.
Needham, MA 02492
781-449-3235
781-400-1305
www.copperharborconsulting.com

Crisis Management International Inc
8 Piedmont Center
Suite 420
Atlanta, GA 30305-1533
404-841-3400
800-274-7470
www.CMIATL.com

DaVinci Technology Corporation (DaVinciTek)
89 Headquarters Plaza
North Tower, 14th Floor
Morristown, NJ 07960
973-993-4860
www.davincitek.com

EBC Partners, Inc.
6753 Thomasville Rd.
Suite 108
Tallahassee, FL 32312
850-894-4043
www.ebcpartners.com

Eyeview Recovery Consulting
8923 W Sunset dr
Wonder Lake, IL 60097
815-653-4045
www.eyeviewrecovery.com

Globe Midwest Adjusters Intl.
25800 Northwestern Highway
Southfield, MI 48075-8403
800-445-1554
248-352-2100
www.globemw-ai.com

IBM Canada Ltd.
3500 Steeles Avenue, East
Markham, ON
Canada
905-316-2067

IBM Global Services
10 North Martingale Road
Woodfield Prese
Schaumburg, IL 60173
1-800-IBM-7080
www.ibm.com

KETCHConsulting
P.O. Box 641
Waverly, PA 18471
888-538-2492
570-563-0868
www.ketchconsulting.com

La Société Prudent inc
2075 rue Victoria bureau 113
St-Lambert, QC J4S 1H1
Canada
450-672-7966
www.prudent.qc.ca

Mikron Consulting
1073 Oakwood Ct.
Chanburgh, IL 60193
847-909-9516
847-846-5519
www.mikronconsulting.com

Phoenix Consulting Services
4450 California Avenue
Suite K-285
Bakersfield, CA 93309-1152
661-396-8336

Pitney Bowes Inc.
1 Elmcroft Road - World Headquarters
Stamford, CT 06926-0700
888-245-PBMS
www.pb.com

Protiviti Inc.
5720 Stoneridge Drive
Pleasanton, CA 94588
888-556-7420
www.protiviti.com

R&A Crisis Management Services
650 South River Road
#713
Des Plaines, IL 60016-8344
847-827-4267
www.raconsulting.net

Recovery-Plus Planning Products & Svcs.
304 Circle Drive
Suite 117
Algonquin, IL 60102-2126
847-658-1300

RSM McGladrey Inc.
801 Nicollet Avenue
11th Floor West Tower
Minneapolis, MN 55402
800-648-4030
www.RSMMCGLADREY.com

Sage Business Associates, Inc.
6156 Powell Road
Parker, CO 80134
303-841-4467
720-989-5039

SEM3 Solutions
19 Jackson Drive
Raynham, MA 02767
508-717-7208
www.sem3solutions.com

Siegel Rich Division-Rothstein, Kass and
Company, D.C.
1350 Avenue of the Americas
Floor 15
New York, NY 10019
212-997-0500
www.rkco.com

Systems Audit Group, The
25 Ellison Road
Newton, MA 02459-1434
617-332-3946
www.Disaster-Risk-Planning.com

The Revere Group
325 N. LaSalle
Suite #325
Chicago, IL 60610
888-473-8373
312-873-3400
www.reveregroup.com

Continuity research analysis firms

Continuity Research
P.O. Box 5849
Baltimore, MD 21282
215-968-2300
www.continuityresearch.com

COOP (continuity of operations)

CEM Associates, Inc.
2218 Little John Trail
Newton, NC 28658
828-465-0874
828-310-2859
CEMAssociates.org

Criterion Strategies Inc
580 Broadway
Suite 305
New York, NY 10012
212-343-1134
www.criterionstrategies.com

EBC Partners, Inc.
6753 Thomasville Rd.
Suite 108
Tallahassee, FL 32312
850-894-4043
www.ebcpartners.com

Excelliant
1201 Lee Branch Lane
Birmingham, AL 35242
888-675-6627
205-313-9180
www.excelliant.com

KETCHConsulting
P.O. Box 641
Waverly, PA 18471
888-538-2492
570-563-0868
www.ketchconsulting.com

Knight-Star Enterprises, Inc.
HUB/Woman-Owned Business
P.O. Box 7873
Waco, TX 76714
866-776-1996
254-776-1996
www.knightstar.us

National Security Research
2231 Crystal Drive
Suite 500
Arlington, VA 22202
703-647-2200
www.nsrinc.com

TDG, Inc
82 Sorrentino Way
Mays Landing, NJ 08330
609-476-2055
www.tdginc.com

URS Corporation
200 Orchard Ridge Dr.
Suite 101
Gaithersburg, MD 20878
301-258-6554
www.urscorp.com

Crisis management

ALSO SEE CRISIS MANAGEMENT SERVICES IN MISC. SERVICES SECTION

Agnes Huff Communications Group, LLC
Howard Hughes Center
6601 Center Drive West, Suite 100
Los Angeles, CA 90045
310 641-2525
www.ahuffgroup.com

Allan Bonner Communications Management
393 King St. W.
Suite #701
Toronto, ON M5V 3G8
Canada
877-484-1667
416-961-3620
www.allanbonner.com

Bernstein Crisis Management LLC.
1013 Orange Avenue
Monrovia, CA 91016-3724
626-305-9277
www.BERNSTEINCRISISMANAGEMENT.com

Childress Duffy Goldblatt, Ltd.
515 N State
Suite 2200
Chicago, Il 60610
312-494-0200
www.ChildressLaw.net

COPE Solutions Inc
3274 Rosedale Rd North
Smiths Falls, ON K7A 4S7
Canada
613-223-1128
416-89-4737
www.copesolutions.com

Crisis Response Planning Corporation
464 Gowland Crescent
Milton, ON L9T 4E5
Canada
905-876-0229
www.crpc.com

Globe Midwest Adjusters Intl
25800 Northwestern Highway
Southfield, MI 48075-8403
800-445-1554
248-352-2100
www.globemw-ai.com

**IBM Global Services
10 North Martingale Road
Woodfield Prese
Schaumburg, IL 60173
1-800-IBM-7080
www.ibm.com**

Incident Mitigation, Inc.
17340 W. 12 Mile Rd., Suite 101
Southfield, MI 48076
248-552-0821
www.incidentmitigation.com

Institute for Crisis Management
950 Breckenridge Lane
Suite 140
Louisville, KY 40207
502-891-2507
888-708-8351
www.crisisconsultant.com

Int'l. Critical Incident Stress Foundation
3290 Pine Orchard Lane
Suite 106
Ellicott City, MD 21042-2254
410-750-9600
www.ICISF.org

KETCHConsulting
P.O. Box 641
Waverly, PA 18471
888-538-2492
570-563-0868
www.ketchconsulting.com

Oppenheimer Wolff & Donnelly LLP
Plaza VII, Suite 3300
45 South 7th Street
Minneapolis, MN 55402
612-607-7204
612-607-7000
www.oppenheimer.com

**Pitney Bowes Inc.
1 Elmcroft Road - World Headquarters
Stamford, CT 06926-0700
888-245-PBMS
www.pb.com**

PricewaterhouseCoopers LLP
300 Madison Avenue
24th Floor
New York, NY 10017
646-471-4000
www.PWC.com/US

**Protiviti Inc.
5720 Stoneridge Drive
Pleasanton, CA 94588
888-556-7420
www.protiviti.com**

R&A Crisis Management Services
650 South River Road
#713
Des Plaines, IL 60016-8344
847-827-4267
www.raconsulting.net

Raido Response
1109 First Avenue
Suite 212
Seattle, WA 98101
206-628-9156
www.raidoresponse.com

The Redfern Group
14450 T.C. Jester Blvd.
Suite 205
Houston, TX 77014
281-866-9451
http://www.redferncpr.com

**URS Corporation
200 Orchard Ridge Dr.
Suite 101
Gaithersburg, MD 20878
301-258-6554
www.urscorp.com**

Data protection & storage

Datalink
8170 Upland Circle
Chanhassen, MN 55317
952-944-3462
800-448-6314
www.datalink.com

Disaster avoidance

Comprehensive Solutions
250 N Sunny Slope Road
Suite 300
Brookfield, WI 53005
262-785-8101
www.COMP-SOLN.com

Computersite Engineering
1347 Tano Ridge Road
Santa Fe, NM 87506
505-982-8300
www.UPSITE.com

Consonus AllWaysOn Data Centers
180 East 100 South
Questar Building
Salt Lake City, UT 84111
888-452-8000
www.consonus.com

Contingency Management Consultants
4 Shawnee Lane
Orinda, CA 94563-3217
925-254-1663
925-766-3466
www.BUSINESSCONTINUITY.com

Emotional Continuity Management
Inner Directions, LLP
2815 Van Giesen
Richland, WA 99354
509-942-0443
509-948-3593
www.emotionalcontinuity.com

IBM Global Services
10 North Martingale Road
Woodfield Prese
Schaumburg, IL 60173
1-800-IBM-7080
www.ibm.com

Landslide Observatory
JCET
University of Maryland Baltimore County
Baltimore, MD 21250
410-455-5834
www.jcet.umbc.edu

Oppenheimer Wolff & Donnelly LLP
Plaza VII, Suite 3300
45 South 7th Street
Minneapolis, MN 55402
612-607-7204
612-607-7000
www.oppenheimer.com

RecoveryPlanner
2 Enterprise Drive
Shelton, CT 06484
203-925-3950
866-925-3950
www.RECOVERYPLANNER.com

Triangle Resource Group
5510 Six Forks Road
Raleigh, NC 27609
919-841-0175
800-213-7168
www.alertnowusa.com

TSC Consulting Inc.
5030 Champion Blvd.
G6-205
Boca Raton, FL 33496
800-658-7606
561-829-8118
www.THESECURECOMPUTER.com

Disaster recovery planning & emergency preparedness

2bcool Enterprises Inc.
503-333 2 Avenue NE
Calgary, AB T2E 0E5
Canada
403-276-3855
www.2bcool.ca

ACS Image Solutions
102 Business Park Drive
Suite I
Ridgeland, MS 39157
601-977-4000

Advanced Process Solutions Inc.
2416 Basil Drive
Raleigh, NC 27612
919-844-1625
www.aps4you.com

Agility Recovery Solutions
7621 Little Avenue
Suite 218
Charlotte, NC 28226
866-364-9696
704-341-8700
www.agilityrecovery.com

Agility Recovery Solutions
2281 N. Sheridan Way
Mississauga, ON L5K 2S3
Canada
800-567-5001
www.AGILITYRECOVERY.com

AMTI
2900 Sabre Street
Suite 800
Virginia Beach, VA 23452
757-431-8597
703-415-4406
http://www.amti.net

Arlington Associates, LLC
770 Arlington Circle
Novato, CA 94947-4976
415-883-0884

AXCESS Disaster Consulting Group
P.O. Box 91825
West Vancouver, BC V7V 4S1
Canada
604-657-6760
www.strategis.ca.gc

BearingPoint Inc.
1676 International Drive
McLean, VA 22030
703-747-3000
www.BEARINGPOINT.com

BOOZ-ALLEN & HAMILTON Inc.
8283 Greensboro Drive
McLean, VA 22102-3838
703-902-5000
www.BOOZALLEN.com

Business & Government Continuity Services
P.O. Box 1706
Oklahoma City, OK 73101
405-737-8348
www.businesscontinuity.info

Business Contingency Group
18034 Ventura Blvd Suite 333
Encino, CA 91316
818-784-3736
www.BUSINESSCONTINGENCYGROUP.com

CAPS Business Recovery Services
2 Enterprise Drive
Suite 200
Shelton, CT 06484
800-542-2773
www.CAPSBRS.com

CGI
1130 Sherbrooke St. West 7th Floor
Montreal, QC H3A 2M8
Canada
514-841-3200
www.CGI.com

Chubb Group of Insurance Companies
55 Water St
New York, NY 10041
212-612-4000
800-884-4669
www.CHUBB.com

Comprehensive Solutions
250 N Sunny Slope Road
Suite 300
Brookfield, WI 53005
262-785-8101
www.COMP-SOLN.com

Consolidated Risk Management
1717 East 9th Street
Suite 1125
Cleveland, OH 44114-2804
216-623-1777
www.RISK-MANAGE.com

Contingency Planning Solutions Inc.
1400 South Van Dyke Road
Appleton, WI 54914
920-734-0241
www.contingencyplans.com

Curtis 1000
1725 Breckinridge Parkway
Duluth, GA 30096
678-380-9095
www.CURTIS1000.com

Damicon, LLC
13 Jackson Road
Burlington, MA 01803
781-789-8238
www.damicon.com

DataCenterManager.com
P.O. Box 805975
Chicago, IL 60680
312-451-1052
www.DATACENTERMANAGER.com

Disaster Recovery Planning Services
429 Archers Way
Madisonville, LA 70447-9472
985-845-0771
985-264-0476

Disaster Recovery System
1732 Remson Avenue
Merrick, NY 11566-2611
516-623-2038
www.DRSBYTAMP.com

Disaster Resource Mgmt
11700 Mountain Park Road
Roswell, GA 30075
678-277-9860
770-605-6477

DPS Management Consultants
2320 Gravel Drive
Fort Worth, TX 76118-6950
817-284-7711
800-776-1574
www.DPSCONSULTANTS.net

Dreamcatcher Disaster Resilience LLC
1647 Dancer Drive
Rochester Hls, MI 48307
248-650-9900
www.DREAMCATCHER-DR.com

Eagle Rock Alliance LTD.
80 Main Street
West Orange, NJ 07052
973-325-9900
www.EAGLEROCKALLIANCE.com

EBC Partners, Inc.
6753 Thomasville Rd.
Suite 108
Tallahassee, FL 32312
850-894-4043
www.ebcpartners.com

Elliot Consulting Services
10238 Woodford Bridge Street
Tampa, FL 33626
813-792-8833
http://www.elliot-consulting.com

Emergency Visions
2110 Spring Hill Court
Smyrna, GA 30080
770-436-2474
http://www.emergencyvisions.com

Emotional Continuity Management
Inner Directions, LLP
2815 Van Giesen
Richland, WA 99354
509-942-0443
509-948-3593
www.emotionalcontinuity.com

Enterprise Connections
1800 Century Park E Suite 600
Los Angeles, CA 90067
310-229-5744
www.EnterpriseConnections.com

Enterprise Risk Worldwide, Inc
551 Fifth Avenue, Suite 3025
New York, NY 10176
212-599-1878
www.enterpriseriskworldwide.com

Equivus Consulting
4238b N. Arlington Heights Rd #361
Arlington Heights, IL 60004
847-956-3322
866-378-4887
http://www.equivus.com

Ernst & Young LLP
1401 McKinney Street
Houston, TX 77010
713-750-1500
713-750-8147
www.EY.com

First General Enterprises, Inc.
2455 E. Sunrise Blvd., Suite 1201
Fort Lauderdale, FL 33304-3115
800-523-3680
954-537-5556
www.firstgeneralservices.com

Gerard Group International LLC
164 Westford Road
Suite 15
Tyngsborough, MA 01879
978-649-4575
www.GERARDGROUP.com

Globe Midwest Adjusters Intl
25800 Northwestern Highway
Southfield, MI 48075-8403
800-445-1554
248-352-2100
www.globemw-ai.com

Grant Thornton LLP
18400 Von Karman Avenue
Irvine, CA 92612
949-553-1600
www.GT.com

Greenley & Associates Incorporated
5 Corvus Court
Ottawa, ON K2E 7Z4
Canada
613-247-0342
www.greenley.ca

HAN Consulting
4960 Almaden Expressway
Suite 243
San Jose, CA 95118
408-474-2106
925-352-5447
www.HAN-CONSULTING.com

Harland Finanacial Solutions
312 Plum Street
Cincinnati, OH 45202
513-381-9400
www.INTRIEVE.com

Healy & Associates Banking Services
P.O. Box 2143
Asheboro, NC 27204-2143
336-629-0153

Hour Zero Crisis Consulting Ltd.
9914 - 86 Avenue
Edmonton, AB T6E 2L7
Canada
780-439-0999
www.hour-zero.com

IBM Global Services
10 North Martingale Road
Woodfield Prese
Schaumburg, IL 60173
1-800-IBM-7080
www.ibm.com

Idea Integration
1899 Wynkoop Street
Denver, CO 80202
303-571-4557
www.IDEA.com

IEM Inc.,
8555 United Plaza Boulevard
Suite 100
Baton Rouge, LA
800-977-8191
225-952-8191
www.ieminc.com

International Dynamics Research Corp
1266 West Paces Ferry Rd
Suite 207
Atlanta, GA 30327
770-723-9785
http://www.goATAB.org

Intrado
1601 Dry Creek Dr
Longmont, CO 80503
877-262-3775
720-494-5800
www.intrado.com

J&H Marsh & McLennan Inc
212 Carnegie Center
Princeton, NJ 08543
609-520-2900
www.MARSH-FINANCIAL.com/risk.html

Janus Associates
River Plaza
9 West Broad Street - 9th Floor
Stamford, CT 06902
203-251-0200
www.JANUSASSOCIATES.com

KETCHConsulting
P.O. Box 641
Waverly, PA 18471
888-538-2492
570-563-0868
www.ketchconsulting.com

Knight-Star Enterprises, Inc.
HUB/Woman-Owned Business
P.O. Box 7873
Waco, TX 76714
866-776-1996
254-776-1996
www.knightstar.us

McWains Chelsea Inc
53 Center Ave
Morristown, NJ 07960
973-993-5700
www.MCWAINS.com

Multi Risk Strategies
6955, boul. Taschereau, 210
Brossard, QC J4Z 1A7
Canada
450-443-2500
www.multirisques.net

National Insitute for Occupational Safety and Health
200 Independence Ave, SW
Hubert H. Humphery Bldg 715H
Washington, DC 20201
202-260-9727
www.cdc.gov/niosh

Oppenheimer Wolff & Donnelly LLP
Plaza VII, Suite 3300
45 South 7th Street
Minneapolis, MN 55402
612-607-7204
612-607-7000
www.oppenheimer.com

Pearces 2 Consulting Corporation
5730 Sunshine Falls Lane
North Vancouver, BC V7G 2T9
Canada
604-929-4560
www.pearces2.com

Phoenix Consulting Services
4450 California Avenue
Bakersfield, CA 93309
661-396-8336

Phoenix Continuity Solutions, LLC
25800 Northwestern Highway
Suite L-60
Southfield, MI 48075
248-263-3855
www.PCSPHOENIX.com

Phoenix Disaster Services
10221 Desert Sands Street
Suite 111
San Antonio, TX 78216-3944
210-541-0505
www.PDSTX.com

Pitney Bowes Inc.
1 Elmcroft Road - World Headquarters
Stamford, CT 06926-0700
888-245-PBMS
www.pb.com

Pre-Emergency Planning, LLC
P.O. Box 75
Lodi, WI 53555
608-592-2511
www.pre-emergency.com

Professional Loss Adjusters
343 Washington Street
Newton, MA 02458
617-850-0477
www.pla-us.com

SERVICES

Reynolds Bone & Griesbeck
5100 Wheelis Drive
Suite 300
Memphis, TN 38117
901-682-2431
www.rbgcpa.com

Sage Business Associates, Inc.
6156 Powell Road
Parker, CO 80134
303-841-4467
720-989-5039

Scanlon Associates Inc.
117 Aylmer Ave.
Ottawa, ON K1S 2X8
Canada
1-613-730-9239
011-44-20-7483-3036

Science Applications Intl. Corp. (SAIC)
301 Laboratory RD P.O.Box 2501
Oak Ridge, TN 37831
865-482-9031
www.SAIC.com

Short Elliott Hendrickson, Inc.
Butler Square Building, Suite 710-C
100 North Sixth St.
Minneapolis, MN 55403-1515
612-758-6700
866-830-3388
www.sehinc.com

SRA International Inc.
4300 Fair Lakes Court
Fairfax, VA 22033
703-803-1500
www.sra.com

Stephens Associates, Inc
157 Broad Street
Suite 202
Red Bank, NJ 07701
732-842-1903
www.stevensassocinc.com

Stratford Solutions
2988 Monmouth Rd.
Cleveland Hts., OH 44118
216-932-5690
www.stratfordsolutions.com

Strohl Systems
631 Park Avenue
Kng of Prussa, PA 19406
610-768-4120
800-634-2016
www.strohlsystems.com

TAMP Computer Systems Inc.
1732 Remson Avenue
Merrick, NY 11566-2611
516-623-2038
www.DRSBYTAMP.com

The Revere Group
325 N. LaSalle
Suite #325
Chicago, IL 60610
888-473-8373
312-873-3400
www.reveregroup.com

The Steele Foundation
388 Market St. 5th Floor
San Francisco, CA 94111
415-354-3846
415-225-0914
www.steelefoundation.com

The Systems Audit Group Inc.
25 Ellison Road
Newton, MA 02459-1434
617-332-3496
www.Disaster-Risk-Planning.com

TRC
5709 E. I-240 Service Rd
Suite D
Oklahoma City, OK 73135
405-736-1990
www.trcdisastersolutions.com

Turnbull Consulting Inc.
P.O. Box 475
Wallace, NC 28466-0475
910-285-8606
888-TCI-DRP1
www.TURNBULLCONSULTING.us

USG Recovery Centers
7831 East Bush Lake Road
Suite 100
Edina, MN 55439
612-874-6500
www.usgrecoverycenter.com

USG University
7831 East Bush Lake Road
Suite 100
Edina, MN 55439
612-874-6500
www.usguniversity.org

USG, Inc.
5775 Wayzata Boulevard
Suite 700
Minneapolis, MN 55416
612-874-6500
www.usg-inc.com

Disaster recovery planning & emergency preparedness, for academic institutions

Disaster Management Inc.
1531 SE Sunshine Avenue
Port St. Lucie, FL 34952-6011
772-335-9750
www.DISASTERMGT.com

J. Berra Engineering Inc.
333 N Sam Houston Parkway E
Suite 230
Houston, TX 77060
281-447-8300
www.crisisplans.com

Disaster recovery planning & emergency preparedness, for utilities

Blue Heron Consulting Corp.
300 Airpark Drive
Suite 80
Rochester, NY 14624
800-253-3449
www.BLUEHERON-CONSULTING.com

JALCO Services, Inc
521 Helena Avenue
Wyckoff, NJ 07481
201-847-2019
www.jalcoservices.com

SEH Inc.
6418 Normandy Lane #100
Madison, WI 53719
608-274-2020
608-270-5364
www.sehinc.com

The National Environmental Services Center
West Virginia University
P.O. Box 6064
Morgantown, WV 26506
800-624-8301

Earthquake

Anderson Niswander Construction Inc.
3620 Haven Ave.
Redwood City, CA 94063
650-369-9443
www.ANDERSONNISWANDER.com

California Seismic Safety Commision, The
1755 Creekside Oaks Drive
Suite 100
Sacremento, CA 95833
916-263-5506
www.seismic.ca.gov

Construction Technology Laboratories Inc (CTL)
5400 Old Orchard Road
Skokie, IL 60077
847-965-7500
www.CTLGROUP.com

Dynamic Isolation Systems Inc
3470 Mt Diablo Boulevard
Lafayette, CA 94549
925-283-1166
www.DIS-INC.com

Strand Earthquake Consultants
1436 S Bentley Avenue
Apt. 6
Los Angeles, CA 90025-3400
310-473-2316
www.STRANDEARTHQUAKE.com

URS Corporation
200 Orchard Ridge Dr.
Suite 101
Gaithersburg, MD 20878
301-258-6554
www.urscorp.com

Education (also see Training)

Active Canadian Emergency Training Inc.
695 McMurray Road
Unit # 3
Waterloo, ON N2V 2B7
Canada
800-205-3278
www.activecanadian.com

Judith Eckles & Partners
2042 Old Gulph Road, Suite 100
Villanova, PA 19085
610-527-1982
610-766-0053
www.juditheckles.com

KETCHConsulting
P.O. Box 641
Waverly, PA 18471
888-538-2492
570-563-0868
www.ketchconsulting.com

Restoration Alliance
1414 Meador Ave
Suite 104
Bellingham, WA 98229
877-693-0111
www.restorationalliances.com

Strohl Systems
631 Park Avenue
Kng of Prussa, PA 19406
610-768-4120
800-634-2016
www.strohlsystems.com

TecAccess
18122 Vontay Road
Rockville, VA 23146
804-749-8646
http://www.TecAccess.net

The Institute of Terrorism Research and Response
P.O. Box 56555
Philadelphia, PA 19111
866-778-1871
267-688-8344

Emergency & crisis management

Asesores en Emergencias y Desastres
Paseo Jurica 105-25PB
Jurica, Querétaro/Mexico
Queretaro, TX 76100
442-218-4424
http://www.asemde.com

Barron Emergency Consulting
33 Gaskins Road
Milton, MA 02186
617-298-8265
www.barronemergencyconsulting.com

C4CS, LLC
5625 Hempstead Road
Suite 101
Pittsburgh, PA 15217
412 421-0433
412-708-0940
www.c4cs.com

Crisis Consulting Group
P.O. Box 84153
Fairbanks, AK 99708
888-439-6898
848-333-1376
www.fwep.org

**Criterion Strategies Inc
580 Broadway
Suite 305
New York, NY 10012
212-343-1134
www.criterionstrategies.com**

Earthquake Solutions
940 E. Union Street
Suite 202
Pasadena, CA 91106
626-795-4000
www.earthquakesolutions.com

**EBC Partners, Inc.
6753 Thomasville Rd.
Suite 108
Tallahassee, FL 32312
850-894-4043
www.ebcpartners.com**

EnviroMED INC
4400 E Broadway Boulevard
Tucson, AZ 85711
520-881-1000

Envision - Planning Solutions Inc.
131 Scenic Hill Close NW
Calgary, AB T3L 1R1
Canada
403-241-8883

FIRECON
P.O. Box 231
East Earl, PA 17519
717-354-2411
http://www.FIRECON.com

FirstCall Network, Inc.
5423 Galeria Drive
Baton Rouge, LA 70816
800-653-9232
225-295-8123
www.firstcall.net

Frontline Corporate Communications Inc.
650 Riverbend Drive
Kitchener, ON N2K 3S2
Canada
888-848-9898
www.fcc.onthefrontlines.com

Global Impact Inc
21 Gardiner Dr
Bradford, ON
Canada
416 791 6109
www.riskandthreat.net

Hazmat DQE
8112 Woodland Drive
Indianapolis, IN 46278
800-355-4628
www.DQEREADY.com

**IBM Canada Ltd.
3500 Steeles Avenue, East
Markham, ON
Canada
905-316-2067**

KETCHConsulting
P.O. Box 641
Waverly, PA 18471
888-538-2492
570-563-0868
www.ketchconsulting.com

**National Notification Network (3N)
505 North Brand Blvd
Suite 700
Glendale, CA 91203
818-230-9700
888-366-4911
www.3NONLINE.com**

R.D. Zande & Associates, Inc.
1500 Lake Shore Drive
Suite 100
Columbus, OH 43204
614-486-4383
www.zande.com

Strategic Teaching Associates, Inc.
4158 Forestbrook Drive
Liverpool, NY 13090
315-622-5924
www.drpwithdrtom.com

**URS Corporation
200 Orchard Ridge Dr.
Suite 101
Gaithersburg, MD 20878
301-258-6554
www.urscorp.com**

Environmental strategies peer reviews

Hydro Geo Chem Inc
51 W Wetmore Road
Suite 101
Tucson, AZ 85705
520-293-1500
800-727-5547
www.HGCINC.com

**Rimkus Consulting Group Inc.
8 E Greenway Plaza
Floor 5
Houston, TX 77046
713-621-3550**

**URS Corporation
200 Orchard Ridge Dr.
Suite 101
Gaithersburg, MD 20878
301-258-6554
www.urscorp.com**

Equipment restoration

**BELFOR
185 Oakland Avenue
Suite 300
Birmingham, MI 48009
800-856-3333
www.belfor.com**

BELFOR (**◉**)

PROPERTYRESTORATION

BELFOR is the global leader in integrated disaster recovery and restoration services.

185 OAKLAND AVE, STE. 300 | BIRMINGHAM, MI 48009
PHONE: 800.856.3333 | FAX: 248.594.1133
www.belfor.com

Continental Machinery Company Inc.
10382 Miller Road
Dallas, TX 75238
800-616-8600
www.CONTINENTALMACHINERY.com

MET Electrical Testing Co Inc.
3700 Commerce Drive
Suite 901
Baltimore, MD 21227
410-247-3300
800-275-8378
www.MET-TEST.com

Technical Restoration Services Inc
5620 NW 12th Avenue
Fort Lauderdale, FL 33309
954-351-0301
800-423-3182
www.LOSS-RECOVERY.com

Fire protection

Certified Firestop, LLC
1868 Forsyth Ave, c/o 101
Monroe, LA 71201
318-665-2060
800-286-4006

Fyrsafe Engineering Inc.
1225 Carnegie Street Suite 108
Rolling Meadows, IL 60008-1032
847-392-1111

Haberill Contracting
40 Lynch Lane
Everett, ON L0M1J0
Canada
416-709-2460
705-435-4219

Harrington Group Inc
3055 Breckinridge Boulevard
Duluth, GA 30096
770-564-3505
www.HGI-FIRE.com

Loss Control Assoc. Inc.
172 Middletown Boulevard
Langhorne, PA 19047
215-750-6841
www.losscontrolassociates.com

MATRIX Risk Consultants Inc
3130 S Tech Boulevard
Miamisburg, OH 45342-4882
937-886-0000
www.MATRIXRC.com

Risk, Reliability, and Safety Engineering
2525 South Shore Blvd.
Suite 206
League City, TX 77573
281-334-4220
www.RRSENG.com

SERVICES

SERVICES

Rolf Jensen & Assoc. Inc
600 West Fulton Street
Suite 500
Chicago, IL 60661
312-879-7200
www.rjainc.com

Rollinger Engineering Inc
2000 S Dairy Ashford Street
Suite 455
Houston, TX 77077-5727
281-558-5000
www.REIFIREPRO.com

The Deatherage Companies
1805 N. 16th St.
Broken Arrow, OK 74012-9339
918-355-2344

TriData Corporation
1000 Wilson Boulevard
Arlington, VA 22209-3927
703-351-8308

Healthcare, HIPAA compliance

EBC Partners, Inc.
6753 Thomasville Rd.
Suite 108
Tallahassee, FL 32312
850-894-4043
www.ebcpartners.com

IT GlobalSecure
P.O. Box 53330
Washington, DC 20009-9330
202-332-5106
www.ITGLOBALSECURE.com

KETCHConsulting
P.O. Box 641
Waverly, PA 18471
888-538-2492
570-563-0868
www.ketchconsulting.com

Knight-Star Enterprises, Inc.
HUB/Woman-Owned Business
P.O. Box 7873
Waco, TX 76714
866-776-1996
254-776-1996
www.knightstar.us

LearnSomething, Inc.
2457 Care Drive
Tallahassee, FL 32308
850-385-7915
www.learnsomething.com

Insurance

Adjusters International
126 Business Park Drive
Utica, NY 13502
800-382-2468
315-797-3035
www.adjustersinternational.com

AIG eBusiness Risk Solutions
175 Water Street
New York, NY 10038
212-458-3695
www.aigebrs.com

Berman Adjusters, Inc.
1155 Walnut Street
Newton, MA 02461
617-964-0000
877-964-0000
www.bermanadjusters.com

Charles R. Tutwiler and Associates Inc.
5401 W. Kennedy Boulevard
Suite 757
Tampa, FL 33609
800-321-4488
813-287-8090
www.publicadjuster.com

Childress Duffy Goldblatt, Ltd.
515 N State
Suite 2200
Chicago, Il 60610
312-494-0200
www.ChildressLaw.net

Figlin & Associates, Inc.
8400 Bustleton Ave.
Suite 204
Philadelphia, PA 19152
215-342-8514
800-292-9090
www.figlinassoc.com

Finnicum Adjusting Company, Inc.
4268 Erie Avenue S.
P.O. Box 10
Navarre, OH 44662
800-359-2201

FM Global
1301 Atwood Ave
P.O. Box 7500
Johnston, RI 02919
401-275-3000
www.fmglobal.com

Insurance Claim Consultants - Public Adjusters
320 Coleman Blvd.
Suite M
Mt. Pleasant, SC 29464
843-971-1561
800-428-8583
www.claimassist.com

justclaims
200 White Horse Pike
Haddon Heights, NJ 08035
866-411-2524
609-410-1922
www.justclaims.net

McNeary
6525 Morrison Boulevard
Suite 200
Charlotte, NC 28211
704-365-4150
www.MCNEARY.com

NICE Network Inc.
2613 Crescent Springs Pike
Crescent Spgs, KY 41017
859-814-0061
800-837-6423
www.NICENETWORK.com

Nonprofit Risk Management Center
1001 Connecticut Avenue NW
Washington, DC 20036
202-785-3891
www.nonprofitrisk.org

Professional Loss Adjusters
343 Washington Street
Newton, MA 02458
617-850-0477
www.pla-us.com

Safeware The Insurance Agency Inc
6500 Busch Boulevard
Columbus, OH 43229
614-781-1492
800-722-0385
www.SAFEWARE.com

Loss prevention & investigation

Cannon Cochran Management Services Inc
2 E Main Street
Danville, IL 61832
217-446-1089
800-252-5059
www.CCMSI.com

Cap Index, Inc.
The Commons at Lincoln Center
150 John Robert Thomas Dr.
Exton, PA 19341
610-903-3000
800-227-7475
www.capindex.com

Childress Duffy Goldblatt, Ltd.
515 N State
Suite 2200
Chicago, Il 60610
312-494-0200
www.ChildressLaw.net

Gallagher Bassett Services Inc (National HQ)
2 Pierce Place
Itasca, IL 60143
630-773-3800

Helmsman Management Services Inc
9 Riverside Road
Weston, MA 02493
617-243-7985
www.HELMSMANTPA.com

JMG Consultants, Inc.
330 Jervis Avenue
Copiague, NY 11726
631-842-8847
631-495-1051
www.ienga.com

Madsen Kneppers & Associates Inc
1855 Olympic Boulevard
Suite 310
Walnut Creek, CA 94596
800-822-6624
www.MKAINC.com

Meadowbrook Insurance Group Inc
26600 Telegraph Road
Southfield, MI 48034
800-482-2726
www.meadowbrook.com

Overland Solutions Incorporated
11880 College Boulevard
Suite 400
Overland Park, KS 66210
913-451-3222
www.olsi.net

Regional Reporting Inc
40 Fulton Street
New York, NY 10038
212-964-5973
www.regionalreporting.com

Risk Consultants Inc
P.O. Box 490850
Atlanta, GA 30349
770-964-1226
800-644-7475
www.RISKCON.com

Schirmer Engineering Corp
707 Lake Cook Road
Deerfield, IL 60015
847-272-8340
www.schirmerengineering.com

Spybusters.com
P.O. Box 668
Oldwick, NJ 08858-0668
908-832-7900
http://www.spybusters.com

The Paragon Group
12722 Highway 3
Suite D
Webster, TX 77598
281-218-6373
www.origin-cause.com

SERVICES

URS Corporation
200 Orchard Ridge Dr.
Suite 101
Gaithersburg, MD 20878
301-258-6554
www.urscorp.com

Network recovery

Deloitte & Touche LLP
10 Westport Road
Wilton, CT 06897
203-761-3000
www.DELOITTE.com

IBM Global Services
10 North Martingale Road
Woodfield Prese
Schaumburg, IL 60173
1-800-IBM-7080
www.ibm.com

Premiere Network Services Inc
1510 N Hampton Road
Desoto, TX 75115
972-228-8885
www.rewireit.com

SECTOR, Inc.
90 Broad Street
New York, NY 10004
866-383-3315
www.sectorinc.com

ServePath
SF2 Data Center & Office
360 Spear Street, 2nd Floor
San Francisco, CA 94105
866-321-PATH
415-869-7000
www.servepath.com

Outside audit of disaster plan adequacy

Business & Government Continuity Services
P.O. Box 1706
Oklahoma City, OK 73101
405-737-8348
www.businesscontinuity.info

Comprehensive Solutions
250 N Sunny Slope Road
Suite 300
Brookfield, WI 53005
262-785-8101
www.COMP-SOLN.com

Criterion Strategies Inc
580 Broadway
Suite 305
New York, NY 10012
212-343-1134
www.criterionstrategies.com

Disaster Management Inc.
1531 SE Sunshine Avenue
Port St. Lucie, FL 34952-6011
772-335-9750
www.DISASTERMGT.com

EBC Partners, Inc.
6753 Thomasville Rd.
Suite 108
Tallahassee, FL 32312
850-894-4043
www.ebcpartners.com

IBM Global Services
10 North Martingale Road
Woodfield Prese
Schaumburg, IL 60173
1-800-IBM-7080
www.ibm.com

Jack Henry & Associates Inc. - Centurion Disaster
Recovery
663 West Highway 60
P.O. Box 807
Monett, MO 65708
800-299-4411
417-235-6652
www.jackhenry.com

KETCHConsulting
P.O. Box 641
Waverly, PA 18471
888-538-2492
570-563-0868
www.ketchconsulting.com

MLC & Associates, Inc.
P.O. Box 635
Port Orchard, WA 98366-0635
253-857-3124
949-222-1202
mlscandassociates.com

The Revere Group
325 N. LaSalle
Suite #325
Chicago, IL 60610
888-473-8373
312-873-3400
www.reveregroup.com

URS Corporation
200 Orchard Ridge Dr.
Suite 101
Gaithersburg, MD 20878
301-258-6554
www.urscorp.com

Power protection & continuity

Majorpower Corporation
7011 Industrial Drive
Mebane, NC 27302
800-931-4919
www.majorpower.com

MCCM
509 Londontown Road
Edgewater, MD 21037
410-591-5648
www.mccm.us

Power & Systems Innovations Inc.
P.O. Box 590223
Orlando, FL 32859
407-380-9200
www.psihq.com

Power Service Concepts Inc
599 Albany Ave North
Amityville, NY 11701
631-841-2300
www.powerserviceconcepts.com

U.S. Dept. of Energy Efficiency & Renewable Energy
P.O. Box 3048
Merrifield, VA 22116
877-337-3463
www.eere.energy.gov

Vital Records Control of Arkansas
1401 Murphy Drive
Maumelle, AR 72113
501-374-7775
www.VRCofAR.com

Vital Records Control of Florida
2801 Michigan Avenue
Fort Myers, FL 33916
239-337-4030
www.VRCofFL.com

Vital Records Control of South Carolina
255 Eagle Road
Goose Creek, SC 29445
843-566-7650
www.VRCofSC.com

Vital Records Control of Tennessee
4011 E Raines Road
Memphis, TN 38118
901-363-6555
www.VRCofTN.com

Records management

Advanced Records Management Services, Inc.
249 North Street
Danvers, MA 01923
888-869-2767
www.ARMSRECORDS.com

Archive Document Storage Inc.
345 10th Street
Jersey City, NJ 07302
201-716-7900
www.ARCHIVEDOCUMENTSTORAGE.com

Pitney Bowes Inc.
1 Elmcroft Road - World Headquarters
Stamford, CT 06926-0700
888-245-PBMS
www.pb.com

SECTOR, Inc.
90 Broad Street
New York, NY 10004
866-383-3315
www.sectorinc.com

Technology Today, Inc.
41 Peaslee Crossing
Newton, NH 03858
603-382-8116
www.tectoday.org

Vault Management Inc.
1805 W Detroit
Broken Arrow, OK 74012
918-258-7781
www.vault-tulsa.com

Risk analysis, environmental

ACM Environmental Inc
26598 U.S. 20 West
South Bend, IN 46628
574-234-8435
www.ACMENV.com

Alternative Environmental Solutions, Inc.
2217 Liberty Street
Monroe, LA 71201
318-388-4833
318-348-5038

Bercha Group
P.O. Box 61105
Calgary, AB T2N 4S6
Canada
403-270-2221
www.BERCHAGROUP.com

Braun Intertec Corp.
11001 Hampshire Ave S
Minneapolis, MN 55438
952-995-2000
800-279-6100
www.BRAUNCORP.com

Calvin, Giordano & Associates
1800 Eller Drive
Ft. Lauderdale, FL 33316
954-921-7781
www.calvin-giordano.com

CDM
1 Cambridge Place 50 Hampshire St
Cambridge, MA 02139
617-452-6000
800-243-2677
www.CDM.com

CH2M Hill
9189 South Jamaica St.
Englewood, CO 80112
303-771-0900
www.ch2m.com

Clayton Group Services Inc.
P.O. Box 8008
Novi, MI 48376-8008
888-357-7020
248-344-8550
www.CLAYTONGRP.com

EBC Partners, Inc.
6753 Thomasville Rd.
Suite 108
Tallahassee, FL 32312
850-894-4043
www.ebcpartners.com

Ecology & Environment Inc
368 Pleasantview Dr
Lancaster, NY 14086
716-684-8060
www.ENE.com

EMG
11011 McCormick Road
Hunt Valley, MD 21031
800-733-0660
www.EMGCORP.com

ENSR Consulting and Engineering
2 Technology Park Drive
Westford, MA 01886
978-589-3000
www.ENSR.com

Environmental & Occupational Risk Management
283 E Java Drive
Sunnyvale, CA 94089
408-822-8100
www.EORM.com

Environmental Management & Engineering Inc
5242 Bolsa Avenue
Huntington Beach, CA 92649
714-379-1096
www.emeiaq.com

Environmental Resources Management (ERM)
350 Eagleview Boulevard
Exton, PA 19341
610-524-3500
www.ERM.com

Fehr-Graham Assoc
221 E Main Street
Suite 200
Freeport, IL 61032
815-235-7643
www.FEHR-GRAHAM.com

First Environmental Nationwide
5223 Riverside Drive
Macon, GA 31210
478-477-2323
888-720-1330
www.FIRSTENVIRONMENTAL.com

Golder Associates Corp
3730 Chamblee Tucker Road
Atlanta, GA 30341
770-496-1893
www.GOLDER.com

Green Environmental Inc
52 Accord Park Drive
Norwell, MA 02061
617-479-0550
www.greenenvironmental.com

HWS Consulting Group Inc
825 J Street
Lincoln, NE 68508
402-479-2200
www.HWS-CON.com

Integrated Environmental Services
1445 Marietta Blvd.
Atlanta, GA 30318
800-409-8474
www.IESCYLINDERS.com

O'Connor Associates Environmental Inc
318 11th Ave SE Suite 200
Calgary, AB T2G 0Y2
Canada
403-294-4200
www.OCONNOR-ASSOCIATES.com

PerkinElmer
45 William Street
Wellesley, MA 02481
781-237-5100
www.PERKINELMER.com

PSI
1901 S.Meyers Blvd
Suite 400
Oakbrook Terrace, IL 60181
800-548-7901

Quality Inspection Service
7420 Stanford Avenue
La Mesa, CA 91941
619-466-2581

Safety & Environmental Management Planning, Inc.
235 Antigua Dr.
Lafayette, LA 70503
337-981-5391
www.semp.com

Shaw Environmental & Infrastructure Inc.
2790 Mosside Boulevard
Monroeville, PA 15146
412-372-7701
www.SHAWGRP.com

Shaw Environmental Inc.
88C Elm Street
Hopkinton, MA 01748
508-435-9561
www.shawgrp.com

Shaw Group
4171 Essen Lane
Baton Rouge, LA 70809
225-932-2500
800-562-2953
www.SHAWGRP.com

Superior Environmental Corp
1128 Franklin Street
Marne, MI 49435
616-677-5255
www.superiorenvironmental.com

Terracon Environmental Inc
16000 College Boulevard
Lenexa, KS 66219
800-593-7777

Tetra Tech Inc
3475 E Foothill Boulevard
Pasadena, CA 91107
626-351-4664
www.TETRATECH.com

Trinity Consultants
2311 W 22nd Street
Suite 315
Oak Brook, IL 60523
630-574-9400
www.TRINITYCONSULTANTS.com

URS Corporation
200 Orchard Ridge Dr.
Suite 101
Gaithersburg, MD 20878
301-258-6554
www.urscorp.com

Washington Group International
720 Park Blvd
P.O. Box 73
Boise, ID 83729
208-386-5000
www.wgint.com

xl insurance
520 Eagleview Boulevard
Exton, PA 19341
610-458-0570
800-327-1414
www.xlenvironmental.com

Risk analysis, information systems

Coffing Corporation
5336 LeSourdsville West Chester Road
Hamilton, OH 45011
513-755-8866
www.coffingco.com

DaVinci Technology Corporation (DaVinciTek)
89 Headquarters Plaza
North Tower, 14th Floor
Morristown, NJ 07960
973-993-4860
http://www.davincitek.com

EBC Partners, Inc.
6753 Thomasville Rd.
Suite 108
Tallahassee, FL 32312
850-894-4043
www.ebcpartners.com

Forsythe Solutions Group
7770 Frontage Road
Skokie, IL 60077
847-675-8000
www.FORSYTHESOLUTIONS.com

Hospitech Solutions
150 River Road
Suite G4B
Montville, NJ 07045
973-263-9800
www.hospitechsolutions.com

IBM Canada Ltd.
3500 Steeles Avenue, East
Markham, ON
Canada
905-316-2067

IBM Global Services
10 North Martingale Road
Woodfield Prese
Schaumburg, IL 60173
1-800-IBM-7080
www.ibm.com

InfoSENTRY Services, Inc.
434 Fayetteville Street
Suite 2330
Raleigh, NC 27601
919-838-8570
www.infosentry.com

MLC & Associates, Inc.
P.O. Box 635
Port Orchard, WA 98366-0635
253-857-3124
949-222-1202
mlscandassociates.com

SECTOR, Inc.
90 Broad Street
New York, NY 10004
866-383-3315
www.sectorinc.com

Sigma Business Solutions Inc.
55 York Street,
Suite 1100
Toronto, ON M5J 1R7
Canada
416-594-1991
202-756-4993
www.sigma-sbs.com

SRA International Inc.
4300 Fair Lakes Court
Fairfax, VA 22033
703-803-1500
www.sra.com

Risk analysis, management & control

1SecureAudit LLC
1600 Tysons Boulevard
8th Floor
McLean, VA 22102
703-245-3020
www.1secureaudit.com

ABD Insurance & Financial Services
305 Walnut Street
Redwood City, CA 94063
650-839-6000
www.cybersure.com

ABS Consulting
16800 Greenspoint Park Drive
Houston, TX 77060-2393
281-673-2800
www.ABSCONSULTING.com

Albert Risk Management Consultants
72 River Park
Needham Heights, MA 02494-2631
781-449-2866
www.ALBERTRISK.com

Alpha Risk MGMT. Inc.
60 Cuttermill Road
Great Neck, NY 11021
516-829-3500
www.ALPHARISKMANAGEMENT.com

Applied Risk Control Corp.
15 N Mill Street
Nyack, NY 10960
845-365-2444
www.appliedriskcontrol.com

Arup Risk Consulting
1500 W Park Drive Suite 180
Westborough, MA 01581-3966
508-616-9990
www.ARUP.com/risk

Business & Government Continuity Services
P.O. Box 1706
Oklahoma City, OK 73101
405-737-8348
www.businesscontinuity.info

Cardinal Risk Management Alternatives, Inc.
13140 Coit Road Suite 113
Dallas, TX 75240
214-365-0055
www.cardinalriskmanagement.com

CGI Adjusters Inc.
90 Allstate Pkwy
Markham, ON L3R 6H3
Canada
905-474-0003

Clair Odell Group
2 West Lafayette Street
Norriftwn, PA 19401
610-825-5555
800-220-3008
www.CLAIRODELL.com

Comprehensive Solutions
250 N Sunny Slope Road
Suite 300
Brookfield, WI 53005
262-785-8101
www.COMP-SOLN.com

Crain Langner & Co.
P.O. BOX 531
Richfield, OH 44286
330-659-3142

Criterion Strategies Inc
580 Broadway
Suite 305
New York, NY 10012
212-343-1134
www.criterionstrategies.com

Custard Insurance Ajusters
1 Dunwoody Park suite 204
Atlanta, GA 30338
770-551-2050
www.custard.com

DelCreo, Inc.
256 N. Main Street
Suite B
Alpine, UT 84004
801-756-4180
866-335-2736
www.DELCREO.com

Deloitte & Touche LLP
City Place 1 185 Asylum Street
Hartford, CT 06103
860-280-3000
www.DELOITTE.com

EBC Partners, Inc.
6753 Thomasville Rd.
Suite 108
Tallahassee, FL 32312
850-894-4043
www.ebcpartners.com

Fenwal Protection Systems
400 Main St
Ashland, MA 01721
800-336-9251
www.fenwalcontrols.com

First Response Management LLC
71 Krestview Lane
Golden, CO 80401
303-526-2550
www.FIRSTRESP.com

GatesMcDonald
215 N Front St
Columbus, OH 43215
614-677-3700

Hartford Financial Services Group Inc
Hartford Plaza
Hartford, CT 06106
860-547-5000
www.thehartford.com

IBM Global Services
10 North Martingale Road
Woodfield Prese
Schaumburg, IL 60173
1-800-IBM-7080
www.ibm.com

Iron Mountain
4002 Industry Drive
Chattanooga, TN 37416
423-894-4828
800-899-IRON
www.ironmountain.com

Iron Mountain Offsite Data Protection
5455 Kearny Villa Road
San Diego, CA 92123
858-576-9400
800-750-5455
www.ironmountain.com

Johnsonite
16910 Munn Road
Chagrin Falls, OH 44023
800-899-8916
440-543-8916
www.johnsonite.com

KETCHConsulting
P.O. Box 641
Waverly, PA 18471
888-538-2492
570-563-0868
www.ketchconsulting.com

KPMG, LLP
Risk Advisory Services
345 Park Avenue
New York, NY 10154
212-872-4380
www.kpmg.com

Louis A. Hellming Co.
5710 Wooster Pike
Suite 110
Cincinnati, OH 45227
513-922-2261

MATRIX Risk Consultants Inc
3130 S Tech Boulevard
Miamisburg, OH 45342-4882
937-886-0000
www.MATRIXRC.com

MLC & Associates, Inc.
P.O. Box 635
Port Orchard, WA 98366-0635
253-857-3124
949-222-1202
mlscandassociates.com

RiskCap
1655 Lafayette Street Suite 200
Denver, CO 80218
303-388-5688
www.riskcap.com

Safety & Risk Control Services Inc.
395 Main Street
Suite 4
Metuchen, NJ 08840-1875
800-466-4025
732-906-2244
www.SAFETYRISK.com

Safty Insurence
20 Custom House St
Boston, MA 02110
617-960-5700
www.saftyinsurence.com

Stevenson & Associates
8205 Spain Blvd. NE
Suite 208
Albuquerque, NM 87109
505-822-8510

Sweet Claims Company
65 North Moore Street
New York, NY 10013
212-226-4500
www.sweetclaims.com

T.E.Brennan Co.
2025 N Summit Avenue
Milwaukee, WI 53202
414-271-2232
www.tebrennan.com

Taylor Risk Consulting
16415 Addison Road
Suite 800
Addison, TX 75001
972-447-2055
214-274-7111
www.taylorrisk-ctc.com

The Revere Group
325 N. LaSalle
Suite #325
Chicago, IL 60610
888-473-8373
312-873-3400
www.reveregroup.com

Tristar Risk Management
2835 Bristol Parkway
Signal Hill, CA 90755
310-342-0500

URS Corporation
200 Orchard Ridge Dr.
Suite 101
Gaithersburg, MD 20878
301-258-6554
www.urscorp.com

SERVICES

SERVICES

Vance International
10467 White Granite Drive
Suite 210
Oakton, VA 22124-2700
703-592-1400
www.VANCEGLOBAL.com

Willis
7 Hanover Square
New York, NY 10004
212-344-8888
www.willis.com

Willis of Pennsylvania Inc.
BLdg 5 Suite 200 100 Matsonford Rd
Radnor, PA 19087
610-964-8700
www.willis.com

Roofing

Primero Engineering
1747 Citadel Plaza, Suite 204
San Antonio, TX 78209
210-829-5499

Safety

Acordia
24 E Greenway Plaza
Suite 1100
Houston, TX 77046
713-507-9476
800-364-9476
www.acordia.com

Claims Administrative Services Inc.
501 Shelley Drive
Fl Second
Tyler, TX 75701
903-509-8484
800-765-2412
www.cas-services.com

COMCO Safety Consulting Inc.
4412 E. Village Road
Long Beach, CA 90808
562-981-5335
www.safetydynamicsgroup.com

Compaudit Services
266 Harristown Road
Suite 200
Glen Rock, NJ 07452
201-689-4040
800-285-1948
www.NATIONALRISK.com

Executive Environmental Services Corp.
507 Mission Street
South Pasadena, CA 91030
626-441-7050
www.EXECENV.com

Inservco Insurance
2 N 2nd Street
Harrisburg, PA 17101
717-230-8300
www.INSERVCO.net

KEMPER INSURANCE COMPANIES
One Kemper Drive
Long Grove, IL 60049
847-320-2026
www.kemperinsurance.com

Liberty International Risk Services
175 Berkeley Street
Boston, MA 02116
617-574-5601
www.LIBERTYINTERNATIONAL.com

MEMIC Safety Services
261 Commercial Street
Portland, ME 04104
207-791-3480
207-791-3300
www.MEMIC.com

National Floor Safety Institute
P.O. Box 92628
Southlake, TX 76092
817-749-1700
www.nfsi.org

North American Risk Services
P.O. Box 49228
Sarasota, FL 34230
941-907-2200
www.narisk.com

Octagon Risk Services
2101 Webster Street
Suite 645
Oakland, CA 94612
510-452-9300
www.octagonrs.com

Pooler Consultants Ltd.
321 Upland Drive
Lafayette, LA 70506
337-984-1601

Railroad Safety Consultants, Inc.
P. O. Box 22746
Lake Buena Vista, FL 32830
407-319-4819
www.RailroadSafetyConsultants.com

SAIC
10260 Campus Point Drive
San Diego, CA 92121
858-826-6000
www.SAIC.com

Short Elliott Hendrickson, Inc.
Butler Square Building, Suite 710-C
100 North Sixth St.
Minneapolis, MN 55403-1515
612-758-6700
866-830-3388
www.sehinc.com

Specialty Risk Services
225 Asylum Street
Floor 16th
Hartford, CT 06103
860-520-2599

Sarbanes-Oxley compliance

Daniel S. Willard, P.C.
51 Monroe Street
Penthouse IV
Rockville, MD 20850
800-310-1178
301-424-1177
dswlaw@willardlaw.com

EBC Partners, Inc.
6753 Thomasville Rd.
Suite 108
Tallahassee, FL 32312
850-894-4043
www.ebcpartners.com

Security, general

Allied Security
3606 Horizon Drive
Kng of Prussa, PA 19406
800-437-8803
www.ALLIEDSECURITY.com

Competitive Insights Inc
24 Valencia Street
Ottawa, ON K2G 6T1
Canada
613-843-9944
www.competitiveinsightsinc.com

Gerard Group International LLC
164 Westford Road
Suite 15
Tyngsborough, MA 01879
978-649-4575
www.GERARDGROUP.com

HMA Consulting
2929 Briarpark Drive
Suite 325
Houston, TX 77042
832-242-1600
www.hmaconsulting.com

Honeywell Access Systems
135 West Forest Hill Avenue
Oak Creek, WI 53154
414-766-1700
www.honeywellaccess.com

Initial Security
1771 Diehl Road
Suite 200
Naperville, IL 60563
630-369-6761
800-942-9394
www.INITIALSECURITY.com

Initial Security
3355 Cherry Ridge Street
Suite 200
San Antonio, TX 78230-4818
210-349-6321
800-683-7771
www.INITIALSECURITY.com

IT Matters Inc.
412, 1000 8th Avenue SW
Calgary, AB T2P 3M7
Canada
403-503-0772
www.ITMATTERS.ca

KETCHConsulting
P.O. Box 641
Waverly, PA 18471
888-538-2492
570-563-0868
www.ketchconsulting.com

MERIT SECURITY
P.O. BOX 7236
REDWOOD CITY, CA 94063
650-366-0100
www.meritsecurity.com

MLC & Associates, Inc.
P.O. Box 635
Port Orchard, WA 98366-0635
253-857-3124
949-222-1202
mlscandassociates.com

Network Systems Architects
14 Page Terrace
Stoughton, MA 02072
781-297-5300
www.nsaservices.com

Protective Counter Measures and Consulting, Inc.
70 West Red Oak Lane
White Plains, NY 10604
914-697-4777
www.protectivecountermeausres.com

Protiviti Inc.
5720 Stoneridge Drive
Pleasanton, CA 94588
888-556-7420
www.protiviti.com

Sako & Associates
600 West Fulton Street
Suite 500
Chicago, IL 60661
312-879-7230
www.sakosecurity.com

Strategic Technology Group
100 Medway Rd, Suite 3000
Milford, MA 01757
508-473-4949
617-429-4445
www.drthermos.com

SERVICES

SERVICES

Walker International LLC
P.O. Box 4311
Manchester, NH 03108
603-930-4141
www.WalkerIntl.com

Security, information systems

Anteon
3211 Jermantown Road
Suite 700
Fairfax, VA 22030
703-246-0200
www.anteon.com

Bocada, Inc.
10500 NE 8th Street
Bellvue, WA 98004
425-818-4400
www.bocada.com

CERIAS: Cent. for Information Assurance & Security
Purdue University
656 Oval Dr
West LaFayette, IN 47907-2086
765-494-7841
www.CERIAS.purdue.edu

CERT Coordination Center
Software Engineering Institute
Carnegie Mellon University
Pittsburgh, PA 15213-3890
412-268-7090
www.CERT.org

Damicon, LLC
13 Jackson Road
Burlington, MA 01803
781-789-8238
www.damicon.com

DaVinci Technology Corporation (DaVinciTek)
89 Headquarters Plaza
North Tower, 14th Floor
Morristown, NJ 07960
973-993-4860
www.davincitek.com

Guardium
Prospect Place
230 Third Avenue
Waltham, MA 02451
877-487-9400
781-487-9400
www.guardium.com

IBM Global Services
10 North Martingale Road
Woodfield Prese
Schaumburg, IL 60173
1-800-IBM-7080
www.ibm.com

MLC & Associates, Inc.
P.O. Box 635
Port Orchard, WA 98366-0635
253-857-3124
949-222-1202
mlscandassociates.com

Murray Associates
P.O. Box 668
Oldwick, NJ 08858-0668
908-832-7900
www.spybusters.com

PC SYSWARE Inc.
57 Squires Avenue
Toronto, ON M4B 2R6
Canada
416-951-0110
www.securesmb.ca

Sarcom, Inc.
8337-A Green Meadows Dr. N
Lewis Center, OH 43035
800-326-3962
614-845-1300
www.sarcom.com

Science Applications International Corporation
Justice and Security Solutions
8301 Greensboro Drive
McLean, VA 22102
703-676-6046
www.saic.com

SecureWorks
11 Executive Park Drive
Atlanta, GA 30329
404-327-6339
www.secureworks.com

Securify Inc.
20425 Stevens Creek Boulevard
200
Cupertino, CA 95014
650-812-9400
www.SECURIFY.com

TechGuard Security
St. Louis West County Office
743 Spirit 40 Park Dr. Suite 206
Chesterfield, MO 63005
636-519-4848
www.techguardsecurity.com

TriAxis Inc.
23 Midstate Drive
Suite 106
Auburn, MA 01501
508-721-9691
www.triaxisinc.com

Security, mailing systems

U.S. Postal Inspection Service
P.O. Box 2000
Pasadena, CA 91102-2000
626-405-1200

SERVICES

U.S. Postal Inspection Service
1745 Stout St
St 900
Denver, CO 80299-3034
303-313-5320

U.S. Postal Inspection Service
3400 Lakeside Dr, Fl 6
Mirimar, FL 33027-3242
954-436-7200

U.S. Postal Inspection Service
433 W. Harrison St. Fl6
Chicago, IL 60699-0001
312-983-7900

U.S. Postal Inspection Service
495 Summer Street, Suite 600
Boston, MA 02210-2114
617-556-4400

U.S. Postal Inspection Service
10500 Little Patuxent Pkwy, Suite 200
Columbia, MD 21044-3509
410-715-7700

U.S. Postal Inspection Service
P.O. Box 555
New York, NY 10116-0555
212-330-3844

U.S. Postal Inspection Service
P.O. Box 7500
Phildelphia, PA 19101
215-895-8450

U.S. Postal Inspection Service
P.O.Box 1276
Houston, TX 77251-1276
713-238-4400

U.S. Postal Inspection Service
P.O. Box 400
Seattle, WA 98111-4000
206-442-6300

Security, network testing

BOOZ-ALLEN & HAMILTON Inc.
8283 Greensboro Drive
McLean, VA 22102-3838
703-902-5000
www.BOOZALLEN.com

Conqwest, Inc.
84 October Hill Road
Building 7
Holliston, MA 01746
508-893-0111
888-234-7404
www.conqwest.com

International Network Services Inc.(INS)
1600 Memorex Drive
Suite 200
Santa Clara, CA 95050
408-330-2700
www.INS.com

Network Systems Architects
14 Page Terrace
Stoughton, MA 02072
781-297-5300
www.nsaservices.com

SurfControl
1900 West Park Drive
Suite 180
Westborough, MA 01581
831-440-2500
www.surfcontrol.com

**TriAxis Inc.
23 Midstate Drive
Suite 106
Auburn, MA 01501
508-721-9691
www.triaxisinc.com**

SERVICES, Data & Records Storage and Recovery

Data recovery from broken hard disks

Data Mechanix
18271 W McDurmott
Suite B
Irvine, CA 92614
949-263-0994
800-886-2231
www.DATAMECHANIX.com

**Eco Data Recovery
4115 Burns Road
Palm Bch Gdns, FL 33410-4605
561-691-0019
800-339-3412
www.EcoDataRecovery.com**

Kenai Computer Forensics
P.O. Box 304
Carlisle, MA 01741
978-394-2728
http://www.kenaicomputerforensics.com

Subterranean Data Service Company
16713 NE 12th St.
Vancouver, WA 98684
360-604-0411
www.trueevaulting.com

Vantage Technologies, Inc.
4 John Tyler Street
Merrimack, NH 03054-4885
800-487-5678
603-883-6249
www.vantagetech.com

Data recovery from damaged media, misc.

CBL Data Recovery Technologies, Inc.
800-551-3917
www.cbltech.com

Datasafe Recovery Services Ltd
703 6th Avenue SW
Calgary, AB t2p 0t9
Canada
403-269-9128
www.DATASAFE.ca

Drivesavers Data Recovery
400 Bel Marin Keys Boulevard
Novato, CA 94949
415-382-2000
800-440-1904
www.DRIVESAVERS.com

Eagle Software
123 Indiana Avenue
Salina, KS 67401
785-823-7257
www.EAGLESOFT.com

E-Mag Solutions
13230 Evening Creek Dr S
Suite 202
San Diego, CA 92128-4106
858-746-3000
800-328-2911
www.DATA911.net

Excalibur Data Recovery Inc
5 Billerica Avenue
N Billerica, MA 01862
978-663-1700
800-466-0893
www.excaliburdatarecovery.com

Lazarus Data Recovery
379 Clementina Street
San Francisco, CA 94103
415-495-5556
800-341-3282
www.lazarus.com

LXI Corp
391 Las Colinas Boulevard E
130-326
Irving, TX 75039-5526
972-444-2323
www.LXICORP.com

Media Recovery Inc.
Nationwide - offices listed on website
7929 Brookriver Drive, Suite 200
Dallas, TX 75247
800-527-9497
214-630-9625
www.mediarecovery.com

Ontrack Data Recovery
9023 Columbine Road
Eden Prairie, MN 55347
952-937-5161
800-872-2599
www.krollontrack.com

REACT Computer Services
8238 S.Madison Street
Burrridge, IL 60527
630-323-6200
800-662-9199
www.reactnet.com

Techfusion
20 Concord Lane
Cambridge, MA 02138
617-491-1001
877-310-3282
www.TECHFUSION.com

Vantage Technologies, Inc.
4 John Tyler Street
Merrimack, NH 03054-4885
800-487-5678
603-883-6249
www.vantagetech.com

Vogon International
2600 Van Bure Suite 2623/2625
Norman, OK 73072
405-321-2585
800-392-5373
www.VOGON-INTERNATIONAL.com

Data recovery from damaged tape

CBL Data Recovery Technologies, Inc.
800-551-3917
www.cbltech.com

E-Mag Solutions
13230 Evening Creek Dr S
Suite 202
San Diego, CA 92128-4106
858-746-3000
800-328-2911
www.DATA911.net

Integra Manufufacturing
34 Linnell Circle
Billerica, MA 01821
978-671-0009

Vantage Technologies, Inc.
4 John Tyler Street
Merrimack, NH 03054-4885
800-487-5678
603-883-6249
www.vantagetech.com

Data recovery from failed servers

ActionFront Data Recovery Labs Inc.
Technology Park
2 Sun Court - Suite 375
Norcross, GA 30092
905-474-2220
800-563-1167
www.ACTIONFRONT.com

Adaptive Data Storage
P.O. Box 3399
Cinnaminson, NJ 08077
856-764-8401
www.adaptivedata.com

CBL Data Recovery Technologies, Inc.
800-551-3917
www.cbltech.com

Eco Data Recovery
4115 Burns Road
Palm Bch Gdns, FL 33410-4605
561-691-0019
800-339-3412
www.EcoDataRecovery.com

Totally Connected Security Ltd.
1312 SE Marine Dr.
Vancouver, BC V5X 4K4
Canada
604-432-7828
www.totallyconnectedsecurity.com

Vantage Technologies, Inc.
4 John Tyler Street
Merrimack, NH 03054-4885
800-487-5678
603-883-6249
www.vantagetech.com

Data recovery from optical disks

CBL Data Recovery Technologies, Inc.
800-551-3917
www.cbltech.com

Vantage Technologies, Inc.
4 John Tyler Street
Merrimack, NH 03054-4885
800-487-5678
603-883-6249
www.vantagetech.com

Information management & protection

AISG
11315 Corporate Blvd
Suite 210
Orlando, FL 32817
407-581-2929
www.aisg.com

Coffing Corporation
5336 LeSourdsville West Chester Road
Hamilton, OH 45011
513-755-8866
www.coffingco.com

Iron Mountain
3502 Bissonet Street
Houston, TX 77005
713-628-8732

National Security and Trust
868 Mount Moriah Road
Memphis, TN 38117
901-685-1177
www.NationalSecurityTrust.com

TriAxis Inc.
23 Midstate Drive
Suite 106
Auburn, MA 01501
508-721-9691
www.triaxisinc.com

Vital Records Control of Arkansas
1401 Murphy Drive
Maumelle, AR 72113
501-374-7775
www.VRCofAR.com

Vital Records Control of Florida
2801 Michigan Avenue
Fort Myers, FL 33916
239-337-4030
www.VRCofFL.com

Vital Records Control of South Carolina
255 Eagle Road
Goose Creek, SC 29445
843-566-7650
www.VRCofSC.com

Vital Records Control of Tennessee
4011 E Raines Road
Memphis, TN 38118
901-363-6555
www.VRCofTN.com

Microfilm drying & re-wash service

Midwest Freeze-Dry, Ltd.
7326 N. Central Park
Skokie, IL 60076
847-679-4756
www.midwestfreezedryltd.com

Microfilming & record copying

American Micro Data
4950 E 41st Avenue
Denver, CO 80216
303-322-4008
www.AMERICANMICRODATA.com

Anacomp Inc.
39 Brooks Drive
Braintree, MA 02184
781-843-5650
800-884-5858
www.anacomp.com

ArchivesOne
777 N James Road
Columbus, OH 43219
614-235-7000
www.ARCHIVESONE.com

Assured Micro-Services Inc
659 Lakeview Plaza Boulevard
Worthington, OH 43085
614-431-1818
513-591-0880
www.ASSUREDMICRO.com

BELFOR
185 Oakland Avenue
Suite 300
Birmingham, MI 48009
800-856-3333
www.belfor.com

Central States Microfilming Inc
302 Cary Point Drive
Cary, IL 60013
847-639-0443

Columbus Microfilm Inc
1600 Universal Road
Columbus, OH 43207
614-443-7825

CriticalControl
2400,205 5th Ave SW
Calgary, AB T2P 2V7
Canada
403-705-7500
www.criticalcontrol.com

Lason
10515 E 40th Avenue Unit #105
Denver, CO 80239
303-371-7755
www.LASON.com

Lason
450 Franklin Rd
Suite 100
Marietta, GA 30067
770-952-8094
www.LASON.com

SERVICES

Lason
161 Tower Drive
Suite A
Burr Ridge, IL 60527
630-654-2393
800-330-6724
www.lason.com

Leet-Melbrook Inc
18810 Woodfield Road
Gaithersburg, MD 20879-4715
301-670-0090
www.REPRO-TECH.com

Metroplex Office Systems
1100 Valwood Parkway
Carrollton, TX 75006
972-242-2062
www.mossolutions.com

Microsystems Inc
625 Academy Drive
Northbrook, IL 60062
847-205-1986
www.microsystemsinc.com

New England Archives
624 Hampden Street
Holyoke, MA 01040
800-225-2405

Western Micrographics & Imaging Systems
4320 Viewridge Avenue
Suite B
San Diego, CA 92123
858-268-1091
www.westernmicrographicsimaging.com

Offsite record & hard-copy storage

Archive Management Inc
6455 Box Springs Boulevard
Riverside, CA 92507-0725
951-656-2238
800-660-2724
www.ARCHIVEMANAGEMENT.com

CDI Vaults
P.O. Box 22308
Eugene, OR 97402
541-344-7890
www.CDIVAULTS.com

Datasafe
574 Eccles Avenue
South San Fran, CA 94080
650-875-3800
www.DATASAFE.com

Infoguard Inc
2563 Industry Lane
Norristown, PA 19403
800-446-8998
610-631-1312
www.INFOGUARDINC.com

Kentucky Underground Storage Inc
3830 High Bridge Road
Wilmore, KY 40390
859-858-4988
859-858-4407

Peak 10
8910 Lenox Pointe Drive
Suite A
Charlotte, NC 28273-3432
866-473-2510
866-4-PEAK10
www.PEAK10.com

Recall
#2 Executive Dr. Concourse Level
Fort Lee, NJ 07024
201-592-7868
www.recall.com

Underground Vaults & Storage. Inc
P.O. Box 1723
Hutchinson, KS 67504
620-662-6769
800-873-0906
www.uvsinc.com

Vault Management Inc.
1805 W Detroit
Broken Arrow, OK 74012
918-258-7781
www.vault-tulsa.com

VeriTrust
P.O. Box 22737
Houston, TX 77227-2737
713-263-9000
www.VeriTrust.net

Offsite tape, film, optical, etc. data storage

Adaptive Data Storage, Inc.
P.O. Box 3369
Cinnaminson, NJ 08077-3369
856-764-8401
www.adaptivedata.com

Compu Vault
515 S Lindbergh Boulevard
Saint Louis, MO 63131
314-991-3858
www.COMPUVAULTSTL.com

DataSite Northwest
12000 NE 8th Street
Bellevue, WA 98005
425-455-1198
www.DATASITENW.com

IG2 Data Security, Inc.
451 North Paulina Street
Chicago, IL 60622
312-850-4421
www.ig2data.com

Information Vaulting Services
301 Louisiana Street
Suite 14
Little Rock, AR 72201
501-455-4300
www.IVSofAR.com

Iron Mountain
4002 Industry Drive
Chattanooga, TN 37416
423-894-4828
800-899-IRON
www.ironmountain.com

Iron Mountain (Nationwide offices)
745 Atlantic Avenue
Boston, MA 02111
800-935-6966
www.IRONMOUNTAIN.com

National Security and Trust
868 Mount Moriah Road
Memphis, TN 38117-5705
901-685-1177
www.NationalSecurityTrust.com

Perm-A-Store Inc
6325 Sandburg Road
Suite 1100
Golden VALLEY, MN 55427
763-230-3911
800-366-7535
www.turtlecase.com

Perpetual Storage Inc.
6279 E Little Cottonwood Road
Sandy, UT 84092-6006
801-942-1950
800-753-2200
www.perpetualstorage.com

Recall
P.O. Box 27035
Kitchener, ON N2M 5P2
Canada
519-895-1213
www.DRIE.org

William B. Meyer, Inc.
255 Long Beach Blvd
Stratford, CT 06615
800-use-meyer
203-375-5801
http://www.williambmeyer.com/

William B. Meyer, Inc.
181 Route 117 Bypass Road
Bedford Hills, NY 10507
800-554-2673
914-242-8637
http://www.williambmeyer.com/

Oversized documents scanning & archiving

SCP America
799 CR 305
Rockdale, TX 76567
512-446-7988
310-876-0237
www.scp-america.com

Recovery of water-damaged books/documents

American Freeze-Dry Inc.
39 Lindsey Ave.
Runnemede, NJ 08078
800-817-1007
609-458-0510
www.americanfreezedry.com

BELFOR
185 Oakland Avenue
Suite 300
Birmingham, MI 48009
800-856-3333
www.belfor.com

BELFOR Canada Inc.
2625 Skeena St.
Vancouver, BC V5M 4T1
Canada
866-366-0493
www.belfor.com

Central Data Processing, Inc.
8007 Cryden Way
Forestville, MD 20747
301-568-4900

Freezedry Specialties Inc
4875 70th Avenue
Princeton, MN 55371
800-362-8380
www.FREEZEDRY.com

Midwest Freeze-Dry, Ltd.
7326 N. Central Park
Skokie, IL 60076
847-679-4756
www.midwestfreezedryltd.com

NMT Corporation
P.O. Box 2287
La Crosse, WI 54602
800-236-0850

Ronsin Photocopy Micro-50
215 Lemon Creek Drive
Walnut, CA 91789
909-598-0027
800-331-0006
www.RONSIN.com

The Rosco Group - Document Restoration Inc.
225 Lindsay Avenue
Dorval, QC H9P 1C6
Canada
514-931-7789

Remote software-backup/recovery services

AmeriVault Corp.
60 Hickory Drive
Waltham, MA 02451-1013
781-890-8690
800-774-0235
www.amerivault.com

AmeriVault Corp.
130 Turner Street
Building 3
Waltham, MA 02451
800-774-0235
www.amerivault.com

CBL Data Recovery Technologies, Inc.
800-551-3917
www.cbltech.com

CWRBS Backup Inc.
255 Queens Avenue
Suite 2330
London, ON N6A 5R8
Canada
888-558-9786
519-435-9225
www.cwrbs.com

Data Ensure, Inc.
P.O. Box 1234
Norton, VA 24273
276-679-7900
www.dataensureinc.com

Data Storage Corporation
One Penn Plaza
Suite 3600
New York, NY 10119
212-564-4922
www.dscorp.net

EVault Inc
2421 Bristol Cr.
Oakville, ON L6H 5S9
Canada
905-844-4453
www.EVAULT.com

eVAULT Remote Backup Facility
6121 Hollis St
EMERYVILLE, CA 94608
925-944-2422
www.EVAULT.com

Holben Webdesigns
18 Colonial Avenue
Haddonfield, NJ 08033
856-428-1004
888-403-8343
www.sosds.com

Hollywood Vaults Inc
742 Seward Street
Los Angeles, CA 90038-3504
323-461-6464
800-569-5336
www.HOLLYWOODVAULTS.com

IBM Canada
1360 Rene Levesque West
Suite 400
Montreal, QC H3G 2W6
Canada
514-964-1616
www.ibm.com

IBM Global Services
10 North Martingale Road
Woodfield Prese
Schaumburg, IL 60173
1-800-IBM-7080
www.ibm.com

Lockstep Systems Inc.
P.O. Box 1906
Scottsdale, AZ 85252
480-596-9432
877-932-3497
www.LOCKSTEP.com

Pitney Bowes Inc.
1 Elmcroft Road - World Headquarters
Stamford, CT 06926-0700
888-245-PBMS
www.pb.com

Recovery Point Systems
75 West Watkins Mill Road
Gaithersburg, MD 20878
240-632-7000
877-445-4333
www.RECOVERYPOINT.com

Subterranean Data Service Company, LLC
2033 3rd Ave Nt
Lewiston, ID 83501
208-746-2188
www.trueevaulting.com

Topio, Inc.
5201 Great America Parkway
Suite 340
Santa Clara, CA 95054
408-350-9800
www.topio.com

VaultLogix
78B Turnpike Rd.
Ipswich, MA 01938
877-VAULTLOGIX
877-828-5856
www.vaultlogix.com

VERITAS Software
Canadian Head Office
3381 Steeles Av
Toronto, ON M2H 3S7
Canada
416-774-0000
800-327-2232
www.VERITAS.com

SERVICES, Miscellaneous

Actuaries

Aon Risk Services Inc
1330 Post Oak Boulevard
Suite 900
Houston, TX 77056
832-476-6000
www.AON.com

Arthur Andersen LLP
33 W. Monroe
Chicago, IL 60603
312-580-0033
www.arthurandersen.com

Air ambulance evacuation

Critical Care Medflight
P.O. Box 245
Lawrenceville, GA 30046
770-513-9148
800-426-6557
www.GAJET.com

Animal & pet services

ACES - Animal Care Equipment & Services, Inc.
4920-F Fox Street
Denver, CO 80216
303-296-9287
800-338-2237
www.animal-care.com

American Humane
63 Inverness Drive East
Englewood, CO 80112
303-792-9900
www.americanhumane.org

Code 3 Associates
P.O. Box 1128
Erie, CO 80516
303-772-7724
www.code3associates.org

Humane Society of the United States, The
700 Professional Drive
Gaithersburg, MD 20879
301-258-3103
www.hsus.org

Minnesota Animal Disaster Coalition (MN-ADC)
MACA
13416 Xerxes Ave. S.
Burnsville, MN 55337-2140
952-563-4940
www.minnesotaanimalcontrol.org/

Noah's Wish
POB 997
Placerville, CA 95667
530-622-9313
www.noahswish.org

United Animal Nations (UAN)
Emergency Animal Rescue Service (EARS)
P.O. Box 188890
Sacramento, CA 95818
916-429-2457
www.uan.org

Auction firms

BSC America - Atlantic Auctions
P.O. Box 516
Bel Air, MD 21014
410-803-4160
www.ATLANTICAUCTIONS.com

Meyers Auctions & Appraisals Service
Box 221
Arden, MB R0J 0B0
Canada
204-368-2333
204-476-6262
www.meyersauctions.com

Ballast recyclers

ALSO SEE SCRAP FLUORESCENT LAMPS &
BALLASTS - BUYERS IN MISC. SERVICES SECTION

AERC Recycling Solutions
2591 Mitchell Avenue
Allentown, PA 18103
800-554-2372
610-797-7602
www.aercrecycling.com

Northeast Waste Management Officials Association
(NEWMOA)
129 Portland Street
Suite 602
Boston, MA 02114-2014
617-367-8558
www.NEWMOA.org

Bird/pest control

Avian Flyaway
500 Turtle Cove Boulevard
Rockwall, TX 75087
800-888-0165
www.AVIANFLYAWAYINC.com

Pest Control Services Inc.
469 mimosa circle
kennett square, PA 19348
610-284-6249

Charities: donations of surplus equipment accepted

Kirsha Foundation
2815 Van Giesen
Richland, WA 99354
509-942-0443
509-948-3593
www.kirshafoundation.org

Conservation: art, library & museum

American Institute for Conservation of Historic & Artistic Works
1717 K Street NW Suite 200
Washington, DC 20036-5346
202-452-9545
www.AIC-FAIC.org

Art Conservation Services of Sarasota
813 Hudson Ave
Sarasota, FL 34236
941-366-6194
www.ART-CONSERVATION-SARASOTA.com

Artifex Equipment, Inc.
P.O. Box 319
Penngrove, CA 94951
707-664-1672
www.artifexequipment.com

Better Image, The
P.O. Box 48
37 Carpenter Street
Milford, NJ 08848
908-995-2600
www.THEBETTERIMAGE.com

Chicago Conservation Center, Inc.
730 N. Franklin
Suite 701
Chicago, IL 60610
312-944-5401
800-250-6919
www.chicagoconservation.com

Conservation Ctr for Art and Historic Artifacts
264 S 23rd Street
Philadelphia, PA 19103-5530
215-545-0613
www.CCAHA.org

ESIS Inc.
1601 Chestnut Street
Philadelphia, PA 19103
215-640-1324
215-640-1000
www.ESIS.com

Gilman Studios
20 Market Street
P.O. Box 350
Amesbury, MA 01913
978-388-5204
www.gilmanstudios.com

Heritage Preservation
1012 14th st NW
suite 1200
Washington, DC 20005
202-634-1422
www.HERITAGEPRESERVATION.org

Northeast Document Conservation Center
100 Brickstone Square
Andover, MA 01810
978-470-1010
www.nedcc.org

O'Toole-Ewald Art Associates Inc
1133 Broadway
New York, NY 10010
212-989-5151
www.OTOOLE-EWALD.com

Pick Up The Pieces Art Restoration
711 W 17th Street
Suite C12
Costa Mesa, CA 92627
800-934-9278

Susan L. Duhl Art Conservation
206 Marywatersford Road
Bala Cynwyd, PA 19004
610-667-0714
610-563-8876

Construction, emergency

Nationwide Electrical Contractor & Engineering
58 Jennifer Ln
Calumet City, IL 60409
708-829-6512
708-359-4265

Cooling services

Atlas Cold Storage
215 Industrial Park Road NE
Cartersville, GA 30121
770-382-5115
www.atlascold.com

Atlas Cold Storage
2006 Industrial Boulevard
Douglas, GA 31533
912-384-7272
www.atlascold.com

Jaxport Refrigerated Services Inc.
2701 Talleyrand Avenue
Jacksonville, FL 32206
904-786-8038
www.icslogistics.com

Spot Coolers (nationwide service)
444 E Palmetto Park Road
Boca Raton, FL 33432
800-367-8675
www.SPOT-COOLERS.com

Crisis management services

ALSO SEE CRISIS MANAGEMENT IN CONSULTING
SERVICES SECTION, AND PSYCHOLOGICAL
SERVICES SECTION

Crisis Care Network
2855 44th St. SW
Suite 360
Grandville, MI 49418
888-736-0911
www.crisiscare.com

IBM Global Services
10 North Martingale Road
Woodfield Prese
Schaumburg, IL 60173
1-800-IBM-7080
www.ibm.com

KI Canada Ltd.
707 Alness Street #206
Toronto, ON M3J 2H8
Canada
416-857-4464
416-661-1818
www.kicanada.com

URS Corporation
200 Orchard Ridge Dr.
Suite 101
Gaithersburg, MD 20878
301-258-6554
www.urscorp.com

Damage assessment

EGP & Associates Inc.
300 Clay Street
Sutie 600
Oakland, CA 94612
510-446-7722
800-435-8744

EGP & Associates Inc.
1715 Avenida Del Sol
Boca Raton, FL 33432
561-392-0094
800-435-8744

EGP & Associates Inc.
6075 Roswell Road
Suite 210
Atlanta, GA 30328
678-904-8730
800-435-8744

FenceClaim.com
2835 Contra Costa Blvd.
Pleasant Hill, CA 94523
877-693-3623
www.fenceclaim.com

First Response
1919 South Michigan Street
South Bend, IN 46613
574-288-0500
www.firstresponseDRS.com

URS Corporation
200 Orchard Ridge Dr.
Suite 101
Gaithersburg, MD 20878
301-258-6554
www.urscorp.com

Data center operation, outsourced

Alicomp
2 Christie Heights
Leonia, NJ 07605
800-274-5556
www.alicomp.com

Lee Technologies
400 Continental Blvd.
El Segundo, CA 90245
310-426-2590
www.leetechnologies.com

Lee Technologies
1600 Parkwood Cr.
Atlanta, GA 30339
770-427-7178
www.leetechnologies.com

Lee Technologies
P.O. Box 2398
Columbia, MD 21045
443-535-0670
www.leetechnologies.com

Lee Technologies
4510 Cox Road
Glen Allen, VA 23060
804-747-8684
www.leetechnologies.com

Lee Technologies
12150 Monument Dr.
Suite 150
Fairfax, VA 22033
703-968-0300
877-654-9662
www.leetechnologies.com

Roan Solutions, Inc.
143 Pine Street
Belmont, MA 02478
877-774-4647
www.roansolutions.com

Education, training & awareness

ALSO SEE TRAINING & CONFERENCES SECTION

Business Recovery and Continuity Education
P.O. Box 26
Mount Ephraim, NJ 08059
856-635-9770
www.BRACEONLINE.com

Contingency Planning Exchange
11 Hanover Square
Suite 501
New York, NY 10005
212-344-4003
www.CPEWORLD.org

Frontline Corporate Communications Inc.
650 Riverbend Drive
Kitchener, ON N2K 3S2
Canada
888-848-9898
www.fcc.onthefrontlines.com

Mennonite Disaster Service
1018 Main St
Akron, PA 17501
717-859-2210
717-859-4910
www.MDS.MENNONITE.net

MIS Training Institute
498 Concord Street
Framingham, MA 01702-2357
508-879-7999
www.MISTI.com

Natural Haz. Research & Applications Info. Center
University of Colorado
482 UCB
Boulder, CO 80309-0482
303-492-6818

Northwest Weather and Avalanche Center
7600 Sandpoint Way NE
Seattle, WA 98115-6349
206-526-6677
503-808-2400
www.nwac.us

SOLO Wilderness & Emergency Medicine
P.O. Box 3150
621 Tasker Hill Road
Conway, NH 03818-3150
603-447-6711
www.SOLOSCHOOLS.com

Strohl Systems
631 Park Avenue
Kng of Prussa, PA 19406
610-768-4120
800-634-2016
www.strohlsystems.com

URS Corporation
200 Orchard Ridge Dr.
Suite 101
Gaithersburg, MD 20878
301-258-6554
www.urscorp.com

Emergency response logistics

ALSO SEE TRANSPORTATION IN MISC. SERVICES SECTION

FedEx Custom Critical
1475 Boettler Road
Uniontown, OH 44685-9584
800-762-3787
customcritical.fedex.com

Hurricane Watch Net, Inc.
10374-178th Ct. So.
Boca Raton, FL 33498
561-487-9208
www.hwn.org

Ethical hacking

ALSO SEE SECURITY - NETWORK TESTING IN CONSULTING SERVICES SECTION

Digital Defense, Inc.
1711 Citadel Plaza
San Antonio, TX 78209
888-273-1412
210-822-2645
www.digitaldefense.net

Facilities preparation for data processing equipment

Weston Solution Inc.
P.O. Box 2653
West Chester, PA 19380
610-701-3000
www.westonsolution.com

Fleet services, accident related

PHH Vehicle Management Services
940 Ridgebrook Road
Sparks Glenco, MD 21152
800-392-7751

Forensic accountants

American Express Tax & Business Service
2850 Ocean Park Blvd. Suite 240
Santa Monica, CA 90405
818-466-2100
www.americanexpress.com

Carranza Cowheard & Associates
3625 NW 82nd Avenue Suit 306
Doral, FL 33166
305-463-7978
www.CCVCPA.com

Lurie Besikof Lapidus & Company LLP (LBLCO)
2501 Wayzata Blvd
Minneapolis, MN 55405
612-377-4404
www.lblco.com

RGL Forensic Accountants and Consultants
5619 DTC Parkway
Suite 1010
Englewood, CO 80111
888-RGl-4-CPA
303-721-2970
www.rgl.com

Rimkus Consulting Group Inc.
8 E Greenway Plaza
Floor 5
Houston, TX 77046
713-621-3550

Siegel Rich Division-Rothstein, Kass and
Company, D.C.
1350 Avenue of the Americas
Floor 15
New York, NY 10019
212-997-0500
www.rkco.com

Forensic analysts, computer systems

Computer Forensics
1749 Dexter Ave N
Seattle, WA 98109
206-324-6232
www.FORENSICS.com

Electronic Evidence Discovery Inc
Plaza Yarrow Bay Suite 200
Kirkland, WA 98033
206-343-0131
www.EEDINC.com

Price Hollingsworth
2625 American Lane
Elk Grove Vlg, IL 60007
800-568-5865

Schaefer Engineering
23109 55th Avenue W
Mountlake Ter, WA 98043
425-775-5550
800-711-0704
www.forensic-engrs.com

Forensic analysts, fires

BCI Engineers & Scientists Inc
2000 East Edgewood Drive
Suite 215
Lakeland, FL 33803
877-550-4224
863-667-2345
www.bcieng.com

Haag Engineering
2455 McIver Lane
Carrollton, TX 75006
281-313-9700
www.HAAGENGINEERING.com

Hall and Foreman
20950 Warner Center lane
Woodland Hills, CA 91367
818-251-1200
www.hallandfareman.com

Interscience Inc
7705 Ann Ballard Road
Tampa, FL 33634
813-885-4774
www.inerscienceinc.com

MDE Inc.
700 S Industrial Way
Seattle, WA 98108
206-622-2007
www.MDE.com

Packer Engineering Inc
P.O. Box 353
Naperville, IL 60566
630-505-5722
800-323-0114
www.PACKERENG.com

Rimkus Consulting Group Inc.
8 E Greenway Plaza
Floor 5
Houston, TX 77046
713-621-3550

Rudick Forensic Engineering
855 Tod Avenue
Youngstown, OH 44502
800-966-5392

SEA Limited
7349 Worthington Galena Road
Columbus, OH 43085
614-888-4160
800-782-6851
www.sealimited.com

SERVICES

SERVICES

Forensic analysts, structures

Forcon International
1534 Dunwoody Village Parkway
Suite 105
Atlanta, GA 30338
770-390-0980
www.forcon.com

**Rimkus Consulting Group Inc.
8 E Greenway Plaza
Floor 5
Houston, TX 77046
713-621-3550**

Rothfuss Engineering
10610 Iron Bridge Road
Suite 5
Jessup, MD 20794
301-725-6544
www.rothfussengineering.com

**URS Corporation
200 Orchard Ridge Dr.
Suite 101
Gaithersburg, MD 20878
301-258-6554
www.urscorp.com**

Forensic analysts, water damage

**Rimkus Consulting Group Inc.
8 E Greenway Plaza
Floor 5
Houston, TX 77046
713-621-3550**

Forensic engineers

**BCI Engineers & Scientists Inc
2000 East Edgewood Drive
Suite 215
Lakeland, FL 33803
877-550-4224
863-667-2345
www.bcieng.com**

EFI Global (Engineering & Fire Investigations)
2218 Northpark Drive
Kingwood, TX 77339
281-358-4441
888-888-2467
www.EFIGLOBAL.com

Forensic Analysis & Engineering Corp
5301 Capital Boulevard
Suite A
Raleigh, NC 27616-2956
919-872-8788
www.FORENSIC-ANALYSIS.com

Garrett Engineers Inc
P.O. Box 91659
Long Beach, CA 90809
562-308-4150
800-229-3647
www.garrett-engineers.com

Halliwell Engineering Associates Inc.
865 Waterman Avenue
East Providence, RI 02914
401-438-5020
800-394-9680
www.HEAINC.com

Investigative Engineers Association Inc.
2455 E. Sunrise Blvd.
Suite 1201
Ft. Lauderdale, FL 33304
954-537-5556
800-523-3680
www.CLAIMSSUPPORT.com

Riddick Engineering Corp.
4600 West Markham
Little Rock, AR 72205
501-666-7300

**Rimkus Consulting Group Inc.
8 E Greenway Plaza
Floor 5
Houston, TX 77046
713-621-3550**

Robson Lapina
354 North Prince Street
Lancaster, PA 17603
800-813-6736

SEA Ltd.
955 Hurricane Shoals Road
Suite 102
Atlanta, GA 30043
800-782-6851
www.SEAlimited.com

System Engineering & Laboratories
12785 State Highway 64 E
Tyler, TX 75707-5333
903-566-1980
www.SEALCORP.com

Tighe & Bond
53 Southampton Road
Westfield, MA 01085
413-562-1600
www.TIGHEBOND.com

**URS Corporation
200 Orchard Ridge Dr.
Suite 101
Gaithersburg, MD 20878
301-258-6554
www.urscorp.com**

Western Engineering & Research Corp
2175 S Jasmine Street
Suite 119
Denver, CO 80222
303-757-4000
www.WERC.com

Government services—U.S.
(see Canadian services, next section)

Alabama Emergency Management Agency
Post Office Drawer 2160
Clanton, AL 35046-2160
205-280-2200
www.aaem.us/links.htm

Alaska Dept. of Military and Veteran Affairs
P.O. Box 5750
Ft Richardson-Camp Denali, AK 99505-5750
907-428-7000

Alaska Division of Emergency Services
P.O. Box 5750
Fort Richardson, AK 99505-5750
907-428-7000
www.ak-prepared.com

Alaska State Emergency Response Commission
P.O. Box 5750
Fort Richardson, AK 99505-5750
907-428-7000
www.ak-prepared.com/serc

Arizona Division of Emergency Management
5636 E. McDowell Road
Phoenix, AZ 85008
602-244-0504
800-411-2336
www.dem.state.az.us

Arkansas Department of Emergency Management
P.O. Box 758
Conway, AR 72033-0758
501-730-9750
www.adem.state.ar.us

Atlanta-Fulton County Emergency Management Agency
130 Peachtree Street
Suite G-157
Atlanta, GA 30303
404-730-5600
www.AFCEMA.net

California Governor's Office of Emergency Services
P.O Box 419047
Rancho Cordova, CA 95741-9047
916-845-8510
www.oes.ca.gov/

City of Detroit Emergency Management Division
250 W Larned St.
Detroit, MI 48226
313-596-5196
www.WAYNECOUNTY.com/emd/default.html

City of Houston Emergency Management
P.O. Box 1562
Houston, TX 77251-1562
713-884-4500
www.CI.HOUSTON.TX.us/eom/hcra.html

Colorado Division of Emergency Management
15075 South Golden Road
Golden, CO 80401-3979
303-273-1622
www.dola.state.co.us/oem/oemindex.htm

Connecticut Office of Emergency Management
Military Department
360 Broad Street
Hartford, CT 06105
860-566-3180
www.mil.state.ct.us/oem.htm

County of Dade Emergency Management
9300 NW 36th Street
Miami, FL 33178
305-468-5400
www.CO.MIAMI-DADE.FL.us/oem/

Delaware Emergency Management Agency
State Emergency Operations Center
165 Brick Store Landing Rd
Smyrna, DE
302-659-3362

Denver Office of Emergency Mgmt
1437 Bannock St.
Denver, CO 80202
720-865-7600
www.DENVERGOV.org/oem

Department of Health and Human Services
Asst. Sec. for Pub. Hlth Emergency Preparedness
200 Independence Avenue SW
Washington, DC 20201
202-205-1300

District of Columbia Emergency Management Agency
2000 14th Street, NW
8th Floor
Washington, D.C. 20009
202-727-2775
www.mema.state.md.us

Emergency Management Institute FEMA
16825 S Seton Avenue
Emmitsburg, MD 21727-8920
301-447-1000
800-238-3358
www.FEMA.gov

FEMA - Caribbean Area Division
New San Juan Building
159 Calle Chardon, 5th Fl
Hato, PR 00918
787-296-3514

EVERY BUSINESS SHOULD HAVE A PLAN.

"It caused destruction to everything in its path. Houses, buildings. Some people lost everything.

But we were prepared for an emergency like that. We knew how to reach our employees, knew what to do. We had emergency supplies on hand. And as a company, we made it through Hurricane Charley because we had a plan."

CHARLES G. BROWN, President & CEO
Charlotte State Bank, Port Charlotte, FL

Whether it's a hurricane, terrorist attack or other disaster, every business needs an emergency plan. A plan can save your entire business, including company assets and most importantly, the lives of your employees – at little or no cost to your company. You can't control what happens. But you can be prepared. Visit www.ready.gov for practical steps you can take now to give your company a better chance of survival.

FEMA - Connecticut
360 Broad Street
Office of Emergency Management
Hartford, CT 06105
860-566-3180
www.ct.gov/oem/site/default.asp

FEMA - Pacific Area Office
546 Bonnie Loop
Ft. Shafter, HI 96858-5000
808-851-7900
http://www.fema.gov/regions/ix/about.shtm

FEMA Region 1
99 High Street
6th Floor
Boston, MA 02110
617-956-7506

FEMA Region II
26 Federal Plaza, Suite 1307
New York, NY 10278-0001
212-680-3600

FEMA Region III
615 Chestnut Street
Philadelphia, PA 19106
215-931-5608

FEMA Region IV
3003 Chamblee Tucker Road
Atlanta, GA 30341
770-220-5200
www.fema.gov/regions/iv/about.shtm

FEMA Region IX
1111 Broadway, Suite 1200
Oakland, CA 94607
510-627-7100

FEMA Region V
6th Floor
536 South Clark St.
Chicago, IL 60605
312-408-5504
www.fema.gov/regions/v/dir.shtm

FEMA Region VI
800 N Loop 288
Denton, TX 76209
940-898-5399
www.fema.gov/regions/vi/about.shtm

FEMA REGION VII (Kansas City
2323 Grand Boulevard
Suite 900
Kansas City, MO 64108-2670
816-283-7061
www.fema.gov/regions/vii/about.shtm

FEMA, Honolulu
Bldg. T-112 - M.S. 120
Fort Shafter
Honolulu, HI 96817-2115
808-851-7900

FEMA, Region VIII (CO, MO, ND, WY)
P.O. Box 25267
Building 710
Denver, CO 80225-0267
303-235-4800
www.fema.gov/regions/viii/env/web.shtm

FEMA, Region X
Federal Regional Center
130 228th Street, SW
Bothell, WA 98021-9796
425-487-4600
www.fema.gov/region/x/

Florida Division of Emergency Management
2555 Shumard Oak Blvd
Tallahassee, FL 32399-2100
850-413-9900
850-413-9969
www.floridadisaster.org

Georgia Emergency Management Agency
P. O. Box 18055
Atlanta, GA 30316-0055
404-635-7001

Government Emergency Telecommunications Service
15000 Conference Center Drive
Chantilly, VA 20151
866-NCS-CALL
703-676-2255
gets.ncs.gov

Governor's Office of Emergency Management
State Office Park South
107 Pleasant Street
Concord, NH 03301
603-271-2231
www.nhoem.state.nh.us

Hawaii State Civil Defense
3949 Diamond Head Road
Honolulu, HI 96816
808-733-4300
www.scd.state.hi.us

Idaho Bureau of Disaster Services
4040 Guard Street
Building 600
Boise, ID 83705-5004
208-334-3460
208-422-5268
www2.state.id.us/bds

Illinois Emergency Management Agency
110 East Adams St.
Springfield, IL 46204
217-782-2700
www.state.il.us/iema

Indiana State Emergency Management Agency
302 West Washington St.
Room E208
Indianapolis, IN 46204
317-232-3980
800-669-7362
www.in.gov/sema

Iowa Homeland Security & Emergency Management Division
Department of Public Defense
Hoover Office Building
Des Moines, IA 50319
515-281-3231
www.iowahomelandsecurity.org/

Kansas Division of Emergency Management
2800 S.W. Topeka Boulevard
Topeka, KA 66611-1287
785-274-1401

Kentucky Emergency Management Agency
100 Minuteman Pkwy
Bldg. 100
Frankfort, KY 40601-6168
502-607-1682
kyem.dma.state.ky.us

Los Angeles Emergency Preparedness Department
200 N. Spring Street
Room 1533
Los Angeles, CA 90012
213-978-2222

Louisiana Office of Emergency Preparedness
P.O. Box 44217
P.O. Box 44217, LA 70804
225-342-5470
www.loep.state.la.u

Maricopa County Emergency Management
2035 North 52nd Street
Phoenix, AZ 85008-3403
602-273-1411
www.MARICOPA.gov/emerg_mgt/

Maryland Emergency Management Agency
Camp Fretterd Military Reservation
5401 Rue Saint Lo Drive
Reistertown, MD 21136
410-517-3600
www.mema.state.md.us/

Massachusetts Emergency Management Agency - MEMA
400 Worcester Rd.
Framingham, MA 01702
508-820-2010

Medical Reserve Corp.
U.S. Dept. of Health & Human Services
5600 Fishers Lane, Room 18-66
Rockville, MD 20857
301-443-4951

MEMA - Maine Emergency Management Agency
State Office Building, Station 72
Augusta, ME 04333
207-626-4503

Michigan Division of Emergency Management
4000 Collins Road
P.O. Box 30636
Lansing, MI 48909-8136
517-333-5042
http://www.michigan.gov/msp/

Michigan State Police, Emergency Mgmt. Div.
714 S. Harrison Road
East Lansing, MI 48823
517-332-2521
http://www.michigan.gov/msp

Minnesota Department of Public Safety
Division of Emergency Management
444 Cedar St., Suite 223
St. Paul, MA 55101
651-296-0450
www.hsem.state.mn.us

Minnesota Division of Emergency Management
Department of Public Safety
444 Cedar Street, Suite 223
St. Paul, MN 55101-6223
651-296-2233
www.dps.state.mn.us/emermgt/

Mississippi Emergency Management Agency
P. O. Box 4501
Jackson, MS 39296-4501
601-960-9000

Missouri State Emergency Management Agency
P.O. Box 116
Jefferson City, MO 65102
573-526-9101
www.sema.state.mo.us/semapage.htm

Montana Disaster and Emergency Services Division
P.O. Box 4789
1900 Williams Street
Helena, MT 59604-4789
406-841-3911
www.discoveringmontana.com/dma/des

Nassau County HazMat/WMD Team
Office of Nassau Fire Marshal
899 Jerusalem Avenue, P.O. Box 128
Uniondale, NY 11553
516-572-1092
516-572-1117

National Disaster Medical System Section
Department of Homeland Security
500 C Street S.W., Suite 713
Washington, DC 20472
800-USA-NDMS (800-872-6367)
ndms.dhhs.gov

National Earthquake Information Center
United States Geological Survey
Box 25046, DFC, MS 966
Denver, CO 80225-0046
303-273-8500
303-273-8516
neic.usgs.gov

National Insitute for Occupational Safety and Health
200 Independence Ave, SW
Hubert H. Humphery Bldg 715H
Washington, DC 20201
202-260-9727
www.cdc.gov/niosh

Nebraska Emergency Management Agency
1300 Military Road
Lincoln, NE 68508-1090
402-471-7430
402-471-7421
www.nebema.org/

Nevada Division of Emergency Mgmt.
2525 South Carson Street
Carson City, NV 89711
775-687-4240
http://dem.state.nv.us/

New Jersey Office of Emergency Management
P.O. Box 7068 Old River Road
West Trenton, NJ 08628-0068

New Mexico Office of Emergency Management
13 Bataan Boulevard
P.O. Box 1628
Santa Fe, NM 87505
505-476-9606
505-476-9635
www.dps.nm.org/emergency/index.htm

New York State Emergency Management Office
1220 Washington Avenue
Building 22, Suite 101
Albany, NY 12226-2251
518-457-2222
www.nysemo.state.ny.us

North Carolina Emergency Management Agency
4713 Mail Service Center
116 W Jones St
Raleigh, NC 27603
919-733-3867
www.dem.dcc.state.nc.us

North Dakota Division of Emergency Management
P.O. Box 5511
Bismarck, ND 58506
701-328-8100
www.state.nd.us/dem/

Office of Civil Emergency Management
Will Rogers Sequoia Tunnel
2401 N Lincoln
Oklahoma City, OK 73152
405-521-2481
www.odcem.state.ok.us/

Office of Emergency Management and Communications
1411 W. Madison Street
Chicago, IL 60607
312-746-9111
www.CITYOFCHICAGO.org

Office of Food Security and Emergency Preparedness
USDA-Food Safety and Inspection Service
901 D St., SW, 3rd Floor, Room 414
Washington, DC 20024
202-690-6514
www.fsis.usda.gov

Office of Security and Emergency Management
509 Main Street
Room 305
Dallas, TX 75202-3545
214-653-7972
www.DALLASCOUNTY.org

Ohio Emergency Management Agency
2855 West Dublin-Granville Rd.
Columbus, OH 43235
614-889-7150
ema.ohio.gov

Okfuskee County Sheriff Dept.
209 N 3rd St
County Courthouse
Okemah, OK 74859
918-623-1122
918-623-0481

Oregon Emergency Management
3225 State Street
P.O. Box 14370
Salem, OR 97309-5062
503-378-2911
800-452-0311
www.osp.state.or.us/oem/

Pacific Disaster Center
590 Lipoa Parkway
Suite #259
Kilhei, HI 96753
808-891-0525
888-808-6688
www.pdc.org

Pennsylvania Emergency Management Agency
2605 Interstate Drive
Harrisburg, PA 17110-9364
717-651-2001
www.pema.state.pa.us

Puerto Rico Emergency Management Agency
Office of the Governor
P.O. Box 966597
San Juan, PR 00906-6597
787-724-0124
http://www.fema.gov/fema/statedr.shtm#p

Rhode Island Emergency Management Agency
645 New London Avenue
Cranston, RI 02920
401-946-9996
www.riema.ri.gov

San Antonio Emergency Mgmt
203 W. Nueva Street
Suite 200
San Antonio, TX 78201-4505
210-335-0300

San Diego Office of Disaster Preparedness
5555 Overland Ave.
Building 19
San Diego, CA 92123
858-565-3490
www.CO.SAN-DIEGO.CA.us

Seattle Emergency Management
2320 Fourth Avenue
Seattle, WA 98121
206-233-5089
www.CITYOFSEATTLE.net/emergency_mgt/

South Carolina Emergency Management Agency
1100 Fish Hatchery Road
West Columbia, SC 29172
803-737-8500

South Dakota Division of Emergency Management
118 West Capitol
Pierre, SD 57501
605-773-3231
www.state.sd.us/dps/sddem/home.htm

Tennessee Emergency Management Agency
3041 Sidco Drive
Nashville, TN 37204-1502
615-741-9303
www.tnema.org/Misc/TN_ES_List.htm

Texas Division of Emergency Management
P.O. Box 4087
Austin, TX 78773-0001
512-424-2138
www.txdps.state.tx.us/dem/

U. S. Small Business Association
130 South Elmwood Avenue
Buffalo, NY 14202
800-659-2955
716-843 - 4100
www.sba.gov/disasterarea1/

U.S. Geological Survey
119 National Center
Reston, VA 20192
703-648-4447
www.usgs.gov

U.S. Small Business Administration
Disaster Area 4 Office
P.O. Box 419004
Sacramento, CA 95841-9004
800-488-5323
www.SBA.gov/disasterarea4

U.S. Small Business Administration
Disaster Area 2
1 Baltimore Pl., Suite 300
Atlanta, GA 30308
800-359-2227
www.SBA.gov/disasterarea2

U.S. Small Business Administration
Disaster Area 1 Office
130 South Elmwood Avenue
Buffalo, NY 14202
800-659-2955
716-843-4100
www.sba.gov/disasterarea1

U.S. Small Business Administration
Disaster Area 3 Office
14925 Kingsport Road
Ft. Worth, TX 76155-2243
800-366-6303
www.SBA.gov/disasterarea3

US Department of Homeland Security
Washington, DC 20528
202-282-8000
202-282-8495
www.dhs.gov

US, EPA: Chemical Emergency Preparedness and Prevention Office
Ariel Rios Federal Building (5104A)
1200 Pennsylvaina Avenue, NW
Washington, DC 02460
1-800-424-9346
1-703- 412-9810
www.epa.gov/swercepp/

Utah Division of Emergency Services and Homeland Security
1110 State Office Building
P.O. Box 141710
Salt Lake City, UT 84114-1710
801-538-3400
www.des.utah.gov

Vermont Division of Emergency Management
Department of Public Safety
103 S. Main Street
Waterbury, VT 05671
802-244-8721
800-347-0488

Virgin Islands Emergency Management Agency
#2C Estate Contant
St. Thomas, USVI 00820
340-774-2244

Virginia Department of Emergency Management
10501 Trade Court
Richmond, VA 23236-3713
804-897-6510
804-674-2400
www.vdem.state.va.us

Washington Emergency Management Division
Washington State Military Department
Bldg 20, MS: TA-20
Camp Murray, WA 98430-5122
800-258-5990
800-562-6108
http://access.wa.gov/emergency/index.aspx

West Virginia Office of Emergency Services
1900 Kanawha Boulevard East
Building 1, Room EB-80
Charleston, WV 25305-0360
304-558-5380
www.state.wv.us/wvoes

Wisconsin Emergency Management
P.O. Box 7865
2400 Wright Street
Madison, WI
608-242-3232

Wyoming Office of Homeland Security, Emerg. Mgmt.
122 West 25th Street
Herschler Bldg, 1st Floor East
Cheyenne, WY 82002
307-777-4663
http://wyohomelandsecurity.state.wy.us/

Government services, Canadian

Canadian Forces Disaster Assistance Response Team
(DART)
Major-General George R. Pearkes Building
101 Colonel By Drive
Ottawa, ON K1A 0K2
Canada
613-995-2534

Canada Public Safety, Security and Emerg. Prep.
Information and Resources
Avail online, free
www.safecanada.ca/menu_e.asp

Canadian Red Cross-Atlantic Zone
70 Lansdowne Avenue
P.O. Box 39
Saint John, NB E2L 3X3
Canada
506-674-6200

Canadian Red Cross-National Office
170 Metcalfe Street
Suite 300
Ottawa, ON K2P 2P2
Canada
613-740-1900

Canadian Red Cross-Ontario Zone
5700 Cancross Court
Mississauga, ON L5R 3E9
Canada
905-890-1000

Canadian Red Cross-Quebec Zone
6, place du Commerce
lle-des-Soeurs Verdun, QC H3E 1P4
Canada
514-362-2930

Canadian Red Cross-Western Zone
100-1305 11 Avenue SW
Calgary, AB T3C 3P6
Canada
403-205-3448

Critical Infrastructure Protection & Emergncy Prep
British Columbia
P.O. Box 10,000
Victoria, BC V8W 3A5
Canada
250-363-3621
www.OCIPEP.GC.ca/home/index_e.asp

Critical Infrastructure Protection & Emergncy Prep
122 Bank Street
Ottawa, ON K1A 0W6
Canada
613-991-7077
www.OCIPEP-BPIEPC.GC.ca

Disaster Services - Alberta Municipal Services
16D Commerce Place
10155 - 102nd Street
Edmonton, AB T5J 4L4
Canada
780-422-9000
www.GOV.AB.ca/ma/ema

Emergency Management Ontario (EMO)
25 Grosvenor Street
Floor 18
Toronto, ON M7A 1Y6
Canada
416-326-5010
416-314-3723
http://www.mpss.jus.gov.on.ca

Emergency Measures- Ontario
25 Grosvenor Street
19th Floor
Toronto, ON M7A 1Y6
Canada
416-314-3723
www.MPSS.JUS.GOV.ON.ca

Emergency Measures Org- New Brunswick
P.O. Box 6000
65 Brunswick St.
Fredericton, NB E3B 5H1
Canada
506-453-2133
800-561-4034
www.GNB.ca/cnb/emo-omu/index-e.asp

Emergency Measures Org- Newfoundland
50 Parade St. 2nd Floor
P.O. Box 8700
St. John's, NF A1B 4J6
Canada
709-729-3703
www.GOV.NF.ca/mpa/emo.html

Emergency Measures Org- Nova Scotia
P.O. Box 2581
21 Mount Hope Avenue, 2nd Floor
Halifax, NS B3J 3N5
Canada
902-424-5620
www.GOV.NS.ca/emo

Emergency Measures Org- Prince Edward Island
P.O. Box 2063
120 Harbour Drive
Summerside, PE C1N 5L2
Canada
902-888-8050
www.GOV.PE.ca/commcul/emo/index.php3

SERVICES

SERVICES

Newfoundland & Labrador
Emergency Measures Organization
P.O. Box 8700, 50 Parade St, 2nd Fl
St. John's, NF A1B 4J6
Canada
613-991-7077
613-996-0995

Nunavut Emergency Management
P.O. Box 1000
Station 700
Iqaluit, NT X0A 0H0
Canada
867-975-5317
867-979-4221
www.NSS.GC.ca

Office of Public Health Security
Centre for Emergency Preparedness and Response
100 Colonnade Road, PL6201A
Ottawa, K1A 0K9
Canada
613 954 8498

Prince Edward Island
Emergency Measures Organization
P.O. Box 2063, 120 Harbour Drive
Summerside, PE C1N 5L2
902-888-8050
www.gov.pe.ca/commcul/emo/index.php3

Provincial Emergency Program-British Columbia
P.O. Box 9201
Stn. Prov. Govt.
Victoria, BC V8W 9J1
Canada
250-952-4913
www.PEP.BC.ca

Public Safety & Emergency Prep.(PSEPC)-Canada
Communications Branch
340 Laurier Avenue West
Ottawa, ON K1A 0P8
Canada
613-991-7000
613-944-4875
www.PSEPC-SPPCC.GC.ca

Quebec Ministère de la Sécurité publique
2525, boul. Laurier, 6 eétage
Sainte-Foy, QC G1V 2L2
Canada
866-776-8345
418 646-5611
www.msp.gouv.qc.ca/secivile/index_en.asp

Saskatchewan Emergency Planning
1855 Victoria Ave.
Room 200
Regina, SK S4P 3V7
Canada
306-787-9563
www.CPS.GOV.SK.ca/safety/emergency/default.shtml

Yukon Emergency Measures Branch
Dept. of Community and Transportation Srvcs.
P.O. Box 2703
Whitehorse, YK Y1A 2C6
Canada
867-667-5220
800-661-0408 (in Yukon)
www.GOV.YK.ca/depts/community/emo

Government services, poison control

Alabama Poison Center
2503 Phoenix Drive
Tuscaloosa, AL 35405
800-222-1222

Animal Poison Control Center
ASPCA
1717 South Philo Road
Urbana, Il 61802
888-426-4435

Arizona Poison & Drug Info Center
1501 North Campbell Avenue
Tucson, AZ 85724
800-222-1222

Arkansas Poison & Drug Information Center
4301 W. Markham
Little Rock, AR 72205
800-222-1222

California Poison Control System
UC Davis Medical Center
2315 Stockton Blvd
Sacramento, CA 95817
800-22-1222

Carolinas Poison Center
Carolinas Medical Center
5000 Airport Center Parkway
Charlotte, NC 28208
800-222-1222

Central New York Poison Center
750 East Adams Street
Syracuse, NY 13210
800-222-1222

Central Ohio Poison Center
700 Children's Drive
Columbus, OH 43205
800-222-1222

Centre antipoison-Québec
Le Centre Hospitalier de l'Université Laval
2705 boul. Laurier
Sainte-Foy, PQ G1V 4G2
Canada
800-463-5060
418-656-8090

Children's Hospital of Wisconsin Poison Center
P.O. Box 1997
Mail Station 677A
Milwaukee, WI 53201
800-222-1222

Connecticut Poison Control Center
263 Farmington Avenue
Farmington, CT 06030
800-222-1222

Emergency Department-Northwest Territories
Stanton Yellowknife Hospital
P.O. Box 10
Yellowknife, NT X1A 2N1
Canada
867-669-4100

Emergency Measures Org- Manitoba
405 Broadway Ave.
Room 1525
Winnipeg, MB R3C 3L6
Canada
204-945-4772
888-826-8298
www.GOV.MB.ca/gs/memo/index.html

Florida Poison Information Center - Miami
P.O. Box 016960 (R-131)
Miami, FL 33101
800-222-1222

Georgia Poison Center
80 Jesse Hill Jr. Drive, SE
P.O. Box 26066
Atlanta, GA 30335
800-222-1222

GNT Emergency Measures-Northwest Territories
600 Northwest Tower
5201 - 50th Avenue
Yellowknife, NT X1A 3S9
Canada
867-920-6133
www.GOV.NT.ca

Hennepin Regional Poison Center
Hennepin County Medical Center
701 Park Avenue
Minneapolis, MN 55415
800-222-1222

Illinois Poison Center
222 S Riverside Plaza
Chicago, Il 60606
800-222-1222

Indiana Poison Center
I-65 at 21st Street
Indianapolis, IN 46206
800-222-1222

Iowa Statewide Poison Control Center
2910 Hamilton Boulevard Lower A
Sioux City, IA 51104
800-222-1222

Kentucky Regional Poison Center
234 East Gray Street
Lousiville, KY 40202
800-222-1222

Louisiana Drug and Poison Information Center
University of Louisiana at Monroe
College of Pharmacy
Monroe, LA 71209
800-222-1222

Maryland Poison Control
University of MD at Baltimore
20 North Pine Street, PH 772
Baltimore, MD 21201
800-222-1222

Michigan Regional Poison Control Center
4160 John R Harper Professional Office Bldg
Detroit, MI 48201
800-222-1222

Mid-America Poison Control Center
3901 Rainbow Blvd.
Kansas City, KS 66160
800-222-1222

Middle Tennessee Poison Center
501 Oxford House
1161 21st Avenue South
Nashville, TN 37232
800-222-1222

Mississippi Regional Poison Control Center
University of Mississippi Medical Center
2500 N State Street
Jackson, MS 39216
800-222-1222

Missouri Regional Poison Center
7980 Clayton Rd., Suite 200
St. Louis, MO 63117
800-222-1222

National Capital Poison Center
3201 New Mexico Avenue, NW
Washington, DC 20016
800-222-1222

Nebraska Regional Poison Center
8200 Dodge Street
Omaha, NE 68114
800-222-1222

New Hampshire Poison Information Center
Dartmouth-Hitchcock Medical Center
One Medical Center Drive
Lebanon, NH 03756
800-222-1222

New Jersey Poison Info & Education System
Univ of Medicine & Dentistry at NJ
65 Bergen Street
Newark, NJ 07107
800-222-1222

SERVICES

New Mexico Poison & Drug Info Center
University of New Mexico
Albuquerque, NM 87131
800-222-1222

New York City Poison Control Center
NYC Bureau of Labs
455 First Avenue
New York, NY 10016
800-222-1222

North Texas Poison Center
Parkland Memorial Hospital
5201 Harry Hines Blvd.
Dallas, TX 75235
800-222-1222

Northern New England Poison Center
22 Bramhall Street
Portland, ME 04102
800-222-1222
207-871-2879

Oklahoma Poison Control Center
Children's Hospital at OU Medical Center
940 N.E. 13th Street
Oklahoma City, OK 73104
800-222-1222

Oregon Poison Center
Oregon Health Services University
3181 SW Sam Jackson Park Road, CB550
Portland, OR 97201
800-222-1222

Palmetto Poison Center
College of Pharmacy
University of South Carolina
Columbia, SC 29208
800-222-1222

Poison and Drug Information Centre-B.C.
St. Paul's Hospital
1081 Burrand Street
Vancouver, BC V6Z 1Y6
Canada
800-567-8911
604-682-5050

Poison and Drug Information Services-Calgary
Foothills General Hospital
1403 - 29th St. N.W.
Calgary, AB T2N 2T9
Canada
800-332-1414
403-670-1414

Poison Control Centre
The Moncton Hospital
135 McBeath Avenue
Moncton, NB E1C 6Z8
Canada
506-857-5555
506-857-5353

Poison Control Centre-Nova Scotia
The Izaak Walton Killam Children's Hospital
P.O. Box 3070
Halifax, NS B3J 3G9
Canada
800-565-8161
902-428-3213

Poison Control Centre-Ontario
The Hospital for Sick Children
555 University Avenue
Toronto, ON M5G 1X8
Canada
416-813-5900
800-268-9017 (Ontario only)

Poison Emergency Department-Saskatchewan
Regina General Hospital
1440 14th Ave.
Regina, SK S4P 0W5
800-667-4545
306-359-4545

Poison Emergency Department-Yukon Territory
Whitehorse General Hospital
5 Hospital Road
Whitehorse, YT Y1A 3H7
Canada
403-667-8726

Provincial Poison Control Centre-Newfoundland
The Dr. Charles A. Janeway Child Health Center
710 Janeway Place
St. John's, NF A1A 1R8
Canada
709-722-1110

Provincial Poison Information Centre-Manitoba
Children's Hospital Health Sciences Centre
840 Sherbrook Street
Winnipeg, MB R3A 1S1
Canada
204-787-2591
204-787-2444

Puerto Rico Poison Center
Calle San Jorge #252
Santurce, PR 00912
800-222-1222

Regional Cntr for Poison Control & Prevention for
Massachusetts and Rhode Island
300 Longwood Avenue
Boston, MA 02115
800-222-1222

Rocky Mountain Poison & Drug Center
777 Bannock Street
Denver, CO 80204
800-222-1222

The Poison Control Center
Children's Hospital of Philadelphia
34th & Civic Center Blvd
Philadelphia, PA 19104
800-222-1222

Utah Poison Control
585 Komas Drive
Suite 200
Salt Lake City, UT 84108
800-222-1222

Virginia Poison Center
Medical College of Virginia Hospitals
P.O. Box 980522
Richmond, VA 23298
800-222-1222

Washington Poison Center
155 NE 100th Street
Seattle, WA 98125
800-222-1222

West Virginia Poison Center
3110 MacCorkle Ave, S.E.
Charleston, WV 25304
800-222-1222

Guard services

All State Guard Service Inc
P.O Box 7449
Houston, TX 77248-7449
713-526-7171
www.allstateguard.com

Alliance Detective & Security Service Inc
930 Broadway
Everett, MA 02149
617-387-1261
800-287-1261

Allied Security
147 E 2nd Street
Mineola, NY 11501
516-877-0500
800-645-6366
www.DALESECURITY.com

Chamberlain Paul International
9454 Wilshire Boulevard
Beverly Hills, CA 90212
310-276-2601
800-227-4421

Corporate Protective Solutions
409-1500 Hornby St
Vancouver, BC V6Z 2R1
Canada
604-915-7538
866-824-9025
www.corpprotect.com

Corporate Security Service Inc
5 3rd Street
San Francisco, CA 94103
415-543-3460
www.CSSSECURITY.com

Elite Protective Services
255 Commandants Way
Chelsea, MA 02150
617-739-0100
www.ELITEPROTECTIVE.com

Executive Security
2 Henry Adams Street
San Francisco, CA 94103
415-626-1011

Fort Knox Protection Inc
111 Executive Way
DeSoto, TX 75115
972-298-6991

Guardsmark llc
22 S 2nd Street
Memphis, TN 38103
901-522-6000
800-238-5878
www.GUARDSMARK.com

Industrial Patrol Service
1900 N Austin Avenue
Chicago, IL 60639
773-235-2181

Initial Security
265 S Anita Drive
Orange, CA 92868
714-464-4005
www.INITIALSECURITY.com

Initial Security
3355 Cherry Ridge Street
Suite 200
San Antonio, TX 78230-4818
210-349-6321
800-683-7771
www.INITIALSECURITY.com

Integrity International Security Services
P.O. BOX 274
Clarksville, TN 37041
931-647-5384
www.isssecurity.com

Intercon Security
40 Sheppard Ave West
Toronto, ON M2N 6K9
Canada
416-229-6811
www.intercon.com

Midwest Security Agency
235 E 35th Street
Chicago, IL 60616
312-842-7033

Murray Guard Inc
58 Murray Guard Drive
Jackson, TN 38305
731-668-3400
www.MurrayGuard.com

N. Shore Protection
25 Waverly Street
Stoneham, MA 02180-1614
781-279-0127
800-750-0127
www.northshoreprotection.com

New Orleans Private Patrol Service Inc
1661 Canal Street
New Orleans, LA 70112
504-525-7115

Publicover Security Service
P.O. Box 149
Arlington, MA 02476
781-643-6673

Securitas
4330 Park Terrace Drive
Westlake Vlg, CA 91361
818-706-6800
www.SECURITASINC.com

Securitas
1 Harborside Drive
Boston, MA 02128
617-568-8700
www.securitasinc.com

Securitas Security Services USA Inc.
500 Main Street
Orange, CA 92868
714-541-4277
www.SECURITASINC.com

Securitas Security Services USA Inc.
400 Chastain Center Boulevard NW
Suite 410
Kennesaw, GA 30144
770-426-5262
www.SECURITASINC.com

Securitas Security Services USA Inc.
9265 Counselors Row
Suite 106
Indianapolis, IN 46240
317-569-1149
www.SECURITASINC.com

Securitas Security Services USA Inc.
2 Campus Drive
Parsippany, NJ 07054
973-397-2276
www.SECURITASINC.com

Securitas Security Services USA Inc.
3 Parkway Center
Suite G 5
Pittsburgh, PA 15220
412-919-0146
www.SECURITASINC.com

Securitas Security Services USA Inc.
16801 Greenspoint Park Drive
Suite 100
Houston, TX 77060
281-875-2237
www.SECURITASINC.com

SilverSEAL Corporation
45 John Street
Suite 800
New York, NY 10038
212-732-1897
888-542-9155
www.SilverSEAL.net

Special Response Corp.
10612 Beaver Dam Road
Hunt Valley, MD 21030
410-494-1900
www.specialresponse.com

The Officers Group
270 N. Canon Drive #1225
Beverly Hills, CA 90210
310-470-6802
800-407-0578
www.theofficersgroup.com

U S Security
5301 TACONY Street
Philadelphia, PA 19137
215-535-4782

Wackenhut Corp The
4200 Wackenhut Drive
Palm Beach Gardens, FL 33410
561-622-5656
www.WACKENHUT.com

Heating

Foley Rents
833 Centennial Ave
Piscataway, NJ 08855
732-885-5555
www.Foleyinc.com

Housing services

ALSO SEE HOUSING, TEMPORARY IN MOBILE BUILDINGS SECTION

Marriott Execustay Insurance Housing Solutions
Nationwide Service
1020 Serpentine Lane
Pleasanton, CA 94566
800-990-9292
www.marriottinsurancehousing.com

Hydraulic hose repair

Pirtek-Clearwater
10780 47th St. North
Unit A
Clearwater, FL 33762
727-573-8522
727-573-8513
www.PIRTEKUSA.com

Insurance adjusters, public

Adjusters International
17130 Dallas Parkway
Suite 210
Dallas, TX 75248
800-992-7771
www.ai-texas.com

Alex N. Sill Company
6000 Lombardo Center
Suite 600
Cleveland, OH 44131-2579
216-524-9999
www.SILL.com

Allmark Services, Inc.
10805 Sunset Office Drive
Suite 304
St. Louis, MO 63127
314-966-8976
888-672-8494
www.allmarkasi.com

Berman Adjusters
1155 Walnut Street
Newton, MA 02461
617-964-0000
www.bermanadjusters.com

Carolina Claims Service
111 Executive Center Drive
Suite 250
Columbia, SC 29210
803-731-4005
www.carolinaclaims.com

Colonial Adjustment, Inc.
P.O. Box 9528
Westbrook, ME 04098-5028
207-797-9036
www.colonialadj.com

Cox Pierce & Associates Inc
1315 Deer Park Boulevard
Omaha, NE 68108
402-734-0754
www.COX-PIERCE.com

Crawford & CO Risk Management Services
5620 Glenridge Dr NE
Atlanta, GA 30342
404-256-0830
www.crawfordandcompany.com

Crawford & CO Risk Mgmt. Svc.
P.O.270427
Fort Collins, CO 80527
970-225-9733

Crocker Claims Service
4521 Leavenworth Street
Suite 30
Omaha, NE 68106
402-558-4447
www.CROCKERCLAIMS.com

Dallmer Adjusters
1023 Bristol Pke
Bensalem, PA 19020
215-245-4504
877-885-1751

Federated Adjustment Co Inc
1 Linden Place
Great Neck, NY 11021
516-466-6900

Frontier Adjusters Inc
45 E Monterey Way
Phoenix, AZ 85012
800-528-1187
www.FRONTIERADJUSTERS.com

GAB Robins N. America
7600 E Eastman Avenue
Denver, CO 80231
303-831-7222
800-747-7222
www.GABROBINSNA.com

GAB Robins N. America
4080 Woodcock Drive
Jacksonville, FL 32207
904-396-2841
www.GABROBINSNA.com

GAB Robins N. America
4360 Chamblee Dunwoody Road
Atlanta, GA 30341
770-457-9555
800-766-9550
www.GABROBINSNA.com

Gallagher Bassett Services Inc
1650 Des Peres Road
Saint Louis, MO 63131
314-965-7810
www.GALLAGHERBASSETT.com

Golub and Associates Inc
130 S Bemiston Avenue
Clayton, MO 63105
314-725-6610
888-424-6582
www.GOLUBPA.com

Goodman-Gable-Gould Company
133 Rollins Avenue
Suite 1
Rockville, MD 20852-4040
800-858-3900
301-881-9230
www.ggg-ai.com

Heavy Equipment Claims Service
2441 South State Rd 7
Ft. Lauderdale, FL 33317
954-583-2989
www.heavyequipment.com

Hospital Insurance Systems Inc
771 S Kirkman Road
Orlando, FL 32811
407-293-7120
800-327-8905

Howarth, Keys & Associates Inc.
137 Third Avenue North
Franklin, TN 37064
800-647-2236
615-550-5500
www.hkai.biz

Howarth, Keys & Associates Inc.
137 3rd Avenue North
Franklin, TN 37064
800-647-2236
615-550-5500
www.hkai.biz

Insurance Claim Services, Inc.
12 North 64th St.
Suite 4
Belleville, IL 62223-3809
618-397-8800
888-920-1946
www.icsadjusters.com

Insurance Recovery Inc
1778 Park Ave N Suite 111
Maitland, FL 32751
407-539-1946
www.ADJUSTERSITE.com

InterClaim
4640 Valis Ct.
Suite 204
Alpharetta, GA 30022
404-875-5866
www.interclaim.com

Jansen International LLC
922 West Greens Road
Suite 100
Houston, TX 77067
1-800-779-8714
281-873-8700
www.jansenco.com

National Fire Adjustment Co., Inc.
1 NFA Park
10 John James Audubon
Amherst, NY 14228
716-689-7700
800-777-3333
www.nfa.com

Neaman A.H. Co Inc
5362 Steubenville pike
Pittsburgh, PA 15136
412-787-7775

New York Public Adjusters Association
299 Broadway
New York, NY 10007
212-285-0510
www.NYPAA.com

Newsam-Harp Inc. General Adjusters
20201 E. Jackson Drive
Suite 460
Independence, MO 64057
816-753-4285
www.NEWSAM-HARP.com

Paul Guttman & Co
203 Rockaway Avenue
Valley Stream, NY 11580
516-825-4800

Pearce & Frankman Inc
2380 Junipero Serra Boulevard
Daly City, CA 94015
650-756-7400
800-794-7606
www.CLAIMSADJUSTER.com

Permanent Claims Service Inc
4912 William Arnold Road
Memphis, TN 38117
901-761-1670

Personal Public Adjusters Inc
1200 Bustleton Pke Suite #8
Feasterville, PA 19053
215-355-8488
www.PERSONALADJUSTERS.com

Policyholders Adjusting Service
4540 Kearny Villa Road
San Diego, CA 92123
858-569-9190

Professional Loss Adjusters
343 Washington Street
Newton, MA 02458
617-850-0477
www.pla-us.com

Property Damage Appraisers
13975 Connecticut Avenue
Silver Spring, MD 20906
301-871-1500

RAC Adjustments
1410 Auburn St.
P.O. Box 1839
Rockford, IL 61110
815-968-7686
www.racadj.com

Rittel Hill and Zimmerman Ins Svcs Inc
4920 Reed Road
Columbus, OH 43220
614-457-7765

Seltser & Goldsteen Public Adjusters Inc.
900 Cummings Center
Suite 309 U
Beverly, MA 01915
978-921-2926

Settipane Richard Public Insurance Adjusters
1 Longfellow Place
Boston, MA 02114
617-523-3456

Stephen R. Figlin & Associates Inc.
8400 Bustletons Avenue
Suite 204
Philadelphia, PA 19152
215-342-8514
800-292-9090
www.FIGLINASSOC.com

Swerling Milton & Winnick Public Adjusters Inc.
36 Washington Street
Suite 310
Wellesley Hls, MA 02481
781-416-1000
800-677-5454
www.SWERLING.com

The Greenspan Co.
400 Oyster Point Boulevard
South San Fran, CA 94080
650-583-4300
800-248-3888
www.greenspan.com

Insurance, special situations

Haynes Insurance Group
1000 N Walnut Creek Drive
Suite E
Mansfield, TX 76063
817-477-1455
www.HIG-ins.com

McLarens Brouwer International
5925 Airport Rd.
Suite 1000
Mississauga, ON L4V 1W1
Canada
905-671-0185
800-668-6100
www.mbii.ca

Swett & Crawford Group
21650 Oxnard Street
Suite 1400
Woodland Hls, CA 91367
818-593-2008
www.SWETT.com

Language translating

Bowne Global Solutions
132 W 31st Street
Floor 12th
New York, NY 10001
917-339-4700
800-608-6088
www.BERLITZGLOBALNET.com

Ectaco
31-21 31st Street
Long Island City, NY 11106
800-710-7920
718-728-6110
www.speechguard.com

Integrated Wave Technologies, Inc.
4042 Clipper Court
Fremont, CA 94538
510-353-0260
www.i-w-t.com

Japan Communication Consultants LLC
350 5th avenue
Suite 3304
New York, NY 10118
212-759-2033
www.JAPANCC.com

Language Line Service
1 Lower Ragsdale Drive
Bldg 2
Monterey, CA 93940
800-752-0093
www.LANGUAGELINE.com

Legal issues, disaster-related

Burns and Levinson LLP
125 Summer Street
Boston, MA 02110
617-345-3000
www.BURNSLEV.com

Childress Duffy Goldblatt, Ltd.
515 N State
Suite 2200
Chicago, Il 60610
312-494-0200
www.ChildressLaw.net

FEMA Law Associates, PLLC
The Southern Building - Suite 510
805 15th Street, NW
Washington, DC 20005
202-326-9319
www.fema-law.com

Governo Law Firm LLC
260 Franklin Street
Boston, MA 02110
617-737-9045
www.GOVERNO.com

Kroll Associates
900 3rd Avenue
New York, NY 10022
212-593-1000
888-209-9526
www.KROLLWORLDWIDE.com

Oppenheimer Wolff & Donnelly LLP
Plaza VII, Suite 3300
45 South 7th Street
Minneapolis, MN 55402
612-607-7204
612-607-7000
www.oppenheimer.com

SERVICES

SERVICES

Wilkofsky, Friedman, Karel & Cummins Attorneys
299 Broadway
Suite 1700
New York, NY 10017
212-285-0510
www.WFKCLAW.com

Legal issues, environmental

Bingham McCutchen
150 Federal Street
Boston, MA 02110
617-951-8000
202-822-9320
www.BINGHAM.com

Burns and Levinson LLP
125 Summer Street
Boston, MA 02110
617-345-3000
www.BURNSLEV.com

Childress Duffy Goldblatt, Ltd.
515 N State
Suite 2200
Chicago, Il 60610
312-494-0200
www.ChildressLaw.net

Robinson & Cole
1 Boston Place
Boston, MA 02108
617-557-5900
www.rc.com

Serafini Serafini Darling and Correnti
63 Federal Street
Salem, MA 01970
978-744-0212

Wilmer Cutler Pickering Hale and Dorr
1455 Pennsylvania Avenue NW
Suite 1000
Washington, DC 20004
202-942-8400
www.wilmerhale.com

Legal issues, insurance

MJM Investigations Inc.
910 Paverstone Drive
Raleigh, NC 27615
800-927-0456
919-846-0997
www.mjminc.com

Pre-Paid Legal Services, Inc.
2855 E Broadway Rd #220
Mesa, AZ 85204
480-228-3758
888-211-5812
http://www.prepaidlegal.com/info/ryancrow

Wilkofsky Friedman Karel & Cummins Attorneys
299 Broadway
Rm 1700
New York, NY 10007
212-285-0510

Legal-fee management

Allegient Systems Inc
15 River Road
Suite 300
Wilton, CT 06897
203-761-1289
www.ALLEGIENTSYSTEMS.com

Libraries & information centers

Earthquake Hazards Program
345 Middlefield Rd
Menlo Park, CA 94025
650-329-5020
http://pasadena.wr.usgs.gov/step/

Environmental Health Services Branch
Centers for Disease Control and Prevention
4770 Buford Highway, Mail Stop F-28
Atlanta, GA 30341
770-488-7476
www.cdc.gov/nceh/ehs/ETP/

National Center for Food Protection and Defense (NCFPD)
University of Minnesota - Twin Cities Campus
925 Delaware St. SE - Suite 200
Minneapolis, MN 55455
612-624-2458
www.ncfpd.umn.edu

National Vulnerability Database (NVD)
NIST Computer Security Division
100 Bureau Drive
Gaithersburg, MD 20899
301-975-2934
nvd.nist.gov

Natural Hazards Center
Geosciences Department - Penn State University
210 Research West Building (Mail 540 DK)
University Park, PA 16802
814-863-0567
www.essc.psu.edu/hazards

Natural Hazards Research and Applications Information Center
University of Colorado
482 UCB
Boulder, CO 80309-0001
303-492-6818
www.colorado.edu/hazards

Pan American Health Organization
Emergency Preparedness Program
525 Twenty-third Street, NW
Washington, DC 20037
202-974-3520
202-974-3399
www.paho.org/english/ped/pedhome.htm

Southern California Earthquake Center
University of Southern California
3651 Trousdale Parkway
Los Angeles, CA 90089
213-740-5843
www.scec.org

University of Pittsburgh Medical Center
Clinicians' Biosecurity Network
200 Lothrop St.
Pittsburgh, PA 15213-2582
443-573-3304
www.upmc-cbn.org/dmz/about_network.html

USGS Earthquake Hazards Program
U.S. Geological Survey Geologic Hazards
1711 Illinois St.
Golden, CO 80401
303-273-8579
http://pasadena.wr.usgs.gov/step/

USGS Earthquake Hazards Program Office
12201 Sunrise Valley Drive
MS 905
Reston, VA 20192
703-648-6714
703-648-6696
http://pasadena.wr.usgs.gov/step/

Liquidators & salvage buyers

ALSO SEE SALVAGE IN MISC SERVICES SECTION

Air Salvage of Dallas
1361 Ferris Road
Lancaster, TX 75146
800-336-6399
www.AIRSOD.com

Allied Salvage Co
7943 Parke West Drive
Glen Burnie, MD 21061
410-760-8350

American Salvage
70001 NW 27TH Avenue
Miami, FL 33147
305-691-7001
www.americansalvage.com

Blue Metals
18 North State Street
Newtown, PA 18940
215-860-2345
www.bluemetals.com

Houston General Salvage
10307 Airline Drive
Houston, TX 77037
281-445-6696
888-826-6696

Northshore International Insurance Services
199 Rosewood Drive
Danvers, MA 01923
978-745-6655
www.niis.com

Lodging, long-term

Extended Stay Hotel
100 Dunbar Street
Spartanburg, SC 29306
864-573-1600
800-EXT-STAY
www.EXTSTAY.com

Oakwood Worldwide - Nationwide Locations
2222 Corinth Avenue
Los Angeles, CA 90064
310-478-1021
www.OAKWOOD.com

Mailing, printing, & inserting services

Adwest Mailers Inc.
13013 Saticoy Street
N Hollywood, CA 91605
818-982-3720
www.ADWEST.com

Aero Fulfillment Services
3900 Aero Drive
Mason, OH 45040
800-225-7145
www.AEROFULFILLMENT.com

Apple Direct Mail
225 Varick Street
New York, NY 10014
212-924-4488
www.APPLEMAIL.com

Atlanta Marketing Solutions Inc.
5001 McNeel Industrial Boulevard
Powder Spgs, GA 30127
770-439-6173
www.amsolutions.com

Aus-Tex Printing & Mailing
2431 Forbes Drive
Austin, TX 78754
512-476-7581
www.AUSTEX.com

SERVICES

Bender Direct Mail Service
2201 S Jackson Avenue
Tulsa, OK 74107
918-583-1171
www.BENDERDIRECTMAIL.com

Bowe & Bell & Howell
795 Roble Road
Allentown, PA 18109
610-264-4510
800-723-2338
www.BELLHOWELL.com

Brokers Worldwide
701 Ashland Avenue
Folcroft, PA 19032
610-461-3661
800-624-5287
www.brokersworldwide.com

Conder Direct
22967 La Cadena Drive
Laguna Hills, CA 92653
949-855-8300
www.CONDERDIRECT.com

Crossroads Industries Inc.
2464 Silver Fox Trail
Gaylord, MI 49734
989-732-1233
www.CROSSROADSINDUSTRIES.com

D3Logic
89 Commercial Way
East Providence, RI 02914
401-435-4300
888-624-5672
www.d3logic.com

Data-Mail Inc.
240 Hartford Avenue
Newington, CT 06111
860-666-0399
www.data-mail.com

Direct Mail of Maine
Scarborough, ME 04070
800-883-6930
www.thinkdmm.com

Diversified Direct Mailing Services Inc.
1301 Burton Street
Fullerton, CA 92831
714-776-4520
www.DIVERSIFIED-DIRECT.com

DST Output
2534 Madison Avenue
Kansas City, MO 64108
816-435-3070
www.dstoutput.com

High Cotton Direct Marketing
2901 Alton Way
Birmingham, AL 35210-4328
205-838-2345
877-838-2345

I.C. System Inc.
444 Highway 96 E
Saint Paul, MN 55127
800-443-4123
www.ICSYSTEM.com

International Postal Systems Inc
1916 Wilson Boulevard Suite 100
Arlington, VA 22201
703-522-8338
703-522-7800
www.action.com

JLS Mailing Services Inc.
672 Crescent Street
Brockton, MA 02302-3360
508-313-1024
508-313-1000
www.jlsms.com

Lee Marketing Services
8801 Autobahn Drive
Dallas, TX 75237
972-293-5000
www.LEEMARKETING.com

Mail Communications
22 Digital Drive
Novato, CA 94949
415-883-2383
www.MAILCOMUSA.com

Mail Mogul
25115 Avenue Stanford
A-111
Valencia, CA 91355
800-589-2525
www.mailmogul.com

Mail Tech Enterprises
1115 W Detweiller Drive
Peoria, IL 61615-2077
309-691-6600
www.mailtechenterprises.com

Mail-Gard
65 Steamboat Dr.
Warminster, PA 18974
267-960-3119
www.MAIL-GARD.com

Modern Mailers Inc.
P.O. BOX 5376
Tallahassee, FL 32314
850-877-0613
www.MODERNMAILERS.com

Newchannel Direct
2659 Center Road
Hinckley, OH 44233
330-225-8950

Pitney Bowes Inc.
1 Elmcroft Road - World Headquarters
Stamford, CT 06926-0700
888-245-PBMS
www.pb.com

Pitney Bowes Management Services
One Elmcroft Road
Stamford, CT 06926
800-672-6937
888-245-7267
www.PITNEYBOWES.com

Summers Mailing Company
4850 W Ledbetter Drive
Dallas, TX 75236
972-296-9871

The Jackson Group
5804 Churchman Bypass
Indianapolis, IN 46203
317-781-4600
www.jacksongroup.com

The Mail Room Inc.
2110 Busch Avenue
Colorado Spgs, CO 80904
719-636-1303
www.THEMAILROOMINC.COM

United Wire Service
8600 N. Industrial Rd.
Peoria, IL 61615
309-689-6160
www.unitedwire.net

Universal Mailing Services
10 New England Avenue
Piscataway, NJ 08854-4101
732-981-9100
www.UMSMAIL.com

US Web Mailing Services
780 Park Avenue
Huntington, NY 11743
631-427-5200
www.USWEBINC.com

Vencenveo
3001 Lakeview Road
Memphis, TN 38116
901-396-9904
www.cenveo.com

Maintenance policies, specialty

Computers Inc
120 Turnpike Road
Southborough, MA 01772
508-871-6800
www.geac.com

Guardian Computer Support Inc.
5637 La Ribera Street
Number BNC
Livermore, CA 94550
800-752-8733
www.gardian-computer.com

NCE Computer Group
1973 friendship dr
El Cajon, CA 92020
800-446-6456

Medical assistance, overseas travelers

International SOS Assistance, Inc.
3600 Horizon Boulevard
Suite 300
Philadelphia, PA 19053
215-942-8000
www.internationalsos.com

International SOS Assistance, Inc.
2211 Norfolk
Suite 517
Houston, TX 77098
713-521-7611
www.internationalsos.com

Museum services

ALSO SEE CONSERVATION IN MISC. SERVICES SECTION

University Products, Inc.
517 Main Street
Holyoke, MA 01040
800-336-1847
413-532-3372
www.universityproducts.com

Outside audit of disaster plan adequacy

The Systems Audit Group Inc.
25 Ellison Road
Newton, MA 02459-1434
617-332-3496
www.Disaster-Risk-Planning.com

URS Corporation
200 Orchard Ridge Dr.
Suite 101
Gaithersburg, MD 20878
301-258-6554
www.urscorp.com

Public relations/crisis communications

Frontline Corporate Communications Inc.
650 Riverbend Drive
Kitchener, ON N2K 3S2
Canada
888-848-9898
www.fcc.onthefrontlines.com

SERVICES

Godec Randall & Associates
3944 N 14th Street
Phoenix, AZ 85014
602-266-5556
www.GODECRANDALL.com

Hennes Communications
2841 Berkshire Road
Cleveland, OH 44118
216-321-7774
www.hennescommunications.com

PR Direct
36 King St., East
Toronto, ON M5C 2L9
Canada
416-507-2028
866-736-3779
www.prdirect.ca

Ten United
375 N Front Street
Suite 400
Columbus, OH 43215
614-221-7667
www.tenunited.com

**URS Corporation
200 Orchard Ridge Dr.
Suite 101
Gaithersburg, MD 20878
301-258-6554
www.urscorp.com**

Weber Shandwick
101 Main Street
Floor 8th
Cambridge, MA 02142
617-661-7900
www.WEBERSHANDWICK.com

William Russell & Associates, Inc.
305 W. Masonic View Avenue
Alexandria, VA 22301-2418
703-739-6277

Recruiting/employment/ personnel

**BC Management, Inc
2082 Business Center Drive, #254
Irvine, CA 92612
949-250-8172
888-250-7001
www.bcmanagement.com**

Key Strategies LLC
100 Eagle Rock Avenue
East Hanover, NJ 07936
973-887-2300
www.KEYSTRATEGIES.com

Salvage & surplus specialists & buyers

A. D. I.
1056 So. Lewis Street
Mesa, AZ 85210
480-539-4555
480-226-9097
http://www.HeavyEquipmentGuide.com

All States Ag Parts, Inc
221 S. Phillips Ave. Suite 201
Sioux Falls, SD 57104
605-359-2447
www.asapagparts.com

Callan Salvage & Appraisal Co
P.O. Box 190
Eads (Menphis), TN 38028
901-867-3300
www.callansalvage.com

Continental Jewelry Replacement Co.
4427 W Kennedy Boulevard
Suite 300
Tampa, FL 33609
800-282-5182

Electronic Salvage Resources Inc
460 Penny Lane
Suite 100
Grayslake, IL 60030
847-548-7627
www.ESRINCORPORATED.com

Garvin-Fram
809 Albion Avenue
Schaumburg, IL 60193
800-351-5516

Greer & Kirby Co., Inc.
14714 Industry Circle
La Mirada, CA 90638-5817
562-802-2883
714-670-7721
www.GREERANDKIRBY.com

Greer & Kirby Co., Inc.
2706 McCone Avenue
Hayward, CA 94545-1615
510-786-1671
www.GREERANDKIRBY.com

Greer & Kirby Co., Inc.
4220 Steve Reynolds Blvd.
Suite 19
Norcross, GA 30093-3325
770-921-5959
www.GREERANDKIRBY.com

Greer & Kirby Co., Inc.
2234 Landmeier Road
Elk Grove Village, IL 60007-2617
847-956-7180
www.GREERANDKIRBY.com

Greer & Kirby Co., Inc.
1133 Third Avenue S.W.
Carmel, IN 46032-2565
317-575-4293
www.GREERANDKIRBY.com

Greer & Kirby Co., Inc.
6989 Washington Avenue
Edina, MN 55439-1506
952-829-1682
www.GREERANDKIRBY.com

Greer & Kirby Co., Inc.
387 Moutain View Road
Glade Valley, NC 28627-8951
336-363-9292
www.GREERANDKIRBY.com

Greer & Kirby Co., Inc.
219 Homestead Road
Building 2, Unit 2
Hillsborough, NJ 08844-1900
908-431-4050
www.GREERANDKIRBY.com

Greer & Kirby Co., Inc.
P.O. Box 510
453 Millers Run Road
Morgan, PA 15064-0510
412-220-9163
www.GREERANDKIRBY.com

Greer and Kirby Co., Inc.
491 Maple Street
Suite 107
Danvers, MA 01923-4024
978-646-9600
978-475-2864
www.GREERANDKIRBY.com

Greer Kirby & Co.
14714 Industry Circle
La Mirada, CA 90638
714-670-7721
www.greerandkirby.com

I. V. Auto Inc
11625 Vanowen Street
N Hollywood, CA 91605
818-982-9053
www.IVAUTOINC.com

Insurance Auto Auctions
2 West Brook Corporate Center Suite 500
Westchester, IL 60154
847-839-3939
www.iaai.com

Insurance Salvage Buyers of America
1299 Coney Island Avenue
Brooklyn, NY 11230
718-377-6515
www.aaacloseout.com

Mainline Metals
21 Bala Avenue
Bala Cynwyd, PA 19004
610-668-0888
www.mainmetals.com

Manasseh Truck & Equipment
426 Hlavek Road
Decatur, TX 76234
940-627-6102

Nardone & Co.
838 Ritchie Hwy
Suite 2
Severna Park, MD 21146
800-315-8200
www.nardonenet.com

R & R Salvage Corp
P.O. Box 1073
Rahway, NJ 07065
800-732-6837

The Salvage Group
24025 Greater Mack Avenue
Suite 203
St. Clair Shores, MI 48080
800-524-7246
00-800-4263-8263
www.salvagegroups.com

Weller/salvage
2525 Chicago Drive
Grand Rapids, MI 49509
616-538-5000
www.weller/salvage.com

West Side Salvage
P.O. Box 9129
Cedar Rapids, IA 52409
800-747-0104

Scrap computer & banking equipment buyers

ALSO SEE SALVAGE, LIQUIDATORS IN MISC. SERVICES SECTION

A-1 Teletronics
1010 118th Avenue N
St. Petersburg, FL 33716
800-736-4397
www.a1teletronics.com

Business Equipment Unlimited
43540 Blacksmith Square
Ashburn, VA 20147
703-626-1643

Chase Electronics Inc
166 Academy Lane
Upper Darby, PA 19082
610-449-8160
www.chaserecycling.com

ECS Refining
705 Reed Street
Santa Clara, CA 95050-3980
408-988-4386
800-469-9277
www.ECSREFINING.COM

Scrap fluorescent lamps & ballasts buyers

ALSO SEE BALLAST RECYCLERS IN MISC. SERVICES SECTION

Air Cycle Corp.
2000 S 25th Avenue
Broadview, IL 60155
800-909-9709
www.AIRCYCLE.com

The USA Lamp & Ballast
2010 Rt 9W
Milton, NY 12547
718-328-4667
www.usalamp-ny.com

Search & rescue

Speed Shore Corp
3330 S Sam Houston Parkway E
Houston, TX 77047
713-943-0750
www.SPEEDSHORE.com

Storage, post-disaster

Wells Cargo, Inc.
1503 W. McNaughton St.
P.O. Box 728
Elkhart, IN 46515
800-348-7553
574-264-9661
http://www.wellscargo.com

Transportation, expedited

Active Aero
2068 E Street
Belleville, MI 48111
734-547-7200
800-872-5387
www.activeaero.com

Alliance Air Freight & Logistics, Inc.
13345 Saticoy St.
N. Hollywood, CA 91605
800-684-6359
www.shipalliance.com

FedEx Custom Critical
1475 Boettler Road
Uniontown, OH 44685-9584
800-762-3787
customcritical.fedex.com

Transportation, specialized trucking

ALSO SEE EMERGENCY RESPONSE LOGISTICS IN MISC. SERVICES SECTION

FedEx Custom Critical
1475 Boettler Road
Uniontown, OH 44685-9584
800-762-3787
customcritical.fedex.com

Menlo Worldwide Expedite
10881 Lowell Avenue
Overland Park, KS 66210
800-714-8779
www.menloexpedite.com

Overnite Transportation Co
1000 Semmes Avenue
Richmond, VA 23224
804-231-8646
800-368-5035
www.OVERNIGHT.com

Page Transportation Inc
P.O. Box 920
Weedsport, NY 13166
315-834-6681
800-233-2126
www.pagetran.com

Transportation, temperature control

FedEx Custom Critical
1475 Boettler Road
Uniontown, OH 44685-9584
800-762-3787
customcritical.fedex.com

Tree removal services

American Tree Experts LLC
1180 Greenspring Rd.
York, PA 17402
717-848-9796

Antietam Tree and Landscape
405 North Buhrans Blvd
Hagerstown, MD 21740
301-791-3500
www.antietamtree.com

SERVICES

Arbor Pro, Inc.
912 NE Kelly Avenue, Suite 219
Portland, OR 97030
503-491-2844
503-710-0815
www.arborpronw.com

ARBORWELL
21638 Redwood Road
Castro Valley, CA 94546
888-969-8733
925-260-6667
www.arborwell.com

Asplundh Tree Expert Co.
708 Blair Mill Road
Willow Grove, PA 19090
215-784-4200
800-248-8733
www.ASPLUNDH.com

Brennan's Tree Service, LLC
218 Holden Drive
Manassas Park, VA 20111
703-393-8861
brennanstreeservice.com

Custom Tree Care, Inc.
5525 SW Auburn Rd
Topeka, KS 66610
785 478-9805
785 221-7550

Davey Tree Expert Company The
Kent, OH 44240
800-445-8733
www.DAVEY.com

Eden Tree & Landscape Inc.
13703 S. 226 Ave
Gretna, NE 68028
402-332-2839
402-510-9853
www.edentreelandscape.com

Green Side Up Landscaping Inc.
P.O. Box 44061
Baltimore, MD 21236
410-256-3328
410-365-0365

Greenskeeper Environmental, LLC
P.O. Box 428
Ashton, MD 20861
301-774-8201

Husqvarna Forest & Garden
7349 Statesville Road
Chain Saw Manufacturer
Charlotte, NC 28269
800-487-5962
800-487-5958
www.usa.husqvarna.com

Lam Tree Service
p.o. box 2486
evergreen, CO 80437
303-674-8733
www.lamtree.com

Peninsula Tree LLC
130 San Ramon Drive
San Jose, CA 95111
408-210-1236
650-941-6627
www. peninsulatree.com

TFR Enterprises, Inc.
10731 E. Crystal Falls Parkway
Leander, TX 78641
512-260-3322
www.tfrinc.com

The Tree Mann Inc.
2367 N US 35
La Porte, IN 46350
219-362-3988
219-325-5349
www.thetreemann.com

Tree Care by Stan Hunt, Inc
53 Boulevard
Queensbury, NY 12804
518-793-0804
800-734-0806
www.treecarebystanhunt.com

Tree Care Industry Association
3 Perimeter Rd
Unit 1
Manchester, NH 03031
603-314-5380
800-733-2622
www.TCIA.org

Tree Care Industry Association
3 Perimeter Rd
Unit 1
Manchester, NH 03031
603-314-5380
800-733-2622
www.TCIA.org

Tree Care Of New York, LLC
P.O. Box 283
Lancaster, NY 14086
716-681-1414

Treescaps Inc.
618 Winwood Rd.
Gastonia, NC 28052
704-867-4100
704 598-6641
www.treescapeonline.com

SERVICES

Under The Needle Tree Service LLC
1244 N 173rd
Shoreline, WA 98133
206-412-7267
206-459-7800
www.41arbor.com

Westcoast Tree Care, Inc
Seattle, Wa
Portland, Or
seattle, WA 98024
425-922-1515
503-807-6601
http://westcoasttree.uswestdex.com/

Tree removal services, utility-line clearance

Asplundh Tree Expert Co.
708 Blair Mill Road
Willow Grove, PA 19090
215-784-4200
800-248-8733
www.ASPLUNDH.com

Vehicles: emergency-service specialty-manufacturer

LDV Inc.
180 Industrial Drive
Burlington, WI 53105
800-558-5986
www.ldvusa.com

Water leak detection

American Leak Detection, Inc.
888 Research Drive
Suite 100
Palm Springs, CA 92262
800-755-6697
www.americanleakdetection.com

Weather forecasting

AccuWeather Inc
385 Science Park Road
State College, PA 16803-2286
314-235-3600
www.ACCUWEATHER.com

Advanced Forecasting Corporation
2711 Centerville Road
Suite 400
Wilmington, DE 19808
305-949-0040
406-651-5085
www.advancedforecasting.com

Climate Prediction Center
5200 Auth Road
Camps Springs, MD 20746
301-763-8000
www.CPC.NCEP.NOAA.gov

DTN MeteorLogix
9110 W Dodge Rd
Omaha, NE 68114
402-255-8489
800-610-0777
www.meteorlogix.com

Florida International University - Hurricane Center
11200 S.W. 8th Street
University Park, MARC 360
Miami, FL 33199-0001
305-348-1607
www.ihrc.fiu.edu

National Hurricane Center
11691 S.W. 17th Street
Miami, FL 33165-2149
305-229-4470
www.nhc.noaa.gov

National Water and Climate Center
USDA/NRCS
Portland, OR 97232
503-414-3055

NOAA National Weather Service
Office of Climate, Water, and Weather Services
1325 East West Highway
Silver Spring, MD 20910
301-713-0090 x150
www.nws.noaa.gov/

North American Weather Consultants
8180 South Highland Dr.
Suite B-2
Sandy, UT 84093
801-942-9005
nawcinc.com

Ocean Prediction Center
5200 Auth Road
Camp Springs, MD 20746
301-763-8441
www.OPC.NCEP.NOAA.gov

Office of Climate, Water and Weather Services
1325 East West Highway
Silver Spring, MD 20910-3283
301-713-4000
www.nws.noaa.gov/os/

Skywatch Weather Center
347 Prestley Road
Bridgeville, PA 15017-1949
412-221-6000
800-SKYWATCH
www.SKYWATCHWEATHER.com

StormNow
DataSwitch Information Services Inc.
316 Burkets Road
Bremen, IN 46506
269-983-6271
www.acp-international.com

Universal Weather
8787 Tallyho Road
Houston, TX 77061
713-944-1622
800-231-5600
www.UNIV-WEA.com

Weather Decision Technologies Inc
1818 W Lindsey
Norman, OK 73069
405-579-7675
www.WDTINC.com

Weather Insight, L.P.
2925 Briarpack Drive
Suite 675
Houston, Texas 77042
713-361-4950
www.weatherinsight.com

WeatherData Inc.
245 N. Waco Street
Suite 310
Wichita, KS 67202-1116
316-265-9127
www.WEATHERDATA.com

WeatherTAP.com
174 Fourth Street
Crossville, TN 38555
800-337-5263
931-484-5137
www.weathertap.com

West National Technology Support Center
USDA/NRCS 5601 Sunnyside Ave
Beltsville, MD 20705-5420
301-504-3946

Weather, historical records

Falconer Weather Information Service, LLC
7 Via Maria Drive
Scotia, NY 12302-5717
518-399-5388
800-428-5621
www.wxscape.com/FWIS

National Climactic Data Center
151 Patton Ave
Asheville, NC 28801-5001
704-271-4800
www.ncdc.noaa.gov

National Ice Center
Federal Building #4
Washington, DC 20395
301-457-5300
www.natice.noaa.gov

National Snow and Ice Data Center
Univ. of Colorado
Campus Box 449
Boulder, CO 80309-0449
303-492-6199
www.nsidc.colorado.edu

Window glass safety film, installed

3M Buildings Safety Solutions Dept
12810 Talley Lane
Gaithersburg, MD 20878
800-940-9142
301-258-8914

3M Canada Company
5520 Explorer Drive
Suite 201
Mississauga, ON L4W 5L1
Canada
905-602-3814
800-561-5115 x3814
www.3M.com/windowfilm

American Window Film Inc
21 Cocasset Street
Foxborough, MA 02035
508-549-0300
800-274-8468

CPFilms Inc.
P.O. Box 5068
Martinsville, VA 24115
800-255-8627
www.llumar.com

Energy Management Systems
4208 Fitch Ave
Baltimore, MD 21236
800-537-3911
410-882-0800
www.emswindowfilm.com

GlassLock, Inc.
301 Steeple Chase Drive
Suite 101
Prince Frederick, MD 20678
410-535-9898
www.glasslock.com

Madico Window Films
64 Industrial Parkway
Woburn, MA 01801
800-225-1926
www.madico.com

Wrapping, roofs, buildings, etc.

Dr. Shrink, Inc.
1606 State St.
Manistee, MI 49660-1855
800-968-5147
231-723-2685
www.dr-shrink.com

Global Wrap and Services, Inc.
102 South St.
St. Augustine, FL 32084
800-972-7120
800-WRA-P120
www.globalwrap.com

SERVICES, Psychological

Crisis management, human factors

Crisis Care Network
2855 44th St. SW
Suite 360
Grandville, MI 49418
888-736-0911
www.crisiscare.com

Crisis Management Group Inc
381 Elliot Street
Newton, MA 02464
617-969-7600
800-444-7262
www.CMGASSOCIATES.com

Crisis Management International Inc
8 Piedmont Center NE
Atlanta, GA 30305
404-841-3400
800-274-7470
www.CMIATL.com

Crisis Recovery Services
10 W Hanover Avenue
Suite 110
Randolph, NJ 07869-4221
973-895-4799

Integrated Insights
9370 Sky Park Court
San Diego, CA 92123
858-278-3626
www.integratedinsights.com

Trauma/crisis counseling & management

Arizona Center for Mental Health
5070 N 40th Street
Suite 200
Phoenix, AZ 85018-2135
602-954-6700

Center Town Psychological Services
Nicol Building
331 Cooper St
Ottawa, ON K2P P0G
Canada
613-235-9196

Crisis Care Network
2855 44th St. SW
Suite 360
Grandville, MI 49418
888-736-0911
www.crisiscare.com

Delta Psychological Services
3865 Rocky River Drive
Cleveland, OH 44111
216-671-4508

Disaster Mental Health Institute - The University of South Dakota
414 E. Clark Street
SDU 114
Vermillion, SD 57069
605-677-6575
800-522-9684
www.usd.edu/dmhi/conf05

Dr. E. A. Ryan
P.O. Box 102
Clarendon Hls, IL 60514
630-887-0413

Emergency Services and Disaster Relief Branch (ESDRB)
Center for Mental Health Services (CMHS)
P.O. Box 42557
Washington, DC 20015
800-789-2647
240-747-5475
www.mentalhealth.samhsa.gov

Emotional Continuity Management
Inner Directions, LLP
2815 Van Giesen
Richland, WA 99354
509-942-0443
509-948-3593
www.emotionalcontinuity.com

Fedoravicius Al S Phd
9426 Indian School Rd
Suite 1
Albuquerque, NM 87112
505-345-6100

FEI Behavioral Health
11700 West Lake Park Drive
Milwaukee, WI 53224
800-987-4368
www.feinet.com

Health Psychology Group
10 W Hanover Avenue
Suite 110
Randolph, NJ 07869-4221
973-895-4799

Int'l. Critical Incident Stress Foundation
3290 Pine Orchard Lane
Suite 106
Ellicott City, MD 21042
410-750-9600
www.ICISF.org

Nordli Wilson Associates
71 Old Coach Highway
Hamden, CT 06518
203-288-7472
www.NORDLIWILSON.com

Northern Wyoming Mental Health Center
1221 W 5th Street
Sheridan, WY 82801
307-674-4405

Otter Creek Associates/Matrix Health Sys
86 Lake Street
Burlington, VT 05401
802-865-3450

Phoenix Mental Health
567 S Governors Avenue
Dover, DE 19904
302-736-6135

Psychiatric Inst. of Wash.
4228 Wisconsin Avenue NW
Washington, DC 20016
202-885-5600
www.psychiatricinstitute.com

ResponseWorks, Inc.
11 Lincoln Avenue
Lambertville, NJ 08530
609-397-9597
www.responseworks.com

SAMHSA's National Mental Health Information Center
P.O. Box 42557
Washington, DC 20015
800-789-2647
240-747-5484
www.mentalhealth.samhsa.gov

Strongsville Pyschological Services
14843 Sprague Road
Strongsville, OH 44136
440-234-9955

Trauma Reduction Inc.
18802 Avenue Biarritz
Lutz, FL 33558
813 335 1143
traumareduction.com

WVU Dept. of Behavioral Medicine
P.O. BOX 1547
Charleston, WV 25326
304-341-1500

Workplace violence consulting

Crisis Prevention Institute Inc.
3315 N 124th Street
Brookfield, WI 53005
262-783-5787
800-558-8976
www.CRISISPREVENTION.com

Huffmaster Crisis Management
1300 Combermere
Troy, MI 48083
800-446-1515
248-588-1600
www.huffmaster.com

SERVICES

SERVICES

SOFTWARE

SOFTWARE, Disaster Recovery Planning

IBM AS400-based

PAE Inc
7 Riverway Road
Salem, MA 01970
978-744-8612
www.PAEINC.com

IBM PC & compatibles-based

Apex Software
6363 DeZavala Suite 200
San Antonio, TX 78249
800-858-9958
210-699-6666
www.apexwin.com

ARCHIBUS, Inc.
18 Tremont Street
Boston, MA 02108
617-227-2508
www.archibus.com

Binomial International
812 Proctor Avenue
Ogdensburg, NY 13669
888-246-6642
www.BINOMIAL.com

BISYS
11 E Greenway Plaza
Houston, TX 77046
713-622-8911
www.BISYS.com

Business Protection Systems International
5041 La Mart Drive
Suite 130
Riverside, CA 92507
800-594-3714
951-341-5050
www.businessprotection.com

Contingency Planning and Outsourcing Inc
P.O. Box 290505
Columbia, SC 29229
803-712-6105
www.CPOTRACKER.com

ContingenZ Corporation
227 Fowling Street
4th Floor
Playa Del Rey, CA 90293
310-306-0166
www.contingenz.com

Deccan International
9860 Mesa Rim Road
San Diego, CA 92121
858 799 7986
858 799 7998
www.deccanintl.com

Defense Group Inc. / CoBRA Software
2034 Eisenhower Ave
#115
Alexandria, VA 22314
703-535-8720
877-233-5789
www.defensegroupinc.com/cobra

DML Consulting
400 Hancock Avenue
East Norriton, PA 19401
267-249-9340

FutureShield
57 Galaxy Blvd.
Unit 6
Toronto, ON M9W 5P1
Canada
416-675-7835
www.futureshield.net

Infotech Century LC
14 Leatherleaf Ct
Gaithersburg, MD 20878
301-258-2653

PaloAlto Software
144 E 14th Ave
Eugene, OR 97401
800-229-7526
541-683-6162
www.scplans.com

Rothstein Catalog on Disaster Recovery
4 Arapaho Road
Brookfield, CT 06804-3104
203-740-7444
888-768-4783
www.DisasterRecoveryBooks.com

RSM McGladrey Inc.
801 Nicollet Avenue
11th Floor West Tower
Minneapolis, MN 55402
800-648-4030
www.RSMMCGLADREY.com

Strohl Systems
631 Park Avenue
Kng of Prussa, PA 19406
610-768-4120
800-634-2016
www.strohlsystems.com

UNISYS Corp
Unisys Way
Blue Bell, PA 19424
215-986-4011
www.UNISYS.com

Unisys Corporation
11720 Plaza America Dr
Reston, VA 20190
703-439-5000
703-439-5185
www.unisys.com

XOsoft
1601 Trapelo Road
Waltham, MA 02451
781-419-5200
www.xosoft.com

IBM System/370 architecture-based

CDB Software Inc
11200 Richmond Ave
Houston, TX 77082
800-627-6561
281-920-3305
www.CDBSOFTWARE.com

Innovation Data Processing
275 Paterson Avenue
Little Falls, NJ 7424
973-890-7300
www.INNOVATIONDP.FDR.com

Mainstar
P.O. Box 4132
Bellevue, WA 98009
425-455-3589
800-233-6838
www.MAINSTAR.com

shaheengagan.com
2200 columbia pike
Suite 909
arlington, VA 22204
703-920-2055
https://www.shaheengagan.com

Internet-based

Buffalo Computer Graphics, Inc.
3741 Lake Shore Road
Blasdell, NY 14219
716-822-8668
www.disasterlan.com

Business Protection Systems International
5041 La Mart Drive
Suite 130
Riverside, CA 92507
800-594-3714
951-341-5050
www.businessprotection.com

COOP Systems
607 Herndon pkwy
Suite 108
Herndon, VA 20170
703-464-8700
www.coop-systems.com

Crisis Management Software LLC
P.O. Box 911
Middlebury, VT 05753
802-388-7379
www.CRISISMANAGEMENTSOFTWARE.com

EmergencyPlan.com
3778 Silverwood Drive
York, PA 17402-4355
717-755-2627
www.emergencyplan.com

Global Security Solutions LLC
12819 SE 38th #389
Bellevue, WA 98006
866-332-3477
425-990-6463
www.globalsecuritysolutions.net

Grapevine Software, LLC
33532 Atlantic Ave
Dana Point, CA 92629
949-697-4517
www.grapevinesoftware.net

MissionMode Solutions
570 Asbury Street N.
Suite 203
St. Paul, MN 55104
612-822-4800
www.missionmode.com

Optinuity, Inc.
7101 Wisconsin Ave.
Suite 1100
Bethesda, MD 20814
202-292-4920
www.optinuity.com

Pitney Bowes Inc.
1 Elmcroft Road - World Headquarters
Stamford, CT 06926-0700
888-245-PBMS
www.pb.com

RecoveryPlanner
2 Enterprise Drive
Shelton, CT 06484
203-925-3950
866-925-3950
www.RECOVERYPLANNER.com

Strohl Systems
631 Park Avenue
Kng of Prussa, PA 19406
610-768-4120
800-634-2016
www.strohlsystems.com

TAMP Computer Systems Inc.
1732 Remson Avenue
Merrick, NY 11566-2611
516-623-2038
www.DRSBYTAMP.com

Twenty First Century Communications
760 Northlawn Dr
Columbus, OH 43214
614-442-1215
800-382-8356
www.tfcc.com

Running on LINUX systems

NovaStor Corp.
80 W Cochran Street
Suite B
Simi Valley, CA 93065
805-579-6700
www.NOVASTOR.com

SOFTWARE, Erased & Damaged File Recovery Utilities

IBM AS400

TechAssist Inc
31115 US Highway 19 N
Palm Harbor, FL 34684
727-547-0499
800-274-3785
www.TOOLSTHATWORK.com

IBM PC & compatibles

Bright Tools, Inc.
P.O. Box 7034
Boca Raton, FL 33431
616-949-2177
877-512-4134
www.brighttools.com

File & Data Backup/Recovery

DEC

Bear Computer Systems Inc
12315 Califa Street
2
Valley Vlg, CA 91607
818-832-5548
800-255-0662
www.BEARCOMP.com

Hewlett-Packard

21st Century Software Inc.
940 W Valley Road
Suite 1604
Wayne, PA 19087-1853
800-555-6845
610-971-9946
www.21STCENTURYSOFTWARE.com

Orbit Software USA Inc
315 Diablo Road
Danville, CA 94526
925-837-4143
www.ORBITSOFTWARE.com

TriAxis Inc.
23 Midstate Drive
Suite 106
Auburn, MA 01501
508-721-9691
www.triaxisinc.com

IBM AS400

Application Design Services, Inc.
250 A Centerville Road
Warwick, RI 02886
401-737-2040
866-423-7400
www.adsapps.com

Help Systems Inc
6101 Baker Road
Suite 210
Minnetonka, MN 55345-5981
952-933-0609
www.HELPSYSTEMS.com

Lakeview Technology Inc.
1901 South Meyers Road
Suite 600
Oakbrook Terrace, IL 60181
630-282-8100
www.lakeviewtech.com

PAE Inc
7 Riverway Road
Salem, MA 01970
978-744-8612
www.PAEINC.com

SOFTWARE

SOFTWARE

IBM DB2/MVS-specific

Advanced Software Products Group, Inc.
3185 Horseshoe Drive South
Naples, FL 34104
800-662-6090
239-649-1548
http://www.aspg.com

CDB Software Inc
11200 Richmond Ave
Houston, TX 77082
800-627-6561
281-920-3305
www.CDBSOFTWARE.com

Recovery Knowledge
P.O. Box 20870
Long Beach, CA 90801
800-754-2201

IBM large systems

21st Century Software Inc.
940 W Valley Road
Suite 1604
Wayne, PA 19087-1853
800-555-6845
610-971-9946
www.21STCENTURYSOFTWARE.com

Ciber Inc
5251 Dtc Parkway
Greenwood Vlg, CO 80111
303-220-0100
www.CIBER.com

Mainstar
P.O. Box 4132
Bellevue, WA 98009
425-455-3589
800-233-6838
www.MAINSTAR.com

New Era Software Inc
18625 Sutter Boulevard
Morgan Hill, CA 95037
800-421-5035
www.newera.com

SERENA Software
2755 Campus Drive
San Mateo, CA 94403
650-522-6600
800-457-3736
www.SERENA.com

Systems/Software Engineering
940 W Valley Road
Wayne, PA 19087
610-341-9017
800-555-6845
www.SSE.com

Universal Software Inc
304 Federal Road
Brookfield, CT 06804-2418
203-792-5100
800-333-4567
www.UNIVERSALSOFT.com

IBM PC & compatibles

Darryl Thompson
P.O. Box 12408
Durham, NC 27709
919-210-3737
919-484-1453
www.prepaidlegal.com/hub/darrylthompson

Lockstep Systems Inc.
P.O. Box 1906
Scottsdale, AZ 85252
480-596-9432
877-932-3497
www.LOCKSTEP.com

Pitney Bowes Inc.
1 Elmcroft Road - World Headquarters
Stamford, CT 06926-0700
888-245-PBMS
www.pb.com

LINUX systems

21st Century Software Inc.
940 W Valley Road
Suite 1604
Wayne, PA 19087-1853
800-555-6845
610-971-9946
www.21STCENTURYSOFTWARE.com

Red Hat Linux, Inc.
1801 Varsity Drive
Raleigh, NC 27606
866-273-3428 x45555
919-754-3700
www.redhat.com

Networks

CommVault Systems Inc
P.O. Box 900
Oceanport, NJ 07757
732-870-4000
www.COMMVAULT.com

CommVault Systems Inc
200 Elgin St. Suite 1105
Ottawa, ON K2P 1L5
Canada
613-231-2800
www.COMMVAULT.com

EVault, Inc.
6121 Hollis St.
Emeryville, CA 94608
877-382-8581
www.evault.com

LiveVault Corporation
201 Boston Post Road West
Marlborough, MA 01752-4667
508-460-6670
800-638-5518
www.LIVEVAULT.com

Storage Soutions Group
222 S15th Street Suite 3B
Omaha, NE 68102
888-884-7967
402-884-7967
www.storsolgroup.com

Syncsort Inc.
50 Tice Boulevard
Woodcliff Lk, NJ 07677
201-930-9700
201-930-8200
www.SYNCSORT.com

UltraBac Software
15015 Main Street
Suite 200
Bellevue, WA 98007-5229
425-644-6000
www.ultrabac.com

VERITAS
350 Ellis Street
Mountain View, CA 94043
650-527-8000
800-327-2232
www.VERITAS.com

Sun

21st Century Software Inc.
940 W Valley Road
Suite 1604
Wayne, PA 19087-1853
800-555-6845
610-971-9946
www.21STCENTURYSOFTWARE.com

Legato Software
2350 W El Camino Real
Mountianview, CA 94040
925-556-4100
650-210-7000
www.legato.com

TriAxis Inc.
23 Midstate Drive
Suite 106
Auburn, MA 01501
508-721-9691
www.triaxisinc.com

UNIX

21st Century Software Inc.
940 W Valley Road
Suite 1604
Wayne, PA 19087-1853
800-555-6845
610-971-9946
www.21STCENTURYSOFTWARE.com

aivant L.P.
2780 Bert Adams Road
Suite 315
Atlanta, GA 30339
770-435-1101
www.aivant.com

SOFTWARE

ALCIE Integrated Solutions
300 Marcelalurin Blv
Saint Lauro, QC H4M 2L4
Canada
514-744-3440

BMC Software Inc.
2101 Citywest Boulevard
Houston, TX 77042
713-918-8800
www.BMC.com

Cactus International
509 E Ridgeville Boulevard
Mount Airy, MD 21771
301-829-1622
800-525-8649
www.CACTUS.com

Lone Star Software Corporation
509 E Ridgeville Blvd
Mount Airy, MD 21771
301-829-1622
www.cactus.com

Select Sales Inc
31 Dartmouth Street
Westwood, MA 02090
781-326-8600
800-634-1806
www.select.com

TriAxis Inc.
23 Midstate Drive
Suite 106
Auburn, MA 01501
508-721-9691
www.triaxisinc.com

SOFTWARE, File Transfer

AS400-SUN

TriAxis Inc.
23 Midstate Drive
Suite 106
Auburn, MA 01501
508-721-9691
www.triaxisinc.com

PC-HEWLETT-PACKARD

WRQ Inc
1500 Dexter Ave N
Seattle, WA 98109
206-217-7100
800-872-2829
www.WRQ.com

PC-IBM large systems

TriAxis Inc.
23 Midstate Drive
Suite 106
Auburn, MA 01501
508-721-9691
www.triaxisinc.com

PC-Macintosh

Laplink Software Inc
10210 NE Points Drive
Suite 400
Kirkland, WA 98033
425-952-6000
www.LAPLINK.com

Unipress Software Inc
2025 State Route 27
Edison, NJ 08817
732-287-2100

PC-UNIX

TriAxis Inc.
23 Midstate Drive
Suite 106
Auburn, MA 01501
508-721-9691
www.triaxisinc.com

SOFTWARE, Mirror Imaging

Running on IBM AS400

Application Design Services, Inc.
250 A Centerville Road
Warwick, RI 02886
401-737-2040
866-423-7400
www.adsapps.com

Barsa Consulting Group, LLC
2900 Westchester Ave.
Purchase, NY 10577
914-251-1234
212-579-9442
www.barsaconsulting.com

Lakeview Technology Inc.
1901 South Meyers Road
Suite 600
Oakbrook Terrace, IL 60181
630-282-8100
www.lakeviewtech.com

Running on IBM large systems

CDB Software Inc
11200 Richmond Ave
Houston, TX 77082
800-627-6561
281-920-3305
www.CDBSOFTWARE.com

TriAxis Inc.
23 Midstate Drive
Suite 106
Auburn, MA 01501
508-721-9691
www.triaxisinc.com

Running on IBM PCs & compatibles

Digital Forensics Canada Inc.
16715 - 12 Yonge St
P.O. Box 1079
Newmarket, ON L3X 1X4
Canada
905-836-0393
416-428-7369
www.digitalforensics.ca

Syncsort Inc.
50 Tice Boulevard
Woodcliff Lk, NJ 07677
201-930-9700
201-930-8200
www.SYNCSORT.com

Running on UNIX-based systems

TriAxis Inc.
23 Midstate Drive
Suite 106
Auburn, MA 01501
508-721-9691
www.triaxisinc.com

SOFTWARE, Miscellaneous

Bank contingency planning software

Computer Security Consultants Inc
590 Danbury Road
Ridgefield, CT 06877
800-925-2724
www.CSCIWEB.com

RecoveryPlanner
2 Enterprise Drive
Shelton, CT 06484
203-925-3950
866-925-3950
www.RECOVERYPLANNER.com

Strohl Systems
631 Park Avenue
Kng of Prussa, PA 19406
610-768-4120
800-634-2016
www.strohlsystems.com

Business continuity planning software

Binomial International
812 Procter Ave.
Ogdensburg, NY 13669
888-246-6642
www.binomial.com

Business911 International Inc
7710-T Cherry Park Drive
Suite 206
Houston, TX 77095-2725
281-550-4995
www.BUSINESS911.com

COOP Systems
607 Herndon pkwy
Suite 108
Herndon, VA 20170
703-464-8700
www.coop-systems.com

Disaster Management Inc.
1531 SE Sunshine Avenue
Port St. Lucie, FL 34952-6011
772-335-9750
www.DISASTERMGT.com

Evergreen Data Continuity Inc
28 Green Street
Newbury, MA 01951-1711
978-499-7722
800-727-4664
www.EVERGREEN-DATA.com

PaloAlto Software
144 E 14th Ave
Eugene, OR 97401
800-229-7526
541-683-6162
www.scplans.com

Paradigm Solutions International
2600 Tower Oaks Blvd
Suite 500
Rockville, MD 20852
800-679-2856
301-468-1200
www.paradigmsolutions.com

RecoveryPlanner
2 Enterprise Drive
Shelton, CT 06484
203-925-3950
866-925-3950
www.RECOVERYPLANNER.com

SOFTWARE

TAMP Computer Systems Inc.
1732 Remson Avenue
Merrick, NY 11566-2611
516-623-2038
www.DRSBYTAMP.com

Business impact analysis software

COOP Systems
607 Herndon pkwy
Suite 108
Herndon, VA 20170
703-464-8700
www.coop-systems.com

Disaster Management Inc.
1531 SE Sunshine Avenue
Port St. Lucie, FL 34952-6011
772-335-9750
www.DISASTERMGT.com

PaloAlto Software
144 E 14th Ave
Eugene, OR 97401
800-229-7526
541-683-6162
www.scplans.com

RecoveryPlanner
2 Enterprise Drive
Shelton, CT 06484
203-925-3950
866-925-3950
www.RECOVERYPLANNER.com

Strohl Systems
631 Park Avenue
Kng of Prussa, PA 19406
610-768-4120
800-634-2016
www.strohlsystems.com

Business resumption planning software

BCP Tools
1623 Military Road # 377
Niagara Falls, NY 14304-1745
800-461-3095
www.BCPTools.com

COOP Systems
607 Herndon pkwy
Suite 108
Herndon, VA 20170
703-464-8700
www.coop-systems.com

eBRP Solutions
7895 Tranmere Drive
Unit 25
Mississauga, ON L5S 1W9
Canada
905-677-0404
888-480-3277 (eBRP)
www.ebrp.net

Persson Associates
P. O. Box 1163
Huntley, IL 60124
847-732-6500
www.perssonassociates.com

RecoveryPlanner
2 Enterprise Drive
Shelton, CT 06484
203-925-3950
866-925-3950
www.RECOVERYPLANNER.com

Strohl Systems
631 Park Avenue
Kng of Prussa, PA 19406
610-768-4120
800-634-2016
www.strohlsystems.com

Credit Union contingency planning software

RecoveryPlanner
2 Enterprise Drive
Shelton, CT 06484
203-925-3950
866-925-3950
www.RECOVERYPLANNER.com

Strohl Systems
631 Park Avenue
Kng of Prussa, PA 19406
610-768-4120
800-634-2016
www.strohlsystems.com

USERS Inc.
1250 Drummers Lane
Valley Forge, PA 19482
610-687-9400
800-523-7282
www.users.com

Electronic vaulting/remote backup

ALSO SEE REMOTE SOFTWARE
BACKUP/RECOVERY SERVICES IN DATA &
RECORDS STORAGE SECTION

Advanced Systems Concepts Inc.
1 Gatehall Drive
Suite 210
Parsippany, NJ 07054
201-798-6400
800-229-2724
www.ADVSYSCON.com

Backup Inc
10350 Science Center Drive
Build14 Suit153
San Diego, CA 92121
858-320-4800
www.BACKUP.com

Legato Software
2350 W El Camino Real
Mountianview, CA 94040
925-556-4100
650-210-7000
www.legato.com

LightEdge Solutions
666 Walnut St. Suite 1900
Des Moines, IA 50309
612-252-2300
877-771-EDGE
www.lightedge.com

LiveVault Corporation
201 Boston Post Road West
Marlborough, MA 01752-4667
508-460-6670
800-638-5518
www.LIVEVAULT.com

Recall
2109 Bering Drive
San Jose, CA 95131
408-453-2753
www.recall.com

Recall
P.O. Box 1365
Saint Louis, MO 63043
314-991-5992
www.recall.com

Recall SDS.
522 Cottage Grove Road
Suite D1
Bloomfield, CT 06002
860-243-1311
800-233-8810
www.Recall.com

Recall Total Information Management
180 Technology Parkway
Norcross, GA 30092
770-776-1000
www.RECALL.com

Recall Total Information Management
5286 Timberlea Blvd
Mississauga, ON L4W 2S6
Canada
905-629-8440
www.RECALL.com

Rimage
7725 Washington Ave S
Edina, MN 55439
952-944-8144
www.rimage.com

TriAxis Inc.
23 Midstate Drive
Suite 106
Auburn, MA 01501
508-721-9691
www.triaxisinc.com

Emergency management software

Agency for Healthcare Research and Quality
Office of Communications and Knowledge Transfer
540 Gaither Road, Suite 2000
Rockville, MD 20850
301-427-1364
www.ahrq.gov

Amcom Software Inc
5555 W 78th Street
Minneapolis, MN 55439-2702
952-829-7445
800-852-8935
www.AMCOMSOFT.com

Anti Terrorism Accreditation Board
1266 West Paces Ferry Rd
Suite 207
Atlanta, GA 30327
703-880-5212
877-6507190
http://www.goATAB.org

BuildingReports.com
4475 River Green Parkway
Suite 200
Duluth, GA 30096
770-495-1993
www.BUILDINGREPORTS.com

E Team Inc.
21700 Oxnard St
Suite 950
Woodland Hills, CA 91367
818-932-0660
877-546-7892
www.ETEAM.com

SOFTWARE

EmerGeo Solutions, Inc.
555 Burrard St
Suite 900
Vancouver, BC V7X 1M8
Canada
604-443-5025
www.emergeo.com

ESi - Emergency Systems Integrators
699 Broad Street
Suite 1100
Augusta, GA 30901
706-823-0911
www.esi911.com

ESRI
380 New York Street
Redlands, CA 92373-8100
909-793-2853
www.esri.com

ESS
1700 Research Blvd.
Rockville, MD 20850
301-556-1700
www.ess-home.com

GeoAge, Inc.
3740 St. Johns Bluff Rd. S
Suite 9
Jacksonville, FL 32224
866-565-9855
904-565-9855
http://www.geoage.com

Paul Consulting Inc.
1342 Timberlane Road
Suite 201
Tallahassee, FL 32312
850-523-9626
850-510-6216
www.paulconsulting.com

RecoveryPlanner
2 Enterprise Drive
Shelton, CT 06484
203-925-3950
866-925-3950
www.RECOVERYPLANNER.com

SoftRisk Technologies Inc
P.O. Box 20163
St. Simons Island, GA 31522
912-634-1700
912-638-0820
www.sotfrisk.com

WeatherBug Government Services
2-5 Metropolitan Court
Gaithersburg, MD 20878
301-258-8390
800-544-4429
www.weatherbuggovernment.com

Facility management software

MicroMain Corporation
5100 Bee Caves Road
Austin, TX 78746
512-328-3235
www.micromain.com

Hazardous material management software

Quantum Complience Systems
2111 Golfside Drive
Ypsilanti, MI 48197
734-572-1000
www.QCS-FACTS.com

Incident management & planning software

Amcom Software Inc
5555 W 78th Street
Minneapolis, MN 55439-2702
952-829-7445
800-852-8935
www.AMCOMSOFT.com

COOP Systems
607 Herndon pkwy
Suite 108
Herndon, VA 20170
703-464-8700
www.coop-systems.com

EmerGeo Solutions, Inc.
555 Burrard St
Suite 900
Vancouver, BC V7X 1M8
Canada
604-443-5025
www.emergeo.com

ESRI
380 New York Street
Redlands, CA 92373-8100
909-793-2853
www.esri.com

FieldSoft Inc.
P.O. Box 1378
Chandler, AZ 85244-1378
480-899-2128
www.fieldsoft.com

Gemini Systems
61 Broadway
Suite 925
New York, NY 10006
212-480-3960
www.gemini-systems.com

PaloAlto Software
144 E 14th Ave
Eugene, OR 97401
800-229-7526
541-683-6162
www.scplans.com

RecoveryPlanner
2 Enterprise Drive
Shelton, CT 06484
203-925-3950
866-925-3950
www.RECOVERYPLANNER.com

Send Word Now
224 West 30th Street
Suite 301
New York, NY 10001
800-388-4796
www.sendwordnow.com

Serena Software
2755 Campus Drive
3rd Floor
San Mateo, CA 94403-2538
650-522-6600
503-645-1150
http://serena.com

Strohl Systems
631 Park Avenue
Kng of Prussa, PA 19406
610-768-4120
800-634-2016
www.strohlsystems.com

Systems Documentation, Inc (SDI)
1001 Durham Avenue
South Plainfield, NJ 07080
908-754-9500
800-SDI-1170
www.sdicorp.com

TRA, Inc.
1608 Walnut Street, Suite 1602
Philadelphia, PA 19103
215-546-9110
www.traonline.com

Information integrity verification software

Unitech Systems Inc
1240 E Diehl Road
Naperville, IL 60563
630-505-1800
www.UNITECHSYS.com

Network backup/recovery

Application Design Services, Inc.
250 A Centerville Road
Warwick, RI 02886
401-737-2040
866-423-7400
www.adsapps.com

Cambridge Computer Services, Inc.
271 Waverley Oaks Road
Suite 301
Waltham, MA 02452
781-250-3000
www.cambridgecomputer.com

Exagrid Systems
2000 West Park Drive
Wesboro, MA 01581
508-898-2872
www.exagrid.com

TriAxis Inc.
23 Midstate Drive
Suite 106
Auburn, MA 01501
508-721-9691
www.triaxisinc.com

Zetta Systems, Inc.
16928 Woodinville Redmond Road NE
Suite B210
Woodinville, 98072 98072
425-485-5548

Network census & inventory

Magee Enterprises Inc
2909 Langford Road
Norcross, GA 30071
770-446-6611
www.MAGEE.com

Tally Systems Corp
P.O. Box 70
Hanover, NH 03755
603-643-1300
www.TALLYSYSTEMS.com

Network problem management

Acterna
20410 Observation Drive
Germantown, MD 20876
800-638-2049
866-228-3762
www.acterna.com

AdRem Software, Inc.
410 Park Avenue, 15th Floor
New York, NY 10022
212-319-4114
www.adremsoft.com

Advanced Electronic Support Products
1810 NE 144th Street
North Miami, FL 33181
800-446-2377
www.AESP.com

Argent
6 Forest Park
Drive
Framington, CT
860-674-1700
www.argent.com

Crosstec Corporation
500 NE Spanish River Blvd.
Suite 201
Boca Raton, FL 33431
800-675-0729
561-391-6560
www.crossTecCorp.com

CXR Digilog
2360 Maryland Road
Willow Grove, PA 19090
800-344-4564
www.digilog.com

Enterasys
35 Industrial Way
Rochester, NH 03867
603-332-9400
www.enterasys.com

Fluke Corporation
P.O. Box 9090
Everett, WA 98206
425-347-6100
800-443-5853
www.fluke.com

Madge Ltd.
39293 Plymouth Rd Suite 107 h
Livonia, MI 48150
734-266-1915
www.MADGE.com

Neon Software
244 Lafayette Circle
Lafayette, CA 94549
925-283-9771
www.neon.com

NEP Manage
35 New England Business Center
Suite 140
Andover, MA 01810
978-685-4000
www.nepmanage.com

Nortel Networks
8200 Dixie Rd. Suite 100
Brampton, ON L6T 5P6
Canada
905-863-0000
800-466-7835
www.NORTELNETWORKS.com

Novell Inc.
1800 South Novell Place
Provo, UT 84606
801-861-7000
www.NOVELL.com

Tekelec
26580 W. Agoura Road
Calabasas, CA 91302
800-835-3532
www.TEKELEC.com

Network problem management, UNIX systems

TeamQuest Corporation
One TeamQuest way
Clear Lake, IA 50428
641-357-2700
www.teamquest.com

Password management

AccessData Corp
384 South 400 West
Lindon, UT 84042
801-377-5410
www.ACCESSDATA.com

Power-loss-detect-&-shutdown utility software

New Generation Software Inc.
3835 N Freeway Boulevard Suite 200
Sacramento, CA 95834
916-920-2200
www.NGSI.com

Works Right INC.
P.O. Box 1156
Madison, MS 39130
601-853-1189
www.worksright.com

Risk analysis software

IBM Global Services
10 North Martingale Road
Woodfield Prese
Schaumburg, IL 60173
1-800-IBM-7080
www.ibm.com

Palisade Corporation
798 Cascadilla Street
Ithaca, NY 14850
607-277-8000
800-432-7475
www.PALISADE.com

PaloAlto Software
144 E 14th Ave
Eugene, OR 97401
800-229-7526
541-683-6162
www.scplans.com

RiskWatch Inc.
2553 Housley Rd
Suite 100
Annapolis, MD 21401
410-224-4773
www.RISKWATCH.com

SafeNet, Inc
4690 Millennium Dr.
Belcamp, MD 21017
410-931-7500
www.safenet-inc.com

Securac, Inc.
2500, 520 -5th Avenue S.W.
Calgary, AB T2P 3R7
Canada
403-225-0403
877-328-7220
www.securac.net

Strohl Systems
631 Park Avenue
Kng of Prussa, PA 19406
610-768-4120
800-634-2016
www.strohlsystems.com

SunGard Availability Services
680 E Swedesford Road
Wayne, PA 19087
800-468-7483
800-523-4970
www.availability.sungard.com

Security & access control, Hewlett Packard

Davis Systems Software Inc
6411 Ivy Lane
Greenbelt, MD 20707
301-486-4600

Security & access control, UNIX

S4Software
6633 Convoy Court
San Diego, CA 92111
858-560-8112
www.s4software.com

Security & authentication software

Los Altos Technologies
111 corning road, suite 160
Cary, NC 27511
1-800-999-8649
1-919-233-9889
www.lat.com

MAXxess Systems, Inc
1515 S. Manchester Ave
Anaheim, CA 92802
800-842-0221
www.maxxess-systems.com

RSA Security
174 Middlesex Turnpike
Bedford, MA 01730
781-687-7000
www.RSASECURITY.com

Security Defense Systems Corp
160 Park Avenuereet
Nutley, NJ 07110
973-235-0606
www.securitydefense.com

Softsystems Inc
1 Summit Avenue Suite 1007
Fort Worth, TX 76102
817-877-5070

TriAxis Inc.
23 Midstate Drive
Suite 106
Auburn, MA 01501
508-721-9691
www.triaxisinc.com

VIACK Corporation
14811 N Kierland Blvd
Suite 100
Phoenix, AZ 85254
480-735-5900
866-265-8060
www.viack.com

SOFTWARE

SOFTWARE

Security policies

BindView Corp
5151 San Felipe Street
Houston, TX 77056
713-561-4000
800-813-5869
www.BINDVIEW.com

NetIQ Corp.
1233 West Loop S
Houston, TX 77027
713-548-1700
888-323-6768
www.NETIQ.com

Strategy evaluation software

NIST- National Insitute of Standards and Technology
Building and Fire Research Laboratory
100 Bureau Drive, Stop 8600
Gaithersburg, MD 20899-8600
301-975-5900
www.nist.gov

Tape library management system (barcode-based)

Cartagena Software Limited
101 Drawbridge Drive
Markham, ON L6C 2N5
Canada
888-USE-TAPE
905-887-0755
www.cartagena.com

**TriAxis Inc.
23 Midstate Drive
Suite 106
Auburn, MA 01501
508-721-9691
www.triaxisinc.com**

SOFTWARE, Remote Operation

Data General

SENTRY
4261-A14 Hwy. #7, Suite #180
Toronto, ON L3R 9W6
Canada
416-270-5574
403-8800102
www.SentryCorp.CA

IBM AS400

Help Systems Inc
6101 Baker Road
Suite 210
Minnetonka, MN 55345-5981
952-933-0609
www.HELPSYSTEMS.com

Vision Solutions
17911 Von Karman Avenue
Floor 5th
Irvine, CA 92614
949-253-6500
800-683-4667
www.VISIONSOLUTIONS.com

IBM PC & compatibles

Century Software
5284 South Commerce Dr
Salt Lake City, UT 84107
801-268-3088
www.CENTURYSOFTWARE.com

ConvergingTechnologies Inc.
3760 N Commerce Drive
Suite 100
Tucson, AZ 85705
800-846-9726
520-629-9810
www.SPARTACOM.com

Excelltech
812 W 3rd Street
Yankton, SD 57078
605-665-8324

Norton-Lambert
P.O. Box 4085
Santa Barbara, CA 93140
805-964-6767
www.norton-lambert.com

Stampede Technologies Inc
80 Rhoades Center Drive
Dayton, OH 45458
937-291-5035
800-763-3423
www.stampede.com

Networks

InoStor Corporation
13000 Gregg Street
Poway, CA 92064
858-726-1800
www.inostor.com

SOFTWARE, Virus Detection/Prevention/ Recovery

IBM PC & compatibles-based

Authentium
7121 Fairway Drive
Suite 102
Palm Beach Gardens, FL 33418
800-423-9147
www.authentium.com

Computer Associates International Inc.
1 Computer Asso
Islandia, NY 11749
800-841-8743
www.CA.com

Microsoft Corp
1 Microsoft Way
Redmond, WA 98052
425-882-8080
800-642-7676
www.MICROSOFT.com

Securify
20425 Stevens Creek Blvd
Cupertino, CA 95014
408-343-4300
www.securify.com

Software Security Solutions
1425 Brentwood St.
Suite 12
Lakewood, CO 80214
303-232-9070
303-233-2371
www.SoftwareSecuritySolutions.com

SYTEX Inc
1934 Old Gallows Rd
Vienna, VA 22182
703-893-9095
http://www.sytex.com

Touchstone Software Corp
1530 Temporary St.
Andover, MA 01845
800-531-0450

Macintosh-based

Apple Computer Inc
1 Infinite Loop
Cupertino, CA 95014
408-996-1010
www.APPLE.com

SYMANTEC Corp
20330 Stevens Creek Bvld
Cupertino, CA 95014
408-253-9600
800-441-7234
www.symantec.com

SOFTWARE

SOFTWARE

SUPPLIES

SUPPLIES, Covers

Waterproof emergency covers, custom-fit

Bamberger Industries Inc
564 Leheigh Lane
Woodmere, NY 11598-1020
516-295-3170

COVERGUARD Corp
1431 Dewey Street
Hollywood, FL 33020
954-923-5550
800-244-7891
www.COVERGUARDCORP.com

Kappler
115 Grimes Drive
Guntersville, AL 35976
800-600-4019
256-505-4005
www.kappler.com

SUPPLIES, Miscellaneous

Business forms

Mortgage Production
601 Magnetic Drive Suite 26
Toronto, ON M3J 3J2
Canada
416-835-4836
www.mortgageproduction.ca

Rite in the Rain, Division of J. L. Darling Corp.
2614 Pacific Highway E
Tacoma, WA 98424-1001
253-922-5000
www.RITEINTHERAIN.com

Cables, fire-safe

DuPont Safety & Environmental Mgmnt. Svcs
1007 Market Street
Wilmington, DE 19898-0001
302-774-1000
www.DUPONT.com

Clothing, protective

Draeger Safety Inc.
101 Technology Drive
Pittsburgh, PA 15275
412-787-8383
800-615-5503
www.DRAEGER-SAFETY.com

LIon Apparel
6450 Poe Avenue
Dayton, OH 45413-0576
937-898-1949
www.lionapparel.com

Coatings, protective

Energy Management Systems
4208 Fitch Ave
Baltimore, MD 21236
800-537-3911
410-882-0800
www.emswindowfilm.com

Grace Constructions Products .
1330 Industry Road
Hatfield, PA 19440
215-362-9020

Containers, contamination storage - HAZMAT

Airgas, Inc.
259 North Radnor-Chester Rd.
Radnor, PA 19087-5283
800-255-2165
www.airgas.com

Hazmat Medical Associates
P.O. BOX 483
New Lenox, IL 60451
815-485-0096
800-462-4002
www.HAZMATMEDICAL.com

Containers, miscellaneous types

Flambeau Inc
100 Grace Drive
Weldon, NC 27890
252-536-2171
www.flambeau.com

Specialized Products Company
1100 S Kimball Avenue
Southlake, TX 76092
817-329-6647
800-866-5353
www.SPECIALIZED.net

Containers, ruggedized

Ameripack
70 South Main Street
P.O. Box 457
Cranbury, NJ 08512
609-395-6969
800-456-7963
www.ameripack.com

SUPPLIES

Hardigg
147 North Main Street
South Deerfield, MA 01373
413-665-2163
800-542-7344
www.militarycases.com

UK
13400 Danielson Street
Poway, CA 92064
858-513-9100
800-327-7388
www.ukbright.com

Westamerican Custom Case Corp
Unit 10-91 Golden Dr.
Coquitlam, BC V3K 6R2
Canada
877-668-2273
604-718-4181

Zero Manufacturing
500 W 200 N
N Salt Lake, UT 84054
801-298-5900
www.ZEROCASES.com

Containers, storage for electronic equipment

Plug-In Storage Systems Inc
70 Industry Dr
West Haven, CT 06477
800-231-5952
pluginstorage.com

UK
13400 Danielson Street
Poway, CA 92064
858-513-9100
800-327-7388
www.ukbright.com

Cots, beds, blankets, tents, etc.

ALSO SEE SHELTERS, PORTABLE IN MOBILE
BUILDINGS SECTION

Coleman Company
Wichita, KS 67201
800-633-7155
www.COLEMAN.com

E-Z Up International, Inc
1601 Iowa Avenue
Riverside, CA 92507
951-781-0843
800-45-SHADE
www.ezup.com

Facility Supply
81 Loudville Road
Easthampton, MA 01027
800-981-8128
413-527-6265
www.FACILITYSUPPLY.com

Festive Tents, LP
10934 Hazelhurst Drive
Houston, TX 77043-3910
713-468-3687
800-391-0448
www.FESTIVETENTS.com

Northwest Woolen Mills
235 Singleton Street
Woonsocket, RI 02895
401-769-0189
800-848-9665
www.northwestwoolen.com

ProPac Inc.
5601 Rivers Avenue
N Charleston, SC 29406
843-308-0994
800-345-3036
www.propacusa.com

Simpler Life Emergency Provisions
2035 Park Avenue
Suite 1
Redlands, CA 92373
909-798-8108
800-266-7737
www.simplerlife.com

Taylor Rental / Party Plus
225 E. Buckingham Rd.
Garland, TX 75040
972-530-6334
www.TAYLORRENTALGARLAND.com

Fasteners, earthquake-proof

Fastening Solutions Inc
19458 Ventura Boulevard
Suite 6
Tarzana, CA 91356-3056
800-232-7836
818-996-1977
www.FASTENINGSOLUTIONS.com

Q-Safety
1760 Evergreen Street
Duarte, CA 91010-2845
800-997-2338
www.qsafety.com

QuakeHold! by Trevco
1150 Simpson Way
Escondivo, CA 92029
760-510-4969
www.earthquakeinfo.com

SUPPLIES

Trevco
1150 Simpson Way
Escondido, CA 92029
760-466-1060
www.TREVCO.net

WORKSAFE TECHNOLOGIES
25133 Avenue Tibbitts
Valencia, CA 91355
661-257-2527
www.WORKSAFETECH.com

Fasteners, hurricane-proof, for windows

Plylox
P.O. Box 1749
Friendswood, TX 77549-1749
281-996-6903
800-583-4289
www.plylox.com

Window Lock Products
4541 White Feather Trail
Daytona Beach, FL 33436
888-228-1600

Fasteners, security

Lakeside True Value
2221 Stevenson Dr.
Springfield, IL 62703
217-529-2987
217-529-5032

Secure-It Inc.
18 Maple Court
East Longmeadow, MA 01028
413-525-7039
www.SECURE-IT.com

Fireproof containers & bags

BAGMASTERS
1160 California Avenue
Corona, CA 92881
800-843-2247
951-280-2400
www.BAGMASTERS.com

DEW Filing Systems and Storage
1525 E. Apache Blvd.
Tempe, AZ 85281
877-933-7238
480-858-0024
www.thefilestore.com

Media Protection Products
P.O. Box 632
Buffalo, NY 14215
716-835-0729
800-445-3309
www.FIRECOOLER.com

Schwab Corp
110 Professional Court
Lafayette, IN 47905
765-447-9470
800-428-7678
www.SCHWABCORP.com

Food & water in emergency rations

AlpineAire Foods
8551 Cottonwood Road
Bozeman, MT 59718
406-585-9324
406-585-9324
www.ALPINEAIRE.com

Aqua Blox Beverage Inc
12000 Slauson Avenue
Suite 3
Santa Fe Spgs, CA 90670
562-693-9599
www.aquablox.com

Be Ready Inc.
602 Garrison Street
Suite 101
Oceanside, CA 92054
760-966-3600
www.bereadyonline.com

Emergency Lifeline
P.O. Box 15293
Santa Ana, CA 92735
714-558-8940
800-826-2201
www.EMERGENCYLIFELINE.com

HeaterMeals
311 Northland Blvd
Cincinnati, OH 45246
800-503-4483
513-772-3066
www.heatermeals.com

IMAC: International Management Assistance Corp.
15830 Foltz Industrial Parkway
Strongsville, OH 44149
440-878-7600
www.IMACSERVICES.com

Nitro-Pak Preparedness Center Inc.
147 N main
Heber City, UT 84032
800-866-4876
www.NITRO-PAK.com

Oregon Freeze Dry Inc.
P.O. Box 1048
Albany, OR 97321
800-547-0244
www.mountainhouse.com

SUPPLIES

SUPPLIES

Ponderosa Sports
6854 Highway 55
Horseshoe Bnd, ID 83629
208-793-3121
www.PONDEROSASPORTS.com

Reliable Restaurant Supplies Co., LTD
3477 Kennedy Road
Unit 2
Scarborough, ON M1V 3Z7
Canada
416-297-9612
647-288-2338
www.reliablesupplies.com

Simpler Life Emergency Provisions
2035 Park Avenue
Suite 1
Redlands, CA 92373
909-798-8108
800-266-7737
www.simplerlife.com

Wornick Company The
4701 Creek Road Suite 200
Cincinnati, OH 45242
513-552-7415
www.WORNICK.com

Gas masks, smoke hoods, personal

Brookdale (A DuPont Canada Company)
1-8755 Ash Street
Vancouver, BC V6P 6T3
Canada
800-459-3822
604-324-3822
www.evacsafety.com

Bullard Co.
1898 Safety Way
Rutland, KY 41031
800-227-0423
859-234-6611
www.bullard.com

Extreme Safety, LLC
1123 E. Dominguez St. Suite F
Carson, CA 90746
310-632-5671
www.extremesafety.com

Gentex Corporation
324 Main Street
Simpson, PA 18407
570-282-3550
www.gentexcorp.com

Safety Express
10441-172 Street
Edmondton, AB T5S 1K9
Canada
780-486-4889
www.safetyexpress.com

Safety Express
104-2971 Viking Way
Richmond, BC V6V 1Y1
Canada
514-422-8886
www.safetyexpress.com

Safety Express
4060B Sladeview Cres.
Unit 2
Mississauga, ON L5L 5Y5
Canada
905-608-0111
www.safetyexpress.com

Safety Express
754 Rue Lajoie
Dorval, QB H9P 1G8
Canada
604-244-8005
www.safetyexpress.com

Simpler Life Emergency Provisions
2035 Park Avenue
Suite 1
Redlands, CA 92373
909-798-8108
800-266-7737
www.simplerlife.com

Xcaper Industries, LLC
1929 Main Street
Suite 102
Irvine, CA 92614
949-852-2021
www.xcaper.com

ID badges, self-expiring

TEMTEC Inc (TEMPbadge)
P.O. Box 823
20 Thompson Rd.
Branford, CT 06405-0823
845-368-4040
800-628-0022
www.tempbadge.com

Kits, emergency/disaster survival

A Royal Wolf Portable Storage
23422 Clawiter Rd
Hayward, CA 94545
800-447-7223
www.ROYAL-WOLF.com

Black Mountain Stores, Inc.
1721 N Texas Ave
Odessa, TX 79761-1226
800-760-7942
432-580-7175
www.survivalequiptment.net

SUPPLIES

Chinook Medical Gear, Inc.
120 Rock Point Drive
Unit C
Durango, CO 81301
970-375-1241
800-766-1365
www.chinookmed.com

Conquest International
1109 SW 8th Street
Plainville, KS 67663
785 434 2483
785 434 4540
www.conquestinc.com and www.NaturalPureWater.com

CPR Savers & First Aid Supply
300 Carlsbad Village Drive
Suite 108A -217
Carlsbad, CA 92008
800-480-1277
760-720-6277
www.cpr-savers.com

DisasterNecessities.com
1267 S. 1125 W.
Orem, UT 84058
801-361-7017
www.DisasterNecessities.com

Emergency Lifeline
POB 15293

Santa Ana, CA 92735
714-558-8940
800-826-2201
www.EMERGENCYLIFELINE.com

Evergreen Fire & Safety Inc
3618 164th Street SW
Lynnwood, WA 98037
206-368-3921
www.evergreenfireandsafety.com

F.A.S.T. Limited
8850 River Rd
Delta, BC V4G 1B5
Canada
604-540-8300
www.fastlimited.com

iPrepare Emergency Supplies
P.O. Box 344
Roseville, CA 95678
707-982-7292

Meridian Medical Technologies, Inc.
10240 Old Columbia Rd.
Columbia, MD 21046
443-259-7800
800-638-8093
www.meridianmeds.com

Peace of Mind USA
1512 Encino Ave #D
Monrovia, CA 91016
626-298-6231
www.peaceofmindUSA.com

ProText Inc
POB 30423
Bethesda, MD 20824
301-320-7231
www.PROTEXT.net

Quest Technologies, Inc.
1060 Corporate Center Dr.
Oconomowoc, WI 53066
262-567-9157
800-245-0779
www.quest-technologies.com

Simpler Life Emergency Provisions
2035 Park Avenue
Suite 1
Redlands, CA 92373
909-798-8108
800-266-7737
www.simplerlife.com

Survivor Industries Inc
4880 Adohr Lane
Camarillo, CA 93012-8508
805-498-6062
www.SURVIVORIND.com

Unlimited Resources Inc. - Florida Office
6014 Bridgewater Circle
Ponte Vedra Beach, FL 32082
703-622-6946
888-340-8010

World Prep
2620-T Centennial Road
Toledo, OH 43617
419-843-3869
888-263-3416
www.worldprep.com

Lighting

Big Beam Emergency Systems Inc.
290 East Prairie Street
P.O. Box 513
Crystal Lake, IL 60039-0518
815-459-6100
www.BIGBEAM.com

Ericson Manufacturing Company
4215 Hamann Parkway
Willoughby, OH 44094
440-951-8000
http://www.ericson.com

SUPPLIES

Simpler Life Emergency Provisions
2035 Park Avenue
Suite 1
Redlands, CA 92373
909-798-8108
800-266-7737
www.simplerlife.com

Streamlight, Inc.
30 Eagleville Rd
Eagleville, PA 19403
800-523-7488
610-631-0600
www.streamlight.com

UK
13400 Danielson Street
Poway, CA 92064
858-513-9100
800-327-7388
www.ukbright.com

WPS Disaster Management Solutions
10900 NE 8th Avenue
Suite 900
Bellevue, WA 98005
800-545-9028
425-450-3260
www.wps-plan.com

Medical supplies

Airgas, Inc.
259 North Radnor-Chester Rd.
Radnor, PA 19087-5283
800-255-2165
www.airgas.com

Alliance Medical
P.O. Box 147
Russellville, MO 65074
888-633-6098
800-4ALLMED
www.allmed.net

Ambu, Inc.
6740 Baymeadow Drive
Glen Burnie, MD 21060
800-262-8462
410-768-6464
www.AmbuUSA.com

Armstrong Medical Industries, Inc.
575 Knightsbridge Parkway
P.O. Box 700
Lincolnshire, IL 60069-0700
800-323-4220
847-913-0101
www.armstrongmedical.com

Chinook Medical Gear, Inc.
120 Rock Point Drive
Unit C
Durango, CO 81301
970-375-1241
800-766-1365
www.chinookmed.com

Disaster Management Systems
2651 Pomona Boulevard
Pomona, CA 91768
909-594-9596

Emergency Medical Products
1711 Paramount Ct
Waukesha, WI 53186
800-558-6270
www.BuyEMP.com

Masune First Aid & Safety
500 Fillmore Avenue
Tonawanda, NY 14150
716-695-4999
800-831-0894
www.MASUNE.com

Matrx Medical, Inc
P.O. Box 210
Ballentine, SC 29002
800-845-3550
803-781-3370
www.matrxmedical.com

Medprotect Inc
1900 Preston Road
Plano, TX 75093
800-945-4158
www.MEDPROTECT-INC.com

Northern Safety Co., Inc.
232 Industrial Park Drive
Frankfort, NY 13340
800-631-1246
www.northernsafety.com

Simpler Life Emergency Provisions
2035 Park Avenue
Suite 1
Redlands, CA 92373
909-798-8108
800-266-7737
www.simplerlife.com

Rags, towels

ERC Wiping Products, Inc.
19 Bennett Street
Lynn, MA 01905
800-225-9473
781-593-4000
www.ERCWIPE.com

Sandbags

Breedon Bag & Burlap Co. Inc.
2937 Strickland Street
Jacksonville, FL 32254
904-389-8085
888-428-7527
www.BREEDONBAG.com

Dayton Bag & Burlap
322 Davis Avenue
Dayton, OH 45403
800-543-3400
www.DAYBAG.com

Nier Systems Inc
6678 Newport Lake Circle
Boca Raton, FL 33496
561-989-0049
niersyst@bellsouth.net

The Sandbagger Corp.
P.O. Box 607
Wauconda, IL 60084
815-363-1400
www.THESANDBAGGER.com

Sanitation

Enviro Pump Plus, Inc.
1018 CO Rd 63
P.O. Box 376
Balation, MN 56115
507-734-4661

Porta-John
Shelby Twp, MI 48318
800-521-6310

Simpler Life Emergency Provisions
2035 Park Avenue
Suite 1
Redlands, CA 92373
909-798-8108
800-266-7737
www.simplerlife.com

Search & rescue kits & supplies

ACR Electronics, Inc.
5757 Ravenswood Road
Ft. Lauderdale, FL 33312
954-981-3333
www.acrelectronics.com

Chinook Medical Gear, Inc.
120 Rock Point Drive
Unit C
Durango, CO 81301
970-375-1241
800-766-1365
www.chinookmed.com

Emergency Lifeline
POB 15293
Santa Ana, CA 92735
714-558-8940
800-826-2201
www.EMERGENCYLIFELINE.com

Fraser-Volpe LLC
1025 Thomas Drive
Warminster, PA 18974
215-443-5240
http://www.fraser-volpe.com

Hale Products
700 Spring Mill Avenue
Conshohocken, PA 19428
610-825-6300
800-220-4253
www.haleproducts.com

Simpler Life Emergency Provisions
2035 Park Avenue
Suite 1
Redlands, CA 92373
909-798-8108
800-266-7737
www.simplerlife.com

SUPPLIES

TRAINING & CONFERENCES

TRAINING & CONFERENCES

Certification, professional: disaster/emergency

1st Responder Consultants
112 Keasler
Hughes Springs, TX 75656
903-639-3596

American Public University System
111 West Congress Street
Charles Town, WV 25414
877-468-6862
www.apus.edu

Board of Certified Safety Professionals (BCSP)
208 Burwash Avenue
Savoy, IL 61874
217-359-9263
www.bcsp.org

Boston University
755 Commonwealth Avenue
Boston, MA 02215
617-353-6000
www.bu.edu/disted/emoc

Clover Park Technical College
4500 Steilacoom Blvd SW
Lakewood, WA 98499
253-589-5862

College of Lake County
19351 W. Washington Street
Social Science Division, Room A-244
Grayslake, IL 60030
847-543-2047
www.clcillinois.edu

Columbus State Community College
Continuing Professional Education Department
550 E. Spring Street
Columbus, OH 43215
614-287-2576
www.cscc.edu/

Community College of Rhode Island
1762 Louisquisset Park
Lincoln, RI 02865
401-333-7102

CompTIA
1815 South Meyers Road
Suite 300
Oakbrook Terrace, IL 60181
630-678-8300
www.comptia.org

Continuing Challenge HazMat Workshop
5770 Freeport Blvd
Suite 200
Sacramento, CA 95822
916-433-1688
www.hazmat.org

Delgado Community College
2600 General Meyer Ave.
New Orleans, LA 70114
504-361-6246
www.dcc.edu/

DRI International
201 Park Washington Court
Falls Church, VA 22046-4527
703-538-1792
www.DRII.org

Fairleigh Dickinson University
1000 River Road
Teaneck, NJ 07666
201-692-7172
www.fdu.edu/homeland

Florida Atlantic University
P O Box 3091
Boca Raton, FL 33431-0991
561-297-0052
www.fau.edu/crisismgt

Florida State University
Florida Public Affairs Center
Center for Disaster Risk Policy
Tallahassee, FL 32306-2250
850-644-9961
www.fsu.edu/

Frederick Community College
7932 Oppossumtown Pike
Frederick, MD 21702
301-846-2635
www.frederick.edu/

Frontier Community College
Lot 2 Frontier Drive
Fairfield, IL 62837
618-842-3711
www.iecc.cc.il.us/fcc/

Gwinnett Technical College
5150 Sugarloaf Parkway
P O Box 1505
Lawrenceville, GA 30046-1505
770-962-7580 x232
www.gwinnetttechnicalcollege.com

Hennepin Technical College Campus
1450 Energy Park Drive
Suite 100-B
St Paul, MN 55108-5265
651-649-5411
800-311-3143
www.hennepintech.edu

IAQ Trainging Institute
46 South Linden Street
Duquesne, PA 15110
866-427-4727
www.IAQtraining.com

TRAINING & CONFERENCES

Institute of Hazardous Materials Management
11900 Parklawn Drive
Suite 450
Rockville, MD 20852-2676
301-984-8969
www.IHMM.org

Institute of Inspection, Cleaning, and Restoration
Certification (IICRC)
2515 E. Mill Plain Blvd.
Vancouver, WA 98661
360-693-5675
www.iicrc.com

Jacksonville State University
700 Pelham Road North
Jacksonville, AL 36265
800-231-5291 x5926
256-782-5926
http://iep.jsu.edu

Lakeland Community College
7700 Clocktower Drive
Kirtland, OH 44094
440-953-7252
www.lakeland.cc.oh.us/

Lamar Institute of Technology
855 East Lavaca
P O Box 10043
Beaumont, TX 77710
409-880-8093
www.lit.edu/currentlinks.asp?PageID=153

Lynn University
3601 North Military Trail
Boca Raton, FL 33431
561-237-7146
www.lynn.edu/

Metropolitan Community College
P. O. Box 3777
Omaha, NE 68103-0777
402-457-2756
www.mccneb.edu/

MLC & Associates, Inc.
P.O. Box 635
Port Orchard, WA 98366-0635
253-857-3124
949-222-1202
mlscandassociates.com

Montgomery County Community College
240 Parkhouse Hall
Blue Bell, PA 19422
215-641-6428
www.mc3.edu

Norwich University
Online Graduate Programs
158 Harmon Drive
Northfield, VT 05663
802-485-2001
800-468-6679
www.NORWICH.edu/index.html

Purdue University, Calumet
2200 169th Street
Hammond, IN 46323-2094
219-989-2596
www.calumet.purdue.edu

Red Rocks Community College
13300 West Sixth Avenue
Lakewood, CO 80228
303-914-6404
www.ccconline.org

Shenandoah University
1460 University Drive
Winchester, VA 22601
540-665-4584
800-665-5640

Sonoma University
1801 East Cotati Ave.
Rohnert Park, CA 94928-3609
415-265-1662
www.sonoma.edu/

SUNY Maritime College
6 Pennyfield Avenue
Bronx, NY 10465
718-409-7341
www.sunymaritime.edu

The Center for Continuity Leadership
P.O. Box 1566
Edmonds, WA 98020
425-210-9900
www.continuityleadership.com

Ultrasonics International
104-1414 Meador Ave
Bellingham, WA 98229
800-500-2544
www.sonicpro.com

Univ. of Richmond-School of Continuing Studies
Special Programs Building
28 Westhampton Way
Richmond, VA 23173
804-289-8133
www.oncampus.RICHMOND.edu/academics/scs/emermg
mt/

University of Findlay
1000 North Main Street
Findlay, OH 45840
419-434-4588
866-424-5747
http://seem.findlay.edu

University of Hawaii- West Oahu
96-129 Ala Ike
Building C-140C
Pearl City, HI 96782
808-454-4712
866-299-8656
wwwuhwo.hawaii.edu

TRAINING & CONFERENCES

University of Idaho
1776 Science Center Road
Idaho Falls, ID 83402
208-282-7718

University of Michigan- Flint
516 William Murchie Science Building
Flint, MI 48502-1950
810-762-3355
www.umflint.edu

University of Missouri
Fire and Rescue Training Institute, 201 S. Seventh
240 Heinkel Building
Columbia, MO 65211-1342
573-884-8984
www.mufrti.org/emmag.htm

University of North Carolina at Chapel Hill
Community Preparedness and Disaster Management
Campus Box 7411 (HPAA)
Chapel Hill, NC 27599-7411
919-843-1219
http://DisasterManagement.unc.edu

University of Texas at Dallas
P.O. Box 830688, SM 10
Dallas, TX 75083-0688
972-883-2562
www.som.utdallas.edu/executive/cert/emp/

University of Utah
260 South Central Campus Drive
Room 270
Salt lake City, UT 84112-9155
801-581-7930
www.utah.edu/

University of Wisconsin - Green Bay
Outreach and Extension
2420 Nicolet Drive
Green Bay, WI 54311-7001
920-465-2468
www.uwgb.edu/em

URS Corporation
200 Orchard Ridge Dr.
Suite 101
Gaithersburg, MD 20878
301-258-6554
www.urscorp.com

USG University
5775 Wayzata Blvd.
Suite 700
Minneapolis, MN 55416
612-874-6500
www.usguniversity.org

Western Washington University-EESP
516 High Street
Mail Stop 5293 WWU
Bellingham, WA 98225-5946
360-650-3717
www.ACADWEB.WWU.edu/eesp/certificates/default.asp

Disaster planning & emergency management training

AED Instructor Foundation
600 N. JACKSON ST. SUITE 1
MEDIA, PA 19063
610-566-2824

Albert Einstein Healthcare Network
WMD Training and Education
One Penn Boulevard
Philadelphia, PA 19144
215-951-8145
215-951-8195
www.AEMC-emergency.com

American Safety & Health Institute
4148 Louis Avenue
Holiday, FL 34691
800-246-5101
800-682-5067
www.ashinsitute.org

Arizona State University
Office of Hazard Studies
Tempe, AZ 85287-0703
480-965-4505

Arkansas Tech University
Dean Hall
Room 110
Russellville, AR 72801-2222
479-968-0318
commed.ATU.edu

Attainium Corp
14540 John Marshall Highway
Suite 103
Gainesville, VA 20155
571-248-8200
703-941-8462
www.attainium.net

California Specialized Training Institute
P.O. Box 8123
San Luis Obispo, CA 93403
805-549-3535
www.oes.ca.gov

California State University, Long Beach - Occupational
Studies Dept.
E-Tech 224, CSULB
1250 Bellflower Blvd
Long Beach, CA 90840-5601
888-999-9935
www.csulb.edu/depts/ocst/DL/Masters/masters.htm

Center for Disaster Research & Education (CDRE)
Millersville University, P.O. Box 1002
1 South George Street
Millersville, PA 17551
717-872-3568
muweb.MILLERSVILLE.edu/~CDRE/index.html

Center for Harzards Reaserch
California State University - Chico
Chico, CA 95929-0425
530-898-4953
www.csuchico.edu/geop/chr/chr.html

Central Georgia Technical College
3300 Macon Tech Drive
Macon, GA 31206
478-757-6688
www.cgtcollege.org

Central Missouri State University
323A Humphreys
Warrensburg, MO 64093
660-543-4971
www.cmsu.edu/sst

CertTest Training Center Inc.
1340 S. Main St, Suite 100
Grapevine, TX 76051
817-410-8000
888-923-7883
www.CertTest.com

Coastal Hazards Assessment and Mitigation Program
Clemson University
Department of Civil Engineering
Clemson, SC 29634-0911
864-656-5941

Commonwealth Films Inc
223 Commonwealth Avenue
Boston, MA 02116-1700
617-262-5634
www.COMMONWEALTHFILMS.com

CRI Network Inc
suite 401- 901 Gordon Street
Victoria, BC V8L 2K6
Canada
250-889-5030
www.crinetwork.com

Criterion Strategies Inc
580 Broadway
Suite 305
New York, NY 10012
212-343-1134
www.criterionstrategies.com

Delaware County Community College
85 N. Malin Road
Broomall, PA 19008
610-359-7387
610-359-5127
www.dccc.edu/academics/depts/teched/psafety.html

Delaware Technical & Community College
Stanton Campus
400 Stanton-Christiana Road
Newark, DE 19713
302-454-3933
www.dtcc.edu

Disaster Preparedness Academy
P.O. Box 11364
Santa Ana, CA 92711
714-481-5300
www.OC-REDCROSS.org

Discover Living
101 W. McKnight Way, B-21
Grass Valley, CA 95949
530-432-7530
www.discoverliving.com/education.html

Doyle Group/CSERT Inc., The
401 Marsh Lane
Suite 1
Newport, DE 19804
302-993-9081
888-927-3789
www.CSERT.com

Drexel University Goodwin College
3001 Market Street (One Drexel Plaza)
Suite 100
Philadelphia, PA 19104
215-895-0909
www.drexel.edu

Durham Technical Community College
2401 Snowhill Road
Durham, NC 27712
919-686-3520

Earthquake Engineering Research Institute
499 14th Street
Suite 320
Oakland, CA 94612
510-451-0905
www.eeri.org

Earthquake Solutions
940 E. Union Street
Suite s 102 and 202
Pasadena, CA 91106
626-795-4000
www.earthquakesolutions.com

East Tennessee State University
P.O. Box 70674
Johnson City, TN 37601
423-439-4332
423-439-4243
www.etsu.edu/cpah/pubheal/ugoverview.asp

Eastern Michigan University
Roosevelt Hall
Room 8
Ypsilanti, MI 48197
734-487-1590
www.emich.edu/

EducExpert
105 cote de la Montagne, suite 500
Quebec, QC G1K 4E4
Canada
418-694-2115
www.educexpert.com

Emergency Management Ontario (EMO)
25 Grosvenor Street
Floor 18
Toronto, ON M7A 1Y6
Canada
416-326-5010
416-314-3723
www.mpss.jus.gov.on.ca

Emergency Medicine Learning & Resource Center
3717 South Conway Road
Orlando, FL 32812
407-281-7396
800-766-6335
www.emlrc.org

Emergency Response Educators and Consultants, Inc.
5980 NE 57th Loop
Silver Springs, FL 34488
352-236-5348
www.erecinc.com

EMI Independent Study
16825 S Seton Avenue
independent.study@dhs.gov
Emmitsburg, MD 21727
301-447-1200
www.training.fema.gov/emiweb/is/

Emotional Continuity Management
Inner Directions, LLP
2815 Van Giesen
Richland, WA 99354
509-942-0443
509-948-3593
www.emotionalcontinuity.com

Empire State College
Center for Distance Learning
3 Union Avenue
Saratoga Springs, NY 12866-4391
518-587-2100 x775
www.esc.edu/esconline/online2.nsf/ESChome.html

fire etc. Emergency Training Centre, Lakeland College
5704 - 47 Avenue
Vermilion, AB T9X 1K4
Canada
780-853-5800
www.fire-etc.ca

Frontline Corporate Communications Inc.
650 Riverbend Drive
Kitchener, ON N2K 3S2
Canada
888-848-9898
www.fcc.onthefrontlines.com

George Washington University
900 23rd Street, NW
Suite 6142
Washington, DC 20037
202-741-2941
http://gwumc.edu/ems

Georgia State University - Andrew Young School of Policy Studies
14 Marietta Street, NW
Room 337
Atlanta, GA 30302-3992
404-651-4592
www.GSU.edu/~wwwsps

Gerard Group International LLC
164 Westford Road
Suite 15
Tyngsborough, MA 01879
978-649-4575
www.GERARDGROUP.com

Global Strategic Resources
1725 S. Rainbow Blvd., Suite 2, Box 171
Las Vegas, NV 89146
702-259-9579
www.globalstrategicresources.com

Hazards Research Lab, University of South Carolina
Department of Geography
University of South Carolina
Columbia, SC 29208
803-777-1699
www.cas.cs.edu/geog/hrl/index.htm

HazMat Solutions, Inc.
13623 Lakeshore Dr.
Grand Haven, MI 49417
616-850-9036
616-886-4448
www.hazmatsolutions.net

Indiana State University
Health, Safety & Environment Health Sciences Dept.
200 North Seventh Street
Terre Haute, IN 47809
812-237-3104
www.INDSTATE.edu/hsehs/

Industrial Emergency Council
P.O. Box 686
San Carlos, CA 94070
650-508-9008
www.iectraining.org

Institute for Business Continuity Training
1623 Military Road, # 377
Niagara Falls, NY 14304-1745
800-461-3095
www.IBCT.com

Institute for Crisis, Disaster and Risk Management
George Washington University
1776 G. St. NW, Suite 110
Washington, DC 20052
202-994-6736
www.GWU.edu/~icdrm/

International Assn of Emergency Managers (IAEM)
201 Park Washington Court
Falls Church, VA 22046-4527
703-538-1795
www.IAEM.com

Jim Stanton & Associates
2415 Dunbar Street
Vancouver, BC V6R 3N2
Canada
604-737-1612
778-772-3717
www.jim-stanton.com

John Jay College, City University of NY
445 West 59th Street
New York, NY 10019
212-237-8834
http:web.jjay.cuny.edu/~prt_mgt/index.htm

Kaplan College - School of Criminal Justice
Terrorism & National Security Management Prgrm.
6409 Congress Avenue
Boca Raton, FL 33487
866-523-3473
866-572-6026
www.KAPLANCOLLEGE.edu/terrorism

Knight-Star Enterprises, Inc.
HUB/Woman-Owned Business
P.O. Box 7873
Waco, TX 76714
866-776-1996
254-776-1996
www.knightstar.us

Life Goes On
28494 Westinghouse Place
Valencia, CA 91355
661-298-4277

Life Safety Associates
53A Bonaventura Drive
San Jose, CA 95134
408-577-1929
www.LIFESAFETY.com

Louisiana State University
119b Hodges Hall
Baton Rouge, LA 70803
225-578-1075
www.LSU.edu

Massachusettes Maritime Academy
101 Academy Drive
Buzzards Bay, MA 02532
508-830-5011
www.maritime.edu/

Meridian Community College
910 HWY 19N
Meridian, MS 39307
1-800-622-8431 x842
601-484-8842
www.mcc.cc.ms.us/newhome/anewpage2.htm

Metropolitan College of New York
75 Varick Street
New York, NY 10013-1919
646-243-7608

Millersville University of Pennsylvania
Center for Disaster Research and Education
P.O. Box 1002
Millersville, PA 17551
717-872-3568
muweb.millersville.edu/~cdr

Mission-Centered Solutions
P.O. Box 969
Franktown, CO 80116
303-646-3700
www.MCSolutions.com

MLC & Associates, Inc.
P.O. Box 635
Port Orchard, WA 98366-0635
253-857-3124
949-222-1202
mlscandassociates.com

Nash Community College
P.O. Box 7488
522 N. Old Carriage Road
Rocky Mount, NC 27804-7488
252-443-4011 x312
www.nash.cc.nc.us

National American University- Albuquerque Campus
4775 Indian School Road, NE
Suite 200
Albuquerque, NM 87110
505-265-7517
www.national.edu/AlbuquerqueCampus/Index.htm

National College of Business &Technology
P.O. Box 2036
Bayamon, PR 00960
787-740-4627
www.nationalcollege.com

Natural Haz. Research & Applications Info. Center
University of Colorado
482 UCB
Boulder, CO 80309-0482
303-492-6818

North Dakota State University
402 C. Minard Hall
Fargo, ND 58102
701-231-8657
http://emgt.ndsu.nodak.edu

Norwich University
Online Graduate Programs
158 Harmon Drive
Northfield, VT 05663
802-485-2001
800-468-6679
www.NORWICH.edu/index.html

Oklahoma State Univ
Department of Political Science
535 Math Sciences
Stillwater, OK 74078
405-744-5606
405-744-6534
http://polsci.okstate.edu/graduate/femp/

Onondaga Community College
4969 Onondaga Road
Syracuse, NY 13215
315-498-6046
www.pstc.sunyocc.edu

Palisade Corporation
798 Cascadilla Street
Ithaca, NY 14850
607-277-8000
800-432-7475
www.PALISADE.com

Park University
934 Wyandotte
Kansas City, MO 64105
816-421-1125
www.park.edu/MPA

Pikes Peak Community College
5675 S. Academy Blvd
Colorado Springs, CO 80906
719-540-7345
800-456-6847
www.ppcc.edu

Quincy College
34 Coddington Street
Quincy, MA 02169
617-984-1640
www.quincycollege.edu/

Rochester Institute of Technology
31 Lomb Memorial Drive
Rochester, NY 14623-5603
585-475-4999

San Antonio College
1300 San Pedro Avenue
San Antonio, TX 78212
210-733-2187

Scott Community College
500 Belmont Road
Bettendorf, IA 52722-6804
563-441-4001
www.EICC.edu/hset/

Sentryx
1812 Samuelson Circle
Mississauga, ON L5N 7Z5
Canada
905-565-6013
www.sentryx.com

Slippery Rock University
1 Morrow Way
Slippery Rock, PA 16057
412-738-2260
www.sru.edu

Southwestern College
2040 South Rock Road
Wichita, KS 67207
316-684-5335
www.sckans.edu/ps/majors/secmgmt.html

St Edward's University
3001 S. Congress Avenue
Austin, TX 78704-9841
512-428-1063
www.stedwards.edu/pacepsm

St. Petersburg College
P.O. Box 13489
St. Petersburg, FL 33733-3489
727-341-4479
www.SPCOLLEGE.edu/ac/

SUNY at Stony Brook
School of Health Technology and Management HSC
Level 2, Room 452
Stony Brook, NY 11794-8200
631-444-6158
631-444-7887

SUNY Ulster County Community College
Nursing & Public Safety, Hardenburgh 120
Stone Ridge, NY 12484
800-724-0833
www.sunyulster.edu/catalog/emergmgmt.asp

Texas A&M Univ.
Hazard Reduction & Recovery Center
College Sta, TX 77843-3137
979- 862-3969
http://hrrc.tamu.edu

Texas A&M University
Hazard Reduction and Recovery Center
TAMU MS 3137
College Station, TX 77842-3137
979-845-7813
www.TAMU.edu

Texas Tech University Institute for Disaster Resea
Civil Engineering Department
P.O. Box 41023
Lubbock, TX 79409-1023
806-742-3476

**TRAINING &
CONFERENCES**

The Institute of Terrorism Research and Response
P.O. Box 56555
Philadelphia, PA 19111
866-778-1871
267-688-8344

Thomas Edison State College
101 West State Street
Trenton, NJ 08608-1176
888-442-8372
www.TESC.edu

Touro University International
5665 Plaza Drive
3rd Floor
Cypress, CA 90630
714-226-9840
www.tourou.edu/CHS/emergencyM.htm

UCLA Center for Public Health and Disasters
1145 Gayley Avenue
Suite 304
Los Angeles, CA 90024
310-794-0864
www.cphd.ucla.edu

University of Akron
Polsky Building 161
Akron, OH 44325-4304
330-927-7789
330-972-8317
www.uakron.edu

University of CA Riverside Extension
1200 University Avenue
Riverside, CA 92507
909-787-5804
www.UCREXTENSION.net

University of California at San Diego
Environmental and Safety Department
9500 Gilman Drive
La Jolla, CA 92093
619-622-5712

University of Delaware
276 Graham Hall
Newark, DE 19716-7381
302-831-8405
www.udel.edu/ceep

University of Florida
Bureau of Fire Standards and Training
11655 N.W. Gainesville Road
Ocala, FL 34482-1486
352-369-2800
www.fldfs.com/sfm/bfst/index.shtml

University of Maine at Fort Kent
23 University Drive
Fort Kent, ME 04743
1-888-TRY-UMFK
207-834-7563
www.umfk.maine.edu/

University of Nevada at Las Vegas
ECEM Degree Program
4505 Maryland Pkwy, Box 45037
Las Vegas, NV 89154-2037
702-939-4631
http://iss.unlv.edu/index.html

University of New Orleans
College of Urban and Public Affairs
351 Mathematics Building
New Orleans, LA 70148
504-280-6521
504-280-6277
www.uno.edu/cupa/pages/degreeMPA.html

University of North Carolina
School of Public Health
Rosenau Hall, CB# 7400
Chapel Hill, NC 27599-7400
919-966-7676
www.SPH.UNC.edu/hpaa/academic/disaster.htm

University of North Texas
Emergency Administration and Planning
P.O. Box 310617
Denton, TX 76203-0617
940-565-2996
www.UNT.edu/eadp

University of Tennessee at Chattanooga
615 McCallie Avenue
Chattanooga, TN 37403
423-425-2150
www.utc.edu

University of Tennessee, Knoxville
1914 Andy Holt Avenue
Knoxville, TN 37993-2710
865-974-1108
www.utk.edu

University of Washington
Department of Urban Design & Planning
410 Gould, Box 355740
Seattle, WA 98195
206-543-4190
www.caup.washington.edu/html/urbdp/

University of Wisconsin-Disaster Management Center
Department of Engineering Professional Development
432 North Lake St
Madison, WI 53706
608-262-5441
800-462-0876
dmc.ENGR.WISC.edu

URS Corporation
200 Orchard Ridge Dr.
Suite 101
Gaithersburg, MD 20878
301-258-6554
www.urscorp.com

UTD Engineering and Computer Science
The University of Texas at Dallas
P.O. Box 830688
Richardson, TX 75083-0688
972-883-2874
www.som.utdallas.edu/erc/

Vincennes University
1200 North 2nd Street, Davis Hall
Room 411
Vincennes, IN 47591
812-888-5137
www.vinu.edu

Wayne Community College
3000 Wayne Memorial Drive
P.O. Box 8002
Goldsboro, NC 27534
919-735-5151
www.waynecc.edu

West Texas A&M University
WTAMU Box 60807
Canyon, TX 79016-0001
806-651-2436
979-458-1821

Western Carolina University
105A Belk Building
Cullowhee, NC 28723
828-227-2815
http://www.wcu.edu/

Western Washington University-EESP
516 High Street
Mail Stop 5293 WWU
Bellingham, WA 98225-5946
360-650-3717

Disaster planning & emergency management training, taught in Spanish

**Binomial International
812 Proctor Avenue
Ogdensburg, NY 13669
888-246-6642
www.BINOMIAL.com**

Fire, Etc.
Lakeland College
5707 47 Ave. West
Vermilion, AB T9X 1K5
Canada
780-853-8400
800-661-6490
www.fire-etc.ca

Med-E-Train
382 San Claudio Ave.
PMB #33
San Juan, PR 00926-9910
787-630-6300
787-335-0026
www.medetrain.com

National College of Business &Technology
P.O. Box 2036
Bayamon, PR 00960
787-740-4627
www.nationalcollege.com

**URS Corporation
200 Orchard Ridge Dr.
Suite 101
Gaithersburg, MD 20878
301-258-6554
www.urscorp.com**

Earthquake engineering training

Canadian Association For Earthquake Engineering
The University of Ottawa
161 Louis Pasteur St.
Ottawa, ON K1N 6N5
Canada
613-562-5800
www.caee.uottawa.ca

Center for Earthquake Research and Information
University of Memphis
3892 Central
Memphis, TN 38152
901-678-2007
www.ceri.memphis.edu

Consortium of Universities for Research in Earthquake Engineering (CUREE)
1301 S. 46th Street
Building 420
Richmond, CA 94804
510-231-9557
www.curee.org

Earthquake Engineering Center for the Southeastern United States (ECSUS)
Department of Civil and Environmental Engineering
111B Patton Hall, Virginia Tech University
Blacksburg, VA 24061
540-231-6635
ecsus.ce.vt.edu

Earthquake Engineering Research Center
Univeristy of California, Berkley
1301 S. 46th RFS 451
Richmond, CA 94804
510-231-9554
eerc.berkeley.edu

Mid-America Earthquake Center
1241 Newmark Civil Engineering Laboratory, MC-250
205 North Matthews
Urbana, IL 61801
217-244-6302
mae.cee.uiuc.edu

Multidisciplinary Center for Earthquake Engineering
University at Buffalo
State University of New York
Buffalo, NY 14261
716-645-3391
http://mceer.buffalo.edu/default.asp

Ottawa Carleton Earthquake Engineering Research
Centre
The Department of Earth Sciences
140 Louis Pasteur
Ottawa, ON K1S 5B6
Canada
613-520-2600
www.genie.uottawa.ca/oceerc

The John A. Blume Earthquake Engineering Center
Department of Civil and Environmental Engineering
Stanford University MC: 4020, Building 540
Stanford, CA 94305-4020
650-723-4150
blume.stanford.edu

Environmental safety training

Canberra Industries Training & Tech. Svcs. Dept.
800 Research Parkway
Meriden, CT 06450-7127
800-255-6370
203-238-2351
www.ATCANBERRA.com

Center for Hazards and Risk Research
Columbia University
230 Seismology - Route 9W
Palisades, NY 10964
845-365-8909
www.ldeo.columbia.edu/CHRR/

Chemical Stockpile Emergency Preparedness Program
Dept. of Homeland Security/FEMA
500 C St. SW
Washington, DC 20472
202-646-2734
emc.ORNL.gov/CSEPPweb/FEMACSEPPHome.html

Clayton Group Services Inc.
P.O. Box 8008
Novi, MI 48376-8008
888-357-7020
248-344-8550
www.CLAYTONGRP.com

Colorado Alliance for Environmental Education
15260 S. Golden Rd.
Golden, CO 80401
303-273-9527
www.caee.org

Field Safety Corporation
101 C Fowler Road
North Branford, CT 06471
888-964-9199
203-483-6003
www.fieldsafety.com

Hazardous Material Training Program
University of Illinois ILIR.
1705 North Country Club Road
Decatur, IL 62521
217-333-0640
www.ILIR.UIUC.edu/extension/hazmat

The National Environmental Services Center
West Virginia University
P.O. Box 6064
Morgantown, WV 26506
800-624-8301

URS Corporation
200 Orchard Ridge Dr.
Suite 101
Gaithersburg, MD 20878
301-258-6554
www.urscorp.com

Fire training & towers

Fire, Etc.
Lakeland College
5707 47 Ave. West
Vermilion, AB T9X 1K5
Canada
780-853-8400
800-661-6490
www.fire-etc.ca

MSU Fire Services Training School
Montana State University
750 6th Street SW, Suite 205
Great Falls, MT 59404
406-761-7885
800-294-5272
www.montana.edu/wwwfire/

WHP Trainingtowers
9121 Bond
Overland Park, Ka 66214
800-351-2525
www.TRAININGTOWERS.com

Fire/water damage restoration training

Bolden's Mfg / Hydro-Lab
20799 Riverwood Ave
Building B
Noblesville, IN 46062
888-776-6708
317-776-8787
www.hydro-systems.com

Center for Disaster Recovery
259A Innisfil Street
Barrie, ON L4N 3G2
Canada
877-792-6569
705-792-0307
www.centerfordisasterrecovery.com

IOT - Interactive Occupational Training
171 S. Van Gordon Street
Suite C
Lakewood, CO 80228
303-984-4671
866-665-5566
www.iot-edu.com

Restoration College
16 Thornhedge Court
Ottawa, ON K1T 3E4
Canada
613-227-3141
www.restorationcollege.com

Safety training

AED Instructor Foundation
600 N. JACKSON ST. SUITE 1
MEDIA, PA 19063
610-566-2824

American Safety & Health Institute
4148 Louis Avenue
Holiday, FL 34691
800-682-5067
www.ashinstitute.org

Compliance Solutions
10515 E. 40th Avenue
Suite 116
Denver, CO 80239
800-711-2706
www.CSREGS.com

Emergency Preparedness Systems LLC
2720 Hickory Dr.
Plover, WI 54467
715-321-1800
http://www.eps411.com

International Fire Service Training Assn.
930 N Willis Street
Stillwater, OK 74078
800-654-4055
www.IFSTA.org

JoshuaCasey Corporate Training
915 E. Katella Ave
200
Anaheim, CA 92805
714-245-9440
www.joshuacasey.com

LifeSafe Services, LLC
5971 Powers Ave
Suite 108
Jacksonville, FL 32217
888-767-0050
904-730-4800
www.lifesafeservices.com

Med-E-Train
382 San Claudio Ave.
PMB #33
San Juan, PR 00926-9910
787-630-6300
787-335-0026
www.medetrain.com

MLC & Associates, Inc.
P.O. Box 635
Port Orchard, WA 98366-0635
253-857-3124
949-222-1202
mlscandassociates.com

NEHA Training LLC
720 S Colorado Blvd
Suite 900-S
Denver, CO 80246-1960
303-756-9090
http://www.nehatraining.com

SafeX
140 N. Otterbein Avenue
Westerville, OH 43081
614-890-0800
866-SafexUS
www.safex.us

Short Elliott Hendrickson, Inc.
Butler Square Building, Suite 710-C
100 North Sixth St.
Minneapolis, MN 55403-1515
612-758-6700
866-830-3388
www.sehinc.com

The MARCOM Group, Ltd.
20 Creek Parkway
Boothwyn, PA 19061
800-654-2448
610-859-8989
www.marcomltd.com

URS Corporation
200 Orchard Ridge Dr.
Suite 101
Gaithersburg, MD 20878
301-258-6554
www.urscorp.com

Security training

Bioterrorism and Emerging Infections
John N. Whitaker Building, Suite 406
500 22nd Street South
Birmingham, AL 35294-4551
205-934-2687
www.bioterrorism.uab.edu

Commonwealth Films Inc
223 Commonwealth Avenue
Boston, MA 02116-1700
617-262-5634
www.COMMONWEALTHFILMS.com

Gerard Group International LLC
164 Westford Road
Suite 15
Tyngsborough, MA 01879
978-649-4575
www.GERARDGROUP.com

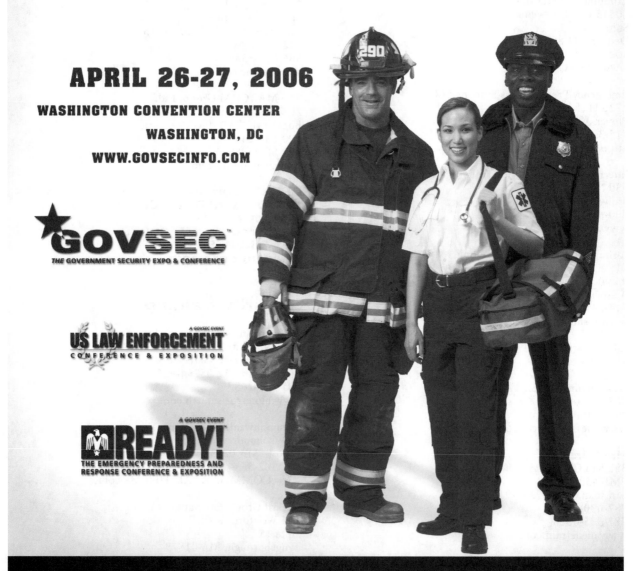

YOU ARE AMERICA'S FIRST RESPONDERS

HOMELAND SECURITY BEGINS AT THE LOCAL LEVEL.

When a terrorist attack, natural disaster or accident strikes police, fire and EMS are the first on the scene; on the front lines of America's war on terror. GovSec, U.S. Law and Ready! is the only event to unite first responders with law enforcement and government security professionals in a forum that also includes more than 500 industry manufacturers presenting the newest products, cutting edge technologies and critical solutions for securing America's citizens and critical assets.

APRIL 26-27, 2006

WASHINGTON CONVENTION CENTER
WASHINGTON, DC
WWW.GOVSECINFO.COM

GOVSEC
THE GOVERNMENT SECURITY EXPO & CONFERENCE

US LAW ENFORCEMENT
A GOVSEC EVENT
CONFERENCE & EXPOSITION

READY!
A GOVSEC EVENT
THE EMERGENCY PREPAREDNESS AND RESPONSE CONFERENCE & EXPOSITION

AMERICA'S PREMIER HOMELAND SECURITY EVENT

GOVSEC, U.S. LAW and READY
313 South Patrick Street
Alexandria, VA 22314
800-687-7469
703-683-8500
www.govsecinfo.com

J.J. Keller & Associates Inc.
P.O. Box 368
Neenah, WI 54957-0368
800-327-6868
www.jjkeller.com/jjk

MIS Training Institute
498 Concord Street
Framingham, MA 01702-2357
508-879-7999
www.MISTI.com

Simulations & exercises, emergency

Crisis Simulations International, LLC
279 Veleros Court
Coral Gables, FL 33143
305-205-5042
www.crisissimulations.com

Crisis Simulations International, LLC
1673A SW Montgomery Drive
Portland, OR 97201
503-248-2233
www.crisissimulations.com

Disaster Survival Planning Network (DSPN)
5352 Plata Rosa Court
Camarillo, CA 93012
800-601-4899
www.DSPNETWORK.com

JS Training Institute
16940 B Street
Rm 1
Huntingtn Bch, CA 92647-4846
714-375-0059
www.JSTI.com

Telecommunications training

Sterling Commerce
4600 Lakehurst Court
Dublin, OH 43016
614-793-7000
800-677-3342
www.STERLINGCOMMERCE.com

Trade shows & conferences, misc.

Annual International Disaster Management Conf
Florida Emergency Medicine Foundation
3717 South Conway Road
Orlando, FL 32812
407-281-7396
800-766-6335
www.femf.org

ASSE Annual Conference
The American Society of Safety Engineers
1800 E. Oakton Street
Des Plaines, IL 60018
847-699-2929
www.asse.org/index.html

Association of Contingency Planners National HQ
7044 S 13th Street
Oak Creek, WI 53154-1429
414-768-8000 x116
800-445-4227
www.ACP-INTERNATIONAL.com

Business Continuity & Infrastructure Security Conf
Flagg Management, Inc.
353 Lexington Ave
New York, NY 10016
212-286-0333

Business Continuity Planning Conference
Securities Industry Association
120 Broadway 35th floor
New York, NY 10271-0080
212-608-1500
www.sia.com

Business Continuity, Security & Crisis Mgmt. Conf.
The Conference Board
845 Third Avenue
New York, NY 10022
212-339-0345
www.conference-board.org

California Seismic Safety Commision, The
1755 Creekside Oaks Drive
Suite 100
Sacremento, CA 95833
916-263-5506
www.seismic.ca.gov

Canadian Centre for Emergency Preparedness
860 Harrington Ct
Burlington, ON L7N 3N4
Canada
905-331-2552
www.CCEP.CA

Contingency Planners of Ohio
P.O. Box 340825
Columbus, OH 43234-0825
614-249-9339
614-331-8417
www.CPOHIO.org

TRAINING & CONFERENCES

TRAINING & CONFERENCES

Contingency Planning & Management Expo
WPC Expositions
20 Commerce Street
Flemington, NJ 08822
908-788-0343
www.contingencyplanningexpo.com

Continuity Insights Management Conference
Communications Technologies, Inc.
301 South Main Street
Doylestown, PA 18901
215-230-9556
www.continuityinsights.com

CPM Group
20 Commerce Street
Flemington, NJ 08822
908-788-0343
www.CONTINGENCYPLANNING.com

Disaster Preparedness & Business Continuity Conf.
American Red Cross of Central New Jersey
707 Alexander Road Suite 101
Princeton, NJ 08540
609-951-2106
www.njredcross.org

DRIE Ottawa Annual Conference
Disaster Recovery Information Exchange-Ottawa
P.O. Box 20518, 390 Rideau St.
Ottawa, ON K1N 1A3
Canada
613-238-2909
www.drieottawa.org

DRIE Toronto Quarterly Seminar
Disaster Recovery Information Exchange (DRIE)
2175 Sheppard Ave. East, Suite 310
Toronto, ON M2J 1W8
Canada
416-491-2420
www.drie.org/toronto

DRJ World Conference
11131 E. South Town Sq.
St. Louis, MO 63123
314-894-0276
www.wrj.com

Florida Emerg. Prep. Assn.
3015 Shannon Lakes North
Tallahassee, FL 32309
850-906-0779

Gartner IT Security Summit
Gartner Events
56 Top Gallant Road
Standford, CT 06904
203-316-6757
www3.gartner.com/Init

Government Security Expo & Conference
313 South Patrick Street
Alexandria, VA 22314
703-683-8500

Governor's Hurricane Conference
P.O. Box 279
Tarpon Springs, FL 34688
727-944-2724
800-544-5678
www.flghc.org

IAEM Annual & EMEX Emergency Mgt. Conference
International Association of Emergency Managers
201 Park Washington Court
Falls Church, VA 22046-4527
703-538-1795
www.iaem.com

Institute for Catastrophic Loss Reduction
20 Richmond Street East
Suite 210
Toronto, ON M5C 2R9
Canada
416-364-8677
www.iclr.org

Institute for Crisis, Disaster and Risk Management
George Washington University
1776 G. St. NW, Suite 110
Washington, DC 20052
202-994-6736
www.GWU.edu/~icdrm/

International Disaster Recovery Assn. (IDRA)
P.O. Box 4515
Shrewsbury, MA 01545-7515
508-845-6000
www.IDRA.com

International Security Conference West
Reed Exhibitions
383 Main Avenue
Norwalk, CT 06851
203-840-5602
800-840-5602
www.iscwest.com

Kansas Emergency Management Annual Conference
115 North 4th Street
Manhattan, KS 66502
785-537-6333

Long Island/NYC Emergency Management Conference
State Emergency Management Office
1220 Washington Avenue, Suite 101, Building 22
Albany, NY 12226-2251
631-436-4228
518-457-2200
www.linycemconference.com

National Earthquake Conference
644 Emerson Street
Palo Alto, CA 94301
650-330-1101
www.wsspc.org

National Emergency Management Annual Conference
National Emergency Management Association
P.O. Box 11910
Lexington, KY 40578
859-244-8000
www.nemaweb.org

National Hurricane Conference
2952 Wellington Circle
Tallahassee, FL 32308
850-906-9224
www.hurricanmeeting.com

NEDRIX - New England Disaster Recovery Information Exchange
P.O. Box 52120
Boston, MA 02205
781-485-0279
www.NEDRIX.com

NFPA World Annual Safety Conference
National Fire Protection Association
1 Batterymarch Park
Quincy, MA 02169-7471
617-770-3000

OC Disaster Preparedness Academy Conf.
Orange County Red Cross
P.O. Box 11364, 601 North Golden Circle Drive
Santa Ana, CA 92711-1364
714-481-5300
www.oc-redcross.org

Parma Annual Risk Managers Conference
Public Agency Risk Managers Association
P.O. Box 6810
San Jose, CA 95150
888-907-2762
www.parma.com

PRIMA Annual Conference
Public Risk Management Association
500 Montgomery Street
Alexandria, VA 22314
703-528-7701
www.primacentral.org

Risk & Ins. Mgmt. Society Annual Conference
655 Third Avenue
2nd Floor
New York, NY 10017
212-286-9292
www.rims.org

The Pacific Security Expo
Association of Bay Area Governments
510-464-7968
www.pacificsecurityexpo.com

The UCLA Center for Public Health and Disaster Relief
UCLA Center for Public Health and Disasters
1145 Gayley Avenue, Suite 304
Los Angeles, CA 90024
310-794-0864
www.ph.ucla.edu/cphdr

Total Facility Management Show
Group C Communications, Inc.
44 Apple Street, Suite #3
Tinton Falls, NJ 07724
800-524-0337
www.tfmshow.com

TRAINING & CONFERENCES

Windstorm Insurance Conference
P.O. Box 30486
Pensacola, FL 32503
850-473-0601
www.windnetwork.com

World Conference on Disaster Management
Absolute Conferences & Events Inc.
144 Front St. W., Suite 640
Toronto, ON M5J 2L7
Canada
905-331-2552
www.wcdm.org

Workplace violence control, training

Business & Government Continuity Services
P.O. Box 1706
Oklahoma City, OK 73101
405-737-8348
www.businesscontinuity.info

Emotional Continuity Management
Inner Directions, LLP
2815 Van Giesen
Richland, WA 99354
509-942-0443
509-948-3593
www.emotionalcontinuity.com

TRAINING &
CONFERENCES

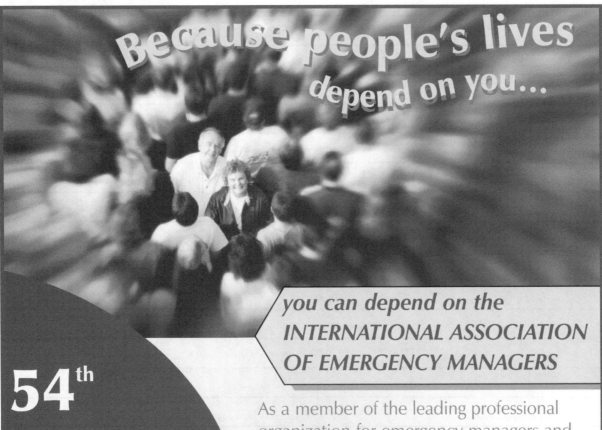

Because people's lives depend on you...

you can depend on the **INTERNATIONAL ASSOCIATION OF EMERGENCY MANAGERS**

54th IAEM Annual Conference & EMEX 2006

November 4-8, 2006

Orlando Convention Center Orlando, Florida

As a member of the leading professional organization for emergency managers and homeland security officials, you can depend on IAEM to deliver:

- ◆ Largest experts network offering solutions, guidance and assistance.
- ◆ Job opportunities – extensive online compilation.
- ◆ Unified voice on policies and legislation.
- ◆ Information updates – monthly newsletter, and e-mail notifications.
- ◆ Professional tools and discussion groups on www.iaem.com.
- ◆ Certified Emergency Manager® and Associate Emergency Manager programs.
- ◆ Scholarship program.

iAEM
International
Association of
Emergency Managers

JOIN IAEM TODAY!
201 Park Washington Ct. • Falls Church, VA 22046-4527
703-538-1795 • www.iaem.com • www.emex.org

TRAINING &
CONFERENCES

COMPANY LISTINGS ALPHABETICALLY

Our customers would hire us again!

We survey all our customers to ask them how well we performed while on their disaster recovery project.

Here's what our customers told us:

- 96% said they would enthusiastically hire us again!

- 94% said we provided services beyond their expectations.

- 96% said they were impressed with how quickly we arrived.

- 99% said we were prepared and started the recovery quickly.

- 95% said we quoted the job accurately and clearly.

- 94% said our services were a good value.

If you want to know about Munters, don't ask us. Ask our customers. Here's how: We've published the results of our survey for the most recent 250 disaster recovery services customers in a booklet called: "What Our Customers Think." We'll be pleased to send it to you, so that you can read for yourself exactly what our customers are saying. We know that when you are under pressure to hire a disaster recovery company, you won't have time to check references. So, do it now. Just e-mail us and we will send you our booklet. You'll be glad you did, because planning for a disaster is an essential part of recovering from it.

**mcsinfo@munters.com
or call 1-800-MUNTERS**

1-800-BoardUp Inc.
St. Louis, MO 63126
800-585-9293

1SecureAudit LLC
McLean, VA 22102
703-245-3020

1st Responder Consultants
Hughes Springs, TX 75656
903-639-3596

21st Century Computer
Keller, TX 76244
817-379-6603

21st Century Software Inc.
Wayne, PA 19087-1853
800-555-6845

2bcool Enterprises Inc.
Calgary, AB T2E 0E5
Canada
403-276-3855

308 Systems, Inc
Fort Collins, CO 80525
970-282-7006

360 Surveillance, Inc.
Victoria, BC V8Z 1B5
Canada
250-388-7232

3D Disaster Kleenup of Columbus
Columbus, OH 43228
614-351-9695

3E Company
Carlsbad, CA 92008
800-360-3220

3M Buildings Safety Solutions Dept
Gaithersburg, MD 20878
800-940-9142

3M Canada Company
Mississauga, ON L4W 5L1
Canada
905-602-3814

4 - Star TrueValue Builing Center
Seymour, MO 65746
417-935-4384

410 Rentals
Buckley, WA 98321
253-826-7671

9-1-1 MAGAZINE
Tustin, CA 92780
714-544-7776

A & I Fire & Water Restoration
Myrtle Beach, SC 29577
843-448-8485

A & I Fire & Water Restoration
Wilmington, NC 28405
910-799-5135

A & M Disaster Services
Minneapolis, MN 55406
612-722-0137

A Practical Guide for University Crisis Response
Commack, NY 11725
631-543-2217

A Rental Service Division of Wirtz Rentals
Chicago, IL 60609
773-247-2443

A Royal Wolf Portable Storage
Hayward, CA 94545
800-447-7223

A to Z Equipment Rentals & Sales
Phoenix, AZ 85032
602-992-1150

A. D. I.
Mesa, AZ 85210
480-539-4555

A. L. E. Mobile Housing
Carrollton, TX 75011-7715
888-921-5749

A.R.S. Services Inc.
Newton, MA 02458
800-298-6660

A-1 Flood Tech
Manassas, VA 20110
703-631-0400

A-1 Glass Services Inc
Covington, LA 10433
985-892-5312

A1 Restoration Inc.
Pocatello, ID 83201
208-237-0033

A-1 Teletronics
St. Petersburg, FL 33716
800-736-4397

AAA Commercial Products
Mayfield Hts, OH 44124
877-536-0808

AAA Painters
Phoenix, AZ 85017
602-242-7248

A-AAACORN Glass & Board Up Service
Chicago, IL 60632
773-776-5000

AAAction Cleaning and Restoration
Pflugerville, TX 78660
512-837-1470

AAR Divison Indeck Power
Wheeling, IL 60090
847-541-8300

Abatement Technologies, Inc.
Duluth, GA 30096
800-634-9091

ABC Chem-Dry
Utica, NY 13502
800-FOR-ABC1

ABD Insurance & Financial Services
Redwood City, CA 94063
650-839-6000

ABEC
McMinnville, OR 97128
503-434-9100

Able Mobile Housing
Flint, MI 48504
800-273-5774

Able Restoration Inc.
Weymouth, MA 02189
781-335-0000

ABM/Disaster Recovery SVCS.
King of Prussia, PA 19406
610-275-6200

Abney Construction Inc.
Ada, OK 74820
580-332-6229

ABS Associates Inc
Rolling Mdws, IL 60008
847-437-8700

ABS Consulting
Houston, TX 77060-2393
281-673-2800

ABTECH Systems Inc.
Carlsbad, CA 92008
760-827-5110

Academy of Certified Hazardous Materials Managers, Inc.
Rockville, MD 20849
800-437-0137

AccessData Corp
Lindon, UT 84042
801-377-5410

AccessIT
Morristown, NJ 07960
973-290-0093

AccessPoint Business Recovery Services
Port Moody, BC V3H 1K3
Canada
604-250-4829

AccuForm Signs
Brooksville, FL 34604
800-237-1001

Accurate Construction
Harbor City, CA 90710
800-696-1977

Accutech Restoration & Remodeling
Sarasota, FL 34240
941-378-0700

AccuWeather Inc
State College, PA 16803-2286
314-235-3600

Ace Tool Rental
Falls Church, VA 22046
703-532-5600

ACES - Animal Care Equipment &
Services, Inc.
Denver, CO 80216
303-296-9287

ACM Environmental Inc
South Bend, IN 46628
574-234-8435

Acordia
Houston, TX 77046
713-507-9476

ACP
Santa Ana, CA 92705
714-558-8822

ACR Electronics, Inc.
Ft. Lauderdale, FL 33312
954-981-3333

ACS Image Solutions
Ridgeland, MS 39157
601-977-4000

ACSI - Advanced Containment Systems
Houston, TX 77075
800-927-2271

Acterna
Germantown, MD 20876
800-638-2049

Action Catastrophe
Denver, CO 80211
303-964-1188

Action Chem-Dry
Lewiston, NY 14092
716-754-7700

Action Cleaners Restoration
Wheeling, IL 60090
847-658-8988

Action Fire InStar Services
Chicopee, MA 01020
413-594-7800

Action Pro Air Duct Cleaning
Allentown, PA 18109
610-821-8338

ActionFront Data Recovery Labs Inc.
Norcross, GA 30092
905-474-2220

Active Aero
Belleville, MI 48111
734-547-7200

Active Canadian Emergency Training Inc.
Waterloo, ON N2V 2B7
Canada
800-205-3278

Adapt Inc.
Front Royal, VA 22630
800-243-2665

Adaptive Data Storage, Inc.
Cinnaminson, NJ 08077-3369
856-764-8401

Adjusters International
Dallas, TX 75248
800-992-7771

Adjusters International
Utica, NY 13502
800-382-2468

AdRem Software, Inc.
New York, NY 10022
212-319-4114

Adtranstore, Inc.
Sparta, NJ 07871
888-328-2266

Advance Companies Inc
Fridley, MN 55432
763-572-2000

Advanced Continuity
Haymarket, VA 20169
800-299-5235

Advanced Digital Information Corp.
(ADIC)
Redmond, WA 98073
425-881-8004

Advanced Electronic Support Products
North Miami, FL 33181
800-446-2377

Advanced Engineering Solutions Inc
Canton, MI 48187-2600
734-459-9948

Advanced Enviromental Consultants
Torrance, CA 90503
310-347-3347

Advanced Forecasting Corporation
Wilmington, DE 19808
305-949-0040

Advanced Input Systems
Coeur d'Alene, ID 83815
800-444-5923

Advanced Process Solutions Inc.
Raleigh, NC 27612
919-844-1625

Advanced Records Management
Services, Inc.
Danvers, MA 01923
888-869-2767

Advanced Restoration Corporation
West Babylon, NY 11704-4903
631-422-2100

Advanced Restoration Specialists Inc.
South El Monte , CA 91733-2020
626-442-7700

Advanced Restoration Technologies Inc
Clifton Heights, PA 19018
610-626-9002

Advanced Software Products Group, Inc.
Naples, FL 34104
800-662-6090

Advanced Systems Concepts Inc.
Parsippany, NJ 07054
201-798-6400

Advantaclean
Charlotte, NC 28208
704-391-3330

AdvantaClean
Orlando, FL 32810-4224
407-839-0088

Advantec Computer Company
Fremont, CA 94538
510-440-9700

Adwest Mailers Inc.
N Hollywood, CA 91605
818-982-3720

AED Instructor Foundation
MEDIA, PA 19063
610-566-2824

AERC Recycling Solutions
Allentown, PA 18103
800-554-2372

Aerial Access Equipment
Baton Rouge , LA 70817
225-753-2332

Aero Fulfillment Services
Mason, OH 45040
800-225-7145

AFCOM
Orange, CA 92866
714-997-7966

Affiliated Warehouses Companies, Inc.
Hazlet, NJ 07730-0295
732-739-2323

After Disaster
Greensboro, NC 27404
800-948-0242

After Disaster Housing Co
Jackson, NJ 08527
732-928-8100

Agency for Healthcare Research and
Quality
Rockville, MD 20850
301-427-1364

Aggreko Rental
New Iberia, LA 70560-9134
800-258-4874

Agility Recovery Solutions
Charlotte, NC 28226
866-364-9696

Agility Recovery Solutions
Mississauga, ON L5K 2S3
Canada
800-567-5001

Agnes Huff Communications Group, LLC
Los Angeles, CA 90045
310 641-2525

Aiex Co.
Belmont, CA 94002
650-591-3700

AIG eBusiness Risk Solutions
New York, NY 10038
212-458-3695

Air & Electric Equipment Co.
Philadelphia, PA 19133
215-425-8500

Air Cycle Corp.
Broadview, IL 60155
800-909-9709

Air Flow Systems
Dallas, TX 75243
214-503-8008

Air Quality Engineering
Brooklyn Park, MN 55428
763-531-9823

Air Salvage of Dallas
Lancaster, TX 75146
800-336-6399

Air Systems International, Inc.
Chesapeake, VA 23320
800-866-8100

Aire Master of America Inc.
Nixa, MO 65714
417-725-2691

Airgas, Inc.
Radnor, PA 19087-5283
800-255-2165

AirPac Inc.
Front Royal, VA 22630
888-324-7722

Airstar America, Inc.
N. Hollywood, CA 91601
800-217-9001

Airworx Construction Equipment & Supply
Indianapolis, IN 46225
317-471-1272

AISG
Orlando, FL 32817
407-581-2929

aivant L.P.
Atlanta, GA 30339
770-435-1101

Akibia
Westborough, MA 01581
508-621-5100

Alabama Emergency Management
Agency
Clanton, AL 35046-2160
205-280-2200

Alabama Poison Center
Tuscaloosa, AL 35405
800-222-1222

Alacrity Services LLC
Atlanta, GA 30328
770-953-3220

Alan Plummer Associates Inc
Fort Worth, TX 76118
817-284-2724

Alaska Dept. of Military and Veteran
Affairs
Ft Richardson-Camp Denali, AK 99505-5750
907-428-7000

Alaska Division of Emergency Services
Fort Richardson, AK 99505-5750
907-428-7000

Alaska State Emergency Response
Commission
Fort Richardson, AK 99505-5750
907-428-7000

Albert Einstein Healthcare Network
Philadelphia, PA 19144
215-951-8145

Albert Risk Management Consultants
Needham Heights, MA 02494-2631
781-449-2866

ALCIE Integrated Solutions
Saint Lauro, QC H4M 2L4
Canada
514-744-3440

Alex N. Sill Company
Cleveland, OH 44131-2579
216-524-9999

Alexander Equipment
Lisle, IL 60532
630-663-1400

Alicomp
Leonia, NJ 07605
800-274-5556

All American Cleaning
Idaho Falls, ID 83403
208-529-8179

All Care Chem-Dry
Miami, FL 33177
305-969-3733

All Clean Restoration Services Inc.
Belleville, IL 62220-2803
800-422-3944

All in One Rentals
East Northport, NY 11731
631-499-5151

All Pro Chem-Dry
Jacksonville, FL 32259
904-230-9918

All State Guard Service Inc
Houston, TX 77248-7449
713-526-7171

All States Ag Parts, Inc
Sioux Falls, SD 57104
605-359-2447

All Ways ChemDry
Carpentersville, IL 60110
630-377-7417

Allan Bonner Communications
Management
Toronto, ON M5V 3G8
Canada
877-484-1667

Allegient Systems Inc
Wilton, CT 06897
203-761-1289

Allen Restoration & Construction
Denton, TX 76208
940-320-1900

Allen-Vanguard Corp.
Ottawa, ON K1J 9M3
Canada
613-747-3590

AllerAir Industries Inc.
Laval, QC H7L 5P1
Canada
888-852-8247

Alliance Air Freight & Logistics, Inc.
N. Hollywood, CA 91605
800-684-6359

Alliance Detective & Security Service Inc
Everett, MA 02149
617-387-1261

Alliance Environmental Group
Azusa, CA 91702
626-633-3500

Alliance Medical
Russellville, MO 65074
888-633-6098

Alliance of Professional Restoration
Drycleaners
Nashville, TN 37205
615-230-5966

Allied Environmental Group Inc
Merrick, NY 11566
516-867-6452

Allied Restoration Specialists
Charlotte, NC 28205
704-377-1661

Allied Salvage Co
Glen Burnie, MD 21061
410-760-8350

Allied Security
Kng of Prussa, PA 19406
800-437-8803

Allied Security
Mineola, NY 11501
516-877-0500

Allmand Bros., Inc.
Holdrege, NE 68949
800-562-1373

Allmark Services, Inc.
St. Louis, MO 63127
314-966-8976

AllPro Cleaning & Restoration Services
Elmsford, NY 10523
800-352-7886

Allstate Power Vac
Rahway, NJ 07065
908-862-3800

Allstream ITS
Toronto, ON M5V 1J9
Canada
416-591-7220

AllTech Communications
Tulsa, OK 74127
918-576-0000

Alpha Communications
Farmingdale , NY 11735
631-777-5500

Alpha Omega Environmental Services Inc.
Pompano Beach, FL 33069
954-427-8586

Alpha Risk MGMT. Inc.
Great Neck, NY 11021
516-829-3500

Alpha Technologies
Bellingham, WA 98226
360-671-7703

Alpine Air Corp.
Los Angeles, CA 90042
310-862-4019

Alpine Portable Restrooms
Sterling, VA 20166
540-905-0847

AlpineAire Foods
Bozeman, MT 59718
406-585-9324

AltaTech Technologies Inc
Plymouth, MN 55447
763-475-2900

Altered Standards of Care in Mass
Casualty Events
Rockville, MD 20850
800-358-9295

Alternative Environmental Solutions, Inc.
Monroe, LA 71201
318-388-4833

AlturnaMATS, Inc.
Titusville, PA 16301
888-544-6287

Aluma Tower Company Inc.
Vero Beach, FL 32961-2806
772-567-3423

Alvin L Davis Inc
Savannah, GA 31406
912-352-2666

Ambu, Inc.
Glen Burnie, MD 21060
800-262-8462

Amcom Software Inc
Minneapolis, MN 55439-2702
952-829-7445

Amec Earth & Environmental
Calgary, AB T2E 6J5
Canada
403-248-4331

America Prepared Campaign
New York, NY 10111
212-332-6302

American Academy of Experts in
Traumatic Stress
Commack, NY 11725-4322
631-543-2217

American Academy of Sanitarians
Denver, CO 80246
678-584-9127

American Association of Homeland
Security Professionals
Washington, DC 20036
866-722-4774

American Bio-Recovery Association
Ipswich, MA 01938
888-979-2272

American Classic Chem-Dry by Morley
Moreno Valley, CA 92552
951-601-3775

American Express Tax & Business
Service
Santa Monica, CA 90405
818-466-2100

American Fire Restoration
Roslyn Heights, NY 11577-2107
516-484-1777

American Freeze-Dry Inc.
Runnemede, NJ 08078
800-817-1007

American Humane
Englewood, CO 80112
303-792-9900

American Industrial Hygiene Assn
Fairfax, VA 22031-4340
703-849-8888

American Industrial Hygiene Association
Fairfax, VA 22031
703-849-8888

American Innotek Inc.
Escondido, CA 92029
760-741-6600

American Institute for Conservation of
Historic & Artistic Works
Washington, DC 20036-5346
202-452-9545

American LaFrance Corporation
Ladson, SC 29456
888-253-8725

American Leak Detection, Inc.
Palm Springs, CA 92262
800-755-6697

American Micro Data
Denver, CO 80216
303-322-4008

American Mobile Homes Inc
East Weymouth, MA 02189-2305
781-331-0333

American Permalight Inc
Torrance, CA 90505
310-891-0924

American Planning Association
Chicago, IL 60603-6111
312-431-9100

American Power Conversion Corp
West Kingston, RI 02892
401-789-5735

American Psychological Association
Washington, DC 20002-4242
800-374-2721

American Public University System
Charles Town, WV 25414
877-468-6862

American Public Works Association
Kansas City, MO 64108-2641
816-472-6100

American Red Cross BICEPP Program
Cleveland, OH 44115
216-431-3311

American Red Cross Disaster Services
Washington, DC 20006
703-206-6000

American Red Cross National Headquarters
Washington, DC 20006
202-303-4498

American Risk & Insurance Association
Malvern, PA 19355-3402
610-640-1997

American Safety & Health Institute
Holiday, FL 34691
800-246-5101

American Salvage
Miami, FL 33147
305-691-7001

American Science and Engineering Inc.
Billerica, MA 01821
978-262-8700

American Signal Corp.
Milwaukee, WI 53218-1417
800-243-2911

American Society for Industrial Security
(ASIS)
Alexandria, VA 22314-2882
703-519-6200

American Society of Appraisers
Herndon, VA 20170
703-478-2228

American Society of Safety Engineers
Des Plaines, IL 60018-2100
847-699-2929

American Superconductor
Middleton, WI 53562
608-831-5773

American Trauma Society
Upper Marlboro, MD 20772
301-420-4189

American Tree Experts LLC
York, PA 17402
717-848-9796

American Water Works Association, AWWA
Denver , CO 80235
800-926-7337

American Window Film Inc
Foxborough, MA 02035
508-549-0300

America's Personal Security, Inc.
Clearwater, FL 33767
727-443-6603

Americlean Corporation
Billings, MT 59101
406-256-9113

Americlean Services Corp.
Manassas Park, VA 20111
703-551-2903

Americold Logistics Inc. Headquarter Office
Atlanta, GA 30328
678-441-1400

Ameripack
Cranbury, NJ 08512
609-395-6969

Ameritec Corp
Covina, CA 91722
626-915-5441

AmeriVault Corp.
Waltham, MA 02451
800-774-0235

AmeriVault Corp.
Waltham, MA 02451-1013
781-890-8690

Amerizon Wireless
Fort Wayne, IN 46808
260-484-0466

Amerizon Wireless Communication Service
Fort Wayne, IN 46808
260-484-0466

Ames Sciences Inc.
Easton, MD 21601
410-820-8100

Ametek HDR Power Systems
Columbus, OH 43204
614-308-5500

AMS Alltronics Inc.
Oakville, ON L6M 3H2
Canada
905-844-5772

Amtelco
McFarland, WI 53558
800-356-9148

AMTI
Virginia Beach, VA 23452
757-431-8597

An Ounce of Prevention: Disaster Planning for Archives
Lenexa, KS 66215
913-341-3808

Anacomp
San Diego, CA 92128
858-716-3400

Anacomp Inc.
Braintree, MA 02184
781-843-5650

Anco Environmental
Berkeley Heights, NJ 07922
908-464-3511

Anderson Niswander Construction Inc.
Redwood City, CA 94063
650-369-9443

Angelus Mobileasing Co. Inc
South El Monte, CA 91733
626-443-1715

Animal Poison Control Center
Urbana, Il 61802
888-426-4435

Ankeny Rental Center
Ankeny, IA 50023
515-964-5400

Anniversary Reactions to a Traumatic Event
Washington, DC 20015
800-789-2647

Annual International Disaster Management Conf
Orlando, FL 32812
407-281-7396

Ansul Inc.
Marinette, WI 54143
715-735-7411

Anteon
Fairfax, VA 22030
703-246-0200

'Anthrax Video'
Santa Ana, CA 92704
800-468-4296

Anti Terrorism Accreditation Board
Atlanta, GA 30327
703-880-5212

Antietam Tree and Landscape
Hagerstown , MD 21740
301-791-3500

Antique & Personal Property Appraisals
El Cajon, CA 92019
619-670-4455

ANVIL Technologies Inc.
North York, ON M2K 1E3
Canada
905-887-7535

AOK Global Products Limited (RESCUE CHAIRS)
Deer Park, NY 11729
631-242-1642

Aon Risk Services Inc
Houston, TX 77056
832-476-6000

APC
West Kingston, RI 02892
877-272-2722

Apex Software
San Antonio, TX 78249
800-858-9958

Apple Computer Inc
Cupertino, CA 95014
408-996-1010

Apple Direct Mail
New York, NY 10014
212-924-4488

Application Design Services, Inc.
Warwick, RI 02886
401-737-2040

Applied Risk Control Corp.
Nyack, NY 10960
845-365-2444

Applied Technology Council
Arlington, VA 22201
703-351-5052

Applied Technology Council
Redwood City, CA 94065-1191
650-595-1542

Appropriate Systems, LLC
Wayne, NJ 07470
973-904-1547

Aqua Blox Beverage Inc
Santa Fe Spgs, CA 90670
562-693-9599

Aramsco
Thorofare, NJ 08086
856-848-5330

Arbor Pro, Inc.
Portland, OR 97030
503-491-2844

ARBORWELL
Castro Valley, CA 94546
888-969-8733

Arch Wireless
Columbia, MD 21046
800-340-4732 x8555

ARCHIBUS, Inc.
Boston, MA 02108
617-227-2508

Archive Document Storage Inc.
Jersey City, NJ 07302
201-716-7900

Archive Management Inc
Riverside, CA 92507-0725
951-656-2238

ArchivesOne
Columbus, OH 43219
614-235-7000

Argent
Framington, CT
860-674-1700

Arizona Center for Mental Health
Phoenix, AZ 85018-2135
602-954-6700

Arizona Division of Emergency
Management
Phoenix, AZ 85008
602-244-0504

Arizona Poison & Drug Info Center
Tucson, AZ 85724
800-222-1222

Arizona State University
Tempe, AZ 85287-0703
480-965-4505

Arkansas Department of Emergency
Management
Conway, AR 72033-0758
501-730-9750

Arkansas Poison & Drug Information
Center
Little Rock, AR 72205
800-222-1222

Arkansas Tech University
Russellville, AR 72801-2222
479-968-0318

Arlington Associates, LLC
Novato, CA 94947-4976
415-883-0884

ARMA International
Lenexa, KS 66215
913-341-3808

ArmaKleen Company, The
Princeton, NJ 08543
800-332-5424

Armstrong Medical Industries, Inc.
Lincolnshire, IL 60069-0700
800-323-4220

ARS Advanced Restoration Solutions
Houston, TX 77066
281-397-0184

Art Conservation Services of Sarasota
Sarasota, FL 34236
941-366-6194

Arthur Andersen LLP
Chicago, IL 60603
312-580-0033

Artifex Equipment, Inc.
Penngrove, CA 94951
707-664-1672

Arup Risk Consulting
Westborough, MA 01581-3966
508-616-9990

Ascendent Systems
San Jose, CA 95110
888-507-1777

ASCO Power Techonologies
Florham Park, NJ 07932
800-800-2726

Asesores en Emergencias y Desastres
Queretaro, TX 76100
442-218-4424

AshBritt Environmental
Lake Arrowhead, CA 92532
909-336-6464

Asplundh Tree Expert Co.
Willow Grove, PA 19090
215-784-4200

ASSE Annual Conference
Des Plaines, IL 60018
847-699-2929

Asset Recovery Technologies Inc.
Elk Grove Village, IL 60007
847-758-1985

Assisting People with Disabilities in a
Disaster
Washington, DC 20472
202-566-1600

Assoc. of State & Territorial Health
Officials
Washington, DC 20005-4006
202-371-9090

Associated Records and Information
Services
Caddo Mills, TX 75135-0937
214-675-9598

Association for Facilities Engineering
Cincinnati, OH 45242
513-489 2473

Association for Information & Image
Mgmt. (AIIM)
Silver Spring, MD 20910-5616
301-587-8202

Association of Contingency Planners
National HQ
Oak Creek, WI 53154-1429
414-768-8000 x116

Association of Contingency Planners
National HQ
Oak Creek, WI 53154-1429
414-768-8000 x116

Association of Contingency Planners (ACP)
Arlington, VA 22216
301-931-2050

Association of Contingency Planners (ACP)
Austin, TX 78711-3371
512-473-4072

Association of Contingency Planners (ACP)
Bethlehem, PA 18020
610-867-9839

Association of Contingency Planners (ACP)
Bloomington, IL 61704
309-828-1313

Association of Contingency Planners (ACP)
Chicago, IL 60606
312-875-1069

Association of Contingency Planners (ACP)
Clearwater, FL 33762-0111
727-567-4777

Association of Contingency Planners (ACP)
Davie, FL 33329
954-383-4031

Association of Contingency Planners (ACP)
Englewood, CO 80155-3943
720-889-2020

Association of Contingency Planners (ACP)
Houston, TX 77095
281-550-4995

Association of Contingency Planners (ACP)
Irving, TX 75016
214-820-0899

Association of Contingency Planners (ACP)
Jacksonville, FL 32241-3556
904-281-3271

Association of Contingency Planners (ACP)
Little Rock, AR 72222-7587
501-220-6258

Association of Contingency Planners (ACP)
Nashville, TN 37219-8050
615-401-2275

Association of Contingency Planners (ACP)
Orange, CA 92856-1842
626-537-2712

Association of Contingency Planners (ACP)
Phoenix, AZ 85026-7434
480-557-1132

Association of Contingency Planners (ACP)
Port Hueneme, CA 93041-2171
805-984-9547

Association of Contingency Planners (ACP)
Redmond, WA 98073-2346
425-580-8095

Association of Contingency Planners (ACP)
Salt Lake City, UT 84147-1434
801-902-4508

Association of Contingency Planners (ACP)
San Diego, CA 92142
858-385-2700

Association of Contingency Planners (ACP)
Satellite Beach, FL 32937
321-554-1922

Association of Contingency Planners (ACP)
Sioux Falls, SD 57101-0884
605-782-5020

Association of Contingency Planners (ACP)
Tulsa, OK 74101-0776
918-835-0435

Association of Contingency Planners; LA
Chapter
Westlake Village, CA 91361-3508
805-332-5400

Association of Specialists in Cleaning &
Restoration (ASCR)
Millersville, MD 21108
800-272-7012

Association of State Dam Safety Officials
Lexington, KY 40507-1544
859-257-5140

Association of State Floodplain Managers
(ASFPM)
Madison, WI 53713
608-274-0123

Assured Micro-services Inc
Worthington, OH 43085
614-431-1818

Assurity River Group
Minneapolis, MN 55424-0506
612-435-2170

AstroCare Fire & Water
Orange, NJ 07050-3529
973-677-1234

AT&T
Bedminster, NJ 07921
800-222-0400

ATF Bomb Threat and Detection, Athena
Global
Montreal, QC H4A 2Z3
Canada
514-488-3867

Atilla Technologies, LLC
Hoboken, NJ 07030
201-216-5029

Atlanta Marketing Solutions Inc.
Powder Spgs, GA 30127
770-439-6173

Atlanta-Fulton County Emergency
Management Agency
Atlanta, GA 30303
404-730-5600

Atlantic Builders
Charleston, SC 29413
843-554-2065

Atlantic Detroit Diesel Allison Inc
Lodi, NJ 07644
718-665-1500

Atlantic Oceanographic and
Meteorological Laboratory
Miami, FL 33149
305-361-4450

Atlantic Scientific
Melbourne, FL 32904
800-544-4737

Atlantic Scientific Corp
West Melbourne, FL 32904-1527
321-725-8000

Atlantix Global Systems Inc
Norcross, GA 30092
770-248-7700

Atlas Cold Storage
Cartersville, GA 30121
770-382-5115

Atlas Cold Storage
Douglas, GA 31533
912-384-7272

ATM Exchange Inc. The
Cincinnati, OH 45227
513-272-1081

A-Town Hi-Tech LP
Abilene, TX 79605-7238
325-692-1893

Attainium Corp
Gainesville, VA 20155
571-248-8200

AudienceCentral
Bellingham, WA 98225
360-756-9090

Aura Systems, Inc.
El Segundo, CA 90245
310-643-5300 x213

Aus-Tex Printing & Mailing
Austin, TX 78754
512-476-7581

Austin Power Equipment
Legander, TX 78641
512-260-3333

Authentium
Palm Beach Gardens, FL 33418
800-423-9147

Auto Supply True Value
Johns Island, SC 29455
843-559-1555

Automated Mailing Systems Corp.
Dallas, TX 75220
800-527-1668

Avian Flyaway
Rockwall, TX 75087
800-888-0165

Avoid Disaster: Keep your business going
Indianapolis, IN 46256
877-762-2974

AXCESS Disaster Consulting Group
West Vancouver, BC V7V 4S1
Canada
604-657-6760

Ayers Professional Services
College Station, TX 77845
979-776-5800

Az Carpet & Restoration Co.
Phoenix, AZ 85034
602-257-8444

Backup Inc
San Diego, CA 92121
858-320-4800

BAGMASTERS
Corona, CA 92881
800-843-2247

Baker Safety Equipment
Townsend, DE 19734
302-652-7080

Bamberger Industries Inc
Woodmere, NY 11598-1020
516-295-3170

Banaher Power Solutions
Richmond, VA 23231
804-236-3326

Bank - In - A - Box
Pittsburgh, PA 15232
412-681-1091

Bank Administration Institute
Chicago, IL 60606
312-553-4600

BankSystems
Eagan, MN 55121
651-686-1400

Barco
Dallas, TX 75207
214-428-5691

Barney F. Pelant & Associates
Bloomingdale, IL 60108-2141
630-894-6989

Barrett Cleaning and Restoration
Hatboro, PA 19040
215-715-3544

Barron Emergency Consulting
Milton, MA 02186
617-298-8265

Barsa Consulting Group, LLC
Purchase, NY 10577
914-251-1234

Basement Systems
Seymour, CT 06483
800-541-0487

Base-X Expediation Shelters
Fairfield, VA 24435
800-969-8527

Bay Area Clean Care
Petoskey, MI 49770-9263
231-347-7707

Bay Area Disaster Kleenup
Oldsmar, FL 34677
800-362-8453

Bay Metro Corporation
San Francisco, CA 94107
415-626-4067

Bay Restoration & Air Duct Services
Lively , VA 22482
800-438-2436

Bayside Chem-Dry
Cedar Point, NC 28584
252-393-7580

Bayside Equipment Co.
Redwood City, CA 94063
650-368-3955

BC Management, Inc
Irvine, CA 92612
949-250-8172

BCI Engineers & Scientists Inc
Lakeland, FL 33803
877-550-4224

BCP Media
St. Louis, MO 63151
314-894-0276

BCP Tools
Niagara Falls, NY 14304-1745
800-461-3095

Be Alert, Be Aware, Have a Plan: Guide
to Safety
Guilford , CT 06437
203-458-4500

Be Ready Inc.
Oceanside, CA 92054
760-966-3600

Bear Carpet & Restoration
Albuquerque, NM 87107
505-888-1164

Bear Computer Systems Inc
Valley Vlg, CA 91607
818-832-5548

Bearcom Wireless Worldwide Inc.
Garland, TX 75041
800-541-9333

BearingPoint Inc.
McLean, VA 22030
703-747-3000

Begal Enterprises, Inc. Fire & Water
Restoration Specialists
Rockville, MD 20852
301-984-8566

Behlman Electronics
Ventura, CA 93003
805-642-0660

Bel Esprit Partners
Eden Prairie, MN 55344
952-223-5404

BELFOR
Birmingham, MI 48009
800-856-3333

BELFOR
Seattle , WA 98103
800-775-0806

BELFOR Canada Inc.
Vancouver, BC V5M 4T1
Canada
866-366-0493

Belkin Components
Compton, CA 90220
310-898-1100

Belyea Company Inc
Easton, PA 18045
610-515-8775

Benchmark Technology Group
Alpharetta, GA 30004
678-319-3999

Bender Direct Mail Service
Tulsa, OK 74107
918-583-1171

Bennett's Trailer Co.
Aston, PA 19014
800-735-5820

Bercha Group
Calgary, AB T2N 4S6
Canada
403-270-2221

Berman Adjusters
Newton, MA 02461
617-964-0000

Berman Adjusters, Inc.
Newton, MA 02461
617-964-0000

Bernstein Crisis Management LLC.
Monrovia, CA 91016-3724
626-305-9277

Better Floors & Restorations
Placentia, CA 92870
714-524-8500

Better Image, The
Milford, NJ 08848
908-995-2600

Betty Brite Cleaners
Windsor, NJ 08561
609-426-4600

Beverly Bremer Silver Shop
Atlanta, GA 30305
404-261-4009

Bierschbach Equipment & Supply
Sioux Falls, SD 57106
605-332-4466

Big Beam Emergency Systems Inc.
Crystal Lake, IL 60039-0518
815-459-6100

bigbyte.cc
Albuquerque, NM 87012
505-255-5422

BindView Corp
Houston, TX 77056
713-561-4000

Bingham McCutchen
Boston, MA 02110
617-951-8000

Binomial International
Ogdensburg, NY 13669
888-246-6642

BioCare Inc.
Easley, SC 29641-0817
864-855-3400

BIOPRO, LLC
Gilbert, AZ 85233
877-492-7549

Bio-Recovery Corporation
Long Island City, NY 11101-2011
718-729-2600

Biosystems
Middletown, CT 06457
860-344-1079

Bioterroism Preparedness and Response
Planning
Atlanta, GA 30333
800-CDC-INFO

Bioterror Preparedness, Attack and
Response
St. Louis, MO 63146
800-545-2522

Bioterrorism and Emerging Infections
Birmingham, AL 35294-4551
205-934-2687

Bioterrorism Preparedness Program
Providence, RI 02908
401-222-6868

Birch Equipment Rental & Sales
Bellingham , WA 98226
866-722-4724

Bishop Companies The
Goldendale, WA 98620
800-443-3473

Bishop Services
Goldendale, WA 98620
509-773-4707

BISYS
Houston, TX 77046
713-622-8911

Bizco
Lincoln, NE 68510
877-2B-TOUGH

Black & Veatch
Kansas City, MO 64114
913-458-2000

Black Box Corp
Lawrence, PA 15055
724-746-5500

Black Box Corp.
Duluth, GA 30096
678-475-5500

Black Mountain Stores, Inc.
Odessa, TX 79761-1226
800-760-7942

Blackmon Mooring Steamatic
Fort Worth, TX 76107
877-730-1948

Blanchard Machinery Inc.
North Miami, FL 33181
305-949-2581

BLI International, Inc. - Priority Start!
Granada Hills, CA 91344
818-363-5390

Blindsided: Managers Guide to
Catastrophic Incidents
The Woodlands, TX 77387

Blue Heron Consulting Corp.
Rochester, NY 14624
800-253-3449

Blue Metals
Newtown, PA 18940
215-860-2345

BlueBridge Networks, LLC
Cleveland, OH 44115
216-621-BLUE

BlueStar Construction Co
Loganville, GA 30052
770-736-9202

Blu-Med Response Systems
Kirkland, WA 98033
425-739-2795

BMC Software Inc.
Houston, TX 77042
713-918-8800

BMS Catastrophe Inc. (BMS CAT)
Fort Worth, TX 76107-2352
800-433-2940

Board of Certified Safety Professionals (BCSP)
Savoy, IL 61874
217-359-9263

Bocada, Inc.
Bellvue, WA 98004
425-818-4400

Bolden's Mfg / Hydro-Lab
Noblesville, IN 46062
888-776-6708

Bolden's Mfg / Xtreme Products
Noblesville, IN 46062
888-776-6708

Bomb Threat Management and Policy
St. Louis, MO 63146
800-545-2522

Boomerang.com
Palo Alto, CA 94303
800-779-7792

Boone's Restoration Technologies
Conroe, TX 77385
281-444-5959

BootSector Industries
Farmingdale, NY 11735
631-249-2700

BOOZ-ALLEN & HAMILTON Inc.
McLean, VA 22102-3838
703-902-5000

Borden/Lee Consulting
North Hills, CA 91343
818-893-2552

Boston Financial Data Services
North Quincy, MA 02171
617-483-5000

Boston Financial Data Services
North Quincy, MA 02171
617-483-5000

Boston University
Boston, MA 02215
617-353-6000

Bostonian Cleaning Services
Braintree, MA 02184-4404
781-340-1252

Bowe & Bell & Howell
Allentown, PA 18109
610-264-4510

Bowles Construction Inc.
Augusta, GA 30909
800-738-9446

Bowne Global Solutions
New York, NY 10001
917-339-4700

Braley Communication Systems Inc
MIDLAND, MI 48640
989-687-6319

Braun Intertec Corp.
Minneapolis, MN 55438
952-995-2000

Bravo Communications, Inc.
San Jose, CA 95135
408-297-8700

Breedon Bag & Burlap Co. Inc.
Jacksonville, FL 32254
904-389-8085

Brennan's Tree Service, LLC
Manassas Park, VA 20111
703-393-8861

Bright Tools, Inc.
Boca Raton, FL 33431
616-949-2177

Britannia Inc.
South San Francisco, CA 94080-6305
650-742-6490

Britz-Heidbrink, Inc.
Wheatland, WY 82201
307-322-4040

BRM Disaster Recovery Services Inc
Pittsburgh, PA 15233-2024
412-249-1200

Brokers Worldwide
Folcroft, PA 19032
610-461-3661

Brookdale (A DuPont Canada Company)
Vancouver, BC V6P 6T3
Canada
800-459-3822

Brothers ChemDry & Oceanfront ChemDry
Virginia Beach, VA 23452
757-498-3439

Brown's Cleaners
Ottawa, ON K1R 7R7
Canada
613-235-5181

BRProactive Inc.
Glendora, CA 91741
626-852-0412

BSC America - Atlantic Auctions
Bel Air, MD 21014
410-803-4160

Buffalo Computer Graphics, Inc.
Blasdell, NY 14219
716-822-8668

Building Owners & Managers Association (BOMA)
Washington, DC 20005
202-408-2662

Building Service Contractors Assn. Intl.
Fairfax, VA 22030
703-359-7090

BuildingReports.com
Duluth, GA 30096
770-495-1993

Bullard Co.
Rutland, KY 41031
800-227-0423

Burch Manufacturing Company, Inc.
Fort Dodge , IA 50501
515-573-4136

Burns and Levinson LLP
Boston, MA 02110
617-345-3000

Business & Government Continuity Services
Oklahoma City, OK 73101
405-737-8348

Business Contingency Group
Encino, CA 91316
818-784-3736

Business Continuity & Infrastructure Security Conf
New York, NY 10016
212-286-0333

Business Continuity Planners Association
St. Paul, MN 55175-0930
651-223-9801

Business Continuity Planners, Inc (BCPI)
Maryland Heights, MO 63043
314-541-4913

Business Continuity Planning Conference
New York, NY 10271-0080
212-608-1500

Business Continuity, Security & Crisis Mgmt. Conf.
New York, NY 10022
212-339-0345

Business Continuity: Best Practices
Brookfield, CT 068094-3104
203-740-7444

Business Disaster Preparedness Council, The
Ft. Myers, FL 33902-0398
941-477-3600

Business Equipment Unlimited
Ashburn, VA 20147
703-626-1643

COMPANY LISTINGS ALPHABETICALLY

Business Network of Emergency
Resources, Inc.
New York, NY 10176
888-353-BNET

Business Protection Systems International
Riverside, CA 92507
800-594-3714

Business Recovery and Continuity
Education
Mount Ephraim, NJ 08059
856-635-9770

Business Recovery Center, Inc.
Parsippany, NJ 07054
973-299-0302

Business Recovery Consultants Inc.
Hockessin, DE 19707-2059
800-795-5985

Business Recovery Managers Association
San Francisco, CA 94126
925-355-8660

Business Recovery Planners Assoc of WI
Madison, WI 53705-4456
608-231-7502

Business Recovery Planners Association
of SE WI
West Allis, WI 53219-1011
414-543-8100

Business911 International Inc
Houston, TX 77095-2725
281-550-4995

Butler Manufacturing Co.
Kansas City, MO 64102
816-968-3000

Buzco Construction Co. Inc.
Torrance, CA 90505
310-326-8139

BWT Associates
Shrewsbury, MA 01545
508-845-6000

C & E Services Inc.
Phoenix, AZ 85063
602-246-2483

C&G Chem-Dry
Odenton, MD 21113
410-674-4240

C&T Systems
Saint Paul, MN 55107
800-472-2081

C4CS, LLC
Pittsburgh, PA 15217
412 421-0433

Cables-to-go
Salt Lake City, UT 84119
801-973-6090

Cactus International
Mount Airy, MD 21771
301-829-1622

California Diesel and Power
Martinez, CA 94553
925-229-2700

California Governor's Office of
Emergency Services
Rancho Cordova, CA 95741-9047
916-845-8510

California Poison Control System
Sacramento, CA 95817
800-22-1222

California Rental Association
Sacramento, CA 95834
800-272-7400

California Restoraton Contractors
Ventura, CA 93003-6671
805-650-1209

California Seismic Safety Commision, The
Sacremento, CA 95833
916-263-5506

California Specialized Training Institute
San Luis Obispo, CA 93403
805-549-3535

California State University, Long Beach -
Occupational Studies Dept.
Long Beach, CA 90840-5601
888-999-9935

Callan Salvage & Appraisal Co
Eads (Memphis), TN 38028
901-867-3300

Calvin, Giordano & Associates
Ft. Lauderdale, FL 33316
954-921-7781

Cambridge Computer Services, Inc.
Waltham, MA 02452
781-250-3000

Cameo Services Inc.
York, PA 17403-5303
717-843-8893

Can Am Computer Inc.
Mahwah, NJ 07430
201-512-1414

Canada Public Safety, Security and
Emerg. Prep., Canadian Association For
Earthquake Engineering
Ottawa, ON K1N 6N5
Canada
613-562-5800

Canadian Centre for Emergency
Preparedness
Burlington, ON L7N 3N4
Canada
905-331-2552

Canadian Emergency Preparedness
Association
Chilliwack, BC V2R 2C2
Canada
604-858-7092

Canadian Environmental Auditing
Association
Mississauga, ON L5N 5M3
Canada
905-814-1160

Canadian Red Cross-Atlantic Zone
Saint John , NB E2L 3X3
Canada
506-674-6200

Canadian Red Cross-National Office
Ottawa, ON K2P 2P2
Canada
613-740-1900

Canadian Red Cross-Ontario Zone
Mississauga, ON L5R 3E9
Canada
905-890-1000

Canadian Red Cross-Quebec Zone
lle-des-Soeurs Verdun, QC H3E 1P4
Canada
514-362-2930

Canadian Red Cross-Western Zone
Calgary, AB T3C 3P6
Canada
403-205-3448

Canadian Society for Industrial Security Inc.
Ottawa, ON K2E 6T7
Canada
613-274-3022

CANBERRA Co. - Canada
Concord, ON L4K 4N8
Canada
905-660-5373

Canberra Industries Training & Tech
Svcs. Dept.
Meriden, CT 06450-7127
800-255-6370

Cannon Cochran Management Services Inc
Danville, IL 61832
217-446-1089

Cans-To-Go, LLC
Milwaukee, WI 53224
414-447-9000

Canvas Systems, Inc.
Norcross, GA 30071
770-662-1881

Cap Index, Inc.
Exton, PA 19341
610-903-3000

Capital Card Systems
Rockville, MD 20855
888-645-0727

Capital City Restorations
Rockville, MD 20850
800-785-8810

Capital Data
Lansing, MI 48917
517-371-7100

CapRock Communications
Houston, TX 77048
832-668-2300

CAPS Business Recovery Services
Shelton, CT 06484
800-542-2773

Captain Clean Inc.
Sheridan, WY 82801
307-672-0726

Cardiac Science
Irvine, CA 92614
949-797-3800

Cardinal Risk Management Alternatives,
Inc.
Dallas, TX 75240
214-365-0055

Carlin MFG.. LLC
Fresno, CA 93711-3602
559-276-0123

Carner Brothers Environmental
Excavating
Roseland, NJ 07068
973-226-1840

Carolina Claims Service
Columbia, SC 29210
803-731-4005

Carolinas Poison Center
Charlotte, NC 28208
800-222-1222

Carpet & FabriCare Institute The
Mission Viejo, CA 92690
800-227-7389

Carpet Revival Centre Ltd. The
Brockville, ON K6V 5T4
Canada
613-342-4967

Carr Hardware
Pittsfield, MA 01202
413-443-5611

Carranza Cowheard & Associates
Doral, FL 33166
305-463-7978

Cartagena Software Limited
Markham, ON L6C 2N5
Canada
888-USE-TAPE

Carter Burgess Inc
Little Rock, AR 72211
501-223-0515

Cascade - Phillips Co.
Clackamas, OR 97015
800-726-4768

Castay Inc
La Place, LA 70068
504-524-8444

Cat 5 Disaster Services / Nationwide
Decaturville, TN 38329
731-852-2560

Cat Rental Power
Mossville, IL 61552
1-800-RENT CAT

Catalano's Cleaning Services
Metairie, LA 70001
504-885-7417

Catastrophe Services, Inc. (CSI)
Columbia, SC 29224
803-788-1800

Caterpillar Power Quality Protection
Systems
Peoria, IL 61629-0001
309-578-6298

Catholic Relief Services
Baltimore, MD 21201-3443
410-625-2220

CBL Data Recovery Technologies, Inc.
800-551-3917

C-COM Satllite Systems Inc.
Ottawa, ON K1B3V7
Canada
877-463-8886

CDB Software Inc
Houston, TX 77082
800-627-6561

CDCLarue Industries, Inc.
Sand Springs, OK 74063
866-954-9700

CDI Vaults
Eugene, OR 97402
541-344-7890

CDM
Cambridge, MA 02139
617-452-6000

CDS
Oakhurst, NJ 07755
732-517-0919

Celebrity Services Group, LLC.
Fishers, IN 46038
317-578-2822

Cell-Tel Government Systems
Jacksonville, FL 32256
904-363-1111

CEM Associates, Inc.
Newton, NC 28658
828-465-0874

Center for Development and Disability
Albuquerque, NM 87107
505-272-2990

Center for Disaster Recovery
Barrie, ON L4N 3G2
Canada
877-792-6569

Center for Disaster Research &
Education (CDRE)
Millersville, PA 17551
717-872-3568

Center for Domestic Preparedness
Anniston, AL 36205-5100
256-847-2225

Center for Earthquake Research and
Information
Memphis, TN 38152
901-678-2007

Center for Harzards Reaserch
Chico, CA 95929-0425
530-898-4953

Center for Hazards and Risk Research
Palisades, NY 10964
845-365-8909

Center Town Psychological Services
Ottawa, ON K2P P0G
Canada
613-235-9196

Centers for Disease Control and
Prevention
Atlanta, GA 30333
800-311-3435

Central Data Processing, Inc.
Forestville, MD 20747
301-568-4900

Central Georgia Technical College
Macon, GA 31206
478-757-6688

Central Missouri State University
Warrensburg, MO 64093
660-543-4971

Central New York Poison Center
Syracuse, NY 13210
800-222-1222

Central Ohio Poison Center
Columbus, OH 43205
800-222-1222

Central States Microfilming Inc
Cary, IL 60013
847-639-0443

Centre antipoison-Québec
Sainte-Foy, PQ G1V 4G2
Canada
800-463-5060

Centre for Emergency Preparedness and
Response
Burlington, ON L7N SN4
Canada
905-331-2552

Centurian Surplus Inc.
Morgan Hill, CA 95037
408-778-2001

Century Software
Salt Lake City, UT 84107
801-268-3088

CERIAS: Cent. for Information
Assurance & Security
West LaFayette, IN 47907-2086
765-494-7841

CERT Coordination Center
Pittsburgh, PA 15213-3890
412-268-7090

Certified Disaster Services
Ogden, UT 84401
801-399-9996

Certified Firestop, LLC
Monroe, LA 71201
318-665-2060

Certified Restoration and Construction Inc.
Sacramento, CA 95828-1027
916-386-4811

Certified Restoration and Remediation
Services
Las Vegas, NV 89123
702-837-6653

Certified Restoration Drycleaning
Network (CRDN)
Ann Arbor, MI 48108
888-379-2532

Certified Restoration Drycleaning of
Denver
Highlands Ranch, CO 80126
303-991-0600

Certified Restoration Services Inc.
Holbrook, NY 11741
631-737-5050

Certified Risk Managers Intl.
Austin, TX 78755
800-633-2165

CertTest Training Center Inc.
Grapevine, TX 76051
817-410-8000

Cervalis
Stamford, CT 06905
866-602-2020

CESCO
North Charleston, SC 29418
888-772-3726

Ceva Computer Corp
Brooklyn Heights, OH 44131
216-749-7300

CGI
Montreal, QC H3A 2M8
Canada
514-841-3200

CGI Adjusters Inc.
Markham, ON L3R 6H3
Canada
905-474-0003

CGI-AMS
Fairfax, VA 22033
800-255-8888

CH2M Hill
Englewood, CO 80112
303-771-0900

Chamberlain Paul International
Beverly Hills, CA 90212
310-276-2601

Champion Solutions Group
Boca Raton, FL 33487
561-997-2900

Charles R. Tutwiler and Associates Inc.
Tampa, FL 33609
800-321-4488

Chase Electronics Inc
Upper Darby, PA 19082
610-449-8160

Chem Dry - By Moore
Yonkers, NY 10704
914-843-8062

Chem-Dry of Boise
Boise, ID 83706
208-322-7771

Chem-Dry of Brazos County
College Station, TX 77845
979-776-9833

Chem-Dry of Lafayette
West Lafayette, IN 47906
765-423-1166

ChemDry of Long Beach
Long Beach , CA 90815
562 437-7000

Chem-Dry of Marin
Novato , CA 94949
415-382-8196

Chem-Dry of North Valley
Chico, CA 95973
530-891-6747

Chem-Dry on the No. Shore
Reading, MA 01867
781-670-9169

Chemdry Tricity Carpet Cleaning
Allentown, PA 18109
610-821-4916

Chemical Manufacturers Association
Arlington, VA 22209-2323
703-741-5000

Chemical Stockpile Emergency
Preparedness Program
Washington, DC 20472
202-646-2734

Chemical Waste Management
Model City, NY 14107
716-754-8231

Chicago Cash Register
Morton Grove, IL 60053
312-666-5555

Chicago Conservation Center, Inc.
Chicago, IL 60610
312-944-5401

Children's Hospital of Wisconsin Poison
Center
Milwaukee, WI 53201
800-222-1222

Childress Duffy Goldblatt, Ltd.
Chicago, Il 60610
312-494-0200

Chinook Medical Gear, Inc.
Durango, CO 81301
970-375-1241

Chubb Group of Insurance Companies
New York, NY 10041
212-612-4000

Church World Service Emergency
Response Program
New York, NY 10115
212-870-3151

Ciber Inc
Greenwood Vlg, CO 80111
303-220-0100

CIS Steeplejack
Medina, OH 44256
216-395-5663

CITEL Inc
Miami, FL 33169-5100
305-621-0022

City of Detroit Emergency Management
Division
Detroit, MI 48226
313-596-5196

City of Houston Emergency Management
Houston, TX 77251-1562
713-884-4500

City TrueValue Just Ask Rental
Bristol, CT 6010
860-582-7166

City Watch by AVTEX
Bloomington, MN 55437
952-831-0888

Claimlink
Red Bank, NJ 07701
800-537-4700

Claimlink Jewelry Solutions
Red Bank, NJ 07701
800-537-4700

Claims Administrative Services Inc.
Tyler, TX 75701
903-509-8484

'Claims Magazine'
Erlanger, KY 41018
800-543-0874

Clair Odell Group
Norriftwn, PA 19401
610-825-5555

Clamshell Buildings Inc
Ventura, CA 93003
805-650-1700

Clark - Devon Hardware Co.
Chicago, IL 60626
773-764-3575

Clary Corp
Monrovia, CA 91016-4847
800-442-5279

Classic Furniture Services
Franklin, MA 02038
800-834-6016

Clean Aire Inc.
Hopkins, SC 29061
803-776-1117

Clean Care of New England
Warwick, RI 2886
401-736-5420

Clean Harbors Environmental Services, Inc.
Braintree, MA 02184-9048
781-849-1800

Clean Sweep Restoration Services of New England
Wallingford, CT 06492
800-952-0556

Clean Tech Restoration
Wichita, KS 67203
316-729-8100

Cleancare Services
Owen Sound, ON N4K 5N7
Canada
519-376-9932

Cleaning Genie Inc.
Sylvania, OH 43560
419-885-5511

Cleaning Services Group CSG
Danvers, MA 01923
800-683-6572

Cleaning Specialists Magazine, ICS
Woodland Hills, CA 91364
818-224-8035

Cleaning Unlimited Inc
Harahan, LA 70123
504-832-1636

Clean-Scene Restorations
Castlegar, BC V1N 4B3
Canada
800-414-8890

Cleary Cleaners
Rochester, NH 03839
603-332-2374

Cleveland Brothers Equipment Company
Harrisburg, PA 17111
800-482-2378

Climate Prediction Center
Camps Springs, MD 20746
301-763-8000

Clothes Call
Crofton, MD 21114
877-721-7445

Clover Park Technical College
Lakewood, WA 98499
253-589-5862

CM Services & Security
Taunton, MA 02780
508-989-3528

CMS Restoration
Lakeland, FL 33811
863-644-2958

CNT
Lumberton, NJ 08048
609-518-4000

Coakley & Williams Construction Co Inc
Gaithersburg, MD 20877
301-963-5000

Coastal Hazards Assessment and Mitigation Program
Clemson, SC 29634-0911
864-656-5941

Coastal Training Technologies
Virginia Beach, VA 23452
800-767-7703

COCAT Inc.
Denver, CO 80239
303-333-0392

COCAT.INC
Denver, CO 80237
303-333-0392

Code 3 Associates
Erie, CO 80516
303-772-7724

Coffing Corporation
Hamilton, OH 45011
513-755-8866

Coit Restoration Services
Woodinville, WA 98072
800-367-2648

Coleman Company
Wichita, KS 67201
800-633-7155

College of Lake County
Grayslake, IL 60030
847-543-2047

Collocation Solutions
Dallas, TX 75207-3139
214-231-0162

Colonial Adjustment, Inc.
Westbrook, ME 04098-5028
207-797-9036

Colorado Alliance for Environmental Education
Golden, CO 80401
303-273-9527

Colorado Catastrophe Inc.
Denver, CO 80209
303-333-0392

Colorado Division of Emergency Management
Golden, CO 80401-3979
303-273-1622

ColoSpace Inc.
Rockland , MA 02370
888-583-9200

Columbia Chem-Dry
Longview, WA 98632
360-423-5754

Columbus Microfilm Inc
Columbus, OH 43207
614-443-7825

Columbus State Community College
Columbus, OH 43215
614-287-2576

ComCARE Alliance
Washington, DC 20006
202-429-0574

COMCO Safety Consulting Inc.
Long Beach, CA 90808
562-981-5335

Comlanta
Norcross, GA 30092
770-449-6116

Commercial Paving & Recycling Company LLC
Scarborough, ME 04074
207-883-3325

Commercial Property Guide: Earthquake Safety
Sacramento, CA 95833
916-263-5506

Commonwealth Films Inc
Boston, MA 02116-1700
617-262-5634

Communications-Applied Technology
Reston, VA 20190-5202
800-229-3925

Community Alert Network Inc.
Albany, NY 12205-6000
800-992-2331

Community College of Rhode Island
Lincoln, RI 02865
401-333-7102

CommVault Systems Inc
Oceanport, NJ 07757
732-870-4000

CommVault Systems Inc
Ottawa, ON K2P 1L5
Canada
613-231-2800

Compaudit Services
Glen Rock, NJ 07452
201-689-4040

Competitive Insights Inc
Ottawa, ON K2G 6T1
Canada
613-843-9944

Compleat Restorations
Dallastown, PA 17313
800-699-1176

Compleat Restorations
Ephrata, PA 17522
800-699-1176

Compliance Solutions
Denver, CO 80239
800-711-2706

Comprehensive Solutions
Brookfield, WI 53005
262-785-8101

CompTIA
Oakbrook Terrace, IL 60181
630-678-8300

Compu Vault
Saint Louis, MO 63131
314-991-3858

CompuCom Systems
Dallas, TX 75230
972-856-3600

Compurex Systems Inc(CSI)
South Easton, MA 02375
508-230-3700

Computech Systems Corp.
Kirkland, WA 98034
800-882-0201

Computer Air and Power Systems, Inc.
Santa Clara, CA 95051
408-748-0200

Computer Associates International Inc.
Islandia, NY 11749
800-841-8743

Computer Clearing House
Rochester, NY 14623
585-334-0550

Computer Connection Corp
Minneapolis, MN 55420
952-884-0758

Computer Connection of NY Inc.
Utica, NY 13502
315-724-2209

Computer Engineering Associates
Millersville, MD 21108
410-987-7003

Computer Forensics
Seattle, WA 98109
206-324-6232

Computer Horizons - Headquarters
Mountain Lks, NJ 07046
973-299-4000

Computer Security Consultants Inc
Ridgefield, CT 06877
800-925-2724

Computer Security Institute
San Francisco, CA 94107-1387
917-305-3390

Computer Site Technologies Inc
Stuart, FL 24997
954-425-0638

Computer Wholesalers
Sarasota, FL 34237
800-229-2897

Computers Inc
Southborough, MA 01772
508-871-6800

Computersite Engineering
Santa Fe, NM 87506
505-982-8300

Computex Support Services
Plano, TX 75074
972-424-4011

Comservco Ent. Corp
Brooklyn, NY 11229-0702
718-332-2300

Concept Computer Inc
Buffalo, NY 14209
716-884-8220

Concord Communications Inc.
Marlborough, MA 01752
508-460-4646

Conder Direct
Laguna Hills, CA 92653
949-855-8300

Congressional Hazards Caucus
Alexandria, VA 22302
703-379-2480

Connecticut Office of Emergency Management
Hartford, CT 06105
860-566-3180

Connecticut Poison Control Center
Farmington, CT 06030
800-222-1222

Conquest International
Plainville, KS 67663
785 434 2483

Conqwest, Inc.
Holliston, MA 01746
508-893-0111

Conservation Ctr for Art and Historic Artifacts
Philadelphia, PA 19103-5530
215-545-0613

Consolidated Risk Management
Cleveland, OH 44114-2804
216-623-1777

Consonus AllWaysOn Data Centers
Salt Lake City, UT 84111
888-452-8000

Consortium of Universities for Research in Earthquake Engineering (CUREE)
Richmond, CA 94804
510-231-9557

Con-Space Communications Ltd.
Richmond , BC V6V 2M2
Canada
800-546-3405

Construction Data Service Inc
Temple City, CA 91780
626-401-0039

Construction Technology Laboratories Inc (CTL)
Skokie, IL 60077
847-965-7500

Con-Tech Restorations Ltd.
Toronto, ON M1P 3A6
Canada
416-288-9932

Contemporary Computer Services
Bohemia, NY 11716
631-563-8880

Continental Jewelry Replacement Co.
Tampa, FL 33609
800-282-5182

Continental Machinery Company Inc.
Dallas, TX 75238
800-616-8600

Continental Overspray Rempoval
San Diego, CA 92109
800-459-5772

Continental Restoration Consulting
Dallas, TX 75355
214-342-8910

Contingency Management Consultants
Orinda, CA 94563-3217
925-254-1663

Contingency Planners of Ohio
Columbus, OH 43234-0825
614-249-9339

Contingency Planners, Inc.
Conway, AR 72032-0958
501-329-0958

Contingency Planning & Management Expo
Flemington, NJ 08822
908-788-0343

Contingency Planning & Recovery Institute (CPR-I)
Wellesley Hills, MA 02481
781-235-2895

Contingency Planning and Disaster Recovery
Indianapolis, IN 46256
877-762-2974

Contingency Planning and Outsourcing Inc
Columbia, SC 29229
803-712-6105

Contingency Planning Association of the Carolinas
Charlotte, NC 28232-2492
704-906-1158

Contingency Planning Exchange
New York, NY 10005
212-344-4003

Contingency Planning Solutions Inc.
Appleton, WI 54914
920-734-0241

ContingenZ Corporation
Playa Del Rey, CA 90293
310-306-0166

Continuing Challenge HazMat Workshop
Sacramento, CA 95822
916-433-1688

Continuity Centers
Woodbury, NY 11797
516-622-0200

Continuity First
Richmond, VA 23228
804-559-6623

Continuity Insights
Doylestown, PA 18901
215-230-9556

Continuity Insights Management
Conference
Doylestown, PA 18901
215-230-9556

Continuity Research
Baltimore, MD 21282
215-968-2300

Continuity Shield
Toronto, ON M5E 1W7
Canada
416-483-0464

Continuity Solutions Inc
Worthington, OH 43085-4004
614-885-5001

Continuity Solutions, Inc.
Worthington, OH 43085
614-885-5001

ContinuityPlanner.com
Hamilton, ON L8S 4S3
Canada
800-461-3095

Continuous Solutions Inc.
Albuquerque, NM 87113
505-228-2438

Controlled Power Company
Troy, MI 48083
248-528-3700

Controls & Power Systems
Boxford, MA 01921
978-887-8525

ConVault Florida
Wildwood, FL 34785
352-748-6462

ConvergingTechnologies Inc.
Tucson, AZ 85705
800-846-9726

COOP Systems
Herndon, VA 20170
703-464-8700

COPE Solutions Inc
Smiths Falls, ON K7A 4S7
Canada
613-223-1128

Coping With Technological Disasters
Anchorage, AK 99503
907-277-7222

Copper Harbor Consulting, Inc.
Needham, MA 02492
781-449-3235

Corby M & Associates
Worcester, MA 01609-1953
508-792-4320

Corey InduServe
Williamston, NC 27892
252-809-9022

CorigElan, LLC
Chicago, IL 60607
312-563-1430

Cornell Communications
Milwaukee, WI 53223-3830
414-351-4660

Corner Construction Co Inc
Los Angeles, CA 90019
323-965-1999

Cornerstone Appraisal and Restoration
Princeton, NJ 08540
609-520-8877

Corporate Protective Solutions
Vancouver, BC V6Z 2R1
Canada
604-915-7538

Corporate Risk Solutions, Inc.
Lenexa, KS 66215
913-422-0410

Corporate Security Service Inc
San Francisco, CA 94103
415-543-3460

CORT Furniture Rental -
Commercial/Residential
Fairfax, VA 22030-7400
703-968-8500

County of Dade Emergency Management
Miami, FL 33178
305-468-5400

Cousino Construction Company, Inc.
Perrysburg, OH 43551
800-874-2122

COVERGUARD Corp
Hollywood, FL 33020
954-923-5550

Cox Pierce & Associates Inc
Omaha, NE 68108
402-734-0754

CPFilms Inc.
Martinsville, VA 24115
800-255-8627

CPM Group
Flemington, NJ 08822
908-788-0343

CPR Savers & First Aid Supply
Carlsbad, CA 92008
800-480-1277

CRA Inc.
Phoenix, AZ 85029
602-944-1548

Crain Langner & Co.
Richfield, OH 44286
330-659-3142

Crawford & CO Risk Management
Services
Atlanta, GA 30342
404-256-0830

Crawford & CO Risk Mgmt. Svc.
Fort Collins, CO 80527
970-225-9733

CRDN of the Midsouth
Collierville, TN 38017
901-850-1611

Crete True Value Just Ask Rental
Crete, NE 68333
402-826-3397

CRI Network Inc
Victoria, BC V8L 2K6
Canada
250-889-5030

Crime and Death Scene Cleaning
Ipswich, MA 01938
877-366-8348

Crisis Care Network
Grandville, MI 49418
888-736-0911

Crisis Consulting Group
Fairbanks, AK 99708
888-439-6898

Crisis Management Group Inc
Newton, MA 02464
617-969-7600

Crisis Management International Inc
Atlanta, GA 30305
404-841-3400

Crisis Management Software LLC
Middlebury, VT 05753
802-388-7379

Crisis Management: Planning for the
Inevitable
Pasadena, CA 91103
626-683-9200

Crisis Prevention Institute Inc.
Brookfield, WI 53005
262-783-5787

Crisis Recovery Services
Randolph, NJ 07869-4221
973-895-4799

Crisis Response in Our Schools
Commack, NY 11725
631-543-2217

Crisis Response Planning Corporation
Milton, ON L9T 4E5
Canada
905-876-0229

Crisis Simulations International, LLC
Coral Gables, FL 33143
305-205-5042

Crisis Simulations International, LLC
Portland, OR 97201
503-248-2233

Criterion Strategies Inc
New York, NY 10012
212-343-1134

Critical Care Medflight
Lawrenceville, GA 30046
770-513-9148

Critical Infrastructure Protection &
Emergncy Prep
Ottawa, ON K1A 0W6
Canada
613-991-7077

Critical Infrastructure Protection &
Emergncy Prep
Victoria, BC V8W 3A5
Canada
250-363-3621

Critical Situation Management Inc.
Bala Cynwyd, PA 19004
610-617-9988

CriticalControl
Calgary, AB T2P 2V7
Canada
403-705-7500

Crocker Claims Service
Omaha, NE 68106
402-558-4447

Crossroads Industries Inc.
Gaylord, MI 49734
989-732-1233

Crosstec Corporation
Boca Raton, FL 33431
800-675-0729

CRS Temporary Housing
800-968-0848

CRYSTAL RESTORATION
Carle Place, NY 11514
516-333-7070

CSU Industries
Cedarhurst, NY 11516
516-239-4310

CUBIX Corp
Carson City, NV 89706
775-883-7611

Cummins NPower LLC
Hodgkins, IL 60525
651-636-1000

Cummins Power Rent
Minneapolis, MN 55432
623-572-4940

Cummins Rocky Mountain LLC
Avondale, AZ 85323
800-800-2345

Cura Emergency Services
Plano, TX 75093
800-486-7117

Curtis 1000
Duluth, GA 30096
678-380-9095

Curtis Engine & Equipment Inc
Baltimore, MD 21227
410-536-1203

Curtis L.N. & Sons
Oakland, CA 94607
800-443-3556

Custard Insurance Ajusters
Atlanta, GA 30338
770-551-2050

Custom Commercial Fabric Restoration
Services
Hayward, CA 94545
510-723-1000

Custom Tree Care, Inc.
Topeka, KS 66610
785 478-9805

CWK Construction Co. Inc
Hyattsville, MD 20781
301-927-7033

CWRBS Backup Inc.
London, ON N6A 5R8
Canada
888-558-9786

CXR Digilog
Willow Grove, PA 19090
800-344-4564

Cyberex Inc
Richmond, VA 23231
800-238-5000

Cycle City
Broomall, PA 19008
610-356-2662

CYN Environmental Services
Stoughton, MA 2072
781-341-1777

Cypress Bend Construction, LLC
Cookeville, TN 38502
9313720092

Cypress Technology Inc.
Largo, FL 33773
727-557-0911

D & S Professional Services
Minoa, NY 13116
800-359-2534

D3Logic
East Providence, RI 02914
401-435-4300

Daisy Disc Corp
Newburyport, MA 01950
978-462-3475

Dallmer Adjusters
Bensalem, PA 19020
215-245-4504

Dalworth Restoration
Euless, TX 76040-5250
817-355-8625

D'Ambra Construction Co. Inc
Warwick, RI 02886
401-737-1300

Damicon, LLC
Burlington, MA 01803
781-789-8238

Daniel S. Willard, P.C.
Rockville, MD 20850
800-310-1178

Darryl Thompson
Durham, NC 27709
919-210-3737

'Data Center Management Magazine'
(DCM)
Orange, CA 92866
714-997-7966

Data Clean Corp
Des Plaines, IL 60016-6511
847-296-3100

Data Clean Inc.
Anaheim, CA 92805
800-328-2256

Data Ensure, Inc.
Norton, VA 24273
276-679-7900

Data Exchange Corporation
Camarillo, CA 93012
805-388-1711

Data Mechanix
Irvine, CA 92614
949-263-0994

Data Storage Corporation
New York, NY 10119
212-564-4922

Data393
Englewood, CO 80112-5816
303 268-1470

DataCenterManager.com
Chicago, IL 60680
312-451-1052

Dataco DeRex Inc
Pompano Beach, FL 33069
954-977-6362

Dataco DeRex Inc
Shawnee Msn, KS 66215
913-438-2444

Datalink
Chanhassen, MN 55317
952-944-3462

Data-Mail Inc.
Newington, CT 06111
860-666-0399

Dataprobe
Paramus, NJ 07652
201-967-9300

Datasafe
South San Fran, CA 94080
650-875-3800

Datasafe Recovery Services Ltd
Calgary, AB t2p 0t9
Canada
403-269-9128

DataSite Northwest
Bellevue, WA 98005
425-455-1198

Datatrend Technologies Inc
Minnetonka, MN 55305
952-931-1203

Datatronics Inc
Conroe, TX 77385
281-367-0562

Dataware Systems Lease Inc
Staten Island, NY 10301
718-447-4911

Davey Tree Expert Company The
Kent, OH 44240
800-445-8733

David Clark Company Incorporated
Worcester, MA 01615-0054
508-751-5800

DaVinci Technology Corporation (DaVinciTek)
Morristown, NJ 07960
973-993-4860

Davis Systems Software Inc
Greenbelt, MD 20707
301-486-4600

Daycom Systems Inc.
San Diego, CA 92121
858-200-3100

DaySpring Restoration
Missoula, MT 59801
800-555-3803

Dayton Bag & Burlap
Dayton, OH 45403
800-543-3400

DBSi
Bethlehem, PA 18017
610-691-8811

DD1 Computers
Irving, TX 75062
972-570-1227

Dealing With Problem Employees: A Legal Guide
Berkeley, CA 94710-2524
800-728-3555

Deccan International
San Diego, CA 92121
858 799 7986

Decision One
Frazer, PA 19355
610-296-6000

Decision One
Hayward, CA 94545
800-345-7950

Decisive Technologies Inc.
Ottawa, ON K4A 2P8
Canada
613-824-3719

Defense Group Inc. / CoBRA Software
Alexandria, VA 22314
703-535-8720

Defibtech, LLC
Guilford, CT 06437
203-453-6654

Definitive Handbook of Business Contingency Management
Indianapolis, IN 46256
877-762-2974

DeFranco True Value/Rental
Niagara Falls, NY 14301
716-285-3393

Dehumidification Technologies, Inc.
Houston, TX 77011
713-939-1166

Delaware County Community College
Broomall, PA 19008
610-359-7387

Delaware Emergency Management Agency
Smyrna, DE
302-659-3362

Delaware Technical & Community College
Newark, DE 19713
302-454-3933

DelCreo, Inc.
Alpine, UT 84004
801-756-4180

Delgado Community College
New Orleans, LA 70114
504-361-6246

Delmarva Trailer Rentals
Baltimore, MD 21227
410-799-1185

Delmhorst Instrument Co.
Towaco, NJ 07082-1025
973-334-2557

Deloitte
Chicago, IL 60601
312-946-3000

Deloitte & Touche LLP
Hartford, CT 06103
860-280-3000

Deloitte & Touche LLP
Wilton, CT 06897
203-761-3000

Delta Psychological Services
Cleveland, OH 44111
216-671-4508

Demos Restoration Services
Chicopee, MA 01020
413-594-7801

Denver Office of Emergency Mgmt
Denver, CO 80202
720-865-7600

Department of Health and Human Services
Washington, DC 20201
202-205-1300

Dependable Power Systems
Fredericktown, OH 43019
740-694-0496

DEPOT AMERICA
Farmingdale, NJ 07727-1602
732-919-0209

Design Shelter Inc.
Mississauga, ON L4Y 4G2
Canada
604-921-8805

Deskco Office Furniture
Farmdale, NY 11735
631-753-3601

Detail Masters Inc
San Antonio, TX 78258
210-490-1155

Deucalion Inc.
Hillsboro, OR 97123
866-269-2150

Developing Mental Health Crisis Response Plan
Albany, NY 12203
800-732-3933

DEW Filing Systems and Storage
Tempe, AZ 85281
877-933-7238

Dialogic Communications Corp
Franklin, TN 37067
615-790-2882

Diamond National Glass Co.
Paramount, CA 90723
562-634-2100

Dick Moore Housing
Millington, TN 38053
901-873-4663

Diebold Inc
North Canton, OH 44720
330-490-4000

Digital Courier Systems
San Jose, CA 95160
877-WARNFAST

Digital Defense, Inc.
San Antonio, TX 78209
888-273-1412

Digital Forensics Canada Inc.
Newmarket, ON L3X 1X4
Canada
905-836-0393

Direct Mail of Maine
Scarborough, ME 04070
800-883-6930

Disability Preparedness Center
Washington, DC 20007
202-338-7158

Disaster Forum Association
Edmonton, AB T5K 0L5
Canada
780-424-8742

Disaster Kleenup Canada
Mississauga, ON L53 2J3
Canada
905-564-0188

Disaster Kleenup Canada - Shamrock
Services (Sarnia)
Sarnia, ON N7S 5N5
Canada
519-337-4192

Disaster Kleenup International
Bensonville, Illinois 60106
630-350-3000

Disaster Kleenup Serving Treasure Valley
Nampa, ID 83687
208-887-0004

Disaster Management in
Telecommunications
Indianapolis, IN 46256
877-762-2974

Disaster Management Inc.
Port St. Lucie, FL 34952-6011
772-335-9750

Disaster Management Systems
Pomona, CA 91768
909-594-9596

Disaster Masters
Flushing, NY 11367-1203
718-939-5800

Disaster Mental Health Institute - The
University of South Dakota
Vermillion, SD 57069
605-677-6575

Disaster News Network
Columbia, MD 21045
410-884-7350

Disaster Preparedness & Business
Continuity Conf.
Princeton, NJ 08540
609-951-2106

Disaster Preparedness Academy
Santa Ana, CA 92711
714-481-5300

Disaster Preparedness of North Texas
Denton, TX 76209
817-271-0077

Disaster Recovery Consultants, LLC
Montville, NJ 07045
908-328-7719

Disaster Recovery for LANS
Phoenix, AZ 85076-1108
800-322-2202

Disaster Recovery Info Exchange-Ottawa
Ottawa, ON K1N 1A3
Canada
613-238-2909

Disaster Recovery Info. Exchange (DRIE-
SWO)
Kitchener, ON N2M 5P2
Canada
519-895-1213

Disaster Recovery Information Exchange
(DRIE)
Toronto, ON M5H 4E7
Canada
647-299-9743

Disaster Recovery Information Exchange
(West)
Calgary, AB T2P 3B9
Canada
403-543-4695

Disaster Recovery Institute
Toronto, ON M2J 1W8
Canada
416-491-5335

Disaster Recovery Journal
Saint Louis, MO 63151
314-894-0276

Disaster Recovery Planning Services
Madisonville, LA 70447-9472
985-845-0771

Disaster Recovery System
Merrick, NY 11566-2611
516-623-2038

Disaster Recovery System (DRS)
Merrick, NY 11566
516-623-2038

Disaster Recovery Testing
Brookfield, CT 06804-3104
203-740-7444

Disaster Research Center
Newark, DE 19716-2581
302-831-6618

Disaster Resource Guide
Santa Ana, CA 92735
714-558-8940

Disaster Resource Mgmt
Roswell, GA 30075
678-277-9860

Disaster Response
Redding, CA 96002
800-368-3693

Disaster Restoration Inc
Denver, CO 80216
800-475-FIRE

Disaster Restoration Solutions, Inc.
Ijamsville, MD 21754
301-926-0000

Disaster Services - Alberta Municipal
Services
Edmonton, AB T5J 4L4
Canada
780-422-9000

Disaster Services Inc
Atlanta, GA 30360
770-446-5300

Disaster Services, Inc. (Temporary
Housing)
Annapolis, MD 21403
410-974-8090

Disaster Specialists
Sandwich, MA 02563
800-675-3622

Disaster Survival Planning Network (DSPN)
Camarillo, CA 93012
800-601-4899

DisasterNecessities.com
Orem, UT 84058
801-361-7017

Discover Living
Grass Valley, CA 95949
530-432-7530

District of Columbia Emergency
Management Agency
Washington, D.C. 20009
202-727-2775

Diversified Direct Mailing Services Inc.
Fullerton, CA 92831
714-776-4520

Diversified Telecom Solutions-DTS
Temple, TX 76504
254-760-7710

DJS Technology Solutions
Colmar, PA 18915
215-822-5515

DK Services
Redding, CA 96002
530-224-2323

DKI/Better Floors & Restorations
Placentia, CA 92870
800-655-2005

DMA Insurance Housing Assistants,
National HQ
Solana Beach, CA 92075
800-550-1911

DML Consulting
East Norriton, PA 19401
267-249-9340

Document Reprocessors
Middlesex, NY 14507
888-437-9464

Document Reprocessors - West Coast
Operations
Burlingame, CA 94010
650-401-7711

Don J. Brooks Holdings Ltd.
London, ON N6H 4Y7
Canada
519-657-5472

Donjean's Cleaning & Restoration Inc.
Merced, CA 95340
209-383-2880

Dorlen Products
Milwaukee, WI 53220-4564
262-282-4840

Doyle Group/CSERT Inc., The
Newport, DE 19804
302-993-9081

DPS Management Consultants
Fort Worth, TX 76118-6950
817-284-7711

DR Information E-Change Group
Woonsocket, RI 02895
401-765-1500

Dr. E. A. Ryan
Clarendon Hls, IL 60514
630-887-0413

Dr. Shrink, Inc.
Manistee, MI 49660-1855
800-968-5147

Draeger Safety Inc.
Pittsburgh, PA 15275
412-787-8383

Dranetz Technologies
Edison, NJ 08817-2216
732-287-3680

DRC Inc
Ellicott City, MD 21023
410-750-7131

Dreamcatcher Disaster Resilience LLC
Rochester Hls, MI 48307
248-650-9900

Dressler Consulting Engineers Inc.
Overland Park, KS 66207-4013
913-341-5575

Drexel University Goodwin College
Philadelphia, PA 19104
215-895-0909

DRI International
Falls Church, VA 22046-4527
703-538-1792

DRIE Ottawa Annual Conference
Ottawa, ON K1N 1A3
Canada
613-238-2909

DRIE Toronto Quarterly Seminar
Toronto, ON M2J 1W8
Canada
416-491-2420

Dri-Eaz Corp.
Burlington, WA 98233-9656
800-932-3030

Dripping Springs Hardware & Rental
Dripping Springs, TX 78620
512-858-5601

Drivesavers Data Recovery
Novato, CA 94949
415-382-2000

DRJ World Conference
St. Louis, MO 63123
314-894-0276

DRS, Disaster Recovery Services, Inc.
Charlotte, NC 28220
704-525-0096

DryTech Co, LLC
Hugo, MN 55038
651-429-8444

DST Output
Kansas City, MO 64108
816-435-3070

DTN MeteorLogix
Omaha, NE 68114
402-255-8489

Du All Service Contractors Inc.
Columbia Heights, MN 55421
763-788-9411

DuPont Safety & Environmental Mgmnt. Svcs
Wilmington, DE 19898-0001
302-774-1000

Duraclean Professional Services
Irmo, SC 29063
803-732-2000

Durham Technical Community College
Durham, NC 27712
919-686-3520

Duthie Power Services
Long Beach, CA 90805
562-432-3931

Dutil's Home Repair / Water Out of Oklahoma
Lawton, OK 73505
580-536-3649

Dynamic Isolation Systems Inc
Lafayette, CA 94549
925-283-1166

Dynamic Restoration
West Chester, PA 19382
888-760-2842

Dynamic Systems
Nesconset, NY 11767
800-422-0708

Dynamic Systems, Inc.
Los Angeles, CA 90045
877-DSI-2-BUY

E Team Inc.
Woodland Hills, CA 91367
818-932-0660

E. V. Bishoff Company
Columbus, OH 43215
614-221-4736

E.V. Bushoff Company
Columbus, OH 43215
814-221-4736

Eagle Rock Alliance LTD.
West Orange, NJ 07052
973-325-9900

Eagle Software
Salina, KS 67401
785-823-7257

Earthquake Anxiety in Children
Memphis, TN
901-544-3570

Earthquake Engineering Center for the Southeastern United States (ECSUS)
Blacksburg, VA 24061
540-231-6635

Earthquake Engineering Consultants
San Anselmo, CA 94960
415-457-7777

Earthquake Engineering Research Center
Richmond, CA 94804
510-231-9554

Earthquake Engineering Research Institute
Oakland, CA 94612
510-451-0905

Earthquake Hazards Program
Menlo Park, CA 94025
650-329-5020

Earthquake Preparedness Handbook (online, PDF), Earthquake Preparedness: for Childcare Providers
Washington, DC 20472
202-566-1600

Earthquake Safety Systems Inc
Los Osos, CA 93402
805-534-1582

'Earthquake Safety Video-reducing employee expos.'
Santa Ana, CA 92704
800-468-4296

Earthquake Solutions
Pasadena, CA 91106
626-795-4000

Earthquakes Canada (East)
Ottawa, ON K1A 0Y3
Canada
613-995-5548 [en]

Earthquakes Canada (West)
Sidney, BC V8L 4B2
Canada
250-363-6500

East Coast Computer Inc
Pompano Beach, FL 33060
954-463-7300

East Hazel Crest P.D.
East Hazel Crest, IL 60429
708-798-2186

East Tennessee State University
Johnson City, TN 37601
423-439-4332

East Valley Disaster Services Inc.
Mesa, AZ 85210
480-833-4538

Eastco Enterprises Inc.
San Antonio, TX 78260
830-980-4771

Eastern Diversified Services Inc.
Souderton, PA 18964
215-723-1920

Eastern Michigan University
Ypsilanti, MI 48197
734-487-1590

Eaton Corp Powerware
San Diego, CA 92110
619-291-4211

Eaton Corporation Powerware
Raleigh, NC 27615
919-872-3020

EBC Partners, Inc.
Tallahassee, FL 32312
850-894-4043

eBRP Solutions
Mississauga, ON L5S 1W9
Canada
905-677-0404

Eco Data Recovery
Palm Bch Gdns, FL 33410-4605
561-691-0019

Ecology & Environment Inc
Lancaster, NY 14086
716-684-8060

E-commerce Security: Weak Links, Best Defenses
Indianapolis, IN 46256
877-762-2974

ECS Refining
Santa Clara, CA 95050-3980
408-988-4386

Ectaco
Long Island City, NY 11106
800-710-7920

Eden Tree & Landscape Inc.
Gretna, NE 68028
402-332-2839

Edenvale Restoration Specialists
Burnaby, BC V5J 5E6
Canada
604-436-1440

EducExpert
Quebec, QC G1K 4E4
Canada
418-694-2115

Edwards & Cromwell Spill Control
Baton Rouge, LA 70810
225-292-3377

Effective Physical Security
St. Louis, MO 63146
800-545-2522

EFI Electronics Corp
Salt Lake Cty, UT 84104
801-977-9009

EFI Global (Engineering & Fire Investigations)
Kingwood, TX 77339
281-358-4441

eGlobalReach, Inc
Acton, MA 01720
978-635-9542

EGP & Associates Inc.
Atlanta, GA 30328
678-904-8730

EGP & Associates Inc.
Boca Raton, FL 33432
561-392-0094

EGP & Associates Inc.
Oakland , CA 94612
510-446-7722

Electric Power Research Institute (EPRI)
Palo Alto, CA 94304-1395
650-855-2000

Electric Tool & Supply Co.
Peoria, AZ 85345
623-878-0777

Electrical Safety Foundation International
Arlington, VA 22209
703-841-3229

Electronic Decontamination Specialists
Draper, UT 84020
801-553-1087

Electronic Evidence Discovery Inc
Kirkland, WA 98033
206-343-0131

Electronic Renaissance Corp.
Edison, NJ 08837
732-417-9090

Electronic Salvage Resources Inc
Grayslake, IL 60030
847-548-7627

Electronic Specialists Inc
Natick, MA 01760-0004
800-225-4876

Electronic Systems International
Santa Margarita, CA 92688
800-843-7749

ELI Systems Inc
Cambridge, MA 02139
617-547-1113

Elite Protective Services
Chelsea, MA 02150
617-739-0100

Elliot Consulting Services
Tampa, FL 33626
813-792-8833

Em & M's Restoration
Santa Ana, CA 92707
714-434-6577

E-Mag Solutions
San Diego, CA 92128-4106
858-746-3000

Emercon Construction Inc
Anaheim, CA 92806-2501
714-630-9615

Emergency Department-Northwest Territories
Yellowknife, NT X1A 2N1
Canada
867-669-4100

Emergency Film Group
Edgartown, MA 02539
508-627-8844

Emergency Lifeline
Santa Ana, CA 92735
714-558-8940

Emergency Management Association of Texas
Richmond, TX 78611
512-473-4072

Emergency Management Canada Magazine
Dundas , ON L9H 1V1
Canada
905-628-4309

'Emergency Management for Records & Information Programs'
Lenexa , KS 66215
913-341-3808

Emergency Management Institute FEMA
Emmitsburg, MD 21727-8920
301-447-1000

Emergency Management Ontario (EMO)
Toronto, ON M7A 1Y6
Canada
416-326-5010

Emergency Measures- Ontario
Toronto, ON M7A 1Y6
Canada
416-314-3723

Emergency Measures Org- Manitoba
Winnipeg, MB R3C 3L6
Canada
204-945-4772

Emergency Measures Org- New Brunswick
Fredericton, NB E3B 5H1
Canada
506-453-2133

Emergency Measures Org- Newfoundland
St. John's, NF A1B 4J6
Canada
709-729-3703

Emergency Measures Org- Nova Scotia
Halifax, NS B3J 3N5
Canada
902-424-5620

Emergency Measures Org- Prince Edward Island
Summerside, PE C1N 5L2
Canada
902-888-8050

Emergency Medical Products
Waukesha, WI 53186
800-558-6270

Emergency Medicine Learning & Resource Center
Orlando, FL 32812
407-281-7396

Emergency Planning Handbook, 2nd
Alexandria, VA 22314-2818
703-519-6200

'Emergency Preparedness at Work Video'
Santa Ana, CA 92704
800-468-4296

Emergency Preparedness Systems
Elkhart , IN 46516
800-478-2363

Emergency Preparedness Systems LLC
Plover, WI 54467
715-321-1800

Emergency Response Educators and Consultants, Inc.
Silver Springs, FL 34488
352-236-5348

Emergency Response Planning
St. Louis, MO 63146
800-545-2522

Emergency Restoration Specialists Inc.
South Milwaukee, WI 53172
414-571-9977

Emergency Services and Disaster Relief Branch (ESDRB)
Washington, DC 20015
800-789-2647

Emergency Visions
Smyrna, GA 30080
770-436-2474

EmergencyPlan.com
York, PA 17402-4355
717-755-2627

EmerGeo Solutions, Inc.
Vancouver, BC V7X 1M8
Canada
604-443-5025

Emergin, Inc
Boca Raton, FL 33487
866-eme-rgin

EMG
Hunt Valley, MD 21031
800-733-0660

EMI Independent Study
Emmitsburg, MD 21727
301-447-1200

Emotional Continuity Management
Richland, WA 99354
509-942-0443

Empire State College
Saratoga Springs, NY 12866-4391
518-587-2100 x775

EMSCO, Electric Motor Supply Co.
Fridley, MN 55421
800-328-1842

Enera Inc
Chicago, IL 60615
866-463-6372

Energy Management Systems
Baltimore, MD 21236
800-537-3911

Energy Systems
Stockton, CA 95206
209-983-6900

Engage Technologies Inc.
Tampa, FL 33634
813-885-6615

ENPRO Services Inc
Newburyport, MA 01950
800-966-1102

EnSafe Inc
Memphis, TN 38134
800-588-7962

ENSR Consulting and Engineering
Westford, MA 01886
978-589-3000

Enterasys
Rochester, NH 03867
603-332-9400

Enterprise Connections
Los Angeles, CA 90067
310-229-5744

Enterprise Risk Worldwide, Inc
New York, NY 10176
212-599-1878

Enviro Pump Plus, Inc.
Balation, MN 56115
507-734-4661

EnviroDri, Inc.
Fort Myers, FL 33912
239-482-2169

Enviro-Energy Technologies
Markham, ON L3R 1N1
Canada
416-927-7690

EnviroMED INC
Tucson, AZ 85711
520-881-1000

Environment One Corp.
Niskayuna, NY 12309
518-346-6161

Environmental & Occupational Risk Management
Sunnyvale, CA 94089
408-822-8100

Environmental Health Services Branch
Atlanta, GA 30341
770-488-7476

Environmental Management & Engineering Inc
Huntington Beach, CA 92649
714-379-1096

Environmental Products & Services of Vermont Inc.
Syracuse, NY 13204-1129
315-471-0503

Environmental Quality Company
Wayne, MI 48184
734-329-8000

Environmental Resources Management(ERM)
Exton, PA 19341
610-524-3500

Environmental Services Inc.
South Windsor, CT 06074
1-800-486-7745

Envirotech Clean Air Inc.
Stoneham, MA 02180
781-279-2900

Envision - Planning Solutions Inc.
Calgary, AB T3L 1R1
Canada
403-241-8883

EnvoyWorldWide Inc
Bedford, MA 01730-1438
781-482-2100

Equivus Consulting
Arlington Heights, IL 60004
847-956-3322

ERC Parts
Kennesaw, GA 30152
770-984-0276

ERC Wiping Products, Inc.
Lynn, MA 01905
800-225-9473

Ericson Manufacturing Company
Willoughby, OH 44094
440-951-8000

Erie County Emergency Services
Buffalo, NY 14202
716-858-8477

Erlad Inc.
North Andover, MA 01845
978-975-3336

Ernst & Young LLP
Houston, TX 77010
713-750-1500

ESi - Emergency Systems Integrators
Augusta, GA 30901
706-823-0911

ESIS Inc.
Philadelphia, PA 19103
215-640-1324

ESRI
Redlands, CA 92373-8100
909-793-2853

ESS
Rockville, MD 20850
301-556-1700

Ethix Consulting, LLC
Harrisburg, PA 17112
717-651-1520

Eton Corporation
Palo Alto, CA 94303
800-872-2228

Eurodata Inc
Ottawa, ON K1B 3V7
Canada
613-745-0921

Evac+Chair Corporation
New York, NY 10021-5818
212-734-6222

Evans Restoration Services Inc.
Springfield, IL 62707
217-528-2878

EVault Inc
Oakville, ON L6H 5S9
Canada
905-844-4453

eVAULT Remote Backup Facility
Emeryville, CA 94608
925-944-2422

EVault, Inc.
Emeryville, CA 94608
877-382-8581

Evergreen Data Continuity Inc
Newbury, MA 01951-1711
800-727-4664

Evergreen Fire & Safety Inc
Lynnwood, WA 98037
206-368-3921

'Every Second Counts' Emergency Response Magazine
Itasca, IL 60143-3201
630-285-1121

Evolving Solutions, Inc
Hamel, MN 55340
800-294-4362

Exabyte Corp
Boulder, CO 80301
303-442-4333

Exacom, Inc.
Concord, NH 03301
603-228-0706

Exagrid Systems
Wesboro , MA 01581
508-898-2872

Excalibur Data Recovery Inc
N Billerica, MA 01862
978-663-1700

Excelliant
Birmingham, AL 35242
888-675-6627

Excelltech
Yankton, SD 57078
605-665-8324

Executive Environmental Services Corp.
South Pasadena, CA 91030
626-441-7050

Executive Security
San Francisco, CA 94103
415-626-1011

Explosion Protection
St. Louis, MO 63146
800-545-2522

Exponent Failure Analysis Associates
Menlo Park, CA 94025
650-688-6719

Express Computer Systems
Irvine, CA 92614
800-327-0730

ExpressPoint
Golden Valley, MN 55422
763-543-6000

Extended Stay Hotel
Spartanburg, SC 29306
864-573-1600

Extreme Safety, LLC
Carson, CA 90746
310-632-5671

Eye of the Storm, Inc
Nazereth, PA 18064
610-614-1860

Eyeview Recovery Consulting
Wonder Lake, IL 60097
815-653-4045

E-Z Up International, Inc
Riverside, CA 92507
951-781-0843

F.A.S.T. Limited
Delta, BC V4G 1B5
Canada
604-540-8300

Facility Supply
Easthampton, MA 01027
800-981-8128

Failsafe Air Safety Systems Corp
Tonawanda, NY 14150
716-694-6390

Fairleigh Dickinson University
Teaneck, NJ 07666
201-692-7172

Falconer Weather Information Service, LLC
Scotia, NY 12302-5717
518-399-5388

Fargo Electronics, Inc.
Eden Prairie, MN 55344
952-941-9470

Fastening Solutions Inc
Tarzana, CA 91356-3056
800-232-7836

Federal Engineering Inc.
Fairfax, VA 22030
703-359-8200

Federal Signal Corporation
University Park, IL 60466
800-548-7229

Federated Adjustment Co Inc
Great Neck, NY 11021
516-466-6900

FedEx Custom Critical
Uniontown, OH 44685-9584
800-762-3787

Fedhealth
Tucson, AZ 85710
888-999-4352

Fedoravicius Al S Phd
Albuquerque, NM 87112
505-345-6100

Fehr-Graham Assoc
Freeport, IL 61032
815-235-7643

FEI Behavioral Health
Milwaukee, WI 53224
800-987-4368

FEMA - Caribbean Area Division
Hato, PR 00918
787-296-3514

FEMA - Connecticut
Hartford, CT 06105
860-566-3180

FEMA - Pacific Area Office
Ft. Shafter, HI 96858-5000
808-851-7900

FEMA Region 1
Boston, MA 02110
617-956-7506

FEMA Law Associates, PLLC
Washington, DC 20005
202-326-9319

FEMA Region II
New York, NY 10278-0001
212-680-3600

FEMA Region III
Philadelphia, PA 19106
215-931-5608

FEMA Region IV
Atlanta, GA 30341
770-220-5200

FEMA Region IX
Oakland, CA 94607
510-627-7100

FEMA Region V
Chicago, IL 60605
312-408-5504

FEMA Region VI
Denton, TX 76209
940-898-5399

FEMA REGION VII (Kansas City
Kansas City, MO 64108-2670
816-283-7061

FEMA, Honolulu
Honolulu, HI 96817-2115
808-851-7900

FEMA, Region VIII (CO, MO, ND, WY)
Denver, CO 80225-0267
303-235-4800

FEMA, Region X
Bothell, WA 98021-9796
425-487-4600

FenceClaim.com
Pleasant Hill, CA 94523
877-693-3623

Fenwal Protection Systems
Ashland, MA 01721
800-336-9251

Festive Tents, LP
Houston, TX 77043-3910
713-468-3687

Festvities, LLP
Springdale, AR 72766
866-549-7368

FiberMedia Headquarters
Hollywood, FL 33020
954-367-0416

Field Safety Corporation
North Branford, CT 06471
888-964-9199

FieldSoft Inc.
Chandler, AZ 85244-1378
480-899-2128

Figlin & Associates, Inc.
Philadelphia, PA 19152
215-342-8514

Fike Corporations
Blue Springs, MO 64015
816-229-3405

Film Technology Company Inc.
Los Angeles, CA 90038
323-464-3456

Findlay Dinger (Service Master)
Winter Park, FL 32789
800-237-9688

Fine Wood Solutions
Ephrata, PA 17552
877-837-2105

Finnicum Adjusting Company, Inc.
Navarre, OH 44662
800-359-2201

Fire and Explosion Planning Matrix, Emergency Training Centre, Lakeland College
Vermilion, AB T9X 1K4
Canada
780-853-5800

Fire Restoration Services of New England
Norwood, MA 02062-4765
800-649-5080

Fire, Etc.
Vermilion, AB T9X 1K5
Canada
780-853-8400

FIRECON
East Earl, PA 17519
717-354-2411

FireDEX of Pittsburgh
Allison Park, PA 15101
412-487-3332

FireKing International Inc.
New Albany, IN 47150
812-948-8400

FireSafe Innovations LLC
Rochester, NY 14610-3446
585-385-9007

FireStar Inc.
Savannah, GA 31405
912-232-3473

First Advantage Restoration
South Elgin, IL 60177
800-282-1616

First Alert
Oakmont, PA 15139
800-345-7462 x1217

First Atlantic Restoration
Virginia Bch, VA 23462
757-499-1915

First Coast Chem-Dry
Jacksonville, FL 32257
904-262-2322

First Environmental Nationwide
Macon, GA 31210
478-477-2323

First General Enterprises
Fort Lauderdale, FL 33304-3115
954-537-5556

First General Enterprises, Inc.
Fort Lauderdale, FL 33304-3115
800-523-3680

First General Services Ltd.
Calgary, AB T3E 0B4
Canada
403-229-1479

First General Services (Edm) Inc.
Edmonton, AB T6B 0B7
Canada
780-463-4040

First General Services Canada
Toronto, ON M3J 2T7
Canada
416-736-0395

First General Services of Northeast Texas
Longview, TX 75608
903-759-8803

First General Services of Baton Rouge
Baton Rouge, LA 70806
225-928-7205

First General Services of Central Pa, Ltd.
York, PA 17403
717-845-7391

First General Services of Cleveland & Akron
Westlake, OH 44145
800-943-7054

First General Services of Fort Bend County
Sugar Land, TX 77478
281-933-1244

First General Services of Madison
Madison, WI 53713
800-318-3473

First General Services of N.E. PA
Wilkes-Barre, PA 18702-4309
570-824-0680

First General Services of Pen-Mar Inc.
Waynesboro, PA 17268
717-762-0550

First General Services of SW Florida
Fort Myers, FL 33912
239-454-4402

First General Services of the Panhandle
Santa Rosa Beach, FL 32459
850-622-9700

First General Services of the Quad Cities
Davenport, IA 52807
563-386-7220

First General Services Treasure Valley
Nampa, ID 83687
208-463-2385

First Line Technology
Washington, DC 20037
202-249-8480

First Response
South Bend , IN 46613
574-288-0500

First Response Management LLC
Golden, CO 80401
303-526-2550

First Restoration Services
Charleston, SC 29418
866-844-9FRS

First Restoration Services Inc.
Charlotte, NC 28206-3021
800-743-6717

First Restoration Services of Ashville
Fletcher, NC 28732
800-537-6151

FirstCall Network, Inc.
Baton Rouge, LA 70816
800-653-9232

COMPANY LISTINGS ALPHABETICALLY

FirstMerit Corporation
Brecksville, OH 44141
440-838-4044

Flagship Technologies Inc
Hamel, MN 55340
800-416-8900

Flambeau Inc
Weldon, NC 27890
252-536-2171

Fleet Environmental Services, LLC
Randolph, MA 02368
888-233-5338

Flexlite Inc.
Red Bank, NJ 07701
732-263-1771

Flir Systems, Inc.
North Billerica, MA 01862
800-464-6372

Flood Rescue
St. Louis, MO 63139
314-452-3194

Florida Atlantic University
Boca Raton, FL 33431-0991
561-297-0052

Florida Division of Emergency
Management
Tallahassee, FL 32399-2100
850-413-9900

Florida Emerg. Prep. Assn.
Tallahassee, FL 32309
850-906-0779

Florida International University -
Hurricane Center
Miami, FL 33199-0001
305-348-1607

Florida Poison Information Center -
Miami
Miami, FL 33101
800-222-1222

Florida State University
Tallahassee, FL 32306-2250
850-644-9961

Fluke Corporation
Everett, WA 98206
425-347-6100

FM Emergency Generator
Canton, MA 02021-2502
781-828-0026

FM Global
Johnston, RI 02919
401-275-3000

FoamPro — Hypro/Pentair Water
New Brighton, MN 55125
651-766-6300

Foley Machinery Co.
Monroe Township, NJ 08831
609-443-1991

Foley Power Systems
Piscataway, NJ 08855
732-885-5555

Foley Rents
Piscataway, NJ 08855
732-885-5555

Forbes Services
Plainfield, IL 60544
708-544-1200

Forces Inc
Naperville, IL 60563
800-222-1195

Forcon International
Atlanta, GA 30338
770-390-0980

Forensic Analysis & Engineering Corp
Raleigh, NC 27616-2956
919-872-8788

Forsythe Solutions Group
Skokie, IL 60077
847-675-8000

Fort Knox Protection Inc
DeSoto, TX 75115
972-298-6991

Fortress Technologies
Oldsmar, FL 34677
813-288-7388

Four Star Cleaning & Restoration
Fremont, CA 94538-6309
800-255-3333

Fraser-Volpe LLC
Warminster, PA 18974
215-443-5240

Frederick Community College
Frederick, MD 21702
301-846-2635

Freels Enterprises Inc.
Mays Landing, NJ 08330
609-965-7666

Freezedry Specialties Inc
Princeton, MN 55371
800-362-8380

Freyer & Laureta, Inc.
San Mateo, CA 94401
650-344-9901

Fronte Infrastructure Associates, LLC
Hillsdale, NJ 07642
201-666-8715

Frontier Adjusters Inc
Phoenix, AZ 85012
800-528-1187

Frontier Cleaning and Restoration
Corner Brook, NF A2H 3J7
Canada
709-785-5859

Frontier Community College
Fairfield, IL 62837
618-842-3711

Frontline Corporate Communications Inc.
Kitchener, ON N2K 3S2
Canada
888-848-9898

Frontline First Responder Magazine
Van Nuys, CA 91406
800-224-4367

FrontLine Magazine
Ottawa, ON K1J 6A4
Canada
613-747-1138

Frye Restoration
Monongahela, PA 15063
724-258-7577

FSI North America(r)
Sheffield Lake, OH 44054
440-949-2400

FSP Books and Videos
Hudson, MA 01749
978-562-1289

FSW Cleaners
Bridgeview, IL 60455
708-598-4158

Fundamentals of Aquatic Toxicology
Boca Raton, FL 33431
800-272-7737

Fusepoint Managed Services
Mississauga, ON L5N4J9
Canada
905-363-3737

FutureShield
Toronto, ON M9W 5P1
Canada
416-675-7835

Fyrsafe Engineering Inc.
Rolling Meadows, IL 60008-1032
847-392-1111

G.S. Jones & Sons
Pittsburgh, PA 15202-1451
412-766-6886

GAB Robins N. America
Atlanta, GA 30341
770-457-9555

GAB Robins N. America
Denver, CO 80231
303-831-7222

GAB Robins N. America
Jacksonville, FL 32207
904-396-2841

Gallagher Bassett Services Inc
Saint Louis, MO 63131
314-965-7810

Gallagher Bassett Services Inc (National
HQ)
Itasca, IL 60143
630-773-3800

Galls Incorporated
Lexington , KY 40509
800-477-7766

Garaventa (Canada) LTD.
Surrey, BC V3W 7B3
Canada
604-594-0422

Garrett Engineers Inc
Long Beach, CA 90809
562-308-4150

Gartner IT Security Summit
Standford, CT 06904
203-316-6757

Garvin-Fram
Schaumburg, IL 60193
800-351-5516

GatesMcDonald
Columbus, OH 43215
614-677-3700

GE Capital Modular Space
Bakersfield, CA 93313
661-397-3833

GE Capital Modular Space
Brandywine, MD 20613
301-372-1282

GE Financial Services
Bannockburn, IL 60015
847-615-0992

Geist Manufacturing Inc.
Lincoln, NE 68521
402-474-3400

GemaTech
S, CA 92108
619 283 3765

Gemini Systems
New York , NY 10006
212-480-3960

Generac Power Systems, Inc
Waukesha, WI 53187-0008
262-544-4811

General Atomics Electronic Systems, Inc.
San Diego, CA 92123
858-522-8300

General Monitors
Lake Forest, CA 92630
866-686-0741

GENESYS Software Systems Inc
Methuen, MA 01844
978-685-5400

Genium Publishing Corp
Amsterdam, NY 12010
518-842-4111

GenPrime, Inc.
Spokane, WA 99201
866-624-9855

GenTech
Flint , MI 48507
810-244-7777

Gentex Corporation
Simpson, PA 18407
570-282-3550

GeoAge, Inc.
Jacksonville, FL 32224
866-565-9855

George Washington University
Washington, DC 20037
202-741-2941

Georgia Emergency Management Agency
Atlanta, GA 30316-0055
404-635-7001

Georgia Poison Center
Atlanta, GA 30335
800-222-1222

Georgia State University - Andrew Young
School of Policy Studies
Atlanta, GA 30302-3992
404-651-4592

Gerard Group International LLC
Tyngsborough, MA 01879
978-649-4575

Gilman Studios
Amesbury, MA 01913
978-388-5204

Givens Cleaning Contractors, Inc.
Wichita, KS 67214
316-265-1315

Givens Restoration & Cleaning
Wichita, KS 67214
316-265-1315

GlassLock, Inc.
Prince Frederick, MD 20678
410-535-9898

Glenncarey Restoration Contractors Ltd.
Claremont, ON L1Y 1A2
Canada
905 428-6327

Global Disaster Information Network
GDIN
South Riding, VA 20152
202-647-5070

Global ePoint, Inc.
City of Industry, CA 91789
909-869-1688

Global Impact Inc
Bradford, ON
Canada
416 791 6109

Global Link Communications Inc.
Bensalem, PA 19020-5813
215-633-0300

Global Security Solutions LLC
Bellevue, WA 98006
866-332-3477

Global Strategic Resources
Las Vegas, NV 89146
702-259-9579

Global Technologies Inc.
New Bedford, MA 02745
508-991-3939

Global Water Group Inc
Dallas, TX 75247
214-678-9866

Global Wrap and Services, Inc.
St. Augustine, FL 32084
800-972-7120

GlobalCom Satellite Communication
Decatur, AL 35603-2641
256-432-2685

Globe Midwest Adjusters Intl
Southfield, MI 48075-8403
800-445-1554

GNT Emergency Measures-Northwest
Territories
Yellowknife, NT X1A 3S9
Canada
867-920-6133

Godec Randall & Associates
Phoenix, AZ 85014
602-266-5556

Godwin Pumps of America, Inc.
Bridgeport, NJ 08014
856-467-3636

Golden Office Trailers Inc
Lake Elsinore, CA 92530
909-678-2177

GoldenGate Software, Inc.
San Francisco, CA 94105
415-777-0200

Golder Associates Corp
Atlanta, GA 30341
770-496-1893

Golub and Associates Inc
Clayton, MO 63105
314-725-6610

Goodman-Gable-Gould Company
Rockville, MD 20852-4040
800-858-3900

Gordon Kapes Inc
Skokie, IL 60077
847-676-1750

Gorman-Rupp Company
Mansfield, OH 44901
419-755-1011

Government Emergency
Telecommunications Service
Chantilly, VA 20151
866-NCS-CALL

Government Security Expo & Conference
Alexandria, VA 22314
703-683-8500

Governo Law Firm LLC
Boston, MA 02110
617-737-9045

Governor's Hurricane Conference
Tarpon Springs , FL 34688
727-944-2724

COMPANY
LISTINGS
ALPHABETICALLY

Governor's Office of Emergency
Management
Concord, NH 03301
603-271-2231

GOVSEC, U.S. LAW and READY
Alexandria, VA 22314
800-687-7469

Gower Technical Services Inc
Columbus, OH 43235
614-764-2224

Grace Constructions Products
Hatfield, PA 19440
215-362-9020

GraEagle Consstruction, LLC.
Las Vegas, NV 89102
702-248-0170

GraEagle Construction, LLC.
Sparks, NV 89431
775-851-2722

Graham Restorations
Hamilton, ON L8W 2T7
Canada
905-574-1210

GramTel USA
South Bend, IN 46601
574-472-4726

Grand Rental Station
Chesterton, IN 46304
219-395-9797

Granite State Environmental LLC
Bedford, NH 03110
800-448-2024

Grant Thornton LLP
Irvine, CA 92612
949-553-1600

Grapevine Software, LLC
Dana Point, CA 92629
949-697-4517

Great Lakes Business Recovery Group
Rochester Hls, MI 48307-3312
248-650-9900

Great Plains Contingency Planners
Omaha, NE 68101-0033
402-633-1192

Green Environmental Inc
Norwell, MA 02061
617-479-0550

Green Side Up Landscaping Inc.
Baltimore, MD 21236
410-256-3328

Greenley & Associates Incorporated
Ottawa, ON K2E 7Z4
Canada
613-247-0342

Greenskeeper Environmental, LLC
Ashton, MD 20861
301-774-8201

Greer & Kirby Co., Inc.
Carmel, IN 46032-2565
317-575-4293

Greer & Kirby Co., Inc.
Edina, MN 55439-1506
952-829-1682

Greer & Kirby Co., Inc.
Elk Grove Village, IL 60007-2617
847-956-7180

Greer & Kirby Co., Inc.
Glade Valley, NC 28627-8951
336-363-9292

Greer & Kirby Co., Inc.
Hayward, CA 94545-1615
510-786-1671

Greer & Kirby Co., Inc.
Hillsborough, NJ 08844-1900
908-431-4050

Greer & Kirby Co., Inc.
La Mirada, CA 90638-5817
562-802-2883

Greer & Kirby Co., Inc.
Morgan, PA 15064-0510
412-220-9163

Greer & Kirby Co., Inc.
Norcross, GA 30093-3325
770-921-5959

Greer and Kirby Co., Inc.
Danvers, MA 01923-4024
978-646-9600

Greer Kirby & Co.
La Mirada, CA 90638
714-670-7721

Groundwater & Environmental Services
Inc
Neptune, NJ 07753
732-919-0100

Guardian Computer Support Inc.
Livermore, CA 94550
800-752-8733

Guardium
Waltham, MA 02451
877-487-9400

Guardsmark llc
Memphis, TN 38103
901-522-6000

Gulf Electroquip Inc
Houston, TX 77020
713-675-2525

Gwinnett Technical College
Lawrenceville, GA 30046-1505
770-962-7580 x232

H O Penn Machinery
Hoitsville , NY 11742
631-654-4400

Haag Engineering
Carrollton, TX 75006
281-313-9700

Haberill Contracting
Everett, ON L0M1J0
Canada
416-709-2460

Hahn Equipment Co.
Houston, TX 77007
713-868-3255

Hale Products
Conshohocken, PA 19428
610-825-6300

Hall and Foreman
Woodland Hills, CA 91367
818-251-1200

Halliwell Engineering Associates Inc.
East Providence, RI 02914
401-438-5020

Hammer Restoration Inc.
Saginaw, MI 48603
989-793-5700

HAN Consulting
San Jose, CA 95118
408-474-2106

Hannah-Watrous Continuity Strategies
Chester, CT 06412-1345
860-227-5046

Hanson Data Systems Inc
Marlborough, MA 01752
508-481-3901

Hardigg
South Deerfield, MA 01373
413-665-2163

Hardware & Peripherals Inc.
Cleveland, OH 44128
216-292-9200

Hardware Technology
Morgan Hill, CA 95037
408-776-9920

Harland Finanacial Solutions
Cincinnati, OH 45202
513-381-9400

Harrington Group Inc
Duluth, GA 30096
770-564-3505

Harris Fire & Water Cleaning Specialists
Perrysburg, OH 43551
419-874-9420

Harris Fire and Water Cleaning
Specialists
Perrysburg, OH 43551
877-883-9896

Hartford Computer Group
inverness, IL 60067
224-836-3550

Hartford Financial Services Group Inc
Hartford, CT 06106
860-547-5000

Harwood International Corp
Chattanooga, TN 37343
423-870-5500

Hawaii State Civil Defense
Honolulu, HI 96816
808-733-4300

Haynes Insurance Group
Mansfield, TX 76063
817-477-1455

Hazardous Material Training Program
Decatur, IL 62521
217-333-0640

Hazards Research Lab, University of South Carolina
Columbia, SC 29208
803-777-1699

Hazmat DQE
Indianapolis, IN 46278
800-355-4628

Hazmat Medical Associates
New Lenox, IL 60451
815-485-0096

HazMat Solutions, Inc.
Grand Haven, MI 49417
616-850-9036

HDH Associates
Christiansbrg, VA 24073
540-381-7999

Health Canada, Centre for Emergency Preparedness and Response
Ottawa, ON K1A 0K9
Canada
613-954-8498

Health Psychology Group
Randolph, NJ 07869-4221
973-895-4799

Healy & Associates Banking Services
Asheboro, NC 27204-2143
336-629-0153

HeartSine Technologies, Inc.
San Clemente, CA 92673
949-218-0092

HeaterMeals
Cincinnati, OH 45246
800-503-4483

Heavy Equipment Claims Service
Ft. Lauderdale, FL 33317
954-583-2989

Helmsman Management Services Inc
Weston, MA 02493
617-243-7985

Help Systems Inc
Minnetonka, MN 55345-5981
952-933-0609

Hennepin Regional Poison Center
Minneapolis, MN 55415
800-222-1222

Hennepin Technical College Campus
St Paul, MN 55108-5265
651-649-5411

Hennes Communications
Cleveland, OH 44118
216-321-7774

Herakles , LLC
Sacramento, CA 95834
916-679-2100

Hercules Portable Power Co.
Carson, CA 90745
310-830-2254

Heritage Preservation
Washington, DC 20005
202-634-1422

Hertz Equipment Rental
Park Ridge, NJ 07656
888-777-2700

Hewlett-Packard Canada, Ltd.
Mississauga, ON L4W 5G1
Canada
905-206-4725

Hewlett-Packard Co
Bellevue, WA 98007
425-643-4000

Hewlett-Packard Company
Palo Alto, CA 94304-1185
650-857-1501

High Cotton Direct Marketing
Birmingham, AL 35210-4328
205-838-2345

High Point Solutions Inc
Sparta, NJ 07871
973-940-0040

Hitachi Data Systems
Santa Clara, CA 95050
800-227-1930

Hi-Tech Carpet & Restoration
Rocklin, CA 95677
916-789-9213

Hi-Tech Fire & Water Restoration Inc
Abilene, TX 79605-7238
915-692-1892

Hitran Corp
Flemington, NJ 08822
908-782-5525

Hi-Way Equipment Co., Inc.
Houston, TX 77087
713-649-0940

HMA Consulting
Houston, TX 77042
832-242-1600

HMP Industries
Ansonia, CT 06401
203-734-8201

Hobbs Ultra-Clean Service
Corapeake, NC 27926
252-465-8297

Hogan MFG Inc.
Escalon, CA 95320
209-838-7323

Holben Webdesigns
Haddonfield, NJ 08033
856-428-1004

Holland-Dutch Cleaning/Restoration Services Inc
Tukwila, WA 98188
206-322-7000

Holliday Canopies
Charleston, WV 25311
800-788-3969

Hollywood Vaults Inc
Los Angeles, CA 90038-3504
323-461-6464

Holt Cat Power Systems
Irving, TX 75061
972-721-5800

Home Safety Council
Washington, DC 20006
202-349-1100

Homeland Defense Journal
Arlington, VA 22203-1867
301-455-5633

Homeland Protection Professional
Western Springs, IL 60558
708-246-2525

Homisco Inc
Melrose, MA 02176
781-665-1997

Honeywell Access Systems
Oak Creek, WI 53154
414-766-1700

Horizon Contracting Inc.
sterling, VA 20166
540-338-8989

Hospital Insurance Systems Inc
Orlando, FL 32811
407-293-7120

Hospitech Solutions
Montville, NJ 07045
973-263-9800

Hour Zero Crisis Consulting Ltd.
Edmonton, AB T6E 2L7
Canada
780-439-0999

Housing Headquarters, Inc.
Libertyville, IL 60048
866-918-RELO

Houston General Salvage
Houston, TX 77037
281-445-6696

Howarth, Keys & Associates Inc.
Franklin, TN 37064
800-647-2236

Huffmaster Crisis Management
Troy, MI 48083
800-446-1515

Humane Society of the United States, The
Gaithersburg, MD 20879
301-258-3103

Humidity Control Systems
Vancouver, WA 98668
800-642-7910

Huntington Cleaners
Huntington Wd, MI 48070
248-541-6038

Huntington Power Equipment Inc
Shelton, CT 06484
203-929-3203

Hurricane Protection Magazine
North Palm Beach, FL 33408
561-627-3393

Hurricane Watch Net, Inc.
Boca Raton, FL 33498
561-487-9208

Husqvarna Forest & Garden
Charlotte, NC 28269
800-487-5962

HWS Consulting Group Inc
Lincoln, NE 68508
402-479-2200

Hydration Technologies, Incorporated
Albany, OR 97322
541-917-3335

Hydro Geo Chem Inc
Tucson, AZ 85705
520-293-1500

HZX Computer Systems Consultants - BCP Services
Toronto, ON M2K 1W2
Canada
416-221-6603

I. V. Auto Inc
N Hollywood, CA 91605
818-982-9053

I.C. System Inc.
Saint Paul, MN 55127
800-443-4123

IAEM Annual & EMEX Emergency Mgt. Conference
Falls Church, VA 22046-4527
703-538-1795

IAQ Trainging Institute
Duquesne, PA 15110
866-427-4727

IBM Business Resilience and Continuity Svcs
Sterling Forest, NY 10979
800-599-9950

IBM Canada
Montreal, QC H3G 2W6
Canada
514-964-1616

IBM Canada Ltd.
Calgary, Alberta T2P 4B4
Canada
905-316-2067

IBM Canada Ltd.
Markham, ON
Canada
905-316-2067

IBM Canada Ltd.
Markham, ON L3R 927
Canada
905-316-2067

IBM Canada Ltd.
Montreal, Quebec H2J 2S5
Canada
905-316-2067

IBM Canada Ltd.
Winnipeg, Manitoba R3E 2V7
Canada
905-316-2067

IBM Global Services
Schaumburg, IL 60173
1-800-IBM-7080

IC Engineering, Inc.
Owings Mills, MD 21117
410-363-8748

ICA
Englewood, CO 80110
303-806-9090

Icom America Inc
Bellevue, WA 98004
425-454-8155

ICS Logistics
Jacksonville, FL 32254-2066
904-786-8038

Idaho Bureau of Disaster Services
Boise, ID 83705-5004
208-334-3460

Idea Integration
Denver, CO 80202
303-571-4557

Ideal Drying
South San Fran, CA 94080-4666
800-379-6881

IEM Inc.,
Baton Rouge, LA
800-977-8191

IG2 Data Security, Inc.
Chicago, IL 60622
312-850-4421

Illinois Emergency Management Agency
Springfield, IL 46204
217-782-2700

Illinois Poison Center
Chicago, Il 60606
800-222-1222

Illinois Wholesale Cash Register (IWCR) Corp
Hoffman Estate, IL 60195
800-544-5493

IMAC: International Management Assistance Corp.
Strongsville, OH 44149
440-878-7600

Immediate Environmental Recovery Solutions
Portland, OR 97218
800-369-3214

Immediate Response Service Company
Mission Hills, CA 91346
800-483-9009

IMS Systems Inc
Silver Spring, MD 20904
301-680-0006

Incident Mitigation, Inc.
Southfield, MI 48076
248-552-0821

Indiana Poison Center
Indianapolis, IN 46206
800-222-1222

Indiana State Emergency Management Agency
Indianapolis, IN 46204
317-232-3980

Indiana State University
Terre Haute, IN 47809
812-237-3104

Indoor Enviroment Connections
Rockville, MD 20852
301-230-9606

Industrial Accident Prevention Association
Toronto, ON M5J 2Y3
Canada
416-506-8888

Industrial Emergency Council
San Carlos , CA 94070
650-508-9008

Industrial Patrol Service
Chicago, IL 60639
773-235-2181

Industrial Scientific Corporation
Oakdale, PA 15071
412-788-4353

Industrial Services, Inc.
Chatsworth, CA 91313
818-822-7529

Infocrossing Inc.
Leonia, NJ 07605-2233
866-779-4369

InfoEdge
Cambridge, MA 02139
800-363-7150

Infoguard Inc
Norristown, PA 19403
800-446-8998

Information Station Specialists(ISS)
Zeeland, MI 49464-0051
616-772-2300

Information Technology Association of America
Arlington, VA 22209-2318
703-522-5055

InfoSENTRY Services, Inc.
Raleigh, NC 27601
919-838-8570

Infotech Century LC
Gaithersburg, MD 20878
301-258-2653

Ingersoll-Rand Equipment and Services
Philadelphia, PA 19154
800-679-1951

Ingersoll-Rand Equipment Sales
Southborough, MA 01772
508-481-1350

Initial Security
Naperville, IL 60563
630-369-6761

Initial Security
Orange, CA 92868
714-464-4005

Initial Security
San Antonio, TX 78230-4818
210-349-6321

Injectidry Systems Inc
Kirkland, WA 98033-5749
425-822-3851

Inmarsat, Inc.
Arlington, VA 22209
703-647-4760

Innovation Data Processing
Little Falls, NJ 7424
973-890-7300

Innovative Technology Inc
Brooksville, FL 34604
352-799-0713

InoStor Corporation
Poway, CA 92064
858-726-1800

Input Technologies LLC
Colorado Springs, CO 80903-3314
719-475-7223

Inservco Insurance
Harrisburg, PA 17101
717-230-8300

Insight Public Sector
Tempe, AZ 85283
800-467-4448

Instant Offices
New York, NY 10005
212-918-4640

Instar Services Group
Safety Harbor, FL 34695-3856
727-726-1357

Institute of Internal Auditors Inc
Altamonte Springs, FL 32701
407-830-7600

Institute for Business Continuity Training
Niagara Falls, NY 14304-1745
800-461-3095

Institute for Catastrophic Loss Reduction
Toronto, ON M5C 2R9
Canada
416-364-8677

Institute for Crisis Management
Louisville, KY 40207
502-891-2507

Institute for Crisis, Disaster and Risk
Management
Washington, DC 20052
202-994-6736

Institute of Hazardous Materials
Management
Rockville, MD 20852-2676
301-984-8969

Institute of Inspection, Cleaning, and
Restoration Certification (IICRC)
Vancouver, WA 98661
360-693-5675

Instrumentation & Control Systems(ICS)
Addison, IL 60101
630-543-6200

Insurance Auto Auctions
Westchester, IL 60154
847-839-3939

Insurance Claim Consultants - Public
Adjusters
Mt. Pleasant, SC 29464
843-971-1561

Insurance Claim Services, Inc.
Belleville, IL 62223-3809
618-397-8800

Insurance Contractors Inc
Portland, TN 37148
615-323-8889

Insurance Damage Specialists
York, PA 17403
717-718-1969

Insurance Information Institute
New York, NY 10038
212-346-5500

Insurance Reconstruction Services, Inc.
Smithfield, RI 02917
401-231-3130

Insurance Recovery Inc
Maitland, FL 32751
407-539-1946

Insurance Restoration Services
Cranberry TWP, PA 16066
412-322-1135

Insurance Salvage Buyers of America
Brooklyn, NY 11230
718-377-6515

Integra Manufacturing
Billerica, MA 01821
978-671-0009

Integrated Environmental Services
Atlanta, GA 30318
800-409-8474

Integrated Insights
San Diego, CA 92123
858-278-3626

Integrated Wave Technologies, Inc.
Fremont, CA 94538
510-353-0260

Integrity International Security Services
Clarksville, TN 37041
931-647-5384

Intek Painting Svc.
Sioux Falls, SD 57104
605-334-9716

Intelagard, Inc.
Broomfield, CO 80020
303-309-6309

Intelligent Wireless Solutions
Magnolia, TX 77355
281-356-5689

InterClaim
Alpharetta, GA 30022
404-875-5866

Intercon Security
Toronto, ON M2N 6K9
Canada
416-229-6811

Intergraph Public Safety
Madison, AL 35758
256-730-8911

Interim Housing Solutions
866-279-4471

Interlink Supply
Salt Lake City, UT 84123
800-660-5803

Intermountain Construction & Recovery
Alliance
Draper, Utah 84020
866-483-5911

International Assn of Emergency
Managers (IAEM)
Falls Church, VA 22046-4527
703-538-1795

International Association of Fire Chiefs
Fairfax, VA 22033-2868
703-273-0911

International Association of Professional
Security
Des Moines, IA 50309-4501
515-282-8192

International Computing Systems
Hopkins, MN 55343
952-935-8112

International Disaster Recovery Assn.
(IDRA)
Shrewsbury, MA 01545-7515
508-845-6000

International Dynamics Research Corp
Atlanta, GA 30327
770-723-9785

COMPANY
LISTINGS
ALPHABETICALLY

International Facility Management
Association
Houston, TX 77046
713-623-4362

International Fire Service Training Assn.
Stillwater, OK 74078
800-654-4055

International Hurricane Protection
Assciation World Office
Lantana, Fl 33462
561-433-2101

International Network Services Inc.(INS)
Santa Clara, CA 95050
408-330-2700

International Postal Systems Inc
Arlington, VA 22201
703-522-8338

International Power Technologies
Orem, UT 84058
801-224-4828

International Safety Equipment
Association
Arlington, VA 22209
703-525-1695

International Security Conference West
Norwalk, CT 06851
203-840-5602

International Society of Cleaning
Technicians
Thompson Station, TN 37179
615-591-9610

International SOS Assistance, Inc.
Houston, TX 77098
713-521-7611

International SOS Assistance, Inc.
Philadelphia, PA 19053
215-942-8000

Interscience Inc
Tampa, FL 33634
813-885-4774

Interstate Restoration Group, Inc.
Fort Worth, TX 76140
800-622-6433

Int'l. Critical Incident Stress Foundation
Ellicott City, MD 21042
410-750-9600

INTRA Computer Inc
Jamaica, NY 11434
718-805-3911

Intrado
Longmont, CO 80503
877-262-3775

Investigative Engineers Association Inc.
Ft. Lauderdale, FL 33304
954-537-5556

IOT - Interactive Occupational Training
Lakewood, CO 80228
303-984-4671

Iowa Contingency Planners
Des Moines, IA 50301
515-246-7059

Iowa Homeland Security & Emergency
Management Division
Des Moines, IA 50319
515-281-3231

Iowa Statewide Poison Control Center
Sioux City, IA 51104
800-222-1222

iPower Systems
Brandon, FL 33511-6157
813-685-2424

iPrepare Emergency Supplies
Roseville , CA 95678
707-982-7292

Iron Mountain
Chattanooga, TN 37416
423-894-4828

Iron Mountain
Houston, TX 77005
713-628-8732

Iron Mountain (Nationwide offices)
Boston, MA 02111
800-935-6966

Iron Mountain Offsite Data Protection
San Diego, CA 92123
858-576-9400

ISA International Society of Arborculture
champaign, IL 61826-3129
217-355-9411

ISES CORPORATION
Stone Mountain, GA 30087
770-879-7376

Isonics Corporation
Columbia, MD 21045
410-381-5254

ISSA Information Systems Security
Association
Oak Creek, WI 53154
414-908-4949

IT Business Edge
Louisville, KY 40202
502-583-8024

IT GlobalSecure
Washington, DC 20009-9330
202-332-5106

'IT Handbook InfoBase: Bus. Continuity
Planning'
Arlington, VA 22226
703-516-5588

IT Matters Inc.
Calgary, AB T2P 3M7
Canada
403-503-0772

Item Inc
Alexandria, VA 22310
703-971-5700

J&H Marsh & McLennan Inc
Princeton, NJ 08543
609-520-2900

J. Berra Engineering Inc.
Houston, TX 77060
281-447-8300

J. Bowers Disaster Restoration Specialists
Akron, OH 44312
800-289-9050

J.J. Keller & Associates Inc.
Neenah, WI 54957-0368
800-327-6868

Jack Henry & Associates Inc. - Centurion
Disaster Recovery
Monett, MO 65708
800-299-4411

Jacksonville State University
Jacksonville, AL 36265
800-231-5291 x5926

JALCO Services, Inc
Wyckoff, NJ 07481
201-847-2019

James Cohen Consulting PC
Pennington, NJ 08534
267-757-0710

Janes
Alexandria, va 22314
703 683-3700

Jane's Crisis Communications Handbook
Alexandria, VA 22314-2818
703-519-6200

Jannaway & Associates
Toronto, ON M1L 3T3
Canada
416-694-3274

Jansen International LLC
Houston, TX 77067
1-800-779-8714

Janus Associates
Stamford, CT 06902
203-251-0200

Japan Communication Consultants LLC
New York, NY 10118
212-759-2033

Jaxport Refrigerated Services Inc.
Jacksonville, FL 32206
904-786-8038

JBK True Value & Just Ask Rental
Chestertown, MD 21620
410-778-9600

JC Restoration
Bensenville, IL 60106
800-956-8844

Jim Stanton & Associates
Vancouver, BC V6R 3N2
Canada
604-737-1612

Jim Thompson & Co.
Blackwell, MO 63626
636-337-8200

Jim's Mobile Offices
Marion, IL 62959-9801
618-997-6072

JLS Mailing Services Inc.
Brockton, MA 02302-3360
508-313-1024

JMG Consultants, Inc.
Copiague, NY 11726
631-842-8847

John Jay College, City University of NY
New York, NY 10019
212-237-8834

Johnny's Drycleaning
Phoenix, AZ 85027
623-582-9261

Johns Hopkins Lifeline
Baltimore, MD 21287
410-502-7415

Johnson Machinery Co.
Riverside, CA 92501
951-686-4560

Johnson Power Systems
Riverside, CA 92502
951-683-5960

Johnsonite
Chagrin Falls, OH 44023
800-899-8916

Johnson's Chem-Dry
Crested Butte, CO 81224
970-349-7052

Jonathan Ward & Associates
Toronto, ON M4N 3R8
Canada
416-932-2314

Jon-Don
Roselle, IL 60172
800-556-6366

JoshuaCasey Corporate Training
Anaheim, CA 92805
714-245-9440

Journagan True Value
Aurora, MO 65605
417-678-4488

Journal of Emergency Management
Weston , MA 02493
781-899-2702

JS Training Institute
Huntingtn Bch, CA 92647-4846
714-375-0059

Judith Eckles & Partners
Villanova, PA 19085
610-527-1982

justclaims
Haddon Heights, NJ 08035
866-411-2524

K Manley Trucking
Drewryville , VA 23844
434 658-9349

Kansas Division of Emergency
Management
Topeka, KA 66611-1287
785-274-1401

Kansas Emergency Management Annual
Conference
Manhattan, KS 66502
785-537-6333

Kaplan College - School of Criminal Justice
Boca Raton, FL 33487
866-523-3473

Kappler
Guntersville, AL 35976
800-600-4019

Kawasaki Portable Generators
Punnam, CT 06260
860-928-7565

Kaydon Filtration Group
Lagrange, GA 30240
706-884-3041

Keith Industries
Newark, NJ 07114
973-642-3332

Kelly Generator & Equipment Inc
Uppr Marlboro, MD 20772-2614
301-420-3983

KEMPER INSURANCE COMPANIES
Long Grove, IL 60049
847-320-2026

Kenai Computer Forensics
Carlisle, MA 01741
978-394-2728

Kennedy Restoration Services
Weymouth, MA 02189
781-335-8000

Kent Cleaners Ltd
Peterborough, ON K9J 7P7
Canada
705-745-7904

Kentuckiana Contingency Planner's
Users's Group
Louisville, KY 40233
502-485-3948

Kentucky Emergency Management
Agency
Frankfort, KY 40601-6168
502-607-1682

Kentucky Regional Poison Center
Lousiville, KY 40202
800-222-1222

Kentucky Underground Storage Inc
Wilmore, KY 40390
859-858-4988

Kern Valley Portable Showers, Inc.
Wofford Heights, CA 93285
760-376-3145

Kessler Construction Co., Inc.
Loveland, CO 80538
970-663-4342

KETCHConsulting
Waverly, PA 18471
888-538-2492

Key Strategies LLC
East Hanover, NJ 07936
973-887-2300

Keystone Building Center
Keystone Heights, FL 32656
352-473-9991

Keystone Pump & Power, LLC
Dillsbury, PA 17019
717-502-8500

KI Canada Ltd.
Toronto, ON M3J 2H8
Canada
416-857-4464

KI4U, Inc.
Gonzales, TX 78629
830-672-8734

King Services and Construction
Lewiston, ID 83501
208-746-4192

Kinsley Power Systems
East Granby, CT 06026
860-844-6100

Kirsha Foundation
Richland, WA 99354
509-942-0443

Kitchens to Go
Naperville, IL 60540
630-305-6147

Klein Enterprises Inc
Albuquerque, NM 87109
505-344-3960

Knight-Star Enterprises, Inc.
Waco, TX 76714
866-776-1996

Koxlien Group The
Eau Claire, WI 54703
715-831-5581

KPMG, LLP
New York, NY 10154
212-872-4380

Kraft Powerr
Woburn, MA 01801
781-938-9100

Kroll Associates
New York, NY 10022
212-593-1000

Kulis Freeze Dry
Bedford, OH 44146
440-232-8352

Kullman Industries Inc
Lebanon, NJ 08833
908-236-0220

Kussmaul Electronics Co., Inc.
West Sayville, NY 11796
800-346-0857

L.E.A. International
Hayden, ID 83835
800-881-8506

La Société Prudent inc
St-Lambert, QC J4S 1H1
Canada
450-672-7966

LabelMaster
Chicago, IL 60646
800-621-5808

Laidlaw Inc.
Burlington, ON L7R 3Y8
Canada
905-804-0449

Laidlaw Inc.
Naperville, IL 60563
630-848-3000

Lake Erie Systems and Services Inc
Erie, PA 16510
814-898-0704

Lakeland Community College
Kirtland, OH 44094
440-953-7252

Lakeside True Value
Springfield, IL 62703
217-529-2987

Lakeview Technology Inc.
Oakbrook Terrace, IL 60181
630-282-8100

Lam Tree Service
evergreen, CO 80437
303-674-8733

Lamar Institute of Technology
Beaumont, TX 77710
409-880-8093

Lampe True Value and Just Ask Rental
Bellevue, IA 52031
563-872-4459

Landslide Observatory
Baltimore, MD 21250
410-455-5834

Language Line Service
Monterey, CA 93940
800-752-0093

Lansing Cleaners
Lansing, IL 60438
708-474-2459

Laplink Software Inc
Kirkland, WA 98033
425-952-6000

Lason
Burr Ridge, IL 60527
630-654-2393

Lason
Denver, CO 80239
303-371-7755

Lason
Marietta, GA 30067
770-952-8094

Lazarus Data Recovery
San Francisco, CA 94103
415-495-5556

LDV Inc.
Burlington, WI 53105
800-558-5986

LearnSomething, Inc.
Tallahassee, FL 32308
850-385-7915

Lee Marketing Services
Dallas, TX 75237
972-293-5000

Lee Technologies
Atlanta, GA 30339
770-427-7178

Lee Technologies
Columbia, MD 21045
443-535-0670

Lee Technologies
El Segundo, CA 90245
310-426-2590

Lee Technologies
Fairfax , VA 22033
703-968-0300

Lee Technologies
Glen Allen, VA 23060
804-747-8684

Leet-Melbrook Inc
Gaithersburg, MD 20879-4715
301-670-0090

Legato Software
Mountianview, CA 94040
925-556-4100

Legible Signs, Inc.
Rockford, IL 61111
888-Legi-Sign

LeMaster Restoration, Inc.
Burnsville, MN 55337
952-707-1256

Leppert Nutmeg Inc.
Bloomfield, CT 06002
860-243-1737

Lessons from Oklahoma City Bombing
Reston, VA 20191-4400
800-548-2723

Liberty International Risk Services
Boston, MA 02116
617-574-5601

Liebert Corp
Columbus, OH 43085
614-888-0246

Life Goes On
Valencia, CA 91355
661-298-4277

Life Safety Associates
San Jose, CA 95134
408-577-1929

LifeSafe Services, LLC
Jacksonville, FL 32217
888-767-0050

LifeSavers, Inc.
West Caldwell, NJ 07006
866-641-1200

Lifesaving Systems, Inc.
Roswell, GA 30075
866-OXYLATE

LightEdge Solutions
Des Moines, IA 50309
612-252-2300

Lightning Strike Emergencies
Camarillo, CA 93012
800-737-1825

Lightning Strikes: Staying Safe Under Stormy Skies
Seattle, WA 98134
206-223-6303

Linco Computer Sales and Service
Houston, TX 77090
281 893-8880

Lincoln Environmental Inc.
Smithfield, RI 02917
401-232-3353

Lindstrom Cleaning & Construction Inc
Minneapolis, MN 55441
763-544-8761

Lion Apparel
Dayton, OH 45413-0576
937-898-1949

LiveVault Corporation
Marlborough, MA 01752-4667
508-460-6670

Living with Earthquakes in California
Corvallis, OR 97331
541-737-3166

LNJ Enterprises
Davie, FL 33314
954-525-7339

Lockstep Systems Inc.
Scottsdale, AZ 85252
480-596-9432

Lockwood Greene Engineers Inc.
Spartanburg, SC 29303
864-578-2000

Locus Technologies
Walnut Creek, CA 94596
925-906-8100

Logical Maintenance Solutions Inc.
Irvine, CA 92614
714-549-1608

Lone Star Software Corporation
Mount Airy, MD 21771
301-829-1622

Long Island Production
Durham, NC 27713
800-390-8283

Long Island/NYC Emergency
Management Conference
Albany, NY 12226-2251
631-436-4228

Long Life Food Depot
Richmond, IN 47374-0081
800-601-2833

Longeneckers Just Ask Rental
Manheim, PA 17545
717-665-2020

Lorleberg True Value & Just Ask Rental
Oconomowoc, WI 53066
262-567-0267

Los Altos Technologies
Cary, NC 27511
1-800-999-8649

Los Angeles Emergency Preparedness
Department
Los Angeles, CA 90012
213-978-2222

Loss Control Assoc. Inc.
Langhorne, PA 19047
215-750-6841

Loss Recovery Systems Inc.
Syracuse, NY 13209
315-451-9111

Louis A. Hellming Co.
Cincinnati, OH 45227
513-922-2261

Louisiana Drug and Poison Information
Center
Monroe, LA 71209
800-222-1222

Louisiana Machinery
Carencro, LA 70520
337-896-7211

Louisiana Machinery Co., LLC
Gonzales, LA 70737
1-800-685-4228

Louisiana Office of Emergency
Preparedness
P.O. Box 44217, LA 70804
225-342-5470

Louisiana Rents
Gonzales, LA 70737
225-644-6600

Louisiana State University
Baton Rouge, LA 70803
225-578-1075

LS Chemical Services
Chesterfield, MO 63017
314-576-1877

Lunngroup Consulting Inc
Port Moody, BC V3H SH1
Canada
604-780-4816

Lurie Besikof Lapidus & Company LLP
(LBLCO)
Minneapolis, MN 55405
612-377-4404

Lutheran Disaster Response of New York
New York, NY 10007
866-864-1600

LVI Services, Inc.
New York, NY 10016
888-584-2677

LXI Corp
Irving, TX 75039-5526
972-444-2323

Lynn University
Boca Raton, FL 33431
561-237-7146

Lynne Company
Grover Beach, CA 93483
805-489-1564

Mack Boring & Parts Co.
Union, NJ 07083
908-964-0700

MACTEC Inc
Alpharetta, GA 30004
770-360-0600

MadahCom, Inc.
Sarasota, FL 34240
941-342-9022

Madge Ltd.
Livonia, MI 48150
734-266-1915

Madico Window Films
Woburn, MA 01801
800-225-1926

Madsen Kneppers & Associates Inc
Walnut Creek, CA 94596
800-822-6624

Magee Enterprises Inc
Norcross, GA 30071
770-446-6611

Magna-Dry International Inc.
Jenison, MI 49428
616-457-6664

Magnolia Rental & Sales, Inc.
Batesville, MS 38606
662-563-9373

Magnolia Rental & Sales, Inc.
Oxford, MS 38655
662-236-7368

MagPower Systems Inc
Delta, BC V4K 5B8
Canada
604 940-3232

Maguire J.P. Associates Inc
Waterbury, CT 06708-1426
203-755-2297

Mahaffey Fabric Structures
Memphis, TN 38118-7503
901-363-6511

Mail Communications
Novato, CA 94949
415-883-2383

Mail Mogul
Valencia, CA 91355
800-589-2525

Mail Tech Enterprises
Peoria, IL 61615-2077
309-691-6600

Mail-Gard
Warminster, PA 18974
267-960-3119

Mainline Metals
Bala Cynwyd, PA 19004
610-668-0888

Mainstar
Bellevue, WA 98009
425-455-3589

Mainstay Consulting Group, LLC
San Clemente, CA 92672
949-280-8648

Mainstream Dry Hydrants Inc.
Dunrobin Shores, ON K0A 1T0
Canada
613-832-0300

Majorpower Corporation
Mebane, NC 27302
800-931-4919

Manager's Guide to Contingency
Planning for Disasters
Indianaoplis, IN 46256
877-762-2974

Manasseh Truck & Equipment
Decatur, TX 76234
940-627-6102

MARCOR Environmental
Hunt Valley, MD 21030
410-785-0001

Maricopa County Emergency
Management
Phoenix, AZ 85008-3403
602-273-1411

Marine Pollution Control Corp.
Detroit, MI 48209
313-849-2333

Maritime Telecommunications Network
Miramar, FL 33025
954-538-4000

Marquardt Switches Inc
Cazenovia, NY 13035
315-655-8050

Marriott Executay Insurance Housing
Solutions
Pleasanton, CA 94566
800-990-9292

Marsh Inc.
New York, NY 10036-2774
866-928-7475

Maryland Emergency Management
Agency
Reistertown, MD 21136
410-517-3600

Maryland Poison Control
Baltimore, MD 21201
800-222-1222

Massachusettes Maritime Academy
Buzzards Bay, MA 02532
508-830-5011

Massachusetts Emergency Management
Agency - MEMA
Framingham, MA 01702
508-820-2010

Master Clean Restoration Services Inc
Hingham, MA 02043-2028
781-749-2314

Master Contract Services Ltd.
Surrey, BC V4N 1A2
Canada
1-604-583-7103

MasterPros Emergency Services
Consortium
Toronto, ON M8W4M1
Canada
416-822-3334

MasterWorks Communications
Fallbrook, CA 92028-8040
760-723-8897

Masune First Aid & Safety
Tonawanda, NY 14150
716-695-4999

Mateson Chemical Corp
Philadelphia, PA 19125
215-423-3200

Matrix Business Consulting Inc.
Denver, CO 80202
800-321-5200

MATRIX Risk Consultants Inc
Miamisburg, OH 45342-4882
937-886-0000

Matrx Medical, Inc
Ballentine, SC 29002
800-845-3550

MaximForce Drying
Edison, NJ 08817
732-287-3010

Maxons Restorations Inc
New York, NY 10016-0801
800-362-9667

MAXxess Systems, Inc
Anaheim, CA 92802
800-842-0221

MCCM
Edgewater, MD 21037
410-591-5648

McGrath RentCorp
Livermore, CA 94551
510-276-2626

MCI
Beltsville, MD 20705
240-264-2000

McLarens Brouwer International
Mississauga, ON L4V 1W1
Canada
905-671-0185

McNeary
Charlotte, NC 28211
704-365-4150

McQuade & Bannigan Inc.
Utica, NY 13502
315-724-7119

MCR Technologies
Wakefield, MA 01880
781-438-7801

McWains Chelsea Inc
Morristown, NJ 07960
973-993-5700

MDE Inc.
Seattle, WA 98108
206-622-2007

MDY Advanced Technologies Inc.
Fair Lawn, NJ 07410
201-797-6676

Meadowbrook Insurance Group Inc
Southfield, MI 48034
800-482-2726

MECX, L.L.C.
Bellaire, TX 77401
713-585-7000

Med-E-Train
San Juan, PR 00926-9910
787-630-6300

Media Mastr Computer Products, Inc.
Robbinsville, NJ 08691-1604
609-856-7576

Media Protection Products
Buffalo, NY 14215
716-835-0729

Media Recovery Inc.
Dallas, TX 75247
800-527-9497

Medical Reserve Corp.
Rockville, MD 20857
301-443-4951

Medprotect Inc
Plano, TX 75093
800-945-4158

Medtronic Emergency Response Systems
Redmond, WA 98073
800-442-1142

Mellon Certified Restoration
Huntingdon Vy, PA 19006
215-357-6000

Mellon Certified Restoration
Yeadon, PA 19050
610-622-5860

MEMA - Maine Emergency Management
Agency
Augusta, ME 04333
207-626-4503

MEMIC Safety Services
Portland, ME 04104
207-791-3480

Menlo Worldwide Expedite
Overland Park, KS 66210
800-714-8779

Mennonite Disaster Service
Akron, PA 17501
717-859-2210

Meredith Management Group
Paoli, PA 19301
800-981-1283

Meridian Community College
Meridian, MS 39307
1-800-622-8431 x842

Meridian Medical Technologies, Inc.
Columbia, MD 21046
443-259-7800

MERIT SECURITY
Redwood City, CA 94063
650-366-0100

MessageOne Inc.
Austin, TX 78759-5328
512-652-4500

MET Electrical Testing Co Inc.
Baltimore, MD 21227
410-247-3300

Metro Fire & Safety Equipment
Carlstadt, NJ 07072
201-635-0400

Metroplex Office Systems
Carrollton, TX 75006
972-242-2062

Metropolitan College of New York
New York, NY 10013-1919
646-243-7608

Metropolitan Community College
Omaha, NE 68103-0777
402-457-2756

Metropolitan Fire Restoration Services
Libertyville, IL 60048
847-367-8500

Meyers Auctions & Appraisals Service
Arden, MB R0J 0B0
Canada
204-368-2333

MGE UPS Systems
Costa Mesa, CA 92626
714-557-1636

Michigan Division of Emergency Management
Lansing, MI 48909-8136
517-333-5042

Michigan Regional Poison Control Center
Detroit, MI 48201
800-222-1222

Michigan State Police, Emergency Mgmt Div.
East Lansing, MI 48823
517-332-2521

Micro Technologies International
Georgetown, TX 78628
800-288-1487

MicroMain Corporation
Austin, TX 78746
512-328-3235

Microsoft Corp
Redmond, WA 98052
425-882-8080

Microsystems Inc
Northbrook, IL 60062
847-205-1986

Mid-America Contingency Planning Forum
St. Louis, MO 63138
314-466-3509

Mid-America Earthquake Center
Urbana, IL 61801
217-244-6302

Mid-America Poison Control Center
Kansas City, KS 66160
800-222-1222

Mid-Atlantic Disaster Recovery Assoc., Inc., MADRA
College Park, MD 20743
301-226-9900

Middle Tennessee Poison Center
Nashville, TN 37232
800-222-1222

Mid-Island Emergency Coordinators and Managers
Qualicum Beach, BC V9K 1S7
Canada
250-752-6921

Midwest Contingency Planners
Indianapolis, IN 46206-1632
765-778-8758

Midwest Freeze-Dry, Ltd.
Skokie, IL 60076
847-679-4756

Midwest Security Agency
Chicago, IL 60616
312-842-7033

Mikron Consulting
Chanburgh, IL 60193
847-909-9516

Miller Building Systems
Elkhart, IN 46517
800-423-2559

Millersville University of Pennsylvania
Millersville, PA 17551
717-872-3568

Milto Cleaners
Greenwood, IN 46142
317-888-7396

Milton Cat, Power Systems Division
Milford, MA 01757-1733
508-634-3400

Mindready Solutions Inc(HQ)
Saint-Laurent, QC H4S 2C2
Canada
514-339-1394

Minicomputer Exchange
Sunnyvale, CA 94085
408-733-4400

Minnesota Animal Disaster Coalition (MN-ADC)
Burnsville, MN 55337-2140
952-563-4940

Minnesota Computers Inc
Minneapolis, MN 55441
763-544-7900

Minnesota Department of Public Safety
St. Paul, MA 55101
651-296-0450

Minnesota Division of Emergency Management
St. Paul, MN 55101-6223
651-296-2233

Minuteman UPS
Carrollton, TX 75007
972-446-7363

MIR3
San Diego, CA 92130-2022
858-724-1200

MiraLink Corp
Portland, OR 97204
503-419-1660

MIS Training Institute
Framingham, MA 01702-2357
508-879-7999

Mission-Centered Solutions
Franktown, CO 80116
303-646-3700

MissionMode Solutions
St. Paul, MN 55104
612-822-4800

Mississippi Emergency Management Agency
Jackson, MS 39296-4501
601-960-9000

Mississippi Regional Poison Control Center
Jackson, MS 39216
800-222-1222

Missouri Regional Poison Center
St. Louis, MO 63117
800-222-1222

Missouri State Emergency Management Agency
Jefferson City, MO 65102
573-526-9101

Mitigation and Repair Solutions
Las Vegas, NV 89109
702-257-3955

Mi-T-M Corporation
Peosta, Iowa 52068
563-556-7484

Mitsubishi Generators and Pumps
Portage, IN 46368
888-387-3464

MJM Investigations Inc.
Raleigh, NC 27615
800-927-0456

MLC & Associates, Inc.
Port Orchard, WA 98366-0635
253-857-3124

'Mngr's Guide to Contingency Planning-Disasters'
Lenexa, KS 66215
913-341-3808

Mobile Mini Storage Systems
Rialto, CA 92377
909-356-1690

Mobile Modular
Celebration, FL 34747
321-939-2142

Mobile Modular
Livermore, CA 94551
800-944-3442

Mobile Modular
Mira Loma, CA 91752
951-360-6600

Mobile Modular
Pasadena, TX 77505
281-487-9222

Mobile Office Inc
Alsip, IL 60803-2897
773-735-6500

Mobile Satellite Ventures
Reston, VA 20191
613-742-4168

Moblie Enhanced Situation Network
Washington, DC 20002
202-380-4171

Modern Mailers Inc.
Tallahassee, FL 32314
850-877-0613

Modoc Sanitation
Eagleville, CA 96110
530-279-2025

Modtech Holdings
Glen Rose, TX 76043
254-897-3072

Moldlab
Addison, TX 75001
972-247-9373

Montana Disaster and Emergency
Services Division
Helena, MT 59604-4789
406-841-3911

Monterey Bay Communications
Santa Cruz, CA 95060
831-429-6144

Montgomery County Community College
Blue Bell, PA 19422
215-641-6428

Morgan Building Systems Inc
Garland, TX 75041
972-840-1200

Mortgage Production
Toronto, ON M3J 3J2
Canada
416-835-4836

Motala Tents Inc.
Mission, BC V2V-4J4
Canada
604-826-8368

Motient Corporation
Lincolnshire, IL 60069
800-668-4368

Motorola Inc Special Business Unit
Schaumburg, IL 60196
847-576-5000

Mountaineer Chem-Dry
Morgantown, WV 26501
304-598-3691

MovinCool
Long Beach, CA 90810
800-264-9573

MPA Systems Inc.
Sanger, TX 76266-0838
888-233-1584

Mr.Steam/Ree-Construction
Bellevue, ID 83313
208-788-2220

MSI: Minnesota Systems International. Inc
Minneapolis, MN 55425
952-883-0808

MSU Fire Services Training School
Great Falls, MT 59404
406-761-7885

Multi Risk Strategies
Brossard, QC J4Z 1A7
Canada
450-443-2500

Multidisciplinary Center for Earthquake
Engineering
Buffalo, NY 14261
716-645-3391

Multihazard Mitigation Council of the
National Institute of Building Science
Washington, DC 20005-4905
202-289-7800

Munters
Mississauga, ON L5N 5M2
Canada
905-858-5894

Munters Corporation
Amesbury, MA 01913
800-MUNTERS

Murray Associates
Oldwick, NJ 08858-0668
908-832-7900

Murray Guard Inc
Jackson, TN 38305
731-668-3400

Myers/Abacus Power Products Inc.
Bethlehem, PA 18020
610-868-3500

N. Shore Protection
Stoneham, MA 02180-1614
781-279-0127

Na Technologies
Marietta, GA 30066
770-449-8000

NACOMEX USA
Tivoli, NY 12583
845-757-2626

NACS
Melbourne, FL 32934
888-595-6227

NanoScake Materials, Inc.
Manhattan, KS 66502
785-537-0179

Nardone & Co.
Severna Park, MD 21146
800-315-8200

Nash Community College
Rocky Mount, NC 27804-7488
252-443-4011 x312

Nassau County HazMat/WMD Team
Uniondale, NY 11553
516-572-1092

Nat. Assoc. Waterproofing&Struct.
Repair Contrctrs
Baltimore, MD 21236
410-931-3332

National Air Duct Cleaners Association
(NADCA)
Washington, DC 20005
202-737-2926

National American University-
Albuquerque Campus
Albuquerque, NM 87110
505-265-7517

National Assn. of Public Insurance
Adjusters
Potomac Falls, VA 20165
703-433-9217

National Association for Search and
Rescue
Centreville, VA 20120-2020
877-893-0702

National Association of County and City
Health Officials
Washington, DC 20036
202-783-5550

National Association of Environmental
Professionals
Bowie, MD 20718
888-251-9902

National Association of Flood and Storm
Water Management Agencies
Washington, DC 20005
202-218-4122

National Business Services Inc
El Paso, TX 79901
800-777-7807

National Business Systems
Eagan, MN 55121
651-688-0202

National Capital Poison Center
Washington, DC 20016
800-222-1222

National Center for Food Protection and
Defense (NCFPD)
Minneapolis, MN 55455
612-624-2458

National Climactic Data Center
Asheville, NC 28801-5001
704-271-4800

National College of Business
&Technology
Bayamon, PR 00960
787-740-4627

National Data Systems
Bainbridge Island, WA 98110
206-780-5700

National Defense Industrial Association
Arlington, VA 22201-3061
703-522-1820

National Disaster Medical System Section
Washington, DC 20472
800-USA-NDMS (800-872-6367)

National Drought Mitigation Center -
University of Nebraska, Lincoln
Lincoln, NE 68583-0749
402-472-6707

National Earthquake Conference
Palo Alto, CA 94301
650-330-1101

National Earthquake Information Center
Denver, CO 80225-0046
303-273-8500

National Emergency Management
Annual Conference
Lexington, KY 40578
859-244-8000

National Emergency Management
Association (NEMA)
Lexington, KY 40578
859-244-8000

National Fire Adjustment Co., Inc.
Amherst, NY 14228
716-689-7700

National Fire Protection Agency (NFPA)
Quincy, MA 02169-7471
617-770-3000

'National Fire Protection Association
Journal'
Quincy, MA 02169-7471
617-770-3000

National Floor Safety Institute
Southlake, TX 76092
817-749-1700

National Funeral Directors Assn.
Brookfield, WI 53005
800-228-6332

National Hurricane Center
Miami, FL 33165-2149
305-229-4470

National Hurricane Conference
Tallahassee, FL 32308
850-906-9224

National Ice Center
Washington, DC 20395
301-457-5300

National Insitute for Occupational Safety
and Health
Washington, DC 20201
202-260-9727

National Instructors Resource Center
Holiday, FL 34691
800-246-5101

National Notification Network (3N)
Glendale, CA 91203
818-230-9700

National Response Center
Washington, DC 20593-0001
800-424-8802

National Safety Council
Itasca, IL 60143-3201
800-621-7619

National Security and Trust
Memphis, TN 38117
901-685-1177

National Security Research
Arlington, VA 22202
703-647-2200

National Snow and Ice Data Center
Boulder, CO 80309-0449
303-492-6199

National Voluntary Organizations Active
in Disaster
Alexandria, VA 22315
703-339-5596

National Vulnerability Database (NVD)
Gaithersburg, MD 20899
301-975-2934

National Water and Climate Center
Portland, OR 97232
503-414-3055

NationsRent
Brooklyn, NY 11211
718-387-4872

NationsRent
Ft. Lauderdale, FL 33301
800-667-9328

Nationwide Electrical Contractor &
Engineering
Calumet City, IL 60409
708-829-6512

Nationwide Overspray Network
Farmers Branch, TX 75234
800-345-1269

Natural Haz. Research & Applications
Info. Center
Boulder, CO 80309-0482
303-492-6818

Natural Hazards Center
University Park, PA 16802
814-863-0567

'Natural Hazards Observer'
Boulder, CO 80309-0482
303-492-6818

Natural Hazards Research and
Applications Information Center
Boulder, CO 80309-0001
303-492-6818

NBD International Inc
Ravenna, OH 44266
330-296-0221

NCD: Medical Corporation
Eastlake, OH 44095
440-953-4488

NCE Computer Group
El Cajon, CA 92020
800-446-6456

NCR Business Continuity Solutions
Dayton, OH 45479
800-587-0911

NCRI
Lenexa, KS 66214
913-663-4111

NCRI
Wichita, KS 67226-1344
316-636-5700

Neaman A.H. Co Inc
Pittsburgh, PA 15136
412-787-7775

Nebraska Emergency Management
Agency
Lincoln, NE 68508-1090
402-471-7430

Nebraska Regional Poison Center
Omaha, NE 68114
800-222-1222

Nechama - Jewish Response to Disaster
Minneapolis, MN 55416
763-732-0610

NEDRIX - New England Disaster
Recovery Information Exchange
Boston, MA 02205
781-485-0279

NEHA Training LLC
Denver, CO 80246-1960
303-756-9090

Neon Communications, Inc.
Westborough, MA 01581
800-891-5080

Neon Software
Lafayette, CA 94549
925-283-9771

NEP Manage
Andover, MA 01810
978-685-4000

NES Rentals
Chicago, IL 60631
773-695-3999

Net Synergistics LLC
Basking Ridge, NJ 07920
908-719-9873

Net Telcos, Inc.
Glen Allen, VA 23060
804-270-6063

NetIQ Corp.
Houston, TX 77027
713-548-1700

Network Management Corp.
Chardon, OH 44024
440-285-8400

Network Systems Architects
Stoughton, MA 02072
781-297-5300

Nevada Division of Emergency Mgmt.
Carson City, NV 89711
775-687-4240

New England Archives
Holyoke, MA 01040
800-225-2405

New England Bank Equipment
Glastonbury, CT 06033
800-842-9985

New England Crime Scene Clean-up and
Safety Consulting Services
Hampton, NH 03843
800-524-9591

New England Rest Room's Inc.
North Reading, MA 01864
877-883-5874

New England Satellite Systems Inc
Shrewsbury, MA 01545
508-842-4328

New England Security
Taunton, MA 02780
508-823-6531

New Era Software Inc
Morgan Hill, CA 95037
800-421-5035

New Generation Software Inc.
Sacramento, CA 95834
916-920-2200

New Hampshire Poison Information
Center
Lebanon, NH 03756
800-222-1222

New Heights Manufacturing
Ellaville, GA 31806
800-826-2844

New Image Building Services, Inc.
Mount Clemens, MI 48043
586-465-4420

New Jersey Office of Emergency
Management
West Trenton, NJ 08628-0068

New Jersey Poison Info & Education
System
Newark, NJ 07107
800-222-1222

New Life Service Co.
Eureka, CA 95501
707-444-8222

New Mexico Office of Emergency
Management
Santa Fe, NM 87505
505-476-9606

New Mexico Poison & Drug Info Center
Albuquerque, NM 87131
800-222-1222

New Orleans Private Patrol Service Inc
New Orleans, LA 70112
504-525-7115

New York City Poison Control Center
New York, NY 10016
800-222-1222

New York Public Adjusters Association
New York, NY 10007
212-285-0510

New York State Emergency Management
Office
Albany, NY 12226-2251
518-457-2222

Newchannel Direct
Hinckley, OH 44233
330-225-8950

Newfoundland & Labrador
St. John's, NF A1B 4J6
Canada
613-991-7077

Newground Resources Inc
Chesterfield, MO 63017
314-821-2265

Newsam-Harp Inc. General Adjusters
Independence, MO 64057
816-753-4285

Nexcom International Corp. LTD.
Fremont, CA 94538
510-656-2248

Nextteq, LLC
Tampa, FL 33634
877-312-2333

'NFPA 1600: Standard for Disaster
Planning'
Quincy, MA 02169-7471
617-770-3000

NFPA World Annual Safety Conference
Quincy, MA 02169-7471
617-770-3000

NICE Network Inc.
Crescent Spgs, KY 41017
859-814-0061

Nickell Equipment Rental & Sales
Griffin, GA 30223
770-227-9122

Nickell Equipment Rental & Sales
Newnan, GA 30265
770-253-4242

Nier Systems Inc
Boca Raton, FL 33496
561-989-0049

NIST- National Insitute of Standards and
Technology
Gaithersburg, MD 20899-8600
301-975-5900

Nitro-Pak Preparedness Center Inc.
Heber City, UT 84032
800-866-4876

NMT Corporation
La Crosse, WI 54602
800-236-0850

NOAA National Weather Service
Silver Spring, MD 20910
301-713-0090 x150

Noah's Wish
Placerville, CA 95667
530-622-9313

Nonprofit Risk Management Center
Washington, DC 20036
202-785-3891

NorCo Computer Systems Inc
Brunswick, OH 44212
800-892-1920

Nordic Cold Storage Inc.
Doraville, GA 30340
770-448-7400

Nordli Wilson Associates
Hamden, CT 06518
203-288-7472

Nortel Networks
Brampton, ON L6T 5P6
Canada
905-863-0000

North American Risk Services
Sarasota, FL 34230
941-907-2200

North American Weather Consultants
Sandy, UT 84093
801-942-9005

North Carolina Emergency Management
Agency
Raleigh, NC 27603
919-733-3867

North Dakota Division of Emergency
Management
Bismarck, ND 58506
701-328-8100

North Dakota State University
Fargo, ND 58102
701-231-8657

North Safety Products
Cranston, RI 02921
800-430-4110

North Texas Poison Center
Dallas, TX 75235
800-222-1222

Northeast Document Conservation
Center
Andover, MA 01810
978-470-1010

Northeast Florida Association of
Contingency Planners
Jacksonville, FL 32256
904-281-3271

Northeast States Emergency Consortium
Wakefield, MA 01880-1301
781-224-9876

Northeast Waste Management Officials
Association (NEWMOA)
Boston, MA 02114-2014
617-367-8558

Northern New England Poison Center
Portland, ME 04102
800-222-1222

Northern Safety Co., Inc.
Frankfort, NY 13340
800-631-1246

Northern Wyoming Mental Health
Center
Sheridan, WY 82801
307-674-4405

Northshore International Insurance
Services
Danvers, MA 01923
978-745-6655

Northwest Weather and Avalanche
Center
Seattle, WA 98115-6349
206-526-6677

Northwest Woolen Mills
Woonsocket, RI 02895
401-769-0189

Norton-Lambert
Santa Barbara, CA 93140
805-964-6767

Norwich University
Northfield, VT 05663
802-485-2001

NOTIFIER/Fire-Lite Alarms Inc
Northford, CT 06472
203-484-7161

NovaStor Corp.
Simi Valley, CA 93065
805-579-6700

Novell Inc.
Provo, UT 84606
801-861-7000

NPA Computers
Holbrook, NY 11741
631-467-2500

Nu-Air The Healthy Choice
Pennsawken, NJ 08109
856-317-0500

Nunavut Emergency Management
Iqaluit, NT X0A 0H0
Canada
867-975-5317

NY Grace Realty
Flushing, NY 11354
718-358-6100

NY State Psychological Assn.
Albany, NY 12203
800-732-3933

Oakwood Worldwide - Nationwide
Locations
Los Angeles, CA 90064
310-478-1021

Oakwood Worldwide Headquarters
Los Angeles, CA 90064
310-478-1021

OC Disaster Preparedness Academy Conf.
Santa Ana, CA 92711-1364
714-481-5300

Ocean Prediction Center
Camp Springs, MD 20746
301-763-8441

Oceanside Inc
Hyannis, MA 02601
508-771-3374

O'Connor Associates Environmental Inc
Calgary, AB T2G 0Y2
Canada
403-294-4200

Octagon Risk Services
Oakland, CA 94612
510-452-9300

Odell Electronics Cleaning Stations
Westlake, OH 44145
440-365-5910

Odor Science & Engineering Inc
Bloomfield, CT 06002
860-243-9380

Office Furniture Rental Alliance
Chicago, IL 60108
630-790-9740

Office Furniture Rental Alliance
Dallas, TX 75220
214-358-5990

Office Furniture Rental Alliance
East Hartford, CT 06108
860-528-2000

Office Furniture Rental Alliance
Fullerton, CA 92831
714-447-4023

Office Furniture Rental Alliance
Grand View, OH 43212
614-469-7950

Office Furniture Rental Alliance
Largo, MD 20774
301-333-4116

Office Furniture Rental Alliance
Longwood, FL 32750
407-260-5048

Office Furniture Rental Alliance
Milpitas, CA 95035
408-719-3217

Office Furniture Rental Alliance
Seattle, WA 98108
206-768-8000

Office Furniture Rental Alliance
Tucker, GA 30084
770-491-8896

Office of Civil Emergency Management
Oklahoma City, OK 73152
405-521-2481

Office of Climate, Water and Weather
Services
Silver Spring, MD 20910-3283
301-713-4000

Office of Emergency Management and
Communications
Chicago, IL 60607
312-746-9111

Office of Food Security and Emergency
Preparedness
Washington, DC 20024
202-690-6514

Office of Public Health Security
Ottawa, K1A 0K9
Canada
613 954 8498

Office of Security and Emergency
Management
Dallas, TX 75202-3545
214-653-7972

Office Suites PLUS
Lexington, KY 40504
800-316-7950

Offsite, LLC
Kenosha, WI 53140
312-off-site

Ohio Emergency Management Agency
Columbus, OH 43235
614-889-7150

Okfuskee County Sheriff Dept.
Okemah, OK 74859
918-623-1122

Oklahoma Poison Control Center
Oklahoma City, OK 73104
800-222-1222

Oklahoma State Univ
Stillwater, OK 74078
405-744-5606

OmniClean
Brook Park, OH 44142
216-362-8686

On Side Restoration Services Ltd.
Burnaby, BC V5C 5A9
Canada
604-293-1596

Oneac Corp
Libertyville, IL 60048
847-816-6000

Onondaga Community College
Syracuse, NY 13215
315-498-6046

OnScreen Technologies Inc.
Safety Harbor, Fl 34695
727-797-6664

Ontario Association of Emergency
Managers
Mississauga, ON L5L 5V4
Canada

Ontario Environment Industry
Association
Toronto, ON M2J 1W8
Canada
416-531-7884

Ontario Funeral Service Association
(OFSA)
Etobicoke, ON M9C 5K4
Canada
416 695 3434

Ontrack Data Recovery
Eden Prairie, MN 55347
952-937-5161

Open Solutions
Atlanta, GA 30305
404-262-2298

Oppenheimer Wolff & Donnelly LLP
Minneapolis, MN 55402
612-607-7204

OptiMetrics, Inc.
Ann Arbor, MI 48104-5131
734-973-1177

Optinuity, Inc.
Bethesda, MD 20814
202-292-4920

Orbit Software USA Inc
Danville, CA 94526
925-837-4143

Oregon Emergency Management
Salem, OR 97309-5062
503-378-2911

Oregon Freeze Dry Inc.
Albany, OR 97321
800-547-0244

Oregon Poison Center
Portland, OR 97201
800-222-1222

Osler Hoskin & Harcourt LLP
Montreal, QC H3B 4W5
Canada
514-904-8159

O'Toole-Ewald Art Associates Inc
New York, NY 10010
212-989-5151

Ottawa Carleton Earthquake Engineering Research Centre
Ottawa, ON K1S 5B6
Canada
613-520-2600

Otter Creek Associates/Matrix Health Sys
Burlington, VT 05401
802-865-3450

O-Two Medical Technologies Inc
Mississauga, ON L5S1C8
Canada
905-677-9410

Outfitter Satellite
Nashville, TN 37214
615-889-8833

Overland Solutions Incorperate
Overland Park, KS 66210
913-451-3222

Overnite Transportation Co
Richmond, VA 23224
804-231-8646

Overspray Removal Specialists
Naples, FL 34103-3717
239-435-0511

Overspray Removal Specialists
Sarasota, FL 34238
941-966-8600

Pacific Consolidated Industries (PCI)
Riverside, CA 92503-4820
951-479-0860

Pacific Corporate Housing
Corona Del Mar, CA 92625
949-425-9127

Pacific Disaster Center
Kilhei, HI 96753
808-891-0525

Packer Engineering Inc
Naperville, IL 60566
630-505-5722

PAE Inc
Salem, MA 01970
978-744-8612

Page Transportation Inc
Weedsport, NY 13166
315-834-6681

Palace Construction
Denver, CO 80223
303-777-7999

Palisade Corporation
Ithaca, NY 14850
607-277-8000

Palmer Snyder
Lexington, KY 40502
800-762-0415

Palmetto Poison Center
Columbia, SC 29208
800-222-1222

PaloAlto Software
Eugene, OR 97401
800-229-7526

Pan American Health Organization
Washington, DC 20037
202-974-3520

PanAmSat Corporation
Wilton, CT 06897
203-210-8000

Paradigm Solutions International
Rockville, MD 20852
800-679-2856

Paragon Restoration Group Inc
Depew, NY 14043
716-685-2775

Paramount Computer
Austin, TX 78744
512-263-7010

Park University
Kansas City, MO 64105
816-421-1125

Parma Annual Risk Managers Conference
San Jose, CA 95150
888-907-2762

Partners Remarketing Inc.
Livermore, CA 94550
925-449-2120

Partners' Restoration & Construction, LLC
Dallas, TX 75220-2523
214-366-2528

Partnership for Emergency Planning
Overland Park, KS 66251
913-315-8224

PATLITE USA Corp.
Torrance, CA 90503
310-214-3222

Patriot Antenna Systems
Albion, MI 49224
800-470-3510

Patten Power Systems
Elmhurst, IL 60126
630-530-2200

Patton Electronics Co
Gaithersburg, MD 20879
301-975-1000

Paul Consulting Inc.
Tallahassee, FL 32312
850-523-9626

Paul Davis Restoration
Knoxville, TN 37919
865-584-0216

Paul Davis Restoration of Central New Hampshire
Manchester, NH 03109
603-622-9800

Paul Davis Restoratin of Central Mississippi
Ridgeland, MS 39157
601-605-1717

Paul Davis Restoration
Ann Arbor, MI 48103
734-930-0303

Paul Davis Restoration
Boise, ID 83705
208-429-9992

Paul Davis Restoration
Bowling Green, KY 42103
270-782-0123

Paul Davis Restoration
Branford, CT 06405
203-315-1500

Paul Davis Restoration
Brick, NJ 08723
732-451-1280

Paul Davis Restoration
Carrollton, TX 75006
972-323-6565

Paul Davis Restoration
Chattanooga, TN 37421
423-899-2406

Paul Davis Restoration
Corona, CA 92879
909-270-5304

Paul Davis Restoration
Denver, CO 80231
303-338-8232

Paul Davis Restoration
Des Moines, IA 50322
515-252-0600

Paul Davis Restoration
Fletcher, NC 28732
828-687-7766

Paul Davis Restoration
Glenside, PA 19038
215-887-5991

Paul Davis Restoration
Houston, TX 77081
713-270-6030

Paul Davis Restoration
Jacksonville, FL 32202-5020
888-907-5907

Paul Davis Restoration
Morton , PA 19070
610-328-5901

Paul Davis Restoration
Neenah, WI 54956
920-729-1551

Paul Davis Restoration
Phoenix, AZ 85021
623-445-9922

Paul Davis Restoration
Plainville, CT 06062
860-747-6993

Paul Davis Restoration
Pueblo, CO 81006
719-583-8080

Paul Davis Restoration
Springfield, IL 62705-1001
217-544-4667

Paul Davis Restoration
Stone Mountain, GA 30047
770-985-1727

Paul Davis Restoration
Tampa, FL 33637
813-984-2700

Paul Davis Restoration
W. Jordan, UT 84088
801-561-4900

Paul Davis Restoration
Wilmington, NC 28405
910-452-7290

Paul Davis Restoration - East Bay
San Leandro, CA 94578
510-635-6800

Paul Davis Restoration - Triad
Kernersville, NC 27284
800-951-7881

Paul Davis Restoration - Washtenaw County
Ann Arbor, MI 48103
734-930-0303

Paul Davis Restoration & Remodeling
Dansville, NY 14437
585-335-2780

Paul Davis Restoration & Remodeling
Detroit Lakes, MN 56501
218-847-1800

Paul Davis Restoration & Remodeling
Indian Orchard, MA 01151
413-543-5001

Paul Davis Restoration & Remodeling
Kalamazoo, MI 49001
269-388-3700

Paul Davis Restoration & Remodeling
Lititz, PA 17543
717-291-6000

Paul Davis Restoration & Remodeling
Nixa, MO 65714
417-725-7575

Paul Davis Restoration & Remodeling
Owensboro, KY 42301
270-691-0005

Paul Davis Restoration & Remodeling
West Fargo, ND 58078
701-271-4770

Paul Davis Restoration & Remodeling of Cleveland Metro West
Brunswick, OH 44212
330-221-2002

Paul Davis Restoration & Remodeling of Suburban VA
MANASSAS, VA 20109
703-335-2424

Paul Davis Restoration & Remodeling of Tarrant County
Fort Worth, TX 76117
817-759-2600

Paul Davis Restoration & Remodeling, Mid-Mich
Mason, MI 48854
517-676-8000

Paul Davis Restoration & Remoldeling
Gaithersburg, MD 20879
301-948-8008

Paul Davis Restoration / Denver West
Denver, CO 80231
303 296-8080

Paul Davis Restoration Co. of Collier
Naples, FL 34109
239-598-2426

Paul Davis Restoration Inc. of Southern MD
Clinton, MD 20735
301-856-0090

Paul Davis Restoration Inc. of Volusia County
South Daytona, FL 32119
386-760-8959

Paul Davis Restoration of Akron
Cuyahoga Falls, OH 44221
330-920-1936

Paul Davis Restoration of Baltimore
Baltimore, MD 21228
410-719-8830

Paul Davis Restoration of Bucks County
Telford, PA 18969
215-799-0777

Paul Davis Restoration of Cape Cod & The Islands
Brewster, MA 02631
508-896-1799

Paul Davis Restoration of Central CT
Glastonbury, CT 06033
860-633-7733

Paul Davis Restoration of Central Mississippi
Ridgeland, MS 39157
601-605-1717

Paul Davis Restoration of Central NH
Manchester, NH 03109
603-622-9800

Paul Davis Restoration of Central Orange County
Irvine, CA 92618
949-859-9515

Paul Davis Restoration of Cleveland Metro
Chagrin Falls, OH 44023
440-247-5122

Paul Davis Restoration of Contra Costa & Solano
Concord, CA 94520
925-939-1300

Paul Davis Restoration of Dayton
Dayton, OH 45439
937-436-3411

Paul Davis Restoration of East Central IN
Muncie, IN 47302
765-284-3737

Paul Davis Restoration of Eastern CT.
Old Saybrook, CT 06475
860-388-3444

Paul Davis Restoration of Fox Valley
Appleton, WI 54914
920-882-9287

Paul Davis Restoration of Greater Miami Inc.
Miami, FL 33155
305-260-0034

Paul Davis Restoration of Greater Phoenix
Phoenix, AZ 85040
602-278-8837

Paul Davis Restoration of Greater Richmond, Inc.
Richmond, VA 23236
804-330-9500

Paul Davis Restoration of Greater Tri-Cities
Bristol, VA 24202
276-669-7208

Paul Davis Restoration of Johnson Co. Inc.
Olathe, KS 66062
913-345-2700

Paul Davis Restoration of Lehigh Valley
Allentown, PA 18109
610-433-2212

Paul Davis Restoration of Lexington
Nicholasville, KY 40356
859-885-7653

Paul Davis Restoration of Macomb & St. Clair Counties
Warren, MI 48091
586-755-1700

Paul Davis Restoration of Mercer & Middlesex, Inc.
Ewing, NJ 08628
609-538-8424

Paul Davis Restoration of Michiana
South Bend, IN 46628
574-234-4400

Paul Davis Restoration of Morris County
Florham Park, NJ 07932
973-765-9707

Paul Davis Restoration of N. Fulton & Forsyth
Alpharetta, GA 30004
770-360-7994

Paul Davis Restoration of N.Y.
New York, NY 10033
212-740-6611

Paul Davis Restoration of New Mexico
Albuquerque, NM 87107
505-884-5583

Paul Davis Restoration of Northeast New Jersey
Saddlebrook, NJ 07663
973-546-0203

Paul Davis Restoration of Northeast WI
Appleton, WI 54914
920-882-9287

Paul Davis Restoration of Northwest Mich
Traverse City, MI 49686
231-933-9077

Paul Davis Restoration of Northwest Michigan
Traverse City, MI 49686
231-933-9077

Paul Davis Restoration of Orlando
Winter Park, FL 32789
407-629-6700

Paul Davis Restoration of Palm Beach County
West Palm Beach , FL 33409
561-478-7272

Paul Davis Restoration of Pensacola-Ft. Walton
Pensacola, FL 32501
850-437-0400

Paul Davis Restoration of Rockland and Orange Counties
Middletown, NY 10940
845-361-1840

Paul Davis Restoration of S.W. Chicagoland
Romeoville , IL 60446
630-378-9011

Paul Davis Restoration of Sacramento
Sacramento, CA 95838
916-648-2040

Paul Davis Restoration of San Diego Inc.
San Diego, CA 92123
858-560-0444

Paul Davis Restoration of Sioux City
Sioux City, IA 51106
712-234-0095

Paul Davis Restoration of Somerset, Hunterdon, & Warren Counties
High Bridge, NJ 08829
908-638-8440

Paul Davis Restoration of Southeast Wisconsin
Milwaukee, WI 83202
414-383-3131

Paul Davis Restoration of Southern California
La Mirada, CA 90638
800-325-4636

Paul Davis Restoration of Southern NH & ME
North Hampton, NH 03862
603-964-8484

Paul Davis Restoration of St. Augustine
St. Augustine, FL 32086
904-824-1468

Paul Davis Restoration of Tallahasse
Tallahasse, FL 32303
850-576-7901

Paul Davis Restoration of the MidSouth
Memphis, TN 38134
901-373-5394

Paul Davis Restoration of the Space Coast
Cocoa, FL 32926
321-690-0000

Paul Davis Restoration of the Treasure Coast
Port St. Lucie, FL 34984
772-340-2080

Paul Davis Restoration of the Wiregrass
Dothan, AL 36301
334-702-7379

Paul Davis Restoration of Tucson
Tucson, AZ 85745
520-624-4560

Paul Davis Restoration of Urbandale
Des Moines, IA
515-334-3473

Paul Davis Restoration of Volusia County
South Daytona, FL 32119
386-760-8959

Paul Davis Restoration of W. Middlesex County
Acton, MA 01720
978-264-3141

Paul Davis Restoration of Western Lake Erie
Holland, OH 43528
419-866-9844

Paul Davis Restoration of Western Mass
Springfield, MA 01151
413-543-5001

Paul Davis Restoration of Western Michigan
Grand Rapids, MI 49503
800-676-9118

Paul Davis Restoration of Western NY
Buffalo, NY 14120
800-836-8910

Paul Davis Restoration of Western NY
Buffalo, NY 14231
716-824-2230

Paul Davis Restoration of Western PA
Ellwood City, PA 16117
724-758-6540

Paul Davis Restoration Polk County
Winter Haven, FL 33880
863-299-9688

Paul Davis Restoration, Tampa East
Tampa, FL 33637
813-984-2700

Paul Davis Restoration/Northern Colorado
Fort Collins, CO 80524
970-221-1281

Paul Guttman & Co
Valley Stream, NY 11580
516-825-4800

PAULI ENGINEERING
Fresno, CA 93728
559-237-4408

PC SYSWARE Inc.
Toronto, ON M4B 2R6
Canada
416-951-0110

PCI
Hackensack, NJ 7601
201-646-9000

PCS Restoration
Whiteland, IN 46184
317-535-7007

PDR of Southern NH and ME
North Hampton, NH 03820
603-964-8484

Peace of Mind USA
Monrovia, CA 91016
626-298-6231

Peak 10
Charlotte, NC 28273-3432
866-473-2510

Pearce & Frankman Inc
Daly City, CA 94015
650-756-7400

Pearces 2 Consulting Corporation
North Vancouver, BC V7G 2T9
Canada
604-929-4560

Pearson Electronics Inc
Palo Alto, CA 94303
650-494-6444

Peerless Cleaners
Decatur, IL 62522
217-423-7703

Peninsula Tree LLC
San Jose, CA 95111
408-210-1236

Penn Computer Corporation
Hatboro, PA 19040
215-444-9999

Pennsylvania Emergency Management Agency
Harrisburg, PA 17110-9364
717-651-2001

PentaSafe Security Technologies Inc.
Houston, TX 77027-9106
713-860-9390

PerkinElmer
Wellesley, MA 02481
781-237-5100

Permanent Claims Service Inc
Memphis, TN 38117
901-761-1670

Perm-A-Store Inc
Golden VALLEY, MN 55427
763-230-3911

Perpetual Storage Inc.
Sandy, UT 84092-6006
801-942-1950

Personal Public Adjusters Inc
Feasterville, PA 19053
215-355-8488

Persson Associates
Huntley, IL 60124
847-732-6500

Pest Control Services Inc.
kennett square, PA 19348
610-284-6249

Peterson Power Systems Inc
San Leandro, CA 94577
510-895-8400

PHH Vehicle Management Services
Sparks Glenco, MD 21152
800-392-7751

Philips
Andover, MA 01810
800-934-7372

Phillips and Jordan Inc
Cary, NC 27513
919-388-4222

Phillips and Jordan Inc
Robbinsville, NC 28771
828-479-3371

Phillips and Jordan Inc
Zephyrhills, FL 33541
813-783-1132

Phillips Environmental Products, Inc.
Belgrade, MT 59714
406-388-5999

Philtek Power
Blaine, WA 98231
360-332-7252

Phoenix Consulting Services
Bakersfield, CA 93309
661-396-8336

Phoenix Continuity Solutions, LLC
Southfield, MI 48075
248-263-3855

Phoenix Disaster Services
San Antonio, TX 78216-3944
210-541-0505

Phoenix Mental Health
Dover, DE 19904
302-736-6135

Phonetics Inc
Aston, PA 19014-1597
610-558-2700

Pick Up The Pieces Art Restoration
Costa Mesa, CA 92627
800-934-9278

Pikes Peak Community College
Colorado Springs, CO 80906
719-540-7345

Pinckney Tru-Value Hardware
Pickney, MI 48169
734-878-2000

Pirtek-Clearwater
Clearwater, FL 33762
727-573-8522

Pitney Bowes Inc.
Stamford, CT 06926-0700
888-245-PBMS

Pitney Bowes Management Services
Stamford, CT 06926
800-672-6937

Plantation True Value Hardware
Richmond, TX 77469
281-342-5207

Plug-In Storage Systems Inc
West Haven, CT 06477
800-231-5952

Plylox
Friendswood, TX 77549-1749
281-996-6903

PND Corporation
Bellevue, WA 98007
425-562-7252

Poison and Drug Information Centre-B.C.
Vancouver, BC V6Z 1Y6
Canada
800-567-8911

Poison and Drug Information Services-Calgary
Calgary, AB T2N 2T9
Canada
800-332-1414

Poison Control Centre
Moncton, NB E1C 6Z8
Canada
506-857-5555

Poison Control Centre-Nova Scotia
Halifax, NS B3J 3G9
Canada
800-565-8161

Poison Control Centre-Ontario
Toronto, ON M5G 1X8
Canada
416-813-5900

Poison Emergency Department-Saskatchewan
Regina, SK S4P 0W5
800-667-4545

Poison Emergency Department-Yukon Territory
Whitehorse, YT Y1A 3H7
Canada
403-667-8726

Policyholders Adjusting Service
San Diego, CA 92123
858-569-9190

Ponderosa Sports
Horseshoe Bnd, ID 83629
208-793-3121

Pooler Consultants Ltd.
Lafayette, LA 70506
337-984-1601

Portable Computer Systems, Inc.
Golden, CO 80403
303-346-2487

Portable Sanitation Association International
Bloomington , MN 55425
952-854-8300

Portable Space
Exeter, PA 18643
570-655-4501

Portable Storage Corp
Ontario, CA 91762
800-527-8673

Porta-John
Shelby Twp, MI 48318
800-521-6310

Porta-King Building Systems
Earth City, MO 63045
314-291-4200

Potter Electric Signal Co
Saint Louis, MO 63146
800-325-3936

Powell Decontamination Systems
Lillington, NC 27546
800-800-6296

Power & Systems Innovations Inc.
Orlando, FL 32859
407-380-9200

Power & Systems Innovations, Inc.
Orlando, FL 32859-0223
407-380-9200

Power Equipment Co
Attleboro, MA 02703
508-226-3410

Power Plus
Phoenix, AZ 85027
480-951-9116

Power Service Concepts Inc
Amityville, NY 11701
631-841-2300

Power Systems Specialists, Inc.
Milford, PA 18337
888-305-1555

PowerFlare
San Jose, CA 95120
408-323-2371

Powervar
Waukegan, IL 60085
847-816-8585

Powerware
Necedah, WI 54646
608-565-7200

PR Direct
Toronto, ON M5C 2L9
Canada
416-507-2028

Praetorian Protective Services LLC
Orinda, CA 94563
925-376-7169

Pre-Emergency Planning, LLC
Lodi, WI 53555
608-592-2511

PreEmpt Inc.
Euless, TX 76040
817-685-9765

Premier Cleaning and Restoration
Santa Rosa, CA 95407
707-522-0198

Premiere Network Services Inc
Desoto, TX 75115
972-228-8885

Pre-owned Electronics Inc
Bedford, MA 01730
781-778-4600

Pre-Paid Legal Services, Inc.
Mesa, AZ 85204
480-228-3758

'Preparing for Trial'
Costa Mesa, CA 92626
800-394-2626

Price & Gannon True Value & Just Ask Rental
Centreville, MD 21617
410-758-0730

Price Hollingsworth
Elk Grove Vlg, IL 60007
800-568-5865

Price Wheeler Corp.
San Diego, NJ 92011
800-528-0313

PricewaterhouseCoopers LLP
New York, NY 10017
646-471-4000

PRIMA Annual Conference
Alexandria, VA 22314
703-528-7701

Primero Engineering
San Antonio, TX 78209
210-829-5499

Prince Edward Island
Summerside, PE C1N 5L2
902-888-8050

Prism - Emergency Inflatable Lighting
JACksonville, FL 32257
904-880-9900

PRISM International: Professional Records & Information Services Management
Garner, NC 27529-3905
800-336-9793

Pro Care Services, Inc.
Carefree, AZ 85377
480-488-7800

Process Results, Inc.
Saline, MI 48176
734-429-8900

Productivity Inc.
Shelton, CT 06484-6255
860-225-0451

Proengin, Inc.
Fort Lauderdale, FL 33304
954-760-9990

Professional Insurance Agents Association
Glenmont, NY 12077
800-424-4244

Professional Loss Adjusters
Newton, MA 02458
617-850-0477

ProPac Inc.
N Charleston, SC 29406
843-308-0994

Property Damage Appraisers
Silver Spring, MD 20906
301-871-1500

Property Loss Research Bureau (PLRB)
Downers Grove, IL 60515-1291
888-711-PLRB

Prosys Information Systems
Norcross, GA 30071
888-337-2626 x9011

Pro-Tech Cleaning & Restoration,LLC
Boerne, TX 78006
830-816-3202

Protech Construction
Arcadia, CA 91006
800-884-6999

Protect Environmental Services, Inc.
Haltom City, TX 76117
817-589-9005

Protective Counter Measures and Consulting, Inc.
White Plains , NY 10604
914-697-4777

ProText Inc
Bethesda, MD 20824
301-320-7231

Protiviti Inc.
Pleasanton, CA 94588
888-556-7420

PROTOCOL
Van Nuys, CA 91406
818-782-5705

Provincial Emergency Program-British Columbia
Victoria, BC V8W 9J1
Canada
250-952-4913

Provincial Poison Control Centre-Newfoundland
St. John's, NF A1A 1R8
Canada
709-722-1110

Provincial Poison Information Centre-Manitoba
Winnipeg, MB R3A 1S1
Canada
204-787-2591

PSEG
Newark, NJ 07102
973-430-6725

PSI
Oakbrook Terrace, IL 60181
800-548-7901

P-SPAN
Amery, WI 54001
715-268-8106

Psychiatric Inst. of Wash.
Washington, DC 20016
202-885-5600

Public Entity Risk Institute
Fairfax, VA 22030
703-352-1846

Public Risk Management Association
Alexandria, VA 22314
703-528-7701

Public Safety & Emergency Prep.(PSEPC)-Canada
Ottawa, ON K1A 0P8
Canada
613-991-7000

Publicover Security Service
Arlington, MA 02476
781-643-6673

Puerto Rico Emergency Management
Agency
San Juan, PR 00906-6597
787-724-0124

Puerto Rico Info Security Emergency
Mgmt Assoc.
San Juan, PR 00929-0715
787-768-1115

Puerto Rico Poison Center
Santurce, PR 00912
800-222-1222

Pulcir Incorporated
Oak Ridge, TN 37830
800-862-1390

Purdue University, Calumet
Hammond, IN 46323-2094
219-989-2596

Purified Restoration Fire Smoke & Water
Tulsa, OK 74145
918-610-8173

Puroclean of South Miami
Miami, FL 33193
305-752-4019

Purofirst Disaster Services
Louisville, KY 40223
502-244-1510

Purofirst Div. of Cardan Construction Inc
Pittsfield, MA 01202
413-499-0010

Q-Safety
Duarte, CA 91010-2845
800-997-2338

Quake Kare, Inc.
Moorpark, CA 93020-0013
800-2pre-pare

QuakeHold! by Trevco
Escondivo, CA 92029
760-510-4969

Quality Inspection Service
La Mesa, CA 91941
619-466-2581

Qualstar Corporation
Simi Valley, CA 93063
805-583-7744

Quantum Complience Systems
Ypsilanti, MI 48197
734-572-1000

Quantum Corporation - Storage Devices
Boulder, CO 80303
720-406-5700

Quantum Restoration
Boomington, MN 55438
952-943-4357

Quantum Technology Inc
Elkins Park, PA 19027
215-635-2650

Quarles & Brady LLP
Naples, FL 34109-7874
239-262-5959

Quebec Ministère de la Sécurité publique
Sainte-Foy, QC G1V 2L2
Canada
866-776-8345

QUEST International Inc
Irvine, CA 92618
949-581-9900

Quest Technologies, Inc.
Oconomowoc, WI 53066
262-567-9157

Quincy College
Quincy, MA 02169
617-984-1640

Quinn Power Systems
Selma, CA 93662
559-891-5447

QwikResponse Disaster Control &
Construction
Cerritos, CA 90703
562-809-1532

R & R Salvage Corp
Rahway, NJ 07065
800-732-6837

R&A Crisis Management Services
Des Plaines, IL 60016-8344
847-827-4267

R.D. Zande & Associates, Inc.
Columbus, OH 43204
614-486-4383

R.L. Smith Co. Inc.
Leitchfield, KY 42755-0365
270-259-5684

R.S. Restoration Services, Ltd
Victoria, BC V9A 5V1
Canada
866-313-0030

RAC Adjustments
Rockford, IL 61110
815-968-7686

Radiant Resources Inc
Randolph, NJ 07869
973-442-5555

RAE Systems
San Jose , CA 95134
408-952-8200

Raido Response
Seattle, WA 98101
206-628-9156

Railroad Safety Consultants, Inc.
Lake Buena Vista, FL 32830
407-319-4819

Rain for Rent
Bakersfield, CA 93308
661-399-9124

Rainbow International Carpet Care &
Restoration
Waco, TX 76707
254-745-2444

RainbowBrite
Toronto, ON M8W4M1
Canada
416-255-4248

Rajant Corporation
Wayne, PA 19087
484-582-2200

Rapid Technologies LLC
Portland, OR 97223
503-968-3125

RBF Interiors
Saint Louis, MO 63115
314-383-7003

REACT Computer Services
Burrridge, IL 60527
630-323-6200

Recall
Fort Lee, NJ 07024
201-592-7868

Recall
Kitchener, ON N2M 5P2
Canada
519-895-1213

Recall
Saint Louis, MO 63043
314-991-5992

Recall
San Jose, CA 95131
408-453-2753

Recall SDS.
Bloomfield, CT 06002
860-243-1311

Recall Total Information Management
Mississauga, ON L4W 2S6
Canada
905-629-8440

Recall Total Information Management
Norcross, GA 30092
770-776-1000

Recovery Knowledge
Long Beach, CA 90801
800-754-2201

Recovery Point Systems
Gaithersburg, MD 20878
240-632-7000

Recovery Room Inc.
Chaska, MN 55318
952-361-9355

RecoveryPlanner
Shelton, CT 06484
203-925-3950

Recovery-Plus Planning Products & Sves.
Algonquin, IL 60102-2126
847-658-1300

Red Hat Linux, Inc.
Raleigh, NC 27606
866-273-3428 x45555

Red Rocks Community College
Lakewood, CO 80228
303-914-6404

Redmond Worldwide, Inc
Brooklyn, NY 11220
718-545-0582

Regency Construction Corporation
Clinton Township, MI 48035
586-741-8000

Regional Cntr for Poison Control &
Prevention for
Boston, MA 02115
800-222-1222

Regional Reporting Inc
New York, NY 10038
212-964-5973

Relational Technology Services
Largo, FL 33773
727-524-9668

Reliable Electric Motor Inc
Hartford, CT 06114
860-522-2257

Reliable Restaurant Supplies Co., LTD
Scarborough, ON M1V 3Z7
Canada
416-297-9612

Relocation Housing Specialists
Sacramento, CA 95825
800-690-0070

Remote Satellite Systems
Santa Rosa, CA 95401
707-545-8199

remote-i
Goleta, CA 93117
805-683-3738

Rental Motors Sports
Gorham, ME 04038
207-839-5522

Rental Works
Richmond, VA 23230
804-288-0018

Rental World
McAllen, TX 78501
956-630-5222

RentalMax
Wheaton, IL 60187
630-221-1133

Rent-a-PC
Atlanta, GA 30318
404-352-0900

Rent-a-PC
Culver City, CA 90232
310-237-5324

Rent-a-PC
Englewood Cliffs, NJ 07632
201-568-6555

Rent-a-PC
Plymouth Meeting, PA 19462
610-940-9500

Rent-a-PC
Pompano Beach, FL
954-979-8300

Rent-a-PC
Vienna, VA 22180
703-207-0550

Rent-a-PC
Watertown, MA 02472
617-926-2266

Rent-A-PC / All Service Computer
Rentals
Hauppauge, NY 11788-3609
631-273-8888

Rent-a-Tool Inc
Revere, MA 02151
781-289-3800

Rentex
Boston, MA 02210-1732
617-423-5567

Rentsys Recovery Services
College Station, TX 77845-4468
800-955-5171

Rentsys Recovery Services
Houston , TX 77040
800-955-5171

Rescue U Disaster Systems
Thousand Oaks, CA 91362
805-492-0393

RescueTech
Denver , CO 80260
303-380-1708

Resilience Corporation
Mountain View, CA 94043
888-297-8515

Responder Knowledge Base
Burke , VA 22015
703-641-3731

Response Biomedical Corp.
Burnaby, BC V5J 5J1
Canada
604-681-4101

ResponseWorks, Inc.
Lambertville, NJ 08530
609-397-9597

Restoration Alliance
Bellingham, WA 98229
877-693-0111

Restoration College
Ottawa, ON K1T 3E4
Canada
613-227-3141

Restoration Rental Equipment
Abilene, Tx 79605
325-692-1818

Restoration Specialists
Carle Place, NY 11514
800-432-6243

Restoration Specialists Inc.
Addison, TX 75001
214-637-2200

Restoration Specialists of Greater New York
Carleplace, NY 11514
631-587-3800

Restoration Technologies Inc
Aurora, IL 60504
630-851-1551

Restorx Northern Illinois
Freeport, IL 61032-9327
815-235-9606

RESTORX-BORDER STATES
Sidney, MT 59270
800-578-2113

Restotech Water & Fire Damage
Restoration
Long Beach, CA 90755
800-995-8988

Restronic
Frederick, MD 21701
301-682-9887

Resun Leasing
Dulles, VA 20166
703-661-6190

Resun Leasing
New Britain, CT 06051
800-692-1234

Resun Leasing Inc.
Dulles, VA 20166
866-772-2328

Retail Control Solutions Inc
Needham, MA 02494
781-444-7300

Retrofit Technologies
Milford, MA 01757
508-478-2222

Reverse 911
Indianapolis, IN 46254
800-247-2363

Rex Spencer Equipment Company
Belton, MO 64012
800-878-6078

Reynolds Bone & Griesbeck
Memphis, TN 38117
901-682-2431

RGL Forensic Accountants and
Consultants
Englewood, CO 80111
888-RGl-4-CPA

Rhode Island Emergency Management
Agency
Cranston, RI 02920
401-946-9996

Riddick Engineering Corp.
Little Rock, AR 72205
501-666-7300

Rimage
Edina, MN 55439
952-944-8144

Rimkus Consulting Group Inc.
Houston, TX 77046
713-621-3550

Risk & Ins. Mgmt. Society Annual Conference
New York, NY 10017
212-286-9292

Risk and Insurance Management Society(RIMS)
New York, NY 10017
212-286-9292

Risk Consultants Inc
Atlanta, GA 30349
770-964-1226

'Risk Management Magazine'
New York, NY 10017
212-286-9292

Risk, Reliability, and Safety Engineering
League City, TX 77573
281-334-4220

RiskCap
Denver, CO 80218
303-388-5688

RiskWatch Inc.
Annapolis, MD 21401
410-224-4773

Rite in the Rain, Division of J. L. Darling Corp.
Tacoma, WA 98424-1001
253-922-5000

Rittel Hill and Zimmerman Ins Svcs Inc
Columbus, OH 43220
614-457-7765

River Bend Business Continuity
Stamford, CT 06907
203-978-7444

RJ Cleaning and Restoration
Odenton , MD 21113
410-672-3104

RJS Landscaping
Warren, NJ 07059
908-917-9221

RKI Instruments, Inc.
Union City, CA 94587
800-754-5165

RL Construction.com
Hill City, SD 57745
605-574-9550

RMC Medical
Philadelphia, PA 19154-3201
215-824-4100

Roadmaster LLC
Goshen, IN 46514
574-537-0669

Roan Solutions, Inc.
Belmont, MA 02478
877-774-4647

Robinette Demolition Inc.
Oakbrook Terrace, IL 60181
630-833-7997

Robinson & Cole
Boston, MA 02108
617-557-5900

Robson Lapina
Lancaster, PA 17603
800-813-6736

Rochester Institute of Technology
Rochester, NY 14623-5603
585-475-4999

Rocky Mountain Poison & Drug Center
Denver, CO 80204
800-222-1222

Rolf Jensen & Assoc. Inc
Chicago, IL 60661
312-879-7200

Rollinger Engineering Inc
Houston, TX 77077-5727
281-558-5000

Ronsin Photocopy Micro-50
Walnut, CA 91789
909-598-0027

Ross Environmental Services Inc
Elyria, OH 44035
440-366-2000

Rothfuss Engineering
Jessup, MD 20794
301-725-6544

Rothstein Catalog on Disaster Recovery
Brookfield, CT 06804
203-740-7400

RP Rentals Inc
Ridgewood, NY 11385
718-456-7397

RSA Security
Bedford, MA 01730
781-687-7000

RSM McGladrey Inc.
Minneapolis, MN 55402
800-648-4030

Rudick Forensic Engineering
Youngstown, OH 44502
800-966-5392

Rudox Engine & Equipment Co.
Carlstadt, NJ 07072
201-438-0111

Russelectric Inc.
Hingham , MA 02043
781-749-6000

Ryder Communications Inc
Sparta, NJ 07871
877-RYDRCOM

S4Software
San Diego, CA 92111
858-560-8112

Safe Supervisor
Oroville, WA 98844
800-667-9300

Safecore Inc.
Medford, MA 02155
781-391-1700

SafeNet, Inc
Belcamp, MD 21017
410-931-7500

Safety & Environmental Management Planning, Inc.
Lafayette, LA 70503
337-981-5391

'Safety & Health Magazine'
Itasca, IL 60143-3201
630-285-1121

Safety & Risk Control Services Inc.
Metuchen, NJ 08840-1875
800-466-4025

Safety Express
Dorval, QB H9P 1G8
Canada
604-244-8005

Safety Express
Edmondton, AB T5S 1K9
Canada
780-486-4889

Safety Express
Mississauga, ON L5L 5Y5
Canada
905-608-0111

Safety Express
Richmond, BC V6V 1Y1
Canada
514-422-8886

Safety Storage Inc.
Hollister, CA 95023
831-637-5955

Safety Technology International Inc
Waterford, MI 48327-1209
800-888-4784

Safetyfile, Inc.
Excelsior, MN 55331
800-700-8025

SafetyHQ.com
Bow, NH 03304
603-226-7233

Safety-Kleen System Inc.
Plano, TX 75024
972-265-2000

Safeware
Landover, MD 20785
800-331-6707

Safeware The Insurance Agency Inc
Columbus, OH 43229
614-781-1492

SafeX
Westerville, OH 43081
614-890-0800

Safty Insurence
Boston, MA 02110
617-960-5700

Sage Business Associates, Inc.
Parker, CO 80134
303-841-4467

Sage Landscaping and Tree Service
Watchung , NJ 07069
908-668-5858

Sahara Chem-Dry
Las Vegas, NV 89102
702-242-0500

SAIC
San Diego, CA 92121
858-826-6000

Sako & Associates
Chicago, IL 60661
312-879-7230

SAMHSA's National Mental Health Information Center
Washington, DC 20015
800-789-2647

Samuelson True Value & Just Ask Rental
Craig, CO 81625
970-824-6683

San Antonio College
San Antonio, TX 78212
210-733-2187

San Antonio Emergency Mgmt
San Antonio, TX 78201-4505
210-335-0300

San Diego Office of Disaster Preparedness
San Diego, CA 92123
858-565-3490

Sarcom, Inc.
Lewis Center, OH 43035
800-326-3962

Sargeant Steam Clean
Huntsville, ON P1H 2M3
Canada
705-789-2289

Sarver TrueValue Just Ask Rental
Sarver, PA 16055
724-295-5131

Saskatchewan Emergency Planning
Regina, SK S4P 3V7
Canada
306-787-9563

Satellite Shelters Inc
Minneapalis, MN 55441
763-551-7219

SBP Consulting Services Inc
Toronto, ON M6J3C2
Canada
416-723-7953

'SC Magazine'
New York, NY 10001
646-638-6000

Scanlon Associates Inc .
Ottawa, ON K1S 2X8
Canada
1-613-730-9239

Schaefer Engineering
Mountlake Ter, WA 98043
425-775-5550

Schirmer Engineering Corp
Deerfield, IL 60015
847-272-8340

Schutt Restoration Services (SRS)
Thunder Bay, ON P7C 5H7
Canada
807-624-9080

Schwab Corp
Lafayette, IN 47905
765-447-9470

Science Applications International Corporation
McLean, VA 22102
703-676-6046

Science Applications Intl. Corp. (SAIC)
Oak Ridge, TN 37831
865-482-9031

Scivantage
New York, NY 10005
646-452-0050

Scott Community College
Bettendorf, IA 52722-6804
563-441-4001

Scott Construction
St. Louis Park, MN 55426
612-721-3311

SCP America
Rockdale, TX 76567
512-446-7988

SDN Global
Charlotte, NC 28241
704-587-4868

SEA Limited
Columbus, OH 43085
614-888-4160

SEA Ltd.
Atlanta, GA 30043
800-782-6851

Sean's ChemDry
Smyrna, TN 37167
615-890-8055

'SearchStorage.com Compliance Infoguide'
Needham, MA 02494
781-657-1000

Seattle Emergency Management
Seattle, WA 98121
206-233-5089

SECTOR, Inc.
New York, NY 10004
866-383-3315

Securac, Inc.
Calgary, AB T2P 3R7
Canada
403-225-0403

Secure-It Inc.
East Longmeadow, MA 01028
413-525-7039

SecureWorks
Atlanta, GA 30329
404-327-6339

Securify Inc.
Cupertino, CA 95014
650-812-9400

Securitas
Boston, MA 02128
617-568-8700

Securitas
Westlake Vlg, CA 91361
818-706-6800

Securitas Security Services USA Inc.
Houston, TX 77060
281-875-2237

Securitas Security Services USA Inc.
Indianapolis, IN 46240
317-569-1149

Securitas Security Services USA Inc.
Kennesaw, GA 30144
770-426-5262

Securitas Security Services USA Inc.
Orange, CA 92868
714-541-4277

Securitas Security Services USA Inc.
Parsippany, NJ 07054
973-397-2276

Securitas Security Services USA Inc.
Pittsburgh, PA 15220
412-919-0146

Security and Loss Prevention
St. Louis, MO 63146
800-545-2522

Security Center The
New Orleans, LA 70130
504-522-1254

Security Computer Sales
White Bear Lk, MN 55110
651-653-5200

Security Defense Systems Corp
Nutley, NJ 07110
973-235-0606

Security Industry Association
Alexandria, VA 22314
703-683-2075

'Security Magazine'
Bensenville, IL 60106
630-616-0200

'Security Management Magazine'
Alexandria, VA 22314
703-518-1455

SEH Inc.
Madison, WI 53719
608-274-2020

Select Sales Inc
Westwood, MA 02090
781-326-8600

Selectron, Inc.
Portland, OR 97224
503-639-9988

Seltser & Goldsteen Public Adjusters Inc.
Beverly, MA 01915
978-921-2926

SEM3 Solutions
Raynham, MA 02767
508-717-7208

Send Word Now
New York, NY 10001
800-388-4796

Sentinel Data Centers
Needham, MA 02494
781-444-4348

SENTRY
Toronto, ON L3R 9W6
Canada
416-270-5574

Sentryx
Mississauga, ON L5N 7Z5
Canada
905-565-6013

Serafini Serafini Darling and Correnti
Salem, MA 01970
978-744-0212

SERENA Software
San Mateo, CA 94403
650-522-6600

ServePath
San Francisco, CA 94105
866-321-PATH

Server Technology Inc
Reno, NV 89521
408-988-0142

Service Management Group LLC
Bridgeport, CT 06608
203-333-1707

Service Master
Memphis, TN 38125
901-597-7500

Service Master By Artec
Clifton Heights, PA 19018
610-626-9002

Service Master of Fay-West
Connellsville, PA 15425
724-628-2122

Service Master of Greater Tacoma /
Bremerton
Tacoma, WA 98409
800-339-5720

Service Master of Midland/Orilla
Midland, Ont L4R4P4
Canada
705-527-5722

Service Team of Professionals
Ramsey, MN 55303
763-753-8080

ServiceMaster
Chambusburg, PA 17201
717-267-2223

Servicemaster
Kennewick, WA 99336
509-582-0166

ServiceMaster - At Your Service
Lima, OH 45807
419-339-0871

ServiceMaster - Disaster Associates
Stoneham, MA 02180
781-438-6033

ServiceMaster Absolute Water and Fire
Damage Serv.
Lemon Grove, CA 91945-1438
619-287-7070

ServiceMaster Advanced Cleaning
Theodore, AL 36582
251-653-9333

ServiceMaster Advanced Restorations
Southlake, TX 76092
817-481-0664

ServiceMaster Advantage
Delphi, IN 46923
765-564-1099

ServiceMaster Advantage
Tulsa, OK 74145
918-250-7040

ServiceMaster Advantage Restoration &
Cleaning
Houston, TX 77289
281-332-3900

ServiceMaster Albino Services
Waterbury, CT 06708
203-753-0666

ServiceMaster Allcare Restoration
San Jose, CA 95126
408-885-0280

ServiceMaster Anytime
Redlands, CA 92373
909-796-4939

ServiceMaster At The Valley
Calabasas, CA 91302
818-591-1137

ServiceMaster by Anderson
Louisville, KY 40299
502-261-1755

ServiceMaster by Armstrong
Wheaton, IL 60189
630-562-0600

ServiceMaster by Arrigo Restoration
Pueblo, CO 81007
719-542-2000

ServiceMaster by Avenue of the Saints
Cedar Rapids, IA 52404
319-365-9265

ServiceMaster By Chuck Wallace
Brookhaven, MS 39603
601-835-1000

ServiceMaster by Corbett
Akron, OH 44333
330-864-7300

ServiceMaster by Cornerstone
Cordova, TN 38018
901-624-9200

ServiceMaster by Cypress Bend
Allgood, TN 38506
931-372-8480

ServiceMaster By Ed Smith
Mesa, AZ 85201
480-834-5248

ServiceMaster by Fentz
Greenfield, IN 46140
317-894-2777

ServiceMaster by FloorServe
Memphis, TN 38141
901-363-1331

ServiceMaster by Frintz
Kenosha, WI 53141
262-942-9246

ServiceMaster by Gaudet
Woburn, MA 01801-4325
781-932-1171

ServiceMaster by Holobinko
Bellefonte, PA 16823
814-231-0812

ServiceMaster by Jeff
Tulsa, OK 74145
918-294-8590

ServiceMaster by J-L
Everett, WA 98213
425-353-5586

ServiceMaster by Master and Sons
Santa Clarita, CA 91351
661-299-9090

Servicemaster by Professional Clean
College Point, NY 11356
718-762-5566

ServiceMaster by Reid
Ridgeland, MS 39157
601-853-1615

ServiceMaster by Samburg
Warren, OR 97053
503-366-5390

ServiceMaster by Singer
Baltimaore, MD 21224
410-563-2600

ServiceMaster by TA Russell
Glendora, CA 91741
626-963-4048

ServiceMaster by Towne
Elkhart, IN 46516
574-293-5200

ServiceMaster Chicago Hub
Chicago, IL 60618
800-843-8415

ServiceMaster Clean
Deep River, CT 06417
860-388-0440

ServiceMaster Clean
Memphis, TN 38125
800-633-5703

ServiceMaster Clean
Memphis, TN 38175
800-RESPOND

ServiceMaster Clean
Whittier, CA 90605
562-945-2745

ServiceMaster Clean 24 Hour
Tampa, FL 33610
813-623-6111

ServiceMaster Clean At Irvine
Irvine, CA 92618
949-586-5919

ServiceMaster Clean by Stechyn and Son
Spring Hill, TN 37174
931-840-0065

ServiceMaster Clean In A Wink
Wichita, KS 67219
620-221-1386

ServiceMaster Clean in a Wink - Derby
Wichita, KS 67219
316-788-9654

ServiceMaster Clean Quality Restoration
New Braunfels, TX 78131
830-625-1625

ServiceMaster Cleaning & Restoration
Idaho Falls, ID 83403
208-524-8262

ServiceMaster Cleaning & Restoration
Marysville, CA 95901
530-741-8178

ServiceMaster Cleaning & Restoration
Springtown, PA 18081
610-346-8545

ServiceMaster Cleaning and Restoration
Merced , CA 95344
209-726-9182

ServiceMaster Cleaning Service of Brown Co.
New Ulm, MN 56073
507-354-4233

ServiceMaster Cleaning Services
Skokie, IL 60076
847-329-0044

ServiceMaster CleanWorks, LLC
St. Robert, MO 65584
866-336-5994

ServiceMaster Commercial & Residential
South Yarmouth, MA
800-479-3999

ServiceMaster Complete Restoration
Checktowaga, NY 14211
716-893-9797

ServiceMaster Disaster Restoration and Cleaning
Hot Springs, AR 71913
501-525-3125

ServiceMaster Disaster Restoration Services
Concord, CA 94520
800-480-TIDY

ServiceMaster Disaster Restoration Services
Redwood City, CA 94063
650-299-9080

ServiceMaster Disaster Services
Dothan, AL 36301
334-712-1118

ServiceMaster Disaster Services
Villa Park, IL 60181-1249
630-833-0888

ServiceMaster Eastern Sierra
Mammoth Lake, CA 93546
760-924-2097

ServiceMaster Fire & Water Restoration Inc.
Deltona, FL 32738
386-574-4333

ServiceMaster H.K.H.
Oak Park, IL 60302
708-524-7915

ServiceMaster Home & Office
Alpena, MI 49707
989-358-2600

ServiceMaster Lakeshore
Ferrysburg, MI 49409
616-842-3131

ServiceMaster Napa - Vallejo - Benicia
American Canyon, CA 94503
707-255-5550

ServiceMaster of Aberdeen
Aberdeen, SD 57402
800-700-4528

ServiceMaster of Albuquerque /West Mesa
Albuquerque, NM 87107
505-880-1233

ServiceMaster of Allentown
Emmaus, PA 18049-2098
610-965-6058

ServiceMaster of Amelia Island
Fernandina Beach, FL 32034
904-277-2998

ServiceMaster of Big Rapids West
Big Rapids, MI 49346
231-823-8300

ServiceMaster of Bowling Green
Bowling Green, KY 42103-7170
270-782-8500

ServiceMaster of Brandywine Valley
Wilmington, DE 19804
302-652-4151

ServiceMaster Of Bristol County
Middletown, RI 02842
401-274-9500

Servicemaster of Canada
Mississauga, ON L4W 2T7
Canada
905-670-0000

ServiceMaster of Carroll & Coos County
Center Conway, NH 03813
603-447-5031

ServiceMaster of Chantilly
Chantilly, VA 20151
703-968-0505

ServiceMaster of Chaska/Shakopee
Chaska, MN 55318
952-445-5233

ServiceMaster of Chattanooga
Chattanooga, TN 37404
423-624-0937

ServiceMaster of Cherry Hill
Cherry Hill, NJ 08003
856-751-1577

ServiceMaster of Coachella Valley
Palm Desert, CA 92260
760-568-1227

ServiceMaster of Decatur
Doraville, GA 30340
770-368-1866

ServiceMaster of Effingham
Effingham, IL 62401
217-342-3206

ServiceMaster of Fairfield / Vacaville
Fairfield, CA 94533
707-428-1608

ServiceMaster of Forest Lake
St. Paul, MN 55106
651-464-1214

Servicemaster of FT. Collins
FT. Collins, CO 80524
970-484-0588

ServiceMaster of Gateway
Portland, OR 97206
503-760-2461

ServiceMaster of Germantown
Collierville, TN 38017
901-854-6225

ServiceMaster of Grand Traverse Area
Traverse City, MI 49684
231-943-9191

ServiceMaster of Hendersonville
Hendersonville, NC 28792
828-697-9831

ServiceMaster of Ingham County
Mason, MI 48854
517-676-1626

ServiceMaster of Kalamazoo
Kalamazoo, MI 49006
800-530-7747

ServiceMaster of Kingston
Kingston , NY 12401
845-338-4821

ServiceMaster of Lafayette
Lafayette, LA 70507
337-234-1289

ServiceMaster of LaGrande
LaGrande, OR 97850
541-962-2639

ServiceMaster of Lake Oswego
Portland, OR 97224
503-636-8720

ServiceMaster of Martinsburg
Martinsburg, WV 25401
304-262-2600

ServiceMaster of Milwaukee
Milwaukee, WI 53212
414-962-9910

ServiceMaster of Osseo / Maple Grove
Maple Grove, MN 55369
763-424-4100

ServiceMaster of Ottawa
Ottawa, ON K1G 0Z5
Canada
613-244-1997

Servicemaster of Red Deer
Red Deer, AB T4N 1X6
Canada
403-341-6072

ServiceMaster of Rochester
Rochester, MN 55903
507-282-5747

ServiceMaster of Rochester
Rochester, NY 14618
585-473-3290

ServiceMaster of Santa Fe
Santa Fe, NM 87507
505-473-7789

ServiceMaster of Sarpy County
Bellevue, NE 68123
402-293-1625

ServiceMaster of Somerset
Somerset, PA 15501
814-445-1380

ServiceMaster of Sooland
South Sioux City, NE 68776
402-494-3188

ServiceMaster of St. George and Cedar
City
Washington, UT 84780
435-628-9866

ServiceMaster of Tehachapi
Tehachpi, CA 93561
661-822-9408

ServiceMaster of the Foothills
Grass Valley, CA 95949
530-273-1957

ServiceMaster of the Lake
Linn Creek, MO 65052
573-365-4688

ServiceMaster of the Lakes Area
Alexandna, MN 56308
320-763-5551

ServiceMaster of West Rochester, NY
Rochester, NY 14612
585-227-9900

ServiceMaster Professional Cleaning
Cropwell, AL 35054
205-525-4663

ServiceMaster Professional Cleaning
Miami, FL 33126-2976
305-264-8999

ServiceMaster Professional Cleaning
Yakima, WA 98909
509-452-8906

ServiceMaster Professional Cleaning
Services
Nashua, NH 03060
603-883-4800

ServiceMaster Professional Restoration
Littleton, CO 80125
720-981-8809

ServiceMaster Professional Services
Austin, TX 78720
512-249-8710

ServiceMaster Professional Services
Marble Falls, TX 78654
830-693-3869

ServiceMaster Quality Clean
Elkton, MD 21921
410-392-4900

ServiceMaster Quality Restoration
Las Cruces, NM 88005
505-541-0400

ServiceMaster Quality Restoration
McAllen, TX 78502-4514
956-686-2907

ServiceMaster Quality Services
Cleves, OH 45002
513-353-9238

ServiceMaster Quality Services
Houma, LA 70361-0766
985-872-1029

ServiceMaster Remediation
Pompano Beach, FL 33069
954-969-5906

ServiceMASTER Restoration & Clean
Guntersville, AL 35976
256-582-7778

ServiceMaster Restoration & Cleaning
Baraboo, WI 53913
608-253-2905

ServiceMaster Restoration & Cleaning
Services
Price, UT 84501
435-637-9165

ServiceMaster Restoration by Carroll
Houston, TX 77061
713-667-5052

ServiceMaster Restoration Services
Conyers, GA 30013
770-483-4414

ServiceMaster Restoration Services
Salem, VA 24153
540-375-9411

ServiceMaster Services
Pensacola, FL 32504
850-479-6065

ServiceMaster Services Inc.
Canton, MA 02021
800-734-3315

ServiceMaster Sierras
Sonora, CA 95370
209-532-1700

ServiceMaster South Metro
Farmington, MN 55024
651-463-7700

ServiceMaster SouthWest
Sugar Land, TX 77478
281-242-5777

ServiceMaster Superior Restoration &
Cleaning
McKinney, TX 75070
972-881-2345

ServiceMaster To The Rescue
Vineland, NJ 08362
856-692-4269

ServiceMaster Total Restoration
Temecula, CA 92590
800-486-8717

ServiceMaster Tri-County
New Albany, IN 47150
812-944-5094

ServiceMaster West
Clive, IA 50325
515-274-9109

ServiceMasterClean of Kanawha Valley
Charleston, WV 25312
304-345-9198

Services Conseils
Montreal, PQ H1P 3H3
Canada
514-955-0213

Servpro
Gallatin, TN 37066
615-451-0600

Servpro
Garland, TX 75041
214-343-3973

Servpro
Manassas, VA 20111
703-739-2800

Servpro
Wilmington, DE 19801
302-652-1122

ServPro of El Paso East
El Paso, Tx 79928
915-852-0993

Servpro of North Palm Beach
West Palm Beach, FL 33403
561-881-8784

Servpro of Seal Beach/Cypress/Los
Alamitos
Los Alamitos, CA 90720
562-431-9400

SES America
McLean, VA 22102
703-610-1000

Settipane Richard Public Insurance
Adjusters
Boston, MA 02114
617-523-3456

shaheengagan.com
arlington, VA 22204
703-920-2055

Shaw Environmental
Findlay, OH 45839
800-537-9540

Shaw Environmental & Infrastructure Inc.
Monroeville, PA 15146
412-372-7701

Shaw Environmental Inc.
Hopkinton, MA 01748
508-435-9561

Shaw Group
Baton Rouge, LA 70809
225-932-2500

Shenandoah University
Winchester, VA 22601
540-665-4584

Short Elliott Hendrickson, Inc.
Minneapolis, MN 55403-1515
612-758-6700

Siegel Rich Division-Rothstein, Kass and
Company, D.C.
New York , NY 10019
212-997-0500

Sierra Paul J. Construction Inc
Tampa, FL 33603
800-409-5897

Sigma Business Solutions Inc.
Toronto, ON M5J 1R7
Canada
416-594-1991

Signal Mountain Networks, Inc.
Alpharetta, GA 30022
678-867-0793 x102

SilverSEAL Corporation
New York, NY 10038
212-732-1897

Simmons Enivronmental Svcs Inc
Salisbury, MA 01952
978-463-6669

Simpler Life Emergency Provisions
Redlands, CA 92373
909-798-8108

SimplexGrinnell
Westminster, MA 01441
978-731-2500

Sims City Cleaners Inc
Houston, TX 77096
713-721-3100

Sioux Steam Cleaner Corp
Beresford, SD 57004
605-763-2776

Skill Clean
Pittsburg, CA 94565
925-432-4393

Skywatch Weather Center
Bridgeville, PA 15017-1949
412-221-6000

Slippery Rock University
Slippery Rock, PA 16057
412-738-2260

SmartPower Systems
Houston, TX 77043
800-882-8285

Smith & Sons Disaster Kleenup, Inc.
Arroyo Grand, CA 93421
805-481-2955

SML Industries Inc.
Melrose Park, IL 60160
800-730-3927

Smoke Services
Belleville, IL 62221
618-234-9696

Smolian Sound Restoration Studios
Frederick, MD 21701-3022
301-694-5134

Society for Information Management
Chicago, IL 60611-4267
312-527-6734

Society for Risk Analysis
McLean, VA 22101
703-790-1745

Society of Fire Protection Engineers
Bethesda, MD 20814
301-718-2910

Society of Risk Management Consultants
Milwaukee, WI 53203
800-765-7762

SoftRisk Technologies Inc
St. Simons Island, GA 31522
912-634-1700

Softsystems Inc
Fort Worth, TX 76102
817-877-5070

Software Security Solutions
Lakewood, CO 80214
303-232-9070

Sola Communications LLC
SCOTT, LA 70583
337-232-7039

SOLAR INC
Palm City, FL 34990
772-286-9461

Solar Systems Inc & Peripherals
Preston, WA 98050
800-253-5764

SOLO Wilderness & Emergency
Medicine
Conway, NH 03818-3150
603-447-6711

Sommer and Sons Mobile Leasing Inc
Elyria, OH 44035
800-826-5654

Sonoma University
Rohnert Park, CA 94928-3609
415-265-1662

Sorbent Products Company, Inc.
Somerset, NJ 08873
800-333-7672

SOS Technologies
Concord, CA 94520
925-691-9335

Source Graphics
Anaheim, CA 92807
714-939-0114

Source Systems Inc
Twinsburg, OH 44087
330-963-1001

South Carolina Emergency Management
Agency
West Columbia, SC 29172
803-737-8500

South Dakota Division of Emergency
Management
Pierre, SD 57501
605-773-3231

Southern California Earthquake Center
Los Angeles, CA 90089
213-740-5843

Southwestern College
Wichita, KS 67207
316-684-5335

Southwestern Restoration, Inc.
Houston, TX 77043
713-932-1177

Special Response Corp.
Hunt Valley, MD 21030
410-494-1900

Specialized Products Company
Southlake, TX 76092
817-329-6647

Specialized Services
Little Chute, WI 54140
920-788-1738

Specialty Risk Services
Hartford, CT 06103
860-520-2599

Specs Bros LLC
Ridgefield Park, NJ 07660
201-440-6589

Spectrum Computer Inc
Stanton, CA 90680
714-799-7345

Spectrum Restoration Service
Amora, IL 60501
630-898-3200

Spectrum Restoration Services
Sugar Grove, IL 60554
630-557-2621

Speed Shore Corp
Houston, TX 77047
713-943-0750

Spider, a division of SafeWorks, LLC
Seattle, WA 98188
877-774-3370

Spiegel Certified Restoration
Montclair, CA 91763
909-628-8988

Spill Control Association of America
Franklin, MI 48025
248-851-1936

Spot Coolers (nationwide service)
Boca Raton, FL 33432
800-367-8675

Sprague Magnetics Inc
Sylmar, CA 91342
818-364-1800

Sprung Instant Structures
Calgary, AB T2R 0B7
Canada
403-245-3371

Sprung Instant Structures
West Jordan, UT 84088
801-280-1555

Spybusters.com
Oldwick, NJ 08858-0668
908-832-7900

SRA International Inc.
Fairfax, VA 22033
703-803-1500

St Edward's University
Austin, TX 78704-9841
512-428-1063

St. Croix Sensory Inc.
Lake Elmo, MN 55042
800-879-9231

St. Louis Electronics Inc
Maryland Heights, MD 63043
314-615-3131

St. Petersburg College
St. Petersburg, FL 33733-3489
727-341-4479

Staco Energy Products
Dayton, OH 45403-1391
937-253-1191

Stampede Technologies Inc
Dayton, OH 45458
937-291-5035

Stanley Steemer
Atlanta, GA 30340
770-451-3035

Stanley Steemer International, Inc.
Dublin, OH 43016
800-783-3637

Steam/Ree-Construction
Hailey, ID 83333
800-222-4068

Steamatic Inc. International
Headquarters
Fort Worth, TX 76107
817-332-1575

Steamco
Wakefield, MA 01880
781-391-4133

Steamway/Disaster Restorations
Albany, OR 97321
541-928-7267

Steele's Hardware
Tannersville, PA 18372
570-629-3406

Stefek Restoration Services Inc.
Pflugerville, TX 78660
512-837-5774

Stephen R. Figlin & Associates Inc.
Philadelphia, PA 19152
215-342-8514

Stephens Associates, Inc
Red Bank, NJ 07701
732-842-1903

STERIS Corporation
Mentor, OH 44060
440-354-2600

Sterling Commerce
Dublin, OH 43016
614-793-7000

Stevenson & Associates
Albuquerque, NM 87109
505-822-8510

Stewart & Stevenson
Dallas, TX 75212
866-782-8660

Stewart & Stevenson Services
Harvey, LA 70058
504-347-4326

Stockwood W.B. Inc
Woburn, MA 01801
781-935-8181

StoneHenge Partners, Inc.
Tulsa, OK 74103
888-972-1999

'Storage Magazine'
Needham, MA 02494
781-657-1000

Storage Soutions Group
Omaha, NE 68102
888-884-7967

StorageTek
Louisville, CO 80028
303-673-5151

StormNow
Bremen, IN 46506
269-983-6271

Strand Earthquake Consultants
Los Angeles, CA 90025-3400
310-473-2316

Strategic Teaching Associates, Inc.
Liverpool, NY 13090
315-622-5924

Strategic Technology Group
Milford, MA 01757
508-473-4949

Stratford Solutions
Cleveland Hts., OH 44118
216-932-5690

Streamlight, Inc.
Eagleville, PA 19403
800-523-7488

Streem Communications
Loves Park, IL 61111
800-325-7732

Strohl Systems
Kng of Prussia, PA 19406
610-768-4120

Strongsville Pyschological Services
Strongsville, OH 44136
440-234-9955

Structured Technical Services, LLC
Beaverton, OR 97005-1393
503-449-7703

STS Business Services Inc
Hartford, CT 06106
800-541-4964

COMPANY
LISTINGS
ALPHABETICALLY

Subterranean Data Service Company
Vancouver, WA 98684
360-604-0411

Subterranean Data Service Company, LLC
Lewiston, ID 83501
208-746-2188

Suburban Sanitation Service, Inc.
Canton, CT 06019
860-673-3078

Sullivan's Cleaning and Restoration
Service
Green Bay, WI 54304-5666
920-337-1986

Sulmac Inc
Holyoke, MA 01040
413-533-5347

Summers Mailing Company
Dallas, TX 75236
972-296-9871

Sun Rental Center
Colville, WA 99114
509-684-1522

Sun Valley Technical Repair Inc.
Morgan Hill, CA 95037
408-779-4115

Sunbelt Rentals
Charlotte, NC 28217
866—786-2358

Sunbelt Scaffolding and Supply, Inc.
Orlando, Fl 32804
407-244-5556

Sunbelt Transformer Inc
Temple, TX 76504
800-433-3128

SunGard Availability Services
Wayne, PA 19087
800-468-7483

SUNPRO
North Canton, OH 44720
330-452-0837

Sunrise Cleaning
East Lansing, MI 48823
517-351-4200

Sunrise Energy Systems Inc.
Fort Wayne, IN 46808
260-482-1764

Sunstate Equipment Co.
Phoenix, AZ 85034-2106
888-456-4560

SunWize Technologies Inc
Kingston, NY 12401
800-817-6527

SUNY at Stony Brook
Stony Brook, NY 11794-8200
631-444-6158

SUNY Maritime College
Bronx, NY 10465
718-409-7341

SUNY Ulster County Community College
Stone Ridge, NY 12484
800-724-0833

Superior Electric
Bristol, CT 06010
860-582-9561

Superior Environmental Corp
Marne, MI 49435
616-677-5255

SurfControl
Westborough, MA 01581
831-440-2500

Surfside Chem-Dry
Oxnard, CA 93030
805-485-9595

Surviving the Storm: Guide to Hurricane
Preparation
Washington, DC 20472
202-566-1600

Survivor Depot Inc.
Fort Lauderdale, FL 33355
954-382-3323

Survivor Industries Inc
Camarillo, CA 93012-8508
805-498-6062

Susan L. Duhl Art Conservation
Bala Cynwyd, PA 19004
610-667-0714

Sweet Claims Company
New York, NY 10013
212-226-4500

Sweinhart Electric Co. Inc
Buena Park, CA 90621
714-521-9100

Swerling Milton & Winnick Public
Adjusters Inc.
Wellesley Hls, MA 02481
781-416-1000

Swett & Crawford Group
Woodland Hls, CA 91367
818-593-2008

SYMANTEC Corp
Cupertino, CA 95014
408-253-9600

Symco
Suwanee, GA 30024
770-451-8002

Symitar Systems Inc
San Diego, CA 92108
619-542-6700

Syncsort Inc.
Woodcliff Lk, NJ 07677
201-930-9700

Synergistic Online Solutions
Waterford, MI 48327
248-666-4590

Sysgen Data Marketing Ltd
Melville, NY 11747
631-491-1100

System Engineering & Laboratories
Tyler, TX 75707-5333
903-566-1980

System ID Warehouse
Plano, TX 75074
972-516-1100

Systems Audit Group, The
Newton, MA 02459-1434
617-332-3946

Systems Documentation, Inc (SDI)
South Plainfield, NJ 07080
908-754-9500

Systems/Software Engineering
Wayne, PA 19087
610-341-9017

SYTEX Inc
Vienna, VA 22182
703-893-9095

T.E.Brennan Co.
Milwaukee, WI 53202
414-271-2232

Taction
Waldoboro, ME 04572
207-832-0800

Tactron Inc
Sherwood, OR 97140
800-424-8228

Tailored Technologies Co
New York, NY 10017
212-503-6300

Talk-A-Phone Co.
Chicago, IL 60625
773-539-1100

Tally Systems Corp
Hanover, NH 03755
603-643-1300

TallyGenicom
Chantilly, VA 20151
800-436-4266

TAMP Computer Systems Inc.
Merrick, NY 11566-2611
516-623-2038

Taylor Rental
Nashua, NH 03060
603-888-1670

Taylor Rental
Vestal, NY 13850
607-729-7156

Taylor Rental
Washington, NJ 07887
908-689-4666

Taylor Rental
Webster, NY 14580
585-872-2770

Taylor Rental
Whitesboro, NY 13492
315-736-3232

Taylor Rental / Party Plus
Garland, TX 75040
972-530-6334

Taylor Rental Center
Farmington, NH 03835
603-332-0911

Taylor Rental, Sales & Service
Beaver Dam, WI 53916
920-887-7142

Taylor Risk Consulting
Addison, TX 75001
972-447-2055

TCI Inc.
Hudson, NY 12534
518-828-9997

TCI Inc.
Kirkland Lake, ON P2N 3J5
Canada
705-567-9997

TCI Inc.
Pell City, AL 35125
205-338-9997

TDG, Inc
Mays Landing, NJ 08330
609-476-2055

TEAM-1 Emergency Services
Hamilton Ontario, ON L8W 3P2
Canada
905-383-5550

TeamQuest Corporation
Clear Lake, IA 50428
641-357-2700

TecAccess
Rockville, VA 23146
804-749-8646

Tech Environmental
Waltham, MA 02451
781-718-9305

TechAssist Inc
Palm Harbor, FL 34684
727-547-0499

Techfusion
Cambridge, MA 02138
617-491-1001

TechGuard Security
Chesterfield, MO 63005
636-519-4848

Technical Restoration Services Inc
Fort Lauderdale, FL 33309
954-351-0301

Technology Law Bulletin
Boston, MA 02109
617-350-6800

Technology Today, Inc.
Newton, NH 03858
603-382-8116

Ted's Rental & Sales Inc.
Durango, CO 81303
970-247-2930

Tekelec
Calabasas, CA 91302
800-835-3532

Telax Voice Solutions
Toronto, ON M9C1A3
Canada
416-207-9936

Telecom Source, Inc.
Lexington, KY 40509
800-770-6183

TELEHOUSE America
Staten Island, NY 10311
718-355-2572

Telesat Canada
Ottawa, ON K1B 5P4
Canada
613-748-0123

Tele-Serve
Eau Claire, WI 54701
800-428-8159

Teletrix
Pittsburgh, PA 15239
412-798-3636

Teloquent Communications Corporation
Billerica, MA 01821
800-468-6434

Teltone Corporation
Bothell, WA 98041
800-426-3926

TEL-US Message Center
Beverly Hills, CA 90212
310-552-6000

Temp-Air
Burnsville, MN 55337
952-707-5050

Temporary Housing Directory
Plano, TX 75093
800-817-3220

Temporary Perimeter Systems
Lakeville, MN 55044
952-469-5101

TEMTEC Inc (TEMPbadge)
Branford, CT 06405-0823
845-368-4040

Ten United
Columbus, OH 43215
614-221-7667

Tennessee Emergency Management Agency
Nashville , TN 37204-1502
615-741-9303

Terra Restoration/Steamatic Hamilton
Hamilton, ON L8W 2Y6
Canada
905-387-0662

Terracon Environmental Inc
Lenexa, KS 66219
800-593-7777

Terrorist Incident Response Association
Marietta, GA 30060
678-640-9743

TESSCO Technolgies Incorporated
Hunt Valley , MD 21031
410-229-1000

Tetra Tech Inc
Pasadena, CA 91107
626-351-4664

Texas A&M Univ.
College Station, TX 77843-3137
979-862-3969

Texas Division of Emergency Management
Austin, TX 78773-0001
512-424-2138

Texas Severe Storm Association
Arlington, TX 76012

Texas Tech University Institute for Disaster Resea
Lubbock, TX 79409-1023
806-742-3476

TFR Enterprises, Inc.
Leander, TX 78641
512-260-3322

The Adtran Store
Sparta, NJ 07871-3427
973-940-7351

The American Civil Defense Assn. (TACDA)
Starke, FL 32091-1057
904-964-5397

The ArmaKleen Company
Princeton, NJ 08543
800-332-5424

The BIC Alliance
Baton Rouge, LA 70817
800-460-4242

The Canadian Forces Disaster Assistance Response Team (DART)
Ottawa, ON K1A 0K2
Canada
613-995-2534

The Carpet Market
Stuart, FL 34994
772-692-9970

The Center for Biosecurity of UPMC
Baltimore, MD 21202
443-573-3304

The Center for Continuity Leadership
Edmonds, WA 98020
425-210-9900

The Clothes Doctor
Foothill Rnch, CA 92610
949-206-1557

The Deatherage Companies
Broken Arrow, OK 74012-9339
918-355-2344

The Disaster Recovery Handbook
800-714-6395

The Fire Works Restoration Co./
1-800BOARDUP
St. Louis, MO 63126
314-961-3473

The Gardner Stern Company
Chicago, IL 60608
312-733-0401

The Gimbal Group, Inc.
Arlington, VA 22201
703-351-5054

The Greenspan Co.
South San Fran, CA 94080
650-583-4300

The Hertz Corp.
Park Ridge, NJ 07656
201-307-2000

THE HOWE PARTNERSHIP
Toronto, ON M4T 2T5
Canada
416-721-1053

The Infrastructure Security Partnership
(TISP)
Reston, VA 20191
703-295-6231

The Institute of Terrorism Research and
Response
Philadelphia, PA 19111
866-778-1871

The Jackson Group
Indianapolis, IN 46203
317-781-4600

The John A. Blume Earthquake
Engineering Center
Stanford , CA 94305-4020
650-723-4150

The Keystone Group
Niwot, CO 80544
888-652-6164

'The Law and Procedure of Insurance
Appraisal'
New York, NY 10017
888-791-7781

The Mail Room Inc.
Colorado Spgs, CO 80904
719-636-1303

The MARCOM Group, Ltd.
Boothwyn, PA 19061
800-654-2448

The National Burglar & Fire Alarm
Association
Silver Spring, MD 20910
301-585-1855

The National Environmental Services
Center
Morgantown, WV 26506
800-624-8301

The National Environmental, Safety &
Health Training Association - NESHTA
Phoenix, AZ 85016
602-956-6099

The National Tsunami Hazard
Mitigation Program
Honolulu, HI 96813
808-532-6416

The New Pig Corp
Tipton, PA 16684
800-468-4647

The Newman Group
Dexter, MI 48130
734-426-3200

The Nutheme Company
Elk Grove Village, IL 60007
847-952-1870

The Officers Group
Beverly Hills, CA 90210
310-470-6802

The Pacific Security Expo
510-464-7968

The Paragon Group
Webster , TX 77598
281-218-6373

The Penta Network
New York, NY 10005-3101
212-804-5702

The Poison Control Center
Philadelphia, PA 19104
800-222-1222

The Price-Hollingsworth Company
Lincroft, NJ 07738
732-530-9863

The Redfern Group
Houston, TX 77014
281-866-9451

The Revere Group
Chicago, IL 60610
888-473-8373

The Risk Management Association
Philadelphia, PA 19103
215-446-4000

The Rosco Group - Document
Restoration Inc.
Dorval, QC H9P 1C6
Canada
514-931-7789

The Salvage Group
St. Clair Shores, MI 48080
800-524-7246

The Sandbagger Corp.
Wauconda, IL 60084
815-363-1400

The SANS Institute
Bethesda, MD 20814
301-654-7267

The Steele Foundation
San Francisco, CA 94111
415-354-3846

The Systems Audit Group Inc.
Newton, MA 02459-1434
617-332-3496

The Tree Mann Inc.
La Porte, IN 46350
219-362-3988

The UCLA Center for Public Health and
Disaster Relief
Los Angeles, CA 90024
310-794-0864

The USA Lamp & Ballast
Milton, NY 12547
718-328-4667

The Winsted Corporation
Minneapolis, MN 55438
800-447-2257

Therml Abatement, Inc.
Andalusia, AL 36420
877-718-5837

Thermo Electron Corporation
San Jose, CA 95134
408-965-6022

Thomas Edison State College
Trenton, NJ 08608-1176
888-442-8372

Thompson Building Associates, Inc
Columbus, OH 43232
614-863-9650

Three Rivers Contingency Planning
Association
Pittsburgh, PA 15222-2722
412-762-2614

Thunder Restoration, Inc.
Minneapolis, MN 55427
800-374-8810

Thunderbird Catastrophe Services Inc
Alta Loma, CA 91701
800-897-6532

Tidy Coast Containers, Inc.
Hobe Sound, FL 33475
772-545-4000

TIF Data Recovery Service Specialist
Chatsworth, CA 91311
805-526-1555

Tighe & Bond
Westfield, MA 01085
413-562-1600

Titan #1,LLC
Moses Lake, WA 98837
509-762-1332

Tool and Equipment Service Solutions LLC
Hamden, CT 06514
203-248-7553

Topio, Inc.
Santa Clara, CA 95054
408-350-9800

TOPP Potable Air
Aston, PA 19014
800-892-8677

Toshiba International Corp
Houston, TX 77041
800-231-1412

Total Concept Sales
Glendale, CA 91202
818-547-9476

Total Facility Management Show
Tinton Falls, NJ 07724
800-524-0337

Total Restoration Contracting
Collegeville, PA 19426
800-734-4100

Totally Connected Security Ltd.
Vancouver, BC V5X 4K4
Canada
604-432-7828

Touchstone Software Corp
Andover, MA 01845
800-531-0450

Touro University International
Cypress, CA 90630
714-226-9840

Tower Solutions
Pine City, MN 55063
480-315-8830

TRA, Inc.
Philadelphia, PA 19103
215-546-9110

Tracewell
Cuba, NY 14727
585-968-2400

Trackis
Katy, TX 77450
888-693-8426

Tradewinds Power Corp.
Miami, FL 33166
305-592-9745

Training Manual: Mental Health/Human Serv Workers
Washington, DC 20015
800-789-2647

Trauma Pages, Post Traumatic Stress Disorder
Eugene, OR 97405
541-686-2598

Trauma Reduction Inc.
Lutz, FL 33558
813 335 1143

TRC
Oklahoma City, OK 73135
405-736-1990

Tree Care by Stan Hunt, Inc
Queensbury , NY 12804
518-793-0804

Tree Care Industry Association
Manchester, NH 03031
603-314-5380

Tree Care Of New York, LLC
Lancaster, NY 14086
716-681-1414

Treescaps Inc.
Gastonia, NC 28052
704-867-4100

Trefler & Sons Antique/Fine Art Restoration
Newton, MA 02464
617-965-3388

Trevco
Escondido, CA 92029
760-466-1060

Triangle Resource Group
Raleigh, NC 27609
919-841-0175

TriAxis Inc.
Auburn, MA 01501
508-721-9691

Trico Equipment
Vineland, NJ 08360
800-468-7426

TriCounties CRDN
Santa Barbra, CA 93101
805-962-CRDN

TriData Corporation
Arlington, VA 22209-3927
703-351-8308

Tri-Lift NC Inc.
Greensboro, NC 27406
336-691-1511

Trilogy Magnetics Inc
Quincy, CA 95971
800-873-4323

Trinity Consultants
Oak Brook, IL 60523
630-574-9400

Trinity Rentals/D-C Electric, Inc.
Pittsfield, IL 62363
217-285-5566

Tripp Lite
Chicago, IL 60609
312-329-1777

Tri-S Inc. Environmental Services & Consulting
Ellington, CT 06029
860-875-2110

Tristar Risk Management
Signal Hill, CA 90755
310-342-0500

Tri-Supply & Equipment
New Castle, DE 19720
302-838-6333

Tri-Tech Restoration Co. Inc.
Burbank, CA 91504
800-900-8448

TRS Rentelco
Dollard Des Ormeaux, QC H9B 2C5
Canada
514-683-9400

TSC Consulting Inc.
Boca Raton, FL 33496
800-658-7606

Tuckey Restoration Inc.
Carlisle, PA 17013
717-249-7052

Turnbull Consulting Inc.
Wallace, NC 28466-0475
910-285-8606

TVI Corporation
Glenn Dale, MD 20769
301-352-8800

Twenty First Century Communications
Columbus, OH 43214
614-442-1215

TwoSeven, Inc.
Norfolk, VA 23517
804-339-5890

Tyler Rental Inc
Olympia, WA 98512
800-772-0237

U O Equipment Co.
Houston, TX 77292-4615
800-231-6372

U S Security
Philadelphia, PA 19137
215-535-4782

U. S. Small Business Association
Buffalo, NY 14202
800-659-2955

U.S. Army Corps of Engineers
San Francisco, CA 94105-1905
415-744-2809

U.S. Dept. of Energy Efficiency & Renewable Energy
Merrifield, VA 22116
877-337-3463

U.S. Geological Survey
Reston, VA 20192
703-648-4447

U.S. Netcom Corp.
Joplin, MO 64801
417-781-7000

U.S. Postal Inspection Service
Boston, MA 02210-2114
617-556-4400

U.S. Postal Inspection Service
Chicago, IL 60699-0001
312-983-7900

U.S. Postal Inspection Service
Columbia, MD 21044-3509
410-715-7700

U.S. Postal Inspection Service
Denver, CO 80299-3034
303-313-5320

U.S. Postal Inspection Service
Houston, TX 77251-1276
713-238-4400

U.S. Postal Inspection Service
Mirimar, FL 33027-3242
954-436-7200

U.S. Postal Inspection Service
New York, NY 10116-0555
212-330-3844

U.S. Postal Inspection Service
Pasadena, CA 91102-2000
626-405-1200

U.S. Postal Inspection Service
Phildelphia, PA 19101
215-895-8450

U.S. Postal Inspection Service
Seattle, WA 98111-4000
206-442-6300

U.S. Small Business Administration
Atlanta, GA 30308
800-359-2227

U.S. Small Business Administration
Buffalo, NY 14202
800-659-2955

U.S. Small Business Administration
Ft. Worth, TX 76155-2243
800-366-6303

U.S. Small Business Administration
Sacramento, CA 95841-9004
800-488-5323

UCLA Center for Public Health and
Disasters
Los Angeles, CA 90024
310-794-0864

UK
Poway, CA 92064
858-513-9100

UltraBac Software
Bellevue, WA 98007-5229
425-644-6000

Ultrasonics International
Bellingham, WA 98229
800-500-2544

Under The Needle Tree Service LLC
Shoreline, WA 98133
206-412-7267

Underground Vaults & Storage. Inc
Hutchinson, KS 67504
620-662-6769

Underwater Kinetics
Poway, CA 92064
800-327-7388

Underwood DisasterRecovery, LLC
Brooksville, FL 34601
352-279-1767

Ungerman Construction Co
Minneapolis, MN 55419
612-825-2800

UNICCO Facility Services Canada Co.
Edmonton, AB T5E 1Y6
Canada
403-660-6873

UNICCO Facility Services Canada Co.
Ottawa, ON K1G 4L4
Canada
613-736-5900

UNICCO Facility Services Canada Co.
St-Laurent, QC H4R 2B9
Canada
514-332-2085

UNICCO Facility Services Canada Co.
Toronto, ON M5A 3S5
Canada
416-369-0040

UNICCO Facility Services Canada Co.
Vancouver, BC V6E 2R1
Canada
604-682-4442

UNICCO Service Company
Auburndale, MA 2466
617-527-5222

UNI-COMP Equipment Corp
Hendersonvlle, TN 37075
615-822-8484

Unipress Software Inc
Edison, NJ 08817
732-287-2100

Unison Transformer Svc Inc
Kansas City, KS 66115-1202
913-321-3155

UNISYS Corp
Blue Bell, PA 19424
215-986-4011

Unisys Corporation
Reston, VA 20190
703-439-5000

Unitech Systems Inc
Naperville, IL 60563
630-505-1800

United Animal Nations (UAN)
Sacramento, CA 95818
916-429-2457

United Recovery Services Co.
Cherry Hill, NJ 08034
856-427-5700

United Rentals
Bladensburg, MD 20710-1116
301-864-5100

United Rentals
Greensboro, NC 27405
336-379-9757

United Rentals Inc
Crofton, MD 21114
301-864-5100

United Rentals Inc.
Prince Frederck, MD 20678
800-544-8658

United Rentals Inc.(HQ)
Greenwich, CT 06831-5128
203-622-3131

United Rentals Pumps*Power*HVAC
Bellmawr, NJ 08031
610-972-3642

United Rentals Pumps*Power*HVAC
Forest Park, GA 30297
800-506-5831

United Rentals Pumps*Power*HVAC
Kingston, MA 02364
866-544-7867

United Rentals Pumps*Power*HVAC
Lauderhill, FL 33313
954-797-3867

United Rentals Pumps*Power*HVAC
Orlando, FL 32824
888-269-8292

United Rentals Pumps, Power, HVAC
Pompano Beach, FL 33069
800-462-0994

United Rentals Pumps, Power, HVAC
West Haven , CT 06576
203-937-9953

United Rentals, Inc.
West Haven, CT 06516
866-742-0434

United Restoration Inc.
Virginia Beach, VA 23462
757-490-1966

United Restoration Services Inc
Scarsdale, NY 10583
914-472-5565

United Services DKI
Frederick, MD 20678
800-644-8658

United Services DKI
Griffith, IN 46319-1100
219-972-6300

United Wire Service
Peoria, IL 61615
309-689-6160

Univ. of Richmond-School of Continuing
Studies
Richmond, VA 23173
804-289-8133

Universal Mailing Services
Piscataway, NJ 08854-4101
732-981-9100

Universal Power Systems Inc
Chantilly, VA 20151
800-438-8774

Universal Software Inc
Brookfield, CT 06804-2418
203-792-5100

Universal Weather
Houston, TX 77061
713-944-1622

University of Akron
Akron, OH 44325-4304
330-927-7789

University of CA Riverside Extension
Riverside, CA 92507
909-787-5804

University of California at San Diego
La Jolla, CA 92093
619-622-5712

University of Delaware
Newark, DE 19716-7381
302-831-8405

University of Findlay
Findlay, OH 45840
419-434-4588

University of Florida
Ocala, FL 34482-1486
352-369-2800

University of Hawaii- West Oahu
Pearl City, HI 96782
808-454-4712

University of Idaho
Idaho Falls, ID 83402
208-282-7718

University of Maine at Fort Kent
Fort Kent, ME 04743
1-888-TRY-UMFK

University of Michigan- Flint
Flint, MI 48502-1950
810-762-3355

University of Missouri
Columbia, MO 65211-1342
573-884-8984

University of Nevada at Las Vegas
Las Vegas, NV 89154-2037
702-939-4631

University of New Orleans
New Orleans, LA 70148
504-280-6521

University of North Carolina
Chapel Hill, NC 27599-7400
919-966-7676

University of North Carolina at Chapel
Hill
Chapel Hill, NC 27599-7411
919-843-1219

University of North Texas
Denton, TX 76203-0617
940-565-2996

University of Pittsburgh Medical Center
Pittsburgh, PA 15213-2582
443-573-3304

University of Tennessee at Chattanooga
Chattanooga, TN 37403
423-425-2150

University of Tennessee, Knoxville
Knoxville, TN 37993-2710
865-974-1108

University of Texas at Dallas
Dallas, TX 75083-0688
972-883-2562

University of Utah
Salt lake City, UT 84112-9155
801-581-7930

University of Washington
Seattle, WA 98195
206-543-4190

University of Wisconsin - Green Bay
Green Bay, WI 54311-7001
920-465-2468

University of Wisconsin-Disaster
Management Center
Madison, WI 53706
608-262-5441

University Products, Inc.
Holyoke, MA 01040
800-336-1847

Unlimited Resources Inc. - Florida Office
Ponte Vedra Beach, FL 32082
703-622-6946

Unsmoke/Restorx
Coraopolis, PA 15108
412-351-8686

Urban Clean Ltd.
Bolton, ON L7E 1J7
Canada
905-951-2900

URS Corp.
Gaithersburg, MD 20878
301-258-9780

URS Corporation
Gaithersburg, MD 20878
301-258-6554

US Bunkers, Inc.
Miami, FL 33186
305-971-2511

US Department of Homeland Security
Washington, DC 20528
202-282-8000

US Web Mailing Services
Huntington, NY 11743
631-427-5200

US, EPA: Chemical Emergency
Preparedness and Prevention Office
Washington , DC 02460
1-800-424-9346

USA Glass & Mirror
San Francisco, CA 94103
415-285-1110

USERS Inc.
Valley Forge, PA 19482
610-687-9400

USG Recovery Centers
Edina, MN 55439
612-874-6500

USG University
Edina, MN 55439
612-874-6500

USG University
Minneapolis, MN 55416
612-874-6500

USG, Inc.
Minneapolis, MN 55416
612-874-6500

USGS Earthquake Hazards Program
Golden, CO 80401
303-273-8579

USGS Earthquake Hazards Program
Office
Reston, VA 20192
703-648-6714

Utah Disaster Kleenup
Draper, UT 84020
801-553-1010

Utah Division of Emergency Services and
Homeland Security
Salt Lake City, UT 84114-1710
801-538-3400

Utah Poison Control
Salt Lake City, UT 84108
800-222-1222

UTD Engineering and Computer Science
Richardson, TX 75083-0688
972-883-2874

V & M
San Leandro, CA 94577
510-352-3900

V & M Restoration
Orange, CA 92865
714-970-9140

Van Sangas General Contractor Inc
Port St. Lucie, FL 34952
772-335-1526

Vance International
Oakton, VA 22124-2700
703-592-1400

Vanguard Vaults
Sacramento, CA 95865
916-686-8286

Vantage Technologies, Inc.
Merrimack, NH 03054-4885
800-487-5678

Vaportek Inc.,
Sussex, WI 53089
800-237-6367

Vaportek, Inc.
Sussex, WI 53089
800-237-6367

Varitek
Anaheim, CA 92805
714-283-8980

Vaughn's Power Equipment Inc
Kenner, LA 70062
504-466-8568

Vault Management Inc.
Broken Arrow, OK 74012
918-258-7781

VaultLogix
Ipswich, MA 01938
877-VAULTLOGIX

Vencenveo
Memphis, TN 38116
901-396-9904

Venture Resources Management Systems
(VRMS)
Sacramento, CA 95834
800-570-8767

VeriCenter Inc.
Houston, TX 77079
281-584-4500

VeriCenter, Inc.
Houston, TX 77079
281-584-4500

VERITAS
Mountain View, CA 94043
650-527-8000

VERITAS Software
Toronto, ON M2H 3S7
Canada
416-774-0000

VeriTrust
Houston, TX 77227-2737
713-263-9000

Vermont Division of Emergency
Management
Waterbury, VT 05671
802-244-8721

Vernon Computer Rentals & Leasing
Stamford, CT 06902
800-827-3434

VERSO Technologies
Atlanta, GA 30339
678-589-3500

VIACK Corporation
Phoenix, AZ 85254
480-735-5900

ViaSat, Inc.
Carlsbad, CA 92009
760-476-4796

Vics Computer Service
Houston, TX 77063
713-789-1888

Victor L. Philips Co., The
Brookline Station, MO 64120
800-955-2729

Victor L. Philips Co., The
Garden City, KS 67846
800-511-1435

Victor L. Philips Co., The
Joplin, MO 64802
800-878-8223

Victor L. Philips Co., The
Kansas City, MO 64120
800-878-9290

Victor L. Philips Co., The
Topeka, KS 66609
800-878-4345

Victor L. Philips Co., The
Wichita, KS 67219
800-878-3346

VidiPax
New York, NY 10001
212-563-1999

Viking Electronics Inc
Hudson, WI 54016
715-386-8861

Viking Rentals Inc
Telluride, CO 81435
970-728-0101

Vincennes University
Vincennes, IN 47591
812-888-5137

Virgin Islands Emergency Management
Agency
St. Thomas, USVI 00820
340-774-2244

Virginia Department of Emergency
Management
Richmond, VA 23236-3713
804-897-6510

Virginia Poison Center
Richmond, VA 23298
800-222-1222

Virtela Communications, Inc.
Greenwood Village, CO 80111
720-475-4000

Virtual Corporation
Flanders, NJ 07836
973-927-5454

Virtual Group The
Madison Heights, MI 48071
248-545-3100

Vision Solutions
Irvine, CA 92614
949-253-6500

Vision Systems Inc.
Norwell, MA 02061
781-740-2223

Vital Records Programs: Recovering
Business Critical Records
Lenexa, KS 66215
913-341-3808

VLEC Communications Inc.
Denver, CO 80202
303-530-0206

Vogon International
Norman, OK 73072
405-321-2585

Voice Continuity Services, Inc.
Ramona, CA 92065
866-415-2185

Voice Continuity Services, Inc.
Sonoma, CA 95476
707-939-6707

Voice Continuity Services, Inc.
Tampa, FL 33615
813-887-1070

VoiceGate Corporation
Markham, ON L3R 6A8
Canada
905-513-1403

Voices of Safety International
N. Caldwell, NJ 07006
973-228-2258

Wackenhut Corp The
Palm Beach Gardens, FL 33410
561-622-5656

Wades ServiceMaster Superior
Restoration
Middletown, OH 45044
513-424-9487

Walker International LLC
Manchester, NH 03108
603-930-4141

Wall Street Technology Association
Red Bank, NJ 07701
732-530-8808

Wallace Wireless
Amherst, NY 14228
716-583-1604

Warning Systems Inc.
Huntsville, AL 35805-5189
256-880-8702

\Washington Air Compressor Rental Co.
Chantilly, VA 20105
703-742-6200

Washington Air Compressor Rental Co.
Washington, DC 20002
202-635-1500

Washington Emergency Management
Division
Camp Murray, WA 98430-5122
800-258-5990

Washington Group International
Boise, ID 83729
208-386-5000

Washington Poison Center
Seattle, WA 98125
800-222-1222

Waste Management of Canada
Burlington, ON L7L 5Y7
Canada
905-633-3999

Waste Management(National HQ)
Houston, TX 77002
713-512-6200

Water Out
Jackson, NJ 08527
800-848-1761

Water Out - Atlanta
Duluth, GA 30096
770-613-9525

Water Out of Fort Wayne
Fort Wayne, IN 46808
260-489-2070

Waverly Tool Rental & Sales Inc
Framingham, MA 01702
508-872-8880

Wayne Community College
Goldsboro, NC 27534
919-735-5151

Waypoint Advisory
Concordville, PA 19331
610-358-1202

Weather Decision Technologies Inc
Norman, OK 73069
405-579-7675

Weather Insight, L.P.
Houston, Texas 77042
713-361-4950

WeatherBug Government Services
Gaithersburg, MD 20878
301-258-8390

WeatherData Inc.
Wichita, KS 67202-1116
316-265-9127

Weatherhaven
Burnaby, BC V5J 5C8
Canada
604-451-8900

WeatherTAP.com
Crossville, TN 38555
800-337-5263

Weber Shandwick
Cambridge, MA 02142
617-661-7900

Webster Environmental Associates Inc
Louisville, KY 40223
502-253-3443

WEHSCO Bed Products
Stoughton, MA 02072
800-225-8680

Weil Cleaners Inc.
Monroe, LA 71207
318-325-3162

Weld Power Service Company
Auburn, MA 01501-3211
508-832-3550

Weller/salvage
Grand Rapids, MI 49509
616-538-5000

Wells Cargo, Inc.
Elkhart, IN 46515
800-348-7553

Wesco Rental Businesses, LP
Torrance, CA 90502
310-538-2958

West Coast Computer Exchange Inc
Rncho Cordova, CA 95670
916-635-9340

West National Technology Support
Center
Beltsville, MD 20705-5420
301-504-3946

West Side Salvage
Cedar Rapids, IA 52409
800-747-0104

West Texas A&M University
Canyon, TX 79016-0001
806-651-2436

West Virginia Office of Emergency
Services
Charleston, WV 25305-0360
304-558-5380

West Virginia Poison Center
Charleston, WV 25304
800-222-1222

Westamerican Custom Case Corp
Coquitlam, BC V3K 6R2
Canada
877-668-2273

Westcoast Tree Care, Inc
Seattle, WA 98024
425-922-1515

Wester & Associates
Corte Madera, CA 94925
416-274-8493

Wester & Associates
Toronto, ON M5M 2V2
Canada
416-274-8493

Western Carolina University
Cullowhee, NC 28723
828-227-2815

Western Engineering & Research Corp
Denver, CO 80222
303-757-4000

Western Micrographics & Imaging
Systems
San Diego, CA 92123
858-268-1091

Western Washington University-EESP
Bellingham, WA 98225-5946
360-650-3717

Weston Solution Inc.
West Chester, PA 19380
610-701-3000

Wheeler Machinery Co.
Salt Lake City, UT 84120
801-974-0511

Wheelock
Long Branch , NJ 07740
800-631-2148

Wheelwash Division, Global Equipment
Boca Raton, FL 33481
561-750-8662

Whelen Engineering Co.
Chester, CT 06412
860-526-9504

When Their World Falls Apart: Helping
Families and Children Manage the Effects
of Disaster.
Washington, DC 20002
800-227-3590

Whitehead's Grand Rental Station
Blair, NE 68008
402-426-9011

WHP Trainingtowers
Overland Park, Ka 66214
800-351-2525

Widmer's
Cincinnati, OH 45208
513-321-5100

Wilkinson Mobile Boilers
East Weymouth, MA 02189
800-777-1629

Wilkofsky Friedman Karel & Cummins
Attorneys
New York, NY 10007
212-285-0510

Wilkofsky, Friedman, Karel & Cummins
Attorneys
New York, NY 10017
212-285-0510

Will-Burt Company
Orriville, OH 44667
330-682-7015

William B. Meyer, Inc.
Bedford Hills, NY 10507
800-554-2673

William B. Meyer, Inc.
Stratford, CT 06615
800-use-meyer

William Russell & Associates, Inc.
Alexandria, VA 22301-2418
703-739-6277

Williams Scotsman
Arnold, MO 63010
636-296-1500

Williams Scotsman
Aurora, ON L0H 1G0
Canada
905-726-3551

Williams Scotsman
Baltimore, MD 21236
800-782-1500

Williams Scotsman
Kearny, NJ 07032
973-589-1234

Williams Scotsman
Sarina, ON N7S 4M7
Canada
519-336-1010

Williams Scotsman
West Chicago, IL 60185
630-293-0095

Williams Scotsman Du Canada Inc.
St Eustache, QC J7R 4Z1
Canada
514-634-1220

Willis
New York, NY 10004
212-344-8888

Willis of Pennsylvania Inc.
Radnor, PA 19087
610-964-8700

Wilmer Cutler Pickering Hale and Dorr
Washington, DC 20004
202-942-8400

Winco Inc
Le Center, MN 56057-1805
507-357-6821

Window Lock Products
Daytona Beach, FL 33436
888-228-1600

Windstorm Insurance Conference
Pensacola, FL 32503
850-473-0601

Windstorm Insurance Network, Inc.
Pensacola, FL 32503
850-473-0601

WinStar Communications
Herndon, VA 20171
877-WIN-4GSA

Wisconsin Emergency Management
Madison, WI
608-242-3232

WMI Services Corp. HQ
Downers Grove, IL 60515
708-656-5350

Woodard Cleaning & Restoration Service
Saint Louis, MO 63119
314-961-9102

Works Right INC.
Madison, MS 39130
601-853-1189

WORKSAFE TECHNOLOGIES
Valencia, CA 91355
661-257-2527

World Conference on Disaster Management
Toronto, ON M5J 2L7
Canada
905-331-2552

World Data Products
Minnetonka, MN 55305
952-476-9000

World Marketing of America Inc.
Mill Creek, PA 17060
800-233-3202

World Prep
Toledo, OH 43617
419-843-3869

World Restoration Services Inc.
Ukiah, CA 95482
707-485-5441

World Wide Drying Inc.
Taunton, MA 02780-0750
508-823-0189

Worldwide Financial Systems
Buffalo, NY 14207
716-877-3213

Worldwide Trade Corp
Chanhassen, MN 55317
952-474-0322

Wornick Company The
Cincinnati, OH 45242
513-552-7415

WPS Disaster Management Solutions
Bellevue, WA 98005
800-545-9028

Wright Line LLC
Worcester, MA 01606
800-225-7348

WRQ Inc
Seattle, WA 98109
206-217-7100

WTE/Worldwide Technology Exchange
Decatur, GA 30030
404-378-0990

WVU Dept. of Behavioral Medicine
Charleston, WV 25326
304-341-1500

Wyoming Office of Homeland Security, Emerg. Mgmt.
Cheyenne, WY 82002
307-777-4663

Xand Corporation
Hawthorne, NY 10532
914-592-8282

Xcaper Industries, LLC
Irvine , CA 92614
949-852-2021

Xerxes Computer Corp
Minneapolis, MN 55437
952-936-9280

xl insurance
Exton, PA 19341
610-458-0570

XOsoft
Waltham, MA 02451
781-419-5200

XRoads Networks
Irvine, CA 92614
888-9-XROADS

Xtreme Team / Bolden's Mfg
Noblesville, IN 46062
888-776-6708

xynoMedia Technology
Yonkers, NY 10701
866-4-TECH-PLAN

Your Family Disaster Plan, Yukon Emergency Measures Branch
Whitehorse, YK Y1A 2C6
Canada
867-667-5220

Z.S. Engineering P.C.
Floral Park, NY 11001-1927
516-328-3200

Zebra Restoration Services
Rancho Cordova, CA 95742
916-635-8571

Zellweger Analytics
Sunrise, FL 33325
954-514-2700

Zero Manufacturing
N Salt Lake, UT 84054
801-298-5900

Zero Surge Inc
Frenchtown, NJ 08825
908-996-7700

Zetron Inc.
Redmond , WA 98052
425-820-6363

Zetta Systems, Inc.
Woodinville, 98072 98072
425-485-5548

Zoll Medical Corporation
Chelmsford, MA 01824
800-348-9011

Zonecast, Inc.
Burbank, CA 91504
213-215-2037

Zorix Consultants Inc.
Mississauga, ON L5C 4P9
Canada
905-277-1110

Zumro Inc
Hatboro, PA 19040
800-932-6003

Zycko
Minneapolis, MN 55439
952-944-3440